# History of European Drama and Theatre

This major study reconstructs the vast history of European drama from Greek tragedy through to twentieth-century theatre, focusing on the subject of identity. Throughout history, drama has performed and represented political, religious, national, ethnic, class-related, gendered and individual concepts of identity. Erika Fischer-Lichte's topics include:

- Ancient Greek theatre
- Shakespeare and Elizabethan theatre; Corneille, Racine and Molière
- The Italian *commedia dell'arte* and its transformations into eighteenth-century drama
- The German Enlightenment – Lessing, Schiller, Goethe and Lenz
- Romanticism – Kleist, Byron, Shelley, Hugo, de Vigny, Musset, Büchner and Nestroy
- The turn of the century – Ibsen, Strindberg, Chekhov and Stanislavsky
- The twentieth century – Craig, Meyerhold, Artaud, O'Neill, Pirandello, Brecht, Beckett and Müller

Anyone interested in theatre throughout history and today will find this an invaluable source of information.

**Erika Fischer-Lichte** is professor of theatre research at the Freie Universität Berlin, Germany, and president of the International Federation of Theatre Research. Her numerous publications include *The Show and the Gaze of Theatre: A European Perspective* (1997) and *Semiotics of Theatre* (1992).

# History of European Drama and Theatre

ERIKA FISCHER-LICHTE

Translated by Jo Riley

London and New York

First published 2002
by Routledge
11 New Fetter Lane, London EC4P 4EE

Simultaneously published in the USA and Canada
by Routledge
29 West 35th Street, New York, NY 10001

*Routledge is an imprint of the Taylor & Francis Group*

First published in German in 1990 as *Geschichte des Dramas*
(vols 1 & 2) by A. Francke Verlag, Tübingen and Basel
© 1990 Erika Fischer-Lichte
Translation © 2002 Routledge

Typeset in Plantin by Taylor & Francis Books Ltd
Printed and bound in Great Britain by TJ International Ltd,
Padstow, Cornwall

*British Library Cataloguing in Publication Data*
A catalogue record for this book is available from the British Library

*Library of Congress Cataloging in Publication Data*
Fischer-Lichte, Erika.
[Geschichte des Dramas. English]
History of European Drama and Theatre/Erika Fischer-Lichte.
Includes bibliographical references and index.
1. European drama–History and criticism. 2. Theater–Europe–History.
I. Title.
PN1731 .F513 2001
809.2'0094–dc21    2001034969

ISBN 0–415–18059–7 (hbk)
ISBN 0–415–18060–0 (pbk)

# Contents

# CONTENTS

# Acknowledgements

Every effort has been made to obtain permissions to reprint all the extracts included in this volume. Persons entitled to fees for any extracts reprinted here are invited to apply in writing to the publishers. Permission given by the copyright holders for the following extracts is gratefully acknowledged:

Aeschylus: from *Agamemnon*, trans. R. Lattimore, in *The Complete Greek Tragedies*, eds D. Grene and R. Lattimore, Chicago and London: University of Chicago Press, 1960. By permission of University of Chicago Press. © 1947 Richmond Lattimore.

Aeschylus: from *The Eumenides*, trans. R. Lattimore, in *The Complete Greek Tragedies*, vol. III, eds D. Grene and R. Lattimore, Chicago and London: University of Chicago Press, 1960. By permission of University of Chicago Press. ©1953 University of Chicago.

Aeschylus: from *The Libation Bearers*, trans. R. Lattimore, in *The Complete Greek Tragedies*, vol. II, eds D. Grene and R. Lattimore, Chicago and London: University of Chicago Press, 1960. By permission of University of Chicago Press. © 1953 University of Chicago.

Georg Büchner: from *Danton's Death*, in *Danton's Death, Leonce and Lena, Woyzeck*, trans. Victor Price, Oxford: Oxford University Press, 1971. By permission of Oxford University Press.

Anton Chekhov: from *Three Sisters*, trans. Elisaveta Fen (1951), by permission of Penguin UK. © 1951 Elisaveta Fen. From *The Seagull*, in *Anton Chekhov Plays*, trans. Elisaveta Fen, London: Penguin, 1954. By permission of Penguin UK. © 1954 Elisaveta Fen.

Euripides: from *The Bacchae*, trans. W. Arrowsmith, in *The Complete Greek Tragedies*, vol. III, eds D. Grene and R. Lattimore, Chicago and London: University of Chicago Press, 1960. By permission of University of Chicago Press. © 1959 University of Chicago Press.

Carlo Goldoni: from *The Servant of Two Masters*, trans. J.M. Dent, Cambridge: Cambridge University Press, 1928. By permission of Cambridge University Press.

Jerzy Grotowski: from *Towards a Poor Theatre*, London: Methuen, 1975. By permission of Methuen Publishing Ltd.

Heinrich von Kleist: from *Prince of Homburg*, trans. Martin Greenberg, in *Heinrich von Kleist, Five Plays*, New Haven and London: Yale University Press, 1988. By permission of Yale University Press.

J.M.R. Lenz: from *The Tutor*, in *Lenz. Three Plays*, trans. Anthony Meech, London: Oberon Books, 1993. By permission of Oberon Books.

Gotthold Ephraim Lessing: from *Emilia Galotti*, in *Five German Tragedies*, trans. and with an introduction by F. J. Lamport, Harmondsworth: Penguin, 1969. By permission of Penguin, UK. Translation © 1969 F.J. Lamport.

Heiner Müller: from *Hamlet-Machine*, in *Theatremachine*, trans. Marc von Henning, Boston and London: Faber and Faber, 1995. By permission of Faber and Faber, UK.

Luigi Pirandello: from *Six Characters in Search of an Author, Collected Plays*, vol. 2, trans. Robert Rietty, by permission of the Calder Educational Trust.

Jean Racine: from *Phaedra*, in *Jean Racine: Four Greek Plays*, trans. R.C. Knight, Cambridge: Cambridge University Press, 1982. By permission of Cambridge University Press.

Friedrich Schiller: from *Intrigue and Love*, in *Friedrich Schiller, Plays*, ed. Walter Hinderer, trans. Charles E. Passage, New York: the German Library Continuum, 1984. Reprinted by permission of the Continuum International Publishing Group. © 1981 the Continuum Publishing Company.

Friedrich Schiller: from *Mary Stuart*, trans. F.J. Lamport (first published in *Five German Tragedies*, London, Penguin Classics, 1969; revised edition 1998). By permission of Penguin, UK. © 1969, 1998, F.J. Lamport.

Sophocles: from *Oedipus the King*, trans. D. Grene, from *The Complete Greek Tragedies*, eds D. Grene and R. Lattimore, Chicago and London: Chicago University Press. By permission of University of Chicago Press. © 1942 University of Chicago.

August Strindberg: from Strindberg, *The Road to Damascus. A Trilogy*, trans. Graham Rawson, London: Jonathan Cape, 1939. Reprinted by permission of the Random House Group Ltd.

Where no source for an English translation is given, the translation is by Jo Riley.

# Introduction

## THEATRE AND IDENTITY: THEATRE AS LIMINAL SPACE?

In *Letter to Monsieur d'Alembert* (1758), Rousseau energetically quashed d'Alembert's suggestion (in 'Geneva', *The Encyclopaedia*, vol. 7) that Geneva required a theatre in order to keep up with other European cities. Rousseau's main argument was that the theatre would threaten the identity of the inhabitants of Geneva, perhaps even destroy it altogether. His objections concerned both the structure and the content of theatre. Because theatre encourages both men and women to gather together in public for the sake of entertainment, it would attack the traditional forms of communal life in Geneva such as the strictly separated 'circles' of men and women. Moreover, it would also contravene 'natural' female modesty which forbids females from showing themselves in public: 'A woman outside the hearth loses her most perfect enamel and, robbed of her true naturalness, her appearance is unseemly ... Whatever she does, the gaze of the public eye is not the place for her.'[1] But, for Rousseau, even the male identity is endangered by theatre. Because its 'main interest ... is love' (p. 210), it threatens to weaken the male and make him effeminate: 'The constant outbursts of different emotions to which we are subjected in the theatre disturb and weaken us, making us even less able to control our own passions, and the sterile interest which we take in virtue serves only to satisfy our self-love, instead of forcing us to act in a virtuous way' (p. 210). Thus, he felt that the theatre alienated both men and women from the 'fate determined by Nature' (p. 246) and cut them off from traditional ways of life being passed down to them. It threatened the cultural, gender and, ultimately, also the individual identity of the Genevans. In order to preserve their sense of identity, Rousseau believed, they should not accept theatre into their society.

The concept of identity which Rousseau assumes to be fundamental is clearly a static one: identity is understood as something which is either given by Nature or dictated by society for now and ever more, as something which must be maintained in the individual and social life at whatever cost. It is this which forms the basis of the difference between individuals, between the sexes, between cultures. It is this concept of identity which guarantees such differences and makes any shift from one category to another impossible. It is this which establishes the authenticity of emotions and pre-determined ways of behaving and acting. A change to identity is out of the question; change can only be experienced and lamented as a falsification of that which is authentic, as the loss of identity. And, thus, it is hardly surprising that Rousseau believed that the actor represented a consummate example of one who has no identity of his own:

> What is the actor's talent? The art of deception, to take on another character instead of his own, to appear other than he is, to be passionate in cold blood, to speak other than how he really thinks and to do it as naturally as if he really thinks in that way and finally to forget his own situation so

much that he transforms himself into another. ... What then is this spirit which the actor draws into himself? A mixture of baseness, falseness ... which enables him to play all kinds of role except the most noble which is what he abandons, the role of human being.

(p. 239)

Rousseau believed the actor to be 'inauthentic', that is, he has no clear-cut, unchanging, unchangeable identity, and forfeits any kind of identity so that he has stopped being a person at all.

The concept of identity which developed in the eighteenth century and dominated the European discourse on identity until well into the twentieth century, is now long obsolete. Philosophical anthropology, cultural anthropology, feminism – to name just a few fields – have developed different concepts of identity which not only presume change, but even actually understand change as a precondition to individual biography and to the creation and functioning of communities. Without the potential to transgress certain boundaries and cancel out certain existing differences, identity seems almost an impossibility.

Thus, Helmut Plessner determined the *conditio humana* as the distance of the self from the self, as man's de-centred position. Man confronts his self/the other in order to form an image of his self as an other, which he reflects through the eyes of another, or sees reflected in the eyes of another. Or, to put it another way, man finds himself via the detour of another. He seeks to appear in a distancing and distanced relationship and to observe and watch himself in his actions and behaviour as if he were another.[2]

In this, Plessner describes the basic anthropological condition as a fundamentally theatrical one – in the first instance, from the perspective of one who appears as an actor, in the second as one who watches or observes. The actor seems to be a magical mirror to the spectator, reflecting the spectator's image as that of another, that is, the image of another as his own. In reflecting this image back, in his turn the spectator enters into a specific relationship to himself. Through actions carried out by the actors with their bodies and language, and through the role being played, the actors stage aspects and scenes which the spectators perceive and understand as representative of society in terms of their identity as members of a particular society and as themselves. This means that it is only the distancing of man from himself, and thus the fundamental theatrical condition, which allows him to cultivate his identity in any way. It follows that, for Plessner, the actor is understood to be the very symbol and embodiment of the *conditio humana*.[3]

In this way, the fundamental conditions of the very existence of theatre are to be found in the *conditio humana*, which theatre also symbolises at the same time. For the basic theatrical situation contains all the constitutive factors of the *conditio humana* – the desire to create oneself as another and to act out the other, the ability to act, to represent, to play. Its particular quality lies in thematising and symbolising it. In this sense, it can be argued that theatre thematises and reflects the de-centred position of man and the potential resulting from it – for example, in language, in perceiving the self and the other, in the instrumental, expressive and semiotic use of the body. In theatre it is *always* a question of (in structural terms) the creation of identity and changing identities. Regardless of what actions are involved, it is *always* a matter of certain aspects and factors which allow someone to say 'I', which provide him with an awareness of his self and in this sense, a self-consciousness – whether as member of a culture, a nation, an ethnic group, a religious community, a social class or group, a family, or as an individual. Theatres in different cultures and epochs realise this general condition in very different and specific ways.

The fundamental theatrical situation, therefore, always symbolises the *conditio humana*, regardless of its different culturally-historically determined forms, because it is constituted wherever someone stands as an actor before a spectator in order to perform certain actions. The culturally-historically determined differences must, however, always be taken into account, for it is these which determine whether the fundamental theatrical situation manifests itself in an institution which we now call theatre, or in other genres of cultural performance.

The term 'cultural performance' was introduced by the American anthropologist Milton Singer in the 1950s to describe 'particular instances of cultural organisation, e.g. weddings, temple festivals, recitations, plays, dances, musical concerts etc'. Interestingly, Singer linked his definition of cultural performance to the question of cultural identity. For him, cultural performance was a place where a culture could articulate its image of itself and its self-understanding and display this image before its own members and members of other cultures. 'For the outsider these can conveniently be taken as the most concrete observable units of the cultural structure, for each performance has a limited time space, a beginning and end, an organised programme of activity, a set of performers, an audience, and a place and occasion of performance.'[4] This definition would suggest that not only can theatre be described as a specific genre of cultural performance, which may share individual aspects with other genres or be quite different from them, but also that the fundamental theatrical condition is constitutive of all cultural performance in general. In this sense, it can be understood as the symbolisation of the *conditio humana*. Differences do exist, however – in part deep differences – in the extent to which, and the explicitness with which, the fundamental theatrical situation is used as the potential for creating identity.

In his pioneering study, *Rites de passage* (1908), the Belgian anthropologist Arnold van Gennep analysed extensive ethnological material to show that specific kinds of cultural performance have developed in all cultures whose most important function, if not only function, consists in carrying out a transformation of identity. He termed these cultural performances 'rites de passage' – rites of transition. They trigger the transforming effects which change the identity of individuals, social groups and entire cultures at times of life crisis, change of status, or seasonal cycles. Birth, puberty, marriage, pregnancy, illness, famine, war and death represent certain threshold experiences. They are bound to a highly symbolic experience of transition or transgression of boundaries, which Victor Turner later described as 'liminality'. They are usually organised into three phases:

1   The separation phase, in which the candidate is separated from his/her everyday life and social milieu and distanced from it.
2   The threshold or transformation phase (or liminal phase). Here, the person is brought into a condition 'between' all possible states which allows him/her to make new and in part disturbing experiences, and enables him/her to try on or act out different kinds of identity, until s/he is ready and prepared to take on a new identity.
3   The incorporation phase, in which the candidate is re-integrated into the community, welcomed and explicitly confirmed in his/her new identity.

Van Gennep observed this structure in very different cultures. It is only in the specific content of the rituals that they can be culturally differentiated from one another.

A rite of transition can be described as a process in which social energy[5] circulates in particular concentration among the members of a community so that a change occurs in the identity of an individual or a social group. This energy is released by carrying out specific performative acts, which bring about the creation of a new identity, or change in identity. That is, the new identity seems to be the result of specific performative acts carried out by the candidate and/or his/her helpers, teacher or guide and, in this sense, as the result of a staging, or as Judith Butler suggests in terms of gender identity, as 'a performative accomplishment which the mundane social audience, including the actors themselves, come to believe and to perform in the mode of belief'.[6]

At this point, I do not want to take up the old debate on the relationship between ritual and theatre, recently re-kindled by Schechner and Victor Turner. I do believe, and shall argue, however – as this work seeks to show – that it is not only the rite of transition which represents a genre of cultural performance which is particularly concerned with the formation and transformation of identity, but theatre, too. Here, it is a question of fashioning the self or staging the identity. And here, too, the staging occurs as a sequence of performative acts carried out by the actor – albeit generally not in the 'mode of belief'. In Western theatre – and I shall restrict my analysis to Western culture – actors and spectators are generally well aware that the theatre performance is concerned with staging identity. At first sight, this seems to be a rather paradoxical condition for the spectators if they are to experience theatre as a type of liminal space. As Diderot shows in *Paradox of the Actor* (1769–78), the actor's skill is to create the illusion of a man experiencing certain emotions without being moved by those emotions himself. This is the precondition to stimulating emotions in the spectator and turning the spectator into a feeling being. In terms of our investigation, this would mean the actor's skill in staging the identity of a role outside 'the mode of belief' seems to be the precondition to opening a liminal field to the spectator, which allows him to play with different identities and possibly even encourages him to make a change to his identity. Whilst in rites of transition it is generally the 'actors' who are to be transformed, in theatre, it is principally the spectators who are exposed to the possibility of a change in identity and this happens in a process where, before their gaze, the actors seem to take on the identity of role figures which they in fact only bring forth through performative acts. This does not exclude the possibility that the 'auto-suggestive powers of the actor'[7] might also provoke a 'transformation' in the actor which, however, must be achieved in him in such a controlled way that it can be repeated every evening. In this sense, theatre can be described as a liminal space.

If both the rite of transition *and* the theatre represent a genre of cultural performance concerned with the creation, self-fashioning and transformation of identity, then this opens a whole new perspective on the study of the history of theatre. It would appear both a promising and challenging undertaking to write a history of European theatre as a history of identity. This new perspective on European theatre and culture would certainly have important consequences for the re-writing of history. Any such attempt, however, seems to be faced with overwhelming methodological difficulties. For the self-fashioning of identity occurs when specific performative acts are carried out, but performative acts, due to their transitory, fleeting nature, are neither fixable nor transmittable and are therefore not available to historians born after their occurrence. This begs the question as to how such self-fashioning can be examined. And if certain performative acts do indeed turn theatre into a liminal space which gives the spectator the opportunity of testing new identities and acting them out, how can past processes be assessed, how can they be described and analysed?

We are certainly not in a position to examine performative acts carried out by the actors of, for example, the Dionysus theatre, the Globe theatre, the *commedia dell'arte* or Molière's theatre in order to stage and represent the identity of certain role figures. We lack the tools to answer even tentatively the question of whether, or how, they might have transported the spectator into a condition of liminality which might have brought about the play of identities or even a lasting transformation of identities in the spectator. The surviving sources and documents handed down to us are not sufficient to enable us to formulate answers to our questions with any certainty or satisfaction.

Are we now forced to draw the conclusion that, though the history of European theatre may have been carried out as a history of identity, we must give up the task of examining and writing it as such for mere methodological reasons? We should not be too quick to give a positive answer to this question, as the arguments until now would seem to suggest. For we have yet to take into account the intense correlation between performativity and textuality which is constitutive of European theatre. It is true to say that theatre is a performative art *par excellence*. And I agree with the founder of German theatre studies, Max Herrmann, when he argued with a theatre critic in 1918 that, 'Theatre and drama are, I believe, ... originally such extreme opposites that their symptoms will always reveal themselves; the drama is a linguistic-artistic creation by an individual; the theatre is something achieved by the audience and its servants.'[8] Herrmann emphasises, unlike the theatre critic, that it is not the drama which makes theatre into an art, but only the performance; that it is the performativity of theatre which fundamentally differentiates it from literature or the fine arts. This insight is not threatened by the suggestion that in European theatre, as Herrmann himself explained, drama and performance often belong closely together, that the drama – according to one's perspective – is the pattern or material of any performance.

This tight bond between drama and performance even determines the structure of the dramatic text. As mentioned above, the theatre symbolises the human condition of creating identity to the extent to which it makes the distancing of man from himself the condition of its existence. This is imprinted in the basic structure of drama: the function taken on by the body of the actor in performance with which he lends the role figure the corporeal identity of another who acts as a mirror to the spectator is, at least in part, fulfilled in the literary text of the drama by the names or descriptions of the role figures. The body on stage corresponds to the name in the literary text. As de Levita has shown, in all societies body and name function as fundamental factors of identity, even if over and beyond this, different aspects and elements turn into factors of identity which could drive body and name into the background.[9] Body and name are thus permanently associated with the problem of identity. In this sense, it can be assumed that the fundamental structure of drama, its organisation into names of roles and speech text, is given its signature in the issue of identity.

I maintain that dramas from the European tradition can be read as outlines or sketches of identity. And this being the case, then it is likely that every change to the structure of the drama has carried out a correlative change in the concept of identity; that change to the structure of a drama and change to the concept of identity are directly interdependent. From this, however, one should not conclude that a change to the structure of a drama proposing the outline of a new identity is to be understood as the image of an actual change in identity amongst the theatregoers. A misunderstanding such as this overlooks the dialectical relationship which exists between theatre and the social reality of the theatregoers. For theatre has seldom been satisfied with merely depicting social reality. It is far more to be understood as an integrated and integrating element of social reality, changes in which it can decisively influence by a permanent dynamisation – for example, by offering a critique of the current concept of identity or by proposing alternatives, perhaps even by initiating them. Since theatre is a social institution which is realised in the organisation of public performances, it is guaranteed the possibility of public effect as long as its critique and new alternatives are not neutralised by the censor. Enormous tension can arise between the dominant concept of identity in the social class which supports the theatre and the outline of identity created by a drama – and its performance on stage.

This can happen when the drama criticises the identity adopted and realised by the main body of theatregoers, and also when it creates a wholly new identity which is entirely different from the current social one. In this case, quite different possibilities may arise. Thus, drama is able to design an identity which the spectators can neither agree to in the present nor in any foreseeable future, let alone adopt. Or, it may conceive an identity which, though accepted as an ideal by the spectator, is not realised either in the present or at a future time. Or, the drama creates an identity which the spectators understand and grasp as their future identity and thus, eventually realise. In this case, the performance of a drama does indeed turn theatre into a liminal space which both enables and initiates a change in identity.

At first sight, this apparently systematic analysis reveals two serious problems. On the one hand, it will be almost impossible to decide beyond doubt which of these possibilities is relevant to the drama of the era being analysed. For, in order to investigate and determine the relationship between the identity conceived in the drama and that realised in social reality, one must be in a position to compare the identity abstracted from the drama with the actual identity of the spectator as represented in statements and witness accounts. Such an ideal 'laboratory situation' is almost impossible to achieve. None the less, it would certainly be wise to include as many supplementary documents as possible in analysing the dramas which can be assessed in relation to the actual identity of the spectators, as, for example, witness accounts on the social status of the theatre and its various artistic possibilities, documents of reception and all kinds of accounts which deal with the problem of identity. Thus, studies from social history, the history of mentalities, cultural history and the history of ideas must all be included in the examination.

On the other hand, the concept of 'the' spectator and even 'the' audience proves to be extremely problematic. We may know a great deal about the social origins of the spectators in different eras, and even something about their behaviour at the theatre; there are indeed many reports on the general reactions of the audience. In many cases, we know whether a production was a success or a flop. But witnesses who reported on the effect of a production on single spectators are very rare, and those we do have are of varying quality and value to our study. Thus, some belong more to the region of legend and tradition as, for example, one which seeks to persuade us of a mass conversion of spectators to the monastery after a performance of Bidermann's *Cenodoxus, the Doctor of Paris* in the Jesuit theatre of the seventeenth century – which was probably nothing more than inflated propaganda. Others, on the contrary, are concerned

with witness accounts in letters, memoirs and autobiographies in which individuals report on the effect of theatre productions they have seen. Each individual case is to be questioned in terms of how far it can provide useful information. Such material is certainly wholly unable to provide a general answer to the question as to when, where, how and under which conditions theatre becomes a liminal space or can become one. This issue, therefore, is only picked up sporadically and can only be discussed in certain specific cases.

My discussion in this volume concentrates above all on the creation and staging of identity undertaken by European theatre since ancient Greek theatre. If indeed a close bond exists between change to the structure of a drama and change in the concept of identity, then the structure of a drama and the identity it suggests are directly related, and this identity can only be deduced from an analysis of structure. This means the attempt is *not* made here to (re)construct the history of European drama as a history of identity, but rather, it is an attempt to write a history of drama as a history of identity. Though both systems share some similarities, overlaps and points of agreement, they cannot be considered equal. A history of drama represents only *one* part of a history of theatre. At the same time, it is one part of a history of literature, and as such, it is only relevant in the sense that it contributes to the interpretation of the history of drama as a history of identity.

If the identity created by a drama can only be examined through a structural analysis, it follows that the history of drama can only be (re)constructed as a history of identity in a sequence of analyses of single dramatic texts. The selection of which texts to analyse brings with it severe restrictions and limitations which make the criteria of choice a considerable problem. In this study, I shall only include those dramas that have previously been considered (from a Eurocentric perspective) as the canon of 'world theatre' – such as *Oedipus* and *King Lear*, *Phaedra* and *Iphigenia in Tauris*. This is for several reasons. On the one hand, the history of European drama can be described as a succession of texts in which the most recent offers a response to those preceding it. Thus, it seems justified to concentrate our efforts on those dramas which have had significant intertextual effect. On the other hand, it is precisely these texts in which a new concept of identity was formulated and often, at the same time, which created a new form of drama. The same texts which stimulated each following era to make a new reading seem, therefore, most suitable as material for a distancing and historicising reading. The collective history of identity change in European culture is not created and preserved in serial, trivial drama, but in individual works of art. In terms of our investigation, therefore, it is not a question of 'no more masterpieces' (Antonin Artaud).

For some time, the motto for the mental spirit of our age has been 'the unsaveable ego', introduced by Ernst Mach before the turn of the century, as well as the 'death of the subject', and even the 'disappearance of man'. Foucault ended his examination, *Les mots et les choses* (1966), with the shocking words, 'man has disappeared like a face drawn in the sand on the shore'. These words are not to be understood as Foucault's prophecy of the end of man. Rather, it announces the end of a concept of European man as it has developed since ancient times, and particularly after the Renaissance. If indeed it is true that we stand before the end of European man, it seems vital to remind ourselves of what he once was: to recall the collective history of his changing identities once more through the epochs, before the face of this dying species becomes ultimately unrecognisable in the emptiness of future time and we finally lose all trace of it.

# 1    *Ritual theatre*

## THE TRAGIC HERO

### Theatre and the polis

In early spring, when the sea was navigable again after the stormy winter months, the citizens of Athens gathered in the theatre to celebrate the Great, or City Dionysia, the largest and most important state (polis) Dionysian festival. The most significant element and climax of this festival was the performance of tragedies over a period of three days. The *choregoi* (producers), poets and actors competed in the tragic *agon* (competition), and a victory earned them tremendous prestige and respect from the polis. The winning poets were held in such high regard by their fellow citizens that they would often be elected to important political or military posts. Sophocles, for example, who won twenty victories in the tragic *agon* between 468 BC (the first year he competed) and the year of his death in 406 BC, was awarded the post of Hellonotamias in 443–2. Between 441 and 439, he was awarded a generalship with Pericles during the Samic War, it is claimed due to the enormous success of *Antigone*. In 428 he was awarded another generalship, this time with Thucydides, and in 411 he was finally elected as one of the *probuloi* – all of which is impressive evidence of the effect that performances of the tragedies had on the polis.

The performances were dedicated to Dionysus and, thus, functioned as an integrative part of the cult of the state. The Theatre of Dionysus was situated in a holy area dedicated to the god directly adjacent to the temple of Dionysus Eleuthereos. The organisation of the festival was carried out by the polis under the mantle of the highest state minister, the *archon eponymos*. Preparations for the Great Dionysia lasted many months. Directly after taking up his post in summer, the *archon eponymos* would select three poets from the competitors and, it is recorded, allocate each a chorus. Generally, the poet was responsible for directing the play. Its financing, however – including several months' provisions for the citizens, who volunteered as chorus members and who also received a daily wage to compensate for giving up their regular employment – was provided by the *choregos*, a wealthy Athenian who drew upon personal resources to cover the enormous expenditure involved. The *choregos* was similarly elected by the *archon eponymos*.

There was a law which stipulated that wealthy Athenians should take turns to act as *choregos*, but, although taking on such duties meant a heavy financial burden and only benefited the polis, some *choregoi* even fought over the position out of sequence. Indeed, many *choregoi* lost a fortune by outfitting the chorus in an excessively lavish way in order to impress and win personal prestige. It offered the producer an ideal starting point to a public life in politics, as shown by such well-known politicians as Themistocles, Pericles, Alcibiades and Nicias, all of whom took on the post of *choregos* with great success. In fact, the significance of the *choregos* was such that his name was put first, above that of the poet, in the reports on the dramatic competition.

The preparations for the festival climaxed in the selection and appointment of the judges of

8

the competition. This was an event of great general interest, due to the large number of Athenians who went to the performances. The judges were appointed through a process of elections and the casting of lots in which the Council of Five Hundred undertook the initial selection. The Council elected candidates from each of the ten districts of Athens whose names were kept in ten carefully sealed urns until the beginning of the competition. The name of one candidate was drawn from each urn, and the judges then wrote their choice on tablets which were placed in yet more urns. To establish the final result, five of these ten tablets were drawn and the rest cast aside. This method of selection aimed to guarantee a high degree of non-partisanship; the possibility of manipulating the results in such an important event was, to a large extent, ruled out.

The Great Dionysia was considered the most important cultural event in the polis and represented the politics of the polis to the outside world. Since it was held at the beginning of spring, when the various allies of Athens were obliged to submit their annual taxes, many significant representatives from other states were also present, and were given special seats of honour at the festival. The polis at Athens used this occasion to demonstrate its power and riches. It was also the custom to decorate men who had served the community by awarding them a garland in a special ceremony; the sons of soldiers fallen in battle were given a set of arms on the same occasion when they reached adulthood. At the same time, the annual surplus from the state income was divided into baskets of talents (coins) and presented in the orchestra.

It was a matter of course that every Athenian had the right to participate actively or act as a spectator at the festival in honour of Dionysus. In later years, a *theorikon* or 'spectator's wage' was paid to every spectator (equal to the money paid to councillors or trial jury members) because attending a performance was considered to be the public duty of the citizen towards the polis.

The period of the festival was considered holy: it was forbidden to carry out trials, make arrests or send out the bailiff; and prisoners were released for the duration of the festival. Violation of the rules of the festival was seen as the equivalent to religious sin. Violence during the festival or attempting to break open the urns which held the names of the judges could result in the death penalty.

The festival of the Great Dionysia started on the tenth day of the month *Elaphebolion* (March/April). On the eighth night of the *Elaphebolion* the so-called *proagon* took place, in which the poets presented themselves and their plays to the public. On the eve of the festival proper, the ninth night, the statue of Dionysus Eleuthereos was carried out in a festive procession and brought to his temple in the holy quarter. During the course of the night, the announcement was made that the god had appeared and the festival could commence.

The festival began with a great sacrificial procession on the first day which wound its way through the city towards the temple of Dionysus Eleuthereos. After the carrying out of a sacrifice, it moved into the theatre (which could seat approximately 14,000 spectators) and the ceremonies, described above, took place. This was followed in the afternoon by the competition of the dithyramb chorus, which was divided into one by boys and another by men. The comic *agon*, in which five comedies were presented, took place the following day (from 486 BC). The festival was completed by the tragic *agon* – the most important part of the event. One tetrology by a different poet (three tragedies originally linked thematically and a satyr play) was performed on the third, fourth and fifth days. With the announcement of the victor in the tragic *agon* (after 449 BC an *agon* of the best tragic actor was added to the *agon* of the tragic poet and *choregos*), the Great Dionysia drew to a close. On the following day, a public meeting was held in the theatre in which the correctness of the procedure during the festival and offences to be punished were debated.

In the fifth century BC in Athens, four festivals were held annually in celebration of the god Dionysus: the Rural Dionysia (December/

January), the Lenaea (January/February), the Anthesteria (February/March) and the City or Great Dionysia (March/April). Whilst the first three festivals had a relatively long tradition, whose origins are unknown, the City, or Great Dionysia was a new invention. It was introduced in the second half of the sixth century BC by the tyrant Peisistratos and purposefully organised as the largest and most respected festival in honour of the god. The apparently natural link which came to be made between the cult of Dionysus and the performance of tragedy was in fact a contrivance.

This detail exposes a unique aspect of tragedy, which becomes even more noticeable when ethnological comparisons with other cultures are made. Apparently, similar cult festivals and celebrations exist in widely differing cultures which, like the Great Dionysia devoted to the god Dionysus, are dedicated to a god, hero or even totemic animal. Here, too, theatrical performances are an integral part of the festival; they are based on the biography, or key episodes in the life of the dedicatory figure, or involve actions and characteristics associated with a specific god. In confirming the presence of the god, dedicatory clan father or founder, the performance provides the members of the clan, family or community who attend with a shared identity which emphasises their sense of community. Within the framework of a cult, therefore, performance serves to confirm collective identity and unity: those who attend are reminded of their collective unity which derives from a single being.

Apart from a few exceptions (such as Euripides' The Bacchae), the mythological plots of the Greek tragedies, however, have nothing to do with the dedicatory god of the festival, Dionysus. Similarly, the relatively late and contrived connection between tragedy and the cult of Dionysus, mentioned above, would seem to suggest that the relation between tragedy and Dionysus, the god of metamorphosis, must have been of another kind altogether.

The first records to mention the performance of a tragedy refer to the City or Great Dionysia in the year 534 BC (the Olympics of 536/5– 533/2 BC). The victor of the tragic *agon* is recorded as Thespis who, in ancient Greek texts, was often described as the 'founder' of tragedy. Perhaps it was he who gave Peisistratos the idea of holding performances of tragedy at the planned new Dionysia to make it attractive. In any case, it is believed he was the originator of the idea of placing an actor opposite the chorus, which had a long tradition as a cultural institution, in order to provoke dialogue between them. The second actor was later introduced by Aeschylus; Sophocles introduced the third. Tragedy never stretched beyond this number.

Unfortunately, no tragedy by Thespis has survived, and other than some titles and single verses, nothing remains either of the tragedies by Choirilos, who took part for the first time in 523/20, Phrynichos, who won his first victory in 511/8 or Pratinas, who came to Athens in 515 and made the satyr play popular. The earliest tragedy to have survived is Aeschylus' *The Persians* which was performed in 472, and it is this tragedy that forms the beginning of the history of European drama.

From the beginning, therefore, we find ourselves confronted with a highly developed cultural product, both detached from its past origins, and which has no information to offer about such origins. Certain elements remain hidden from us, such as through which intermediate stages or levels of development it passed, from which rites or customs it developed as, for example, its use of mask, dance or the inclusion of the satyr play in the tragedy as integral elements. The origins of Greek tragedy are unknown and even research into its name has not proved illuminating. The word τραγωδια has been translated as 'song of the goats' as it was thought to refer to the singers who were dressed as goats, or 'songs competing for the prize of a goat' (with the variant 'songs at the goat sacrifice'). Such attempts to discover the origins of tragedy in rural custom and sacrificial rite cannot be confirmed by sufficient material evidence. The same is also true of the endeavour to trace the origins of tragedy back over a sequence of many intermediate stages to initiation rites or totemic rites of a clan cult.

As much as it is regrettable that we shall never be able to explain satisfactorily the origins of tragedy, the lack of material does not impede our own investigations. In any case, the fragments of surviving tragedies do not expose any important insights on the theory of a continuum which would relate tragedy to the rituals of an agricultural community in the distant past. For the tragedies by poets such as Aeschylus, Sophocles and Euripides represent a highly developed, mature product, characteristic of the state of Athens. If we assume that the tragic poets cultivated and articulated the concept of a particular identity in their works, then it is the polis which is more directly in focus and of greater significance to us than the distant origins of tragedy, whatever their nature. Performances of tragedy would hardly have had such significance for the polis if they themselves were not imprinted with the image of the polis and the content of tragedy was not, in some form, drawn from the polis, its citizens and their problems. Indeed, the tragic hero always has something to do with the polis and its demands upon him. The tragedy as we know it owes its entire existence to the polis.

## From curse of the clans to political identity

Aeschylus' Oresteia, the only surviving trilogy, was performed in 458 BC, a time of political instability and change in Athens. In 461 the constitution was radically altered by the removal of power from the Areopagus. Ephialtes ensured that the People's Assembly prevented the ancient senate and supreme judicial court (which had been reinstated by Solon and which was principally made up of nobles) from dealing with political affairs. Instead, their responsibilities were limited to dealing with cases of murder and attempted murder. This change meant that the Assembly, which gradually began to include members of the lower classes, was able to dispose of its most powerful enemy. The most important political organs

were now the Assembly and the Council of Five Hundred.

The oliargic party took bloody revenge: Ephialtes was murdered. It seemed as though individual nobles might conspire with Sparta in order to oust democracy in this radical shape. The threat of civil war was ever present.

On the other hand, the removal of power from the Areopagus had the effect of politicising citizens from the middle and lower classes: since these people could now decide on matters of law that would control the polis, they were forced to become a very different kind of citizen. They were responsible for a sudden change in society, 'politics became, to a greater extent, the business of the citizen, and at the same time, the citizen's business became political ... It was not just that the citizens determined politics, but also that politics determined the lifestyle of the citizens, at the same time, on a new communal level. In this, despite individual differences, loyalty was shown to the polis above all else. Other domestic interests were to come behind it. They were citizens amongst citizens and nothing else.'[1]

The Oresteia is full of references to the political situation in Athens at the time which cannot be overlooked. This is particularly true of the last part of the trilogy, The Eumenides, where Aeschylus' representation of how the Areopagus was set up by Athene, has always been understood and interpreted, to varying degrees, as a response to the disempowering of the Areopagus in Athens.

The references in the Oresteia to the polis, and the actual situation, are not made through word play alone but run much deeper. In the trilogy, Aeschylus transforms the ancient, traditional identity into a wholly new one: in place of an identity which is largely defined by the sense of belonging to a certain 'house', 'family', 'lineage' or 'clan', exists an identity based on belonging to the polis which is formed and shaped by the values it represents.

Aeschylus used the ancient motif of the family curse which hangs over the house of Atreus in order to represent the identity of a 'house' or 'lineage' as an outdated form of identity. Identity as such is neutral, for it is given at birth and, thus, guaranteed by factors which are determined by nature, 'ϛυσει' (physei): the same 'blood' that runs in the veins of all members of the house of Atreus and 'bodies' which are shaped by similar characteristics. It is these characteristic features which allow members of a specific house to be identified with certainty, even if a child has been sent abroad and only returns as an adult. In this way, Orestes' lock of hair lying on Agamemnon's grave and his footprints are the signs by which Electra recognises him. This lock of hair 'matches well … with my own hair' (*The Libation Bearers* 174–5)[2] and 'I step / where he has stepped, and heelmarks, and the space between / his heel and toe are like the prints I make' (208–10). The identity which defines membership of a particular 'house' is thus one which is given at birth, and confirmed and guaranteed by naturally determined physical factors.

The curse that hangs over generations of the house of Atreus causes the natural, and therefore originally neutral, form of identity to be turned into a negative one. It means that the identity of any member of the Atreus family is principally confirmed and guaranteed through an 'act' of violence towards another member of the same lineage: Atreus slaughters the children of his brother, Thyestes, and serves them to him to eat (*Agamemnon* 1095–7, 1217–22, 1590–1602). Agamemnon sacrifices his eldest daughter, Iphigenia, on the altar of Artemis in order to guarantee fair winds for the journey to Troy (*Agamemnon* 205–47). Clytemnestra kills Agamemnon in the bath, with an axe, when he returns from Troy in order to avenge her daughter's death, and finally, Orestes murders his mother in revenge for killing his father. Each act of violence against a 'blood member' proves the avenger to be a 'true' member of the line of Atreus, too. It is 'Alastor', the cursing spirit of the family, who is responsible for these murders (*Agamemnon* 1468, 1476–7, 1508). However, these 'acts' do not entirely arise from nature alone, that is, as shared factors of identity they do not only derive from membership of the house of Atreus, such as physical charac-

teristics, alone. Belonging to the lineage of Atreus does not mean that a member of the house of Atreus has no choice but to act violently against his/her relations. Although the curse puts members of the family in a particularly difficult dilemma, the situation is principally one of choice. The decision for or against murdering a relation is open, though it may have serious consequences for the doer, for 'Who acts shall endure' (*The Libation Bearers* 313). Without exception, the murders are the result of conscious decisions taken by Agamemnon, Clytemnestra and Orestes. Aeschylus particularly emphasises these situations of decision. Agamemnon is faced with the dilemma of whether to give up his return attack on Troy, or sacrifice his daughter Iphigenia:

> The elder lord spoke aloud before them:
> 'My fate is angry if I disobey these,
> but angry if I slaughter
> this child, the beauty of my house,
> with maiden blood staining
> these father's hands beside the altar.
> What of these things goes now without
>   disaster?
> How shall I fail my ships
> and lose my faith of battle?
> For them to urge such sacrifice of innocent
>   blood
> angrily, for their wrath is great – it is right.
>   May all be well yet'.
>
> (*Agamemnon* 205–17)

From both the direct speech and the words Agamemnon recounts, it is clear that he is well aware of the injustice of infanticide, but views it as a lesser sin than failing in his military responsibilities. The honour promised by his leadership of the revenge attack against Troy is more important to him than his own daughter. With this knowledge, he decides for 'action', a deed which confirms his accursed identity as descendent of the house of Atreus:

> But when necessity's yoke was put upon him
> he changed, and from the heart the breath
>   came bitter
> and sacrilegious, utterly infidel,

to warp a will now to be stopped at nothing.
The sickening in men's minds, tough,
reckless in fresh cruelty brings daring. He
  endured then
to sacrifice his daughter
to stay the strength of war waged for a woman,
first offering for the ship's sake.
(*Agamemnon* 218–26)

Similarly, Clytemnestra does not sully her
hands with blood unwittingly, rather, she deliberately plans to murder Agamemnon, for 'he
slaughtered like a victim his own child, my pain
/ grown into love, to charm away the winds of
Thrace' (*Agamemnon* 1419–20). She extols her
'act' as a work of justice:

You can praise or blame me as you wish;
it is all one to me. That man is Agamemnon,
my husband; he is dead; the work of this right
  hand
that struck in strength of righteousness. And
  that is that.
(*Agamemnon* 1402–6)

However, Clytemnestra is well aware of the
curse of the house of Atreus at work in her act:

Can you claim I have done this?
Speak of me never
more as the wife of Agamemnon.
In the shadow of this corpse's queen
the old stark avenger
of Atreus for his revel of hate
struck down this man,
last blood for the slaughtered children.
(*Agamemnon* 1497–504)

Here, Clytemnestra explicitly presents her deed
as one factor of identity which confirms her
membership of the house of Atreus.

The case of Orestes is different, in that it is
Apollo who orders him to commit matricide
and who threatens him with severe punishment
should he not comply with his orders. However, Orestes does not execute his act simply in
answer to the god's command. Rather, it is the
result of a decision based on several reasons:

Shall I not trust such oracles as this? Or if
I do not trust them, here is work that must be
  done.
Here numerous desires converge to drive
  me on:
the god's urgency and my father's passion, and
with these the loss of my estates wears hard
  on me;
the thought that these my citizens, most high
  renowned
of men, who toppled Troy in show of
  courage, must
go subject to this brace of women; since his
  heart
is female; or, if it be not, that soon will show.
(*The Libation Bearers* 297–304)

For these reasons, Orestes decides 'I / turn
snake to kill her' (548–9). He, too, chooses
consciously to act – proof of his membership of
the house of Atreus.

I grieve for the thing done, the death and all
  our race.
I have won; but my victory is soiled and has
  no pride.
(*The Libation Bearers* 1016–17)

The identity of the clan or family in the case of
the Atreus family is not given by nature (ςνσει)
but is explicitly confirmed each time as 'act' i.e.
θυσει (*thesei*). Since these acts of violence derive
from revenge and the escalation of revenge, they
result in a debt of blood or blood-guilt which
'had no right' (641) and they show the form of
identity confirmed by such acts as negative.

However, it would be wrong to assume that
the burden of guilt felt by the three murderers
is equally heavy. Their 'acts' are only comparable in that they confirm the murderers as
members of the clan; such acts are proof of
clan identity. But the murderers, and the
degree to which they are guilty, are differently
judged. These differences are based on their
individual, different relations to the polis.

Agamemnon proves to be a good ruler who
respects the counsel of the People's Assembly.
From the very beginning, in his first speech, he
announces that he intends to call a meeting, for

'The people murmur, and their voice is in great strength' (*Agamemnon* 938).

> Now in the business of the city and the gods
> we must ordain full conclave of all citizens
> and take out counsel. We shall see what element
> is strong, and plan that it shall keep its virtue still.
> But that which must be healed – we must use medicine,
> or burn, or amputate, with kind intention, take
> all means at hand that might beat down
> corruption's pain.
>
> (*Agamemnon* 844–50)

This does not lessen Agamemnon's guilt. But it makes Clytemnestra's action seem particularly serious because it severely damages the interests of the polis. Because, in murdering her husband, Clytemnestra also murders the lawful (democratically minded) ruler of Argos. Tyranny follows. Supported by Clytemnestra, Aegisthus grabs despotic rule.

> The mutinous man shall feel the yoke
> drag at his neck, no cornfed racing colt that runs
> free traced; but hunger, grim companion of the dark
> dungeon shall see him broken to the hand at last.
>
> (*Agamemnon* 1639–42)

In contrast to Clytemnestra, Orestes' action is in accord with the interests of the polis. For, amongst his motives for the deed is the thought that 'these my citizens, most high renowned / of men, who toppled Troy in show of courage, must / go subject to this brace of women ...' (*The Libation Bearers* 302–4). His matricide thus frees the state from tyranny:

> You liberated all the Argive city when
> you lopped the heads of these two snakes
> with one clear stroke.
>
> (1045–6)

Although the consequences of Orestes' deed are seen in a positive light, it cannot hide the fact that it is, primarily, part of the chain of revenge and counter-revenge which concerns the house of Atreus and not the polis:

> You that, deep in the house
> sway their secret pride of wealth,
> hear us, gods of sympathy.
> For things done in the past
> wash out the blood in fair-spoken verdict.
> Let the old murder in
> the house breed no more.
>
> (*The Libation Bearers* 800–6)

Similarly, the chorus hopes that Orestes' deed will deliver the clan from their curse and cleanse them of their sins as a form of ending:

> Divinity keeps, we know not how, strength to resist
> surrender to the wicked.
> The power that holds the sky's majesty wins our worship.
>
> Light is here to behold.
> The big bit that held our house is taken away.
> Rise up, you halls, arise; for time is grown too long
> you lay tumbled along the ground.
> Time brings all things to pass. Presently time shall cross
> the outgates of the house after the stain is driven
> entire from the hearth
> by ceremonies that wash clean and cast out the furies.
> The dice of fortune shall be thrown once more, and lie
> in a fair fall smiling
> up at the new indwellers come to live in the house.
>
> (*The Libation Bearers* 957–70)

The words here are full of tragic irony, since, in place of 'light', the furies appear, invoked by Clytemnestra, and attach themselves to Orestes' heels. Neither Apollo's attempt at atonement nor any other atonement ritual can free him from the 'bloodhounds of my mother's hate' (1054). As long as the 'house' is the most important factor in driving Orestes' actions, the curse and its principle of revenge and counter-revenge will rule. The 'net' (*Agamemnon* 357, 868, 1048, 1375, 1492, 1517; *The Libation Bearers* 984; *The Eumenides* 460)[3] which Clytemnestra threw over Agamemnon has become the 'net of entrapment' (*The Eumenides* 112, 146) with which the furies chase the 'beast' Orestes (*The Eumenides* 131) at Clytemnestra's command. The identity of the Atreus clan is indissolubly bound to the curse. As long as this form of identity holds, the fateful chain of revenge and counter-revenge cannot be broken and the tragic hero cannot find atonement. To find atonement, the 'house' must relinquish its identifying characteristic and allow it to be replaced by another, more powerful, one.

This change is brought about in the third part of the *Oresteia*, *The Eumenides*. It is a result of the process of trial which is carried out between the furies and Apollo over Orestes and the consequences of his actions which are to be judged by Athene. Each of these three agents – the furies, Apollo, Athene – represent a different principle in the trial.

The furies maintain it is their 'honourable duty' to 'overthrow houses' (356) and to drive the 'cursed supplicant' (174) and 'matricides out of their houses' (210) for

Zeus has ruled our blood dripping company outcast, nor will deal with us.

I have chosen overthrow
of houses, where the Battlegod
grown within strikes near and dear
down. So we swoop upon this man
here. He is strong, but we wear him down
for the blood that is still wet on him.
> (*The Eumenides* 365–7)

The furies call upon the 'house', the 'clan' and the 'curse' that lies over it. They represent the identity of the clan which is something given at birth.

Apollo, on the other hand, turns to the gods, the 'sworn faith of Zeus and Hera' (214). He stands for the law set by the gods – the 'new' gods of the Zeus generation. Athene, finally, looks to the 'city' and the well-being of her 'citizens':

The matter is too big for any mortal man
who thinks he can judge it. Even I have not
  the right
to analyse cases of murder where wrath's edge
is sharp, and all the more since you have
  come, and clung
a clean and innocent supplicant, against my
  doors.
You bring harm to my city. I respect your
  rights.
Yet these, too, have their work. We cannot
  brush them aside,
and if this action so runs that they fail to win,
the venom of their resolution will return
to infect the soil, and sicken all my land to
  death.
Here is dilemma. Whether I let them stay or
  drive
them off, it is a hard course and will hurt.
  Then, since
the burden of the case is here, and rests on me,
I shall select judges of manslaughter, and
  swear
them in, establish a court into all time to
  come.

Litigants, call your witnesses, have ready your
  proofs
as evidence under bond to keep this case
  secure.
I will pick the finest of my citizens, and come
back. They shall swear to make no judgement
  that is not
just, and make clear where in this action the
  truth lies.
> (*The Eumenides* 470–89)

Athene represents the principle of the polis in which a dispute is decided by majority vote after the motives have been examined and the arguments weighed. This process stems from a hitherto unprecedented legal constitution. Whilst for both the furies and Apollo there is an automatic obligation to punish because the sacred principles they upheld have been disrespected – Apollo demands revenge for

Clytemnestra's murder of her husband, the furies demand revenge for Orestes' matricide – the newly formed court of justice, the Areopagus, should consider the motives and weigh up the arguments before making its decision on the basis of a majority vote. Here, justice is put into the hands of the citizens; everything depends upon their insights and decision.

Athene wants to introduce this new form of reaching a verdict to the polis in order to overcome the prejudices of the old system, in which two opposing claims stood in uncompromising confrontation, and where only one side could obtain justice at the cost of the other. This prejudice, which in its extreme form endangered the stability of the polis, is demonstrated, for example, in the way Apollo and the furies present the evidence. Both parties call upon the bond between blood relations (and thereby the identity of the clan) which must not be broken at any price. The Eumenides argue that Clytemnestra's victim 'was not of blood congenital' (605), but that Orestes was bound to his mother by a 'blood-bond'. This is the reason why they are obliged to torment Orestes and not Clytemnestra. Apollo argues that Orestes must be considered innocent because he was not a blood relation of his mother but only of his father, whose death he must avenge. For:

> The mother is no parent of that which is
> called
> her child, but only nurse of the new-planted
> seed
> that grows. The parent is he who mounts.
> A stranger she
> preserves a stranger's seed, if no god interfere.
> (*The Eumenides* 658–61)

This argument (which has often been taken as a sign of transition from a matriarchal to a patriarchal society) cannot be reconciled. If no compromise can be found, then unrest and eternal struggle will follow. Both parties refer to a legal principle which, for the people concerned and their identity as clan members, comes into power at birth, and is bound to physical nature which also provides absolute validity. This principle runs against the well-being of the polis. For this reason, Athene offers the possibility of mediation between the two extreme positions: certain elected citizens should decide by majority vote:

> If it please you, men of Attica, hear my decree
> now, on this first case of bloodletting I have
> judged.
> For Aegeus' population, this forevermore
> shall be the ground where justices delib-
> erate. …
>
> Here the reverence
> of citizens, their fear and kindred do-no-
> wrong
> shall hold by day and in the blessing of night
> alike
> all while the people do not muddy their own
> laws
> with foul infusions
> … No anarchy, no rule of a single master. Thus
> I advise my citizens to govern and to grace,
> and not to cast fear utterly from your city.
> What
> man who fears nothing at all is ever righteous?
> Such
> be your just terrors, and you may deserve and
> have
> salvation for your citadel, your land's defence,
> such as is nowhere else found among men …
>
> I establish this tribunal. It shall be untouched
> by money-making, grave but quick to wrath,
> watchful
> to protect those who sleep, a sentry on the
> land.
>
> These words I have unreeled are for my
> citizens,
> advice into the future.
> (*The Eumenides* 681–708)

Athene introduces this new legal system for the 'protection' of the citizens as 'salvation for your citadel' refers to the polis and its stability. For this reason, she retains those elements of the old system whose goals are useful: the 'terrors'. Athene's argument, 'What man who fears nothing at all is ever righteous?', evokes the Eumenides, though in a slightly weaker form:

> There are times when fear is good.
> It must keep its watchful place
> at the heart's controls. There is advantage
> in the wisdom won from pain.
> Should the city, should the man
> rear a heart that nowhere goes
> in fear, how shall such a one
> any more respect the right?
>
> (*The Eumenides* 519–25)

The old traditions are absorbed into a new legal system on the basis of which Orestes is acquitted. For, since Athene ('There is no mother anywhere who gave me birth / and, but for my marriage, I am always for the male / with all my heart, and strongly on my father's side', 736–8) decides for Orestes, he 'wins' even 'if the other votes are even' (741). The citizens of Athens have thus, in equal portion, decided for the arguments put forward by the Eumenides and Apollo. Athene's decision 'if the other votes are equal, then Orestes wins', symbolised in her cast of the vote with the stone, is the decisive factor.

Orestes finds permanent atonement and the curse is broken. The principle of revenge and counter-revenge bound to the clan identity is annulled and replaced by the ruling principle of the polis that the majority vote should decide. The 'house' has stopped being the most important term of reference, and is replaced by the polis. The words of farewell spoken by Orestes as a representative from Argos concern the advantages his acquittal will gain for the polis of Athens: a union with Argos 'into all the bigness of time to be' (764).

On the other hand, Orestes' acquittal hides within it severe dangers for the polis, for the rejected representatives of the clan identity, the Eumenides, threaten the city with drought, sterility, sickness, infirmity and death. The danger of civil war, which seemed to have been avoided through the victory of the new legal system over the old, prejudiced system, will be revived if the Eumenides are not appeased:

> as if plucking the heart from fighting cocks,
> engraft upon my citizens that spirit of war
> that turns their battle fury inward on them-
> selves.
>
> (*The Eumenides* 861–3)

Athene argues that the power which will fall to the Eumenides and which is 'large, difficult to soften' (929), can only be transformed into 'good will' for the citizens (927) if they are also given justice within the polis:

> That man
> who has not felt the weight of their hands
> takes the strokes of life, knows not whence,
>   not why,
> for crimes wreaked in past generations
> drag him before these powers. Loud his voice
> but the silent doom
> hates hard, and breaks him to dust.
>
> (*The Eumenides* 930–5)

The representatives of the clan identity must have their place and position in the polis. Athene succeeds in persuading them: 'Do good, receive good, and be honoured as the good / are honoured. Share our country, the beloved of god' (868–9). The Eumenides declare themselves ready to take up residence in Athens and to pass blessing on the city as well-disposed spirits:

> Civil War
> fattening on men's ruin shall
> not thunder in our city. Let
> not the dry dust that drinks
> the black blood of citizens
> through passion for revenge
> and bloodshed for bloodshed
> be given our state to prey upon.
> Let them render grace for grace.
> Let love be their common will;
> let them hate with single heart.
> Much wrong in the world is thereby healed.
>
> (*The Eumenides* 976–87)

Even if their duty to the 'house' remains within the polis, 'No household shall be prosperous without your will' (895), the concept of 'house' or 'clan' is no longer the most important axis of reference for the representatives of the clan identity. In its place stands the polis and the good of the 'inhabitants of the city', the 'people of the city'. Blessing will fall upon Athens because the old clan identity is dissolved into a new identity oriented around the polis. So long as membership of the polis dominates over other kinds of membership (to the clan, for example), so long as the 'children of Cranaus' (1010) are 'fellow citizens' to each other and 'love be their common will / Let them hate with single heart' (985–6), the danger of civil war is kept at bay and blessings fall on the city.

Athene explicitly demands this new identity as a political one based entirely around the polis. It is not only in harmony with the gods and their world order, but Athene also shows its creation to be a 'victory' for Zeus: 'Zeus, who guides men's speech in councils, was too / strong' (973). The transition from the clan identity to a political one appears, thus, to be a work of the gods, at least as a development which accords with the will of Zeus.

The clan identity is confirmed through physical nature, the 'body' and its 'acts' which in committing 'violence', βια (*bia*), engender more violence. In contrast, the political identity is strengthened through an act of agreement by which Athenians establish their legal system themselves and through the 'promise' that, like Athene's 'promise' to the Eumenides (830, 886, 900), should 'persuade' (885, 968) and 'convince' (Peitho, 885, 968). A true citizen of Athens is someone who participates in upholding the legal system through argumentation and casting votes, who participates in decision-making, who seeks to persuade others who have a different opinion through the power of the word. The identity of the clan shown in the 'act' is discredited as the most important factor of identity and the 'word' appears in the brightest light as the fundamental factor in political identity. The political identity of the Athenians finds its ultimate confirmation in the art of speech.

In his trilogy, Aeschylus gives expression and form to a historical moment which was the basis for the blossoming of a democratic culture in Athens: the moment of birth of a political iden-

tity. In this, Attic citizenship is, as Karl Reinhardt formulated, 'the concept of a substance from which any random quantity can be extracted which displays the same qualities and mix as the whole'.[4] The form of political identity which the Athenians developed while still embracing the old clan identity of the noble houses, and which Aeschylus emphatically demands and presents in *The Eumenides*, appears to be the pre-condition for the success of a historically unique experiment of the time, on which the rule of democracy in Athens was founded.

### Conditio humana

The form of political identity outlined in the section above also represented a valid ideal for Sophocles. Wherever his tragedies deal with the theme of the social life of the polis, it appears as a binding norm which, if broken, can only bring severe consequences for the individual and for the polis.

In *Antigone* (*c.*441) – a play which won Sophocles the post of high commander in the Samic War – the tragic heroine, unlike the rulers of the city, represents those values on which the polis and the political identity of the citizens ought to be founded. Creon disrespects such values on two accounts when he forbids Antigone to bury Polyneices' body. First, his ban seeks to overrule 'the gods' unwritten and unfailing laws' (455)[5] which the polis may never do, according to its own constitution and, second, Creon passed the law without consulting the Assembly. Creon argues like a tyrant, 'Am I to rule by other mind than mine?' (736), and not like a democratic leader of the polis.

HAEMON: No city is the property of a single man.
CREON: But custom gives possession to the ruler.
HAEMON: You'd rule a desert beautifully alone.

(*Antigone* 737–9)

In burying her brother, Antigone is the only citizen of Thebes who follows the god-given commandments which form the binding foundation of the polis. In so doing, she shows her fellow citizens whose 'fear' muted them (505) the duties which are incumbent on members of the polis. She dies because she 'respected the right' (943), as a victim of tyranny and, at the same time, as an expiatory sacrifice which reveals the true values and ideals of the polis.

Even in his final tragedy, *Oedipus at Colonus* (written *c.*406 and produced posthumously by his grandson in 401), the 90-year-old Sophocles sings the praises of the polis. He extols Athens, which Oedipus wants to 'grace' (579)[6] with his body, as 'A state that rules by law, and by law only' (914), and places Thebes in opposition to Athens: a place which is torn apart and destroyed by the self-interest, ambition and egotism of certain individuals (Creon, Eteocles and Polyneices).

At the time that Sophocles was writing, the polis in Athens was on the verge of collapse after twenty-five years of war. In 411 in Colonus, the district where Sophocles was born, democracy was swept aside as the anti-democratic party gained power and forced its citizens to accept the Enabling Act in 'a macabre process': 'The People's Assembly was moved to the edge of the city on the hill at Colonus. The people were herded there like a flock of sheep, guarded by armed men … and once there, were obliged to agree to the *abolition of democracy* without resistance. The abdication of democracy was complete, it collapsed at a moral-political low point which could hardly fall any lower than it was.'[7]

Sophocles described the situation in Thebes to warn Athens of its present reality. At the same time, he evoked the image of mythological Athens under Theseus' rule – an image of a democratic, law-abiding polis as it developed in the mid-fifth century BC, and explicitly emphasised its values and norms as both valid and exemplary.

Without doubt the conclusion can be drawn that, until he died, Sophocles felt the political identity of the citizen oriented around the polis represented a high and binding ideal. Nevertheless, this is not the main issue in his tragedies. Instead, he is more concerned with the question of what decides and defines the identity of the individual as a person – that is, before, or beyond the identity of citizen.

One example of this theme is evident in the tragedy *Oedipus the King*, which was probably performed in 428 BC, a year after the plague had ravaged most of Athens. The plague robbed Athens of its 'best man', Pericles, in a particularly critical situation – the second year of the Peloponnesian War, which ended in 404 with the collapse of Athens. Even before this, some pious citizens had already suspected that Pericles' faith was only superficial and that, in truth, he neither believed in the Oracle nor the soothsayers. Even some of Pericles' closest friends were taken to trial for lack of faith, among them the sculptor Phidias, and the philosopher Anaxagoras, who taught that it was not the gods who steered the world but reason (νους [*nus*]). Because Pericles made the 'great mistake' of not foreseeing the 'scourge of the gods', the plague, and was unable to prevent it, the outraged and embittered Athenians ostracised him. Although he was later reinstated by his rueful subjects, he died shortly afterwards of the plague.

In the play, Sophocles combines the theme of the plague and the well-known Oedipus myth. He thus weaves a web of allusions, full of potential meaning, to actual events in Athens.

The tragedy opens with Oedipus as an exemplary, democratic ruler of the polis of Thebes. The citizens all see him as the 'saviour' (48)[8] of the city which he 'liberated' from the Sphinx by his *nus*, or reason. 'For once / in visible form the Sphinx / came on him and all of us / saw his wisdom and in that test / he saved the city' (508–12). For this reason, they beg him to free the city of the plague as he once freed it from the Sphinx:

Raise up our city, save it and raise it up.
Once you have brought us luck with happy
 omen;
be no less now in fortune.

(*Oedipus the King* 51–3)

Indeed, Oedipus' whole sensibility, anxieties and thoughts are directed towards the well-being of the city. Thus, he answers to their plea:

I pity you, children. You have come full of
   longing,
but I have known the story before you told it
only too well. I know you are all sick,
yet there is not one of you, sick though you are,
that is as sick as I myself.
Your several sorrows each have single scope
and touch but one of you. My spirit groans
for city and myself and you at once.
You have not roused me like a man from
   sleep;
know that I have given many tears to this,
gone many ways wandering in thought,
but as I thought I found only one remedy
and that I took. I sent Menoeceus' son
Creon, Jocasta's brother, to Apollo,
to his Pythian temple,
that he might learn there by what act or word
I could save this city.

           (*Oedipus the King* 58–72)

Oedipus seems to identify himself thoroughly
with the polis. Even in the present situation,
when perhaps many others might be more
concerned to distance themselves and their
families from the citizens, Oedipus' only
thoughts are how to save the city. His 'questing'
reason, which up to this point has led him in all
important issues, leaves him brooding all night
until he comes to the conclusion that the
plague can only be healed with the help of the
gods' counsel. Oedipus is determined to do
everything within his power to save the city.

    Because the polis has absolute priority for
him, he deeply respects openness in all important issues. Whilst Creon, for strategic reasons,
wants to communicate Apollo's command pri-
vately, Oedipus chooses to receive it in public.

Speak it to all;
the grief I bear, I bear it more for these
than for my own heart.

           (*Oedipus the King* 93–4)

This basic belief in democracy also holds in
critical situations. When the chorus – the
Assembly of the Elderly – refer to the city ('But
my spirit is broken by my unhappiness for my
wasting country; and this would but add trou-

bles amongst ourselves to the other troubles'
[663–6]) and beg Oedipus to obey Creon's
promise not to do anything against him, and
neither ban nor execute him, Oedipus agrees,
although he is not convinced:

Well, let him go then – if I must die ten times
   for it,
or be sent out dishonoured into exile.
It is your lips that prayed for him I pitied,
not his; wherever he is, I shall hate him.

           (*Oedipus the King* 669–72)

For Oedipus, the polis and its well-being are of
the highest value. It is for the polis that he puts
his own life and needs to one side. And in so
doing, he represents the ideal embodiment of
the political identity as Aeschylus described
and prescribed.

    Oedipus' political identity is constituted and
confirmed by his words and speech acts.
Oedipus *resolved* the *puzzle* of the Sphinx and
saved the city. He *ordered* Creon to go to Delphi
and ask Apollo for help (69–77); he '*commanded*' (227) the citizens to tell him everything
they knew about the murder of Laius (224–9);
he *cursed* the murderer, his helpers and parti-
sans (236–48). The word, by which a particular
speech act is carried out as the result of his
'questing' thoughts, confirms and guarantees
Oedipus' identity as a thoroughly democratically minded ruler – as an ideal political identity,
in the sense described above.

    Alongside this consciously learned and
hard-earned identity, Oedipus has, as becomes
apparent in the further process of the drama, a
second identity which was ascribed to him by
the gods even before his birth: the identity of a
man who kills his father and marries his mother.
Oedipus' question as to who his parents are –
the question of his 'natural' identity – is
revealed to him by Apollo as his inevitable and
future identity because it is predetermined by
the gods. Oedipus denies it decisively and does
everything within his reason in order not to
have to accept it.

    Yet, as is well known, the identity which the
gods gave him at birth has already taken hold at
the beginning of the drama: he has murdered

his father Laius, he has married his mother Jocasta, and conceived four children with her. His body has completed these acts as purely physical processes: reason, or *nus* was kept at a distance and thus has found no echo in his language. His language draws far more on the murder of Laius as being 'strange' to him ('I say / as one that is a stranger to the story / as stranger to the deed', 219–20) and, later, he speaks of it as a murder executed on a 'stranger', he cannot believe there was 'any tie / of kinship twixt this man and Laius' (813–14). In his language, Oedipus sees no relation between his killing of a stranger and the identity ascribed to him by the gods because his reason does not want to accept this relation. It is solely and exclusively his body which is related to this identity. He confirms it, in fact, as a factual identity without, however, being able to give meaning to the relevant physical actions as acts which will constitute identity; as purely physical acts they remain, in this sense, without function.

Since the identity ascribed to Oedipus by the gods at the beginning of the drama is constituted exclusively by his body and actions, he cannot recognise them as his own, although Teiresias confirms in clear terms:

I say you are the murderer of the king
whose murderer you seek. …

I say that with those you love best
you live in foulest shame unconsciously
and do not see where you are in calamity. …

And of the multitude of other evils
establishing a grim equality
between you and your children, you know
 nothing.
(*Oedipus the King* 362, 366–7, 424–5)

Thus, as long as Oedipus' questioning mind has not yet uncovered and proven this identity as his true one, then physical actions do not have the power to constitute another identity. They remain silent and are irrelevant to Oedipus' self-awareness.

Although in Oedipus' conscious mind the two identities – the one he earned politically as saviour of the city and democratic ruler, and the physical one which he is provided with as 'patricide' and mother's lover – have nothing in common, the fable places them in relation to each other from the very beginning of the tragedy. The plague has befallen Thebes because Oedipus has killed his father, Laius, and married his mother, thus defiling or polluting the city. As saviour and king of the city, that is, in realising his political identity, Oedipus is forced to engage his questioning reason to discover the grounds for this pollution and to 'save' the city once again. In this way, the identity realised by the body and the identity confirmed and constituted through speech acts, by his *nus*, his questioning reason, are gradually brought into relation to each other.

Whilst Oedipus interrogates first Jocasta (700–860), then the messenger from Corinth (950–1050) and finally the herdsman (1112–81), his questioning mind unremittingly connects the different facts which he discovers. Thus, in principle, he is already aware, long before the arrival of the herdsman, that he has indeed realised the identity provided for him by the gods.

This process marks the opposition represented by his *nus*, to Jocasta, on the one hand and, on the other, to Teiresias. Although Jocasta begins to suspect who Oedipus really is when she hears the statement by the messenger from Corinth, she believes it is possible to keep the truth hidden and to go on living as before. Oedipus, on the other hand, refuses to grasp at the escape route which offers itself to him and enter Corinth as king. Thebes would be free of the plague in this case, without his natural and, therefore, his physical identity, having to be exposed. But his reason demands he continue on the path he has started without wavering, despite the consequences: 'I will not be persuaded to let be / the chance of finding out the whole thing clearly' (1065). Accordingly, Oedipus answers the herdsman's 'O God, I am on the brink of frightful speech' with 'And I of frightful hearing. But I must hear' (1169–70). The truth must emerge as the result of *nus* connecting information and drawing conclusions. It is Oedipus' hard-won success, won at the highest cost, a truth which will ultimately destroy him.

On the other side stands the truth seen by Teiresias, the gift of the gods. It is neither something he has earned, nor is there any need to expose it: 'Of themselves things will come, although I hide them / and breathe no word of them' (341). This is the reason why Oedipus remains deaf when Teiresias is angry enough to put it into words. It is only after he has pierced through to his self through the power of his questioning mind to reach this truth, that it can function as part of his identity. Oedipus recognises the identity provided for him by the gods as his own.

> Oh, Oh, Oh, they will all come,
> all come out clearly! Light of the sun, let me
> look upon you no more after today!
> I who first saw the light bred of a match
> accursed, and accursed in my living
> with them I lived with, cursed in my killing.
>
> (*Oedipus the King* 1182–5)

If the tragedy were to end with these words one might come to the conclusion that the identity given to Oedipus even before birth is his true one, and that the identity he gained through using his mind as saviour of the city and democratic ruler was simply a fantasy which dissolves into nothing before the power of the gods. But the tragedy does not end here. Instead, a trial begins in which Oedipus begins to constitute his own individual identity as something which can neither be reduced to the level of the inborn, physical, nor to the hard-won political, identity.

This new identity evolves out of a special relationship which Oedipus creates through the power of his *nus* between the two competing identities and the various factors which define them: on one side, language and speech acts, on the other side, body and physical actions .

The process in which this new identity is constituted takes place in three stages: by carrying physical acts over into speech, in blinding himself, and in his decision to make his blinding a public event. Whilst the patricide and incest have until now been represented as purely physical actions, without any power to constitute identity, they are absorbed into Oedipus' language: 'I who first saw the light bred of a match / accursed ... cursed in my killing' (1184–5). In this, they gain the significance of actions which do indeed define identity. Through them, Oedipus consciously accepts the identity which was accorded to him, as his own.

In the second stage he blinds himself, an act described here by the messenger:

> He tore the brooches –
> the gold chased brooches fastening her robe –
> away from her and lifting them up high
> dashed them on his own eyeballs, shrieking out
> such things as: they will never see the crime
> I have committed or had done upon me!
> Dark eyes, now in the days to come look on
> forbidden faces, do not recognise
> those whom you long for – with such impre-
>   cations
> he struck his eyes again and yet again
> with the brooches. And the bleeding eyeballs
>   gushed
> and stained his beard – no sluggish oozing
>   drops
> but a black rain and bloody hail poured down.
>
> (*Oedipus the King* 1268–79)

In this act of blinding, which is accompanied by words which explain and curse the situation, Oedipus transforms his body, his vulnerable physical nature, into a symbolic order. For blinding oneself is, as the accompanying words show, intended and completed as an action full of implication.

First, the self-blinding represents the punishment on physical nature which was unaware, which carried out the highly significant acts (patricide and incest) as if they were lacking in significance. Second, however, the self-blinding is a symbolic action in two senses. On the one hand, it lends physical expression to this unknowing physical nature, to its 'blindness'. On the other hand, it is the symbolic completion of the physical acts carried out in 'blindness': the repeated stabbing of the eyes implies the killing of the father and incest with the mother. By carrying out the physical action of self-blinding consciously and with the intent that it should represent a symbolic action, the body is inscribed with information and acts which are given meaning as factors confirming identity. The mutilated, but now significant, body gains, thereby, the ability to function as a sign of Oedipus' new identity. For, he created it with the same act as that when he transformed the body into a symbolic order.

In both cases it is Oedipus' *nus* which represents a particular relationship between language and body. Because he has exposed physical actions (killing and sexual intercourse) as actions which form identity (as patricide and incest), now Oedipus' speech refers to them in this way. Because he has recognised the basic 'blindness' of the physical nature of the body, the body metamorphoses into a symbolic system, and his speech reflects this physical defect. In this way, Oedipus' reason is powerful enough to constitute the identity accorded him by the gods consciously as his actual identity, through a shift of significance.

In this way, a fundamentally new relationship between his name (as part of the linguistic order) and his physical nature is created. Whilst Oedipus was given the name meaning 'swollen foot' after a physical characteristic – namely, a swollen ankle after being stung, which points to his origins (1036) – in blinding himself he actualises a second possible interpretation of the name. Since the first part of the name is the Greek word 'οιδα', which can mean 'I know' or 'I have seen', the name can be translated as 'one of crippled knowledge' or 'with distorted sight'. Thus, Oedipus recreates his body according to his name – the relationship between body and name is completely upturned. Both can now be understood as signs of his new identity.

Oedipus completes the third stage by displaying his changed body, transformed through blinding into a sign of his new identity, to the people of Thebes and insists, according to his own curse at the beginning, that he, as murderer of Laius and corrupter of the city should be sent into exile:

He shouts
for some one to unbar the doors and show him
to all the men of Thebes, his father's killer,
his mother's – no I cannot say the word,
it is unholy – for he'll cast himself,
out of the land, he says, and not remain
to bring a curse upon his house, the curse
he called upon it in his proclamation.
(*Oedipus the King* 1287–91)

In this way, Oedipus seeks to relate the newly constituted identity which is symbolic of the 'blind' patricide and incest, to his earlier hard-won, political identity. On the one hand, the implications for the well-being of the polis should be openly acknowledged: the defiler of the city has been found and marked as such. On the other hand, his exile appears to be the direct result of a speech act which Oedipus, as saviour and ruler of the city, himself uttered. Thus, everything that happens to him – blinding and exile – is proven to be the result of his own decision, directed by his own reason, *nus*. The city would not only be liberated from this miasma and thus the plague, and Oedipus confirmed as saviour of the city and the power of his searching mind celebrated but, moreover, through the exile which is both caused and desired by him, Oedipus would consciously turn himself into scapegoat for the city and exorcise the ruin with him; he becomes the sacrificial victim by which the well-being of the polis is restored:

I beg of you in God's name hide me
somewhere outside your country, yes, or kill
  me,
or throw me into the sea, to be forever
out of your sight. Approach and deign to
  touch me
for all my wretchedness, and do not fear.
No man but I can bear my evil doom.
(*Oedipus the King* 1410–15)

No longer as ruler, but solely by uncompromisingly standing up to all that he has *done* and *said*, to his physical being, and to his word, can Oedipus bring blessing on the polis.

However, this is thwarted by Creon. Not only does he forbid Oedipus the right to publicity

('Be quick and take him in. It is most decent / that only kin should see and hear the troubles / of kin', 1429–31), he even disputes the right to self-exile ('Be sure I would have done this had not I / wished first of all to learn from the God the course / of action I should follow', 1438–9). If Oedipus is to be sent into exile, it should be solely as the result of Creon's asking the god's permission. In this, the end of *Oedipus the King* anticipates *Oedipus at Colonus*: through the petty power play of individuals – here Creon, later Eteocles and Polyneices – Oedipus cannot offer himself as expiatory sacrificial victim for the benefit of Thebes and he devotes his benef-icent corpse to the ideal polis Athens. In the face of Creon's attempts to debase him as the object of his strategies of leadership, Oedipus can only maintain human dignity, painfully confirmed through his self-blinding, through total abstinence.

The question remains open as to which role the gods play both in the real events as well as in the way the hero sees himself. In tragedies by both Sophocles and Aeschylus, they do not appear as simple poetic symbols. To a greater extent, they represent actual, effective powers against which mankind is helpless. Whilst in the *Oresteia*, the gods use their power for the benefit of mankind and communicate to him the ideas of Dike and Peitho, right and peaceful persua-sion, for his own good, in Sophocles' tragedies no such interest in mankind is apparent. The gods stand, if not in opposition to, then at least indifferent to, mankind. The reason they use their power in the way that they do is not within the grasp of human understanding. Man cannot expect any help from them in any form. All Sophocles' heroes certainly hold this conviction. Whilst Antigone only bewails the fact that the gods have deserted her, 'Why, in my misery, look to the gods for help? / Can I call any of them my ally?' (922–4),[9] the hero of the much later *Philoctetes* pillories the evilness of the gods with biting words:

… nothing evil has yet perished.
The Gods somehow give them most excellent care.

They find their pleasure in turning back from Death
the rogues and tricksters, but the just and good they are always sending out of the world.
How can I reckon the score, how can I praise, when praising Heaven I find the Gods are bad?
(446–52)[10]

Before his birth, the gods decreed that Oedipus should kill his father and marry his mother. He did everything humanly possible to avoid this. The trap which the gods set, however, is too cleverly constructed: Oedipus will inevitably be caught in it. He is, as all men, simply the toy of the gods, or their puppet; it is they who pull the strings. His 'questioning' reason, which constitutes and forms the basis of his self-understanding, is directed by the gods *ad absurdum* and exposed as laughable.

In this situation, there is only one chance for Oedipus to establish his worth as a self-determining, rational being apart from the gods. He reacts to that which the gods have done to him as if it were known to him all the time and committed by him willingly, and he turns it, through symbolic re-enactment, into his own way of behaving which determines his identity:

It was Apollo, friends, Apollo,
that brought his bitter bitterness, my sorrows
to completion.
*But the hand that struck me*
*was none but my own.*
(*Oedipus the King* 1328–32; my italics)

All that remains for Oedipus and that which raises him in opposition to the gods is his *nus* which allows him to stand up for his blind and vulnerable physis as well as for his words *and* deeds, his conscious and intended speech acts, without consideration for himself, and without compromise. Deserted by gods and mankind, that which remains and will never be lost is his consciousness of his self and his sacrosanct human dignity. Thus, Oedipus, blind and covered in blood, appears – like Heracles roaring in pain because his body was being eaten to the bone by Nessus' poison or Philoctetes suffering from his stinking, infected foot until near physical collapse – as the image of the *conditio humana* in a world determined by the whims and cruelty of the gods.

Sophocles did not win first prize for *Oedipus the King*. Whether, in the opinion of the judges (and spectators), the relevance to recent events in Athens was too acute, or whether they refused to accept a heroic figure who goes beyond the ideal of political identity of a model citizen – a hero who directs himself against the gods and who relies on the power of the human identity founded on *nus*, is impossible for us to know. *Philoctetes*, however, did win first prize. But this was nearly twenty years later when democracy was long obsolete and Athenians had already tasted the suffering of nearly twenty-two years of war. It is certainly possible that these experiences made them more receptive to Sophocles' image of man and to his idea that it is the only remaining chance for man to protect his dignity in the face of an incomprehensible and chaotic world. But this must remain pure speculation on our part.

**Relapse into barbarism**

For Aeschylus and Sophocles, the concept of law, the democratic polis and the form of political identity drawn from it, remained a moral commitment throughout their lives, which they not only defended in the theatre. Aeschylus fought for the polis of Athens at the Battles of Marathon (490 BC) and Salamis (480 BC) – actions which, according to his tomb inscription, he valued more than his many victories (twelve or twenty-eight) in the tragic *agon*. Sophocles served the needs of the polis directly by accepting an important political role. Compared with these activities, Euripides, the youngest of the three tragedians, seems to have had a rather more critically distanced, and not wholly unproblematic relationship both to the polis and to his fellow citizens. Certainly, the many critical attacks by Aristophanes, particularly in *The Frogs*, where he is denounced as someone who undermined ancient customs, lead to the conclusion that he was the focus of public criticism and was probably not particularly popular among the general public.

In 455 BC, the 29-year-old poet was given a chorus for the first time; he was 43 by the time he won first prize, and went on to win it only three more times in his lifetime. Thus, the agreement required between poet and public seems to have functioned only rarely. Aristotle has reported that Sophocles said the most important difference between his own dramas and those by Euripides was that Sophocles 'portrayed men as they ought to be, while Euripides portrayed them as they are' (*Poetics* Chapter 25).[11] Perhaps this was one of the main reasons for Euripides' relative lack of popularity. For his tragedies are conspicuous expressions of the crisis in the polis. In them, he presents his fellow citizens with a very unflattering image of themselves. It is, therefore, hardly surprising that Athenians did not like to see themselves in this light.

Yet even Euripides also occasionally represented and propagated the ideals of the polis. In both *Heraclidae* (*Children of Heracles*, 430 BC) and *Suppliant Women* (424 BC), which are celebrated in the ancient index as the 'encomium of Athens', the polis of Athens claims to protect the rights of its citizens and give assistance to those who are suppressed or in need. Thus, the chorus in *Suppliant Women* rejoices in Theseus' decision in favour of the mothers of Theban men who have been denied burial:

O city of Pallas, protect, protect
a mother: see that the laws
of mortals are not defiled!
You honour justice, paying
no honour to injustice,
and always rescue
all that is unfortunate.
(*Suppliant Women* 377–80)[12]

The citizen of the polis in *Suppliant Women* actualises an ideal political identity. The last thing he wants is to damage the polis of Thebes because he is peace-loving, but he sees himself forced to safeguard human dignity, according to the general Hellenistic custom, by allowing the burial of the dead. In this process, the Athenian appears to be the legitimate representative of the interests of all Greece.

Consequently, Theseus praises the achievements and advantages of law and order in a democratic polis to the Theban herald as, for example, the right to free speech:

> There is nothing more hostile to a city than a tyrant. In the first place, there are no common laws in such a city, and one man, keeping the law in his own hands, holds sway. This is unjust. When the laws are written, both the powerless and the rich have equal access to justice, [and it is possible for the weaker man to address the same words to the fortunate man whenever he is badly spoken of], and the little man, if he has right on his side, defeats the big man. Freedom consists in this: 'Who has a good proposal and wants to set it before the city?' He who wants to enjoys fame, while he who does not holds his peace. What is fairer for a city than this?
>
> (*Suppliant Women* 429–41)

The *Heraclidae* was performed in the first year of the Peloponnesian War. It is suffused with outbursts of national pride which gripped most Athenians at the start of war and led them to believe that their cause was right. It also contains, however, some conspicuous warnings, should the boundaries of a citizen's rights be infringed. The widely accepted date of performance of the *Suppliant Women* is 424 BC. In this year, after a succession of glorious victories, Athens suffered its first defeat at Delius near Thebes. The victorious Thebans refused to hand over the enemy dead which caused outrage in Athens. Alongside this contemporary relevance, another important factor may also have been the widespread hope at this time that peace would soon be declared and the old ideal of the polis could unfold its earlier greatness and glory. It is principally this hope which is expressed by the *Suppliant Women*.

The continuing war mercilessly destroyed that hope forever. The deeds of war became more and more brutal and atrocious on both sides. In 416 BC, Athens attacked the small island of Melos. The Athenians presented the inhabitants of Melos with the choice of either submitting or facing destruction. Because they refused to give up their freedom, the entire male population of the island was ruthlessly killed and women and children were sold into slavery. Clearly, Athens had betrayed the ideal of fighting for what was right. Instead, the rights of the strongest determined the action to be taken.

Euripides' later tragedies deal with this reality. In them, we no longer find a single trace of the ideal form of the polis, its citizens and leaders. In *Phoenician Women* (410 BC), the figures of Eteocles and Polyneices bluntly expose the greed for power and possessions as the sole reason for the motivation behind events in the polis. Although *Orestes*, the last drama to be performed in Athens before Euripides' emigration to Macedonia (408 BC), shows that the People's Assembly has the right to judge and decide legal issues through the casting of stones, it none the less reveals itself to be open to manipulation. The art of speech, *peitho*, which is used in the *Oresteia* as confirmation of political identity and on behalf of the polis and its citizens, has been corrupted into pure demagogic strategy with whose help the speaker can influence the people in favour of his personal interests and shamelessly manipulate them towards the decision he wants. Political reality, as Euripides shows, no longer has anything in common with the old ideal of the polis and the political identity of its citizens. In place of law and the common good are brutal violence and self-interest. This is no longer the polis 'as it should be', to which Euripides gave shape in *Suppliant Women* and which Sophocles will conjure again in his *Oedipus at Colonus*, but rather a polis as it really was, at the time of its collapse in the last years of the Peloponnesian War. Reality allowed the ideal to degenerate into fiction – even if it was the hypocritical, devout fiction of a simple fig leaf. Whilst Sophocles resolutely continued to propagate the ideal despite it all, Euripides paid tribute to the radically changed, but real, situation.

The tendency to expose the truth relentlessly, no matter how awful it may be, and which manifests itself in terms of the polis in Euripides' later tragedies in a deeply moving way, also determines the devices he uses to represent man in his earlier, surviving plays. Euripides presents a conspicuous, almost provocative, opposition to Sophocles' image of man. Whilst Sophocles prefers to present his heroes in situations which point to the *nus* (reason), the mediator between physical body and language as the only guarantee of identity, Euripides allows his heroes to fall into critical situations where, in the battle of passions and desires bound to the physis, *nus* is finally defeated. Physis proves to be stronger than reason, intelligence, sense, insight.

Thus, Medea, in the tragedy of the same name (431 BC), is well aware that her plans to murder her children represent a gruesome crime. But her anger, her θυμός (*thymos*), takes control over all other thoughts and considerations: 'I know indeed what evil I intend to do, / But stronger than all my after thoughts is my fury. / Fury that brings upon mortals the greatest evils (1051–3). Medea is uncompromisingly at the mercy of her *thymos* and the demands it makes on her.

Reason does indeed provide insight into that which is right. But this insight remains without consequence in her actions. For Euripides' heroes, reason is obviously no longer able to mediate between physis and language. Its helplessness in face of the physis is pronounced by Phaedra (*Hippolytus* 428 BC):

I have pondered on the causes of a life's shipwreck.
I think that our lives are worse than the mind's quality
would warrant. There are many who know virtue.
We know the good, we apprehend it clearly.
But we cannot bring it to achievement. Some are betrayed by their own laziness, and others value some other pleasure above virtue.

(376–83)[13]

Reason is subordinate to the physis, its desires and passions. Because of this, it also functions in a fundamentally changed way. It no longer seeks to find 'truth' but, instead, to invent rationalisations for the demands made by the physis to justify its actions and to develop strategies which

will allow it to assert itself and be fulfilled. The opposition 'true' or 'false' no longer operates as a yardstick, but simply the alternative 'successful' or 'unsuccessful'. Medea's strategy to deceive first Creon, and then Jason, succeeds because it gains her the time she needs to realise her plan. However, in *Hippolytus* the nurse's strategy fails: 'Had I succeeded, I had been a wise one. / Our wisdom varies in proportion to / our failure in achievement' (700–1).

The re-evaluation of reason also causes a major change in the evaluation of linguistic functions. Language principally serves to move others towards a specific way of acting according to the strategy developed by reason. Euripides' figures are, thus, incomparable eloquents – 'prattlers' as Aristophanes would joke – far more so than Sophocles' figures. For, whilst Sophocles' heroes carry out speech acts which are either effective as such (pleas, orders, promises, curses, oaths) or which put into words a truth acknowledged by reason, Euripides' heroes deliberately try to influence others with their speech in a certain direction. *Peitho* (the art of speech) has turned into a perfect and convenient dialectical form of argumentation. In Sophocles, the hero's speech is the expression of his final autonomy; in Euripides, it is used deliberately as the instrument by which the physically or socially weaker opponent (for example, the seemingly weaker Dionysus in *The Bacchae*) seeks to influence or manipulate the stronger in favour of his own strategy.

Euripides sets out to denounce and deconstruct the ideals of political and individual identity, represented and presented by his predecessors, as fiction. The way his figures seem to refer to real people as they might have lived in Athens during the nearly thirty years of the Peloponnesian War seems almost programmatic. Nevertheless, the Athenians did not identify with them. This may have been because Euripides preferred to choose female figures as heroines and placed them opposite weaker, less heroic, morally far inferior men – Alcestis and Admetus (*Alcestis* 438); Medea and Jason; Hecabe and Agamemnon or Achilles (*Iphigenia at Aulis* 406 BC). Considering the thoroughly subordinate position into which

Athenian women were forced, without any rights, it may have been difficult for the exclusively male citizens of the polis to find empathy with the predominantly female heroines, let alone to respect or give them recognition, particularly when they dared to violate the male concept of the ideal woman so flagrantly.

On the other hand, Euripides' particular dramatic technique is also blamed for the rejecting attitude of the audience. Euripides preferred the form of a two-part tragedy where the identificatory figure is exchanged mid-way. This might either be a figure which arouses sympathy and compassion in the first half but which forfeits such empathy in the second half (as, for example, Alcmene in *Heraclidae* or Hecabe in *Hecabe*), or a figure which disappears in the second half or falls into the background and is replaced by another (as, for example, Phaedra, who is replaced by Hippolytus, in *Hippolytus* or Electra by Hermione in *Orestes*) or, finally, a figure which is first introduced in a negative way only to gather empathy in the second half (as Pentheus in *The Bacchae*). Very rarely, innocent adolescents are presented as figures of constant positive identification who intend to save the polis or Hellas (such as Macarius in *Heraclidae*, Menoeceus in *The Phoenicians* or Iphigenia in *Iphigenia at Aulis*) through their own self-sacrifice. Clearly, Euripides did everything in his power to prevent acceptance, or lasting identification with his heroes. Rather, he took care to keep the spectator at a critical distance from the hero. For the image of mankind presented by such heroes demands critical appraisal rather than identification determined by emotion – even, and most particularly, at the moment of shocked self-recognition.

In his final tragedy, *The Bacchae*, relentlessly pouring salt on a sore wound, Euripides once again confronts the Athenians with similar images of human behaviour – a custom of which he never tired. The play was written in the last year of his emigration to Macedonia and was performed after his death (406 BC) in Athens, along with *Iphigenia at Aulis* and *Alcmaeon at Corinth* which were also written

abroad. *The Bacchae* is one of the few Greek tragedies to take the celebration of the god of the Great Dionysus festival as its theme. It concerns the episode of the Dionysus legend in which the god takes gruesome revenge for the lack of faith shown to him by the family of his mother, Semele, principally by her sisters and nephew, Pentheus, the ruler of Thebes.

Pentheus is introduced as a tyrant, who reigns through fear and terror. Not only has he disposed with the right to free speech, as the words of the shepherd confirm:

But may I speak freely
in my own way and words, or make it short?
I fear the harsh impatience of your nature, sire,
too kingly and too quick to anger.

(*The Bacchae* 668–71)[14]

but his subjects also fear the outbursts of his uncontrolled, despotic whims because he maintains his control as king exclusively through violence. He orders Teiresia's abode to be demolished with 'crowbars' (346); he sends out soldiers to 'catch' (433) the stranger (Dionysus) and bring him 'in chains' (355); he threatens to execute him, later to stone him and orders him to be locked in the 'stables' (509). He intends to fetch the women who escaped from Thebes to Cithaeron 'out of the mountains' and have them trapped in 'iron nets' (228/9); later, to 'march against them' with 'all heavy armoured infantry' and the 'finest troops among our cavalry' (781–2, 784), and be rid of them through 'a great slaughter in the woods of Cithaeron' (796). He confirms his identity as ruler of Thebes exclusively through acts of raw, military power. Anyone who refuses to comply with his will or opposes him in any way – such as the stranger, the Lydian Bacchae, the Theban women, or Teiresias – is discredited as 'mocking me and Thebes' (503), as 'unruly' (247) and is brutally hunted down. The law and order that Pentheus has established in Thebes is merely a reign of terror. Even if he sees himself as the protector of right and moral good, he is, in fact, nothing more than a wild beast which only knows how to assert itself through physical violence:

With fury, with fury, he rages,
Pentheus, son of Echion,
born of the breed of Earth,
spawned by the dragon, whelped by Earth!
Inhuman, a rabid beast.
A giant in wildness raging,
storming, defying the children of heaven.
(*The Bacchae* 537–44)

Because Pentheus is no more than a 'rabid beast', *nus* cannot provide him with the power to constitute an identity. It has, far more, deteriorated into a purely rationalising instrument. The task of reason consists solely in justifying Pentheus' acts of violence through rationalisation.

Thus Pentheus accuses Teiresias of pure egotistic profit-seeking in following Dionysus: 'Yes, you want still another god revealed to men / so you can pocket the profits from burnt-offerings / and bird-watching (255–7). He believes he can prosecute the women of Thebes who have left 'home' (217) because the cult of the new god is being used solely as an excuse for immoral behaviour:

And then, one by one, the women wander off
to hidden nooks where they serve the lusts of
  men.
Priestesses of Bacchus they claim they are,
but it's really Aphrodite they adore.
… When once you see
the glint of wine shining at the feats of women,
then you may be sure the festival is rotten.
(*The Bacchae* 222–5, 260–2)

When Pentheus learns from the messenger that his suspicions are unfounded, his reason quickly finds a new excuse for violent action against the women: 'Like a blazing fire / this Bacchic violence spreads. It comes too close. We are disgraced, humiliated in the eyes / of Hellas / … Affairs are out of hand / when we tamely endure such conduct in our women' (778–9, 785–6).

Pentheus believes he must take action against the stranger because 'His days and nights he spends / with women and girls, dangling before them the joys / of initiation in his mysteries' (235–6) and, thus, is 'mocking me and Thebes'

(503). He rationalises and legitimises his brutal acts of violence with carefully chosen words, so that Teiresias justly accuses him of being 'The man whose glibness flows / from his conceit of speech declares the thing he is: / a worthless and stupid citizen' (270–1).

Thus, it is only logical that Pentheus' downfall should be caused by a similar strategy of dialectic argument and rationalisation by Dionysus. The god presents him with sound, rational arguments as to why Pentheus should not send soldiers against the Bacchae: 'You will all be routed, shamefully defeated, / when their wands of ivy turn back your shields / of bronze' (798–9); and as to why he should dress himself instead as one of them, 'If they knew you were a man, they would kill you instantly' (823). Pentheus bows to the more reasonable argument, 'True. You are an old hand at cunning, I see' (824), and falls into precisely the situation which, with all his 'clever' strategies, he wanted to avoid: into 'humiliation' and 'mockery', that is, he loses his identity as ruler:

After those threats with which he was so fierce,
I want him made the laughing stock of
  Thebes,
paraded through the streets, a woman.
(*The Bacchae* 854–6)

As instrumentalised reason, *nus*, thus obstructs Pentheus from finding self-confirmation and self-assertion which it should, instead, actually provide. In this way, he is unable to be in a position to acknowledge the 'truth'.

DIONYSUS: … You do not know what you do.
  You do not know who you are.
PENTHEUS: I am Pentheus, the son of Echio
  and Agave.
DIONYSUS: Pentheus: you shall repent that
  name.
(*The Bacchae* 506–8)

In a clear reference to Sophocles' *Oedipus the King*, Dionysus accuses Pentheus of not having recognised the true meaning of his name: 'Pentheus' stems from the word πενθος (*penthos*), meaning 'suffering'. Such insights and, thus, the possibility of knowing oneself and constituting one's own identity remain hidden when reason is instrumentalised in this way. It allows Pentheus to run headlong towards his ill fate where no sudden self-recognition, no meaning, no upholding of human dignity is possible. Like a wild beast he is hunted down by other wild animals, trapped and torn apart. That which he threatened to do to the stranger and the Bacchae – stoning, killing and beheading – is now carried out on him. The representative of political power is killed by the power of the Bacchae.

This alternative form of power is represented principally by the women of Thebes. After they have left their homes and town (217), they take on another way of life in the mountainous forests of Cithaeron.

First they let their hair fall loose, down
over their shoulders, and those whose straps
  had slipped
fastened their skins of fawn with writhing
  snakes
that licked their cheeks. Breasts swollen with
  milk,
new mothers who had left their babies behind
  at home
nestled gazelles and young wolves in their
  arms,
suckling them. Then they crowned their hair
  with leaves,
ivy and oak and flowering bryony. One
  woman
struck her thyrsus against a rock and a fountain
of cool water came bubbling up. Another drove
her fennel in the ground, and where it struck
  the earth,
at the touch of god, a spring of wine poured
  out.
Those who wanted milk scratched at the soil
with bare fingers and the white milk came
  welling up.

(*The Bacchae* 696–712)

After giving up their social duties, the women have become one with nature. Not only do they dress in animal skins, living snakes and plants, they also 'adopt' wild animals by feeding them.

In return, they themselves are 'nurtured' by nature's juices – water, wine, milk, honey. The boundaries of the ego are lifted and any kind of identity of the self is extinguished. In its place is a collective identity with nature, φυσις .

However, there are two sides to nature. At the slightest irritation from outside, the peaceful idyll can turn into an inferno of bloody aggression:

Unarmed, they swooped down upon the
  herds of cattle
grazing there on the green of the meadow.
  And then
you could have seen a single woman with
  bare hands
tear a fat calf, still bellowing with fright,
in two, while others clawed the heifers to pieces.
There were ribs and cloven hooves scattered
  everywhere,
and scraps smeared with blood hung from the
  fir trees.
And bulls, their raging fury gathered in their
  horns,
lowered their heads to charge, then fell, stumbling
to the earth, pulled down by hordes of
  women
and stripped of flesh and skin more quickly,
  sire,
than you could blink your royal eyes.

(*The Bacchae* 734–47)

Like wild beasts, the women not only fall upon the domestic 'herds of cattle … grazing' and tear them up, they also break into the villages, enclosures and houses of the people, 'Everything in sight they pillaged and destroyed. / They snatched the children from their homes' (752–5).

It can hardly be overlooked that, just like Pentheus, the Bacchae operate with brutal aggression against everything which stands in their way. It is only in terms of their motives that a fundamental difference can be identified. Whilst Pentheus is obsessed by his desire for power and uses aggression to confirm his identity as ruler, as one who is physically totally superior, the drive towards aggression in the women arises after they have given themselves up to and have wholly identified themselves with the god, after they have become one with nature, and the physis *per se*. A definition of the self which is too rigid is, like total lack of definition, a release into a 'natural state'. Both positions clearly allow mankind to relapse into naked aggression in which only the strongest counts. When beasts attack one another, the result of the battle is decided solely on physical prowess. And thus, Pentheus dies through his mother Agave, her sisters Ino and Autonoë, and the rest of the Bacchae because of the physical superiority of the pack against the individual:

But she [Agave] was foaming at the mouth,
    and her crazed eyes
rolling with frenzy. She was mad, stark mad,
possessed by Bacchus. Ignoring his cries of
    pity,
she seized his left arm at the wrist; then,
    planting
her foot upon his chest, she pulled, wrenching
    away
the arm at the shoulder – not by her own
    strength,
for the god had put inhuman power in her
    hands.
Ino, meanwhile, on the other side, was
    scratching off
his flesh. Then Autonoë and the whole horde
of Bacchae swarmed upon him. Shouts every-
    where,
he screaming with what little breath was left,
they shrieking in triumph. One tore off an arm,
another a foot still warm in its shoe. His ribs
were clawed clean of flesh and every hand
was smeared with blood as they played ball
    with scraps
of Pentheus' body.

(*The Bacchae* 1122–36)

*Homo homini lupus* (man is a wolf to his fellow man). When animalistic nature is dominant in man, he no longer recognises the closest of human relations and social duties – such as the seed of all social relations, the exemplary relationship of mother and child. Any form of human social relation is thereby made impossible.

The fall into barbarism has no cathartic effect for the person concerned and is powerless to constitute identity. When Agave awakes from her madness, recognises her son's head in the seeming lion's head, and gains insight into the terrible act of killing her own son, there is no possibility that she can find any meaning in it – as Oedipus did after he recognised himself as one who had killed his father and committed incest with his mother. Agave's family – which represents all human society – is dissolved; the family members are dissipated across the world in different directions, into exile. Her father, Cadmus, the founder of the polis of Thebes, is turned into a dragon, the animal from which he won his first inhabitants for the polis. The end of the polis has come full circle as the necessary and logical consequence of a general bestialisation of mankind.

What role is played in this process by Dionysus, the god who, according to myth, was responsible for all this, who decided to punish his mother's family for their lack of faith? In the tragedy, two attributes of the god are continually emphasised: first, he is a 'democratic' god because 'To rich and poor he gives / the simple gift of wine, / the gladness of the grape' (423–5). Second, he has no fixed physical form, but rather takes on different forms at will (478), although his favourite embodiments are three aggressive and dangerous animals, the bull, the snake and the lion.

The first characteristic offers comfort to all 'by inventing liquid wine / as his gift to man. / For filled with that good gift / suffering mankind forgets its grief; from it / comes sleep; with it oblivion of the troubles / of the day' (280–3). Wine releases man from the burden of social pressures and needs and reduces him to a state of physical satisfaction and well-being.

The second characteristic calls up in man the urge to do violence.

O Dionysus, reveal yourself a bull! Be manifest,
a snake with darting heads, a lion breathing
    fire!
O Bacchus, come! Come with your smile!

Cast your noose about this man who hunts
your Bacchae! Bring him down, trampled
underfoot by the murderous herd of your
Maenads!

(The Bacchae 1017–23)

Through this second characteristic, the god
also reduces man to pure physicality – in this
case, his drive to overpower with aggressive,
brutal acts. He evokes the wild beast in man.

In this form, Dionysus appears to be a
natural power, bound to the physis, which
sleeps in all men. It is a power which is neither
good nor bad, but one which, once awoken and
released, may be used both in a positive and in
a negative way. The positive power can raise
man almost to the level of a god.

… His worshippers,
like madmen, are endowed with mantic
 powers.
For when the god enters the body of a man
he fills him with the breath of prophecy.

(The Bacchae 298–300)

The negative power, on the other hand, turns
man into a rabid beast. In both cases, man is
reduced to his physis and is only aware of his
self in as much as he is aware of ςυσιη (nature)
– the dissolution of its boundaries just as the
accumulation of power and strength. Under
these conditions, it is impossible to constitute a
human identity. Man appears, thus, as a purely
natural power – beyond the laws of right and
order, beyond good and evil. Man is not in a
position to found a humane, social community
such as that represented by the polis, which
rests on right and law and order.

The torn body, which remains on the stage
at the end after the members of Cadmus'
family are scattered to the winds, points explicitly to the specific condition of human life.
According to the myth, the god Dionysus is
reborn through a miracle by Zeus, whole and
complete, after the Titans have torn him apart
and killed him, so that sparagmos and resurrection of the god function as symbols of the
eternal regeneration of nature in spring. But
the torn mortal remains a torn corpse which

points to nothing more than the aggression
which was turned on him. Pentheus appears as
the subject and object of violence which has
torn apart the 'body' of social community. So
long as violence rules, a rebirth of the polis is
out of the question.

*The Bacchae* won Euripides his fifth victory,
posthumously. This may have been partly out
of piety towards the dead poet. On the other
hand, the possibility of a broad acceptance of
the play cannot be ruled out altogether. Since
Euripides was not alive to create an 'authentic'
production, it is certainly possible that the
performance was given a more 'pious', more
generally acceptable, interpretation. The majority of the audience would have agreed with the
moral in the play that those who do not believe
in the god cannot escape his punishment. In
this sense, the chorus functions as the voice of
the majority:

– A tongue without reins,
defiance, unwisdom –
their end is disaster. …

whose simple wisdom shuns the thoughts
of proud, uncommon men and all
their god-encroaching dreams.
But what the common people do,
the things that simple men believe,
I too believe and do.

(The Bacchae 384–6, 429–32)

The idea that the tragedy shows the end of the
polis of Athens would have remained obscure
to most spectators.

*The Bacchae* stands, in many respects, at the
end of Greek tragedy. In it, Euripides reflects
on the conditions which underlie the founding
of the polis. For Aeschylus, the renunciation of
violence as a political instrument was the precondition for the grounding of the polis and a
political identity. Euripides diagnosed its end
on the basis of a return to violence. In that
tragedy is based upon the possibility of a
meaningful human identity – as political or
individual identity – which can only be developed under the conditions of the polis, the end
of the polis signifies, at the same time, the end

of tragedy. *The Bacchae* can, therefore, be read as a drama on the death of tragedy.

Theatre continued to be performed in the Dionysus theatre. However, soon after the collapse of Athens, it became the practice to allow repeat performances (from 386 BC). The unique nature of the cult event became obsolete with the fall of the polis and its institutions. Cult theatre was replaced by the arbitrarily transferable institution of a theatre which educated and entertained.

## THE MAGIC BODY

### Between religious and secular culture: the religious play

European drama came alive for the second time in the Christian Middle Ages. Once again, it grew out of cult origins. The medieval religious play originated in the liturgy of the Easter Mass. At its core is the Easter trope, constructed at the beginning of the tenth century, which re-creates the announcement of the resurrection given by the angel to the women who came to anoint the crucified corpse of Jesus at the tomb, in the form of question and answer:

Quem queritis in sepulchro, o christicolae?
Jesum Nazarenum cruzifixum, o caelicolae.
Non est hic, surrexit, sicut praedixerat.
Ite nunciate, quia surrexit.

Whom do you seek in the sepulchre, followers
   of Christ?
Jesus of Nazareth, who was crucified, O
   heaven-dwellers.
He is not here, he has risen, as he had foretold; go,
announce that he has risen from the sepulchre.
   (St Gall. *Quem queritis c*.950)[15]

The trope is based on the Evangelists (Matthew 28:1–7; Mark 16:1–8; Luke 24:1–9), which the author has transformed using the sophisticated device of a dialogue form.

Originally, the Easter trope was one element of the introit of the Easter Mass. However, it

was moved to the Easter Matins and given a place between the last response and the 'Te Deum' which sounded the beginning of the day. At first, the trope functioned in the Mass solely as a reminder of the resurrection, but now the moment of remembrance coincided with the moment of resurrection: the trope made the original Easter event happen in the here and now. This may have been one of the reasons why it quickly developed into a scenic representation of the announcement of resurrection.

The first recorded version of this successful restructuring can be found in the *Regularis Concordia* by Bishop Ethelwold. This collection of liturgical customs, vital in all Benedictine monasteries in England, was written in the second half of the tenth century. In it, the 'Visitatio sepulchri' is brought into relation to three other symbolic events: the 'Adoratio crucis', the 'Depositio crucis' and the 'Elevatio crucis'. The *Regularis Concordia* tied the four events together in a sequence of actions which outline the events from the crucifixion to the announcement of the resurrection.

The Adoratio is carried out on Good Friday and its purpose is to remind the congregation of the crucifixion. In the Depositio, the deacons pray to the cross before wrapping it in a cloth and carrying it to a place either on, or near, the altar, 'si Domini Nostri Jhesu Christi Corpore sepulto' (as if they were burying the corpse of Our Lord Jesus Christ). The Elevatio, the actual celebration of the resurrection, takes place without the congregation, in the peace and quiet before the Easter Mass begins. Finally, at the end of Matins, the Visitatio is presented.

The *Regularis Concordia* proscribes that for this, one of the brothers should put on an 'alba', step to the tomb and sit there quietly as the Easter angel 'manu tenens palmam' ('with a palm in his hand'). Three others then step before the tomb as the three Marys 'cappis induti, turribula cum incensu manibus gestantes ac pedetemptim ad similitudinem querentium quid' ('clothed in white cloaks, carrying plates of smouldering incense and cautiously, as if they were looking for something'). Here, the tomb angel and the three Marys sing in antiphony and announce the resurrection of the Lord. At this point, the old trope seems to have been extended by three phrases. The three Marys transmit the Easter message they receive from the angel 'ad chorum' and stand as if about to leave the tomb. As if calling them back, 'velut revocans illas', the angel sings the antiphon 'Venite et videte' ('come and see') and lifts the curtain which hides the 'tomb' and shows that only the cloth in which the cross was wrapped lies in the tomb, not the cross (that is, not the Lord).

This form of Easter celebration quickly spread throughout the Western church, but principally among the Benedictines. Many textual examples originate from the domain of Benedictine monasteries. Alongside the 'pure' form of the Visitatio, in time two extended versions also developed: first, one Visitatio was based on the so-called 'racing' of the disciples and second, another which extended the scene of Christ arisen, appearing to Mary Magdalene. In the first version, the Marys announce the resurrection to the disciples, 'cernitis, o socii' ('Look, O brothers'), whereupon Peter and John race to the tomb, whilst the chorus sings the antiphon 'Currebant duo simul'. Thus, what happens here is actually a repetition of the announcement scene.

The resurrected Jesus Christ is represented in the scene of Christ's appearance. He appears directly after the Visitatio and asks the weeping Mary Magdalene, 'Mulier, quid ploras? Quem queris?' ('Woman, why are you weeping? Whom are you seeking?'). After she has recognised him with the shout of 'Rabboni', he refuses to let her touch him ('noli me tangere') and gives her the command to announce his resurrection to the disciples. These extended forms also found rapid circulation in the Western church. The various uses of the three types clearly depended upon regional particularities and traditions.

These three types of Easter celebration were, until the sixteenth century and, occasionally even in the seventeenth and eighteenth centuries, a fixed element of the liturgy of the Easter Matins. After the Council of Trent (1545–63), at which the singing of tropes was

forbidden, and following the publication of the service of the Roman Mass in its inalterable form in 1570, the celebrations quickly disappeared from the liturgy. Their disappearance falls almost concurrently with the disappearance of the great vernacular plays which were almost totally banned throughout Europe in the course of the Reformation and Counter-Reformation in the second half of the sixteenth century.

Although the origins and downfall of the religious play in this form are well documented and the surviving sources are reliable, the development which lies between them cannot be exactly determined. It is still not known how the vernacular plays, which were performed in church courtyards or market squares in the city, and which often lasted several days, developed from Latin celebrations in the church. For a long time, it was assumed that the Latin celebrations were first based on supplementary material from the Evangelists (as in the apocryphal Nicodemus from which stems the Descensus ad inferos, or the story of the three Marys buying ointment in Mark 16: 1) and then grew into Latin song-plays, which then, in translation, were transformed by various vernacular dialects into vernacular song-plays. Many objections have been raised against such earlier hypotheses, and none of these objections has yet been convincingly refuted. In the framework of the theory of organic growth, how can a fully developed vernacular Easter play exist – the Easter Play of Muri in the mid-thirteenth century – at a time when the somewhat sparse versions of Latin Easter plays can, in no sense, offer a corresponding level of development?

What explanation is there, on the other hand, for the relatively early adaptation of elements from pagan traditions, which decisively affected the form of scenes such as the buying of ointment, the racing disciples or even the appearance scene? Why is it that, even in the somewhat later Easter plays, such as *Erlau III* from the fifteenth century, the buying ointment scene, which makes generous use of traditional pagan material, is accompanied by both the old Easter trope and the early strophes accompanying the three Marys as they walked along the path, both sung, unchanged, in Latin? These and similar questions can only be answered if the theory of organic growth is dropped altogether.

In its place, perhaps, is the idea that the religious plays enjoyed two different cultures. Doubtless they arose in the context, and as a product, of clerical culture. It is equally certain that the performances of the Passion Plays, which lasted several days (and in fifteenth- and sixteenth-century France, up to a month), must be viewed as an integral element of urban festival culture and thus, as a product of vernacular culture. The move from the clerical to the vernacular sphere will not have taken place abruptly but, instead, gradually. It is in no way comparable to the move of the play out of the church, which began in the thirteenth century, even if this event (which cannot be fixed to a specific time) seems to be an important indication that the move towards vernacular culture had already begun. Even when the plays were performed outside the church, their production and finance was still firmly in the hands of the church. It was held to be very important that Christ, the Marys and the disciples were played exclusively by the clergy. It was only in the fifteenth century that the financing was taken over by the city and the guilds when the plays were often produced by the town clerk or another person of scholarship. At the same time, the performance of the 'holy people' was taken over by respected citizens.

By this time, the plays had already become the expression and product of an urban festival culture. This is shown by countless reports on such events. At an eight-day Passion Play in Reims in 1490, at which it is said 16,000 spectators gathered from the city and surrounding villages (a medieval city had between 10,000 and 20,000 inhabitants!), wine and bread was served to the festive community as a gift from the city. Such events almost inevitably included some rioting, ranging from drinking bouts to fights and murders. In Auxerre, the Passion Plays were traditionally performed in the cemetery. In 1551, at a performance which stretched more than twenty-eight days, it came to such

an escalation of violence and rioting that an expiatory ceremony was carried out at the cemetery and the ground was re-sanctified. This evidence is proof that, at least as far as the participants were concerned, the plays had long finished being a part of clerical culture. The church leaders did not view it differently. In the fifteenth and sixteenth centuries, edicts issued by the church forbidding the staging of the plays greatly increased. It was generally accepted in the church that the plays were out of their hands forever.

Thus, the development of the religious play took place between two extremes. It arose in the tenth century out of a purely clerical-liturgical source and was abused, forbidden and suppressed in the sixteenth century by the church as the expression of a vernacular culture which was marked by both Christian and traditional pagan concepts and customs. In the long stretch of time between its beginnings and its downfall, it was certainly part of both cultures simultaneously – though it varied in combination, and domination of one or the other in different ways at different times and in different places.

## The vital body

The medieval religious plays were not – unlike Greek tragedy and the Renaissance drama which followed them – individual creations. It is more accurate to describe them as works which were created in a production process determined by a collective, even if they were sometimes re-worked by individual, though not always named, authors. This did not prevent an original approach to the traditional material in each case, as is impressively shown, for example, in the Easter Play of Muri (c.1250); the *Redentiner Osterspiel* (Redentin Easter Play), whose text was completed on 20 November 1464; the re-working of the Passion of Arras by Arnoul Gréban (mid-fifteenth century), or that twenty-five years later by Jean Michel (1471).

The material for the plays was derived from the Bible. The most popular theme, after the Easter event, was the story of Christmas, particularly plays about the shepherds and the three Magi. Later came plays on the prophets and legends, the ten vestal virgins, Mary Magdalene, Lazarus and many others. The great vernacular Passion Plays often embraced the entire holy story from the creation of the world to the outpourings of the Holy Ghost.

The stories were presented in a sequence of scenes which were changed and reworked according to regional or seasonal conditions and traditions, and handed down as complete set-pieces. The origin and development of single elements is not always possible to discover.

The vernacular Easter Play consisted of seven such complete set-pieces:

1   Pilate and the guards
2   the resurrection
3   the Devil's play, including the Descensus ad inferos (the descent into Hell, or harrowing of Hell), the deliverance of souls and filling of Hell
4   the Grocer's scene (buying the ointment)
5   Visitatio
6   appearance before Mary Magdalene
7   the disciples' race

Whilst the core of the first three scenes is the resurrection, the remaining four scenes are grouped around the visitation. However, neither the resurrection nor the visitation represent the longest scenes. The scenes of each group are unevenly balanced: the Devil's Play, in the first three scenes, and the Grocer's Play in the four latter scenes, are unquestionably of largest scope. Of the 1317 verses of the *Innsbruck Osterspiel* (manuscript of 1391), 244 are devoted to the Devil's Play and 524 to the Grocer's Play. In the *Redentiner Osterspiel*, which only consists of the first group of scenes, 1292 of the total 2025 verses are devoted to the Devil's Play. In *Erlau III*, which does away with the first group of scenes, the Grocer's Play stretches to 885 of the total 1331 verses. Without question, the Devil's Play and the Grocer's Play are the most popular scenes of the Easter Plays. For this reason, an examination of these plays will provide more information on the mentality of the people for whom (and by whom) the plays were performed on Easter Sunday, the day of resurrection.

As a rule, the Devil's Play is introduced by Jesus' descent into Hell, or 'harrowing of Hell'. Sometimes a scene is added in which the souls are shown anticipating the Saviour, or a scene where Satan tells Lucifer what happened at the crucifixion. The Descensus ad inferos follows the pattern of a fixed liturgical form. In all the plays, it follows a similar structure to that in the *Innsbruck Osterspiel*:

*Adam cantat:*
Advenisti, desiderabilis,
quem expectabamus in tenebris,
ut educeres hac nocte
vinculatos de claustris.
te nostra vocabant suspiria,
te larga requirebant lamenta.
tu factus es spes desperatis,
magna consolatio in tormentis.

You have come the one for whom we have
    longed,
for whom we waited in darkness,
to lead us out this night,
we who are chained up, out of the dungeon.
Our sighs are raised up to you,
our pitiful moans seek you out.
You have become the hope of those who have
    no hope,
great comfort in this torment.

*Angeli cantant:*
A porta inferi eripe nos, domine!

Tear us from the Gates of hell, O Lord.

*Lucifer clamat:*
Push the bolts across the door!
I know not what noise is behind it!

*Angeli cantant:*
Tollite portas, principes, vestras,
et elevamini portae aeternales,
et introibit rex gloriae.

Raise the gates, O Princes,
open, O eternal gates,
the King of Glory is about to enter.

*Lucifer clamat:*
Quis est iste rex gloriae?

Who is this King of Glory?

*Angeli:*
Dominus fortis et potens,
dominus potens in proelio.

The great and mighty Lord,
the Lord mighty in battles.

*Item angelus percutiens dicit:*
Lords, open the gates,
The king of the world stands outside!

*Lucifer dicit:*
Who is this much praised king
who heaves so mightily
against my gates?
The Lord should stay outside!

*Angeli cantant:*
Tollite portas, principes, vestras,
et elevamini portae aeternales,
et introibit rex gloriae.

*Lucifer (ut prius):*
Quis est iste rex gloriae?

*Angeli:*
Tollite portas, principes, vestras,
et elevamini portae aeternales,
et introibit rex gloriae.

*Lucifer (ut prius):*
Quis est iste rex gloriae?

*Ihesus dicit:*
You lords of darkness,
How dreadful your pestilence to look upon,
quickly unbolt the gates:
the king of the world is here!

*Lucifer dicit:*
Push the bolts across the door,
the king of the world is before!
He cries into our ears:

indeed he may rage,
he can shout as much as he wishes.
What is he doing here?
I command him to leave at once,
otherwise there'll be a dreadful storm!
Bring me my fork and spoon,
I shall hold him down till he drowns in Hell.

*Et sic Ihesus frangit tartarum, daemones ulalunt.*
Here, Jesus breaks open the doors of Hell.
    The devils howl.

*Ihesus dicit:*
Now come, my dearest children,
who are born of my father!
You should with me eternally
possess my father's kingdom.

(258–306)

Jesus leads the liberated souls out of Hell and
the devils decide how to replenish the suddenly
empty place. This is generally followed by a
soul-capturing scene played out to the full.

Even in the later plays, the Descensus ad
inferos remains unchanged. After the *canticum
triumphale* (Advenisti, desiderabilis), the angels
sing the challenge 'Tollite portas' three times to
which the devil replies with the question: 'Quis
est iste rex gloriae?' The repetition of the
formula three times, handed down from the
gospel of Nicodemus, was adapted from other
church rituals and added to the Easter Play.
There is much evidence to show that, at least
by the ninth century, the ceremony to sanctify
the church was carried out with this formula,
and it also has a long tradition in formulas
belonging to religious exorcism.

The deliberate inclusion of the Latin formula,
even in the late vernacular plays, seems to
suggest that its unique effect was of great
importance to the Easter plays. The devils and
demons were exorcised and, thus, with the
help of 'white' magic belonging to religious
culture, the coarse comedy of the following
soul-catching scene and the Grocer's scene
(whose 'obscenities' were much reprimanded
by earlier researchers) could be fearlessly
played out to the full and enjoyed by the
spectators. Without this safeguard, the actors

playing the devils might have ended their days in poverty, on the gallows or suicidal, as was reported in many legends. It was with good reason that Geroh von Reichersberg (1093–1169) tried to forbid clerics from taking part in the plays because he was afraid that those who played the devil or the Antichrist would thereby become actual servants to Satan. Since the Descensus ad inferos, however, is performed as a formulaic, liturgical exorcism, the 'play on the resurrection of the Lord' fulfils 'the latent function of ritual release from the pressure of fear of the demons'.[16] Through a long fast, the vital, bodily functions which normally expose man to the influence of the devil are forcefully suppressed, and then, because the devil and his evil spirits have been effectively banished, man can live out those vital functions, both freely and without fear.

This release is particularly clear in the Grocer's Play. The scene seems to have been inspired by Mark 16,1 'emerunt aromata, ut venientes ungerunt eum' ('And when the Sabbath was past, Mary Magdalene, and Mary the mother of James, and Salome, had bought sweet spices, that they might come and anoint him'). It quickly grew to become the largest scene of the play into which is worked much material from earlier traditions which derive from pagan concepts and customs. The characters in the scene consist of the Old Doctor (the Grocer who sells the ointment), his young wife, the knave Rubin and the servants Pusterbalk and Lasterbalk. The unqualified hero is Rubin.

The figure of Rubin, or Robin, may be related, on the one hand, to the Wild Man in fertility rites in the Teutonic age or perhaps to the leader of the wild herds in the death cult. On the other hand, in the sixteenth century his name describes a type of travelling apprentice or vagrant. In any case, the medieval spectator brought a wealth of connotations to the name Rubin. In the process of the play, the associations made by both Rubin and Pusterbalk (whom Rubin has won as knave) always refer to the fertility rites and cults of the pagan spring festival, ostarûn. Thus, from the begin-

ning, Rubin demands a reward for his services from the Doctor/Grocer:

> Sir, let's agree,
> and allow me that
> I should while away the time
> with your young wench
> who sits by the fire
> or my services are given too dear!
>
> (*Innsbruck* 587–92)

And Pusterbalk, who 'has a nose like a cat, is broad-shouldered and has a hunchback' (677–9) introduces his grotesque figure in this way:

> Sir, my name is Pastuche
> and I lie under the hedge
> when the shepherd is out herding in the fields:
> while his maid remains behind,
> then I throw her down
> and ruffle her feathers.
> My rubbing tangles her beard:
> I am called hunchback Eckart.
>
> (*Innsbruck* 682–9)

The way Eckhart appears to the woman he overpowers here is another version of the Wild Man, a hunter in the forest, known as Hacco. At the end of the scene, Rubin usually runs away with the Doctor's wife:

> *Rubinus dicit:*
> … now give me thy hand,
> I want to take you to a land,
> where the roasted goose walks about
> well-spiced with pepper,
> and a knife in its beak
> and herbs in its tail feathers.

> *Medica dicit:*
> Rubein, dear boy,
> you need not take me to school,
> the schoolmaster is a dreadful man,
> he taught me if I should ever
> come in the schoolhouse,
> I shall not come out the schoolhouse more as maid.

*Medica iterum dicit:*
Now, take good heed, my lords
and my ladies fine,
I have made a good exchange,
that for my old man
I have now a young one,
who springs from far away,
with whom I shall tumble
as long as my body keeps up;
if I do not tell a lie,
he stirs it in the works
to my heart's desire;
as never did the old bull.
I do not want to leave you
even if you have finished in the pot.

*Rubinus ducit dominam ad locum cantando:*
In the night, I was ill,
one could not find the path into the other,
today, God help us,
one must shove inside the other.

(*Erlau* 875–904)

Clearly, Rubin represents the sexual desire of youth and its victory over the impotence of age. Moreover, the motive of the old man points to the dying God of the Year, who is cursed by his wife 'you'll not last out the year' (*Innsbruck* 1020). The adultery of Rubin and Medica appears, therefore, to be a ritual marriage by which the fertility of man, beast and field is magically conjured at the pagan spring rites. The exhortation to buy herbs, lotions and skills from the Doctor and his Wife also point in a similar direction, as shown by Rubin and Pusterbalk:

*Pusterbalk ad populum:*
Listen to the teaching of my Lady,
whence comes great strength,
she is one of the best magicians,
on whom the sun shines forever:
if there is a young woman here,
whose husband has run off,
so my Lady can help her,
so that he'll come back speedily
in a short while,
even if he has already gone a hundred miles.
Also, if there is an old maid here

who has been ridden in the woods
at Whitsuntide by many,
whether priest or layman,
she should come to my Lady,
it will bring her great advantage,
she will sit her atop a rosary
and make her whole again,
so that she is like a maid as her mother was,
when she recovered from the birth of her
  third child.
You young maids take heed of me
and take each of you a young knave
at this Easter time,
and if you have not enough with one, then
  take three!

(*Erlau* 476–99)

Love potions, fertility and youth-bringing magic clearly represent Medica's particular speciality. Whether the Christian festival of resurrection returns here to the mythical world of pagan re-incarnation and fertility rituals remains open. In any case, the land of milk and honey (Cockaigne) and the repeated incitement to eat and drink certainly point to the unlimited confirmation of the vital functions of the human body. The affirmation of the magical renewal of vitality goes so far as to influence the scenes of the appearance of Christ and the racing disciples which follow. Jesus appears to Mary Magdalene as a gardener who criticises 'It is not right that pious women / run like knaves/ in the morning in the garden,/ as if they were waiting for boys' (*Sterzinger Osterspiel* 1420–40). He seems to grow precisely those herbs in his garden which the Grocer offers for sale as youth-bringing elixir:

I will share the roots with you,
the long ones and the short ones,
which the old women use
to chase away their wrinkles,
then they can wash with it
and come up as shiny as a beggar's bag.

Even if one does not go so far as to view this Jesus-hortulanus as the 'resurrected Christ and, at the same time, a pagan Year-God', 'who is re-born in the garden where he was buried at the time of Easter, the spring-like *ôstarûn*',[17] the relation presented between the resurrected body and the renewal of vitality (as youth regained) cannot be overlooked.

In the race of the disciples, which ends the play, the weakened vitality is revived through the 'flask':

*Johannes respondit:*
Peter, all your sickness
only needs this little flask!
If you hold it to your lips,
you will surely be healed.
And fill your gullet!
But it should never be forgotten:
you should eat a hard boiled egg.

*Petrus dicit:*
Trusted brother, I do not disagree!
It's not too much for me.
I want to keep the wine,
Or you shall ne'er be my brother!

*Johannes respondit:*
Grumbling and dumb!
That's my brother Peter:
Who takes a little flask of wine
for to keep him company.

*Et tunc porrigit sibi flasculum.*

*Johannes dicit:*
Brother Peter, I say to you:
You slurp a whole wine cart,
you can take a long swig,
but leave me something in the flask
so I've got something to wet my whistle with!
And let us discover the truth,
which Mary told.

*Petrus dicit:*
And now, on this occasion,
O, what a useful, noble ointment it is!
Before I was lame and hunchbacked,
now I am fresh and well!
Now look my dear Johannes,
and taste of this wine,
then let us race to the tomb
to see if Mary is right.

*Tunc Petrus et Johannes posthoc transeunt ad*
*sepulchrum cantates: Cernites, o socii!*
*(Sterzinger Osterspiel)*

In this way, the Easter Plays seem to culminate in the renewal of vitality, (as strengthening, rejuvenation, retrieval of virginity, fertility and procreative power). Man, exposed in the Easter Plays is, above all, identical with the vital functions of his body which is experienced as a body filled with lust and greed.

As Norbert Elias, Arno Borst, Robert Muchembled and others have shown, the urban and rural population in the Middle Ages had an uninhibited attitude to food and sexuality.[18] Provisions were hoarded only to be frittered away at the next opportunity for a feast. Feelings of shame were not extensively known, as is shown by the urban bath houses where men and women bathed and dined together. Even if the church marched into battle against gluttony and sexual excess, it did not seem to influence, let alone change, the behaviour of the people in any lasting way. A huge chasm divided the church laws and the attitudes and beliefs of society.

The Easter Plays succeeded in bridging this gap, at least momentarily. By positioning the Descensus ad inferos at the beginning, the action of the Redeemer, as releaser of souls, is shown to be the explicit precondition of how to act out one's own vitality without fear. Thus, because it was such an integral part of the clerical culture, it was sanctioned on a Christian basis – at least for the duration of the Easter festival. Vernacular and religious culture do not overlap in any way, but they do, at least, come close in a complementary relationship.

## The frail and tortured body

Although the Passion Play came about much later than the Easter Play, it did not develop from it. Nor can the old theory that the vernacular Passion Play drew upon a Latin model be upheld today. In fact, the few Latin Passion Plays which have survived seem to be degenerations of the vernacular play. The rise of the Passion Play can, in some individual cases, be traced back to the fourteenth and even the thirteenth century. But it did not become truly popular until the fifteenth and sixteenth centuries. Its greatest popularity was achieved at about the turn of the century, that is, around the year 1500.

The most widespread distribution of the Passion Play coincided, therefore, with a time of extraordinary mass movements, a time in which clerical and popular cultures seem to have engaged in a unique relationship with one another. Flagellators toured the country and carried out their ceremonies in public, mostly before huge crowds. Preachers who appealed to the masses to convert and announced the end of the world were extremely popular. Frequently, they could not even shake off the repentant crowds who followed them from town to town. In cities, people would run from church to church in order to take the Eucharist several times; court cases were even held to decide who should sit in the seat which had the best view of the altar. This was because many believed in the magical healing potential of witnessing the transformation at the Eucharist, which would guarantee long life, health and well-being. The belief in magic, which greatly defined the secular culture of the Middle Ages, and which even the confessional priests could not restrict despite repeated ecclesiastical punishments (as is recorded in the register of sins), seems, in all these cases, to have usurped the content and rituals of the Christian religion in such a way that it was impossible to separate the two entirely. It became impossible to divide cleanly between that which was just acceptable and that which was certainly unacceptable from an ecclesiastical point of view. Thus, a general ban was the only way the church could assert itself (such as the ban on public flagellation and abuses in the administration of the sacraments).

On the other hand, the era of the great Passion Play was also a time of segregation and persecution of Jews and witches. As early as 1290, the Jews were expelled from England; from France, from 1394. In German-speaking countries, Jews were forced to wear a 'Jew's hat' or a 'yellow patch'. In Augsburg in 1434, a decree was passed which ensured that Jews marked themselves as such by wearing a yellow *Ringel* (circle) on the front of their clothes and obliged Jewish women to wear tapered veils. In 1530, this order was extended to the entire German empire. Running almost parallel to these events was the spread across Europe of witch-hunts. In 1484 Pope Innocence VIII passed the Witch's Bull *Summis desiderantes affectibus* in which the most important misdeeds of witches and magicians were listed. The Pope also appointed Institoris and Sprenger as inquisitors in Germany. In 1487, they published the *Malleus maleficarum*, the so-called *Hexen-hammer* ('witch's hammer'), which concentrated on the persecution of witches.

It is only in this historical context that the immense popularity of the Passion Play of the fifteenth and sixteenth centuries can be understood. Like other mass movements of the time, it presented itself as an extraordinary mixture of elements of clerical and popular culture.

As with all the other religious plays, the Passion Plays find their textual models in the Bible and in liturgy, but also in books which derived from the mystic movement surrounding the Passion, which emphasised compassion, and personal empathy for Jesus the man, such as Bonaventura's *Itinerarium mentis in Deum*, Jacob of Milan's *Stimulus amoris*, Holy Birgitta of Sweden's *Revelationes* or the anonymous *Meditationes vitae Christi*, the *Dialogus beatae Mariae et Anselmi de passione domini* and the *Liber de passione Christi et doloribus et planctibus matris ejus*. These countless theological disputations drew upon theological texts, particularly the disputation between Ecclesia and Synagogue, which neither can, nor tries to, hide its religious origins. Moreover, the religious influence is particularly effective in those Passion Plays which are based on the doctrine of Satisfaction, as for example the reworking of the *Passion Plays of Arras* by Arnoul Gréban. This doctrine proposes that God's honour (*honor Dei*) has been tarnished by mortal sin and that evil can only be made good again by making amends, giving satisfaction, through punishment (*satisfactio aut poena*). Since punishment would upset the harmonious execution of God's plan of creation, the only way to give satisfaction is through the living sacrifice of the God-figure Jesus.

Anselm of Canterbury developed this doctrine in a treatise in 1098, *Cur Deus Homo*. It was taken up by theologians of the Western church from the thirteenth century with ever increasing interest and remained of great importance in the following centuries. It influenced the Passion Plays by placing the crucifix at the heart of all theological thought.

It is also likely that the countless Latin sections of the Passion Plays were both the result and evidence of the influence of religious culture. It is, however, more likely that such passages, which are put into the mouths of characters such as Pontius Pilate, Caiphus or Judas, were used and understood as magical formulas rather than as evidence of the 'holiness' of the various characters. The change in significance made by the Passion Plays, the usurping of elements which originally came from religious culture by a vernacular culture which was dominated by belief in magic, grew to such importance that it could hardly be tolerated by the church in this form.

Unlike the Easter Plays, the Passion Plays did not depend upon a fixed day of performance. The cities responsible for production mostly set the performance for a date when the weather would be favourable. Thus, in Frankfurt, the week after Whitsun was a frequently chosen date. The timing had to be carefully chosen since the plays lasted several days and during the performance period – sometimes including month-long preparations – the people's everyday and working lives were suspended. The long period of performance was necessary because of the huge wealth of material contained in the Passion Plays. Some stretched from the Creation of the world to the Last Judgement, others 'only' took into account the much shorter period from the birth of Christ to his death or resurrection. Many scenes were taken over from other plays, such as the Christmas and Easter plays, plays from the prophets and legends, and plays about Mary Magdalene and Lazarus, and worked into

the existing material. In all this variety, two scene patterns emerge which are generally accorded greater importance in the performance event. These are the scenes of Jesus among the people and the actual Passion scenes.

The three- or four-day event mostly took the following order:

*Day 1*: From the Creation of the world (or the birth of Christ) to the Last Supper.

*Day 2*: The Last Supper, taking Christ prisoner, Jesus before Annas, Caiphas and Pilate.

*Day 3*: The actual Passion up to depositing the corpse in the tomb.

*Day 4*: The Resurrection, descent into Hell (Easter Play) up to the ascension to Heaven or the pouring out of the Holy Spirit.

If the plays went on for longer, then the sections may have varied slightly, but the weight of significance always remained the same: the Passion consumes the most amount of time, and among the other groups, those which show Jesus among the people are particularly emphasised.

In many of the plays, this public display concentrates particularly on Jesus' miracles in healing the sick and awakening the dead. In the *Frankfurter Passionsspiel* (which was performed in 1467, 1492, 1498 and 1506), Jesus heals someone who is 'infirm' and someone who is 'lame' (489–512). He exorcises the daughter of the woman of Canaa (545–629); a deaf mute from possession by the devil (630–47); and heals someone blind from birth (683–923), a cripple (986–1007), a man suffering from dropsy (1008–19), a leper (114–27) and the fatally ill son of a king (1373–406). The high point of this sequence of miracles is undoubtedly the awakening of the dead Lazarus (1407–561).

The people whom Jesus encounters are defined by a physical fragility which makes them helpless in the face of sickness, infirmity and death. 'We are all fragile / and measured by human nature' (*Alsfelder Passionsspiel* 1446–7). The body, whose collapse man knows he must ultimately face, is at first experienced as something to be feared. The significance of Jesus is that he can transform frail and mortal human nature through 'joy and eternal life' (*Alsfeld*, 1203, 1229, 1249, 1542, 2251) into its opposite, and thus dissolve the fear which is fixed on the dangers which threaten the human body such as demons, devils and other mysterious things. This is represented in a particularly drastic way in the *Alsfelder Passionsspiel* (dates of performance are 1501, 1511 and 1517) at the awakening of the dead Lazarus. Here, Death appears and paints a picture of the rotting human body:

Lazarus, I am called Death!
I shall bring you great misery
and beat you with my club,
so that the worms may nibble at you!
No one can hide from me,
who has ever had a life on earth, ...

I shall shoot them with my bow and arrow,
so that the worms may enjoy their flesh,
and shall hunt them down with my clubs
so that the toads and snakes shall gnaw their
    bones! ...

*Et tunc immediate vertit se ad populum et
    dicit:*
Thus, death will strike you also!
The worms and your friends shall fight over
    you!
The evil spirits await the sinners' souls
to decide which part belongs to whom!
The friends take the goods and the kin,
while the worms consume the flesh in the
    grave!
That is all our belief!
No one should approach with pride!
God made you from the slime of the earth,
you shall turn again to ashes:
Death makes all things equal!
Whether rich or poor,
then I shall beat them with my clubs,
so that they'll have to be taken off to the
    graveyard!
I shall shoot them with my bow and arrow,
whether they are friends or have power:
I shall spare no one!
I shall reward them with these clubs,

as I did for Lazarus:
as it always has been!
    (*Alsfeld* 2155–60, 2175–8, 2188–204)

The same fears which made the folk preachers and flagellators at the end of the Middle Ages so popular and which drove some to abuse the administration of the sacraments, found their expression in the Passion Plays. These fears revolved around hunger, sickness, infirmity, death – in short, failings which endanger the survival of the human body and thus which directly imply the inescapable mortality of mankind. There is only one man who might be able to act effectively against it and ban such fears: Jesus Christ. Accordingly, when Death challenges him after he has been called back to life, Lazarus announces:

The almighty god from heaven did this!
From death he awakened me so powerfully
with his great mercy
and also with his commandments!
The worms had eaten me,
and I had turned to ashes in four days,
but then my soul unified with the corpore
    again!
Thus I will always praise and honour him!
    (*Alsfeld* 2301–8)

Thus, in an extraordinary way, Christian religious belief and popular magical concepts have become amalgamated. It is not a question of the eternal life of the soul after death, nor of renouncing earthly pleasures. It is a question of the magical reconstruction of the whole, intact body in the here and now. And, thus, it is hardly surprising that Jesus' healing methods are not that different from the magical folk practices of a miracle doctor or sage. Jesus heals a mute man by a magical formula which bans the spirits:

I conjure you up, you evil spirit,
as you well know,
that your evilness has inhabited long
in this human shell,
therefore, Jesus Christ commands you
that you leave the premises at once!
    (*Frankfurt* 636–41)

Jesus heals the leper through touch (*tangit leprosum*) and the cripple through laying on of hands (*imponat manum claudo*). He heals the blind man by covering his eyes with earth which he has previously mixed with his own spit. Simple magic alone can repair the sick, crippled or even already rotting body to its original condition and thus effectively exorcise the fear of frailty that threatens the human body.

Thus, the Passion Plays undergo an unusual conversion. They allow Jesus to appear as a magic miracle-healer or shaman who is, none the less, explicitly introduced and commented on as the healer and saviour of the Christian religion – as, for example, in the *Frankfurter Passionsspiel*, in which Augustine appears as a kind of theatre director. It is the Jews, on the other hand, who decry Jesus as a 'magician' because of his miracle-working (as, for example, in *Frankfurt* 1153 and *Alsfeld* 1574).

The magic belief in miracles in popular culture, which tries to restore the wholeness and intactness of the human body, is disguised as a belief in the miracles of the Christian church, accepted by and propagated by the church. In this, magical practices are hidden behind the figure of Jesus Christ which is sacrosanct to the church. In contrast, the derision which the church usually reserves for people who use these practices, is put into the mouths of the Jews who obstinately turn away from Jesus, who mercilessly persecute the 'magician' and, thus, are denied the salvation which the church prophesies. Here, too, vernacular culture has succeeded in usurping the concepts and contents of the Christian religion in such a skilful way that a clear distinction between religious and popular culture is barely possible.

The branding of Jesus as 'a magician' by the Jews explicitly refers to the two scene sequences containing Jesus' works in public and the Passion. Caiphas, Annas and other Jews standing before Pilate claim Jesus is a 'magician' (*Frankfurt* 2804–10, 3195–200; *Alsfeld* 3986–93) and suggest that his miracle-working is positive proof of this (*Frankfurt* 2957–66, 2973–4). On the way to Golgotha, Synagogue curses him again as a 'magician' who has been given all that he deserves:

Get up, you magician,
and take your false teaching
and let that help you carry
your cross on this day.

(Alsfeld 5316–9)

Even when Jesus is hanging on the cross, reference is made to his miracle-working as a 'magician',

Are you hanging well, now, you magician?
Are you light or heavy?
Other people, you wicked fool,
you helped, now help yourself too,
and step down from the wide gallows:
then we won't do you any more harm!

(Frankfurt 3859–64)

A unique ambivalence is produced in the torture and Passion scenes which perhaps explains, at least to a small extent, the incredible cruelty with which they are carried out. On the one hand, Jesus is cursed, tormented, tortured and killed as a magician who, through his magic practices, has halted the process of deterioration of the human body. For this reason, his body is now exposed to the same destructive powers which everyone who believes in magic, or practises it, fears – the same powers from which the body must be protected as far as possible. By taking the destruction onto his own body, Jesus acts as a kind of representative, protecting the bodies of the spectators who are present from the same destruction. He frees them of their fear that just such destruction might be turned on them. The more cruelly the torture is executed on the 'scapegoat', the greater the protection accorded the spectator's body in a magical way. On the other hand, it is the Jews and the devils who inspire them, who torment and torture Jesus. This is the reason why the cruelty they show to Jesus is damnable and demands Christian compassion for the one crucified. This aspect is always present, but only comes to the forefront after the torment, torture and crucifixion when the weeping Mary calls upon the spectators – particularly the mothers – to feel compassion for herself and her son.

The imprisonment of Jesus, the trial and the

crucifixion follow, as mentioned above, a cruel ritual in both the French and German Passion Plays. Jesus is cursed (*Frankfurt* 2426ff; *Alsfeld* 3434ff), spat upon (*Frankfurt* 2714ff, 2914ff, 3557ff; *Alsfeld* 5415ff) and beaten (*Frankfurt* 2463, 2544, 2596, 2629, 2913; *Alsfeld* 3557, 5415). A game is repeatedly played with him: his head is covered and he is asked to guess who is beating him (*Frankfurt* 2544–631; *Alsfeld* 3602–5, 4098–149) or who has pulled his hair and beard (*Frankfurt* 3560–4). These games are played in an explicitly ritual manner. They are accompanied by Latin formulas ('*Prophetiza nobis, Criste: quis est, qui te percussit?*') and each action (beating, hair-pulling) is carried out three times while the victim endures in silence. Again and again we hear the words 'Salvator tacet' (for example, *Frankfurt* 2756, 2760, 2856, 2864, 2868, 2884, 3253).

The next high point comes with the scourging of Jesus by Pilate's 'knights':

*Primus miles Schintekrae:*
… with whips and rod we shall beat him,
that he shall quite despair! …

we want to make sure we hit you on the spot,
and by beating make you so hot,
that you shall sweat bloody sweat!

*Secundus miles Rackenbein:*
Come here, Jesus, with me:
we want to beat up your
body right now!
Pity the day that you were born!
And I have never lived a happier day,
as now, because of his sheer wickedness,
to give him such a beating!
take off the robe and undress him!

*Et sic exuunt sibi tunicuam et ligant Jhesum ad statuam, et dicit tercius miles Riberbart habens virgas in brachio:*
Brother Ruckenbein, seek out
the best rod!
And you, Schintekrae,
you take two,
then, dear brothers:

we shall do it like the Jews,
and beat Jesus around the pillar,
that his feathers shudder like an owl!
If one of the rods should break,
do not be afraid,
and if you are tired,
then I'll come and help you at your side!

*Quartus miles Springendantz:*
Ay, how cruelly you beat him:
but you don't know how to do it properly!
Get off, you Ruck-and-bein:
I want to have a go alone
and smash his tool!
If the rods don't help then I'll take the whip!
*Et percucient flagellis.*
(*Frankfurt* 3424–57)

Finally, the four push the crown of thorns with all their might onto the head of their victim. Because Jesus seems hardly 'like a man' any more, Pilate stops the torture:

Ecce homo!
You Jews, look: is he like a man?
Now leave him alone, I beg you.
(*Frankfurt* 3521–1)

Synagogue, however, insists 'Crucifige, crucifige eum' (3526).

The ultimate moment of cruelty is reached at the crucifixion. The 'knights' have made the holes for the nails too far apart. They stretch Jesus' limbs with ropes so that he will fit the holes:

*Tercius miles:*
… bring me a blunt nail:
I shall hammer it into his hand!

*Secundus miles:*
Look here at the side:
this hole is too far away!
The hand cannot reach it:
I need a strong rope,
for to stretch the arms!
Come, friends, and help me to stretch!

*Quartus miles capit funem et dicit:*
Happily, my dear friend:

I shall help you as you please
to stretch him apart,
that his skin shall tear apart
and his veins course into one another!
Now pull, now pull, a bit more!
Hah, hah, that was good tugging!

*Et percuciatur secundus clavis*
(*Frankfurt* 3699–712)

The 'knights' refresh themselves with a mighty gulp from the bottle after this exhausting work, and the same procedure begins again on Jesus' feet.

*… quartus miles dicit:*
Have you already had a drink,
then put it down now and come back to work!
Look, I've got a rope, and not too small,
then throw it around his shin bone!
Stretch his limbs towards that hole!
Really, really what tugging!

*Secundus dicit et habet clavum et mallium in manu:*
Now pull a bit more!
The feet are stretched thus far:
then I can hammer the nail in
that the rogue must despair!
(*Frankfurt* 3729–38)

Finally, the cross is erected and the knights throw dice for Jesus' robe, screaming and cursing. The magical scapegoat ritual on the 'magician' Jesus is complete, the fear that violence could easily be applied to the bodies of the spectators in a similar way is effectively banished. Now in conclusion, the Christian *compassio* can be evoked in the Passion scenes, when we hear Mary's complaint and the heavy burden that her son, and she for his sake, must bear.

The scenes of miracle-healing and the Passion obviously met a deep-rooted need in the spectators, for they saw or understood themselves to be *sub specie corporis* and believed that magic was the only effective means of guaranteeing the wholeness and intactness of the body. Whilst generally speaking, magical practice by a miracle-worker might effectively provide help for the individual body in danger of personal disasters, such as illness, frailty, infirmity or death, dangers which threatened the communal body – such as sorcery – could only be exorcised by social magic, that is, by a scapegoat ritual. The body, which determined the individual as individual, and which led him to understand himself as man, was, in both cases, experienced as something to be deeply feared. The Passion Plays became popular mass events because they were able to give lasting relief from the pressure of the fears burdening the body.

## The end of the plays: the suppression of popular culture

The powerful effect of the religious plays on the spectator was without doubt brought about by the unique relationship between the players and the spectators. There were no professional actors, and a spectator at one performance might appear as an actor in the next performance and vice versa. Thus, in medieval theatre, the terms 'actor' and 'spectator' referred to roles which existed for a short amount of time – the length of one performance. Moreover, the roles were interchangeable. In turn, this resulted in a certain kind of spectatorship. The spectator did not attend the performance in order to make an aesthetic judgment. Thus, in the *Sterzinger Passionsspiel* the Precursor warns:

Therefore, be solemn in God today and do not go about cursing and mocking, as one sees in some boorish men; if one of them notices that someone has made a slip in the text, he mocks him and derides the performance. One should not really do that; for the actors only take on their roles to honour Jesus Christ, not for fun, and certainly not out of boyish mischief, which is how some people behave, though it does not suit them at all. Rather, the actor plays for the sake of God and the suffering of Jesus Christ, so that through this play, every man who absorbs himself in it is moved to far deeper devotion than he would be by the mere narration of the words alone.[19]

Spectator and actor were gathered 'in the service of God'[20] and the performance began either early in the morning (six o'clock, in Alsfeld and Lucerne) or at midday (Frankfurt) with communal prayers and hymns and also ended with a communal parting hymn 'Christ is Risen'. Consequently, the effect on spectator and actor was the same. It is described by the Second Angel in the Redentin Easter Play when he announces the play:

Sit down and enjoy yourselves,
those who are gathered here.
Be joyous at this time:
you can free yourself of sin.
Now God will save all those
who give up evil.
Those who rise up with God,
they shall leave this place free of sin.
In order that all this can happen to you,
each one of you must listen and watch![21]

The performance functions as a kind of sacrament which seems to have a magical effect on all those who participate. It is considered 'a "good work" which is automatically tied to the granting of divine mercy'.[22] Here we find an extraordinary amalgamation between beliefs sanctioned by the church and the magic concepts and practices of popular culture.

It would appear that the church attempted to suppress belief in magic totally by passing a ban on the flagellation ceremonies and abuse of the Mass; but in the case of religious plays, it tried to integrate such beliefs into the framework of religious culture. Mainly because it acknowledged attendance at a religious play as a pious work, and actors and spectators were often granted indulgences; generally to the scale of one Quadragene (a forty-day fast on bread and water in return for divine grace), sometimes, however, on a larger scale: in Lucerne in 1556, seven years and seven Quadragenes were handed down and in Calw, in 1502, 240 years![23]

The readiness of the church to tolerate the popular belief in magic manifested in and by the religious play, which it tried to suppress altogether in the case of flagellation ceremonies and the abuse of the Mass, may be a result of the fact that the plays were less a part of religious culture and more an integral element of urban festival culture. The festival, with its sparkling civic self display to visitors from home and abroad, offered many freedoms which had no place in the everyday city life and which were otherwise unacceptable, as is shown by the amnesty which ruled for the duration of the festivities. The religious play of the late Middle Ages developed into an opportunity for people to display a form of piety that was steeped in the belief in magic. At other times, such belief in magic would not be tolerated by the church and was generally attacked.

The immense popularity of the religious play, particularly the Passion Play, among the urban European population continued unbroken throughout the sixteenth century. However, suddenly at the end of the century, the religious play practically disappeared from all large cities in Europe and, although a few individual plays survived in rural and isolated mountain regions sometimes into the seventeenth and even into the eighteenth centuries, the sudden decrease cannot have been the result of a fundamental change in the tastes of the spectators. The guilds would certainly have continued to perform if they had been allowed.

As early as 1515, an application to perform a Passion Play in Frankfurt was turned down by the city council. Yet, up until 1506, the council had allowed gerüstholz (scaffolding) to be erected for performances, even subsidised the gemeynschaft (guild) which performed the plays at the Römer Square and feasted together with the guild at a great malezyt (feast) afterwards.

In 1522, the Passion Plays were banned in Nuremberg. In Canterbury, the last performances occurred in 1500, and in Beverly in 1520. In 1534, the Bishop of Evora in Portugal forbade the performance of any play in general unless it was given a special licence, 'even if they represent the Passion of our Lord Jesus Christ, His resurrection or Nativity ... because from these plays arises much that is unfitting ['muitos inconvenientes'], and they frequently give scandal to those who are not very firm in our holy Catholic faith, when they see the disorders and excesses of these plays.'[24]

From the middle of the century, the state and church authorities increased the number of bans. In 1548, the Parliament of Paris made an edict which forbade any further performance by the Passion Play guilds (however, they were allowed to perform once more in 1557, and this permission was repeated in 1577). By the end of the 1540s, the religious play had vanished from Florence, although texts of traditional vernacular plays were still being published until the end of the sixteenth century. In 1565, the Archbishop Karl Borromeo of Milan held a diocesan synod whose sole purpose was to ban the performance of religious plays.

Quoniam pie introducta consuetudo representandi populo reverendam Christi Domini Passionem et gloriosa Martyrum certamina, aliorumque Sanctorum res gestas, hominum perversitate eo deducta est, at multis offensioni, multis etiam risui et despectui sit, ideo statuimus ut deinceps Salvatoris Passio nec in sacro nec in profano loco agatur, sed docte et graviter eatenus a conciona-toribus exponatur ... Item, Sanctorum martyria et actiones ne agantur, sed ita pie narrentur, ut audi-tores ad eorum imitationem ... excitentur.[25]

In 1578, the Archbishop of Bologna denounced plays altogether, and in 1583, the Council of Reims banned any kind of performance on festival days. In 1557, the Reformed Church of Scotland felt obliged to take serious steps against the performance of plays at Corpus Christi in Perth:

becaws certane inhabitantis of yis town alsweill aganis ye expres commandment of ye ciuill magistratts in cownsall as aganis ye Ministeris prohibitoun in pulpitt hes playit corpus christeis play upon thursday ye vj of Junij last quhilk day ves vount to be callit corpus christeis day to ye great sklander of ye kirk of god and dishonour to yis haill town. And becaws ye said play is idola-trous superstitiows and also sclanderows alsweill be ressoun of ye Idell day.[26]

In 1601, the government in the Spanish Nether-lands released an edict against religious plays because they contained 'many useless things, dis-honourable and intolerable, serving for nothing but to deprave and corrupt morals ... especially those of simple and good people whereby the common people are shocked or led astray'.[27]

Similar objections were continually raised against the plays. Thus, the Lollard 'Tretise of miracles pleying' accused them of being an excuse for gluttony, drunkenness and pleasure-taking, and even the Minorite, William Melton, who basically meant well towards the plays, complained that in York the local citizens and visitors to the plays had dishonoured the city with their 'revellings, drunkenness, shouts, songs and other insolences'.

Scholars are in general agreement that the Reformation was the principal cause for the abrupt end of the religious plays. Indeed, many Reformist records damning the religious plays have survived. Erasmus wanted to ban them entirely because they contained 'traces of ancient paganism' and because of the opportunity they create to 'shake off the moral bridle'.[28] Luther concentrated on forbidding the playing of the Passion Plays because they evoked a dangerous, false attitude to the Passion of the Lord in the spectators, 'And third, they feel empathy for Christ, bewail him and lament him as an inno-cent man, just like women, ... they should lament their own plight and that of their children.'[29]

It should be noted, however, that in those cities which turned earlier to Protestantism, the plays ended long before those in deeply Catholic Tirol or Bavaria, for example. But even here, as across the rest of Catholic Europe, the religious plays had more or less vanished by the end of the sixteenth century.

On the other hand, it should not be over-looked that the Council of Trent, which was called into being in reaction to the Reformation, was not concerned about vernacular religious plays. Though the Council did prepare the end of the liturgical Easter and Christmas celebra-tions, which were developed from the tropes, by banishing tropes from the liturgy, it made no comment expressis verbis on the religious plays. The official position of the Catholic church which might imply a ban on religious plays was never articulated.

Thus, it would be wise to seek other reasons

for what might have caused the general banning of the plays, besides the Reformation alone. This would seem all the more urgent when one takes into account that from 1500, more so after 1550, – that is, parallel to the decline of the religious plays – a process was begun throughout Western Europe which led to the absolute suppression of vernacular culture, as Robert Muchembled and Peter Burke have so convincingly explained.[30]

The most important argument against the plays was always the 'superstition' which they contained and propagated and the 'immoral behaviour' such superstition encouraged. Through our analysis of the Easter and Passion Plays, it cannot be denied that a belief in magic does indeed exist. The spectator experiences his self, above all, in and through his body, a body which is possessed with either lust or fear, according to various magical effects: if it is the 'black magic' of the devil and demons, the body will be overcome by illness, fragility, infirmity, violence and death. If the so-called 'white magic' of wise women, miracle-healers and Christian saints is at work, he will be re-created in his wholeness and intactness and his vitality fundamentally renewed. The body is, in both cases, totally dependent upon the workings of magic. Within the boundaries set by magic, however, the spectator can use his body with relative freedom. Neither the worldly nor religious authorities have the power to limit the way an individual controls his own body.

The growing suppression of popular culture in the sixteenth century across Europe aimed to change this situation. As Robert Muchembled has shown in France (and in the rest of Europe it would have been the same), sexual repression in the urban and rural population began in 1500 and became increasingly powerful around 1550. Extra-marital and 'abnormal' sexual relations were directly persecuted from then on. In 1556, the king passed a law which threatened women with death if they should attempt 'to abort the fruit of their wombs'. The body of the individual from this moment was seen as belonging to the state.

This goal was also reflected in a decisive change in the handing down of punishments.

Whilst in legal archives between 1300 and 1500 there are hardly any references to bodily mutilations, a drastic increase in physical and pain-inflicting punishments can be found in the sixteenth century: amputation of the ears and hands, piercing of the tongue, gouging out the eyes, shaving or burning hair, branding with a white-hot iron, or whipping at the stocks. 'The body is impressed with the seal of power and even suicides are punished in that their bodies are hung on the gallows as a sign of their shame … As the formula of the apology of Arras prophesied, the body of each individual belongs first of all to God, the King and the Law before its actual owner may dispose of it.'[31]

The witch trials, which spread across Europe from the mid-sixteenth century, also point in the same direction. Whilst in England between 1400 and 1500 there were only 38 trials against witches and magicians, in France 95 and in Germany 80, for the period between 1570 and 1630 in the south-west of the German Empire alone, there exist records of at least 363 trials and 2471 death sentences. Here, the urban and rural belief in magic was mercilessly put on trial. Blown up from secular and religious trials into the satanic religion of the Antichrist, the people's belief in the magic of the human body was systematically brought into disrepute, persecuted, punished and stamped out. The scapegoat ritual of the Passion Play became ineffective; the urban and rural population fell victim to witch-hunts. After the Passion Play was wiped out, belief in magic and the secular culture on which it was based almost ceased to exist. The souls and bodies of the people had become controllable.

It is only in the context of this comprehensive development that the disappearance of the religious play from public life in European cities in the course of the sixteenth century can be understood. The 'civilising process' (Norbert Elias), which had already begun a little earlier among the social élite, now began to affect everyone. Since the image of man propagated by the religious plays opposed this image, the plays were forced to yield to it, despite stubborn resistance from the ordinary citizen.

# 2   *Theatrum vitae humanae*

## THEATRE AS LABORATORY – MAN AS EXPERIMENT

### 'All the world's a stage'

In Elizabethan England, the founding of the first public and commercial theatre run by professional actors' companies coincided approximately with the end of the religious plays. In Coventry, the complete cycle that was typical of the Passion and Corpus Christi Play was performed for the last time in 1580. In theory, Shakespeare could have seen such performances in his youth. In 1576, James Burbage built the first permanent professional public theatre, the Theatre, in London's Shoreditch. It was followed in a relatively short space of time by several others: in 1577 performances were given at the Curtain; 1587, the Rose; 1595, the Swan; 1599, the Globe (which was principally played by the Chamberlain's/King's Men, the troupe to which Shakespeare belonged); 1600, the Fortune; and 1605, the Red Bull. Each of these theatres was situated either south of the River Thames in Southwark or north of the city boundaries. From the start, the city fathers of London took a decisive position on public theatres. In a similar tone to that used by church leaders and city fathers in all large cities in Europe, who from the beginning of the sixteenth century repeatedly turned against religious plays because they contained and propagated things which they considered to be 'immoral', the London city patriarchs also accused the theatre of promoting 'immorality'. On 3 November 1594, the Mayor of London wrote a letter to Westminster on the subject of contemporary drama:

> the same, conteining nothing ells but vnchast fables, lascivious divises shifts of cozenage & matters of lyke sort, which ar so framed & represented by them that such as resort to see & hear the same … drave the same into example of imitation & not avoiding the sayed lewed offences.

At this time, Marlowe's *Tamburlaine* and *Doctor Faustus* were being performed again at The Rose. On 13 September, the new Mayor of London wrote to Westminster that the plays contained

> nothing but profane fables, Lascivious matters, cozonning devizes, & other unseemly & scurrilous behaviours, which ar so sett forthe; as that they move wholy to imitacion & not to the avoyding of those vyces which they represent.

In 1595, *Romeo and Juliet* and *Richard II* were brought into the repertoire. On 28 July 1597, a third Mayor of London sent a third letter to the government. He, too, complained that the plays still consisted of

> nothing but prophane fables, lascivious matters, cozeninge devise, & scurrilus beehaviours, which are so set forth as that they move wholie imitation & not to avoydinge of those faults & vices which they represent.

In this year, *Henry IV* was first performed. Clearly, the moral criticisms of the plays had little to do with the dramas which were actually performed in public. Equally invalid was the political argument that the theatre encouraged rebellion, rioting and a multitude of other crimes because of the numbers of people gathered there, as the Mayor of London maintained in the same letter (28 July 1597). He suggested the theatre was a place for 'contrivers of treason and other idele and dangerous persons to meet together ... and what further danger may bee occaisioned by the broyles plotts or practises of such unrulie multitude of people yf they should gett head, your wisdome cann conceive'.

Surviving documents cannot confirm such fears were ever realised. The judicial authorities dealt with only one case in Middlesex in 1600, which concerned a crime that had occurred in the Curtain; and after that, only once more in 1610. In 1613, there was a case of stabbing at the Fortune theatre (at the same time, in London, there were 11 murders, 12 cases of manslaughter, 28 cases of violent attacks, 3 sword fights and 7 attacks on officers; 72 men and 4 women were condemned to hang to death).

What can be confirmed, however, is the economic argument of the city authorities that the performances led to a 'drawing of the artificers and common people from their labour', that thousands of pennies would be withdrawn from trade and nearby shops and instead would pour into the theatre box offices and affect the competition amongst traders, as Henry Chettle complained in 1592,

Is it not a great shame, that the houses of retaylors near the Townss end, should be by their continuance impouerished: Alas good hearts, they pay great rentes; and pittie it is but they be provided for. While Playes are vsde, halfe the day is by most youthes that have libertie spent vppon them, or at least the greatest company drawne to the places where they frequent. If they were supprest, the flocke of yoong people would bee equally parted. But now the greatest trade is brought into one street. Is it not as faire a way to Myle-end by White-chappell, as by Shorditch to

Hackney? the Sunne shineth as clearly in the one place, as in the other.

Although the city fathers and voices from the pulpits repeatedly railed against the theatre, the public still flocked to performances. Around 1595, the population in London was approximately 150,000. The two acting companies which played the theatres at the time were visited by approximately 15,000 spectators. According to the size of theatre, and from the records of takings which assume the capacity of the theatre to be about 2,500 people and an average attendance to be about 50 per cent, it is estimated that approximately 15 to 20 per cent of the population must have regularly gone to the theatre.

The theatre audience was made up of different social classes. The cheapest places (standing in the 'pit') cost 1 pence – as much as a pint of beer – the plain seats in the gallery cost 2 pence and the most expensive seats, 3 pence (as much as a pipe-full of tobacco or the cheapest dinner at a *table d'hôte*). Other than beggars, pedlars, delivery men or gravediggers, a visit to the theatre was within the reach of most Londoners. Accordingly, the audience was composed of a representative cross-section of the London population: apprentices and students from London University, members and employees of the 'Inns', the largest juridical corporation, craftsmen and traders with their families, seamen, merchants, scholars, members of the lower aristocracy and courtiers. From beer-tapper to prince, every social class was represented. Women visited the public theatres as well as men. For the Puritans, this was reason enough to accuse the theatre of being obscene and to brand women who went to the theatre as whores. In the *Second and Third Blast of Retrait from Plaies and Theatres* (1580), it states:

Whosoever shal visit the chappel of Satan, I meane the Theatre, shal finde there no want of yong ruffins, nor lacke of harlots, utterlie past al shame: who presse to the fore-frunt of the scaffoldes, to the end to showe their impudencie, and to be an object to al mens eies. Yea, such is their open shameless behaviour, as everie man maie perceave by their wanton gestures, wherevnto they are given; yea, they seeme there to be like brothels of the stewes. For often without respect of the place, and company which behold them, they commit that filthines openlie, which is horrible to be done in secret; as if whatsoever they did, were warranted.

Foreign visitors to the public theatres, however, took no offence at the presence of women in the audience. In 1599, Thomas Platter from Basle reported that the English audience in London spent their time 'learning at the play what is happening abroad; indeed men and womenfolk visit such places without scruple, since the English for the most part do not travel much, but prefer to learn foreign matters and take their pleasures at home.'

In 1602, Duke Philip Julius von Stettin-Pommern wrote in his travel journal on the London audience:

there are always a good many people present, including many respectable women because useful argumenta, and many good doctrines, as we were told, are brought forward there.

And in 1614, the Venetian Ambassador wrote about London's theatres:

These theatres are frequented by a number of respectable and handsome ladies, who come freely and seat themselves among the men without the slightest hesitation.[1]

These eyewitness accounts are hardly evidence that the audience of the public theatre was composed of lazy, immoral rebellious and criminal elements. Instead, it confirms the expectation that it represented a cross-section of London society, from which only the very poor and sectarian Puritans were excluded.

If, therefore, the plays performed were not immoral and the audience did not consist of lazy or rebellious elements who had nothing else in mind but to use the theatre as a welcome opportunity to promote obscenities, crimes and rioting, why did the city fathers and the church insist on accusing them of such motives? And why did Londoners attend the theatre in such numbers and so regularly? Which needs were actually satisfied by the theatre?

Both opponents and followers of theatre were united in the belief that theatre had the potential to influence people in a lasting way. In *Anatomy of Abuses* (1583), the Puritan, Philip Stubbs, recommended a theatre visit with biting irony, 'if you will learn falsehood; if you will learn cosenage; if you will learn to deceive; if you will learn to play the Hipocrite, to cogge, lye and falsifie', but in *Apology for Actors* (1612), Thomas Heywood recommended the theatre as a highly effective moral institution:

playes have made the ignorant more apprehensive, taught the unlearned the knowledge of many famous histories, instructed such as cannot read in the discovery of all our English chronicles ... for or because playes are writ with this ayme, and carryed with this methode, to teach the subjects obedience to their king, to shew the people the untimely ends of such as have moved tumults, commotions, and insurrections, to present them with the flourishing estate of such as live in obedience, exhorting them to allegeance, dehorting them from all trayterous and fellonious stratagems. ... If we present a tragedy, we include the fatall and abortive ends of such as commit notorious murders, which is aggravated and acted with all the art that may be to terrifie men from the like abhorred practises. If wee present a forreigne history, the subject is so intended, that in the lives of Romans, Grecians, or others, either the vertues of our countrymen are extolled, or their vices reproved; as thus, by the example of Caesar to stir souldiers to valour and magnamity; by the fall of Pompey that no man trust in his own strength: we present Alexander, killing his friend in his rage, to reprove rashnesse; Mydas, choked wih his gold, to taxe covetousnesse; Nero against tyranny; Sardanapalus against luxury; Ninus against ambition, with infinite others, by sundry instances either animating men to noble attempts, or attacking the consciences of the spectators, finding themselves toucht in presenting the vices of others. If a morall, it is to perswade men to humanity and good life, to instruct them in civility and good manners, shewing them the fruits of honesty, and the end of villainy.

Both Stubbs' and Heywood's arguments relied on the fact that the relationship between theatre and life was generally accepted and that the reader was also familiar with this parallel. The metaphor of life as a performance, or the world as theatre, was, for the Elizabethans, a stock phrase in the repertoire of common concepts present in English drama since the 1560s which obviously found rapid and broad popularity. In a drama by the Oxford scholar, Richard Edward, *The Excellent Comedie of the two most faithfullest Freendes, Damon and Pithias* from 1565, for example, the eponymous hero, Damon, at the beginning of the drama explains his desire to go for a walk in the following way:

Pithagoras said, that this world was like a
  Stage,
Wheron many play their partes: the lookers
  on, the sage
Phylosophers are, saith he, whose parte is to
  learne
The maners of all Nations, and the good
  from the bad to discerne.

Shakespeare made great use of the theatre as metaphor; it appears in all his dramas from *Henry VI* to *The Tempest*. It was not for nothing that the motto which hung over the entrance to the Globe was said to read: 'Totus mundus agit histrionem'. The theatre metaphor was clearly of great significance to the Elizabethans.

The Elizabethan age was, in some ways, an era of transition. Fundamental medieval concepts of man, the world and the universe were still valid and widely accepted; in many fields, however, insecurity began to appear and some crises did erupt. One of the traditional concepts which maintained its validity was that of the great 'Chain of Being' and the theory of analogy or correspondence. The description provided by Higden, the Monk of Chester, in the second volume of the *Polychronicon* on the Chain of Being continued to determine Elizabethan thinking:

In the universal order of things the top of an inferior class touches the bottom of a superior; as for instance oysters, which, occupying as it were the lowest position in the class of animals, scarcely rise above the life of plants, because they cling to the earth without motion and possess the sense of touch alone. The upper surface of the earth is in contact with the lower surface of water; the highest part of the waters touches the lowest part of the air, and so by a ladder of ascent to the outermost sphere of the universe. So also the noblest entity in the category of bodies, the human body, when its humours are evenly balanced, touches the fringe of the next class above it, namely the human soul, which occupies the lowest rank in the spiritual order.

Since the Chain of Being makes relationships between all living things, changes on one level have an effect on all other levels. This is particularly true of the relations between microcosm and macrocosm. In *Treatise of the Laws of Ecclesiastical Polity* (1593), Richard Hooker presents the laws of analogy in the following way:

Now the due observation of this law which reason teacheth us cannot but be effectual unto their great good that observe the same. For we see the whole world and each part thereof so compacted that, as long as each thing performeth only that work which is natural unto it, it thereby preserveth both other things and also itself. Contrariwise, let any principal thing, as the sun the moon any one of the heavens or the elements, but once cease or fail or swerve; and who doth not easily conceive that the sequel therof would be ruin both to itself and whatsoever dependeth on it? And is it possible that man, being not only the noblest creature in the world but even a very world in himself, his transgressing the law of his nature should draw no manner of harm after it?

Even if these medieval ideas were still alive in Elizabethan times (ideas which seem to us in some ways animistic, vital and even magically orientated), they took on a different value. For, in the meantime, some important changes had been taking place in many areas. Many of these changes had to do with man, his position in society, in the cosmos and in relation to God, with his experience and cognitive faculty. For example:

- Greater social mobility within Elizabethan society made the social position of the individual less dependent on the class into which he was born and more on his own abilities and achievements.
- The Reformation challenged the idea of guaranteed salvation through doing good deeds and questioned the concept of God's mercy. Not good deeds alone, but only through close exploration of the conscience could the individual clear his conscience and his own guilt; the question of salvation must remain open until the Day of Judgement.
- The confrontation with the opposition between appearance and reality provoked a growing awareness of the relativity of human perception. This manifested itself in a particularly impressive way in Copernicus' discovery which invalidated the Ptolomaic image of the world which had held for centuries. It was made public to Elizabethan contemporaries in several articles, for example, Thomas Digges' *A Perfit Description of the Coelestiall Orbes, according to the most ancient doctrine of the Pythagoreans: lately revived by Copernicus and by Geometricall Demonstrations approved*, which appeared in 1576, though it did not achieve widespread popularity. The consequences this had in terms of the concept of the status of man are, none the less, abundant in much of the writing of Shakespeare's time.

All these changes made English renaissance man question his identity – something which had been secure for so many centuries. That which had determined and created the self was now no longer valid. The old identity was relinquished, but a new one was yet to be discovered. In this situation, on the one hand, many treatises on self-awareness were published – such as John Frith's *A Mirror or Glasse to Know Thyself* (c. 1533), Sir John Davies' *Nosce Teipsum* (1599) and Phillipe de Mornay's *The True Knowledge of a Mans Owne Self* (translated into English in 1602) – and on the other hand, public theatre performances increased. This was the reason behind the popularity of the theatre and the metaphor of the theatre. Thus, in Bouistuan's work, *Theatrum Mundi. The Theatre or Rule of the World, wherein may be seene the running race and course of every mans life, as touching miserie and felicity*, published in 1581, it states, 'In this Theatre thou maist see and beholde all the universall world thou maist first see thy selfe what thou art.'

The theatre quickly became the complete symbol and image of the world because in the tension between reality and illusion it made the opposition between reality and appearance constitutive and fruitful and, on the other hand, the search for identity in the tension between actor and role could be thematised, reflected and played out.

If, finally, we return to the question as to what drove the people in Elizabethan times to the theatre, it may perhaps be answered in this way: theatre appeared to the spectator as the ideal place in which he could playfully give himself up to the search for identity and experiment with and enact new identities. As a place and medium where identity could be developed, the theatre could be sure of great social importance in such transitional times. Since Elizabethan theatre presented very different identities and, thus, raised and dealt with the question of the search for a new identity openly, it must inevitably draw the hostility of the Puritans: it represented precisely the wide range of possibilities of choice they wanted to restrict. For they had made their choice and determined an identity for themselves once and for all.

Among the Elizabethan dramatists, however, it was mainly Shakespeare who used the stage as a 'laboratory' in which the question of man's identity could be tried out in an experimental manner. He not only raised this question in different ways in different genres, but even found new solutions in different dramas of the same genre. Of the multiplicity of possible solutions on which he meditated and presented to the audience, only three examples will be examined and discussed here: the history, *Richard III* (1592); the comedy, *A Midsummer Night's Dream* (1595); and the tragedy, *King Lear* (1605).

## Creator and destroyer of the self

At the end of the sixteenth century, the histories were one of the most popular dramatic genres. They drew their material from the annals of English history, principally from Edward Halle's *The Union of the Two Noble and Illustre Families of Lancaster and York* of 1548, and Raphael Holinshed's *Chronicles of England, Scotland and Ireland*, which was published in 1577 and reprinted as soon as 1587.

Whilst in the Middle Ages history was principally understood through an interpretation which stressed God's saving grace and, thereby, as the history of mankind, from the beginning of the sixteenth century there arose in England a new desire to record a national history. This development may have been the result of a steadily growing national awareness in England, but it also encouraged the same national feeling. In 1588, when the English fleet defeated the Spanish Armada, national emotion was already so firmly established that the event lifted patriotic feeling to great heights. The dramatists recognised the signs of the times: the history play seemed excellently suited to satisfy the growing need to see England's national greatness celebrated and, equally, to warn impressively of the dangers which could grow out of national ignorance and complacency. The representation of events from English history meant that the theatre could develop in the spectator a feeling, or awareness of national identity, and confirm and encourage it.

Shakespeare's historical plays attained this effect in that they principally presented historic events in terms of how they related to the identity of the king and how kingship affected them in return. They were based on the then widespread concept of 'The King's Two Bodies'.

The Elizabethan legal scholar, Edmund Plowden, formulated this concept in 1588 in French (translated into English in 1799) in the following way:

> For the King has in him two Bodies, viz., a Body natural, and a Body politic. His Body natural (if it be considered in itself) is a Body mortal, subject to all Infirmities that come by Nature or Accident, to the Imbecility of Infancy or old Age, and to the like Defects that happen to the natural Bodies of other People. But his Body politic is a Body that cannot be seen or handled, consisting of Policy and Government, and constituted for the Direction of the People, and the Management of the public weal, and this body is utterly void of Infancy, and old Age, and other natural Defects and Imbecilities, which the Body natural is subject to, and for this Cause, what the King does in his Body politic, cannot be invalidated or frustrated by any Disability in his natural Body … [the Body politic] is not subject to Passions as the other is, nor to Death, for as to this Body the King never dies, and his natural Death is not called in our Law … the Death of the King, but the Demise of the King, not signifying by the Word (Demise) that the Body politic of the King is dead, but that there is a Separation of the two Bodies, and that the Body politic is transferred and conveyed over from the Body natural now dead, or now removed from the Dignity royal, to another Body natural. So that it signifies a Removal of the Body politic of the King of his Realm from one Body natural to another.

The concept of the two bodies of the king theoretically opened the possibility that both might appear in opposition to one another; thus two cases are possible:

1 The body politic is legitimately transferred to another member of the royal family, the body natural is not mature enough to fulfil the standards set by the office of kingship.

2 A member of the royal family possesses a body natural which would ideally be in the position to fulfil the duties of king, but the illegitimacy of his claim distances him

from the body politic, which he seeks to usurp illegally.

In both cases, the identity of the king is split. Shakespeare shapes this tension in the histories, from *Henry VI* (1590/1) to *Henry V* (1599), through the theatre metaphor, as the tension between the person as actor and the role he plays. Whilst the player-kings such as Henry VI or Richard II are given the role of king, they only know how to wear the costume and handle the props and do not know how to play their roles; usurpers such as Richard of York or Bolingbroke, however, appear ideally cast to take on the role of king, but are prevented from this by the law. Shakespeare uses the image of actor and role first as theatrical interpretation of the concept of the two bodies of the king and then develops it into a complete metaphor for kingship.

He uses this metaphor extensively in *Richard III*. The figure of Richard as actor has already been introduced in the third part of *Henry VI*:

Why, I can smile, and murder while I smile,
And cry 'Content!' to that that grieves my
  heart,
And wet my cheeks with artificial tears,
And frame my face to all occasions. ...

I'll play the orator as well as Nestor,
Deceive more slily than Ulysses could,
And, like a Sinon, take another Troy.
I can add colours to the chameleon,
Change shapes with Proteus for advantages,
And set the murderous Machiavel to school.
(*Henry VI*, Part 3, III, 2, 182–93)[2]

Richard of Gloucester possesses a highly developed awareness of the theatricality of his actions and entrances. In the course of the plays *Henry VI*, Part 3 and *Richard III*, he says of himself: 'I play ... the orator' (*Henry VI*, III, 2, 188), 'the dog' (*Henry VI*, V, 6, 77), 'the devil' (*Richard III*, I, 3, 338), 'the maid's part' (III, 7, 51) and the 'eavesdropper' (V, 3, 222). Until Richard is crowned (in IV, 1), the entire *Richard III* seems to be a sequence of playlets and scenes which

Richard has devised, produced and directed, and in which he mainly plays the leading role.

His first 'play' is called 'The Enemy Brothers' and leads to Clarence's death:

Plots have I laid, inductions dangerous,
By drunken prophecies, libels, and dreams,
To set my brother Clarence and the King
In deadly hate, the one against the other:
(I, 1, 32–5)

The next play might bear the title: 'The Languishing and Ingenious Lover'. Here, Richard plays the leading role; he courts Lady Anne whose husband and father-in-law he has murdered. First he appears as the Petrarchan lover:

ANNE: Out of my sight! Thou dost infect
  mine eyes.
RICHARD: Thine eyes, sweet lady, have
  infected mine.
ANNE: Would they were basilisks, to strike
  thee dead.
RICHARD: I would they were, that I might die
  at once;
For now they kill me with a living death.
(I, 2, 152–6)

Next, Richard takes on the part of the repentant sinner:

Lo here I lend thee this sharp-pointed sword,
Which if thou please to hide in this true
  breast,
And let the soul forth that adoreth thee, I lay
  it naked to the deadly stroke,
And humbly beg the death upon my knee
*[Kneels; he lays his breast open, she offers at it
  with his sword]*
Nay, do not pause, for I did kill King Henry –
But 'twas thy beauty that provoked me.
Nay, now dispatch: 'twas I that stabbed young
  Edward –
But 'twas thy heavenly face that set me on.
*[She falls the sword]*
Take up the sword again, or take up me.
(I, 2, 178–87)

Richard acts with overwhelming success, for Anne accepts his courtship:

Was ever woman in this humour woo'd?
Was ever woman in this humour won?
I'll have her, but I will not keep her long.
What, I that kill'd her husband and his father:
To take her in her heart's extremest hate,
With curses in her mouth, tears in her eyes,
The bleeding witness of her hatred by,
Having God, her conscience, and these bars
  against me –
And I no friends to back my suit at all
But the plain devil and dissembling looks –
And yet to win her, all the world to nothing!
                 (I, 2, 232–42)

Before the King, the Queen and their family, Richard plays the part of a plain, open and good-hearted man who is misjudged by everyone:

Because I cannot flatter, and look fair,
Smile in men's faces, smooth, deceive and cog,
Duck with French nods and apish courtesy,
I must be held a rancorous enemy.
Cannot a plain man live and think no harm,
But thus his simple truth must be abus'd
With silken, sly, insinuating Jacks?
                 (I, 3, 47–53)

Richard's masterpiece is the play 'The Holy Richard' (III, 7). It is brilliantly directed: 'Buckingham: Look you get a prayer-book in your hand, / And stand between two church-men' (46–7). And Richard plays the title role so convincingly that the Mayor and the citizens force him to accept his position as the sole worthy heir to the English Crown:

Cousin of Buckingham, and sage grave men,
Since you will buckle fortune on my back
To bear her burden whe'er I will or no,
I must have patience to endure the load. ...

For God doth know, and you may partly see,
How far I am from the desire of this.
            (III, 7, 226–9, 234–5)

Richard, the star actor, has become King of England.

Shakespeare's construal of Richard as an actor means that he consciously places him within a theatrical tradition which was still very relevant to the audience: the figure of Vice in the morality play. Vice, who acts as the embodiment of vice, lies and deceives in order to tempt man from the path of virtue. In the prologue, direct address to the audience and many asides, he seeks to collude with the audience and to make it his accomplice in the knowledge of his depraved plans. Richard's monologues and asides fulfil similar functions; he even explicitly draws on the tradition of Vice himself:

RICHARD [aside]: So wise so young, they say,
  do never live long.
PRINCE: What say you, uncle?
RICHARD: I say, without characters fame
  lives long.
[aside] Thus, like the formal Vice, Iniquity,
I moralize two meanings in one word.
                 (III, 1, 79–83)

Viewed within this tradition, it becomes understandable why Richard, the actor, despite his disgraceful deed, is 'applauded' by the audience and is successful right up until the time of his coronation.

On the other hand, this explicit reference to the figure of Vice illustrates precisely how the character of Richard is basically different. Vice plays a role in order to tempt mankind to commit sins. He always refers to his opponent Virtue and the moral order which Virtue represents. Richard, on the other hand, only knows one reference point: himself. He plays a role in order to recreate himself continually on stage. The roles appear as mirrors in which his self reflects in different ways – just as in Richard's monologue, which closes the courtship scene:

I do mistake *my person* all this while!
Upon *my life*, she finds – although *I* cannot –
*Myself* to be a marvellous proper man.
*I'll* be at charges for a looking-glass,
And entertain a score or two of tailors

57

To study fashions to adorn *my body*:
Since *I* am crept in favour with *myself*,
*I* will maintain it with some little cost.
But first *I'll* turn yon fellow in his grave,
And then return, lamenting, to *my love*.
Shine out, fair sun, till *I* have bought a glass,
That *I* may see *my* shadow as *I* pass.

(I, 2, 257–68; my emphasis)

But what is Richard's self? In his entrance monologue, Richard informs the audience, 'I am determined to prove a villain' (I,1, 30). He designs the self as a villain, the realisation of which will serve the different roles which he plays out, one after the other. Richard is thus his own creator – the creator of his own self.

The idea that man can create himself, or must create himself, had already been formulated by the end of the fifteenth century. In a speech written by Giovanni Pico della Mirandola in 1485, but published after his death in 1494, *On the Dignity of Man*, God speaks to Adam in the following way:

I have appointed no particular place to you, and no individual appearance, I have given you no particular talents which are unique to you alone, because you should obtain and keep the self, Adam, the place, the appearance and the talents which you wish for yourself, according to your own discretion. The restricted nature of other creatures will be limited by the laws which I have given. You should decide your own nature for yourself without restriction and according to your own discretion. I have put you in the middle of the world so that you can learn what is around you in the world all the more easily. I have made you neither heavenly, nor immortal so that through your own power to model yourself and work on yourself, you can build yourself freely into the form you choose. You may degenerate into the lower order, to the animals; but you may also, if you desire, be reborn into the heavenly, the godly world.

Richard misuses the inborn possibility of self-determination implied here to 'degenerate into the lower order, the animals'. He is often given animal descriptions such as 'hedgehog', 'spider',

'toad', 'dog', 'cur', 'hog', 'swine', 'boar', 'tiger'. 'Spider', 'toad', 'swine', and 'dog' are used particularly often, that is, beasts which are situated on the lowest levels on the chain of being.

Though degenerated into the animal order, Richard measures himself against God:

I have no brother, I am like no brother; …

… I am myself alone.

(*Henry VI*, Part 3, V, 6, 80–3)

In *De Amore* (1469), a commentary on Plato's *Symposium* by the Florentine philosopher Marsilio Ficino, whose works were known and widespread among Elizabethan scholars and poets, at the end of the fourth chapter of the fourth speech, it states:

Only God alone, who lacks nothing, and above whom is nothing, may restrict himself to himself and be satisfied with himself.

Richard puts himself in God's place and creates a world according to his vision, 'thou has made the happy earth thy hell' (Anne, I, 2 51); 'Thou cam'st on earth to make the earth my hell' (Duchess of York, IV, 4, 167). Richard's ugly appearance gains great importance in this respect, and he explicitly refers to it in the introductory monologue:

But I, that am not shap'd for sportive tricks,
Nor made to court an amorous looking-glass;
I, that am rudely stamp'd, and want love's
  majesty,
To strut before a wanton ambling nymph:
I, that am curtail'd of this fair proportion,
Cheated of feature by dissembling Nature,
Deform'd, unfinished, sent before my time
Into this breathing world scarce half made
  up –
And that so lamely and unfashionable
That dogs bark at me, as I halt by them –
Why, I, in this weak piping time of peace,
Have no delight to pass away the time,
Unless to spy my shadow in the sun,
And descant on my own deformity.

(I, 1 14–27)

Richard's ugliness places him, on the one hand, in the line of the tradition of Vice, who always appeared as a deformed cripple. On the other hand, however, it justifies the reason why Richard is cursed as a 'spider', 'toad' or 'dog'. For, according to the laws of analogy or correspondence valid at the time, a deformed, ugly body implied a chaotic, evil soul inside. Thus, in *The Courtier* by Baldessare Castiglione (written 1508, published 1528, translated into English in 1561, and immensely popular in the Elizabethan age), paragraphs 57/8 of the fourth book state:

> It is seldom ... that a wicked soul inhabits a beautiful body and outer beauty is a true sign of the inner good; this grace is more or less stamped on the body as a characteristic of the soul whereby it shall be recognised on the surface, as the beauty of the blooms on the tree show the goodness of the fruit. The same is true of bodies as one sees, for the physiognomy of the face reveals the morality and thoughts of the man ... Ugly men are therefore mostly bad and beautiful men are good; one can say that beauty is the countenance/face of all that is pleasing, bright, agreeable and worth longing for and that ugliness is the dark, morose, unfavourable and melancholy face of evil.

It is, therefore, unlikely that Shakespeare's audience interpreted Richard's ugliness in the sense of a psychological release or even feel any sympathy towards him because of it. For them, Richard must not forgo love because he is ugly, but rather, the fact that he is ugly seems to be (ana)logically linked to the fact that his soul knows no need for love: 'I am like no brother ... I am myself alone'.

According to Ficino, love is based on similarity between people. 'Love is founded on agreement. This consists of a certain similarity of species in several subjects. For, if I seem the same as you, then you must necessarily be the same as me. This correspondence which forces me to love you, obliges you to love me too.'[3]

In that Richard negates any similarity between himself and another person, he excludes love. At the same time, however, he threatens his own self. For, as Ficino goes on to explain, the individual only finds himself through the experience of love: 'Namely, by loving you, who loves me, I find myself in you, who thinks of me, and thus I regain my self in you who hold me, after I have given myself up to you.'

The self which Richard has designed for himself and which he realises with his role-play seems, thus, deliberately deceitful and empty, as is made clear by the ambivalent judgement of the plot of the drama.

Richard takes for granted that events which led him to England's throne and which strengthen his leadership are the result of his will, his plans and role-play: Clarence's death, the execution of Vaugham, Rivers, Grey and Hastings, the murder of the two princes and his wife, Lady Anne, the imprisonment and execution of his earlier assistant and prompter Buckingham. The historical facts of his leadership over England are, according to this interpretation, created by Richard himself, and are based on the growth and expansion of his 'self'.

Richard sees himself, therefore, as a ruler in the sense of Machiavelli, to whom he refers, not without reason, in *Henry VI*, Part 3, 'And set the murd'rous Machiavel to school' (III, 2, 193). In Chapter 25 of *The Prince*, written in 1513 and first published in 1532, Machiavelli writes:

> It is not unknown to me how many have been and are of the opinion that worldly events are so governed by fortune and by God, that men cannot by their prudence change them, and that on the contrary there is no remedy whatever, and for this they may judge it to be useless to toil much about them, but let things be ruled by chance. This opinion has been more held in our day, from the great changes that have been seen, and are daily seen, beyond every human conjecture. When I think about them, at times I am partly inclined to share this opinion. Nevertheless, that our free will may not be altogether extinguished, I think it may be true that fortune is the

ruler of half our actions, but that she allows the other half or thereabouts to be governed by us.[4]

According to Machiavelli, history is at least 'half' the result of intended, planned human action. In Richard's case, this would also mean that, though Edward IV's death was caused by 'fortune', Richard's ascension to the throne is determined by his own free will. This interpretation of history, which Richard clearly also shares, was for the Elizabethan audience coloured by a distinctly negative aspect.

Machiavelli's works were accessible in Italian to some Elizabethan scholars. But his ideas only found wide circulation through the so-called anti-Machiavelli, Gentillets, whose *Discours sur les Moyens de bien gouverner et maintenir en bonne paix un Royaume ou autre Principauté. Contre Nicholas Machiavel* (Florentin 1576) was translated into English as early as 1577. Gentillets misrepresented Machiavelli's ideas by citing them out of context, in part changing the content and ignoring Machiavelli's historical context. In so doing, he created the foundation of a new stereotype stage figure – the treacherous atheist, greedy for power, egotistic and scheming, in whom can also be found traces of native Vice and the tyrant as handed down in the 'classics' by Seneca. (Marlowe also based Barabas, in the *Jew of Malta* [1589], for example, on the same pattern.) Richard's interpretation of history had long fallen into disgrace with the audience.

In addition, his understanding of history is relativised by the drama itself. For, all events which Richard believes are the result of his schemes and plotting can also be traced back to other causes. Clarence 'did forsake his father Warwick, / Ay, and foreswore himself' (I, 3, 135/6); Rivers, Grey and Hastings are cursed by Queen Margaret, 'God, I pray him, / That none of you may live his natural age, / But by some unlook'd accident cut off' (I, 3, 212–14); her curse also falls onto the crown prince, 'Edward thy son, that now is Prince of Wales, / For Edward my son, that was Prince of Wales, / Die in his youth, by like untimely violence' (I, 3, 199–201). Anne curses herself as she curses Richard's future wife (I, 2, 26 ff) and Buckingham's own oath is turned against him, as he realises at the execution:

Why then, All-Souls' day is my body's
  doomsday,
This is the day which, in King Edward's time,
I wish'd might fall on me when I was found
False to his children and his wife's allies.
This is the day wherein I wish'd to fall
By the false faith of him whom I most
  trusted.
This, this All-Souls' day to my fearful soul
Is the determin'd respite of my wrongs:
That high All-seer which I dallied with
Hath turn'd my feigned prayer on my head,
And given in earnest what I begg'd in jest.
                                        (V, 1, 12–22)

Under this aspect, Richard appears solely as a tool used by the 'All-seer' to keep his order in the world. Richard's understanding of history as the result of his own deliberate and planned course of action, and his idea of himself as a self-created, self-determining and, in this sense, autonomous individual, is thus revealed to be pure self-deception.

The process of exposing the deception begins with Richard's ascension to the throne. Until now, Richard played various roles in order to realise his creation of himself – a villain. The role of king refutes this intention. It cannot be instrumentalised with respect to individual goals. Here, the concept of the two bodies of the king comes into play: the body politic presents the body natural with objective expectations to which the body natural must subject itself. Although Richard up to this point has realised a self by creating himself and enacting role-plays, when he takes on the role of king, he is denied self-realisation in this sense. Self-designation as villain and the position of king will collide with one another as a matter of course – the process of self-destruction begins.

The role of king creates certain obligations to which Richard cannot react with corresponding role-play. From the moment of his ascension, each of his previously successfully directed plays is now followed by a negative pendant which accelerates his downfall. Whilst Richard directed the play 'The Enemy Brothers', to which the guilty Clarence fell victim, with the sovereignty of a marionette master, he commands the death of the two innocent princes openly and explicitly and loses self-control when Buckingham does not obey immediately, 'The King is angry: see, he gnaws his lip.' (IV, 2, 27). As king, Richard has obviously forfeited his ability as actor.

Whilst the play 'The Languishing and Ingenious Lover' was based on Richard's momentary mood and acted out with virtuosity, the courtship of Elizabeth, the daughter of his dead brother Edward, arises from the obligations tied to the role of king: 'I must be married to my brother's daughter, / Or else my kingdom stands on brittle glass' (IV, 2, 60–1). It ends with an error which is hard to gloss over.

Both actions – the murder of the princes and the courtship of Elizabeth – are neither successfully directed nor brilliantly played roles, but they do not contradict Richard's self-designation as villain. It is contradicted, however, in Richard's language which he must adopt along with the position of king. Thus, before the courtship of Elizabeth, he considers the following:

> Murder her brothers, and then marry her –
> Uncertain way of gain! But I am in
> So far in blood that sin will pluck on sin;
> Tear-falling pity dwells not in this eye.
>                         (IV, 2, 62–5)

Whilst the courtship of Anne, whose husband and father-in-law he has murdered, causes him no moral consideration, he now adopts a Christian terminology which explicitly points to the existence of a moral order. The office of king, the body politic, forces Richard, the body natural, towards a moral order which he implicitly recognises when he calls himself 'the Lord's anointed' (IV, 4, 151).

Richmond, the future King Henry VII, the unifier of the houses of York and Lancaster and founder of the Tudor dynasty, fits perfectly into this order; he calls upon it in his battle against Richard:

> O Thou, whose captain I account myself,
> Look on my forces with a gracious eye;
> Put in their hands Thy bruising irons of wrath
> That they may crush down, with a heavy fall,
> Th'usurping helmets of our adversaries;
> Make us Thy ministers of chastisement,
> That we may praise Thee in the victory.
> To Thee I do commend my watchful soul
> Ere I let fall the windows of mine eyes:
> Sleeping and waking, O defend me still!
>                         (V, 3, 109–18)

In the light of this order, however, Richard's self-designation seems to be null and void. It initiates and justifies the battle of Richard against Richard 'myself myself confound!' (IV, 4, 400) in the course of which, he destroys and dissolves himself.

Opposite the brilliantly directed play 'The Holy Richard' stands the scene in Act V where the souls of the murdered appear to Richard in the night before the battle against Richmond and unanimously curse him: 'despair and die!'. Richard awakes from his dream in fear of his life:

> Give me another horse! Bind up my wounds!
> Have mercy, Jesu! – Soft, I did but dream.
> O coward conscience, how dost thou afflict
>   me!
> The lights burn blue; it is now dead midnight.
> Cold fearful drops stand on my trembling
>   flesh.
> What do I fear? Myself? There's none else by;
> Richard loves Richard, that is, I and I.
> Is there a murderer here? No. Yes I am!
> Then fly. What, from myself? Great reason
>   why,
> Lest I revenge? What, myself upon myself?
> Alack, I love myself. Wherefore? For any good
> That I myself have done unto myself?
> O no, alas, I rather hate myself
> For hateful deeds committed by myself.
> I am a villain – yet I lie, I am not!
> Fool, of thyself speak well! Fool, do not flatter,
> My conscience hath a thousand several
>   tongues,
> And every tongue brings in a several tale,
> And every tale condemns me for a villain:

Perjury, perjury, in the highest degree;
Murder, stern murder, in the direst degree;
All several sins, all us'd in each degree,
Throng to the bar, crying all, 'Guilty, guilty!'
I shall despair. There is no creature loves me,
And if I die, no soul will pity me –
And wherefore should they, since that I myself
Find in myself no pity to myself?

(V, 3, 178–204)

Here, Richard has realised his own self-creation, 'I am a villain'. But the moral order which he is obliged to adopt when he takes on the role of king, and on which he himself explicitly calls, 'Have mercy, Jesu!', does not foresee any role for him in which this self can be reflected. He is, quite simply, 'guilty'. And, thus, the paradoxical situation arises that at precisely the same moment Richard is totally thrown back upon himself, he also loses himself.

Ficino wrote of those who love that they find themselves, for they see their reflection in the other: 'for he who loves must once die in himself, because he gives himself up. At the same time, he is reborn in the object of his love when the latter warms him in the glow of his thoughts for him. He comes to life a second time in that he finally recognises himself in the lover, free of all doubt that he is identical to him' (*Oratio secunda*, VIII). Since Richard loves only himself – 'Richard loves Richard' – he becomes the only mirror to reflect his own image: 'I am I', 'Myself upon myself', 'I fear myself', 'I myself find in myself no pity for myself'. Richard is only identical with himself and thus has no identity: 'his conscience' which arose or was awoken through reference to the moral order allows the 'mirror' to shatter into a 'thousand pieces':

My conscience hath a thousand several
  tongues.
And every tongue brings in a several tale,
And every tale condemns me for a villain.

Because Richard has designated himself a villain – that is, a self which only knows and acknowledges itself and which is exclusively concentrated within itself and for itself – taking on the role of king will inevitably lead to the dissolution and splitting of the self. In that Richard makes his self absolute, he kills it off without giving himself the chance 'to come alive again' in himself, as himself. Richard, the actor, played various roles in order to realise a self. Richard, the king, has shown this self to be invalid and destroys it irretrievably. The self-sufficient, absolute 'I' has consumed itself. Richard is no one. His physical death in the battle simply seals this discovery.

*Richard III* was Shakespeare's first great success. At the première, the title role was played by Richard Burbage, the son of the first founder of the theatre. His performance was apparently so brilliant that many anecdotes and legends have grown up around him. The audience was fascinated by the figure of Richard in all its ambivalence. On the one hand, it demonstrated the high-handedness of the autonomous individual and, at the same time, its destructive and self-destructive potential. It expressed the simultaneous attraction to and horror of this new image of man, whereby at the end, horror was the stronger feeling. It seems extraordinary that Shakespeare only introduced the new concept of man as an autonomous individual to the stage in a negative variant, though Pico della Mirandola clearly formulated it positively because it seemed to him to determine the dignity of a person. The tradition founded with Richard was later continued with Iago and Edmund. The spectator could, thus, only understand and view Richard's downfall and demise in the sense that it maintained and strengthened the old order, and the image of man determined by it, inherited from the Middle Ages. All that was put into question is finally re-confirmed. The victory by Richmond (a figure who has all the traditional qualities of kingship), which ends the family war between the houses of York and Lancaster and unites the English kingdom, linked the audience to its own time in affirmative continuity with a positive line of tradition:

Now civil wounds are stopp'd; peace lives
  again:
That she may long live here, God say Amen!

(V, 5, 40–1)

## Transformation and discovering identity – from the rites of May to 'rite of passage'

It is believed that Shakespeare wrote and produced the comedy *A Midsummer Night's Dream* for a noble wedding – the most often cited occasion is that of the marriage of Elizabeth de Vere to the Earl of Derby on 26 January 1595. Whether this was the wedding in question, however, is not known for sure. However, many performances of the comedy in the public theatre are noted in reliable sources.

Whatever the case, *A Midsummer Night's Dream* combines a princely wedding and a folk seasonal rite. Whilst the wedding between Theseus and Hippolyta sets the frame of the comedy, Midsummer's Night is already hinted at in the title, and the rites of May are referred to, in different ways, in the course of the play (for example, 'Where I did meet thee once with Helena / To do observance to a morn of May' [I,1, 166–7]; and 'No doubt they rose up early to observe / The rite of May' [IV,1, 129–30]).

Research into traditional customs has shown that the English May Rite was not only performed in May, let alone 1 May, but also extended into June. It is, therefore, quite possible that it coincided with celebrations on Midsummer's Eve. Both festivals were associated with marital and fertility rites in the minds of Shakespeare's audience (June was the most popular month for weddings).

Very little is known about the festival of Midsummer's Eve in England. In the sixteenth century, Midsummer's Eve was celebrated in the forest. A bonfire was lit and fern seeds and other plants which were believed to have magical-medical powers were gathered. On the other hand, there is much recorded evidence of the May Rites. The Puritans believed they were heathen customs and fought against them. In *Anatomy of Abuses* (1583), Philip Stubbs provides the following description of this 'repulsive' rite:

> Against May, Whitsunday, or other time all the young men and maids, old men and wives, run gadding over night to the woods, groves, hills, and mountains, where they spend all the night in pleasant pastimes; and in the morning they return, bringing with them birch boughs and branches of trees, to deck their assemblies withal. And no marvel, for there is a great Lord present amongst them, as superintendent and Lord over their pastimes and sports, namely, Satan, prince of hell.
>
> But the chiefest jewel they bring from thence is their Maypole, which they bring home with great veneration, as thus: They have twenty or forty yoke of oxen, every oxe having a sweet nose-gay of flowers placed on the tip of his horns, and these oxen draw home this Maypole (this stinking idol, rather) which is covered all over with flowers and herbs, bound round about with strings, from the top to the bottom, and sometime painted with variable colours, with two or three hundred men, women and children following it with great devotion. And thus being reared up with handkerchiefs and flags hovering on the top, they strew the ground round about, bind green boughs about it, set up summer halls, bowers and arbors hard by it. And then fall they to dance about it, like as the heathen people did at the dedication of the Idols, whereof this is a perfect pattern, or rather the thing itself. I have heard it credibly reported (and that *viva voce*) by men of great gravity and reputation, that of forty, three-score, or a hundred maids going to the wood over night, there have scarcely the third part of them returned home again undefiled. These be the fruits which these cursed pastimes bring forth.

As can be seen in this quotation, the May festivities followed a specific spatial and temporal structure. Young and old left their houses at night and gathered in the forest where they spent the night 'in pleasant pastimes'. In the morning, they returned to the town or village with the maypole where celebrations and dancing around the decorated maypole – the phallic symbol, 'this stinking idol' – formed the high point of the ceremonies.

Shakespeare's comedy is based on a similar structure to the May festivities. It begins during the day in Athens (Act I), from where the young lovers and mechanicals depart to spend the night in the forest (Acts II, III, IV). In the morning, they return to the city (Act IV), where the marriage of the princely pair and the

THEATRUM VITAE HUMANAE

young lovers is celebrated (Act V). This structure creates a complex net of analogies and oppositions between characters and groups of characters. Thus, the young lovers and the mechanicals share the experience of the same spatial and temporal stations. In this respect, the princely couple (Theseus and Hippolyta) and the fairies provide an opposing group. The princely pair is accorded the city and day-time (they only step beyond the borders of the city and forest in daylight), while the fairies are accorded the forest and night-time (they only step between forest and city during the night). The young lovers, however, provide an analogy to the princely pair when they celebrate their marriages after their return from the forest. As far as this aspect is concerned, they also provide a counterpoint to the mechanicals, who do not undergo any change in status on their return from the forest. All these movements across boundaries and/or transformations are given importance through reference to the underlying structure, which is abstracted from the May Rite.

At first, the city of Athens appears to be a place of confused feelings. Both Lysander and Demetrius are in love with Hermia, but Hermia loves only Lysander, whilst Helena loves Demetrius who was earlier in love with her, but now wants nothing more to do with her. Hermia's father tries to solve this confusion through paternal force, 'As she is mine, I may dispose of her' (I,1 42), and demands that Hermia marry Demetrius. He calls upon the Athenian law, as Theseus, the ruler, explicitly reminds him,

> To you your father should be as a god:
> One that compos'd your beauties, yea, and
>   one
> To whom you are but as a form in wax
> By him imprinted, and within his power
> To leave the figure, or disfigure it.
>
> (I, 1, 47–51)

The Athenian law only recognises Hermia as the daughter of her father and does not allow her her own will, her own choice or right to self-determination. When she refuses to obey her father, she gives up the right to life and love:

> Either to die the death, or to abjure
> For ever the society of men.
>
> (I, 1, 65–6)

This law, as Theseus makes clear, will be implemented even on his own wedding day, unchanged and without mercy,

> For you, fair Hermia, look you arm yourself
> To fit your fancies to your father's will;
> Or else the law of Athens yields you up
> (Which by no means we may extenuate)
> To death, or to a vow of single life.
>
> (I, 1, 117–21)

Hermia and Lysander elope from Athens in order to escape the place in which their right to love and self-determination is subjugated to paternal force and the law. After they have stepped over the threshold which divides the city from the forest, 'Through Athens' gates have we devis'd to steal' (I,1, 213), the night wood, to which Helena and Demetrius have also followed them, becomes through Oberon's love potion and Puck's mistaken identity a place where all four are exposed to new experiences. After a period of deep insecurity, they are all finally able to resolve the confusion of feelings in a way which is satisfactory to all four lovers.

When Hermia first enters the forest, she is used to being courted by two men and having to shake off one – Demetrius – by being unfriendly ('I frown upon him'; 'I give him curses' [I,1, 194; 196]), whilst she knows how to keep the other – Lysander – at a distance by mentioning propriety and custom. She justifies well her refusal to allow Lysander to sleep near her, even in the forest:

> But, gentle friend, for love and courtesy,
> Lie further off, in human modesty;
> Such separation as may well be said
> Becomes a virtuous bachelor and a maid,
> So far be distant.
>
> (II, 2, 56–60)

In the night forest, however, clearly other rules are at work. It is precisely this distance Hermia requires of Lysander which leads Puck to make his fateful mistake:

Pretty soul, she durst not lie
Near this lack-love, this kill-courtesy.
Churl, upon thy eyes I throw
All the power this charm doth owe:
When thou wak'st, let love forbid
Sleep his seat on thy eyelid.
(II, 2, 76–81)

A tortuous new experience begins for Hermia. Deserted by Lysander, who runs off, suddenly inflamed with Helena, she wakes from a nightmare:

Help me, Lysander, help me! Do thy best
To pluck this crawling serpent from my
  breast!
Ay me, for pity! What a dream was here!
Lysander, look how I do quake with fear.
Methought a serpent ate my heart away,
And you sat smiling at his cruel prey.
Lysander! What, remov'd? Lysander! Lord!
(II, 2, 144–50)

Hermia is alone with her fear of sexuality, which is indicated clearly by the image of the snake as, in general, animals and animal names in the night wood connote the 'animal' nature in man, his sexual drive – and the experience of Lysander who does not love her. She will soon make the experience which Helena tried to overcome in Athens: to be unloved, cursed and repulsed by the man whom she loves:

Hang off, thou cat, thou burr! Vile thing, let
  loose,
Or I will shake thee from me like a serpent.
… Out, tawny Tartar, out!
Out loathed medicine! O hated potion, hence!
… Get you gone, you dwarf;
You minimus, of hindering knot-grass made;
You bead, you acorn.
(III, 2, 260–1, 263–4, 328–30)

Helena, on the other hand, wished in Athens to be transformed into Hermia, 'Were the world mine, Demetrius being bated, / The rest I'd give to be to you translated' (I, 1, 190–1). She compares the image of herself as she enters the forest to wild animals and monsters:

No, no; I am as ugly as a bear,
For beasts that meet me run away for fear:
Therefore no marvel though Demetrius
Do, as a monster, fly my presence thus.
(II, 2, 93–6)

With the same image of herself, she forces herself upon Demetrius:

I am your spaniel; and, Demetrius,
The more you beat me, I will fawn on you.
Use me but as your spaniel, spurn me, strike
  me,
Neglect me, lose me; only give me leave,
Unworthy as I am to follow you.
What worser place can I beg in your love –
And yet a place of high respect with me –
Than to be used as you use your dog?
(II, 2, 203–10)

But even as a 'spaniel', as a 'dog' – and that means, in the connotation of animal names, as a sexual object – Demetrius turns Helena away. When Helena is actually 'translated' into Hermia, both Lysander and Demetrius fall in love with her because of the effects of the love potion and adore her as a higher being. Lysander calls her 'transparent Helena' (II, 2, 104) and Demetrius addresses her 'O Helen, goddess, nymph, perfect divine!' (III, 2, 137). Helena, who was once unloved, is now courted by two men at once, the 'monster' has been transformed into a 'goddess'.

In both Hermia and Helena these new experiences cause a crisis of identity. Neither can believe what she sees. Hermia doubts herself:

Hate me? Wherefor? O me! what news, my
  love?
Am not I Hermia? Are not you Lysander?
I am as fair now as I was erewhile.
(III, 2, 272–4)

Helena believes that the two men are making fun of her and that Hermia is in collusion with them:

Injurious Hermia! Most ungrateful maid! ...

Is all the counsel that we two have shar'd,
The sisters' vows, the hours that we have spent,
... O, is all forgot?
All school-days' friendship, childhood inno-
cence? ...

... So we grew together,
Like to a double cherry, seeming parted,
But yet an union in partition,
Two lovely berries moulded on one stem;
So, with two seeming bodies, but one heart; ...

And will you rent our ancient love asunder
To join with men in scorning your poor
friend?
(III, 2, 195, 198–9, 201–2, 208–12, 215–16)

The friendship that existed between Helena and Hermia from childhood until their escape to the forest is broken by the new experiences. The old childhood relationship cannot be maintained and is dissolved: Hermia and Helena separate in bitter hatred of each other.

The two young men undergo similar disturbing experiences. Lysander, who has sworn eternal love to Hermia, falls in love with Helena, curses Hermia with the foulest of animal names and justifies his change of feelings, which has actually come about through the love potion, by declaring it the choice of 'reason' and 'maturity':

Not Hermia, but Helena I love:
Who will not change a raven for a dove?
The will of man is by his reason sway'd,
And reason says you are the worthier maid.
Things growing are not ripe until their season:
So I, being young, till now ripe not to reason;
And, touching now the point of human skill,
Reason becomes the marshal to my will,
And leads me to your eyes, where I o'erlook
Love's stories, written in love's richest book.
(II, 2, 112–21)

Demetrius, the 'inconstant man' (I, 1, 140), returns, on the other hand, to his first love:

Lysander, keep thy Hermia; I will none.
If ere I lov'd her, all that love is gone.
My heart to her but as a guest-wise sojourn'd,
And now to Helen is it home return'd,
There to remain.
(III, 2, 169–73)

Demetrius relates his new experiences to the move away from childhood:

... my love to Hermia,
Melted as the snow, seems to me now
As the remembrance of an idle gaud
Which in my childhood I did dote upon;
(IV, 1, 164–7)

Like Helena and Hermia, Lysander and Demetrius also quarrel bitterly. The night in the forest ends in all four singly wandering through a fog 'black as Acheron' (III, 2, 357) and finally, exhausted, they sink to the ground near to each other and sleep. When they awake the next day, the confusion of feelings has disappeared. Hermia and Lysander are in love with each other as are Helena and Demetrius. Together with Theseus and Hippolyta, they return to the city where all three couples 'shall eternally be knit' in the temple (IV, 1, 178).

The experience of the four young lovers can most accurately be described as a *rite de passage* (a term from Arnold van Gennep), that is, a rite of transition. Such rites order the crises in our lives and require that we shed our old identity in favour of a new one – the passage from one kind of life into another (such as birth, initiation, marriage, pregnancy and giving birth, entry into a profession, promotion into a higher social class, death). The rite of passage itself is divided into three parts: separation from the normal situation in life, the threshold, or phase of actual transformation, and the incorporation or re-integration of the transformed person back into society.

The lovers mark their separation by leaving Athens, the place where they spent their childhood and first fell in love, the place which is ruled by the father and the law. In the night wood, the phase of transformation begins. They shed their previous identities as daughter, friend, one who is loved, who is happy in love, one who is rejected and unrequited in love, as loyal lover, as fickle lover. Thus, they experience, on the one hand, a reversal of the roles that they have played so far and, on the other hand, an intensification of experiences undergone up to this point. The 'eye-love' which has directed their emotions until now is taken *ad absurdum* by the magic potion dropped onto their eyelids (the image of the eyes is a leitmotif for relations between lovers: it is used 68 times – including plural and composites – to which can also be added 39 examples of 'see' and 10 of 'sight'). They experience sexual desire dominated by fear and divide love into divine love and sexual love which they cast with various different objects.

The four lovers are transformed by their experiences in the night wood. Out of the 'eye-love' comes enduring love, and thus children become adults. After they have passed through the fog, which is 'black as Acheron' (the river of death), and overcome sleep, their old identities have worn off and they awake with new personal and social identities – as lovers who are constant, and as adults. The phase of transition is complete, the 'trial period' is over, and the newly transformed lovers must take their places in society once again. The incorporation phase can begin.

This commences in the forest in the early morning when Theseus and Hippolyta are out hunting and happen upon the four lovers asleep. They listen to their stories and Theseus decides against his earlier command to put himself, as ruler, above the paternal will and rights of Egeus and the Athenian law:

Egeus, I will overbear your will;
For in the temple, by and by, with us,
These couples shall eternally be knit.
(IV, 1, 178–80)

Society, changed for the better in this way, can now reintegrate the newly adult young lovers. This occurs with a further 'rite de passage' –

the wedding – which creates a married couple out of single people; a final play by the mechanicals, the 'most Lamentable Comedy and most Cruel Death of Pyramus and Thisby', at which the lovers, as spectators (implying a certain distance), follow a love story and comment on it (instead of being involved in it themselves); and, ultimately, the consummation of the marriage on the wedding night. In this manner, Hermia and Lysander, and Helena and Demetrius have been transformed: they have taken on new identities.

The plot of the comedy relates the sequence of action borrowed from the May Rite to the phases of a rite of transition: the escape from the city marks the separation from the usual life situation; the stay in the night forest is realised as a threshold, or liminal phase in which the old identities are dissolved and new experiences lead to taking on new identities; and the return to the city marks the beginning of the incorporation phase, which is passed at the wedding and at the play which follows it, and ends with the wedding night. In this way, the play presents a far-reaching change in the collective experience. Whilst the May Rite – like the Grocer's scene in the Easter Play (see Chapter 1) – is performed in order to guarantee the community a magic renewal of vitality, which can also be executed as the collective-anarchic liberation of youth and sexuality ('of forty, three-score, or a hundred maids going to the wood over night, there have scarcely the third part of them returned home again undefiled'), the rite of transition enables youths to bring their sexuality under control in accordance with society and to live out their sexual desires only in the form of a marriage sanctioned by society. The transformation of a May Rite into a rite of transition, which *A Midsummer Night's Dream* achieves, recovers that which was lost in the suppression of popular culture by Puritan society and brings it back into society in a socially acceptable form. The community, which formerly carried out the May Rite, become spectators who, like the young couple at the play of 'Pyramus and Thisbe', watch others acting as representatives, as it were, in place of them and, thus, can achieve a distance to and distancing consciousness of the (own) actions.

The transition from the May Rite into a rite of transition in *A Midsummer Night's Dream* points to a basic dramatic structure which is characteristic of nearly all Shakespeare's comedies, where initial spatial separation forms the starting point of the phase of transformation – in *As you Like It*, the withdrawal from the court into the forest of Arden, in *Twelfth Night*, the shipwreck which casts Viola up in Illyria. The transformation phase is marked by a confusion of feelings – thus, in *Twelfth Night*, the Duke Orsino is in love with the Countess Olivia who is in love with Viola, disguised as Cesario, who is in love with the Duke. Contrary to *A Midsummer Night's Dream*, in *Twelfth Night* (as in *As You Like It*), it is the heroine who plays out the dissolution of the old identity and the appropriation of new, completely opposite experiences in a conscious role-play which becomes possible through dressing as a boy. The distancing self-awareness which the young lovers only gain as spectators of 'Pyramus and Thisbe' in *A Midsummer Night's Dream* already directs the role-play of Rosalind and Viola in the phase of transition which leads to the conscious acceptance of the new identity. The lovers 'transformed' through constant, mature love are also integrated into society through the rite of transition of a marriage. Thus, the comedies follow the structure of a transition rite of initiation, which helps the young people to separate from their former, child-like identities and move them towards, and create for them new individual and social identities as married adults through a process of separation, transformation and incorporation. In this process, the catalyst is always the transformation of 'eye-love' into constant love. It is this which prepares for and guarantees the new identity.

At the same time, nature, the individual and society are all related to one another in the comedies. The discordant love between Oberon and Titania, and Titania's misdirected love for the 'changeling boy', manifests itself in an overwhelming disturbance in the order of nature:

The seasons alter: hoary-headed frosts
Fall in the fresh lap of the crimson rose;

And on old Hiem's thin and icy crown,
An odorous chaplet of sweet summer buds
Is, as in mockery, set; the spring, the summer,
The chiding autumn, angry winter, change
Their wonted liveries; and the maz'd world,
By their increase, now knows not which is
   which.
And this same progeny of evils comes
From our debate, from our dissension;
We are their parents and original.
                              (II, 1, 107–17)

This imbalance corresponds to the confusion of feelings in the young lovers and the inhumane social order of Athens. Once this is remedied, an appropriate personal and social change can begin. The young lovers find new identities and the social order of Athens is altered for the better. Accordingly, in his blessing of the wedding bed at the end of the comedy, Oberon describes love as a transforming and harmonising power:

So shall all the couples three
Ever true in loving be;
And the blots of Nature's hand
Shall not in their issue stand:
Never mole, hare-lip, nor scar,
Nor mark prodigious, such as are
Despised in nativity,
Shall upon their children be.
                              (V, 1, 401–8)

Constant love guarantees harmony, fertility, physical wholeness and beauty because it produces a happy agreement between social and natural order, between the individual and society. The comedy finishes with an epilogue, spoken by Puck, who is also known by the name of Robin – on the one hand, the name of the knave in the Easter Plays and on the other, a name which suggests Robin Hood, for whom the community gathers hawthorn at the May festival:

If we shadows have offended,
Think but this, and all is mended,
That you have but slumber'd here
While these visions did appear.

And this weak and idle theme,
No more yielding but a dream,
Gentles, do not reprehend: ...

So, goodnight unto you all.
Give me your hands, if we be friends,
And Robin shall restore amends.

(V, 1, 417–23, 430–3)

Here, Puck addresses the actors and their roles as 'shadows' and speaks of the performance of the comedy as a 'dream' which has floated past the dozing spectators. The theme of theatre and the many reflections on theatre which run through the play which, in a sense, already begins with the title of the play *A Midsummer Night's Dream*, reaches here its climax and culmination. Within the comedy, the expression 'dream' is used both by the young lovers when they speak of their experiences in the night wood, 'let us recount our dreams' (IV, 1, 196), and also by Bottom, when he wakes and remembers his night-time experience – his transformation into a donkey and his love affair with Titania,

I have had a most rare vision. I have had a dream, past the wit of man to say what dream it was. Man is but an ass if he go about to expound this dream. Methought I was – there is no man can tell what. Methought I was – and methought I had – but man is but a patched fool if he will offer to say what methought I had. The eye of man hath not heard, the ear of man hath not seen, man's hand is not able to taste, his tongue to conceive, nor his heart to report, what my dream was. I will get Peter Quince to write a ballad of this dream: it shall be called 'Bottom's Dream', because it hath no bottom.

(IV, 1, 203–14)

In both instances, the word 'dream' is used to describe the experience of the speaker in the night wood. These experiences are comparable in that they allow the various dreamers to have wholly new experiences. They are, however, different in that they lead the young lovers towards a transformation which manifests itself in discarding the old and taking on the new

identity, while, for Bottom, it remains without consequence. Titania's efforts to change Bottom, 'I will purge thy mortal grossness so / That thou shalt like an airy spirit go' (III, 1, 146–7), are unsuccessful. Bottom interprets his new experiences in the light of old ones: 'this is to make an ass of me' (III, 1, 110), and remains the silly ass he always was. As his monologue clearly shows, Bottom is wholly unable to name his night experiences, let alone work through them and, thus, to distance himself from his self. The highly unusual experiences cannot lead to a new awareness of self and thus to a new identity. Bottom's 'dream' lacks the transforming power; it remains, indeed, a dream without a 'Bottom'.

In the epilogue, in which Puck equates the performance to a dream, it implies the following interpretation: theatre creates highly unusual situations for the spectators which allow them to experience wholly new things. If the spectators are able to adopt these experiences consciously and, thus, to distance themselves from their previous selves, the performance can lead them to shed the old identity, and take on a new one.

If theatre is to fulfil this function, certain conditions must be provided, not only for the spectator but also for the actor. These 'shadows' (V, 1, 210) must allow the 'imagination' (V, 1, 211–12) room to unfold. The performance by the mechanicals lacks this potential. It stands for the negative example of a theatre with no power to transform.

Peter Quince's long prologue removes any possibility of the spectator becoming involved in the new and unexpected experiences, for he reports everything in advance, 'At the which let no man wonder' (V, 1, 133). In order that the spectators are not given the illusion of real events, Wall reassures them 'That I, one Snout by name, present a wall; / And such a wall as I would have you think' (155–6); and Lion finds the calming words, 'You ladies, you whose gentle hearts do fear' (216). Moon steps out of the role and explains frankly: 'All that I have to say is to tell you that the lanthorn is the moon; I, the Man i'th'Moon; this thorn-bush, my thorn-bush; and this dog, my dog' (250–2); and Thisbe takes her leave politely from the spectators before she dies '[*stabs herself*] And farewell, friends; / Thus Thisbe ends; / Adieu, adieu, adieu [*Dies*]' (336–8). The medieval tradition of direct speech to the audience is exploited here to excess, so that every dramatic illusion is destroyed in the making. The spectators have no choice but to react with ironic commentary:

DEMETRIUS: Well roar'd, Lion.
THESEUS: Well run, Thisby.
HIPPOLYTA: Well shone, Moon. Truly, the
    moon shines with a good grace.

                (V, I, 257–60)

A theatre which is not in a position to create an illusion for its spectators and allow them to participate in imagination in the events shown is also not able to initiate any change or transformation in the ideal spectator, and is thus nothing more than a way of idling away time. If the actors perform in a way that allows the spectators an imaginative, shared experience of the strange events on stage, the visit to the theatre can become a *rite de passage* for the spectators, too. The spectators are separated from their usual lives either by leaving the city (for the theatre in the north) or crossing the river (to visit the theatres in Southwark). The performance is experienced as the threshold or transformation phase which allows the spectator to discard the old identity and try out new ones. The return across the river, or back into the city, is the phase of incorporation where the new experiences are introduced into daily life and where the new identity can be tried out.

It is not only the individual comedy which is based on the underlying structure of a rite of transition, but the process of a theatre visit in general, whereby the *rite de passage* in this case is related to the structure of the May festival. The position of the night wood is taken by the (day-time) performance. In place of the seasonal rite which takes place as communal action, is the rite of transition to be carried out in each individual spectator (who none the less, as a member of the audience, is part of a community). Whilst the May Rite should magically bring about a renewal of the communal vitality in regular, periodic episodes, the theatre

can become a site for the creation of a new identity of the individual at any time.

*A Midsummer Night's Dream* not only represents the gaining or forfeiting of a new identity of the people who act, but, at the same time, also reflects on the conditions under which theatre itself can function as a social institution, which can effectively change the individual.

### The loss of identity in chaos: the end of the world

Elizabeth I died in 1603 after forty-five years on the throne. Her death almost coincided with the turn of the century, interpreted by many as a time of change. James VI of Scotland, from the House of Stuart, followed her, as James I, onto the throne of England. It was to his pride and credit that he united the three kingdoms of England, Scotland and Wales under one Crown, as the Kingdom of Great Britain.

The plague, which spread throughout London in 1603, meant the closure of all public theatres, and the official coronation of James, which was to have been held in London, was postponed until March 1604. For the occasion of the coronation, seven triumphal arches were built in the city of London, through which James I would travel on his way to Whitehall. The arches were designed in an Italian baroque style and announced the beginning of a new court aesthetic. Its most magnificent manifestations were found in the great court masques which were performed under the direction of the stage designer, Inigo Jones, in 1605: the 'Masques of Blackness' (5 January) and 'Arcadia Reformed' (30 August). The influence of this new genre on the public theatres should not be overlooked.

James I supported the acting companies in the public theatres to a far greater extent than Elizabeth had ever done. He declared that the old licences were invalid and renewed them in his name, in the name of his wife and his son, Prince Henry. Shakespeare's company, until then known as the 'Lord Chamberlain's Men', was promoted to the 'King's Men'. Renowned actors such as Shakespeare, Burbage, Henslowe and Alleyn were awarded coats of arms. The battle against the depravity of the theatre was for the moment won, for, as John Webster in a clever pun on royal patronage suggests in *The Overbury Character*, 'rogues are not to be imployde as maine ornaments to his Majesties Revels'. The average number of court performances by such troupes each year rose dramatically from three (under Elizabeth) to thirteen, and, naturally, the income of the troupes also rose significantly. Under James' rule, theatre was provided with favourable conditions which allowed it to develop.

As is often the case at the turn of a century, there were people at this time who proclaimed the decay of nature and civilisation and prophesied the approaching end of the world. In 1572, a new star appeared in Cassiopeia. The renowned Danish astronomer, Tycho Brahe, interpreted it as a positive sign which announced the birth of a new age of peace and surplus in approximately fifty years. Although Tycho Brahe was held to be an authority in his field, his prophecy did not find wide acceptance. One comet observed in 1577 and a highly unusual abundance of comets which could be observed with the naked eye at the end of the sixteenth and beginning of the seventeenth century – up to the appearance of Halley's comet in the year 1607 – were, for many, a sign of the approaching end of the world. In *Anatomy of Abuses* (1583), Philip Stubbs warns his readers that there is barely any time left for repentance, penitence or conversion:

The day of the Lord cannot be farre of. For what wonderful portents, strong miracles, fearful signes, and dreadful Iudgements hath he sente of late daies, as Preachers & foretellers of his wrath, due unto us for our impertinence & wickedness of life ... have we not seene Commets, blasing starres, firie Drakes, men feighting in the ayre, most fearfully to behold? Hath not dame Nature herselfe denied unto us her operation in sending foorth abortives, untimely births, ugglesome monsters and fearful / mishapen Creatures, both in man & beast? So that it seemeth all the Creatures of God are angry with us, and threaten us with destruction, and yet we are nothing at all amended! (alas) what shal become of us!

As the end of the century approached, such views became increasingly widespread. Thus, Joseph Hall, Bishop of Exeter and Norwich, complained in *Virgidemiarum* (1597) that the world is now 'thriving in ill as it in age decays'. Sir Richard Barcklay, in *The Felicities of Man* (1598), lamented that the wickedness of man 'doth presage the destruction of the world to be at hand', so that the universe, the heavens and all 'resembleth a chaine rent in peeces, whose links are many lost and broken, and the rest so slightly fastened as they will hardly hang together'. Robert Pont, a somewhat quirky Scottish reformer, calculated for his readers in *Newe Treatise of the Right of Reckoning of Yeares* (1599) that the year 1600 would be 'the 60 yeare of the blast of the seaventh & last trumpet' a year, therefore, which one must call 'a yeare of the decaying and fading world'. The comets and the eclipse of the sun in 1598 were signs of a decaying world and 'the age of the Worlde, be tokeneth the decaying parte thereof, as the eeld or age of a man, is called the latter parte of his life. And indeed it may well be said now, that we come to the decaying parte, and letter age of the World.'

A similar argument can be found in many works from the early seventeenth century. Thus, in *Confutation of Atheism* (1605), John Dove points to the 'irregular & threatning Eclipses', the 'un-usual aspects of the starres', the 'fearful Coniunctions of Planets' and the 'prodigious apparitions of Comets' as 'an argument that shortly the high Arch of heaven which is erected over our heads, will fall & dissolve it selfe'.

It is, therefore, hardly surprising that of all the holy scriptures, St John's *Revelations* was the one most frequently cited. It is interesting to note, however, that these commentaries make a clear and explicit relation between *Revelations* and English national history. As early as 1593, in the commentary *A Plaine Discovery of the Whole Revelation of Saint John*, which was reprinted six times before 1607, John Napier made precisely such suggestions. The work was dedicated to James VI, the heir-designate to Elizabeth. In the dedication, Napier draws attention to the beneficial effect on the nation which a good man at the head of state could have, and urged the interpreters of the apocalypse 'to encourage and inanimate Princes, ... as also to exhort them generally, to remove all such impediments in their Cuntries and commonwealths, as may hinder that work, and procure Gods plagues'. In the commentary, *Sermons upon the Whole Booke of the Revelations* (1599), George Gifford showed that 'while the Kings of England ... in times past were once horns of the beast, and gave their power to him', the younger rulers 'have pulled him downe ... They have ... made the whore desolate and naked'. After James' coronation, William Symonds even went so far as to suggest in *Pisgah Evangelica* (1606) that although the apocalypse was still to come, the first resurrection had already begun, as an example, as it were.

The relationship between James I and the apocalypse was frequently played upon and was not coincidental. Even James wrote a commentary, *A Paraphrase upon the Revelation of the Apostle St. John*, first published in 1588 and reprinted in 1603. In the Introduction, James declares that of all the scriptures, *Revelations* has the greatest significance for 'this our last aage ..., as a Prophesie of the latter time'. James' particular competence to interpret *Revelations* was justified and explained by his contemporary, Isaiah Winton:

GOD hath giuen him an vnderstanding Heart in the Interpretation of that BOOKE, beyond the measure of other men. ... God hath in this aage stirred up Kings to deliuer his People from a Scriptural Egypt and Babylon ... That Kings have a kinde of interest in that Booke beyond any other: for as the execution of the Prophecies of that Booke is committed vnto them; So, it may be, that the Interpretation of it, may more happily be made by them: And since they are the principall Instruments, that God hath described in that Booke to destroy the Kingdome of Antichrist, to consume his state and Citie; I see not, but it may stand with the Wisdome of GOD, to inspire their hearts to expound it; ... For from the day that S. John writ the

Booke to this present houre; I doe not thinke that euer any King took such paines, or was so perfect in the Reuelation, as his Maiestie is.[5]

Through his commentary, James gave *Revelations* previously unheard of official approval; at the same time he used the prophesy as a kind of touchstone with which to test loyalty towards him. The apocalypse gained an exceptionally important position in the writing, philosophy and lifestyle of English society during the reign of James I.

The last years of Elizabeth's reign and the first years of James' rule mark a period in which Shakespeare wrote nearly all his great tragedies: *Hamlet* (1601), *Othello* (1604), *King Lear* (1605), *Macbeth* (1606), *Antony and Cleopatra, Coriolanus* and *Timon of Athens* (1607). It therefore seems reasonable to suppose that tragedies in general must be related to the 'end-of-the-world' atmosphere and the debate on the apocalypse. This is particularly true of *King Lear*, which, in a wealth of images, use of word and speech, openly and directly takes up motifs from *Revelations* and draws upon the dramatic events at the world's end, the 'promis'd end' (V, 1, 263).

The play was written probably in 1605, the year in which not only an eclipse of both the sun (October) and the moon (September) occurred, but also the Gunpowder Plot (November) took place. The precise date of the première is not known. At court, however, the tragedy was performed on 26 December 1606. Shakespeare once again used Holinshed as a source, as well as the Lear drama performed in 1594, *The True Chronicle History of King Leir and his Three Daughters* (which first appeared in print in 1605) and, for the plot concerning Gloucester, Edgar and Edmund, Philip Sidney's *Arcadia*.

The tragedy *King Lear* – like Shakespeare's comedies – follows the structure of a rite of transition. The elderly King Lear falls into a crisis of identity (caused by stepping down from the throne, Cordelia's curse and the banishment of Kent [I,1]). This initially forces him to slowly discard his old identity (reduction through Goneril and Regan [Acts I and II]) and allows him to undergo new experiences (on the heath [Act III], madness [Act IV]) which finally lead to him taking on a new identity (reunion with Cordelia [Act IV]). Whilst the parallel procedural structure seems to point to an analogy with the comedies, other characteristics of the structure unmistakably mark out one principal difference: Lear does not pass through any of the stations twice; thus, he neither returns to his starting position nor to any point on his journey so far. Above all, Lear is no young hero on the threshold to adulthood, but rather an old man of over 80 years, on the threshold of death: 'while we / Unburthen'd crawl toward death' (I, 1, 40–1). The journey which he makes in his *rite de passage* completes the transition towards death.

At the beginning, Lear's identity is determined by the consciousness of being 'king' and 'father' – head of state and the family. As early as the first scene, he initiates the three actions which dissolve his identity in that they annul the conditions on which his identity is founded, the conditions through which alone it is secured.

First, Lear abdicates and divides the kingdom:

... Know that we have divided
In three our kingdom; and 'tis our fast intent
To shake all cares and business from our age,
Conferring them on younger strengths...
(I, 1, 36–9)

It would have been obvious to any spectator at the time of James I, the unifier of the kingdom, that Lear undermines the order of the state which rests on the rule of the 'anointed' king and the unity of the kingdom.

Second, he curses his youngest daughter, Cordelia, because she refuses to provide an exaggerated, rhetorical public demonstration of her love for him as his daughter:

For by the sacred radiance of the sun,
The mysteries of Hecate and the night,
By all the operation of the orbs
From whom we do exist and cease to be,
Here I disclaim all my paternal care,
Propinquity and property of blood,
And as a stranger to my heart and me

Hold thee from this for ever. The barbarous
  Scythian,
Or he that makes his generation messes
To gorge his appetite, shall to my bosom
Be as well neighboured, pitied, and relieved,
As thou my sometime daughter.
(I, 1, 110–21)

In this, Lear severs the natural 'bond' (93) on which the cohesion and order of the family depends, as Cordelia describes:

Good my lord,
You have begot me, bred me, loved me. I
Return those duties back as are right fit,
Obey you, love you and most honour you.
(I, 1, 95–8)

Finally, Lear banishes the loyal Kent when he tries to prevent him from dividing the kingdom and cursing Cordelia:

Hear me, recreant, on thine allegiance, hear
  me:
That thou hast sought to make us break our
  vows,
Which we durst never yet, and with strained
  pride
To come betwixt our sentences and our power,
Which nor our nature, nor our place can bear,
Our potency made good, take thy reward.
Five days we do allot thee for provision,
To shield thee from disasters of the world,
And on the sixth to turn thy hated back
Upon our kingdom. If on the next day
  following
Thy banished trunk be found in our domin-
  ions,
The moment is thy death. Away! By Jupiter,
This shall not be revoked.
(I, 1, 168–80)

Lear severs the social bond of loyalty which binds those who have a high social position in mutual dependency and obligation to those who occupy the lower positions, and thus destroys the foundation of social order. With these three actions, Lear undermines the order of the family, the society and the state on which both his identity and the identity of others is founded. A situation of insecurity is established which shakes the ground under his feet and which, in a short time, turns all into chaos. For those without a firm social position, such as the bastard Edmund, a self-made man in the true sense of the word, as is Richard III, the hour of promotion is come: 'I grow, I prosper: / Now gods, stand up for bastards!' (I, 2, 21–2).

Lear's two identities, as king and father, manifested when he divides the kingdom, curses Cordelia and banishes Kent, are revealed in elements which Shakespeare's spectators do not usually read into such role definitions so that they draw even more attention. Lear clearly identifies himself as an omnipotent god, and appears as such in his Old Testament-style rage. He gives the land away forever 'to thine and Albany's issues / Be this perpetual'; 'To thee and thine hereditary ever' (I, 1, 66–7, 79), curses and banishes into eternity (116, 179), and makes his word final (168–9, 179). The gods – Sun, Hecate, Jupiter, Apollo – are united with him and guarantee his oaths.

The image of the almighty god is, on the other hand, tied to the image of a dragon, a monster who tears humans into pieces (116–19; 176–8): 'Come not between the Dragon and his wrath' (121). The image of the dragon is not evoked in vain: in the twelfth book of *Revelations* it is represented as the embodiment of Satan. This all-swallowing monster also demands exclusive love from his daughters and public expression of that love, 'Which of you shall we say doth love us most?' (51).

Alongside these clearly manifested elements of identity can be heard the quiet murmur belonging to the opposite image of the self, though Lear is not yet fully conscious of it, 'while we / Unburdened *crawl* toward death' (39–40); 'I ... thought to set my rest / On her *kind nursery*' (123–4) (my italics). The terms 'crawl' and 'kind nursery' point to a small child who is dependent on a mother's care. The extent to which Lear actually feels his role as child, as one who must be cared for, and sees his daughter as mother, cannot be more clearly conceived.

The reduction of Lear from all-powerful king and father to naked creature, to 'unaccom-modated man' (III, 4, 106), begins directly after the division of the kingdom. At the abdication, Lear clearly assumed that the body politic of the king can be separated from the body natural while still maintaining the king's identity because the body natural secures it through 'The name, and all th'addition to a king' (I, 1, 137). Both assumptions are challenged. To his rhetorical question to Goneril's servant, Oswald, 'Who am I, sir?' (I, 4 76), Oswald answers, 'My lady's father' (77). And the 'addition', his entourage of 100 knights, are reduced by Goneril and Regan in a short time to fifty, twenty-five ten, five, one, none. At the end of Act II, Lear neither bears the 'name' nor commands the 'respect' of a king; in the sense that his identity is guaranteed by these things, he has stopped being king. He is, far more, as the Fool determines, 'an O without a figure', 'nothing' (I, 4, 183; 185).

In a similarly radical way, Lear's identity as father is undone. Goneril views him as an 'Idle old man, / That still would manage those authorities / That he hath given away. Now by my life / Old fools are babes again and must be used / With checks as flatteries, when they are abused' (I, 3, 17–21). After his abdication, he is no longer a father to Goneril, either. She sees him far more in the role of 'babe', whom she is not prepared to look after as caring mother, but thinks of punishing, as a wicked mother, as the Fool remarks sarcastically:

... nuncle, e'er since thou mad'st thy
daughters thy mothers; for when thou gav'st
   them the
rod and putt'st down thine own breeches.

(I, 4, 163–5)

Regan, too, does not enjoy the idea of the role of loving daughter; she also takes on the role of strict mother,

O, sir, you are old:
Nature in you stands on the very verge
Of her confine. You should be ruled and led
By some discretion that discerns your state
Better than you yourself.

(II, 2, 339–42)

Both daughters prove to be 'unnatural hags' (II, 2, 470): they do not recognise the 'bond' by which nature binds father and daughter in loving and mutual obligation to one another. Lear has stopped being a father.

The situation which Lear creates in abdicating, cursing Cordelia and banishing Kent now has effect on his self-awareness. Although he still rages and seeks to insist on his identity as king and father, 'The King would speak with Cornwall, the dear father / Would with his daughter speak, commands – tends – service' (II, 2, 293–4), he must finally accept that he cannot find recognition, either as king or as a father, in a world with no state or family order. He has lost his identity:

Does any here know me? Why, this is not
   Lear.
Does Lear walk thus, speak thus? Where are
   his eyes? …

Who is it that can tell me who I am?
                    (I, 4, 217–18, 221)

In this phase of reduction, the first components of identity which Lear enacts are those which are based on his identification with the 'dragon'. He damns Goneril to remain childless:

Into her womb convey sterility,
Dry up in her the organs of increase,
And from her derogate body never spring
A babe to honour her.
                    (I, 4, 270–3)

It is Regan who is to carry out the act of tearing her apart for him:

When she shall hear this of thee, with her nails
She'll flay thy wolfish visage…
                    (I, 4, 299–300)

The more clearly Lear sees the image of the 'sea-monster' in Goneril (I, 4, 253; I, 5, 18), the 'snake' (II, 2, 353), the 'wolf' (I, 4, 300), the 'vulture' (II, 2, 327), the more clearly he sees himself in relation to his own 'dragon' nature:

But yet thou art my flesh, my blood, my
   daughter,
Or rather a disease that's in my flesh,
Which I must needs call mine. Thou art a boil,
A plague sore, or embossed carbuncle
In my corrupted blood…
                    (II, 2, 413–16)

The process by which Lear arrives at this position exorcises the 'dragon' in him. Lear gives up his identification with it. In its place comes the next phase, in the storm on the heath; he turns solicitously to his companion in misfortune, the Fool:

Come on, my boy. How dost my boy? Art cold?
I am cold myself. [to Kent] Where is this straw
   my fellow? …

[to the Fool] Poor fool and knave. I have one
   part in my heart
That's sorry yet for thee. …

[to the Fool] In boy, go first …
                    (III, 2, 69–70, 72–3; III, 4, 26)

The 'topsy-turvy world' which Lear unmistakably presents to every early seventeenth-century spectator in allowing the Fool to go first – something which is only otherwise possible during the Feast of Fools, the feast of the topsy-turvy world – shows the suspension of the old order for the first time not as something negative, as the destruction of the old identity, but as a positive thing, too, as the potential for a new, better order. For, amongst other things, it allows Lear to see his fellow human beings independent of his position in the social hierarchy.

[Kneels] Poor naked wretches, whereso'er you
   are,
That bide the pelting of this pitiless storm,
How shall your houseless heads and unfed
   sides,
Your looped and windowed raggedness,
   defend you
From seasons such as these? O, I have ta'en
Too little care of this. Take physic, pomp,
Expose thyself to feel what wretches feel,

That thou mayst shake the superflux to them
And show the heavens more just.

(III, 4, 28–36)

On the other hand, Lear keeps his identification with the 'all-powerful'. Not only in cursing Goneril does he see himself in harmony with the gods ('Hear, Nature, hear, dear goddess, hear' [I, 1, 267]), but also – despite the grammatical limitation contained in the 'if' – in his confrontation with Regan (O Heavens! / If you do love old men if your sweet sway / Allow obedience, if you yourselves are old, / Make it your cause. Send down and take my part!' [II, 2, 381–4]) and in his threat of revenge against both,

I will have such revenges on you both
That all the world shall – I will do such things
–
What they are yet I know not, but they shall
be
The terrors of the earth!

(II, 2, 471–4)

Moreover, in the storm on the heath, it is Lear who commands the elements,

Blow winds and crack your cheeks! Rage blow!
You cataracts and hurricanoes, spout
Till you have drenched our steeples, drowned
the cocks!
You sulpherous and thought-executing fires,
Vaunt-couriers of oak-cleaving thunderbolts,
Singe my white head! And thou, all shaking
thunder,
Strike flat the rotundity o'the world,
Crack nature's moulds, all germens spill at once
That make ingrateful man!

(III, 2, 1–9)

Even in his discovery of his own human nature, Lear still acts out his 'likeness to God' in that he claims for himself the right to be 'more just than heaven'. It is only in the meeting with Edgar, dressed as bedlam beggar Tom, that Lear relinquishes his identification with the almighty:

Is man no more than this? Consider him well. Thou ow'st the worm no silk, the beast no hide, the sheep no wool, the cat no perfume. Ha? Here's three on's us are sophisticated; thou art the thing itself. Unaccommodated man is no more but such a poor, bare, forked animal as thou art. Off, off, you lendings: come, unbutton here. [*Tearing at his clothes, he is restrained by Kent and the Fool*].

(III, 4, 101–8)

In place of the gods, Lear now identifies himself with 'the thing itself', the 'unaccommodated man'; the all-powerful king clothed in all the pomp of the first scene has turned into a naked, unprotected man.

After this transformation, Lear reaches a new station on the journey from himself to himself, 'his wits are gone' (III, 6, 85); he enters the 'underworld' of madness. Here, the Fool leaves him because his work is done: he has accompanied Lear safely through the phase of dissolution of the old identity with ironic remarks and songs, has awoken feelings of consideration for his fellow men through his mere presence, and led him to the hovel from which Edgar arose as from the 'grave' (III, 4, 100), as 'the thing itself' and provoked a new source of identification. As a naked creature, 'cleansed' from all that is superfluous, Lear must now enter the 'underworld' alone and prepare himself for a 'rebirth'. The 'leader of souls', the Fool, has played his part.

In his madness, Lear seeks to bind his new identity with his old one. The 'thing itself' should be, at the same time, 'the king himself' (IV, 6, 84) – 'Ay, every inch a king' (107). This trying out of a new composite identity, allows him insight into the decay of society, whose representative he was as king. He sees its manifestation and the fateful consequences it brings, on the one hand, in unrestrained sexuality which upset the family (as in Gloucester):

Behold yon simp'ring dame,
Whose face between her forks presages snow,
That minces virtue and does shake the head
To hear of pleasure's name –

The fitchew, nor the soiled horse, goes to't
  with a more riotous appetite.
Down from the waist they are centaurs,
  though women all above. But to
the girdle do the gods inherit, beneath is all
  the fiend's: there's a hell,
there's darkness, there is the sulpherous pit,
  burning, scalding, stench,
consumption! Fie, fie, fie! Pah, pah!
                                    (IV, 6, 116–25)

On the other hand, he blames the injustice of
the state which only corrects the insignificant
sins of the poor and overlooks the villainy of
the rich:

… the great image of authority: a dog's
  obeyed in office.
Thou, rascal beadle, hold thy bloody hand;
Why dost thou lash that whore? Strip thine
  own back,
Thou hotly lusts to use her in that kind
For which thou whipp'st her. The usurer
  hangs the cozener.
Through tattered clothes great vices do appear;
Robes and furred gowns hide all. Plate sin
  with gold,
And the strong lance of justice hurtless breaks;
Arm it in rags, a pigmy's straw does pierce it.
                                    (IV, 6, 154–63)

The growing consciousness of an identity
which means that he is both 'king' and the
'bare, forked animal' opens Lear's eyes to a
wholly new perspective, on the one hand, of
kingship, on the other, of the human condition.
He finally understands the difficult dialectic of
the principle of the two bodies of the king
through his own body.

GLOUCESTER: O, let me kiss that hand!
LEAR: Let me wipe it first, it smells of
  mortality.
                                    (IV, 6, 128–9)

For Lear, human life appears, from the very
beginning, to be determined by suffering,
inconsistency, role-play and transience:

LEAR: Thou must be patient. We come crying
  hither:
  Thou knowst the first time that we smell
  the air
  We wawl and cry. I will preach to thee:
  mark me.
GLOUCESTER: Alack, alack the day!
LEAR: When we are born we cry that we are
  come
  To this great stage of fools.
                                    (IV, 6, 174–9)

Man may claim no rights other than the
sympathy of his fellow human beings.

  With the insights gained in madness, the
phase of transformation is ended. Lear now
can be 'reborn' into the new identity which was
previously tried and acted out. His rebirth is
the result of the 'good mother', Cordelia. She
was already described in the first scene as
Lear's 'physician' (Kent, 164) and the 'balm of
your age' (France, 216) and has travelled to
England with her army to help Lear – 'No
blown ambition doth our arms incite, / But
love, dear love, and our aged father's right' (IV,
4, 26–7) – and is explicitly described as his
redeemer:

… Thou hast one daughter
Who redeems nature from the general curse
Which twain have brought her to.
                                    (IV, 6, 201–3)

The rebirth is prepared by the 'long sleep' (IV,
7, 18), by dressing in 'fresh garments' (22) and
by 'music' (25). On waking, when Cordelia
says 'How does my royal Lord? How fares your
majesty?' (44), Lear believes that he is still mad
and in the underworld of the 'grave' and 'hell':

You do me wrong to take me out o' the grave.
Thou art a soul in bliss, but I am bound
Upon a wheel of fire that mine own tears
Do scald like moulten lead.
                                    (IV, 7, 45–8)

When he finally recognises Cordelia, 'For, as I
am a man, I think this lady / To be my child
Cordelia' (68–9), after a phase of uncertainty

and doubt about his status ('Would I were assured / Of my condition' [56–7]; 'for I am mainly ignorant / What place this is and all the skill I have / Remembers not these garments' [65–7]), and after she assures him of her love ('no cause, no cause' [75]) and Kent confirms he is, 'In your own kingdom, sir' (77), Lear is reborn as father and king. Now the incorporation phase must begin in which the transformed Lear will be reintegrated into society in his new identity, won through the storm on the heath and experimented with and tried out in madness.

However, this phase is not completed. Cordelia's army is defeated, and Lear and Cordelia are imprisoned. In this situation, Lear himself reduces his identity: he relinquishes his role as king and limits himself to the role of father:

… Come, let's away to prison;
We two alone will sing like birds i' the cage.
When thou dost ask me blessing I'll kneel down
And ask of thee forgiveness. So we'll live
And pray, and sing, and tell old tales, and laugh
At gilded butterflies, and hear poor rogues
Talk of court news; and we'll talk with them
  too –
Who loses and who wins, who's in, who's out –
And take upon's the mystery of things
As if we were god's spies. And we'll wear out
In a walled prison packs and sets of great ones
That ebb and flow by the moon.
                (V, 3, 8–19)

But Lear cannot even realise this reduced identity. Cordelia is hanged. Although Albany addresses him again as king with 'absolute power' (V, 3, 299), Lear no longer reacts,

And my poor fool is hanged. No, no, no life!
Why should a dog, a horse, a rat have life
And thou no breath at all? O thou'lt come no
  more,
Never, never, never, never, never.
[to Edgar?] Pray you undo this button.
  Thankyou, sir. O, O, O, O.
Do you see this? Look on her: look her lips,
Look there, look there! [He dies]
                (V, 3, 304–9)

When Lear dies, he is neither king nor father; he dies as an 'unaccommodated man' who begs an act of love from his fellow man, to 'undo this button'. The transformed Lear is not incorporated back into society.

And thus, equally, his transformation and death cannot lead to a renewal of society. The tragedy ends with Edgar's words – in another quarto given to Albany – which leave the future open:

The weight of this sad time we must obey,
Speak what we feel, not what we ought to say.
The oldest hath borne most; we that are
  young
Shall never see so much, nor live so long.
                (V, 3, 322–5)

The only certainty is that an epoch has come to an end and it is final.

The ending of King Lear forms an unmistakable opposition to the other Shakespearean tragedies. In the earlier tragedies Hamlet and Othello, the death of the hero leads to reintegration into society and, at the same time, renewal – as the marriage of the hero does in the comedies. In the later tragedy, Macbeth, the hero loses his identity and his death seals his ultimate exclusion from society; but, on the other hand, it also provides the conditions for the renewal of Scotland. It is only in King Lear that the death of the hero implies neither his reintegration into society nor the renewal of society.

In King Lear, Shakespeare works with a series of patterns whose sequence continually awakens or creates in the spectator certain expectations in the first four acts which then, at the end, are radically disappointed. Even different kinds or sections of the audience would have been aware of one or other pattern, so that it is certain that at least one of these patterns was familiar to every spectator: the effect of disappointed expectation was, thus, guaranteed.

One of these patterns is provided through knowledge of the earlier play, King Leir, in which Cordelia's army is helped to victory by the French army. Leir is re-enthroned as king and reigns several years more in peace.

Another pattern is provided by a chemical process, as described in various books on alchemy. Between 1602 and 1605, many influential works were published in this field, such as the popular anthology, *Theatrum Chemicum* (edited by Lazarus Zetzner, 1602), the English translation of Basil Valentine's *Zwölf Schlüssel* (*Twelve Keys*, Ersleben, 1599), Thomas Sendivogius' *Novum Lumen Chemicum* (Prague, 1604) and Thomas Tymme's *Practise of Chymicall Physiche* (London, 1605). A basic knowledge of alchemy was relatively widespread in Jacobean England, and thus, we can assume that many spectators were familiar with the concept. Thomas Tymme defined the process of chemical change thus:

> By transmutation I meane, when any thing so forgoeth his outward forme, and is so changed, that it is utterly unlike to his former substance and woonted forme, but hath put on another forme, and hath assumed another essence, another colour, another vertue, and another nature and property.

It was the goal of this process to turn ordinary gold (*aurum vulgi*) into philosophical gold (*aurum nostrum*). In literature of the time, the ordinary gold is symbolised by the king, the philosophical gold – or sage's stone – by the reborn 'red king'. In the process of transmutation, the 'king' must descend into 'nigredo' in which he is dissolved and out of which he will be newly reconstructed – 'solve et coagula' – in order to be unified with virginal mercury as the sage's stone or 'red king' and be reborn. The *longissima via*, by which the *magnum opus* is completed, is described by Sendivogius in the following way:

> *His life and body are both devoured*
> *Until at last his soul to him restored*
> *And his volatile Mother is made one,*
> *And alike with him in his own Kingdome.*
> *Himself also vertue and power hath gained*
> *And far greater strength than before attained.*
> *In old age also doth the Son excell*
> *His own Mother, who is made volatile*
> *By Vulcan's Art.*

In *King Lear*, as Charles Nicholl has shown,[6] Lear's transformation is clearly related to the chemical process of turning gold into the sage's stone through the systematic use of alchemic symbols (such as the dragon, the wolf, fire, etc.), and thus keeps the expectation of Lear's re-enthronement alive in those spectators with knowledge in this field.

Another pattern is revealed in the story of the Passion, both in scriptural form as well as in the version based on the Passion Play. Caroline Spurgeon has argued convincingly that the images and metaphors of the tragedy as a whole create the image of a 'human body in anguished movement' – 'tugged, wrenched, beaten, pierced, stung, scourged, dislocated, flayed, gashed, scalded, tortured, and finally broken on the rack'.[7] This is true of both Lear and Gloucester at whose 'torturing' clear references can be found to parallels in the Passion Play: 'By the kind gods, 'tis most ignobly done / To pluck me by the beard' (III,7, 35–6). Equally, Lear is 'upon the rack of this tough world / Stretch him out longer' (V,3, 313–14). He is – like Jesus – a derided king, and Goneril and Regan prepare his Passion so that he sinks, naked and unprotected, into a death-like sleep ('Oppressed nature sleeps' [Kent, III,6, 95]) and descends into the 'hell' of madness and arises again from the dead ('You do me wrong to take me out o'th'grave' [IV,7, 45]). But as little as Lear appears in his Passion as healer, and after it, as redeemer – these parts are exclusively given to Cordelia – as little does his death function as a socially cleansing scapegoat ritual (as in the Passion Play), nor does Lear experience an 'ascension into heaven', a re-enthronement (as in the scriptures and in the Passion Play).

The almost demonstrative divergence of the play's ending from the standard pattern which *King Lear* actualises for the spectator through the multiplicity of patterns which all awaken similar expectations, is given exceptional importance.

On the other hand, the divergence is not totally unexpected. For another well-known text continually runs against these expectations: the Apocalypse. In the play, references to

*Revelations* stretch from allusions such as the 'dragon and his wrath' (I, 1, 122), the 'late eclipses in the sun and moon' (I, 2, 106), the 'seven stars' (I, 5, 36), the 'prince of darkness' (III, 4, 139), the 'lake of darkness' (III, 6, 7), the 'monsters of the deep' (IV, 2, 51), the 'sulpherous pit' (IV, 6, 124), the 'defiled' and 'fresh garments' (IV, 7, 22), the 'wheel of fire' (IV, 7, 47), the trial scene to the judgement of the 'she-foxes' (III, 6) and the sound of trumpets (V, 3, 217), to this direct reference:

KENT: Is this the promised end?
EDGAR: Or image of that horror?
ALBANY: Fall and cease.

(V, 3, 261–2)

Lear's confrontation with the elements, cited above ('Blow winds...' [III, 2, 1–9]), contains the end of the sixth chapter of *Revelations*, 12–15, which reads, almost word for word:

And I beheld when he opened the sixth seal, and lo, there was a great earthquake; and the sun became black as sackcloth of hair, and the moon became as blood; / And the stars of heaven fell unto the earth ... / And the heaven departed as a scroll when it is rolled together; and every mountain and island were moved out of their places. / And the kings of the earth ... hid themselves in the dens and in the rocks of the mountains.

Such constant analogy forces the structure of the tragic plot and *Revelations* together in such a way that they commentate upon each other. Just as reference to the Apocalypse counteracts the expectations awoken by other underlying and known patterns, the tragedy actualises a secular reading of *Revelations*.

The gods with whom Lear at first identifies, whom Gloucester, Edgar and Albany call upon, never interfere in the actual happenings on stage – neither positively, nor negatively. If they do exist, they remain hidden and leave the world to man. The end of the world, constantly pronounced in the play, is certainly not caused by them – man alone is responsible. It is a world in which there is no valid order and each

individual is champion only of his own well-being, his promotion and the satisfaction of his lusts, a world in which 'homo homini lupus', man is a wolf to other men (as Edmund, Goneril, Regan, Cornwall), which implies degeneration into chaos and barbarism. When a king has learnt to perceive himself as a 'bare, forked animal', to show feelings of empathy for his fellow human beings and ensure justice in social institutions, but who can only act out this humane identity when he is mad, then it means nothing more than the end of human history.

In *King Lear*, Shakespeare confronts James I's reading of the Apocalypse, coloured as it is by national, political and religious concerns, with a secular, humanist one. The history of man can only develop in a new era when feelings of humanity and justice are recognised as the most important values.

Whether this must remain a utopia, or whether it can be realised, is left unanswered at the end of the play. Only in the romances, principally in *The Tempest* (1611), which combines crucial elements from *A Midsummer Night's Dream* with those from *King Lear*, does Shakespeare allow them to become reality, at least on stage.

Shakespeare died 23 April 1616 in Stratford-upon-Avon, where he was born fifty-two years before.

## THE SEDUCER, THE MARTYR AND THE FOOL – THEATRICAL ARCHETYPES IN THE *SIGLO DE ORO*

### 'The great theatre of the world'

In the seventeenth century, the topos of the *theatrum mundi* and the *theatrum vitae humanae* underwent an extraordinary generalisation. 'Theatre' and 'world' or 'life' now appeared as two fundamentally related dimensions which could only be characterised and understood properly through reference to this mutual relationship. This development manifested itself, above all, in two extraordinary processes: in the theatricalisation of life and in the expansion of theatre into a world theatre with a universal aspect.

Life at the European courts was increasingly staged like theatre performance. Whether it was the strict, often bizarre, Spanish court ceremony which was the form in Madrid and Vienna, or the French court ritual, which determined every move from the king's *levée* onwards, in all cases, presence at court was managed as if it were an appearance on stage. This theatricality of life found its greatest exaggeration at court feasts. Here, every festival hall became a stage: members of court appeared as actors; the king or emperor had his own role to play; and the other court members were not addressed according to their social position but, rather, according to the roles they were playing, even off-stage. As Richard Alewyn has remarked, the court feast principally served the court's theatrical self-fashioning:

> When, on the occasion of a wedding, the whole court garden is transformed into Mount Olympus in the *Armida*; when the meeting of two Princes is staged as an *entrevue*, then it is more than a mere theatrical masque. It is nothing less than the expression of a social and political need. It is only in the festival that the court society reached the form it desired. In the festival, it presents itself as it perhaps believes itself to be, and certainly as it would like to be.[8]

In Catholic countries, alongside the stagings of the court were religious stagings. The most important Christian celebrations were accompanied by magnificent processions as were the special festive canonisation celebrations or processions of reliquaries. In Spain, moreover, the Corpus Christi celebrations and the *auto-da-fé*, burning of heretics, which were commonly held at the same time as other great events, presented impressive examples of religious self-fashioning. Court and church staged both single actions and feasts, lasting over several days, as theatrical events.

At the same time, the theatricalisation of life corresponded to a sudden blossoming of theatre. Performances were given throughout Europe, in both urban and rural areas and across all social classes: permanent troupes in the permanent theatres of the bigger cities; wandering troupes on roughly constructed board stages in smaller towns and in the countryside; at court and church festivals; in Protestant schools and in Catholic monasteries. It was only the Puritan citizens in Protestant cities who cut themselves off from the passion of the era for theatre whilst, on the other hand, it was principally the Jesuits who activated all within their power to enable the great spectacles to unfold. Everything which existed in the world (in the universal sense) – whether 'real' event or fiction – could serve the theatre as object or material.

> There is ... nothing, absolutely nothing on, above, or under the earth, in nature, history or society which was excluded from the baroque stage: pagan tales and biblical stories, Roman emperors and Christian saints, the god Apollo on Parnassus and the country bumpkin from Bergamo, the Princess of Byzantium and the professor from Bologna, the cedars of Lebanon and the Holy Ghost as dove, yes, even the invisible movements of the soul and the incomprehensible mysteries of belief – but also the newest things of the day: the massacre of Paris, and the last martyr in China.[9]

In short, the whole cosmos was put on stage.

While the *commedia dell'arte* and Elizabethan theatre dealt with a horizontal perspective on human daily life, that is, with things which concerned life on earth, the new theatre interpeted the world on a vertical line as well, that is, it also took into account the dimension between heaven and hell. The baroque theatre stretched 'From heaven through the world and down to hell', as Goethe described it in 'Prelude in the Theatre' in *Faust*. It recreated the transcendent cosmos of the Middle Ages. The tension between immanence and transcendence formed the basis of baroque theatre and illustrated every happening on stage as an integral part of the history of salvation: theatre became world theatre with a universal aspect.

On the one hand, therefore, the 'world' itself became theatre, a stage where court and religious performances could put themselves on show, and on the other hand, the theatre became the perfect symbol of the 'world'. This mutual relationship is beautifully illustrated on stage by Pedro Calderón de la Barca in his *auto sacramental* (Corpus Christi play), *El gran teatro del mundo* (*The Great Theatre of the World*, 1645). God, the highest Master of Ceremonies, or Director, intends to produce a play himself; the world is the stage, the people are actors; their roles are the different social 'positions' – King, Sage, Beauty, Richman, Peasant and Beggar. The play to be performed is Life:

DIRECTOR: I mean to celebrate
My power infinitely great:
For does not mighty Nature find her sole
    delight
In showing forth my might?
Now as we know
That the most pleasing entertainment is a
    show,
And since we can
Interpret this the entire Life of Man,
I choose that Heaven shall today
Upon your stage witness a play.
I, being audience and manager together,
Can make the company perform this, whether
They would or not. ...

Each player I shall cast as I deem best,
And to ensure the play is to advantage
    dressed
With splendid costumes and with every
    machine
That may adorn the scene,
I wish you presently
To equip the stage with such machinery
As shall with fair effects take every eye,
Causing all doubt to fly
And giving the spectators certainty
Of faith in all they see.
And now it's time that we began –
I the Director, you the stage, the actor, Man.
                              (37–49, 55–66)[10]

Death calls the actors from the stage and when the play is over, God gives each one his wages according to the measure of his efforts:

It matters in no way
If you play Pauper or King;
As long as the Poor Man bring
Lively action to the play,
The King's equal he may
Be at last when they lay by
Their parts and distinctions fly.
If you play as well as your lord
You shall have your due reward
When I raise you up as high. ...

Each actor shall be paid
According to how he played,
And each in his part can
Earn well, the *Life of Man*
*Being all Show and Parade.*

And at the end of the play
The actors who never erred
And never forgot a word
Of the lines they had to say,
Will in my company stay
And have supper at my board
Where rank will be ignored.
                              (409–18, 424–35)

Calderón's *Great Theatre of the World* thus presents itself as a play within a play and, in this way, every play as play within a play. For when 'the reality of the spectator itself is merely a play, as the metaphor of world as theatre implies, then theatre is actually a play within a play'.[11] The boundaries between life and theatre dissolve and are melted away. Life means playing a transitory role, and theatre becomes an allegory of life, that is, it both empowers and exposes appearance, deception and the transience of life.

It is no coincidence that it was a Spanish playwright who articulated and explained such a correlation by means of theatre. This was because in Spain both processes, the theatricalisation of life and the expansion of theatre into world theatre, was realised in a pronounced way. The Spanish baroque coincided with the last days of the so-called 'Golden Age', or *siglo de oro*. This term is used to describe the long era from Charles I (1519–56) to the Treaty of the Pyrenees between Spain and France (1659).

Gold and silver from the Americas enabled Spain to make enterprises beyond its national borders and, thus, expand its power throughout Europe. However, at the end of the reign of Philip II (1598), there were already clear signs of economic weakness at the heart of the empire which escalated drastically under Philip III (1598–1621) and Philip IV (1621–1665). In Spain, the splendour and pomp of baroque theatricalisation unfolded before a background of domestic decay and an increasingly crumbling empire. Extraordinary contradictions define the image of this epoch. Whilst Don Jerónimo de Barrionuevo reported in *News* in 1658 that the Queen must now forgo the sweets with which she liked to end a meal because the confectioner 'no longer wanted to give her any, since she owed him so much and refused to pay', Calderón, who had been employed as court poet since 1635, was commissioned to organise extravagant and magnificent fiestas. The theatricalisation of life and the golden age of theatre effectively gloss over a background of misery, social decline and collapse. And yet, or even, precisely because of this, it was never so greatly magnificent as here.

The extent of the theatricalisation of life is shown by an anecdote recorded and commented on by Ortega y Gasset, in *Papeles sobre Velázquez y Goya*. Don Rodrigo Calderón, Marqués de Siete Iglesias, made himself the most unpopular man in Spain through his rash social promotion and the splendour with which he surrounded himself and was sentenced to death for immoral dealings. The day of his execution, 21 October 1621, became, as Ortega y Gasset wrote in his diary, the 'most glorious day the century has seen'. Not, however, because of the justice dealt out to the man, but rather because of a theatrical gesture made by Don Rodrigo as he climbed the scaffold: 'he climbed up without stumbling, elegantly tossed the hem of his cloak over one shoulder and maintained dignity and noble self-control right to the terrible end'. Immorality, the trial, and unpopularity are forgotten in one moment. A theatrical 'gesture on climbing the scaffold wipes away, destroys all his unpopularity in a moment and trans-

forms Don Rodrigo into the most popular man in the whole of Spain'.[12] Don Rodrigo understood how to direct his last appearance on the stage of the scaffold.

The art of self-representation in public did not stop in the face of death. As many different testaments show, the last fitting-out, the last appearance in the funeral procession, was pre-arranged to the tiniest detail. Calderón created his own funeral as one scenario of an act in *The Great Theatre of the World*, in which his corpse acts as a protagonist that exposes the transience of life and, thus, life as theatre. In his will, drawn up four days before his death (26 May 1681), he determined that he should be carried to the grave in an open coffin so that he might have the opportunity of compensating for the 'public worthlessness' of his 'terrible life' with the 'public warning' of death: *memento mori* – remember, you must die.

Amid this strong sense of the theatrical, it is hardly surprising that seventeenth-century theatre in Spain is described and understood as a phenomenon of mass culture. Performances were given from Easter to the beginning of Lent. Whilst in the sixteenth century, performances were held only on Sundays and feast days, by the beginning of the seventeenth century, two more days were added until, around 1640 in Madrid, performances were held daily in some months (particularly in January and February – carnival time – and in May, the month of Whitsun, October, November and December). The theatre became the 'daily bread' of the Spanish people, as one contemporary observer suggested critically in 1620.

Performances were held in three genres in the *corrales*, on the Corpus Christi stage and in court theatres. The *corrales* theatres – named after the inner courtyard, enclosed on all sides by buildings or walls, open to the air, or covered with a tarpaulin, where a primitive wooden stage was erected for performances – were first organised by *cofradías*, charitable brotherhoods who devoted themselves to the ill, orphaned, old and poor (in 1630, six hospitals depended on the income from theatres in Madrid). In Madrid, there were two *corrales de* comedias: the Corral de la Cruz (built 1579) and the Corral del Principe (opened 1583), both of which provided approximately 2,000 seats for spectators. Performances were mostly sold out. The theatrical troupes were engaged for the duration of a performance period by the various brotherhoods.

If one takes into consideration the frequency of performances, the size of the theatres and the fact that all the seats were sold out, and the size of the population in Madrid (in 1594, 37,500 inhabitants; in 1630, 180,000 residents and 20,000 non-residents, such as foreigners, visitors, vagabonds and beggars), then one must assume that a high percentage of the population regularly went to the theatre. The audience at the corrales was made up of all social classes. The different categories of seating and the gradation of prices accurately reflect the strictly hierarchical organisation of Spanish society. The cheapest were the standing places where mostly the young mosqueteros squeezed together – delivery boys and men in service, such as lackeys, runners, simple craftsmen, traders and opportune workers. François Bertaut, spiritual adviser to the Parliament of Rouen, wrote in his travel journal, Journal du voyage d'Espagne (1659), on the mosqueteros: 'Amongst them can be found all kinds of traders and craftsmen. They leave their shops and come with capes, swords and daggers and call themselves, even the simplest shoe-maker, caballero. They are the ones who decide whether a play is good or not.' Seats in the cazuela ('basket' or 'hutch') – the balcony lying opposite the stage, reserved for the female audience of the lower and middle classes – were also relatively cheap. Seats for the male audience, the gradas, on the long sides of the courtyard, preferred by members of the bourgeoisie, and the bancos, which were principally occupied by members of the lower nobility, were considerably more expensive. Since there were neither tickets nor numbered places, there were often fights over seats, some of which were decided by the sword. In Avisos, by José Pellicer, the following entry, dated 29 December 1643, reads: 'Yesterday Don Pablo de Espinosa killed a nobleman of the name

Diego Abarca at the comedy, and the swordsman himself was so badly wounded that his condition is hopeless.' The most expensive places were the aposentos, the boxes, which were often rented for the entire duration of the festival and occupied by the highest nobility (up to the royal family), important men of the church, high-ranking officials (for example, representatives of the various consejos) and the rich. Whilst the prices for the bancos, gradas and aposentos continually rose between 1608 and the ban on all theatre performances imposed by Philip IV in 1646 (which was lifted only five years later), the prices for the standing places and seats in the cazuela remained relatively stable. Playwrights were always given free entry.

The audience at the corrales de comedias was composed of a representative cross-section of the population of the capital. Extraordinarily, however, the rich nobility and even the king, visited this theatre, although they also commissioned troupes to so-called particulares (private performances) in their mansions and palaces. This seems all the more unusual since there was very little difference between the corrales theatre and the court theatre. The same plays were performed both in the corrales and at court by the same actors, with the sole difference that in the corrales, the performance was given in daylight and at court under artificial light. This changed, however, when a new palace stage was built in Buen Retiro, which opened in 1640. This theatre was equipped with wings – a device invented in 1618 by Aleotti and first installed in the Teatro Farnese in Parma, Italy, as well as with the latest theatrical machinery. It therefore called for plays which could make use of such machines. From this point, the comedia of the corrales theatres and the fiestas of the court theatre began to develop in different directions, even though the same playwrights wrote for both.

They also wrote the autos sacramentales, which were performed at Corpus Christi on cart-stages before the king and the president of the council of Castille, and at various market squares in the city for the general public. The actors who were hired by the church for this purpose belonged to the regular troupes which had fixed contracts at the *corrales*. The 'interchangeability' of the three genres of theatre was relatively great.

A visit to a *comedia* performance promised an entertainment that stretched between three to four hours. Although the performance did not begin before two o'clock, entry was permitted from midday. The time was passed in eating and drinking – every theatre had its own traders who wandered about among the crowd – and with the telling of risqué jokes, which were directed at the women in the *cazuela*, who, in turn, would revenge themselves by throwing nuts, shells and other projectiles. The performance began with a shrill, whistling noise (since there was no curtain to signal that a play was about to start) and music. One actor would appear to speak the *loa*, a form of prologue which flattered the audience, presented the company and the play, and begged the audience's attention, interspersed with witty stories and puns. This was proceeded by a mixed programme that always followed the same sequence: the first act of the *comedia* (which always consisted of three acts, *jornadas*), a farce as interlude with a realistic caricature of a certain social type; the second act of the *comedia*; the performance of a dance; the third act of the *comedia*; and finally, a Mummer's play with animal masks and other costumes, to escort the audience out of the *corrales*. The performances always ended in time for the female spectators to return home before dusk fell.

The entertainment value of the theatre depended, to a large extent, on its ability to offer its audience new and different things. This was achieved by a colourful mixture of individual pieces in the programme, as well as a repertoire which was continually renewed. The plays were quickly exhausted and had to be replaced by new ones. The incredible breadth of material in the baroque theatre helped to guarantee its audience plays filled with the suspense and excitement of the unknown. The playwrights tried to keep up with the rapid consumption of individual plays with an incredible rate of production. Playwright Lope de Vega estimated that at 41 years of age, he had written 230 plays and at 47 years, 483; by the age of 56, 800 and two years later, at 58 years, 900. In 1632, at the age of 70, he could look back on a total production of 1,500 plays, to which can be added 400 *autos sacramentales*. Next to this, Tirso de Molina's output seems modest. In twenty years, he wrote 'only' 400 plays. Like cinema and television today, seventeenth-century *corrales* theatre was obliged to find new plays to serve the audience ever new productions.

Such constant changes, both to the repertoire and to the sequence of single performances, fulfilled very different functions. First, the audience was entertained and diverted from an increasingly desolate reality. At the same time, the theatre provided a model of changeability and continual change, in the same way that fortune was believed to control all human relations. Finally, it confirmed the unchanging importance of certain values and ideals contained and realised in all the plays, despite their great differences. These values and ideals clearly defined an identity which all spectators recognised as binding and controlling in their lives, regardless of their social position and despite, or even precisely because of, the economic depression and political crisis in the Spanish empire.

The system of possible identities in the Spanish *comedia* is, unlike that in Elizabethan theatre, relatively simple and straightforward. It is described in its entirety in the play *The Great Theatre of the World*. Put simply, there are only two kinds of identity: one that is earthly, which is transient and temporary, and another, which is a permanent, true identity in the life after death. Both are determined once and for all by entry into each world (one immanent and one transcendent). The earthly identity is defined by the social 'role' which God has given each person before birth 'according to his nature and orientation'. How it is to be played out is clearly directed by the norms of behaviour which are dictated by the social order to members of the different social levels.

Eternal identity – as God's table companion, or as the damned – depends, on one hand, on how well the social 'role' is played and, there-fore, to what extent the earthly identity is realised and, on the other hand, on God's mercy. Thus, the law of mercy enters as Prompt in the play the *Great Theatre of the World*:

> The Law of Grace, I appear
> To speak the prologue here.
> Lest the actors go astray,
> This my prompt-book does the play
> As written by Thee, O Lord,
> In only two lines record
> That each can apply himself;
> [*Sings*] Love your neighbour as yourself –
> 'Do good, for God is the Lord'.
>
> (659–67)

Both identities are related to one another through the 'free will' of man:

> I easily might correct
> The errors I behold;
> With free will to control
> Their human passions, thus
> Giving them fullest scope
> To gain merit by their roles
> Wholly in their own hands.
>
> (929–37)

Here, a clear boundary is drawn between baroque theatre and the theatre of the Middle Ages. The position occupied in this case by free will was, in the Middle Ages, occupied by the magic of the body. Whilst in medieval theatre, the magic of the body allowed an unrestricted living out of the vital urges under certain conditions and, on the other hand, the magic of the body could only have effect through the physical suffering of a scapegoat, in the baro-que *comedia*, physical needs and drives and physical suffering and pain are both subject to the 'dictation' of the free will of each individual. In this, the responsibility for realisation of the earthly and eternal identity is placed squarely on the shoulders of the individual.

From this starting point, there are four possible ways in which earthly and eternal identities can be related to one another in the theatre:

1 The individual plays his earthly role well and enters the house of God.
2 The individual plays his earthly role well but is damned.
3 The individual plays his earthly role badly but enters the house of God.
4 The individual plays his earthly role badly and is damned.

The dramas can only differ in whether they lay importance on the earthly role (the so-called 'dramas of honour', for example, Lope de Vega's *Castigo sin venganza*, (*Punishment Without Revenge*, 1635) or Calderón's *El médico de su honra* (*Physician to His Own Honour*, 1637) or on the identity in eternity (the rather more 'religious dramas', for example, Tirso de Molina's *El condenado por desconfiado* (*Damned for Lack of Faith*, 1615/18)). Thus, in the *comedia* there are two kinds of hero: the ideal, exemplary one and the negative one who sets a bad example. In each group, one further differ-entiation is possible:

- the hero is judged unanimously by society and God in a positive or negative way (nos 1 and 4).
- mortal and divine judgement on the hero diverges because mortals orientate them-selves on appearance, which can deceive, while God has the whole view of the real being (nos 2 and 3).

Despite the great multiplicity of materials, genres, situations and characters which the Spanish baroque theatre brings to the stage, it always follows the same objective: to confirm for the spectator a fixed social role in his earthly identity and to prepare him for his per-manent identity in eternity, both by presenting models to emulate and, also, by presenting some negative examples to avoid.

### Honour disgraced and the forfeit of mercy

Don Juan, one of the most influential figures in theatre, a literary myth equivalent to Oedipus,

Hamlet or Faust, appears in the history of literature and theatre as a negative example. Later writers who re-worked and interpreted the figure have presented him as a social and metaphysical rebel, a romantic with a restless yearning for an ideal, as the 'absurd' hero *per se*. However, none of this later interpretation touches the first Don Juan. The Mercedarian monk, Gabriel Tellez, who wrote for the theatre under the pseudonym Tirso de Molina, composed the *comedia*, *El Burlador de Sevilla y Convivado de piedra* (*The Trickster of Seville and the Stone Guest*, performed sometime between 1619 and 1624, and printed in 1630) and furnished Don Juan with an inconstant nature from which later interpretations took their starting point. In this first Don Juan, however, his inconstant nature leads him to play a poor social role and gamble away his eternal spiritual salvation. His inconstant nature allows him to become a deterrent example in theatre.

The social order to which the dramatis personae of the *Trickster of Seville* refers is, above all, determined by the ruling law of *honour*. All characters in the play – with the exception of the servants Catalinón and Ripio, who function as *gracioso*, or fools – speak constantly of 'honour', and they only take action for the sake of protecting it, revenging the loss of it or, alternatively, insulting or slandering that of someone else. The question of honour characterises the whole social life of the *comedia*.

This statement can be applied almost without restriction to all Spanish *comedia*. It was not without reason that Lope de Vega explained, in his sole theoretical work, *El arte nuevo de hacer comedias en este tiempo* (*New Art of Play-writing for Today*), that 'cases which deal with honour are the best, for they are powerful in moving people of all social standing'. This reveals that the *comedia* only dealt with the question of honour because it played a dominant role in Spanish seventeenth-century public life and consciousness. The importance of honour for the Spanish way of thinking was almost incomprehensible to citizens outside the Spanish realm. Barthelémy Joly, the 'adviser

and mentor to the King of France', travelled to Spain in 1603/4. Disconcerted, he wrote in his diary, 'Keeping intact one's honour, which they call *sustentar la honra*, is the only thing honour is about. It is useless and responsible for the infertility of Spain.' In the social life of the golden age, honour came to represent the most absolute and highest value. One definition provided by the Castilian statutes, *Las Partidas*, as early as the thirteenth century, was still valid and possibly even more rigorously interpreted in the seventeenth century:

Honour lives in the name which a man has gained for himself through the position he takes up in life, through heroic deeds, or through his worthy character which makes him stand out from the crowd … And there are two things which are of equal weight: killing a man and slandering a man; for a man whose honour is besmirched, even if it is unjustified, is a dead man in terms of the esteem and honour the world shows him; for him, death would be preferable to life.

(Book II, xiii, 4)

Honour, therefore, contains two different aspects. On the one hand, it functions as the expression of personal value and, on the other hand, as the expression of a specific social value which an individual can lose through the actions of others. The Spanish *comedia* deals mainly with this second aspect, honour as a social value, which it holds to be absolute. Thus, in Lope de Vega's *comedia*, *Los Comendadores de Córdoba* (*The Knights-Commander of Cordoba*), he writes:

No man is honourable through his own
   actions,
He is apportioned honour by others.
A man who is virtuous and commendable
May not yet be called honourable. And thus,
Honour lives in others and not
In oneself.

In the Spanish *comedia* of the seventeenth century, honour seldom appears as something earned by personal achievement, rather it is almost exclusively a social value. The loss of honour implies the loss of life. The social identity of the individual is defined and guaranteed solely by his honour. Without honour, he no longer exists as a person. Honour is vital to all members of all social classes. In the *Trickster of Seville*,[13] the fisherman's daughter, Thisbe and the peasant girl, Aminta, bewail the loss of their honour no less vehemently than do the noble ladies, Isabel and Doña Anna. The Duke Octavio sees his honour as much endangered through the behaviour of his bride, the Duchess, as does the peasant Patricio through the supposed wrong-doing of his bride, Aminta. Honour is determined according to the family into which the individual is born, according to his 'blood'. Thus, Don Diego trusts in the honour of his son, Don Juan, and points to his heritage, 'No, his blood's too noble' (III, p. 358), just as the peasant Gaseno believes in his daughter, Aminta, in his reference to the 'purity of her blood' ('limpieza de sangre'), since she stems from an 'ancient Christian' family in which there are no 'moriscos' (baptised Arabs) or Jews.

> Most honourable,
> … she is by lineage.
> One of the non-converted ancient Christians.
> (III, p. 359)

One *has* honour, it cannot be earned and yet it can be lost at any time. Mere doubt about someone, whether founded or unfounded, is reason enough to rob them of their honour and turn them into a social nonentity. The system of social identity is precariously balanced. It can only function smoothly when an individual is prepared to keep his desires and emotions under the control of his free will and is able to avoid harming anyone else's honour. However, such perfect self-control is hardly a general quality. It is far more the exception than the rule. In cases of lack of self-control, society has two possibilities. If a young unmarried girl has been dishonoured, the loss of honour which affects not only the girl but also her family, can be redressed by marriage to the seducer. (Accordingly, marriage in the *comedias* always represents the re-building – or strengthening – of the disturbed social order.) In all other cases,

on the other hand, the loss of honour must be revenged by the death of the one who has caused the dishonour.

Even Don Juan unconditionally recognises the law of honour. He often refers to it in different ways. Thus, he answers the stone statue, 'And as a Gentleman, you'll keep your word? / I keep my word, with men, being a knight' (III, p. 356). He has high hopes that his honour will increase when he receives the invitation to supper in Don Gonzalos' crypt:

> Tomorrow I will go there to the Chapel
> Where he invited me, that all of Seville
> May make a living legend of my valor.
> (III, p. 356)

Thus, the expectation that Don Juan only dishonours women because he seeks to rebel against valid norms and values, is firmly refuted. Tirso de Molina's Don Juan is no social revolutionary.

Unlike the Don Juans who follow him, the first Don Juan seldom comments on the reason for his repeated seductions. The reader/spectator discovers nothing about his motives for dishonouring the Duchess Isabel. In the case of the fisherman's daughter, Thisbe, Don Juan blames it all on sexual desire, explaining to his servant Catalinón, 'Why for her love I'm almost dying / I'll have her now, then scamper flying' (I, p. 305); 'I'm on the verge / Of dying for her. She's so good' (I, p. 311). Similarly, he justifies the seduction of Aminta by equating the sudden outbreak of desire with love: 'Love guides me to my joy. None can resist him. / I've got to reach her bed' (III, p. 341). As for Doña Anna, on the other hand, of whom he only knows that she is 'Nature's masterpiece' (II, p. 322) without even having seen her, he gives the enjoyment of a successful trick as his motive:

> In Seville
> I'm called the Trickster; and my greatest pleasure
> Is to trick women, leaving them dishonoured.
> (II, p. 323)

Wherever the code of honour stands in opposition to Don Juan's individual preferences, emotions and desires, and threatens to restrict him, he does not have the least scruple in contravening it. For him, his own individual person carries the highest value. He is neither willing, nor able, to control his desires for the sake of social honour – unless his own honour is at stake – and instead, allows himself to be blown to and fro by his emotions. Don Juan's lack of constancy stems from misusing his free will; this is the reason for the loss of his social identity.

In order to satisfy his emotions and desires, Don Juan turns to deception, disguise and role-play in which words serve as an effective mask. To the Duchess Isabel and Doña Anna he plays the role of fiancé – either as Duke Octavio or the Marquis de la Mota. He also promises marriage to the two peasant girls, Thisbe and Aminta. Thus, in each case, Don Juan provides a negative self-definition: either he plays the role of someone of a different standing than his own, or he executes a speech-act which does not agree with his social role (marriage between members of the nobility and ordinary citizens was forbidden). In order to satisfy his individual needs and to show himself off to advantage, Don Juan paradoxically dissolves his own social identity and thereby the single factor which would create and maintain his honour and, consequently, his social status as a person. He becomes a 'man without a name' (I, p. 288), he reduces himself to a simple biological being when he reacts to the Neapolitan king's question as to his identity, with the words, 'Why can't you see – / A man here with a woman? Her and me' (I, p. 288).

At first, society allows itself to be deceived by Don Juan. Its highest representative, the king, intends to honour and reward the respected Don Juan Tenorio, son of the First Chamberlain, Don Diego Tenorio, with the hand of Doña Anna. After he learns of Isabel's seduction, he sees it as a single crime against honour which can be made good through marriage. He even gives Don Juan the title, Count of Lebrija, in order to console Isabel for losing a Duke (Octavio). It is only when all those who have been dishonoured and deceived by Don Juan appear before the king and demand their rights, that the extent of his crimes comes to light. Finally, the king orders him to be put to death.

In the meantime, however, divine justice already plays a part, for God cannot be deceived and, through the hand of the deceased Don Gonzalo de Ulloa, has shown Don Juan the torments of eternal damnation in hell, 'God ordered me to kill you thus, and punish / Your monstrous crimes. For what you've done, you pay' (III, p. 367). There can be no doubt now that Don Juan's crimes against society – dishonouring women, betraying a friend, offending a host, killing Don Gonzalo in a duel, showing lack of respect for the sacraments of marriage (Aminta), deceiving the king – are also sins in the eyes of the Catholic faith. Nevertheless, Don Juan is not judged primarily for this reason.

The dramatic characters of the *Trickster of Seville* are all sinful people. Isabel allows her supposed fiancé entry to her private quarters, just as Doña Anna calls the Marquis de la Mota to her in order to rebel against her father and the king. Thisbe behaves arrogantly to her suitors and gives herself up to Don Juan, and the Marquis de la Mota is known to stroll the alleyways with prostitutes. As it is described by the honourable Don Gonzalo (Act I), Seville is a veritable hotbed of vice, quite the opposite of the Christian city Lisbon. Nevertheless, God's divine judgement does not fall upon any other figure but Don Juan alone.

In terms of Spanish Catholicism in the seventeenth century, even the serial repetition of Don Juan's sins is insufficient cause for damnation. Divine mercy, provided by recommendations by the saints and the soldiers of the church, can wash away every stain of sin, so long as the sinning soul reconciles itself with heaven in the last hour through true repentance, confession and absolution. Eloquent proof of this interpretation of sin and death is provided by numerous reports in the 'news' and 'sketches' of the Spanish capital, detailing fights which ended fatally, for example: 'Last night, Fernando Pimental was killed with a sword before he was even able to draw his own. He called for confession. He died with a great show of repentance for his sins by calling loudly "misere mei Deus" and later, weeping many tears as he died, "In te, Domine, Speravi"' (August 1622); 'At eight o'clock in the evening, some members of the nobility were waiting in front of the entryway of the house of Diego de Avila, in order to kill him. They threw themselves upon him and beat him down. He called loudly for confession' (1 September 1624); 'In the Calle Paredes, Cristóbal de Bustamante was killed, before he was able to make confession' (3 October 1627).

As these records show, Don Juan's crime lies mainly in his lack of willingness to repent. Although he is constantly warned by various people and urged to convert and repent, he refuses to do so and shifts the repentance necessary for his salvation into the far distant future. His servant Catalinón reproaches him: 'Those who cheat women with base sham – / In the long run, their crime will damn, / After they're dead' (I, p. 312). Thisbe also warns him, 'But oh remember God exists – and Death' (I, p. 313). And his father, Don Diego, tries to persuade him:

May God reward you as your sins deserve.
Listen, for though it now appears that God
Puts up with you, consenting to your crimes –
That punishment is certain – and how fearful
For those who have profaned his name in
  vows!
His justice is tremendous after death!

(II, p. 326)

Don Juan throws all these warnings and admonitions to the winds with words which almost become a leitmotif: 'A long, long time, before I need repentance' ('¡Qué largo me lo fiáis!' and '¿Tan largo me lo fiáis?').

He does not refuse to repent on the grounds that he is a heretic (Protestant) or even an atheist. He certainly does believe in hell and in divine mercy; eagerly, he seeks to question the dead Don Gonzalo:

Are you in the Grace
Of God? Or was it I that killed you recklessly
In a state of mortal sin. Speak! I am anxious.

(III, p. 354)

Don Juan is, therefore, no more a metaphysical rebel than he is a social revolutionary. He only shifts the necessary repentance to a later date because he relies on God's patience. The expression '¿Tan largo me lo fiáis?' belongs to the world of economics: a borrowed sum of money must be repaid by a certain date. Don Juan is counting on the fact that God will hold good his debt until his death, which he believes is far off in the future: 'A long, long time, before I need repentance'. In the meantime, however, he does not see any obstacle which might prevent him from satisfying all his various desires, feelings and inclinations; he misuses free will by deliberately leading a life of sin and hopes to negotiate God's mercy through confession and, ultimately, formal repentance at the actual moment of death.

At the beginning of the seventeenth century, the relationship between divine mercy and human freedom was a point of heated and controversial discussion among Spanish theologians. Luis de Molina (whose name Tirso de Molina borrowed as his pseudonym) taught that God only awards mercy to those who are prepared to ask for it. The Dominican friars opposed this idea as a belittling of God, a restriction of his almighty power. This argument was debated in all social classes in Spain so passionately that in 1602 the Papal Curia felt it necessary to forbid any further public discussion of the matter.

Tirso de Molina took up the theme in *Condenado por desconfiado* (*Damned for Lack of Faith*) and reanimated discussion in the theatre in *Trickster of Seville*, where he proposes a specific viewpoint on the matter. Don Juan, the *burlador* (someone who tricks, deceives and mocks) is torn out of his young, sinful life and damned to the eternal tortures of hell because, despite many admonitions, he shows no willingness to repent and undertakes nothing to ask for God's forgiveness, but rather views it as a kind of mercantile object which can easily be redeemed at the moment of death through confession and absolution.

Even if Don Juan exercised a certain fascination on his spectators – particularly the young men who felt their individuality restricted by the Castilian code of honour and whose secret desires he embodies – there can be no doubt that he was not put on the stage to be received as a figure of identification but, rather, as a deterrent example. Don Juan deliberately and energetically breaks the social and divine order, the law of honour and mercy. In putting his own person at the highest value, he practises no control over his desires, feelings and needs and they lead him hither and thither; he does not even regret his all too human lack of self-control and refuses to do repentance. Social disrepute, death and eternal damnation are the necessary consequences of such behaviour. It is expected and demanded of the individual that he subjects his free will to the earthly and divine order and adapts himself to them. In this, crimes and sins are viewed as 'normal' ('to sin and repent and sin again seem to be almost programmatic for some sections of Spanish society, particularly among the higher classes').[14] An individual who holds himself up to be absolute, however, falls irretrievably out of the system.

## The transitory social role and the eternal self

The dramatists of the golden age not only used the *corrales* theatre as a public forum for the discussion of generally important issues, such as the teaching of mercy, but also, and more frequently, for personal feuds. In early 1629, the actor Pedro de Villegas wounded Calderón's brother, José, in an argument at a gathering of theatre artists in Madrid and fled to the nearby convent of the Barefoot Nuns. During the chase, Calderón forcefully entered the convent with several policemen and ruthlessly searched the cells for the culprit. The case aroused much outrage, not least in Lope de Vega, whose daughter, Marcella, entered the convent at the age of 17 in 1623. The head of the convent, the

court chaplain Fray Hortensio Paravicino de Arteage, exploited the situation at a commemorative service for Philip III on 11 January 1629 in order to rail against actors and playwrights from the pulpit as disturbers of the peace and troublemakers. At the same time, Bartolomé Romeros' company was rehearsing a new play by Calderón, *El príncipe constante* (*The Constant Prince*). Calderón reacted to the sermon by creating a few extra verses for the Fool in the *comedia* and adding them to the speech in which the Fool jokes about a ship coming in:

> A commemorative speech is hammered out,
> Which is a sermon full of nonsense:
> It is a eulogy which I shall declaim to water,
> and I complain with Hortensian railing,
> for my rage has its source
> in watered down wine; it remains and yet is
> old already.
>
> (I, 2)

The audience shrieked with delight, the king found it amusing, but Fray Hortensio was infuriated and wrote a letter in protest to his majesty. Calderón, he explained,

> took revenge last Friday in a *comedia* entitled *The Constant Prince*; he dragged my name across the stage and introduced it through a corrupter of good morals, a foolish servant (or *gracioso* as they are called) who represents an eternal insult to god and man, to make jokes about my sermon – particularly the funerary orations and eulogies that I have, at various times, held for Your Majesty in honour of your glorious father.[15]

Calderón was sentenced to several days' house arrest and was obliged to delete the offending verses. The performances which had already taken place, however, had certainly provided more than adequate public satisfaction.

This episode throws light on one characteristic of Spanish baroque theatre. Neither Calderón nor his contemporaries felt it was a contradiction to use a *comedia* such as *The Constant Prince* which, like no other, preaches the transitory nature of all that is earthly, as an instrument of debate in a very earthly feud against a priest and court chaplain. A public attack from the pulpit could be countered by a public attack from the stage. In this, theatre slapstick and *memento mori*, that which was all too human and that which was all too eternal, found their natural place next to each other on the stage without one disturbing the effect of the other, or even influencing it. The sideswipes against the court chaplain Fray Hortensio did not affect the exemplary, stoically borne suffering of Prince Fernando for the sake of Catholic faith.

*The Constant Prince* involves an episode of Portuguese history which was first reported in a chronicle by João Alvarez (first edition 1527, second edition 1577) and which became the subject of various poetic and historic works in the sixteenth and seventeenth centuries. It concerns the Portuguese expedition to Tangier in 1437, during which the Infante Fernando is imprisoned by the Moors in ransom for the city of Ceuta, and dies. The historical events are interesting to Calderón only in that they allow him to interpret and present history in the light of religious salvation.

The historical events are controlled by fortune, to which both Christians and Moors must bow ('For, in the world of chance / These are the objectionable pranks of fortune' [Fernando: I, 925–6]; 'This inconstancy of the times, / This angry chance, / This stormy fortune, this bitter / Example of the way of the world' [Muley: II, 741–5]; 'false / transitory fortune, / Which plunges me into this state' [King: III, 778–80]). It is a turn in fortune which causes the downfall of Prince Fernando; it transforms the Infante into a prisoner, a slave, and finally, into a cripple and beggar. As Fernando himself comments:

Born as the Infante,
I have become a slave: it teaches me,
That from this state I
Could fall still further into deeper misery.
For, from the rights of an Infante,
To slave, as I am already,
Is much further,
Than it is from slave to most miserable slave.
(II, 151–8)

The stability of the social role which guarantees the individual his identity in the cloak and dagger, or moral and honour plays has become invalid. The social role is subject to fortune and the transitory nature of the world, and is no longer an identificatory factor. This suggests a new constellation in the question of identity.

At first, Fernando finds a solution in drawing upon certain roles, as 'noble' (to Muley [I, 825]), as 'knight' (to the King [I, 906]), as 'Infante', 'Master of the Order', 'Portuguese' (to his brother, Enrique [I, 864–5]). When, however, the Christian city Ceuta is to be handed over to the heathen Moors as ransom for his life, he rejects it all by referring to the vanity of the social role and defining himself as man:

Who am I, more than just a man?
If the ransom could make it happen,
I would be Infante: prisoner
Am I now, such heights
Are beyond the reach of a slave;
And, as I am, he who wants
To call me Infante deceives himself.
(II, 391–7)

Fernando maintains this self-definition up to his last role, that of the beggar:

Look, I am a man and have
Nothing, to refresh my hunger:
Have pity and compassion,
You folk! For even an animal
Has mercy on another animal.
(III, 371–6)

In coming to understand himself as a person, he gains insight into his own mortality:

Yet, should Death never approach,
Although we men are only mortal? ...
Men must not be carefree and blind,
But think of this, in the time allotted,
That there is a life eternal.
(III, 609–10, 614–16)

Eternal life can only be won by bearing witness to the Catholic faith as a Christian; whether as a soldier of Christ, 'Spreading the word of God' (I, 552), or as a martyr who is prepared 'to die / for his belief' (III, 524–5). In refusing to exchange the Christian Ceuta for his freedom 'Because it belongs to God, not me' (II, 485), Fernando freely chooses the earthly lot of the martyr and calls upon the universe to witness his choice:

> King, brother, moors, Christians,
> Sun, moon and starry canopy,
> Heaven, earth, wind and sea,
> Beast, and mountain, hear ye all!
> A constant prince consolidates
> Today the Catholic faith
> In torment and suffering,
> And honours the Almighty Law.
>
> (II, 437–44)

The only way to combat the changeability of life is to own a Christian identity, which is constant. Even if it can only be maintained at the price of suffering and death, it must be paid with stoic patience ('My patience is greater than his anger' [II, 546]). God will then gloriously approve this identity, as the apparition of the dead Fernando reports: 'For so many temples, God shall give one temple to me – rare example!' (III, 707–8). Fernando opposes the transitory nature of the social role with the eternity of his self in God, with his death for the Catholic faith.

It is interesting that Fernando's insight into the vanity of the social role, and the equality of all men in death ('And since all our affairs / are made equal by death, if not today then tomorrow' [II, 618–19]), does not disregard the rules valid to each social role while it is being played. As in social life, Fernando's social identity on stage is clearly marked for the spectator through appropriate costume. As Infante and Master of the Order, Fernando wears a cloak of the Order with a cross over the chest; the king commands the slave to have 'chains' put 'Round his neck … and ankles', 'He shall no longer wear robes of silk / But meagre, rough cloth' (II, 510–11), and as the poor cripple and beggar, Fernando is finally thrown on the 'dungheap'. The change in costume or outward

appearance unmistakably points to the changes in social role dictated by fortune. Each of these roles corresponds to a specific way of behaving to which Fernando strictly adheres. As 'noble' and 'knight' he complies with the knightly code of honour when he generously releases the imprisoned Muley to his Lady Fénix:

> Return home, tell your Lady:
> A Portuguese knight sends
> You to her, as slave.
>
> (I, 805–7)

As slave, Fernando shows himself more than willing to serve: 'For I should be the first to serve well' (II, 613). As beggar he allows the Fool character, Brito, to teach him how to beg correctly:

> If I could
> Raise my voice to move
> Someone to give,
> So that I live yet another moment
> In this misery!
>
> (III, 358–62)

Exact obedience of the rules of the various social roles and upholding the eternal identity as Christ are not mutually exclusive, rather, they are closely related to one another. The role can only be broken if a conflict arises between the transitory role and the eternal identity, as Fernando comments:

> That which is right,
> So heaven decrees, in this
> The slave must obey his Lord.
> But if the Lord orders
> His slave to commit a sin,
> He is not obliged by duty
> To obey, for he who demands the evil act,
> Commits the evil act.
>
> (II, 489–96)

At the end of the *comedia*, when the image of the dead Fernando enters with the cloak of the Order around his shoulders, it functions as a manifest sign which confirms the principal agreement between Fernando's original social role as Infante and Master of the Order, and his eternal identity in God. The repeated imagery of the three crowns also points to this agreement: the crown of the prince, the martyr's crown of thorns and the heavenly crown in eternity.

Through an ingenious play on correspondence and opposition, the other dramatic characters in the play are used as mirrors to Fernando, reflecting various different aspects of the tense relationship between the social role and eternal identity.

The correspondence between Fernando and the King of Fez is determined by the fact that both are princes, even if they are opposed as the Christian and the heathen prince. The superior position of king is unaffected in this, for kingship is founded on and guaranteed by the laws of nature. Here, Fernando tells the king:

I called you king, although you
Are king of a foreign teaching.
Royal divinity is so superior,
So natural,
That it produces a mild spirit …
This name even stands on that noble height
Among animals and wild beasts,
A name which stems from the right
Of Nature and demands
Obedience.

(III, 408–20)

However, though the Christian prince, Fernando, becomes a martyr, the heathen King of Fez proves to be a tyrant, for he puts him in chains and allows him to starve. As Walter Benjamin has explained, 'Tyrants and martyrs … in the baroque are the Janus heads of one crown. They are the inevitable extreme characteristics of royal nature.'[16] In the same way that constancy is characteristic of the prince as martyr, so the tyrant is characterised by the fact that he allows his feelings uncontrolled free reign:

Silence! Speak no more!
For your voice is poison
To me, filled with furious wrath,

Every word brings me near death.
I shall make Africa a graveyard
For your defiant hordes.

(I, 381–6)

The King of Fez embodies the negative side of royalty, Fernando the positive side, which bears on eternity.

Although Muley, as heathen, also stands in opposition to Fernando, he also presents a correspondence. This first becomes apparent in the social role as 'noble'; Fernando and Muley both recognise the knightly code of honour: 'Love and friendship must / Take second place after duty and honour' (II, 880–2). Both meet the changeability of fortune with constancy for what they believe in: just as Fernando proves himself constant in faith, so Muley shows constancy in his love for Fénix. Whilst Fernando battles with the King of Fez for the possession of the Christian city Ceuta, 'which … translated from the Arabic / Into Hebrew means Beauty' (I, 179–81), Muley fights with Tarudante (who, like the king, allows himself to be carried away by his feelings and is a braggart and boaster) for possession of the king's daughter, Fénix, who is introduced as 'hermosura', as 'beauty' and 'beautiful'. The virtues which Fernando shows in the battle and suffering for the Catholic faith, that is, on an eternal level, are reflected in Muley's love for Fénix on an earthly level.

As 'prize for the dead' (II, 647), Fénix is related to Fernando through equivalence to his corpse. Even if her name, a bird who is reborn out of the ashes ever more beautiful, points to the resurrection and allows her to appear, in this respect, in correspondence to Fernando, her actual characteristic is transitoriness, for which both the corpse, flowers and stars provide the most penetrating emblems of the epoch: 'The roses came to bloom so soon, / And bore blossoms as they aged, / Which sprang from the cradle and grave of the bud' (II, 690–2); 'They only live in flower-mourning. / They are night blossoms: … For if a day lasts as long as a blossom, / Then a lifetime of the stars endures but a night' (II, 719–23). It is beauty especially which suffers in the transitory nature of human life revealed in these emblems. On the other hand, it must not be overlooked that it is precisely this beauty which embodies a quality in earthly life which corresponds to enduring faith, or Ceuta.

The earthly qualities of constancy in love, honour and beauty are explicitly reinforced in the marriage of Muley and Fénix at the end. Although these earthly qualities are subject to the passage of time, and though they are transitory they may, as the play of correspondences and parallels shows, be seen as allegories of the eternal qualities of faith, honour in God or the honour of being a Christian and having constancy in faith – in the same way that it was thought that the events of the Old Testament were allegories of those in the New Testament. Earthly qualities gain importance and dignity because, as signs, they are able to refer to the immortal and immaterial; through their sign character, immanence is related to transcendence, social order to divine order, and the social role of man to his eternal identity in God. The strength of the human self is measured according to the constancy with which it meets the various twists of fate. The highest ideal is embodied by the martyr Fernando, who proves his virtue in suffering for the Catholic faith. Whilst in the medieval theatre, physical suffering was only expected of the divine scapegoat, the human self in the baroque theatre is seen to be strong enough to take over as successor to Christ. The Christian prince, as no other, seems most suited to show this human strength and bear witness in an almost representative way.

In other *comedias*, the constant lover is opposed to the seducer, who is also subject to changing affections and desires; here, it is the tyrant who stands in the opposite corner, as deterrent example, as one who allows himself to be controlled by his feelings. Inconstancy, being enslaved by emotion and the lack of self-control consistently characterise negative characters. There is, however, one important exception to this rule, the *gracioso* – the Fool, in

the *comedia*. The *gracioso*'s very element is one of constant change, to which he adapts for the sake of survival and physical intactness, without even thinking. Thus, Brito pretends he is dead as he lies amongst the corpses of the battle field ('For a while / I shall settle myself down and seem dead, / And take it for death in the future [*He throws himself down on the ground*]' [I, 883–5]); he would prefer to let himself be trampled on by the soldiers in battle than be drawn into the chaos of battle itself. When the Moors intend to throw him into the sea as a corpse, he sees no other chance of saving himself than to draw his sword: 'If I cut your heads to threads, / in slice and slash, / Then it proves in death we are still Portuguese' (I, 869–70). In the Moorish prison, he teaches the martyr Fernando how to beg,

Say:
Moors, Let yourselves be begged,
To give alms to the poor,
So that he may stop his hunger
For the sake of the prophet Mohammed's
Holy Big Toe.

(III, 378–83)

The Fool embodies inconstancy *per se*, not as a deterrent or negative figure, but as a comic one. He gives the spectators the opportunity of laughing about (his/their own) human weaknesses and, in so doing, to lift themselves above it. Certainly, the primary function of the *gracioso* is release in the face of the strict demands which honour and faith require.

The strength of the self in the Spanish baroque theatre is not shown in rebellion, nor in the way an individual might rise up against the restrictive order, but rather in his willingness and ability to practise self-control, to follow the rules valid at the time and so adapt himself to the social and divine order. In the world of history, with its changeability of fortunes, only constancy as total self-control, as the martyr Fernando shows, can overcome the transitoriness of life and secure the self an identity in eternity.

## Popular theatre between religious and court theatre

The dramatic characters that inhabit the Spanish popular stage in the seventeenth century are saints and sinners, gentlemen of honour and tricksters, with personalities which are constant or cunning, always ready to defend their honour, to lie, to deceive, even to kill for it; eager to bear public witness to their religious belief, to fight for it and, if necessary, to suffer and die for it. It would be quite wrong to take them for true images of real Spanish people in the golden age. As fictive characters, they much more represent the way in which Spanish society wanted to see itself in theatre. Alewyn's description of the court festival can also be applied to Spanish popular theatre: in theatre, society presents itself 'as it perhaps believes itself to be, and certainly as it would like to be'. In the *comedia* and its characters, Spanish society created an image of itself in which to reflect and recognise itself. The plays of the time, even the cloak and dagger plays and the so-called moral dramas (*comedias de costumbre*), which were also performed at this time in Spain, provide less insight into the life of real Spanish society than into the values to which it adhered and which it propagated – regardless of the extent to which the individual was actually prepared or able to accept and realise such values in his own life.

One extraordinary fact makes seventeenth-century Spanish society unique: the values which the popular *corrales* theatre never ceased to embody and propagate – the Catholic faith and the question of honour – were also continually promoted by the two leading social institutions, the church and the court. This is the basis of the affinity between *corrales* theatre, Corpus Christi stages and court theatre.

The mixture of the sacred and the profane, characteristic of such *comedia* performances as *The Trickster of Seville* or *The Constant Prince*, were equally characteristic of the religious Corpus Christi performances. Even the one-act *auto* (Corpus Christi play) was followed by a comic interlude, and dances by actors and professional dancers were performed within the framework of the procession:

> The celebration and honour of the Eucharist – as object of the procession and the *autos* – is accompanied by overwhelming joy at the salvation given through taking the Eucharist; and the same audience which cheers and applauds the dragon and the giant as they pass by in the procession – symbol of sin and the demon defeated by the sign of the cross – is ultimately called upon in the Corpus Christi play (which revives the fundamental dogmas of the Catholic church in allegorical form) to remember and learn through it.[17]

The Corpus Christi plays, therefore, were slightly weighted in favour of the sacred, in simple opposition to the *comedia* performances; both forms, however, propagated the Catholic faith.

Throughout the rest of seventeenth-century Europe, honour represented a value which was only valid for members of the nobility, but the Spanish popular theatre refers to honour as something beyond social class. The honour of the peasants is – irrespective of real social relations – no less important than that of the nobility. In Lope de Vega's *Fuenteovejuna* (written *c*.1612/14 and first published in 1619) and Calderón's *El alcalde de Zalamea* (*The Mayor of Zalamea*, *c*.1642), the honour of the peasants is not only equal to that of the noble seducer and oppressor but, as insulted honour, given even higher worth. For, as the peasant Pedro Crespo reasons, 'honour ... is in the possession of the soul, / And the Lord of the soul is God' (*The Mayor of Zalamea*, I, 874–6). The noble concept of honour which was originally tied to social position is placed on an equal level to the dignity of man, which God gives to every individual.

If popular theatre consistently deals with the question of honour, it does not follow that it propagates a courtly value, but rather a basic human value; possession of this value guarantees everyone dignity as a human being. This expansion of the concept of honour opened a utopian dimension to the rather conservative form of the *comedia*.

Whilst the Corpus Christi plays show respect to the sacraments, and the court fiestas function as a mythological celebration of the Spanish ruling house, the *comedias* in the *corrales* theatre present a baroque world theatre in its broadest sense. In them, Spanish society created a mirror of itself, in a time of economic decline, social crisis and political collapse of the empire, which reflected its image in a way that it could be proud of itself: the image of a society which is defined by its Catholic faith and belief in the system of honour. Religion increasingly degenerated into mere outward form – Philip IV ordered the nuns of Agreda to do penitence to redeem the sins to which he felt himself drawn by his insatiable sensuality. The concept of honour is increasingly misunderstood and distorted:

Recently, I heard that someone tried to persuade another man to forgive his friend and calm down; and what did he answer? 'And what about honour?' Another was advised to give up his lover for good, and end the scandalous situation of so many years, and he said 'What about honour?' A blasphemer was told to stop cursing and committing perjury, and answered 'What's the honour in that?' A wastrel was counselled to think about the future, and he replied, 'No, it's a question of my honour'. Finally, a man who occupied an official post was told he should not compete with procurers and murderers and he said 'That has nothing to do with my honour'. And everyone was amazed by what the other understood by the term honour.

(Baltasar Gracián, *El Criticón*, 1651–7)

The image of Spanish society created by and reflected in the *comedia* is not, however, clouded by such degenerative misinterpretation. It reflects a dying world as if it were going to last forever.

## MASK AND MIRROR

### The court as stage – the self-fashioning of court society

The great age of French theatre in which Molière and Racine celebrated their triumphs, coincided with the first fifteen years of the reign of Louis XIV. During this period, there was an almost endless string of court festivities, celebrations and extraordinary feasts.

On 26 August 1660, the king entered Paris. By this time, the Frondeur (the uprising of the nobles in 1648–52) had been defeated and the Pyrenean Treaty had achieved a settlement with Spain and France which was gloriously confirmed through the marriage of the young king to the Spanish Infanta.

The *entrée* ceremony was carried out in two phases. In the morning, members of various corporations left Paris, as *membra disiecta* which the king would then reunite. In a long, four-hour procession, King Louis XIV joined these corporations which, according to the teaching of the two bodies of the king, were to be re-integrated through contact with his symbolic body. In this way, the king tied himself absolutely to his people, as the Dean of the University confirmed in a ritual speech:

It is difficult to know whether it is the triumph of Your Majesty, or that of your subjects ... Let us say, that it is one and the other, both together, and that today all that is good, virtuous and majestic in the Prince triumphs in the hearts of his subjects, and that the love, submission and obedience of Your subjects triumphs in the heart of the Prince.[18]

This was followed by the second phase – the organised, re-united corporations returned to the city with the king. The king was now representative of the people, the state and the government.

On 5 and 6 June 1662, Louis XIV organised a so-called carousel in the Tuileries. Five quadrilles, consisting of one commander and ten knights, competed against each other in strength and skill. Each quadrille represented a nation: first, the Romans, whose leadership the king himself adopted, second, the Persians, commanded by Monsieur, the king's brother, third, the Turks, led by the Prince of Condé, fourth, the Indians, gathered under the banner of the Count of Enghien, and fifth, the 'savage Americans', led by the Count de Guise.

Louis XIV, dressed in the costume of a Roman emperor, carried a shield with the emblem of the sun driving away the clouds. The shield bore the inscription *Ut vidi, vici* ('Once seen, then conquered'), a reference to his first diplomatic success after the Vatteville affair. The shields and inscriptions of the other leaders all represented references to the fact that they gained their light and warmth from the sun. The carousel seems, in this respect, to have been a homage to the king: as emperor he was shown subjugation by other great kingdoms. In the role of Roman emperor, Louis XIV also created for himself the greatly more glorious role of the Sun King, the *roi-soleil*.

Another event was the 'Plaisirs de l'île enchantée', which was held from 7 to 13 May 1664 in Versailles. It was intended that this event would actualise the myth of the golden age by drawing it into an allegory on the reign of Louis XIV. In a great parade in the main avenue at the gardens of Versailles, the king in Greek costume strolled amongst the actors of Molière's company, the shining centre of attention, marking the theme at the beginning of the festival. The mask gave the royal person a mythological dimension, which Louis XIV had not yet achieved in his deeds. It represented a prefiguration of what the king wanted to be, the *imago* of the absolute ruler. The function of the costume was both to illuminate and to mystify at the same time; to create a dazzling spectacle to clothe the king, who – as sun god – embodies the state. The king was made into an exemplary figure on the threshold between fiction and reality – an ambiguous, mysterious person who alone was in the position to bring about a golden age.

On 18 July 1668, Louis XIV compressed a great festival into one single night of illusions. The event was conceived as a *grand mise en scène*, as a series of *coups de théâtre*, showing scenes and acts of a performance in which the invited guests transformed themselves into actors. They played their roles without knowing it, in rooms filled with deception and illusion which the great director, the king, had created for them. They believed themselves to be free as they explored rooms of surprises, and yet were nothing more than marionettes in a royal spectacle. The king held the court by the strings of his power.

The last great festival of the Sun King was held between 4 July and 31 August 1674 in Versailles – the 'Fêtes de l'Amour et de Bacchus'. Once again, it propagated the image of the king as sun god, while at the same time introducing a new image. The fireworks display on 18 August showed how the king crossed the Rhine at the head of his army and, at the same time, repeated the allegories to classical history that had dominated the last fourteen years. A chronicler of the festival, André Félibien, described the scene:

> All the decorations were provided with a symbolic and mystical meaning. The obelisk and the sun represented the glory of the king, blazing with light, and firmly in place above his enemies, despite 'Envie', represented by the dragon. The figure of Hercules underlined the invincible power and the largesse of His Majesty's actions, the figure of Pallas showed his courage and his prudent action in all his enterprises.[19]

By 1674, the figure of the sun god represented only a minor element of the decoration. Louis XIV no longer identified himself with it – the memory of the image of the king as it developed and became popular during the early years of his reign was kept alive by an opera figure, Apollo. The king now became Louis le Grand.

The festivals which Louis XIV organised between 1660 and 1674 explicitly represent his talent for putting himself and the state on stage – the city festivals from 1660 to 1662, and the feasts at Versailles, where he and the court presented themselves as on a stage, offer further proof. Paris and Versailles became theatres in which Louis XIV represented himself in the role of sun god and handed out roles to members of 'la cour et la ville'. As director and leading actor, he created an imposing performance in which the different, partly opposing, interests were transformed into a multi-voiced, but harmonious, concert. As the Abbé Cotin explained:

> the King sees that his spirit is, in some way, the spirit of the state, just as the first spirit is the spirit of the world. If such a spirit cannot reduce all oppositions into a perfect temperament which creates the harmony of the universe, the universe would dissolve; and if the intelligence of the monarch does not engage all the machinery of government, the machine will fall to pieces.[20]

In this way, the Sun King's festivals interpret the earlier metaphor of *theatrum mundi* in a new and characteristic way: 'la cour et la ville' function as stage; the king acts as the almighty and creative director, he hands out the roles both to himself and to all members of the court, and oversees the ensemble; he rewards and punishes by sending out or cancelling invitations to the next event. Thus, in the spectacles of the royal festivals, the king succeeded in creating a perfect representation and self-fashioning of court society.

Theatre performances made up an important and integral part of these spectacles. At the 'Plaisirs de l'île enchantée', two of Molière's plays were premièred: the ballet comedy, *La Princesse d'Elide*, on 8 May, and *Tartuffe*, on 12 May. *Les Fâcheux* (*The Bores*) and *Le Marriage Forcé* (*The Forced Marriage*) were also given repeat performances on this occasion.

On the night of the great illusions, 18 July 1668, Molière's *George Dandin* was performed. On 4 July, during the 'Fêtes de l'Amour et de Bacchus', the opera *Alceste ou le triomphe d'Alcide* by Quinault and Lully was performed, and on 19 July, Molière's last play, *Le Malade Imaginaire* (*The Imaginary Invalid*). On 28 July, another Quinault and Lully opera, *Les fêtes de l'amour et de Bacchus*, and on 18 August, the only première at this occasion, Racine's *Iphigénie*, were given. It can hardly be doubted, then, that the theatre played a vital function in terms of royal and court self-representation.

On the other hand, it should not be overlooked that this was not the only function of theatre. In terms of frequency, performances at court fell far behind performances in public theatres.

When Molière came to Paris with his company in 1658, at the age of 36, there were two public theatres. The first, the Hôtel de Bourgogne, was established in 1548 and first belonged to the Confrérie de la Passion and, after 1629, to the Comédiens du Roi. It was originally led by Gros-Guilllaume, from 1634 by Bellerose, and from 1647 by Josias de Soulas, known as Floridor. The second, the Théâtre du Marais, opened in 1629, was where Montdory's company (under changing management) played. Whilst the Hôtel de Bourgogne mostly played tragedies (although there were occasional comedies), after its renovation in 1644, the Théâtre du Marais specialised in baroque machine plays.

Alongside these two public theatres there also existed space for theatre performances in the Louvre, in the Petit Bourbon and in the Palais Royal, over which the king had rights of disposal and which, at specific times or for certain reasons, could be given to individual performing companies. In 1658, the Comédie Italienne played the Petit Bourbon. After Molière came to Paris, the king also allowed his company to play there so that it was alternately used by both companies. After the destruction of the Petit Bourbon on 10 October 1660, both companies settled in the theatre at the Palais Royal furnished by Cardinal Richelieu.

Thus, around 1660, there were three theatres which were constantly in use throughout the performance period (which began just after Easter and closed at Lent the following year, shortly before Easter). Taking the only available statistics for this period as representative – Molière's theatre in the season 1672–3 – the following picture emerges: the number of spectators at one performance was, at the most, 925, on average, just above 400, but occasionally only 68. Even when this number is multiplied by three for the three theatres, the section of the population which regularly visited the theatre in a population of 500,000 was not very high, especially when one takes into consideration the fact that many visitors came from the provinces and abroad and included a visit to the theatre as an indispensable part of their programme of things to do and see during their stay in Paris. A playwright could expect, at best, a new play to draw between 10,000 and 12,000 spectators. Between ten and fifteen performances was viewed as a minor success, thirty to forty a unique success, which was seldom achieved. If one compares these figures with those from London or Madrid, one can conclude that either the enthusiasm of the Parisians for the theatre was limited or, perhaps, that a visit to the theatre was reserved for a relatively small section of society.

Let us return to the figures for Molière's company in the season 1672–3. The greatest number of tickets sold at any performance were: 36 for seats on the stage, 99 for the boxes, 124 for the amphitheatre, 206 for the upper boxes, 78 for the boxes on the third level, and 514 for standing places in the parterre. The majority of the spectators thus, stood in the parterre, which was almost exclusively occupied by men.

Even though some members of the lower nobility, mainly officers, bought tickets for the parterre (15 sous; at a première, 30 sous), the audience in the parterre was principally composed of members of the middle classes: merchants, traders, various professionals, writers and soldiers. A particular role was clearly played by the traders. As Chappuzeau noted in *Théâtre français* (1674), the theatre avoided playing on Wednesdays and Saturdays, because these days were 'market and business days where the bourgeoisie is more occupied than on other days'. Thursday was also considered a bad performance day, 'being, in many places, dedicated to taking a promenade, and this was particularly true of the Academies and colleges'.[21] On the other hand, the theatre faced fierce competition by entertainments which tended to attract the traders and shopkeepers from the rue St Denis. Thus, the parterre at the première of Racine's *Britannicus* (13 December 1669) remained empty because

the Marquis de Courboyer was being executed at the same time. Boursault reports:

> I found a place for myself in the stalls so that I could have the honour of being suffocated by the masses. But since the Marquis de Courboyer ... had attracted all the traders from the rue Saint Denis who usually go to the Hôtel de Bourgogne to have first sight of all the dramas presented there, I felt so at ease, that I decided to beg Monsieur Corneille, whom I spotted all alone in a box, to have the kindness to fling himself at me as soon as infuriation should come upon him.[22]

Nevertheless, the visitors to the stalls generally formed the majority of the audience. Despite this, it was not the stalls who decided on the success of a play (as in Madrid), but the spectators in the more expensive stage, balcony and box seats, occupied by members of the richer bourgeoisie and aristocracy as well as middle-class ladies. Whether *la cour et la ville* was considered more important because of its more refined tastes, or whether its higher station, influence and wealth made its judgement more weighty, is impossible to decide. The future founder (1672) of the *Mercure Galant*, Donneau de Visé, at least, seems not to have rated their ability to appreciate drama very highly. On the success of Molière's troupe after arriving in Paris with the two plays already tried out in the provinces, *L'Étourdi* (*The Blunderer*) and *Le Dépit amoureux* (*The Lover's Quarrel*), he wrote:

> After the success of these two plays his theatre began to be filled with men of high quality, not just because of the entertainment promised to them (for only old plays were performed there), but also, because it had become the fashion to go there. Those who enjoyed company and liked to show themselves off found more than enough to satisfy them. Thus, it was the custom to go without any intention of listening to the comedy or without even knowing what was being played.[23]

Boileau also judged the aesthetic appreciation of *la cour et la ville* as being similarly meagre in *Épître à M. Racine* (1677), where he points out the hostile attitude which a part of the nobility liked to show towards Molière's masterpieces:

> In ignorance or misunderstanding his
> previous plays,
> Dressed as a marquis, in the robes of a
> countess,
> They came to denounce his newest master-
> piece,
> And shook their heads at the best places.
> The commander wished the scene were more
> precise:
> The indignant viscount left in the second act;
> Another, defender of bigots, portrayed in the
> play,
> Condemned it as the prize for his wit, to burn
> on the fire,
> Another, the impetuous Marquis, declaring
> war,
> Wanted to take revenge for the court, which
> was sacrificed in the stalls.

In *The Bores* (1661), Molière also made fun of the artistic judgement of the young nobility, who sprawled about the stage and disturbed the performance – a bad habit which, if one believes the chroniclers of the time, began at the première of Corneille's *Le Cid* (1637) because it was overfilled – whilst, on the other hand, in *Critique de L'École des Femmes* (1663), the *raisonneur* Dorante is provided with high praise of court taste when he gives the unsuccessful poet Lysidas a dressing down:

> Enough, Monsieur Lysidas. I quite see that you want to say that the court knows nothing about these things and your usual route of escape, my dear authors, is to blame the miserable success of your plays on the injustice of the century and the court's meagre knowledge. But please take heed of this, Monsieur Lysidas, the court has eyes as good as any other; one can be just as clever with lace and feathers as with a short wig and a plain Geneva band; the greatest test for all your comedies is the judgement of the court; and it is their taste which one must study to find the art of success; there is no other place where deci-

sions are so just; not even counting all the academics at court, for one learns a special way of thinking from an easy, natural, healthy human understanding and from mixing with better society, which leads to an incomparably better judgement than anything the whole rusty knowledge of pedants could ever offer.

> (Scene 6)

The Abbé de Villiers expressed himself similarly in *Entretiens sur les tragédies de ce temps* (1675):

> If you please the literati, then you will quickly please the court, where there are literati just as anywhere else, and I can say that the literati at court are equal to all others, since their learning provides them with a particularly sensitive and delicate wit which serves good judgement perfectly. It is no longer temperament which hands out praise and applause from the court, but common sense.

To what extent such comments are to be understood as strategic flattery, and to what extent as an embroidered or idealised description of the actual situation, cannot be determined with any certainty. There cannot be any doubt, however, of the great importance which the members of the court in the audience had for the success of the play. Even though the Paris theatres at the time of Molière and Racine had a mixed audience, which was composed of members of the nobility and the middle classes, and even to some extent included lackeys and servants, the theatre cannot be classified as a popular theatre, but rather as the theatre of court society.

The court society at the time of Louis XIV represents, when viewed historically, the culmination of a relatively young development. Norbert Elias dates its actual creation as occurring during these years:

> A new court society was formed and developed at the court of Louis XIV. Here, a process came to an end which had been long in preparation: here, knights and courtly imitators of the knighthood finally turned into court people in the real sense

of the word, people whose social existence and, more often than not, whose income, was dependent on their prestige, their status at court and the court society.[24]

The old nobility, the *noblesse d'épée*, had already been politically disempowered to such an extent that it was dysfunctional by the reign of Louis XIII. The aristocratic rebellion, the Fronde, represented the last attempt to win back political rights and leadership for the nobility but was ultimately defeated. Now all rights of leadership belonged irrefutably to the king alone. The status earned by the individual was now no longer handed out according to heroic deeds in battle but rather according to the king's whim. To win the king's favour, members of the *noblesse d'épée* had to compete with members of the new nobility, the *noblesse de robe*, bureaucrats who had risen out of the bourgeoisie:

> The competitive pressure for prestige and the king's favour is great. The 'affairs', the battles for position and favour never cease. When the sword no longer plays such a great role as a means of earning honour, it is replaced by intrigue, and battles in which success in one's career and in society are fought with words. This demands and breeds other qualities than those needed by battles which are fought with weapons: consideration, long-term strategy, self-control, careful control of one's own emotions, knowing the enemy and the whole territory become the imperative preconditions of any social promotion.[25]

The position allocated someone in the court hierarchy was very unstable and subject to continual shifts. In order to fix one's position in some way, two basic patterns of behaviour were required: first, almost perfect control over one's emotions, and second, the ability to interpret the behaviour of others in the correct way:

> In full emotion it is difficult to control the correct dosage of expression. It reveals the true feelings of the person concerned to such an extent that, because unexpected, it can be harmful; perhaps it plays trumps of favour and prestige into the

enemy's hand. It is ultimately, and above all, a sign of inferiority, and that is precisely the position which the person at court most fears. Competition in court life thus forces one to master the emotions in favour of an exactly calculated and thoroughly nuanced behaviour in all social intercourse.[26]

Court rationalism forces the individual to wear a mask and to play a role whose effect on others is calculated to the last detail. As La Bruyère shows in *Caractères* (1688), the mask appears to be vitally necessary to a successful existence at court:

> A man who knows the court is master of his movements, his eyes and his face. He is deep, opaque, he covers up false deeds, smiles at his enemies, constrains his temperament, disguises his passions, denies his heart, speaks and acts against his own feelings.[27]

On the other hand, it was also important to be able to judge the motives, feelings, abilities and boundaries of others in order not to make any fatal mistake in communicating with them. In *Mémoires* (1694), Saint Simon provides many examples of how to interpret other people's behaviour. He writes:

> I quickly saw that he froze; my eyes followed his behaviour carefully so that I did not deceive myself about that which could, by chance, appear in a man doing dangerous business and that which I suspected. My suspicions were confirmed. This led me to distance myself wholly from him and I acted as if nothing had happened.[28]

Other people functioned as a kind of mirror which reflected back the image of the self according to their particular status. The behaviour which the courtly person held towards another was, both for himself and all other observers, an exact indication and measure of how highly that person was regarded in the eyes of the society at that particular moment. And, since this regard was identical to the social existence of the individual, the nuances with which individuals dressed their mutual respect for each other, gained enormous importance.

Not only Louis XIV's spectacular festivals are to be understood as theatrical representations of life at court. Court life itself unfolded as the result of a highly artistic self-fashioning and theatricalisation, in which only the clever choice of the right mask guaranteed that one could play the desired role, and in which every other player was not only to be thought of as a co-player but also as critical and competent spectator in whose gaze the role and the extent of success in realising the role was mirrored. Only a man who was totally in charge of his art, both as actor and spectator, could reckon with social success in lasting terms. The form of court society which, as theatre audience, decided the success of plays and actors was to a great extent itself deeply theatrical. The members of court society needed the court stage and its centre occupied by the king, because this theatrical existence was the only kind of existence possible.

> It was only in this court society that people who belonged could maintain that which gave their lives sense and direction in their own eyes, their social existence as court members, distance from all others, prestige, and thereby the key to their image of themselves, their personal identity. They did not come to court because they were dependent on the king but, rather, they remained dependent on the king because only through entry to court and living in the midst of court society could they keep that distance from all others on which the salvation of their souls, their prestige as court aristocrats, in short, their social existence and their personal identity, depended.[29]

People in court society lived in a tight web of mutual interdependencies. On one hand, their position in the court hierarchy was constantly in danger and therefore extremely unstable, on the other hand, however, their social existence and personal identity depended on this position. This meant that awareness of the permanent danger to the self and the need to create the most stable representation possible

for the labile self, was greatly heightened. This function was fulfilled, amongst other things, through baroque clothing. For not only could it increase the length and breadth of the body considerably through the help of high heels or a tall hair-style, through padding or girdles, and thus emphasise outward appearance as something of great importance, but it also enabled the wearer to hide characteristics of the physical body dictated to him by the whims of nature and in this way to create himself anew as a social body. The ladies, for example, wore an iron corset to push up their breasts and tighten the waist:

> They must have been torture because of their mere weight, but they gave the upper body the elegant form of an upturned sugarloaf. The tip of the cone rests on a half sphere which stands for the lower body. The hooped skirt consists of a frame of wire and fishbone which, padded with horse hair, rests on the hips, and rich materials are laid or stretched over it. These are then covered with embroideries and lace and are stiff with gold and glittering stones. The head and hands peep out like prisoners from a cage. Outside the house, even these are covered with masks and gloves.[30]

Even the ladies' hair-style, the 'fontange' (tower), allowed, as far as it was not wholly replaced by a wig, no trace of its natural – that is, random – nature to show. Through frames made of wire formed into various shapes, the 'fontange' aspired to vertiginous heights, topped by models of coaches, frigates, bird cages and pavilions which pitched and swayed. Similarly, the skin was covered; both sexes made excessive use of make-up and painted beauty spots.

The representation of the self through outward appearance, through baroque dress, was powerful and important, even 'royal'. It was, at the same time, the only stable and reliable item upon which the court people could depend. Thus it is only to be expected that in *Pensées* (1657–62), Pascal raises the question, 'What is the self?', and replies:

What is the self?

A man goes to the window to see the people passing by; if I pass by, can I say he went there to see me? No, for he is not thinking of me in particular. But what about a person who loves someone for the sake of her beauty; does he love *her*? No, for smallpox, which will destroy beauty without destroying the person, will put an end to his love for her.

And if someone loves me for my judgement or my memory, do they love me? *me*, myself? No, for I could lose these qualities without losing my self. Where then is this self, if it is neither in the body nor the soul? And how can one love the body or the soul except for the sake of such qualities, which are not what makes up the self, since they are perishable? Would we love the substance of a person's soul, in the abstract, whatever qualities might be in it? That is not possible, and it would be wrong. Therefore we never love anyone, but only qualities.

Let us then stop scoffing at those who win honour through their appointments and offices, for we never love anyone except for borrowed qualities.

(323)[31]

Theatre reveals these 'borrowed qualities' as masks, theatrical representations of a deeply theatrical existence in which court members found themselves reflected. If the mirror reflects an image in which they did not recognise, or did not want to recognise themselves, unlike life at court, they were free to declare the mirror blemished, dirty or false. A judgement on the theatre is, thus, almost always a judgement on the courtier's own self image.

### *L'honnête homme* or the end of social intercourse through noble 'amour propre'

In the mid-1660s (1664–6) the sun of royal favour seemed to be shining over Molière. In January 1664, Louis XIV agreed to act as godfather to Molière's first son, Louis. In August 1665, he awarded his own royal patronage to Molière's troupe, which until then had been under the protection of his brother under the name 'troupe de Monsieur', and

sponsored Molière to the sum of 6,000 livres annually. In May 1664, Molière and his company were extensively involved in the festivities of the 'Plaisirs de l'île enchantée'. Moreover, Molière was often commissioned to act at court. The première of his *The Forced Marriage* took place on 29 January 1664 in the Louvre. *L'Amour médecin* (*Love's the Best Doctor*) was first performed on 15 September 1665 at Versailles and, on 2 December 1666, Molière produced the ballet comedy *Melicerte* for the 'Ballet des Muses' at the château of Saint-Germain-en-Laye.

How much more extraordinary must it seem, then, that the three masterpieces which Molière wrote in these years were not successful at court. On 12 May 1664, the première of *Tartuffe* took place as part of the 'Plaisirs de l'île enchantée'. It was banned the next day. On 5 August 1667 a revised version was performed, but was again banned the following day. It was only in February 1669 that the king lifted the ban on the third version after many petitions by Molière.

On 15 February 1665, *Don Juan* was premièred at the Palais Royal. After fifteen performances, Molière found himself forced to bow to court pressure and took the play out of the repertoire. It was never performed again in his lifetime (he died 17 February 1673). It was only in modified form (by Thomas Corneille in 1674) that it returned to the stage, where it remained until the mid-nineteenth century in the repertoire at the Comédie Français, which was founded in 1680.

*The Misanthrope* was given its first performance on 4 June 1666 at the Palais Royal. The play was a minor success, and only remained in the repertoire because, from August, it accompanied the newly written *Médecin malgré lui* (*A Doctor in Spite of Himself*). It was never performed at court during Molière's lifetime.

In order to understand what at first appears to be a paradoxical parallel development, one must take into consideration the fact that Molière created a wholly new type of comedy in the history of French theatre. On the one hand, he combined the national tradition of farce with non-French traditions such as Roman comedy, the Italian *commedia erudita* and *commedia dell'arte* as well as the Spanish comedies of the *siglo de oro* to create a kind of all-embracing European comedy of the century. On the other hand, he gave the comic theatre a new impulse through his desire to be the mirror and critic of his time, and thus to 'faire rire les honnêtes gens' (*Critique de l'École des Femmes*, Scene 6).

Molière's contemporaneity was aggressive, unlike in Renaissance comedy, which also understood itself to be a *speculum consuetudinis*, but which actually based itself upon a fundamental sympathy with the audience. Molière's comic mirrors of social relationships are caricatures containing a strongly polemic element. Any empathy the audience may feel is continually dissolved. Certain social groups, which were certainly represented among the spectators, were exposed to merciless mocking: the conceited, foppish 'petit marquis' and the provincials, the prude and coquettish woman, the sanctimonious hypocrites and the bluestockings, the doctors, the ambitious merchant and the unscrupulous grandseigneur. Scandal was unavoidable. Whilst those who were not affected were greatly amused, those who felt attacked defended themselves with all available means. The more powerful and influential they were, the more Molière had cause to fear them, despite his favour with the king. Scandals could have a vitalising effect and be good for business, but they could also be ruinous and even end in death.

Molière discovered this for himself for the first time with *Tartuffe*. Though he succeeded in winning the first 'querelle' ignited by *École des Femmes* (*School for Wives*, 1662) by offering the two plays *Critique de l'École des Femmes* (1 June 1663 at the Palais Royal) and *L' Impromptu de Versailles* (14 October 1664 before the king in Versailles), the 'querelle du Tartuffe' stirred up far greater enemies.

The king was enthusiastic about *Tartuffe*, but the Archbishop of Paris turned to the king's mother and persuaded her to encourage Louis XIV to ban the play. Molière, who felt supported by the king, had the play performed in the same year before the papal legate, Cardinal Chigi, who condoned it. Many higher aristocrats also commissioned private performances and readings. Molière's opponents, the 'dévots' and among them, particularly, members of the secret society founded in 1627, the 'Compagnie du Saint-Sacrement', who felt themselves particularly affected by *Tartuffe* without wanting to recognise themselves in it, prepared for the counter-attack. A clergyman, Pierre Rouillé, a member of the 'Compagnie', distributed a pamphlet in which he described Molière as 'a man, or rather a demon in the flesh dressed as a man, scarred by impiety and dissipation'. Without any ado, he demanded the burning of the heretic Molière. The danger facing Molière is only clear when one remembers that, as late as 1662, Claude le Petit was burnt at the stake for writing an impudent verse against religion. Molière's entire existence was at stake. If his opponents succeeded in suppressing *Tartuffe* for good, he must reckon with a judicial trial led by the 'dévots' at any time. The 'placets', or petitions, which Molière addressed to the king to beg him to release the ban, allow no doubt that he was very much aware of the risks involved. Thus, in his first 'placet' (1664) he emphasises the fact that the play is not aimed against true piety but rather against the 'faux monayeurs en devotion':

> [His Majesty] can doubtless judge how trying it is for me to find myself exposed daily to the insults of these gentlemen: how harmful such calumnies will be to my public reputation, should they be allowed to pass uncorrected, and how concerned I must be to clear myself of this slander and demonstrate to the public that my play is not at all what it is made out to be.[32]

In his second petition (1667), on the other hand, Molière explicitly states that the triumph of his enemies would mean the end of his theatre:

> I await respectfully such decision as Your Majesty may deign to give on the matter, but one thing is beyond question, Sire, that it is useless for me to

think of writing any more for the theatre if the Tartuffes are to gain the day, for if they do, they will assume the right to persecute me more than ever and contrive to find something to condemn in the most innocent works of my pen.

May your bounty deign to accord me protection, Sire, against their venomous rage and so enable me, when you return from your triumphant campaign, to afford Your Majesty diversion after the fatigues of your conquests, provide you with innocent pleasures after your noble exertions, and bring a smile to the countenance of the Monarch before whom Europe trembles.

*(Ibid.*, p. 108)

The arguments involved in the 'querelle du Tartuffe' are given in the third surviving edition of the play. The merchant, Orgon, who is prepared to sacrifice his family for Tartuffe, and Tartuffe himself, are both exposed as sanctimonious hypocrites who use piety solely as a mask, even if Orgon is not aware of doing so. Orgon lives in the illusion that God has sent Tartuffe as a sign of his special mercy so that he will relieve him of all burdensome commitments to this earth and his dissatisfaction with life. When his hopes for social recognition and promotion are betrayed by social developments, he flees in the illusion of being the chosen one in the after-life. His piety is, thus, to be understood as a mask, in the sense that it enables him to close his eyes to the social reality around him.

Tartuffe, on the contrary, puts on a mask of piety for strategic reasons. Thus, he is introduced as an actor:

Lui, qui connaît sa dupe et qui veut en jouir,
Par cent dehors fardés a l'art d'éblouir.

(Lines 199–200)

He has a hundred ways of deceiving him, gets money out of him constantly by means of canting humbug, and assumes the right to take us to task.

(1, p. 115)

In the seventeenth century, 'l'art d'éblouir' (the art of deception) was a generic term for the art of the actor; 'dehors fardés' describes ways (more than mere make-up) in which disguise was used right down to the last detail in order to fool the spectator. Tartuffe uses the mask of piety consciously and deliberately as a means to enrich himself and to satisfy his desires.

Both Tartuffe and Orgon are, therefore, false 'dévots' as the *raisonneur* of the piece, Cléante, clearly recognises. He claims he has the ability 'd'avoir de bons yeux'. He 'sees', or recognises the truth, and can distinguish appearance and reality. At the beginning of *Discours de la méthode* (1637), Descartes determined 'bons sens' as having the capacity to 'distinguer le vrai d'avec le faux'. The right view of the world enables the right behaviour towards one's fellow human beings. Despite this right view, Cléante remains totally powerless in the face of Orgon's sanctimonious hypocrisy and Tartuffe's intrigues, however. Only the king can bring about a change for the good:

We live under the rule of a prince inimical to fraud, a monarch who can read men's hearts, whom no impostor's art deceives.

(V, p. 162)

Molière ended his first petition to the king with the words, 'with monarchs as enlightened as you, Sire, there is no need to elaborate one's requests. They perceive, like God, what our needs are and know better than we do what should be accorded to us.' These words find their echo in the unlikely *deus ex machina* ending of the comedy. It appears, thus, at the same time, to be the end of the 'querelle du Tartuffe' and a realistic image of the actual balance of power: it is not enough to expose the hypocrite, it also needs the power of the king to render such people harmless.

Whilst in the 'querelle du Tartuffe' Molière 'only' had the 'dévots' against him, with *Don Juan* (subtitled *Festin de Pierre*) he drew the rage of the the aristocracy as well. The Prince de Conti, in earlier years a powerful patron of Molière before he converted to Jansenism in 1657, showed his rage for the play in *Traité de la comédie* (1666):

Is there a more openly atheist school than that in *Festin de Pierre*, where, after a most spirited atheist is made to utter the most dreadful impieties, the playwright confines God's cause to the valet who, to support this, he makes speak the greatest nonsense in the world? And he pretends to justify the end of this blasphemous comedy with a farce which has the ridiculous ministry of God's revenge and worse, in order to strengthen the impression of foolery and confusion represented in this way in the minds of the spectators, he makes the servant utter all kinds of idiocy imaginable on this adventure.

Molière's Don Juan is an egomaniac who seeks to boost his ego with each one of his conquests and prove the extraordinary importance of his own self:

> There is no pleasure to compare with the conquest of beauty, and my ambition is that of all great conquerors who could never find it in them to set bounds to their ambitions, but must go on from conquest to conquest. Nothing can restrain my impetuous desires. I feel it is in me to love the whole world, and like Alexander still wish for new worlds to conquer.
>
> (Act I)[33]

Molière's aim is made very clear in this confession by Don Juan; it is not a question of the common seducer who, coincidentally – because tradition will have it – is a grandseigneur. The tradition is chosen far more because it allows a whole social class to be pilloried. For the old *noblesse d'épée*, the age of territorial conquests and a political claim to power was, in the reign of Louis XIV, only a memory. Conquests were now only possible in love; domination could only be exercised in seduction. Releasing the sexual drive was the only possible way of maintaining the ancient feudal claim to an identity determined by domination. That which piety offers the merchant Orgon in compensation for his frustrated social ambitions arouses sexual insatiability in the politically frustrated noble, Don Juan: all women appear as 'une conquête à faire'.

Don Juan's cold, superior art of strategic seduction and his free spirit, his 'libertinage', seem to be the sole guarantees of an élite, exclusive lifestyle even under changed political and social conditions:

> How delightful, how entrancing it is to lay siege with a hundred attentions to a young woman's heart; to see, day by day, how one makes slight advances; to pit one's exaltation, one's sighs and one's tears, against the modest reluctance of a heart unwilling to yield; to surmount, step by step, all the little barriers by which she resists; to overcome her proud scruples and bring her at last to consent.
>
> (I, p. 203)

The positive representative of the old nobility, Don Juan's father, Don Luis, thus names his son a monster 'against nature' in disgust (IV, 2, p. 237).

As if Molière wanted to crown this already severe critique of nobility, at the beginning of Act 5, he gives Don Juan the choice of taking on the mask of Tartuffe in order to continue his changed life unchecked:

> When I talked of mending my ways and living an exemplary life it was a calculated hypocrisy, a necessary pretence, which I had to assume for my father's benefit because I need his help, and as a protection against society and the hundred-and-one tiresome things that may happen to me.
>
> (V, p. 243)

Under cover of hypocrisy, Don Juan can feel safe in a society in which hypocrisy has become a fashionable vice: 'hypocrisy is a fashionable vice and all vices pass for virtues once they become fashionable' (V, p. 243). Here, only heaven itself can intervene and reinstate the moral order perverted by Don Juan (and his like).

Molière was wise enough not to insist on competing with those powerful opponents who felt themselves provoked by *Don Juan*, nor on proving that it was they who were 'libertins' and hypocrites rather than himself. After the Easter break (21 March–13 April 1665), the play was not taken up into the repertoire at his theatre again.

Compared to the stormy reaction which *Tartuffe* and *Don Juan* engendered, the scandal caused by *The Misanthrope* seems almost harmless. D'Olivet reports:

When he played *The Misanthrope*, Father Cotin and Ménage were at the première, and after they left, they went directly to the Hôtel de Rambouillet to ring the alarm. They said that Molière was publicly mimicking the Duke de Montausier, whose actual rigidity and inflexible attitude on virtue was not warmly received by some followers because it was interpreted, to some extent, as misanthropy. The more delicate the accusation, the greater Molière felt the blow. But he had anticipated it by giving the play to Monsieur de Montausier personally before it was performed, and he was not in the least offended and praised the play, quite rightly, as one of the author's greatest masterpieces.[34]

Thus the scandal was stopped in its seed. But what remained, however, was the extraordinary fact that *The Misanthrope* was never performed at court in Molière's lifetime.

The play is set in a noble milieu: the place of action is the salon of the young, elegant, intelligent and much courted widow, Célimène, where the *jeunesse dorée* like to meet and converse. The young noble Alceste, the title figure, suffers misanthropic fits at what he views as man's basic evil. He is in love with Célimène, and wants to marry her. For the moment, he is tied up in an unpleasant trial.

At first sight, Alceste, who appears in opposition to false hypocrites as their enemy and who insists on *sincérité*, seems to be diametrically opposed to Don Juan, the seducer with no conscience. But on a closer look, an amazing similarity reveals itself between them: both are egomaniacs who seek to impose an unconditional demand for exclusivity and dominance in all situations. Whilst Don Juan chases after erotic victories in order to exercise his dominance, Alceste brings *sincérité* into play to this

effect. Whilst Don Juan shows off his vice to others to gain attention, Alceste seeks admiration for his virtue, 'I want to be singled out' (1, p. 26).[35] 'Seducer of no conscience' and 'moral misanthrope' seem, in this respect, simply two roles which are played to achieve the same end: to represent and validate a colossal (feudal) ego to the full.

The mask which Alceste puts on in order to carry out his claim to power over the others is one called '*sincérité*'. Whilst Don Juan plays his role knowingly and, thus, with the same sovereignty as a great actor who knows how to change his mask and costume at any time, Alceste is imprisoned in his role. He does not recognise '*sincérité*' as a mask – as Orgon does not recognise his piety in *Tartuffe* as a mask or the fact of his being chosen as an illusion – he identifies himself with the role and cannot, therefore, distance himself from it; like Orgon, he becomes a comic figure (both characters were played by Molière).

In the name of *sincérité*, Alceste refuses to adorn his feelings with 'vain compliments' for the sake of politeness, or to put on any kind of mask:

I want us to be men and say what we really mean on all occasions. Let us speak straight from the heart and not conceal our feelings under a mask of vain compliment.

(I, p. 26)

For this reason, he also intends to forbid his friend Philinte from carrying out the polite embrace fashionable at the time:

I expect you to be sincere and as an honourable man never to utter a single word that you don't really mean … I can't bear these despicable mannerisms that so many of our men of fashion put on. There's nothing I hate more than the contortions of these protestation mongers, these affable exchangers of fatuous greetings, polite mouthers of meaningless speeches – who bandy civilities with all comers and treat everyone, blockhead and man of sense and discernment alike. What satisfaction can there be in having a man express his consideration for you, profess friendship, faith, affection, esteem, and praise you up to the skies when he'll hasten to do as much for the first worthless scoundrel he comes across? No, no! No man with any self respect wants that sort of debased and worthless esteem. There's precious little satisfaction in the most glorious of reputations if one finds that one has to share it with the whole universe. Esteem must be founded on some sort of preference. Bestow it on everybody and it ceases to have any meaning at all. Surrender to the foolish manners of the age and, by Gad, you are no friend of mine! I spurn the all-embracing, undiscriminating affection which makes no distinction of merit. I want to be singled out and, to put it bluntly, the friend of all mankind is not my line at all.

(I, p. 26)

In this speech, a deeper reason as to why Alceste denies social role-play with such vehemence becomes apparent. If politeness and respect is shown to everyone, how can one tell if one is really respected or not? And how, then, can one express the fact that he, Alceste, is more highly respected than all the others and is not to be confused 'avec tout l'univers'?

Herein lies Alceste's dilemma. On the one hand, he needs the others – the world – to confirm his fundamental superiority. On the other hand, he refuses to acknowledge the rules of their game, which gives each player his position. Instead of keeping his feelings under control and secret from other people – as Saint-Simon and La Bruyère recommend – Alceste reveals his true feelings, 'I will get annoyed' (p. 25), and in this way, differentiates himself. Rather than practising the skill of observing mankind and drawing conclusions from the tiny nuances of mimic, gesture and behaviour, he demands that everyone else lay bare their 'hearts' so that he can read in them, unmediated and without distraction, how much more they respect him than all others.

Alceste's struggle for dominance does not permit him to be satisfied with conventional admiration. He demands true adoration. But

because the world refuses to make an exception for him, he decides to turn his back on it:

It breaks my heart to see how men compound with vice! There are times when a sudden longing comes over me to seek some solitary place and flee the approach of men.

(I, p. 28)

Alceste's misanthropy is, thus, less a consequence of the 'inferiority' of the world and more the result of its refusal to recognise his superiority. Accordingly, he is not shocked by Philinte's 'falsehood' because it is 'amoral' but because it puts him, Alceste, on the same level as all other men. His hatred of mankind is the expression of the irreconcilable dilemma in which he finds himself: Alceste wants to break with his friend, give up all social contact and turn his back on social life because the others refuse to accept his claim to exclusivity and superiority. On the other hand, however, he robs himself thereby of the only chance of finding his ego appropriately represented and enforced because he is dependent on the respect, confirmation and recognition of the others. Alceste's misanthropy is, thus, to be understood as the sign and result of the dilemma that society withholds from him his true identity – as someone who is superior and exclusive – and yet there is no place outside society in which these things could actually be realised.

This dilemma also determines Alceste's love for Célimène. Célimène has everything which Alceste desires: she occupies the centre 'stage' of her salon, she is admired and adored by all. To own her would mean to usurp her position. In this sense, Alceste's love for Célimène appears to be just a means of accomplishing his claim to superiority. This highlights the contradiction that Alceste loves Célimène because she is the shining, adored centre of her world and yet, on the other hand, he wants to rob her of precisely this occupation of the centre and make her totally dependent on him:

Yes, I would have you unloved, reduced to misery or born to indigence, without rank or birth or fortune so that I might in one resounding act of loving sacrifice repair the injustice of your fate and enjoy the joy and satisfaction of knowing that you owe everything to my love.

(IV, p. 64)

When, finally, Célimène does lose her place in the centre and is deserted by all those who once courted her, marriage alone cannot satisfy him, because it would not bring with it the admiration of society any more. Now he can only achieve superiority through Célimène's total and exclusive dependency on him – he would literally become her whole world:

ALCESTE: Yes, perfidious creature, I'm willing to forget your misdeeds. I'll contrive to excuse or condone them as youthful frailties into which the evil manners of the age have led you – provided you'll agree to join me in my plan of fleeing from all human intercourse and undertake to accompany me forthwith into the rustic solitude to which I have sworn to repair. Thus, and only thus, can you make public reparation for the harm done by your letters. Thus after all the scandal so abhorrent to a noble mind I may be permitted to love you still.
CÉLIMÈNE: Me? Renounce the world before I'm old and bury myself in your wilderness!
ALCESTE: Ah! If your love would but respond to mine what would the rest of the world matter? Can I not give you everything you desire?
CÉLIMÈNE: The mind shrinks from solitude at twenty. I don't feel I have the necessary fortitude to bring myself to take such a decision. If the offer of my hand would content you I would consent and marriage
...
ALCESTE: No! Now I abhor you! This refusal is worse than all that has gone before. Since you can't bring yourself to make me your all in all as you are mine, I renounce you! This dire affront frees me from your ignoble fetters for ever.

(V, p. 74)

Célimène clearly recognises that she would lose her identity if she is removed from social life, because it is only in society that she can play a role. But Alceste remains blind to any insight into the role and mask-play of his own behaviour. His wounded self-love leads him to turn his back on social life and to take on the part of the misunderstood misanthrope. He is not aware that this is also a role to play and that it can only be played within the social sphere. His self-exclusion from the social sphere might liberate society from his company – which is both tiresome as well as amusing – but it cannot create for him the longed-for identity, something which can only be developed and earned within the social frame.

Molière classified this type of asocial behaviour as pathological by giving *The Misanthrope* the subtitle *L'Atrabilaire amoureux* (atrabilious – melancholy, ill-tempered, from the Latin 'black bile'). In the medical and psychological view of the time, melancholy and misanthropy are caused by too much black bile. Alceste himself makes a pun on this relationship:

I have seen and suffered too much. Court and city alike provoke me to fury. It fills me with depression ['m'échauffer la bile'] – reduces me to utter despair ['une humeur noire'] to see men living as they do.

(I, p. 27)

In this process, two aspects can be distinguished. First, the view of social life and the insight into the way it functions, and second, the reaction to that view. The reaction is decided through 'black bile' – through Alceste's egomania. His view is, however, not clouded by it; he sees things the same way as Philinte, as the latter explains:

I notice, as you do, a hundred times a day, things which could be done differently, but whatever I happen to see I don't show my irritation openly, as you do. ...

Yes, I look upon these faults which you are so concerned about as defects inseparable from human nature; it disturbs me no more to find men base, unjust, or selfish than to see apes mischievous, wolves savage, or the vulture ravenous for its prey.

(I, p. 29)

Thus, Alceste and Philinte have the same 'insight' into social life of *la cour et la ville*; they only differ in their reactions to it, as Philinte, with a further reference to the teaching of the tempers and humours, illustrates:

I take men as they are, school myself to bear with what they do, and, in my opinion, my self-possession is no less philosophical than your intemperate spleen ['votre bile'].

(I, p. 29)

In this way, Alceste's critique of the social life of *la cour et la ville* is not challenged, despite his exaggerated reactions. It is far more confirmed and legitimated through what goes on in Célimène's salon.

The figures who come and go in Célimène's salon are, as they never tire of repeating, regularly at court and boast about having a certain influence on the king. Oronte comments that, 'If there is anything I can do for you at court I am known to cut some figure with His Majesty, I have his ear and he treats me with the greatest possible consideration' (I, p. 32).

That which Oronte, Clitandre and the prudish Arsinoé seek in Célimène's salon does not differentiate them fundamentally from Alceste's goal: they, too, want to stand out from all the others and win Célimène's place on the centre stage. Whilst the men want to achieve this goal through marriage to Célimène, Arsinoé tries to shift Célimène from the centre with intrigues and by defaming her character. However, in the duel of the gossips to which she challenges Célimène (III, 4), she is defeated by Célimène and elegantly put in her place.

Alceste seeks to distinguish himself from the others through his *sincérité*. Likewise, Oronte wants to earn distinction with his unutterably mediocre sonnets, and both 'petits marquis', Clitandre and Acaste, want the same with their foolish fashionable turn-out – the 'length' of the little finger-nail, the 'wide frills at the knee', 'accumulation of ribbons', 'massive *Rhingrave*'

(wide, highly be-ribboned breeches) and 'blond periwig' (II, pp. 38–9). Their behaviour is driven by the love of self as defined by Pascal, 'The nature of self-love and of this human self is to love only self and consider only self' (*Pensées*, Fragment 100, p. 347).

For Célimène, the salon fulfils a wealth of functions. On the one hand, it protects her from being alone. She always tries to keep several men about her. When Alceste tries to distance himself, she insists he remain ('But I want you to' [II, p. 41]) and then, almost by the way, asks, 'Haven't you gone?' Social intercourse drives away her boredom, for she knows how to entertain the gentlemen with her conversation: the wicked portraits she draws of acquaintances who are not present (II, 4) create a *pièce de resistance* of social *divertissements*. Not least, finally, Célimène's salon provides her with the opportunity and the satisfaction of knowing herself to be the centre of the world.

Célimène has, therefore, a justified interest in maintaining the social life of her salon. Since her admirers only frequent the salon because they are hopeful of a happy end to their courtship of her, it must be Célimène's goal to keep all of them in limbo as long as possible. She hands out little favours which strengthen the conviction of each vain admirer that he is the chosen one she loves. The delicate balance which Célimène maintains with great aplomb in her salon, is strikingly similar to the conditions which Louis XIV knew how to create and maintain at court. As Saint-Simon reports in his memoirs, no one knew 'as well as he, how to sell himself through words, smiles, looks. Everything he gave was valuable, because he showed differentiation.' Louis XIV even laid importance on firing up or dampening down rivalries and jealousies:

The frequent feasts, the private royal walks at Versailles, and his journeys were the means by which the king distinguished or mortified people by naming those who would come along, and it kept everyone attentive of him and assiduous towards him. He knew that he did not own enough charm to keep the impression going forever. In place of true ideals, he artfully encouraged jealousy, and little preferences, which one finds every day and, in some ways, at every moment. No one was as ingenious as he in tirelessly inventing this sort of thing to engender hope from such little preferences and distinctions and the respect gained from it.[36]

Both at the court of Louis XIV and in Célimène's salon, it is solely the visitor's love of himself (*amour-propre*) which keeps the empty social intercourse going, just as it is maintained, on the other side, by the central figure's fear of emptiness and loneliness, as Pascal explained of the king:

> Yet if you imagine one with all the advantages of his rank, but no means of diversion, left to ponder and reflect on what he is, this limp felicity will not keep him going; he is bound to start thinking of all the threats facing him, of possible revolts, finally of inescapable death and disease, with the result that if he is deprived of so-called diversion he is unhappy, indeed more unhappy than the humblest of his subjects who can enjoy sport and diversion.
>
> (*Pensées*, Fragment 139, p. 67)

Whilst the real power of the king is, none the less, in a position to integrate the different self-interests of the court members in a shared interest and, thus, to provide empty social interaction with some sense, in Célimène's salon, social life disintegrates as soon as each admirer realises that she has only played with him and his goal to excel above all others by marrying her cannot be reached. The game in Célimène's salon is over; the admirers force Célimène out of the centre (Act V) and leave her alone. She leaves the 'stage'. The social life in her salon is dead.

According to this interpretation, *The Misanthrope* appears to be a play on the sociability of man; on the sensitive balance of power in social life and the dangers to which it is constantly exposed. On the one hand, it is threatened by the misanthropic tendency of individuals to escapism, on the other hand, by the emptiness of social relations in the salon. Both dangers are founded in the need of an overreaching ego for admiration and superiority. To quote once again from Pascal's *Pensées*:

> The self is hateful ... It is unjust in itself for making itself centre of everything: it is a nuisance to others in that it tries to subjugate them, for each self is the enemy of all the others and would like to tyrannize them.
>
> (Fragment 455, p. 229)

The self is, in this sense, the ultimate cause of the permanent danger facing social life. On the other hand, social life presents the only conceivable place in which the self can be given respect and find recognition. And herein lies the dilemma of the man at court, as *The Misanthrope* shows in much subtlety: the affirmation of the self and the identity can only exist for the individual within the framework of social life. If the self, however, makes an over-exaggerated claim for respect and confirmation – as expressed in empty social intercourse and misanthropy – it threatens to dissolve social life altogether and thus destroy the basic foundation of the own identity.

One possible way out of this dilemma is shown by Molière in the figures of Philinte and Eliante, who are the playwright's gesture towards identificatory figures. Philinte 'sees' the morals and habits of *la cour et la ville* in a similar way to Alceste, but he tries to make the viewpoint of 'reason' the only valid one:

> Good Lord! Let us worry less about the manners of the age and make more allowance for human nature. Let us judge it less severely and look more kindly on its faults. What is needed in society is an accommodating virtue. It's wrong to be too high principled. True reason lies in shunning all extremes; we should be wise in moderation. This rigorous passion for the antique virtues runs counter to the age and customary usage. It demands too much perfection of mere mortals. We need to move with the times and not be too inflexible, and it's the

height of folly to take upon oneself the burden of the world's correction.

(I, pp. 28–9)

Philinte is thus prepared to bear the price of the 'customary usage' in his behaviour – not, however, in order to achieve advantage for himself, but rather out of consideration for his fellow beings. He embraces those who embrace him in order not to hurt their feelings (p. 30) and praises Oronte's mediocre sonnet in order to soften the scourge he expects from Alceste which must make Oronte rage against Alceste and oblige him to seek revenge. In the portrait scene (II, 4), in which Célimène gives free rein to her brilliant wit, Philinte tries to intervene and lead the conversation towards a more friendly tone by turning the conversation to Damis and, at the same time, to introduce his own judgement in the room as a guiding principle: 'I think he's a sound, sensible fellow' (II, p. 43).

In a similar way, in the same scene, Eliante tries to give substance to empty social relations. In the conversation on Alceste's possessive and bare-faced declaration of love, she proposes an opposite kind of love whose view is clouded, a love which is blind to the weaknesses of the loved one and which always 'sees' its object in a positive way:

That isn't really how love works at all. You find that a lover always justifies his own choice. He's blind to all faults ... for him everything in the loved one is loveable. Her very blemishes he counts as perfections or contrives to find flattering names for; should she be pale it's the pale beauty of the jasmine flower; she may be swarthy enough to frighten you, but for him she's an adorable brunette. ... So the true lover worships the very faults of his beloved.

(II, 4, pp. 45–6)

Eliante and Philinte play the social role only so far as is necessary to be considerate towards others and command 'bienséance' (p. 77) without raising the claim of centre stage for themselves. In this way, they keep the social life going

without being dependent on it to the extent that the others are. Philinte and Eliante have

Gentle spirits and tender hearts; they are proud yet polite, bold yet modest, who are neither greedy nor ambitious, who do not struggle for power and the first place nearest the king. Their only goal is to propagate joy everywhere they go and their greatest care lies in earning respect and love from others ... It is, therefore, their only profession to be honourable, and if someone were to ask me what makes an honourable man, then I would say that it is nothing more than to excel in everything which has to do with the pleasures and propriety of life. This is what, it seems to me, the most perfect and gentle way in the world depends upon.[37]

Philinte and Eliante embody the social ideal of *honnête homme* and *honnête femme* as it was represented by the experienced theoretician and practitioner of *honnêteté*, Antoine Gombaud, Chevalier de Méré (1607–84). This concept of ideal behaviour, independent of social rank, had already begun to be developed during the reign of Louis XIII, less so at court than in the salons where, for example, the Marquise de Rambouillet (at the Hôtel de Rambouillet) gained particular fame.

From 1630, many 'theoreticians' wrote books on *honnêteté* with reference to Castiglione's *Cortegiano*, such as Nicolas Faret (*L' Honnête homme, ou l'Art de plaire à la Cour*, 1630, reprinted 1631, 1634, 1636, 1640, 1656, 1658, 1660 and later) or Le Sieur de Grenailles, who wrote the *Honnête Fille* (1640) and the *Honnête Garçon* (1642), both of which are bursting with moral banalities.

The social ideal of *honnêteté* developed alongside court society. It was understood at the time of Louis XIV in a way formulated and propagated by Chevalier de Méré in his letters and work. Its social function extensively consisted of softening the claim for supremacy of the feudal ego and, in this way, to allow a form of social life as it developed in the court society. In embodying this idea in *The Misanthrope* in the figures of Philinte and Eliante, Molière maintains its possibility and unlimited value: the *honnête homme* and the *honnête femme* are the sole guarantee of social life even if they are pushed away by society in the comedy and represent only secondary figures. It is instead society that is judged.

The critique of court society, as it is represented by Célimène's salon, stood quite obviously in the foreground of reception of the time. Alceste, the misanthrope, was certainly not received as a negative figure. Not for nothing was M. de Montausier exceptionally satisfied with Molière's interpretation of the character on the stage. In *Lettres en vers* (12 June 1666), Robinet writes:

And this *Misanthrope* is so wise,
In countering the morals of our age,
That one would say, my dear reader,
That you are listening to a preacher.

The comedy appeared in print in 1667 with a 'Lettre sur la comédie du Misanthrope' by Donneau de Visé as foreword. In it, the author particularly emphasises the fact that it is a question of a critique of the 'moeurs du siècle' ('morals of the age'):

Molière certainly did not want to write a comedy full of incidents, but simply, a play where *he could speak against the morals of the age*. This is what made him choose a misanthrope as hero ... His choice is most extraordinary for theatre ... It is the most brilliant character ever to be performed on stage ...

It is it entirely ... the marquis who represent the court: so much so, that in this comedy one sees everything which one can say against the morals of this century.

His conclusion on Alceste reads:

*The misanthrope, despite his madness, if one may describe his humour thus, has the character of a man of honour and a great deal of steadfastness* ... The author does not only present the misanthrope through this characteristic he also allows his hero to speak some of the morals of the times, and it is extraordinary that *although he appears quite ridiculous in some ways*, what he says is very just. It does

seem that he demands too much, but one must ask a great deal if one is to achieve something, and it is necessary to make these men appear enlarged in order to oblige them to improve their ways even a little. Molière, through his unique skill, allows us to guess more than he says.

Whilst the audience of the middle classes felt themselves barely touched by the comedy, the spectators from *la court et la ville*, according to reception documents of the time, showed themselves much more deeply affected. A great success in this case was hardly to be expected. Thus, it comes as no surprise to learn that the play was never performed at court during Molière's lifetime and even failed in the Palais Royal after the first four, poorly attended performances. It was only after Molière's death that the play grew in popularity. In the last fifteen years of the rule of Louis XIV (1680–1715), *The Misanthrope* was performed nineteen times at court and at the Comédie Français it advanced to become one of Molière's ten most popular plays. It was performed 265 times in this period. The question is, had the 'morals' changed, or did the audience no longer perceive the theatre as its mirror?

## The gaze of the other and the gaze of the king

Ten years after his theatrical début at Molière's theatre with *La Thébaïde ou les Frères Ennemis* (*The Thebaïd, or The Enemy Brothers*, 1644), Jean Racine, at the age of 35, seemed to have reached the pinnacle of his career as tragic dramatist. His eighth tragedy, *Iphigénie en Aulide* (*Iphigenia*) was premièred at the 'Fêtes de l'Amour et de Bacchus' on 18 August 1674, and widely applauded by the audience at *la cour*. Robinet writes in a letter of 1 September 1674:

The greatly moving Iphigenia,
This masterpiece of genius
By Racine, delighted the court ...
The author was applauded greatly ...
And even our august Sire,
Praised him for it, that says it all!

Four months later, *Iphigenia* was presented to the Parisian audience at the Hôtel de Bourgogne, where it enjoyed unusual success. It remained three months in the repertoire without a break. Whilst there are no records of the first performances, reports from the following months are unanimous in claiming the triumph of *Iphigenia* and its author. *La Gazette d'Amsterdam* reports in the edition of 7 March 1675 that *Iphigenia* was 'the finest play I have ever seen in French theatre ... and that is no surprise, for the illustrious Racine is its author'. The two conversationalists of the *Entretiens sur les tragédies de ce temps* of March/April 1675 are united in their admiration of the tragedy, in particular the ability of the poet to paint the passions of love: 'Have you seen *Iphigenia*?', asks one. 'It's a play that has completely charmed everyone.' 'I found it very pleasing', answers the other, 'and I am not ashamed to say that once or twice, I could not stop my tears as I watched.' The author of *Remarques sur l'Iphigénie de M. Racine*, published in May 1675, notes on the poet, among other things, 'I hold him in the highest esteem which one must have for one of the most delicate pens of our times, and I will continue to put it in print that no one has written better in our language than he.' Pierre Bayle wrote a letter to his brother on 26 June that *Iphigenia* 'was greatly applauded last winter at the Hôtel de Bourgogne for forty consecutive performances'. The almost legendary success of the tragedy put all others in the shade. The great tragic actress La Champmeslé was also responsible for its success; she was known for her creation of the role of Bérénice (in the play of the same name, 1670), Roxane (in *Bajazet*, 1672) and Monime (in *Mithridate* 1673), and Racine specifically wrote the role of Iphigenia for her. At the end of 1675, La Fontaine wrote to her: 'I hope that [M. Racine] will tell me of your triumphs; of which I am sure, since he does not lack the materials.'

Through the overwhelming success of *Iphigenia*, Racine realised the secret goal of triumphing over his old rival, Pierre Corneille, the creator of the French tragic theatre. Before *Iphigenia* was performed at the Hôtel de Bourgogne in December 1674, the first première of the autumn/winter season had been Corneille's last play, *Suréna*. It was seen by only a very few.

The fact that it was the last play by the 68-year-old playwright, whose greatest successes were in the 1640s, following his *Le Cid* (1637), was not acknowledged, and the audience seemed wholly indifferent to his departure from the theatre. Racine's tragedy, on the contrary, became the talk of the town.

Racine's 'bourgeois' private career also reached great heights in 1674. Thanks to a recommendation by Colbert, he was elected to Trésorier de France en la généralité de Moulins, which secured him an extra income of 2,400 livres annually, enough so that he could easily afford a decidedly luxurious lifestyle. Racine might well have seen this period as the culmination of a major phase in his life or, at least, his career. For, at the end of 1675, he compiled a complete collection of his works which was conceived as a finished work.

In any case, after the première of *Iphigenia*, it was another two and a half years before Racine brought a new tragedy to the stage which, however, led him to his final retirement from the theatre. As in *Iphigenia*, Racine turned to a Greek model – this time Euripides' *Hippolytus*. His adaptation was premièred on 1 January 1677 at the Hôtel de Bourgogne, entitled *Phèdre et Hippolyte* (it was only in the 1687 edition that Racine retitled it *Phèdre – Phaedra*).

This particular material was very popular in the seventeenth century. Of the many adaptations, the most outstanding are *Hippolyte* by Gabriel Gilbert (1647), *Bellérophon* by Quinault (1671) and Bidar's *Hippolyte* (1674). But such popularity can hardly be the reason why, alongside Racine, the mediocre playwright, Jacques Pradon, also reworked it. His *Phaedra* was premièred on 3 January 1677 at the Théâtre de Guénégaud (a result of the merging of Molière's troupe with the Théâtre de Marais in 1673). This seemingly timely coincidence in fact did not happen by chance – it was the result of an intrigue which was the daily menu of literary and court life at the time of Louis XIV. The followers of Racine and Boileau who, at the same time, were followers of the 'anciens', stood for the literary side, in opposition to the followers of Corneille, who represented the viewpoint of the 'modernes'. Racine was the protégé of Madame de Montespan, the king's favourite, whereas Pradon was sponsored by members of the Mazarin family, such as the Duc de Nevers, the Duchesse de Bouillon and the Comtesse de Soissons. When Pradon discovered that Racine was working on a version of *Phaedra*, he also turned to the same material. Racine tried to stir up his followers at court to pass a royal ban on Pradon's play being performed at the same time. But Louis XIV, who appreciated the rivalry between his theatres, did not intervene. Thus, two opposing parties were formed, as described in the *Dissertation sur les tragédies de Phèdre et Hippolyte* (April 1677):

> As soon as news of this scheme [Pradon's attempt to compete with Racine] spread,
> Both authors began to intrigue and form a party,
> And each of them instructed his troupes instead of the army.

Racine's tragedy received a frosty reception, even though Champmeslé took the role of Phaedra. Pradon's *Phaedra*, on the other hand, won measurable success, despite the fact that the two best actresses of the Théâtre de Guénégaud, Armande Béjart (Molière's widow) and Cathérine de Brie, refused to play the title roles. *La Gazette d'Amsterdam* of 8 January 1677 reported on both performances by the 'illustre Racine' and Pradon, and declared, 'The first was to the taste of the ancients, but the latter hit the taste of the public.' In a letter by Hansen, Leibniz's informant in Paris, this impression is confirmed: 'Pradon gained victory over Racine, despite the fact that Racine had his play performed at l'Hôtel, where the best actors are.' Pradon's *Phaedra* was given approximately a dozen performances in January and, after a short break, the same number again in February and March. It was indeed for him a pleasant, if not sensational, success.

Public opinion on the two tragedies began to change in March/April as critics began to be involved in the argument. Boileau, a close friend of Racine, had already demonstrated his

viewpoint clearly in February in *Épître VII. à M. Racine*, cited above, where he described Racine as a poet unrecognised by the uneducated audience:

> As soon as a genius inspired by Apollo
> Finds an untrodden path, far from that which is vulgar,
> Intrigues are mounted against him in a hundred places.
> His dark rivals caw around his head,
> And his light, too great, dazzles the eyes
> Even of his own friends, and causes envy.

This is followed by some verses on Molière, and then Boileau draws the conclusion:

> Do not be amazed, if Envy awakened,
> Attaching to your name its filthy reputation,
> And with slander in its hand, pursues you sometimes.

In March and April, Donneau de Visé joined the quarrel over the two tragedies and gave his judgement in the *Mercure Galant*. In a long treatise, he compares both from the perspective of the tragic and comes to the conclusion that Racine's tragedy is far superior: 'Monsieur Racine is always Monsieur Racine, and his verses are too fine not to give the same pleasure in reading them that they give when one hears them being recited in the theatre.' On 1 April, Bayle could still write to his brother that the two tragedies 'divide le Cour et la Ville, some finding more value, poesy or spirit in one of the two plays, others finding it in the other play.' But on 6 May, he was obliged to declare that 'the critics mostly decide vehemently against Pradon'.[38]

In the following six months, Racine's tragedy was performed three times at court, once at Sceaux, where Louis XIV found it worthy 'of particular attention and praise by the audience', and twice at Fontainebleau. The 'querelle' over *Phaedra* was clearly decided in Racine's favour.

At the climax of the 'querelle', both opponents published their versions of the tragedy, Pradon on 13 March 1677, Racine two days later. Pradon referred to the intrigue in his foreword – he complains that the Greeks, so admired by his opponents, 'would never have prevented the best actresses of a company from playing a major role in Athens, as our modern friends have done in Paris at the Théâtre de Guénégaud. It is this which the public regards with indignation and disgust.' But Racine does not allow himself the slightest hint of the débacle in the foreword. He uses it in a far more skilful manner as a means of directing the reception of the reader in a certain way.

Racine bases his divergences from Euripides and Seneca on the demand for 'vraisemblance' and 'bienséance' in the theatre of his time. But he also emphasises unmistakably that his tragedy corresponds to the ancient concepts to a large extent. This is particularly true of the character of Phaedra, which

> has all the qualities which Aristotle demands of a tragic hero, and which provoke empathy and fear. PHAEDRA is neither wholly guilty nor wholly innocent. She is drawn into an illegitimate passion by fate and the anger of the gods and she is the first who is horrified by it. Her whole efforts are directed towards overcoming it … [this] shows very clearly, that her crime is more a punishment by the gods than an action of her own will.

The proximity to the ancients which Racine stresses, is also relevant to the effect he hoped to achieve through the tragedy. For the Greek theatre 'was a school where virtue was not less well taught than in the philosopher's school'. His tragedy should operate in a similar way, and was perhaps, as Racine judged,

> in fact, my best tragedy … I can assure you that I have written no other play where VIRTUE is as prominent as in this drama. The tiniest faults are severely punished. The mere idea of the crime is looked upon with the same horror as the crime itself. Weakness in love is interpreted as true weakness of character, and the passions are only presented so that one sees what chaos they cause.

It is noticeable that both aspects which are taken to prove that Racine's tragedy continues the demands and concepts of the ancients, refer to the 'passions': on the one hand, the 'passion illégitime' that Phaedra feels for her stepson, Hippolytus, is described as the punishment of the gods, for which not she, but her fate, is responsible; on the other hand, reference is made to the 'chaos' caused by the passions. The foreword thus constructs a central perspective from which the reader should view the passions, not just for *Phaedra*, but also for Racine's entire theatrical output – it was not for nothing that his contemporaries saw his 'théâtre des passions' in opposition to Corneille's 'théâtre de la gloire'.

In *Phaedra*, two kinds of passion are given outstanding function and meaning: the 'passion illégitime' of Phaedra for her stepson, Hippolytus, which leads to Phaedra's death, and Theseus' anger over Hippolytus' suspected 'passion illégitime' for his stepmother, which leads to Hippolytus' death. Both passions are placed in direct relation to the gods. Phaedra describes the birth of her love for Hippolytus in the following way:

> I saw and gazed, I blushed and paled again,
> A blind amazement rose and blurred my
> mind;
> My eyes were dim, my lips forgot to speak,
> This, I knew, was the awful flame of Venus,
> The fated torment of her chosen victims. …
>
> No longer is it a secret flame that flickers
> About my veins: headlong in onset Venus
> Hangs on her quarry!
> (275–9, 306–8)[39]

The love which Phaedra feels for Hippolytus did not arise from within, instead, its source is in the goddess Venus. But Venus did not send or kindle this passion, rather the passion *is* Venus. The goddess has taken possession of Phaedra, poured herself into her veins and destroyed her body from the inside out. Thus, Phaedra has no power over her love; will and reason are powerless against her.

In a similar way, Theseus' anger refers to the god Neptune, as Theseus calls upon him:

And now hear, Neptune, hear. If once my
   courage
Scoured off a scum of bandits from thy coasts
Remember thou hast sworn in recompense
To grant one prayer. In long and stern
   confinement
I called not thy undying power; I saved thee
Thrifty of all the aid I hoped for, till
A greater need. Today I pray: avenge
A mourning father. To thy wrath I leave
This profligate. Still his lust in his blood.
Let Theseus read thy kindness in thy rage.

(1086–95)

Theseus' rage is identical to Neptune's 'colère'. He yields control over it and works against Theseus' declared intent towards Hippolytus in a catastrophic way. In vain, Theseus begs 'Neptune, / Delay thy deadly gift, be not too sudden' (1503–4). Theseus is unable either to influence or direct the anger which rages against Hippolytus and leaves nothing behind but 'a ravaged corpse, / The dreadful triumph of an angry Heaven, / Where not a father's eye could undertake / To know his child' (1592–5).

In putting the passions of Phaedra's love and Theseus' rage on the same level as gods who, though one may implore them, cannot be directed or controlled, Racine shows humanity denied the subjugation of the passions to the rule of will and reason. Man is denied conscious control of his emotions.

It is hardly surprising, therefore, that in the foreword, Racine explicitly calls upon the ancients in terms of his representation of the passions. For it stands in striking opposition to the views and persuasions on which court life was founded. Corneille was the first to use the passions as the basis of his drama; his heroes repeatedly demonstrate how they force their most moving and burning passions to submit to the yoke of reason and will with remarkable strength. A prime example of this is provided by Don Rodrigue in *Le Cid* in his famous monologue (I, 7), in which he decides to take revenge on Ximena's father though he loves her, and in so doing denies himself love for ever, for the sake of the honour of his house:

What battles fierce within!
Against my honour passion takes up arms.
If I avenge him, then I must lose her.
One fires me on. The other holds me back.
The shameful choice is to betray my love
Or live in infamy.
In either case, my grief is infinite.
O God! The agony.
I leave an insult unavenged
Or punish my belovèd's father. ...

To die without revenge!
To seek a death fatal to my renown!
To suffer Spain to brand my memory
With a foul stigma that dishonours me!
To cherish still a love my frantic soul
Knows I am bound to lose!
I'll close my ears to these insidious thoughts,
Which merely fan my despair.
Come, save at least my honour, strong right
   arm,
Since after all Ximena's loss is sure.

(*Le Cid* 301–10, 331–40)[40]

Corneille's heroes are autonomous individuals who are centred in their will and reason. Thus, they are ready at any time to bring their passions under control. On the other hand, in *Phaedra*, the figures are totally at the whim of their passions. Without being able to defend themselves, they are forced to observe how their passions culminate in the creation of 'monsters'. Thus, Phaedra describes herself as a monster, after confessing her love for Hippolytus:

Approve yourself a hero's son indeed
And sweep this monster from the universe.
Dare Theseus' widow love Hippolytus?
Truly so vile a monster must not live.

(712–15)

From Theseus' rage grows a veritable monster which Neptune releases out of the flood to destroy Hippolytus:

And now from the level deep immense there
   heaves
A boiling mount of brine, and still it swells,

Rears wave-like foaming down on us and
  breaks
To belch a ravening monster at our feet
Whose threatening brow is broadened with
  huge horns,
Whose body, cased in a golden glint of scales,
Thrashes a train of sinuous writing whorls.
Indomitable bull, malignant dragon,
Its long-drawn bellows rumble down the
  shore;
Heaven quails, earth shudders at the portent,
  air
Reeks with its pestilential breath.

(1535–45)

The 'monsters' which Phaedra's love and
Theseus' anger have called forth, prove to be
merciless, destructive predators.

The word 'monstre' functions as a key word
or leitmotif of the tragedy. It appears again and
again, although it is emphasised that Theseus
has freed the world of its monsters, which
threatened to devastate it with their drive for
destruction. Along with the monsters, Theseus
has banned chaos. In this way, Theseus' function
as the founder of civilisation is emphasised: he
killed the monsters and created order. This
order is based on the political constitution of
the state, as well as on the patriarchal system of
the family: it justifies the law forbidding incest
and adultery. On the basis of this order, a
system of right and law can be created which
represent the conditions of every human
communal life, whether the society as a whole,
smaller groups, or individual interaction.

Among these laws, those which concern
interaction between smaller and middle-size
groups – in the salon or at court – are accorded
special importance for the life at court. The
order which they create is an order of signs.
The most significant theoretician on the
concept of *honnêteté*, Chevalier de Méré, cited
above, describes the rules of conversation in
the following way:

One must observe what is going on in the hearts
and minds of those people with whom one
converses and quickly become accustomed to
recognise the feelings and thoughts through signs

which are barely perceptible. This knowledge,
which is obscure and difficult for those who are not
used to it, will become clearer and easier with time.

It is a science which one must learn like a
foreign language, when one only understands a
little at first. But when one loves and studies it,
one makes swift progress.

This art has something of witchery in it, for it
teaches one divination, and through this, one
discovers many things which one would otherwise
not see at all which can be very useful. Besides, it
is very pleasant to be with people who fulfil one's
wishes without having to ask it of them.[41]

The rules of interaction are comparable to the
rules of a foreign language ('comme une
langue estrangère'). They form a repertoire of
signs and rules concerning certain combina-
tions and applications. A person who knows
these rules, who can read another person's
'thoughts' and 'feelings' through the other's
words, gaze, gestures and movements, is in a
position not only to understand, but also to
manipulate. The art of seeing through another
person's mask and, at the same time, to see it as
the mirror of one's own position in the hierarchy of court life, also provides familiarity
with the rules of interactive signs and their
exact meanings.

Descartes tried to fit the passions into this
rational system of sign interpretation as well. In
his *Traité de passions*, published in 1649, he
starts from the assumption that all mental
conditions to a large extent correspond to
certain modifications in the body. As a result,
such modifications can be read as signs of a
specific mental condition. In order to understand the passions correctly – or to simulate
them – one only has to be aware of the physical
signs in which they are manifested: 'Among
these signs, the most important ones are
actions of the eyes and face, changes in colour,
trembling, languor, fainting, laughter, tears,
groans, and sighs' (article 112, p. 79).[42]

According to Descartes, then, it is not only
the thoughts and feelings of the other person in
the interaction which are open and visible in
outward signs but also the passions. A person
who knows the relevant system of signs can

read them, understand them and, if necessary, manipulate them for specific purposes in a rational and deliberate way.

The 'monster' that the passions release into the world in *Phaedra* breaks these rules of inter-action and destroys the mechanism of its smooth running. They make sure that the signs of passion, to which Descartes refers, are misinterpreted and falsely understood.

After confessing her love to Hippolytus, Phaedra sees him return with the apparently dead Theseus, and cries:

And I see
Hippolytus, and his unflinching eyes
Spell my dishonour.

(930–1)

The 'actions des yeux' to which Descartes refers as sure signs, are interpreted wrongly by Phaedra. She reads in them that Hippolytus intends to betray her, whilst he is actually determined not to speak out, but to flee. This misinterpretation of the gaze proves to be fatal. Because of it, Phaedra agrees to Oenone's plan to accuse Hippolytus of a crime he has not committed.

In a similarly striking way, Theseus misin-terprets Hippolytus' behaviour after he falls into a rage at his supposed 'passion illégitime'.

The perfidy! Yes, for all his craft, he paled;
He quaked with fear, I saw it as he came;
I marvelled then to feel his joylessness
And froze against the chill of his embrace. ...

So, here he comes. Great Gods, that noble
    carriage
Would it not blind another's eye, as mine?
Then sacrilegious and adulterous heads
May flaunt the sacred emblem of the pure?
Why is there no infallible badge to blazon
The minds of our dissembling race of men?

(1045–8, 1057–62)

The 'signes certains' are read wrongly because of his rage. In this case, too, the misinterpreta-tion of signs proves fatal: it allows Theseus to beg Neptune to take revenge and thus sets in motion the uncontrollable machinery which will ultimately crush Hippolytus.

In *Phaedra*, it is the total breakdown of the ability to read mental states and processes in outward signs which leads to catastrophe. The catastrophe is the result of fatal misunder-standing. In this respect, it is noticeable that neither Phaedra's misinterpretation nor Theseus' error lead directly to the use of violence. Both insist: 'my hands are free of evil' (Phaedra, 223), and 'I have kept my hand unstained' (Theseus, 1192). Their hands remain clean. Violence is released through words – words which are spoken out, as well as words which are unspoken. Thus Phaedra's 'crime' consists of speech acts which she should not have uttered, such as confessing her love to Hippolytus, as well as speech acts which she fails to make: she does not obstruct Oenone from the false accusation and out of jealousy does not tell Theseus the truth after she has discovered Hippolytus' love for Arícia. The same is true of Theseus. He refuses to interro-gate his son, and hands over responsibility for death by executing a speech act of request with which he reminds Neptune of his promise. It is not deeds which release their fatal potential in *Phaedra*, but words and looks.

The gaze in the other's eye not only has consequences in that it can perceive the own gaze and distort it. It also accords the other person a far more important meaning which is principally exposed in love.

Hippolytus' first sight of Arícia has an enor-mous impact on him, as Arícia's friend Ismène correctly realises:

I saw a face at variance with the fable;
At once your eyes disturbed that assurance
And his, avoiding you but all in vain,
Melted at once, and could not turn away.

(412–15)

This sight leads him to fall in love and, at the same time, it is the cause of the loss of his own self:

I, long a truant from the law of love
And long a mocker of its votaries,

That stayed ashore watching the luckless sailor
And never thought myself to fight the
   tempest,
Levelled at last beneath the common fate
By strange tides I am borne far from myself.
(534–9)

The sight of Arícia has made Hippolytus a
stranger to himself; he is no longer the man he
was before and thus loses his identity: 'And I,
for all my fruitless pains, look round / To find
Hippolytus, and know him not' (550–1). The
gaze which love releases functions, at the same
time, as a *rite de passage*: it dissolves the old
identity and leads the initiate through a phase
of insecurity before finally according him a
new identity. The sight of Arícia not only turns
a worshipper of Diana into a worshipper of
Venus but it also transforms the obedient son
who is ready and willing to follow his father
(the word 'fils' is used of Hippolytus fifty-two
times!) into an adult man: he loves the woman
forbidden to him by his father for political
reasons and has decided to bear witness to his
independence from his father and declare his
relationship to his lover publicly – at least
under the eyes of the gods – by marriage. In a
similar way, Arícia is also transformed by the
sight of Hippolytus (II, 1; V, 1).

The lovers no longer find their centre within
themselves; instead, they find it in others. It is the
gaze of the other which annuls their identity and,
after a phase of insecurity, provides them with
another identity. In this sense, they are not
autonomous individuals, but heteronomous. The
other's gaze becomes the mirror which dissolves
the old self-image and reflects a new image back
to the one gazing into it.

This dependence of the own identity on the
other, which in the mutual love of Hippolytus
and Arícia leads to a successful rediscovery of
the self in the mirror of the other, has fatal
consequences where love is unrequited.

Phaedra also loses her identity on first
seeing Hippolytus:

I saw and gazed, I blushed and paled again,
A blind amazement rose and blurred my
   mind;

My eyes were dim, my lips forgot to speak.
(275–7)

Venus has taken possession of her so that she
is no longer herself. With no secure identity,
she is torn between contradictory self-images of
herself which are determined by her origins, for
she is 'the child of Minos and Pasiphaë' (36) –
thus her constant reference to her 'blood'.
Consequently, she seeks to balance this contradiction, at least linguistically, in the oxymoron,
'the darkness of these fires' (311). As descendent
of the 'sun' as 'the very blood of Jupiter' (880), as
goddess of the heavens and 'child of Minos'
blood' (770), the god of the underworld, she feels
she belongs to the gods. This self-image is determined by her 'gloire'. As daughter of Pasiphaë,
who desired the bull and bore the minotaur, she
sees herself as 'monster'. This self-image is
marked by her feelings of 'shame'.

Which self-image will finally be actualised
and define her future identity is totally
dependent on Hippolytus' gaze: 'Your eyes can
testify that this is true – / If for one moment
they could bear my sight' (701–2). Hippolytus
does not return Phaedra's love. Thereby her
much longed for 'godly identity' is denied her.
Hippolytus' gaze turns her into a 'monstre
affreux'. In the same process, Phaedra's image
of Hippolytus also changes. Until this point,
she has 'worshipped' him as a god and seen in
him the idealised image of his father,

Yes, Prince, for him indeed I yearn, I
   languish;
I love him – not the man that Hell has claimed,
The butterfly that every beauty lured,
The adulterous ravisher that would have
   stained
The God of Hell's own bed; but faithful, fine,
Sometimes aloof, and pure, gallant and gay,
Young, stealing every heart upon his road –
So do they character our Gods, and so
I see you now.
(639–47)

However, his rejecting, disgusted gaze changes,
in turn, her view of him: 'I see him now / Grim
as a monster and terrible' (903–4). Hippolytus

cannot completely escape the identifying power of her gaze; his self-image is tarnished: 'I cannot see myself without disgust' (731).

The identity of the individual proves to be fundamentally unstable because it is wholly dependent on the other. In *amour tendre*, the mutual attribution of identity can, none the less, succeed because each person reflects a humane image as the mirror of the other. In *amour passioné*, on the other hand, the fundamental danger, which results from the fact that identity only stems from dependency on the gaze of the other, becomes obvious. As a shattered mirror, it reflects different, contradictory images: in love and self-love it reflects the face of a god, in hate and self-hate the grimace of a monster. In both cases, the development of a human identity is made impossible.

The system of mutual attribution of identity on which life at court was based can only really function as long as the individual is in a position to plan his behaviour rationally and steer it with deliberation. Even when this is the case, one still has to be prepared to deceive and be deceived as, unlike Chevalier de Méré, La Rochefoucauld clearly recognises:

> It is as easy to be deceived without realising it as it is difficult to deceive others without them realising it ... It is the subtlest of all refinements to be able to seem to have fallen into the trap others have lain for us, yet one is never so easily deceived as when one believes that one has successfully deceived others ... the intention not to deceive exposes us to the danger of often being deceived ourselves ... True deception is the belief that one is cleverer than the others.
>
> (*Maximes*, 1655, final version 1678)[43]

From this, it follows that the identity of the individual under this system is, in principle, unstable, but not, however, that it is absolutely impossible to develop a personal identity.

In *Phaedra*, on the other hand, the problem of identity is radicalised. The explosion of passion into the symbolic order not only means that the signs are falsely interpreted but it also makes the mutual attribution of identity fail. Hippolytus is blinded by Phaedra's passion and

can only reflect a distorted image of Phaedra; Phaedra's gaze, clouded by passion, can only recognise the image of a monster in this mirror. She is thrown back on herself and remains alone with no acceptable image of herself.

Alongside the lover's gaze, the gaze of the father and the king are given a particularly creative and stimulating power in terms of identity. The first part of the tragedy is carried out in Theseus' absence. He is in the underworld, where he sees things which are normally hidden from human sight. For, 'No man has twice explored the coasts of Death' (628). In Act I, Hippolytus and Phaedra 'break' a long held silence. Hippolytus confesses his forbidden love for Aricia (I, 3) to his teacher and friend, Theramène, and Phaedra tells her maid and friend, Oenone, of her secret love for Hippolytus (I, 3). After Theseus is declared dead (I, 4), both confess their love to their beloved: Hippolytus declares his love to Aricia (II, 2) and Phaedra owns up to Hippolytus (II, 5). The mutual attribution of a new identity between Hippolytus and Aricia succeeds where the mutual attribution of a new identity between Phaedra and Hippolytus fails. In the state of affairs, precisely in the middle of the tragedy, the return of Theseus is announced: 'The King's not dead, and you will see him soon' (III, 3).

Both Phaedra and Hippolytus fall back into a silence which Aricia also does not dare to break, 'Knowing what deference his heart still holds / I should increase his suffering too much / Dared I continue' (1465–7).

> Look to yourself, my lord:
> Your matchless weight of arm redeemed mankind
> From monsters past all counting – but not all,
> The breed is not destroyed, and you have saved
> One – I must say no more; your son forbids me.
> (1460–4)

Thus, Theseus misunderstands the reference to Phaedra and, in his anger towards Hippolytus for the supposed adulterous and incestuous love, attributes him with the identity of a monster:

Dissembler! Dare you come so near to me?
Monster the thunderbolts reprieve too long,
Corrupted stranger of the brigand race.

(1066–8)

In vain, Hippolytus seeks to reveal to the king's gaze an image of a son whose validity is confirmed by his 'blood' inheritance from the chaste Amazon:

Look on my life, consider what I am. …

Like virtue, vice is gradual. No one day
Made any good man vile, murderous, inces-
    tuous,
And innocence is slow to dare, and slow
To push beyond the boundaries of law.
I had a mother, as chaste as she was valiant,
Nor have I derogated from my blood, …

This
Has made Hippolytus his name in Greece.

(1111, 1114–19, 1124–5)

The father's gaze, clouded by rage, dissolves this identity. Like Phaedra after her confession, Theseus sees a monster in Hippolytus. But whilst Phaedra's gaze only has the power to distort Hippolytus' own view of himself, Theseus' gaze proves to be murderous: he relinquishes responsibility for his son to the rage of Neptune, a real monster who tears Hippolytus apart and, thus, destroys his physical identity: all that remains is a 'corps défiguré'.

It is only when Phaedra decides in the last scene 'I have repented of my silence' (1640) that Theseus' eyes are opened to the true identity of his son:

Your son requires his innocence from my lips;
Yes, he was guiltless.

(1641–2)

There is little he can do: 'I must enfold what still remains to touch / Of my dear son, and expiate in tears / The blind curse I shall evermore bewail' (1672–4), but accept his son's lover as his daughter, according to his son's wishes. His gaze has destroyed his son irretrievably.

Theseus' gaze has no power over Phaedra, however. She avoids another's gaze. The father's gaze, which bears down upon her is the gaze of her ancestor, the sun god:

Splendid begetter of a seed afflicted,
Father from whom my mother claimed her
    birth,
O blushing Sun ashamed of my despair,
Now, for the last time, I salute thy face.

(171–4)

Even on her first entrance, Phaedra determines to withdraw herself from the eyes of the sun through death. But this desire is twofold. Thus, Phaedra complains: 'These fripperies, these veils, they hang so heavy!' (160), so that Oenone has to remind her:

Yourself, you rallied your forgotten vigour,
You wanted to be out and see the sunlight.
Now you are here, my lady, and it seems
You loathe the very light that you desired.

(167–70)

Phaedra complains about the weight of the 'veil' which allows her both to show herself to the light of the sun and, at the same time, to hide herself from it. She thus gives expression to the secret wish to be seen and recognised by the sun as who she is – one who, despite her love for Hippolytus, is appropriately named – Phaedra (which means the shining, bright one, granddaughter of the sun, 'blood of Jupiter'). Apart from her beloved Hippolytus, it is only the gaze of the sun – her Ur-father – which can confirm her divine identity. But after Phaedra is carried away by immeasurable jealousy, desired Arícia's downfall and schemed that Theseus should act as the tool of her revenge, she finally gives up this identity for good. The gaze of the sun which exposes her 'shame' and thus denies her any acceptable image of herself, is wholly unbearable:

… and dare I face the sight
Of that sacred Sun, the giver of my life,
I, grandchild of the high Father of the Gods,
My forebears crowding Heaven and all
    creation?

Where may I hide?

(1289–93)

The entire universe appears as Phaedra's divine father whose gaze she seeks to escape because he identifies her with 'shame'. But there is no refuge for Phaedra. The destructive gaze of the father follows her into the underworld:

Flee to the night of Hell?
No, no, not there; for there my father's hands
Inexorably lift the doomsday urn,
They say, and Minos stands in deathly justice
Over the pallid multitudes of men.
Will that great shade not start in ghastly anger
When I in shame before his awful gaze
His daughter, plead my guilt …

Father, what will you say to these? I see
The tremendous urn roll thundering at your
    feet;
I see you ponder unknown penalties
To execute yourself upon your own …

(1293–1302–5)

Condemned by the gaze of her beloved as well as the gaze of her father, who represents divine law, Phaedra can neither find an identity in human society nor in the universe, neither in this world nor the afterworld. As she begins to recognise this, she comes to the decision that she will expose the 'shame' inflicted upon her by the gods, 'The flame of Heaven lighted in my bosom / A fatal fire' (1648–9) and reveal, in doing so, Hippolytus' true identity. By killing herself, Phaedra deliberately and willingly re-establishes the cosmic order of sun and shade, light and darkness which destroyed and injured her 'passion illégitime' against her will.

And death, blurring the sunbeams from these
    eyes
Whose glance polluted them, restores the light
To perfect purity.

(1666–8)

Theseus' reaction is a thorough misunderstanding of the greatness of Phaedra's tragedy which is alone comparable to that of Soph-ocles' Oedipus: 'And would the dark remembrance too might die' (1670). Although Theseus is king and founder of the civilised order, he has shown himself to be incapable of raising himself above events, so to speak, as spectator, and to accord each individual his true identity with both a distancing and totalising gaze. This function is now passed over to the spectators in the auditorium, to whose gaze he remains exposed to the end. It depends on their gaze as to which identity he will finally be given.

This responsibility lies, to a special degree, in the hands of the ideal spectator who sits in the privileged seat with the ideal viewpoint, from which alone an undistorted view (perspective) of the stage can be gained: the royal box of the king, Louis XIV. It is this point which makes direct relations between the play on the gaze in Racine's theatre and the masks and mirrors of court life. In the theatre, as in public life, it is the gaze of the king alone which sees the sense of (historical or dramatic) events as well as the true identities of the actors (on the stage, at court, in the state), which is not dazzled and so views these things distortedly or as through a cloud. The king is the centre whom everyone needs for the development of his own identity which he cannot find for himself in himself; the centre from which the courtier's unstable identity, constantly endangered and threatened by the loss of self, receives a single validity. The gaze of the king is the 'soul' without which 'the machine falls to pieces' (Cotin). The loss of this centre must inevitably explode or collapse the whole complicated system of masking and mirroring in which the mutual attribution of identity is founded. It would no longer be possible for the individual to find an acceptable identity. The parallels between this – wholly plausible – consequence of court life and Racine's *Phaedra* cannot be overlooked. It was not only state theories of the time such as Le Moyne's *Art de reigner* or Bossuet's *Politique tirée des paroles de L'Écriture sainte* which unfolded the theme of the royal gaze and its particular masterly function of giving perspective and stability. It was also a popular topos which found wide acceptance in all writing of the time.

After *Phaedra*, Racine withdrew completely from the theatre. On the wishes of the king, he amended what the bourgeoisie called his chaotic lifestyle and married Catherine de Romanet, who came from an old officials' family, on 1 June 1677. In September, Louis XIV called upon him and his friend Boileau to become the king's historiographers and he bestowed on these posts an annual income of 6,000 livres. Racine became an *honnête homme* and 'le savant de la cour'. Directly in the gaze of the king, he had finally won the social position and personal identity for himself for which he had always striven and for which his career in the theatre had simply provided the springboard.

## The stage world as mirror image of the court

Most of the stages at the time of Louis XIV were built according to the Italian design, in part, with the help of expensive conversions such as at the Théâtre de Marais in 1644 and the Hôtel de Bourgogne in 1647. The stage was separated from the auditorium by a magnificent stage portal. The stage portal was a development of the Renaissance interpretation of the *scenae frons* of Roman theatre, and it encompassed the stage entirely, like a picture frame. This resulted in a major division of the space into two areas: the spectators were seated in the auditorium facing the stage, and the actors performed in front, clearly visible to them. This pleasing arrangement was disrupted, however, by the custom of offering the nobility seats on the stage (a custom which was only banned in 1759).

When the curtain rose at the Hôtel de Bourgogne or at the Palais Royal, the audience was generally confronted with a uniform set before which plays would be performed: a hall in a palace or a salon, a bourgeois interior or a street, a public square or a garden. Some scene changes were used in the comedies, however, and Molière made extensive use of this in *Don Juan*. Frequent scene changes were, none the less, more the realm of the Marais theatre with its machine plays and, later, opera.

The set consisted of painted wings which culminated in a backdrop painted with a view. Since the wings represented a landscape or buildings in complete symmetry, with perspective shortening there could, in principle, be only one point in the theatre to which the stage perspective was oriented and from which alone it could be properly viewed: the ideal viewpoint. This was the royal seat.

The actors entered from between the first pair of wings and performed exclusively on the relatively narrow front stage in order not to break the sense of proportion (by the second pair of wings, a tree might appear smaller than the real actor). At the Hôtel de Bourgogne, with its already small stage, there was not much room left for the actors. Thus, it is hardly surprising that a predominantly statuesque style of acting developed.

The actors generally wore contemporary costume which was mostly very elaborate and costly. As has been variously remarked, they could have appeared at court in the same dress. This is also true of the so-called Turkish, or ancient plays. Here, the contemporary costume, which for the male roles automatically consisted of an *allonge* wig, was given a few meagre accessories, such as a turban or a golden helmet – naturally both with an oversized plume on top. The contemporary costume, none the less, had to fulfil a multiplicity of functions on the stage. Whilst in the tragedies it was mostly restricted to representing the powerful and important royal or heroic roles, in the comedy, costume could imply a wealth of meanings. Particularly creative were the over-exaggerations of certain fashions, such as in Molière's 'petits marquis', or exaggerated details of costume such as the size of the boots or the length of a wig, which could even reach to the floor in the figure of the swaggering boaster. In each case, the over-exaggeration negated the role's demand for recognition and respect: it was obvious to the spectator that such a demand was wholly inappropriate, even absurd. Similarly revealing was the change of costume on the open stage as in Molière's *Précieuses Ridicules* (*The Affected*

Ladies) in front of the spectators. The servants dress themselves as 'marquis' so that the spectator can see through their deceptive manoeuvre right from the start, whilst the two foolish bumpkins, Magdelon and Cathos, celebrate their 'noble' admirers in wonder.

In terms of acting style, there were significant differences between that at the Hôtel de Bourgogne and Molière's Palais Royal. Molière rejected the tragic style, practised by the rival theatre, as stilted, exaggerated and 'unnatural'. In L' Impromptu de Versailles, Molière instructed his actors in the first scene how they should play their roles. As a negative example, he cited the great stars of the Bourgogne and made fun of them: Montfleury in Nicomède, Mlle de Beauchâteau as the Infanta in Le Cid, Hauteroche in Pompée and Villiers in Oedipe (all dramas by Corneille). Molière imitated the way Montfleury declaimed verse 'avec emphase' and put these words into his mouth: 'Do you see this pose? Note it well. Here, give the right stress to the last verse. This is what wins approbation, and makes them roar.' Molière makes one of his own actors complain about Montfleury's 'ton démoniaque', and suggests that a king talking to his guardsman could speak a 'little more humanely'. But Montfleury dispatched him with the comment, 'Go and recite it as you usually do, and you'll see there's no great "Ah!" in the audience'. As well as criticising bombastic declamation aimed at getting the most applause, Molière also condemned the actors' posing, which seemed to him to be the striking opposite of the psychological situation of the role: 'Do you think it is natural and passionate? Are you not amazed by the smiling face she [Mlle de Beauchâteau] maintains despite great changes in emotion?' In contrast to these bad acting habits, Molière insisted his actors should be 'careful to take on the character of your roles and imagine that you are that which you represent. ... I shall tell you all your characters so that they stick firmly in your minds.'

Molière's ideal was clearly a 'natural' style of acting. However, 'natural' is a relative attribute, which changes according to various patterns of social behaviour of the time. Thus, the actor,

du Croisy, who plays the poet, should 'emphasise that all-knowing look, which manifests itself amongst better society, that sententious tone of voice, and exact pronunciation which stresses every syllable and does not allow a single letter to escape the strictest orthography'. Brécourt, who plays an 'honnête homme de cour', should 'take on a calm expression, a natural tone of voice, and ... should gesticulate as little as possible'. All the actors should constantly bear in mind the character of the role they are playing 'in order to make good facial expressions'.

Whilst the audience approved of this acting style in comedy, it was rejected in the playing of tragedy. Thus, Molière was considered to be an 'exécrable tragédien'.

Racine seems to have searched for a style of declamation in tragic theatre which was a middle way between Molière's ideal and the style of the Hôtel de Bourgogne:

> He highly disapproved of the *uniform style* of recitation established in Molière's company. He wanted to give the verses a certain sound which, together with the metre and the rhyme, distinguished it from prose; but he could not bear these drawn out and squawking tones which others wanted to substitute for natural beauty, and which could, as it were, be written down like music.
>
> (Note by his son, J.B. Racine)[44]

As a result, Racine even rehearsed the main female roles of his tragedies with the actresses himself as, for example, Andromaque with Thérèse du Parc and all later roles including Phaedra with Champmeslé.

There are no direct or detailed documents on the acting style practised by the protagonists of the Hôtel du Bourgogne. The *Dissertatio de actione scenica*, published in Munich in 1727 by the Jesuit priest Franciscus Lang, can, however, certainly be viewed as a reliable source, since the Jesuits found the style developed in Paris exemplary and made it the foundation of their own performances in the schools and monastic theatres across Europe.

Lang's basic rule declares that the actors must execute all facial and bodily movements so that the spectator can perceive them without any obstruction. This rule is to be obeyed from the very first entrance:

> As for entrance in the theatre, one must first ensure that when the actor steps out of the wings onto the stage, he immediately turns his face and body to the audience and presents his face in such a way that the spectators can read in his eyes the mood in which he arrives. At the same time, he must take care to step and place the feet in such a way that he always directs his face and eyes towards the spectators ... these are the techniques which will decide on whether the whole performance will succeed.[45]

This rule is particularly important even when several actors have a dialogue on stage at the same time. Since the most important listener is not the partner in dialogue standing on stage but the spectator, the actor in the dialogue must always keep his face, and at least his chest, turned towards the spectator. He must stand in such a way that:

> the mouth of the actor who is speaking is directed to the spectator and not towards the partner to whom he is speaking. The actions may, however, be directed towards the partner, but not the actual face, unless the speech has finished. This will hold the attention of the spectator, for whom the whole performance is taking place. Moreover, it must needs be so. If the actors speak to each other as if there were no listener, and their faces and words were wholly directed at each other, then half of the spectators would be robbed of the sight of that actor whom they can only see either from the side or wholly from behind, which contradicts proper and natural manners and, above all, the respect due to the spectators themselves.
>
> (Lang, *Dissertatio de actione*, p. 193)

Since these aims were not easy to fulfil, specific techniques were developed which would make it possible for the actor to place himself facing the spectator when he spoke. Either the speaker's hand gestures were directed at the dialogue partner, while the face and chest were turned towards the audience and only turned to the partner in pauses in speech. Or, the speaker stood one step behind his partner so that he could direct his words both to the audience and the partner, who, however, must remain with his face to the audience and may only turn around to the speaker now and again, briefly. When it became the partner's turn to speak, then he would take a step backwards and the listener would take a step forward.

Such rules on how the actor must position himself prove, quite clearly, that it was not a question of creating an illusion of reality in theatre. It was far more a question of presenting signs which must be perceived directly and completely so that the spectator can interpret them correctly. Each actor, therefore, claimed a large space for himself on the stage: he could neither stand in front of another, nor allow himself to be even partially hidden by others. If several actors were on stage together, then the semicircle was the most appropriate form, since it allowed each person enough space for the presentation of the signs he wished to produce.

The basic stance taken by each actor was the so-called *crux scenica*. In this position, the feet formed a right-angle and all limbs – shoulders, arms, hands, fingers, hips, legs – were held in *contrapposto*. This was the only bodily position allowed, even if it appeared 'eccentric and artificial' (Lang, *Dissertatio de actione*, p. 173). Steps on the stage should culminate with the actor always returning to this basic position. Lang founded this position on his experience and specialist knowledge and, moreover, suggested that it was appropriate for, 'fitting' and 'becoming of ... a finer way of life'. It would seem that the *contrapposto* position, which underlies all movements on stage, is to be interpreted as the sole, appropriate representation of the self – a way of presenting others with one's own validity.

Particular care is dedicated to the representation of passion. In accord with Descartes, Lang explains that 'all emotions' should 'be apparent in the eyes' which 'are eloquent enough even without a voice, if they have fulfilled their task'. For 'a single blink of the eye in the right way and at the right time often affects feeling more than the poet can ever achieve with a speech no matter how long it is' (pp. 188f). Moreover, for every passion, there exist gestural signs which can easily be identifed by the spectator. As Lang explains (pp. 186f):

1   Admiration: both hands are raised and placed close to the upper part of the chest, whereby the palms are turned towards the spectator.

2   Scorn: the face is turned to the left and the hands are stretched out and slightly raised, shunning the unpleasant object towards the other direction. The same is achieved with the right hand alone, lightly curved towards the wrist and, as if frightened, seeking to dispel that which is abhorred through a repeated movement of defence.

3   Beseeching: both hands with palms together, raised, lowered or clasped.

4   Suffering and despair: both hands are woven together as a comb and either raised to the height of the upper chest or lowered to the level of the belt. The same can be expressed with the right hand stretched out slightly, turning in to the breast.

5   Outcry: both arms are quickly stretched upwards, both hands slightly extended and turned to each other and rounded a little, whereby the meaning of the moment is shown.

6   Accusation: three fingers are bent and the index finger is extended or the middle finger is bent and the other three extended or both middle fingers are bent.

7   Giving encouragement: the arms and hands are slightly open and turned to the person in question as if about to embrace him.

8   Questioning: the right hand, slightly turned, is raised.

9   Regret: with a closed fist resting on the breast.

10  Fear: the right hand is pressed against the breast whereby the first four fingers are shaped to a point; the hand should then be lowered and left hanging down, extended.

Unlike in social life, the spectator in the theatre can know at first sight which passions variously grip the role. Whilst in life at court, the order of signs and exact knowledge of them cannot protect one from being deceived, as La Rochefoucauld recognised, the spectator can never be deceived by the actor. For the signs that the actor uses can always be interpreted correctly.

The signs of the art of acting represent a symbolic system which realises the ideal postulated by Chevalier de Méré for social life: a person who has studied such signs is in a position to interpret them correctly. If, for example, in *Phaedra*, the figures mutually deceive and misunderstand each other, the spectator does not misinterpret the signs given by the actors and is able to draw the actual thoughts, feelings and passions of the figures from the gestures made by the actors.

The theatre thus appears as an idealised mirror image of court life: whilst the spectator remains 'profond' and 'impénétrable', as La Bruyère advised, he may still guess the most secret thoughts and feelings of the figures from the looks, facial expressions, gestures and movements of the actors. Their 'hearts' lie open before him, and he himself can judge whether or not he is looking in a mirror or whether he sees himself confronted by an abhorrent mask.

*Phaedra* ended the glorious epoch in French theatre which had begun forty years earlier with Corneille's *Le Cid*. The 'classical' authors, Corneille, Racine and Molière, would rule the repertoire from now on, without it being extended by other plays which could even remotely measure up to them. For the next thirty years, the field belonged to the producers of a rather limited dramatic menu.

The end of the epoch of classical French theatre coincided with two other intervening events: the birth of the French opera and the merger of the two Parisian theatre companies. On 13 April 1672, Louis XIV gave Lully the privilege of performing opera. This allowed him to 'tenir l'académie royale de musique' in Paris and it also gave him sole rights to perform opera. All other troupes from this period on were forbidden to employ more than two violinists and six singers. Previously, Lully had co-operated with Molière, composed the music for *Psyche* and even played the role of Mufti in *Le Bourgeois Gentilhomme*. Lully succeeded however, in cutting Molière off from the king's favour. Two months after Molière's death, Louis gave the Palais Royal to Lully, and he opened the theatre season in the presence of the king on 27 April with the opera *Cadmus et Hermione*. The opera quickly became the favourite genre of *la cour et la ville*. On the one hand, it offered the opportunity of aestheticising the embodiment of the young *roi-soleil* in the role of Apollo and thus keeping the image alive. On the other hand, the opera was not bound to the rules of *vraisemblance* and satisfied its hungry audiences with elaborate sets, scene changes and machines. In the last forty years of the reign of Louis XIV, the opera became the court genre *par excellence*.

After Molière's troupe was removed from the Palais Royal and lost royal subvention, it joined the remaining members of the Théâtre du Marais, which had been dissolved by royal decree; they inhabited the former Jeu-de-paume hall in the Rue Guénégaud, where they established a new theatre which was both successful and financially secure. It was to this theatre that the most successful tragic actress of the Bourgogne, Mlle de Champmeslé, also transferred in 1679. It only survived seven years, however. On 18 August 1680, the king passed a decree which forced the two remaining dramatic theatres, the Hôtel de Bourgogne and the Théâtre de Guénégaud, to merge. The earlier, fruitful competition between the two stages encouraged by the king was thereby at an end. This was the birth of the Comédie Française. Louis XIV gave the Hôtel de Bourgogne to the Comédie Italienne (which he would finally exile from Paris in 1697). He sponsored the newly founded Comédie Française with 12,000 livres annually, as he had done previously the Hôtel de Bourgogne. It opened on 16 August 1680 in the Hôtel Guénégaud with Racine's *Phaedra*, and a comedy.

In 1683, the queen died. Louis XIV increasingly fell under the influence of the pious-minded Madame de Maintenon whom he secretly married in the same year; he lost all interest in the theatre. In 1687, the Collège des Quatre-nations opened in the neighbourhood of the Hôtel Guénégaud. The principal of the college found the proximity to the theatre intolerable, and in June, Louis XIV ordered the actors to leave and 'chercher à se mettre ailleurs' from October without further ado. The actors decided to move into a new building. After many hindrances and obstructions from the church, they were finally able to find both a suitable location and an architect. On 18 April 1689, the curtain was raised for the first time in the new theatre on the rue des Fossés, St Germain des Près. Once more, the performance was *Phaedra* with Champmeslé in the main role, and Molière's *Le Médecin malgré lui*. The Comédie Française remained in this theatre for nearly a century (until 1770); they not only preserved plays by the great classical authors but also the acting style of the Hôtel de Bourgogne. Thus, in 1748, Diderot could still mock the 'stilted walk of the actors', their 'excessive gestures', 'the extraordinary stress of their rhymed, measured speech' and 'a thousand other inconsistencies' (in *The Affected Ladies*[46]), as Molière had done in 1663. Now however, the time had come when the demands for a 'natural' acting style were to be taken seriously in the tragic theatre.

## FROM THE THEATRICAL TO SOCIAL ROLE-PLAY

### Discovering the identity in transformation: *commedia dell'arte*

In 1750, Carlo Goldoni (1707–93) proposed a programme to reform the Italian theatre in his play *Il teatro comico* (*The Comic Theatre*). Though Carlo Gozzi (1720–1806) later held him responsible for the downfall of *commedia dell'arte*, in fact, the *commedia dell'arte* had long passed its zenith. Although the number of troupes in the eighteenth century increased dramatically – for this period we know of nearly twice as many companies as in the seventeenth century, which records only thirty-six troupes – none of them reached the status or renown of the companies who travelled Italy and Europe in the golden age of *commedia dell'arte*, such as the Comici Gelosi (first documented from 1568), the Confidenti (first recorded in 1574), the Uniti (first mentioned in 1578), the Desiosi (who Montaigne saw perform in 1581), the Accesi (founded in 1590), the Fedeli (founded in 1602) or the Affezionati (which the English traveller, Sir Aston Cockhain, saw perform in Venice in 1632). And yet, in the eighteenth century, there were certainly many excellent actresses and actors, such as Luigi Riccoboni, known as Lelio (1675–1753), at the Comédie Italienne in Paris, who published the first history of the *commedia dell'arte* in 1728 under the title *Histoire du Théâtre Italien*. Others included the Arlecchino actor, Antonio Sacchi, known as Truffaldino (1708–88), his wife Antonia, known as Beatrice (before 1720–88), and his sister Adriana, known as Smeraldina (*c*.1707–76), for whom Goldoni had been writing plays since 1738, amongst them, *Il Servitore di due Padroni* (*The Servant of Two Masters*, 1743), and the first two actresses in Giralomo Medebach's troupe (1706–*c*.1790), Medebach's wife Antonia, known as Rosaura (*c*.1723–61) and Maddalena Marliani, known as Corallina (*c*.1720–after 1782). Goldoni continually supplied this company with plays from the start of the 1748/9 season up to Carnival in 1753 (in the 1750/1 season alone he delivered sixteen comedies). Moreover, the role of Mirandolina in *La Locandiera* (*The Mistress of the Inn*, 1752) was tailormade for Maddalena Marliani. The extremely topical critique on the poor standard of the troupes is, therefore, to be viewed with some scepticism, as is Gottsched's critique of the 'decadence' of the German wandering troupes.[47] The reason for the decline of the *commedia dell'arte* is much more likely to be found in the fact that, during the Enlightenment, it lost the specific function which had guaranteed its vitality and popularity since its beginnings more than one hundred years before. By the middle of the eighteenth century it had outlived itself.

The *commedia dell'arte* was a product of the late Italian Renaissance; it was formed in the second half of the sixteenth century – in the trail of the Council of Trent and the establishment of Spanish rule, in times ravaged by war, plundering, aggression, famines and the plague. Under the terms *commedia all'improvviso*, *commedia mercenaria* and *commedia italiana* (the term *commedia dell'arte* was coined in the eighteenth century) arose widely different forms of a professional, commercial theatre, where performances were given in exchange for money. The earliest contract on the founding of such a professional theatre company is recorded in 1545. It was made between eight actors, for the period of one year, in Padua. Evidence of actresses who, since their first appearance on stage, counted amongst the earliest members and main attractions of their troupes, are frequently to be found from the 1560s. In 1564, a certain 'Donna Lucrezia from Sienna' signed a contract with six male actors to form a troupe for the period of one year in Rome.[48] And in July 1567, a report exists concerning a fight in Mantua between admirers of the famous actresses Vincenza Armani and the 'Roman Flaminia' (whose real name we do not know).

Several theories have been proposed on the origins or founding of the *commedia dell'arte*. Some researchers locate its origins in the Roman comedies or in the *Roman Atellanae*; others see its roots amongst the travelling players, charlatans, mountebanks and so on; and still others believe the *commedia dell'arte* masks derive from masks used at Carnival. Whatever the case, elements of all these aspects can be found in *commedia dell'arte*, though none can be convincingly determined as the sole progenitor.

The term *commedia dell'arte* does not embrace one, wholly specific theatre form; instead, it represents a much more general term for very different theatre forms.[49] The troupes offered their performances at court, in private and public rooms and in the market square. They performed fixed, written texts and improvisations; their repertoire included comedies, pastorals, tragedies, interludes (in amateur performances by the Academy or at court) and later even melodrama. The Comici Gelosi, for example, were extensively involved in the première of Tasso's pastoral *Aminta* in 1573 in Ferrara. The audience was composed of all social classes.

Even when the multiplicity of theatrical forms submerged in the term *commedia dell'arte* is taken into account, two characteristic features stand out which clearly differentiate it from other contemporary, professional theatres. On the one hand, this is the relatively limited set of masks and roles, and on the other, the fact that the *commedia dell'arte* troupes in many, if not most, of their performances performed *all'improvviso*, that is, *ad lib.*

The basic stock of roles consisted of four masks, two elderly men, the Venetian merchant, Pantalone, and the Bolognese lawyer, Dottore, two *zanni*, or servants, from the region near Bergamo, Arlecchino and Brighella, and at least one or two couples, *innamorati* (young lovers), the Spanish Capitano – the braggart soldier – and a maid. Whilst the masked figures made use of local dialect, the lovers spoke pure Tuscany. The masked figures were not only distinguished by their dialect and silk or leather half-masks, but also by a typified and characteristic costume which informed the spectator as to the identity of the role as soon as the actor first appeared. The lovers, on the other hand, wore costly contemporary clothes.

Later, these stock roles were extended by other role-types such as the Neapolitan Pulcinella, which Silvio Fiorello, who was known for his Captain Mattamoro role, is supposed to have created, or the stutterer, Tartaglia, who appeared principally in the southern Italian *commedia dell'arte*, mostly in the form of an official. Even though the role-types of the two elderly figures and the two servants may draw upon earlier examples, they are also recreated in a special, unique way by the actors who derived their stage names from them. The actors did not simply 'inherit' the masks from various, already extant patterns in Carnival or literature; they were far more their

creators. As a rule, an actor played the same role-type for the entirety of his stage career.

Each role-type was furnished not only with a characteristic costume, mask or dialect but also with a specific repertoire of poses, movements, gestures and passages of text. It would be wrong to think that improvisations in movement and gesture, or text, are only thought up by the actor in the process of the performance. A few individual actors and, above all, most actresses were known for improvising highly poetic and complicated passages during the performance.[50] Thus, when Vincenza Armani died, a contemporary emphasised, 'the learned Vincenza imitated the eloquence of Cicero and thereby placed the art of acting on a level with the art of oratory'.[51] And Valerini, another contemporary of Armani, implies that the members of the famous Accademia degli Intronati in Siena held the view that Armani spoke 'far better *ad lib* than any speech which the versed authors could ever write, even after long meditation'.[52] Generally, however, one can assume that the actors had at their disposal a wide repertoire of fixed passages of text which they could insert into the plot as they needed. This is particularly true for all four kinds of text:

1    *tirate*, a long complaint, accusation, eulogy or description which was sometimes directed to another role-type on the stage, such as when the old man gives his son advice, or when the maid turns to one of the suitors, or which is spoken as a thoughtful, reflective and argumentative monologue;

2    *dialoghi amorosi*, a rhetorically brilliant exchange of feeling between lovers who find themselves in a certain situation; rejection, confession, or apology, often taken from the love poetry of the time or from the *commedia erudita* and Renaissance tragedy;

3    *bravure*, masterful, rhetoric boasting by the Capitano, often an element of his dialogue with the servant, but more often carried out as part of a monologue;

4    *lazzi* and *burle*, the witty play on words and movements, mostly used by the *zanni* when they interrupt the scene with comic action.

It is probable that in the early, glorious years of the *commedia dell'arte*, the actors developed and patched together various substitute texts and included them in their repertoire, jealously guarding them from other troupes.

Improvisation is, therefore, to be understood as a combination of elements which were extensively pre-prepared, yet frequently extended and enriched by the ideas and inspirations of the moment.

These characteristics of the *commedia dell'arte* – the fixed set of roles bound to specific actors and the technique of improvisation as well as the staging on simple planks with a single backdrop – allowed the troupes to prepare and perform their plays within the shortest of time. By contrast, performances by the *dilettanti* (amateurs) in the academies and at court generally required several weeks, even months, for their preparation. The *commedia dell'arte* troupes could create the performance 'product' relatively quickly and offer it up for consumption.

Fundamental to the composition of the performance and improvisation were the scenarios – a type of fixed, written summary of the plot in each scene and a general outline of the action. Approximately 800 such scenarios exist today, mostly in manuscript collections. As early as 1611, the actor Flaminio Scala, who was at one time the director of the Confidenti, and himself wrote complete plays and scenarios, published a collection of fifty scenarios entitled, *Il teatro delle Favole rappresentative*. The plots set out in this collection can in no sense be considered naïve or monotonous. They are as multifarious as the sources from which they stem: learned comedy, Roman comedy, novels, foreign plays which were known from texts or performances (for example, *Don Juan*), entertainment spectacles from popular culture and other oral traditions. Despite this multiplicity, certain patterns of action and some structural

elements can be identified which were clearly employed frequently in such scenarios and, thus, extensively determined the unique character and nature of *commedia dell'arte* performances.

Typically, the basic opposition between old and young is emphasised. Time and again, the old men seek to hinder marriage between two young lovers – whether out of greed, or because they themselves have an eye on the lady in question. This raises a further concretisation of the general opposition between old and young: an old character intends to marry a young girl who does not return his love, or he is already married to a young girl who takes on a young lover. A second structural element which is employed in many scenarios concerns the relationship between servant and master. The intrigues of the servants are often directed against their masters – whether these are the two older figures or the *innamorati*. Or else such intrigues are employed for their own private interests. In any case, the master–servant relationship is changed, modified, if not turned upside-down in various ways through the intrigues of the servants. A third important structural element concerns the *innamorati*. The path to finding each other leads through a maze of disguises, deceptions and masking, through magic (in the pastoral) and even madness. It is only after the lovers have passed through a sequence of such transformations that the 'right' partners are united and a marriage can take place.

In all three cases, the structural elements are well known to us in the context of ritual. Their derivation from oral culture makes them seem to be particularly suitable for a *teatro all'improvviso*. The battle between youth and age represents the basic component of many fertility rites.[53] It is found again in the Easter Plays where Robin and Medica elope together.[54] This pattern underlies the reason for actions and events which so many researchers denounce as 'immoral', as when old Pantalone's young wife has no scruples about keeping a lover and remains unpunished for her actions.

The same is also true of the master–servant

relationship. Morality plays no part when the servants seek to upturn the relationship to their masters with their intrigues. Rather, it derives from the 'reverse world' of the Carnival, in which the daily order is temporarily upset and scope for other, alternative orders are opened up.

The series of transformations which the young lovers must pass through in the form of disguise, masquerade, madness, magic and so on, hints at the practices and processes of initiation rituals in which youths lose the identities of girl and boy, and are led towards the changed identities of adult women and men. A particularly notable example is provided by the play *La pazzia d'Isabella* (*Isabella's Madness*), the scenario of which is printed in Scala's collection. Isabella, whose marriage to her beloved Fileno is forbidden by her father, Pantalone de Bisognosi, plans to elope with Fileno. Flavio, who is also in love with Isabella, witnesses their plan and appears in place of Fileno just before the appointed time to give Isabella the secret sign so that he can elope with her instead. As a result, Isabella goes mad, until at the end she is reunited after all with Fileno. This play was the showpiece for Isabella Andreini (1562–1604), in which she could truly unfold the art of transformation for which she was so famous among her contemporaries. One contemporary spectator wrote an entry in his diary on a performance of the play in 1589 in Florence, on the occasion of the marriage between Duke Ferdinand I and Christine von Lothringen:

Meanwhile Isabella, finding herself deceived by Flavio's snare, and not knowing how to remedy her misfortune, became wholly possessed by her grief, and thus dominated by her passion, and allowing herself to be consumed by rage and fury, was beside herself, and like a madwoman wandered through the city stopping now one person, now another, and speaking now in Spanish, now in Greek, now in Italian, and in many other languages, but always without sense. Among other things she began to speak in French, and also to sing songs in the French manner, which gave such pleasure to the Most Serene Bride (the Duke's wife) that no one could have been more delighted. Then she began to imitate the ways of speaking of her fellow-actors – the way, that is, of Pantalone, Gratiano, Zanni, Pedrolino, Francatrippe, Burattino, Capitan Cardone and Franceschina – in such a natural manner, and with so many fine emphases, that no words can express the quality and skill of this woman. Finally, by means of magic arts, and with the aid of certain waters she was given to drink, she was restored to her true self, and expressed at this point, in an elegant and learned style, the passions of love and pains suffered by those caught in its net, thus concluding the comedy. In acting out this madness Isabella demonstrated her wise and rich intellect, prompting so many murmurs of astonishment among her auditors that for as long as the world survives her beautiful eloquence and her worth will ever be praised.[55]

This account clearly emphasises the pattern of disguise, deception and masquerade. After the loss of the old identity, a sequence of new identities are tried on and acted out before the new identity is won, which then appears as the 'true self'. In the union with the beloved, the lovers finally find themselves. In this process of finding the 'true self', echoes of Ficino are unmistakable. His treatise 'On Love, or Plato's Symposium' does not deal with love between a man and a woman. Nevertheless, it was referred to at the end of the sixteenth century in many disputes on the essence of love. In *De amore*, Ficino states: 'for he who loves must once die in himself, because he gives himself up. At the same time, he is reborn in the object of his love when the latter warms him in the glow of his thoughts for him. He comes to life a second time in that he finally recognises himself in the lover, free of all doubt that he is identical to him.'[56] The structural element of the initiation rite points to the concept of the ego and the self as developed by Ficino and, thus, it is concretised and actualised in a specific way.

The question must now arise, how do the structural elements, which suggest ritual contexts, function in relation to the various plots of action? Despite the multiplicity of plots, one particularly frequent pattern can be reconstructed. As a rule, the play deals with one, two or three pairs of lovers who, after a series of tests and obstructions of different kinds, finally find their true partners so that the play ends in the promise of, or actual, marriage. In this – certainly somewhat stereotypical – plot, the ritual structural elements take on various specific functions.

The basic opposition between old and young is based on the 'natural' order. The sterile, old characters must make room for the young so that society can reproduce itself and survive. As long as the old characters obstruct the young from marriage or take the young women for themselves, the natural order is disturbed. When, finally, the lovers find each other – or the young woman gains licence to keep a lover – natural order is restored.

The servants' intrigues, which if they do not upset the master–servant relationship entirely, at least modify it permanently, generally prevent a happy end though in a few cases, they provoke one. The return to social order, which comes about through the happy end, can occur in very different ways. It can mean a return to the original status quo which existed at the beginning of the play; more often, however, it is realised in a marriage between the servants, so that a new, better order is established.

The lovers overcome all obstacles put in their way and survive the tests by undergoing an initiation rite in disguise, masking, mistaken identity, madness and magic, and thus gaining a new identity. This identity fits into the natural and social order and is the driving force behind the restoration of those orders.

It cannot be overlooked that a similar pattern is at work in *A Midsummer Night's Dream* and other Shakespearean comedies. Whilst in Shakespeare's comedies we are provided with a complete text which might offer clues as to the potentially different functions of ritual elements in performance – for example, on the function of play on theatre in the theatre – in the case of the scenarios, we must be satisfied with more cautious conclusions. If we examine the relation to, and

function of, the ritual structural elements in the plot, we can suggest that the performance represents a *rite de passage* – i.e. represents, not carries out – which the lovers undergo in order to become adults in a world in which the natural and social order is in harmony, a *rite de passage* in whose process precisely such order is reconstructed, or – in the case of social order – even improved.

Certainly, there would have been individual performances which did not fulfil this function. Many performances would have fulfilled other functions. Nevertheless, it can be seen that the basic function of the performance consisted of the representation of precisely this process. In this respect, there certainly exists an important shared feature with performances of Shakespeare's comedies in Elizabethan theatre.

One major difference however, arises from the fact that in Elizabethan theatre, the female roles were played by men or boys, whereas in the *commedia dell'arte* they were played by women. This characteristic seems, in many respects, to be constitutive of the *commedia dell'arte*. The special importance which the leading actresses had for their troupes is not only revealed in that they often directed their own troupes, but also, in that it was the habit of the time not to call the troupes by their official names, but rather after their leading actress: 'Signora Vittoria and her acting company', 'Florinda and her troupe' (the first wife of Giovanni Battista Andreini performed under the stage name Florinda, in the troupe, Confidenti) or 'Diana's people' (which referred to the Desiosi). In the minds of spectators of the time, it was the actress who gave the company its profile.

The social background of the actresses is much disputed. For the large part – at least after the second generation – they came from acting families. But on the origin of the first actresses, very little is known. We know nothing about Vittoria Piissimi. Vincenza Armani most probably came from an acting family. Isabella Andreini may have come from a bourgeois family – in any case, she had a good education, which was unusual even for someone from a bourgeois background: she could read and write, and spoke fluent French and Spanish. The great actresses were outstanding not only for their oft admired beauty, but also for their intelligence, and the brilliant and high poetic quality with which they were able to improvise. They were, therefore, put on the same level as the most well-known orators, poets and scholars by their contemporaries. Isabella Andreini, whose writings were published by her husband after her early death, was considered a talented poet even during her lifetime. Alongside Torquato Tasso, she was crowned *poeta laureatus*.

It was these actresses who played the role of the young girl who, on the path of disguise, deceptions and masquerades, etc., finds her true self and her lover. At the same time, some performances certainly reflected on the outrage which many spectators felt for a woman who put herself on show on stage. In the scenarios published by Scala, there are over one hundred scenes in which a woman appears at a window: married women, widows, unmarried girls, servants. In more than half of fifty scenarios the women show themselves at the window – whence they speak to their lovers, husbands and clients, or turn to address the audience directly. And it is exclusively women who appear at the window. The window, as threshold between inside and outside, between the private and the public, can be viewed as the privileged place of women. It is interesting to note that the women who appear at the window are never in disguise. However, if the role is not that of a courtesan, they can only move freely on the piazza and, thus, in public, provided they are disguised as men.[57]

On the fictional level of the plays, the women are given their place on the threshold between private and public. Whilst they are free at any time to withdraw into the privacy of the interior, certain procedures must be met before setting out – escaping – into public life: the woman must dress herself as a man, she must turn herself into a man for others. On the other hand, this transformation acts as a precondition to undergoing a *rite de passage*, at the end of which a new identity will be given and the 'true' self will be discovered.

The actress herself is reflected in this constellation. She cannot endure life indoors, domestic privacy, she is not satisfied with the role of spectator at the window – even if active – so she appears in public on the stage, where she can take on different roles and act them out. In this, she may bring certain components into the play which are viewed by her contemporaries as decidedly male, such as eloquence and intellectual refinement. On the other hand, her appearance on stage might be in the shape of either male or female. She not only plays the lover, who must dress as a man, but also takes on a male role which brings her special applause and great admiration. Thus Isabella Andreini shone in the male title role of Tasso's *Aminta*; Angela d'Orso was celebrated for her acting as 'Capitano Generale', which gave her the opportunity of storming onto the stage at the head of a crew of soldiers; as was Orsola Cecchini, who appeared in a male role bearing a gun, firing all round her.[58] Even in descriptions of the beauty of the actresses, their androgynous nature was emphasised. Thus, Valerini wrote in his obituary of Vincenza Armani:

Signora Vincenza was rather tall in size and her fine limbs were so well proportioned, that no eye had seen such before; there was something manly in her face and conduct so that no one would have thought she were a woman when she appeared on stage in the dress of a youth. She had long hair from the finest gold, which was plaited and tied up, whilst a few strands played about her forehead – as if they had fallen loose, and yet they were arranged with great art.[59]

The public appearance of the actress and her experimentation with various roles allowed her to appear both male and female, arrive at a new identity and to discover her 'true' self, to act out her 'true' self: a permanent stepping over the borders of gender, her androgyny.

In this way, the performance not only *represented* a *rite de passage*, in whose process the disturbed natural and social order was repaired, but it also *executed* a *rite de passage*: a continual transgressing of the borders between the sexes, a permanent transformation of the actress, through which she found her way to her 'true' self. It was this popular ability of the actresses to transform themselves which fascinated the spectators and caused them to heap honours on them which were normally only given to personalities of high rank. In some cities, cannons were fired as a greeting for Vincenza Armani as she entered the city, escorted by the nobility. And when Isabella Andreini died in Lyon, all the inhabitants paid their last respects to her and commemorative coins were minted.[60] This is proof, on one hand, of the great admiration and esteem in which the actresses were held, but, at the same time, points to their ambivalent position between all social classes (which was also true of their male colleagues).

Thus, the stage appeared to be an extraordinary realm of in-between. A rite of passage was played out on the stage, independent of any concrete social relations, and in ever new variations, in the process of which young people were transformed into adults and, thus, a collapsed natural and social order was restored. At the same time, the stage offered the actresses and actors who belonged to no specific social level, the opportunity of winning and acting out a particular identity in the process of permanent transformation. For the spectator, the stage is initially a place of instability, but finally, a place for both spectator and actor to confirm their sense of self.

This function was fulfilled by the *commedia dell'arte* until at least the middle of the seventeenth century. After this, two different developments occurred. The Comédie Italienne in Paris, which shared the Petit Bourbon with Molière's company from 1658, until it was given to the Hôtel de Bourgogne in 1680, increasingly appropriated the tastes, habits and language of the French in order to compete with the French troupes and win an audience for itself. Great changes were made. Thus, the constitutive opposition between the highly poetic and rhetorically brilliant parts of the lovers in Tuscan dialect and the use of different styles, including the 'lowest' forms in the various dialects, was given up. The emphasis increasingly shifted towards physical action. In the collection of plays published by Evaristo Gherardi in 1694, *Le Théâtre Italien*, one can see the gradual changes to the Comédie Italienne until its forced exile from Paris in 1697. Even after 1716, when the *commedia dell'arte* troupe returned to Paris under the leadership of Luigi Riccoboni, these reforms were continued. Thus, although Marivaux continued to write for the new Théâtre Italien, the pantomimic scenes were extended even further.

Similar changes can also be seen in other troupes who principally played abroad. But it must not be forgotten that it was mainly the most outstanding troupes who were invited to foreign courts to perform. Amongst the troupes who performed in Italy at the end of the seventeenth and beginning of the eighteenth centuries there seems, on the contrary, to be no sign of a further development. The old patterns and materials remained in use. The cultural context, however, was rapidly changing. Thus, there was an increasing demand that theatre should represent social reality. In this context, the obscene speeches and gestures of the *zanni* were open to criticism as offences against decent morals, and their relation to the upside-down world of the Carnival was long forgotten. The appearance of young girls in men's clothing in the piazza also appeared to be a violation of the laws of verisimilitude – even here, reference to the initiation rite was lost and forgotten. The *commedia dell'arte* no longer seemed to fulfil its original function in this changed culture; nor was it in a position to undertake a new function. By the time Goldoni began to write for the *commedia dell'arte*, its days were already numbered.

## Theatre as a model of social reality

In 1750/1, Goldoni began to implement his theatre reforms with the aid of sixteen new plays for Medebach's troupe at the Teatro Sant'Angelo in Venice. Up until then, he had already gathered extensive experience of theatre. From 1733, he had co-operated closely with theatre companies, studied the skills and potential of actors and delivered them with plays and rehearsed with them – first Giuseppe Imer's troupe (around 1700–58), then companies led by Sacchi and Medebach. In all the multiplicity of his plays – tragedies, comedies, interludes, opera libretti – he developed certain leading principles of a new dramaturgy which left their traces in the acting style of the troupes concerned. For Goldoni, it was time to take stock.

From September 1750, the first edition of his collected works was published in Venice. In the preface, Goldoni outlines the basic thrust of his dramaturgy. He confesses in all naïveté, so he wrote, that despite attentive study of ancient and modern authors, he was in reality more in debt to two 'books', 'Mondo' ('World') and 'Teatro' ('Theatre').

[The 'World'] shows me a huge, such a huge multiplicity of characters, paints them for me in such a natural way, that it seems specially created to provide me with a wealth of material for charming and instructive comedies. It shows me the signs, power and effect of all human passions, it supplies me with curious events, informs me of current morals, instructs me about the widespread idleness and errors of this century and this nation, which earn disapproval or the scorn of wisdom; and at the same time, it shows me, through some exemplary figures, the means by which virtue can encounter these ruinations. Therefore, I constantly return to and meditate upon this book, to gather all that must be known by one who wishes to take up this profession and succeed in it. The other, finally, the book of the theatre shows me, as it is my business, the colours in which the characters, the passions, the events can be represented on stage in order that they are provided with the best possible contours, and which colours make them most appealing to the delicate eye of the spectator. In short, I learn from theatre, how to recognise that which is most suited to creating an impression on the mind, to achieving amazement or laughter or how to ignite

a certain charming chuckle in the hearts of men which comes about when one hears the mistakes and idiocies of people with whom one constantly converses naturally, represented in the comedies with much skill from their perspective, of course, without shocking too much through offence.[61]

The connection which Goldoni makes between 'world' and 'theatre' seems extraordinary in some respects. Theatre neither represents the world in a way that was the consensus in the eighteenth century, nor does the world appear as theatre, in the sense of the theatre metaphor as it was understood in the seventeenth century. Goldoni, as did his contemporaries, criticised the surviving commedia dell'arte because it was characterised by 'dirty harlequinades, ugly and scandalous love affairs, poorly invented plots acted out even more poorly'.[62] But he still appreciated its potential to provoke self-recognition in the spectator. Goldoni quite deliberately describes the world and the theatre as 'books'. Whilst social knowledge can be gained from the 'book of the world', the 'book of the theatre' provides insight into the different strategies of representation and how to create certain effects. These are the materials of the dramaturgical process. The playwright must choose those elements he finds important from both 'books' and combine them with each other in his unique way. The result is neither an image of reality, nor 'pure' theatrical play, which is cut off from social reality. The relation between world and theatre in Goldoni's comedies can be most easily explained when the process of combination is examined.

One such process consists of moulding certain masks and role-types of the commedia dell'arte, and members of certain social classes and levels into one another as, for example, Pantalone and the bourgeois merchant, or Capitano and a member of the nobility. In Dell'arte rappresentiva premiditiata ed all'improviso (Naples, 1699), Andrea Perucci describes individual masks and roles of the commedia dell'arte. He characterises Pantalone in the following way:

Whoever performs this part should be accomplished in the Venetian language, in all its dialects, proverbs and words, presenting the role of an ailing old man who none the less tries to appear youthful. The actor should memorise various things to say at appropriate moments, like advice to his son, counsel to kings and princes, curses, compliments to the women he loves, and such other matters as he chooses, in order to raise laughter at opportune moments by his respectability and seriousness. He should depict a person of maturity, but one who is all the more ridiculous because while he ought to be a person of authority, setting an example and serving as a lesson to others, he is possessed by love and behaves so like a child that one may say *puer centum annorum*, and his avarice, so typical of old men, is overcome by a greater vice, namely, love, something wholly unsuitable to an elderly person.[63]

Goldoni merged this mask with traces of the ideal merchant, who embodies the most important values of the bourgeoisie, such as uprightness, integrity, thrift. The love for the young girl disappears, greed is modified into thrift, whilst giving advice to the young son, in which exactly these virtues are communicated, remains. In *Il Bugiardo* (*The Liar*, 1750), the Venetian merchant, Pantalone, gives his son Lelio, who has caught himself in a web of lies, a sound scolding:

Well done, my son! Well done! And you thought you could fib like that to your father? Stand up, Sir Schemer, Sir Liar. Is that what you learned in Naples? You have hardly been in Venice long, and before you know it, even before you've greeted your own father, you share company with someone you don't even know, say you are a Neapolitan, Don Asdrubale di Castel d'Oro, millionaire, nephew to the Prince, if not brother to the King. ... What feeds you with such lunatic ideas? Where do you get the inspiration for such damnable lies? A man is not honest by birth, but becomes so through his deeds. The merchant's credibility lies in the fact that he always speaks the truth.

Loyalty and faith are our greatest capital. If you do not enjoy loyalty and faith and undiminished respect, you will always seem suspicious to others and you will be a poor merchant, unworthy of this market, unworthy of my house, unworthy of the honourable name Bisognosi.

(III, 5)

In this speech, Pantalone has been transformed from comic character to a representative of bourgeois values and virtues. But even as respectable merchant, he still provokes a smile. For, without realising it, he provides his son with the cue for his next fabrication. The respectable merchant, Pantalone, is utilised as a positive figure but, because some comic traits remain, it is unsuitable as a figure of identification. This is particularly true of the later embodiments of the respectable merchant. In *I Rusteghi* (*The Boors*, 1760), the protagonists, who are no longer given the name, Pantalone, not only rigidly hold up their professional roles as respectable merchants but also carry this behaviour into their private roles as patriarchs in order to oppress their families. Their total identification with the role of respectable merchant exposes them as ridiculous. Thus, Goldoni uses the reference to traditional masks, on the one hand, to carry the positive values of the bourgeoisie and, on the other, to maintain a certain distance to them which will allow criticism of the way in which these positive values are embodied and executed as, for example, when they are employed as the means of oppression.

The figure of the Capitano is characterised by Perucci in the following way:

The Capitano role is one rich in words and gestures, boastful about beauty, elegance and wealth, but in reality a monster, an idiot, a coward, a nincompoop, someone who should be chained up, a man who wants to spend his life passing himself off as someone he is not, as quite a few do as they journey through this world. ...

All these swashbuckling captains ... may function as second or third lovers, yet in the main they are scorned, rejected, deceived and despised by women, servants and maids, for despite their vigorous side they are in truth lazy, they will pretend to be generous but are in fact mean, they will claim nobility and wealth, but are plebeians, scoundrels and poverty stricken.[64]

Goldoni paints the figure of the Capitano with traces of the fallen nobility – for example, the so-called Barnaboti, parasitic nobles who lived entirely at the cost of state and church and who were given an entire section of Venice – or the rich braggart who could afford to buy himself a peerage. From this arise, for example, the figures of the scandalmonger, Don Marzio in *La Bottega del Caffe* (*The Coffee House*, 1750), the Marquis di Forlipopoli and the Count d'Albafiorita in *La Locandiera* (*The Mistress of the Inn*, 1752), or the fraud Ottavio in *La Cameriera Brillante* (*The Clever Chambermaid*, 1754). In these figures, 'world' and 'theatre' comment on each other. Reference to the Capitano from the *commedia dell'arte* points to someone who, on the one hand, is a comic figure and, on the other, is someone who constantly lives above his means, who pretends to be something other than that which he really is, whose identity is extremely fragile. Interestingly, it is precisely these figures who seek to hide the superficiality of their existence and the questionability of their identity through formulas such as 'I know who I am' or 'I am who I am'.[65] Though they play a role, they are none the less incapable of recognising the fact that it is only a role, or distancing themselves from it; instead, they identify with it wholly. In this respect, the respectable merchant, Pantalone, and the fallen noble parasite, Capitano, are similar to each other: they are not in a position to reflect on the fact that their behaviour is determined by role-play, nor are they able to experiment with role-play. Instead, they identify wholly with the role. References to the mask of Pantalone or the role-type of the Capitano make it obvious to the spectator, however, that they are nothing more than roles.

Another way a relationship is drawn between 'world' and 'theatre' proceeds from the endless sequence of disguises, mistaken identities, masquerades, and magic tricks in the *commedia dell'arte*, where they represent functionally important, but interchangeable, phases of a *rite de passage*. After references to the *rite de passage* had long been forgotten, however, they appear as theatrical elements which drive the play to an end in itself by giving the actors the opportunity of displaying the art of transformation through costume change, powder and make-up, altered voice, linguistic gibberish and so on. Instead, Goldoni refurbishes such elements with clear, precisely formulated goals. After his first comedy, completed in such detail that it was immediately ready for publication, *La Donna di Garbo* (*The Elegant Lady*, 1742), all Goldoni's comedies contain figures who serve to drive the plot forwards by deliberately taking on another or several other roles or patterns of behaviour; who improvise scenes and situations in order to achieve a specific goal: a marriage, unmasking someone, exposing someone, economic advantage, and so on. Frequently it is a female figure whose origins come from the maid in the *commedia dell'arte*, such as in *La Donna di Garbo*, *La Vedova Scaltra* (*The Cunning Widow*, 1748), *La Castalda* (*The Housekeeper*, 1751), *La Locandiera* or *La Cameriera Brillante*. The same function can also be served, however, by male figures such as the liar – Lelio, in *Il Bugiardo* or Arlecchino/Truffaldino in *Il Servitore di due Padroni*. Unlike the 'Pantalone' or 'Capitano' figures, these figures are always aware that they are playing a role; they do not identify themselves with any of the roles they play and keep a constant distance so that they are able to use them with sovereignty and purpose for their own goals. As a rule, other than Lelio, they reach their aims. The fabrications, the role-plays and play-acting appear, thus, as a particularly successful form of rational acting in order to realise a specific aim. In these comedies, two basic preconditions of self-definition in eighteenth-century bourgeoisie seem to stand in unbridgeable opposition: the claim to behave according to rationally mapped out goals collides with the demand for sincerity. Only those figures who abuse the laws of sincerity are successful. And it is precisely these figures *with* whom the audience laughs. On the other hand, the figures who embody and proclaim the values of sincerity are manipulated by them so that the spectators laugh *at* them.

Any clear differentiation between the categories 'positive' and 'negative' seems, thus, impossible.

Both methods qualify the relationship between 'world' and 'theatre' in a special way. Theatre is used as a model of the world – not as its image, or its metaphor, but as a model, through which different constellations can be tried out, experimentally. The model nature of theatre opens the possibility of playing with different concepts of identity as they are articulated with distance, or lack of distance from, the role. At the same time, it allows fundamental bourgeois values to be put on stage and communicated not just in a positive way, but also to test them critically in terms of their being proof of reality. In that theatre becomes the model of social reality, it can integrate 'playful' elements and make them productive as well as 'realistic'. In the model, this opposition is suspended. 'Play' or 'performance' and 'representation of reality' appear far more as two different strategies of modelling which are productive precisely in their interaction. This holds for all Goldoni's comedies, whether they are closer to the 'theatre' extreme as in *Il Servitore di due Padrone*, which Goldoni first wrote as a scenario for Sacchi before he wrote it out fully for publication, or the extreme 'world' as in *Le Baruffe Chiozzote* (*The Chioggian Squabbles*, 1762).

The plot of *Il Servitore di due Padrone* seems to follow the general scheme of a *commedia dell'arte* piece. A young woman, Beatrice, dresses as a man in order to find her lover, Florindo, who was forced to flee from the police because he killed her brother in an argument. The constitutive elements of the *commedia dell'arte*, however, are no longer present. In their place are the methods described above. Thus, the opposition of old and young is not present: the father Pantalone, and the Dottore support the marriage of their children Clarice and Silvio, who love each other. The lovers are not hindered on their path by the fathers, but by another lover, Beatrice, who appears as her own brother, Federigo, to whom Clarice was earlier promised, pretending to insist on the marriage contract.

Indeed, the structure depends far more on the opposition between those figures which totally identify with their roles, such as Pantalone, the Dottore, or even Silvio, and those which act out a certain distance to their roles, such as Beatrice, in part, Clarice and, above all, Truffaldino, the servant of the two masters. Pantalone appears as the respectable Venetian merchant who speaks about money, business, bills, current accounts and balances and who insists on keeping to agreed contracts. This behaviour becomes problematic when it is carried over into the family: upholding the contract which Pantalone agreed with the deceased Federigo would force his own daughter to give up the man she loves and marry someone she does not love. Since Pantalone is not in a position to step back from the role of the respectable merchant and the values bound to it even for a moment, he believes the oppression of his daughter and her wishes is justified:

PANTALONE: That's the long and short of it; Signor Federigo is to be your husband. I have given my word and I am not to be cozened.

CLARICE: You have my obedience, sir; but I beseech you, this is tyranny.

(I, 3, p. 39)[66]

Beatrice, on the other hand, uses role-play deliberately in order to gain advantage for herself. She plays the role of her brother in order to access the money that Pantalone owes him and, thus, to maintain her freedom of movement:

BEATRICE: ... I put on my brother's clothes and followed him. Thanks to the letters of credit, which are my brother's, and thanks still more to you, Signor Pantalone takes me for Federigo. We are to make up our accounts; I shall draw the money, and then I shall be able to help Florindo too, if he has need of it ...

BRIGHELLA: That's all very well, but I don't want to be responsible for Signor Pantalone paying you out the money in good faith and then finding himself made a fool of.

BEATRICE: Made a fool of? If my brother is dead, am I not his heir?

BRIGHELLA: Very true. Then why not say so?

BEATRICE: If I do that, I can do nothing. Pantalone will begin by treating me as if he were my guardian; then they will all worry me and say my conduct is unbecoming and all that sort of thing. I want my liberty.

(I, 1, pp. 17–18)

Beatrice does achieve her goal. However, the action between Beatrice and Florindo is not developed by her role-play, but rather through that of Truffaldino (Arlecchino). It is he who becomes the servant of two masters, Beatrice and Florindo, and it is Truffaldino/Arlecchino who appears as the actual protagonist of the comedy. In him, not only are the traditional masks of Truffaldino-Arlecchino and the traces of the simple, common man who struggles to earn his daily bread, moulded into one another, but he also appears as the dramatic figure through whose fabrications the play is set in motion and kept in motion.

The actor Pier Maria Cecchini describes the masks of the first and second servants, Brighella and Arlecchino, in *Frutti delle moderne comedie et avvisi a chi le recito* (Padua, 1628), thus:

It is essential, and indeed particularly appropriate in comedy, that the part of the astute and ingenious servant, whose business it is to develop the plot-line by the exercise of wit rather than buffoonery, be balanced by another [who is] altogether different. This [servant] should be presented as a clumsy and ignorant person, and he should give every impression of being just that by pretending neither to appreciate nor comprehend what he is told to do. Hence arise comic misunderstandings, absurd errors, and similar contrived confusions which, if they are carried through by

one able to interpret such a role, provide a very delightful part.[67]

Clearly, in Truffaldino, traces of both *zanni* are united, as Beatrice comments: 'He seems a fool at times; but he isn't really a fool' (I, 1, p. 18). At the same time, he appears to be a simple, common man who cannot let slip the chance of better earnings. Thus, he takes up Florindo's offer to serve him although – as the former is naturally unaware – he already serves Beatrice, with the thought, 'Why not? [*Aside*] If his terms are better' (I, 2, p. 22). Thus, he justifies his decision:

There's luck! There are many that look in vain for a master, and I have found two. What the devil am I to do? I cannot wait upon them both. No? Why not? Wouldn't it be a fine thing to wait upon them both, earn two men's wages and eat and drink for two?

(I, 2, p. 25)

It is clearly economic reasons which force the poor, and ever hungry, Truffaldino to become the servant of two masters. In so doing, however, he manoeuvres himself into a situation which constantly puts him before two choices – either to invent a fabrication or to lose the possibility of earning extra money. This means that his fabrications, and his role-play to each of his masters, are a result of concrete constraints. Thus, Truffaldino invents the servant Pasquale because Florindo not only takes the letters addressed to him but also that addressed to Beatrice as well and, in so doing, discovers that Beatrice is in Venice, dressed as a man, looking for him. Each interrogation by Florindo forces Truffaldino to think of something new. In the same way, Truffaldino drives first Florindo, and then Beatrice to distraction, even attempted suicide, with the story of his master's death which he invents in order to explain the exchange of belongings which occurred when he tried to empty both suitcases at once:

FLORINDO: [*To Truffaldino*] Tell me, how ever did this portrait come to be in the pocket of my coat? It wasn't there before.

TRUFFALDINO: [*Aside*] Now what's the answer to that? I don't know. Let me think –

FLORINDO: Come on, out with it, answer me. How did this portrait come to be in my pocket?

TRUFFALDINO: Sir, be kind and forgive me for taking a liberty. The portrait belongs to me, and I hid it there for safety, for fear I might lose it.

FLORINDO: How did you come by this portrait?

TRUFFALDINO: My master left it to me.

FLORINDO: Left it to you?

TRUFFALDINO: Yes, sir; I had a master who died, and he left me a few trifles which I sold, all except this portrait, sir.

FLORINDO: Great heavens! And how long is it since this master of yours died?

TRUFFALDINO: 'Twill be just about a week ago, sir.

[*Aside*] I say the first thing that comes into my head.

FLORINDO: What was your master's name?

TRUFFALDINO: I do not know, sir; he lived *incognito*.

FLORINDO: *Incognito*? How long were you in his service?

TRUFFALDINO: Only a short time, sir; ten or twelve days.

FLORINDO: [*Aside*] Heavens! More and more do I fear that it was Beatrice. She escaped in man's dress; she concealed her name – Oh wretched me, if it be true!

TRUFFALDINO: [*Aside*] As he believes it all, I may as well go on with the fairy-tale.

(III, 2, pp. 91–2)

Truffaldino only returns to being honest when continuing his invented stories means the danger of losing Smeraldina, whom he intends to marry, 'I can boast that nobody would ever have found me out, if I had not given myself away for love of this girl here' (III, 4, p. 125). For Truffaldino, neither fabrication nor honesty are important values in themselves, but both are, instead, employed as rational ways of behaving to achieve certain goals. In the end, Truffaldino is forced to return to being honest.

In his case, story-telling is protected by society, so that the bourgeois laws of honesty are not actually affected by it. For it is his social situation which obliges Truffaldino to fabricate events and play a role: within a specific social background, role-playing and the laws of honesty do not clash.

Quite the opposite is revealed, however in *La Locandiera*.[68] Here, the laws of honesty and role-playing clash irreconcilably together. In some senses, it can be said that Molière's *Misanthrope* is transported here from the court, or noble sphere of the salon, into the bourgeois-mercantile rooms of an inn. The Cavalier di Ripafratta, who justifies his hatred of women by calling on the law of honesty to which women are supposedly not able to adhere, corresponds to the misanthrope, Alceste, who differentiates himself from the others through his honesty. In place of Celimène, who encourages her vain admirers to believe that they are the chosen ones by showing them equal proofs of her favour, and who, thus, keeps the social life of her salon going, is the mistress of the inn, Mirandolina, who greets every guest with the same kindness and accepts presents in order not to offend them, yet without allowing them any freedoms in return. The roles of the two nobles, Marquis Alcaste and Clitandre, are taken over here by the parasitic Marquis di Forlipopoli and the Count d'Albafiorita, who boasts of his wealth. The *honnête gens*, Philinte and Eliante, are replaced by the less honest actresses Ortensia and Deianira. Whilst in the *Misanthrope*, Alceste commands Celimène to declare her love for him publicly and give up the social life of the salon, here, Mirandolina makes the misanthrope Ripafratta fall in love with her and coaxes a declaration from him, without however ever suggesting that she loves him, or even aims to marry him. She agrees, in the end, to marry her servant, Fabrizio.

The shift into the bourgeois-mercantile sphere of the inn changes the basic constellation in a very decisive way. It is no longer a question of the possibility of social life, a question of the rules of *bienséance* and *honnêteté*, but rather the simple law of the market. Everyone at the inn tries to drive his price on the market as high as possible.

In their competition for Mirandolina's favour, the Marquis and the Count offer different services which will decide their market value. The impoverished Marquis continually calls upon the 'protection' which he apparently provides Mirandolina and permanently repeats the formula of his identity, 'I know who I am'. Through these actions, he attempts to give weight to his origin, his title, and the potential they represent. The Count, who has bought himself a title, keeps his side up with expensive presents which his wealth allows. By not rejecting either man, but without favouring either, Mirandolina permits each to believe his market value is the highest. In so doing, she keeps both men at the inn and thus satisfies her own business interests. At the same time, however, she also raises her own price on the market. The two competitors see her as an increasingly expensive item which justifies ever higher investment: the Count heaps more diamond jewellery on top of the diamond pendant and even the penniless Marquis presents Mirandolina with a shawl. Both believe that they have thereby increased their own market value.

To the Cavalier di Ripafratta, on the other hand, Mirandolina is simply 'a woman just like the others' (p. 7).[69] His hatred of women causes him to question their market value, he even greatly diminishes their price.

Indeed, one can't dispute about anything that deserves it less. A woman changes you, a woman upsets you? A woman? What queer things one hears nowadays? As far as I'm concerned there isn't any danger that I'll get into a dispute with anyone about women. I have never loved them, I have never had any use for them, and I have always thought that woman is an unbearable infirmity for man.

(p. 6)

Such devaluation means a severe market loss for the businesswoman, Mirandolina; she can, however, counter-react, by making the Cavalier fall in love with her and ensuring that the other

competitors notice his love for her and see him as a further rival for her favour. At the same time, she provides impressive proof of her own attractions and thus increases her market value considerably.

In order to achieve this goal, Mirandolina begins a role-play which is based on exactly the same value by which the Cavalier sees his own identity guaranteed – honesty.

MIRANDOLINA: Why mention the folly of those two gentlemen? They come to my inn to lodge and then they claim they wish to court the mistress of the inn. I have other things to do besides paying attention to their idle talk. I'm trying to act according to my best interests. If I humour them I do it to keep their custom, and then, to cap the climax, when I see how they're taken in, I laugh like a mad woman.
CAVALIER: Good. Your frankness delights me.
MIRANDOLINA: Oh! I don't have any other good qualities?
CAVALIER: But notwithstanding, you know how to pretend with those who pay you attention.
MIRANDOLINA: I pretend? Heaven help me! Ask these two gentlemen, who are infatuated with me, if I have ever given them a sign of affection; if I have ever jested with them in such a way that they could with reason be flattered. I don't treat them rudely, because my interests won't allow it, but I don't come far from it.

(pp. 21–2)

Mirandolina's interpretation of honesty is given particular credibility in Act III, when the Marquis invites the Cavalier and Mirandolina to taste his Cypress wine in order to confirm its superlative quality:

MARQUIS: [*Pours very slowly and does not fill the glasses; he pours out for the Cavalier, Mirandolina and himself, corking the bottle as well*] What nectar! What ambrosia! What distilled manna! [*Drinks*].
CAVALIER: [*Aside to Mirandolina*] What does this miserable stuff seem like to you?

MIRANDOLINA: [*Aside to the Cavalier*] Rinsings of the flask.

MARQUIS: [*To the Cavalier*] Ah! What are you saying?

CAVALIER: Good! Splendid!

MARQUIS: Are you pleased with it, Mirandolina?

MIRANDOLINA: For my part, sir, I cannot dissimulate. I don't like it; I find it bad and I can't say it's good. I compliment the man who knows how to pretend. But he who can pretend in one thing will know how to pretend in another also.

(pp. 53–4)

Mirandolina's pretend honesty is so perfect that the Cavalier is unable to recognise the fact that she is acting, and he believes it to be the truth. It appears particularly convincing because, curiously, Mirandolina follows the rules of the new aesthetic of eighteenth-century theatre. She creates the same total illusion of reality which Diderot in France, and Lessing in Germany, in the middle of the century, demanded from theatre and the art of acting in particular. However, this illusion is not created on the stage but in the social reality of interaction between people. It is 'play' which does not allow itself to be recognised as such and which, thus, can be mistaken for that which it actually only pretends to be. Mirandolina plays the role of an honest person, while the Cavalier believes her identity is truly founded on honesty.

The two actresses, Ortensia and Deianira, present a revealing opposition to Mirandolina's acts of pretence. Despite being representatives of the professional art of theatre and disguise, they do not succeed in playing the role of ladies at the inn convincingly. They blatantly contravene the rules of probability and naturalness. The story which they invent to explain the lack of a male chaperone sounds thoroughly implausible. Their behaviour ignites suspicion because Deianira giggles each time Ortensia fibs. Thus, their acting is easy to see through for what it is – neither Mirandolina nor the Count fall for it. Deianira acknowledges: 'I could never act off the stage' (p. 31).

Both actresses can only play their roles convincingly on stage; here the spectators know that they are in the theatre and expect role-play and acting. For this reason, role-play and acting do not contravene the laws of honesty or even question them. The spectator is well aware of the context: theatre is being played.

Mirandolina's acting, on the other hand, occurs in a context which does not allow one to expect pretence and role-play: in the social reality of interaction between people for whom the laws of honesty are valid. Here, it is the concrete social reality of the bourgeois-mercantile sphere of the inn, in which the laws of the market rule. The market value of the individual depends upon the respect which he has earned from others and this extensively depends on the style of his acting. Whether he is aware of his acting (as in the case of Mirandolina) or not (as in the case of the Marquis, the Count and the Cavalier) – pretence and role-play become the most important factors in controlling and regulating the market. Since honesty holds a high position in the bourgeois hierarchy of values, the market value of the individual is measured according to whether or not a person seems honest. That is, the law of the market demands a pretend honesty which should be achieved by the most perfect acting possible so that it cannot be recognised as mere acting. In this way, the bourgeois law of honesty is taken *ad absurdum*, to the extreme. Honesty is not in a position to function as a value which stimulates identity. It challenges the idea that the bourgeois identity can be constructed at all if, when and where the laws of the market dominate and control.

Goldoni answers this question through the figure of the businesswoman, Mirandolina. She constructs her identity by taking on different roles and acting in many different ways. In the eighteenth century in general, the view was held – and articulated particularly by Rousseau – that the identity of the individual is founded on a stable core which exposes itself or manifests itself when the laws of honesty, naturalness and authenticity are followed. However, no such stable core can be identified in Mirandolina. Her identity is maintained in the fact that she plays different roles with sovereignty and knows how to put herself on centre stage in many different ways, without settling for any of the roles or fictive scenes which she creates, and without identifying with any of them. She thus shows how others lack distance to their own roles as well as awareness of the theatricality of their own behaviour: honesty, naturalness and authenticity are proved to be (even to those people, such as the Cavalier, who believes such values create identity) the product and result of a process of self-fashioning. Under market conditions, identity can only exist in role-play and fabrications of the self. Theatre appears, therefore, as a highly useful model of social reality for dealing with the bourgeois-mercantile world as it controlled the everyday lives of the ancient merchant city of Venice in the eighteenth century.

These concepts of identity and the self, which seem to us incredibly modern, in no way met with uniform consent among Goldoni's fellow citizens. His plays always found an appreciative audience at the Teatro Sant'Angelo and then, after the break with Medebach, at the Teatro San Luca, which belonged to the patrician family Vendramin – in the case of *La Locandiera*, an enthusiastic audience. But it was precisely Goldoni's most outstanding successes which seem to have challenged his opponents. Their spokesman was the impoverished, but arrogant, Count Gozzi, who branded Goldoni a danger to the traditional order. He maintained that Goldoni destroyed the *commedia dell'arte* with his reforms and thus denied the common people a harmless, theatrical entertainment. In *Ragionamento ingenno e storia sincera delle mei ieci fiabe* (*Naive Comments and the Honest Story of My Ten Fantasy Spectacles*, 1772), he summarises his complaints against Goldoni once more:

He has turned true nobles into a mirror of corruption and, on the other hand, in countless comedies, transformed the simple plebeian into an example of virtue or sincerity. I have the suspicion (but perhaps I am too cruel) that he does this in order to befriend the simple public who

will always rebel against the inevitable yoke of suppression ... Many of his comedies are nothing more than a jumble of scenes which contain such mean, crude, and filthy truths in which, though the actors who played them may have amused me, I cannot understand how a writer can lower himself to such a level, scooping material from the most rancid, plebeian muck; worse, he dares to serve them as trinkets for the theatre and, worse still, how could he be so insolent as to print such shabby stuff as if it were a good example.[70]

As counter-programme to Goldoni's theatre reforms, Gozzi wrote various fantasy spectacles, *L'Amore delle tre Melarance* (*The Love of Three Oranges*), *Il Corvo* (*The Raven*), *Il Re Servo* (*The King Stag*), *Turandot* and others, between 1761 and 1765 for the company of Truffaldino, Antonio Sacchi, at the Teatro San Samuele, with extraordinary success. He intended these plays should elevate the old masks of the *commedia dell'arte* to their former position. Although he wrote the protagonist parts in a highly rhetorical style, he only sketched out the parts of the masks and left their execution to the improvising talents of the actors. He thereby reintroduced single elements of the *commedia dell'arte* without, however, being able to awaken the genre back to new life. The key structural elements of the *commedia dell'arte* cannot be found in Gozzi's fantasy spectacles.

It was certainly this highly unproductive quarrel with Gozzi which caused Goldoni to take up an invitation from the Parisian Comédie Italienne to go to Paris for two years and write for them. After finishing several masterpieces for the Teatro San Luca in the season 1761–2, such as *La Trilogia della Villegiatura* (*Trilogy of Summer*) and *Le Baruffe Chiozzote* (*The Chioggian Squabbles*), Goldoni left Venice in April 1762, and never returned. His last stage success came long after the end of his two-year co-operation with the Comédie Italienne, in 1771, when the Comédie Français premièred *Le Bourru Bienfaisant* (*The Beneficent Bear*). Goldoni died in 1793 impoverished and alone in Paris.

# 3 The rise of the middle classes and the theatre of illusion

## THE MIDDLE-CLASS FAMILY

### From strolling players to moral institution: theatre as one constituent of public life

We have no theatre. We have no actors. We have no audience ... The Frenchman has at least a stage; whilst the German barely has one booth of its own. The French stage exists, at the very least, for the pleasure of a whole, great capital city; whilst in the German cities, the booths are mocked by everyone. The French can at least pride themselves on frequently entertaining their monarch, the whole magnificent court, the greatest and worthiest men of the kingdom, the finest in the world; but the Germans must be satisfied with a few dozen honest private men who have slipped reluctantly into the booth and are willing to watch.

(Gotthold Ephraim Lessing)

Lessing's complaint, in the eighty-first *Literary Letter* of 7 February 1760, appropriately characterised the condition of German theatre in the first half of the eighteenth century. The 'strolling players' still toured the land as they had done one hundred years before with their wagons, from Königsberg – even St Petersburg – and Warsaw in the east to Strasbourg and Colmar in the west, from Flensburg and Schleswig in the north to Bern and Lucerne in the south. In this respect, not much had changed since the days of the English players who came to the Continent under the leader-

ship of Robert Brown and the clown Thomas Saxfield, John Bradstreet and Ralph Reed, John Green and Joris Joliphus (George Jolly), and founded the acting profession in Germany. They also toured across the country and put up stages in the great cities, such as Leipzig, Frankfurt, Cologne, Nuremberg, Munich or Augsburg at trade fairs. Sometimes, they were even invited to the court for a fixed engagement as in Kassel, for Landgrave Moritz and in Braunschweig-Wolfenbüttel, for Duke Heinrich Julius. But their German disciples in the eighteenth century could no longer hope for such strokes of luck. The troupes belonging to Caroline Neuber (between 1727 and 1750), Franz Schuch (1740–70), Johann Friedrich Schönemann (1740–57), Heinrich Gottfried Koch (1750–75), Konrad Ernst Ackermann (1753–67) and Carl Theophil Doebbelin (1756–89) were forced to keep their heads above water by keeping permanently on tour right up to the mid-1760s.

There did exist, however, several large opera houses built on the French model of court theatres as early as the mid-seventeenth century: 1652 in Vienna, 1667 in Nuremberg, 1678 in Hamburg (the 'most spacious'), 1690 in Hanover ('the most attractive'), 1693 in Leipzig, 1667 and 1718 in Dresden. But these theatres, whose stages were equipped with scenery and the latest theatre machinery, remained exclusive to the Italian opera or occasional French acting companies. Neither German acting companies nor the ordinary middle-class public had access to them.

Whilst the Italian opera societies and the French acting companies could perform in technically perfectly equipped theatres and were well paid, the German companies were forced to struggle along on a minimum wage, as socially outcast 'travelling people'. Even in the mid-1750s their pleas to be allowed to perform in the opera houses, such as the one in Nuremberg, were rejected: 'The desire of the German players to act in the opera house as the Italians do, and to be permitted to perform comedies, is denied.'[1]

The travelling troupes did play at the German courts at weddings, birthdays, Carnival, and so on. But their efforts none the less met with deep-rooted suspicion. One director, Schönemann, who had hoped for a permanent home for his German players in Berlin, complained bitterly to the professor of literature in Leipzig, Gottsched (1743), that it was impossible to win the Prussian king over to the German art of acting:

> there is only one obstacle preventing the rise of German theatre and that is the prejudice of Sr. Mayt. according to whom no German is capable of writing anything of meaning or anything of value, let alone does he think it possible that a German player should be able to represent anything of importance on the stage, and thus all my attempts have been rejected. Despite the best performances by the greatest and most respected men, I am unable to persuade the King into the German theatre, yet if this should ever happen, it would have tremendous consequences for me … In the week after Easter we were so close to having the King come to our play, but – it was in German.

The sites where the German companies were permitted to perform were generally rooms in the town hall, in which over the years a certain fund of scenery had often been collected which the troupes could use, or ballrooms. Moreover, in some cities, such as Frankfurt and Hamburg, they were also allowed to build a covered stage, made of wood, in the market square for the duration of the performances – *Spielbude* (performance booths), which had to be pulled down again at the end of the period stipulated.

The repertoire of the touring companies was not large, but it was jealously protected from other companies. Once it was played out, the company travelled on and found a new audience, for whom it still held the appeal of something new. Particularly popular were the so-called *Haupt- und Staatsaktionen*, ('by all accounts a debased form of theatre that encouraged bombastic acting, sensational and gory manifestations on stage, and frequent gross obscenity'[2]), parodies of martyr and tyrant dramas with an obligatory love story, and harlequinades and fooleries by Hanswurst ('Jack Sausage'), as comic interludes. The epilogue mostly took the form of a ballet. Thus, it is hardly surprising that performances by the travelling troupes served as a kind of public entertainment and had high attendance, particularly during trade fairs. Under normal circumstances, however, respectable and educated citizens would rarely consider going to see performances in their leisure time.

As early as the 1730s, there had been attempts to reform the repertoire of the travelling troupes and, thus, to create a theatre for a middle-class audience. In *Versuch einer Critischen Dichtkunst* (*Towards a Critical Art of Poetry*, 1730), Gottsched showed how the 'rules of art' which the artist must follow 'are derived from reason and Nature'.[3] Consequently, everything in the work of art which is contradictory, and in this sense unrealistic, must be excluded. It was assumed that the 'rational citizen' found unrealistic anything which contravened the rules governing natural or social life. In this sense, Gottsched turned against both opera and the court theatre *par excellence*, as well as the *Haupt- und Staatsaktionen* of the travelling troupes. The opera fell victim to his withering verdict as unnatural:

> One thing is certain: the plots and fables from which they are taken have more in common with old tales of knights in armour and poor novels than they do with Nature as it presents itself before our eyes. If we follow an opera in all its coherence, then we must imagine we are in another world: it is so unnatural. The people

think, speak and act quite unlike the way they would in real life: and one would be thought quite mad if one lived only the tiniest part in the way it is proposed in the opera … I have not even mentioned the extraordinary arrangement of music to the words of speech. They do not speak their emotions, or any speech as it would come naturally from their throats, which is the custom of the rest of the nation, but they extend, raise and lower their tone according to the fantasy of another person. They laugh and cry, cough and sneeze according to the notes on the page. They curse and wail in time to the music; and when they kill themselves in desperation, they stretch the heroic deed out until the last warble. What is the example of this form of imitation? Where is Nature, which has something in common with these fables?

(pp. 739f)

Here, Gottsched formulates the fundamental differences between the court theatre and the potential middle-class theatre of which he dreams: the opera, as the embodiment of abnormality and affected artificiality may be seen as an appropriate art form with which to represent the nobility; for the citizen, however, an art form must be developed which is oriented towards reason and nature, which are fundamental to his understanding of the world and himself. For similar reasons, Gottsched also rejected the theatre of the travelling troupes as being unsuitable for a bourgeois audience. The *Haupt- und Staatsaktionen*, which often drew material from Shakespeare adaptations by the English players, contra-vened, as Shakespeare's dramas themselves did, the rules of reality:

The chaos and improbability which arise from not applying the rules, are so overused and ugly even in Shakespeare, that no one who has read anything reasonable can find any virtue in it. … He turns everything inside out. Here come the foolish entrances of mechanicals and such rabble who throw themselves into every villainy and ruffian act and make a thousand fooleries; here come, on the other hand, the greatest Roman

heroes who discourse on the most vital affairs of State.

(*Notes on the 592nd Piece of the Spectator*)

Gottsched suggested taking the 'regular' tragedies of Corneille, Racine and Voltaire as models for the German bourgeois theatre; he wrote the first '*Musterstück*' (model play) of the new genre himself in 1731, *Der Sterbende Cato* (*The Dying Cato*).

Gottsched succeeded in winning over the theatre manageress, Friederike Caroline Neuber, to his ideas on how to reform the repertoire. Her company not only staged *The Dying Cato* (in autumn 1731), but also Corneille's *Le Cid* and *Cinna* as well as Racine's *Iphigenia*. The *Haupt- und Staatsaktionen* did not entirely disappear from the repertoire, but were less often performed. In 1737, Caroline Neuber's troupe even symbolically chased Harlequin from the stage, at Gottsched's suggestion. To counterbalance these less easily digested, classic tragedies, anacreontic, pastoral plays were taken up into the repertoire.

The new repertoire premièred in Leipzig with reasonable success. The initial interest shown by the audience rapidly diminished, however, mainly because the stereotypical chopped Alexandrine verse sounded too monotonous to the German ear. As revealed in a letter by Johann Neuber, even the spectators made suggestions as to how the Alexandrine tirades could be lightened: 'Now Berenice sounds better than in Leipzig; some respected gentlemen who think they understand these things, offered these thoughts: One should only break off here and there in the exceptionally long speeches and allow another person to interject so that the audience may at least enjoy a few changes' (Hamburg, 28 June 1730, 'In der fuhlen Twiete in der Comoedien Bude'). Although in the long term, audience resonance was hollow, Caroline Neuber held firmly to the repertoire inspired by Gottsched. She extended it even further with plays by the young Saxony dramatists Johann Elias Schlegel, Johann Christian Krüger, Christian Leberecht Martini and Adam Gottfried Uhlich. In January 1748, she premièred *Der Junge Gelehrte* (*The Young*

*Scholar*), the first play by a 19-year-old student of theology, Gotthold Ephraim Lessing.

Caroline Neuber's reformed repertoire was continued by Schönemann and his troupe. He entered Neuber's society in 1730 and became independent in 1740 with his own troupe. His repertoire at the time included the following 'regular plays, that we can perform: No. 1 *The Dying Cato* / 2. *Iphigenia* / 3. *Mithridates* / 4. *Polyeucte* / 5. *Cinna* / 6. *The Cid* / 7. *Alzire* / 8 *Machabaer* / 9. *Herod and Mariamne* / 10. *Alexander and Porus* / 11. *L'Enfant Prodigue* / 12. *Le Jaloux* / 13. *Le Malade Imaginaire* / 14. *Orestes and Pylades* / 15. *Der heftige oder ungestüme Freyer* [*The Ardent or Impetuous Suitor*]'. By the end of 1741, Schönemann's repertoire stretched to sixty-two plays, of which seventeen were regular tragedies, nine regular comedies, five harlequinades or *Haupt- und Staatsaktionen*, two pastorals, one *comédie larmoyante* and several prologues and epilogues.

The reformed repertoire inspired by Gottsched was in a good position to bring the new middle-class spectator into performances by the travelling troupes. But it could not provide the foundations for a bourgeois theatre. Lessing thought this failure lay in the fact that Gottsched copied the French theatre for the model of a future German theatre, rather than taking the English theatre:

He understood a little French and began to translate; he encouraged anyone who could understand a little rhyme or Oui Monsieur to translate too; he put 'Cato' together, as a Swiss art critic once said, with scissors and paste; ... he placed a curse on extemporising; he chased Harlequin from the theatre, which was itself the greatest harlequinade ever performed; in short, he wanted less to improve our own, old theatre as to be the creator of a wholly new one. And what kind of new theatre was this to be? A French theatre; without even considering whether this French theatre was appropriate to the German way of thinking or not.

He could easily have seen from the old dramas which he threw out, that we tend far more towards the English taste rather than the French;

... that that which is great, terrible, and melancholic works better for us than that which is charming, tender or amorous.

(Seventeenth *Literary Letter*, 16 February 1759)

The citizen for whom Lessing wanted to create theatre had obviously little in common with Gottsched's rational being.

The second important attempt at reform was undertaken by the actor Conrad Ekhof. As member of the Schönemann society, he founded an acting academy in 1753, in Schwerin. Its purpose was not only to reform the repertoire but also to participate in the discussion raised by major treatises on the art of acting and lead the way towards a theoretically founded, and fundamentally improved, art of acting. Not least, the academy hoped to raise the reputation of the status of actors and thereby bring about a new position for theatre in bourgeois society.

The constitution of the academy, drawn up by Ekhof in twenty-four articles and read and signed at the first meeting on 5 May 1753, proposed that:

Each of the undersigned members of this academy is bound to appear at an agreed place every fourteen days between two and four o'clock...

No member may appear either in the slightest part intoxicated or in any other state of unbalanced reason ...

External, domestic or other subjects which are not appropriate shall not be spoken of at the meeting ...

The main items to be discussed at the meetings should consist of the following: (a) the reading of those plays to be performed ... (b) fundamental and exact researches into the characters and roles of such plays and rational deliberation as to how they can and should be performed. (c) impartial ... critical observations on the plays and their performance shall be carried over from one meeting to another as well as ideas as to how various errors which have occurred can be eradicated or corrected. (d) rational discussion and debate of the art of acting in general, or on particular aspects of it and (e) modest notice of our duties towards the community in terms of how society views ourselves and our theatre. In this process, neither indignation, insult nor over-sensitivity has a place…

Fines will be redeemed annually on the anniversary of the foundation of the academy by all members of the academy and spent in an orderly way; contributions shall be used for various expenses as they are needed, and the rest shall be handed out to needy colleagues who prove themselves worthy.[4]

The acting academy, which Ekhof hoped would make a fundamental improvement and qualitative change to the German theatre, lasted only thirteen months. After that time, the former inefficiency took over again.

A greater success was achieved by an attempt undertaken by several troupe leaders from the 1750s to build a permanent theatre in one of the bigger cities and give up travelling to establish themselves as a permanent company. After Schuch was brutally rejected by the city council in the merchant city, Frankfurt, because of bitter controversy between religious leaders, he succeeded in gaining citizen's rights in Breslau in 1754. He built a theatre there on his own land, and performed regularly from 1755 to 1764. During the same period, Ackermann also built a theatre in Königsberg, which became famous for its superb acoustics. After the Russians occupied Königsberg, Ackermann moved to Hamburg where he applied to the senate:

1    to become a citizen of Hamburg;
2    to be permitted to build a comedy theatre at the Gänsemarkt where, previously, the opera house once stood;
3    to be allowed the privilege of performing German plays for the duration of twelve years. Whilst he and his company are in residence, no other German company shall be permitted to perform in Hamburg.

The building was completed in 1765.

In Berlin in 1765, the impresario and mime artist, Andreas Bergé, built a theatre at Monbijou Square. Franz Schuch's son donated his inheritance towards building a second, private theatre in Berlin. On the initiative of Koch, and with the support of several local merchants, a theatre was built in Leipzig at the Ranstädter Bastei in 1766. Alongside new buildings, renovations were also carried out in some places on buildings which seemed suitable in size and situation: in 1769, in Frankfurt an der Oder, the ballroom was re-designed for this purpose, as was a former hospital in Mannheim in 1776, even a former school church was renovated in Halle, despite the fact that the church had previously always shown itself vehemently opposed to theatre.

The 1760s can generally be held to be a period in which the inhabitants of the city and the acting societies entered into a long-lasting relationship: the leaders of the societies earned themselves citizens' rights – in part, as in Leipzig, with the backing of other citizens – they built permanent theatres in which the troupes performed regularly; ordinary citizens also began to visit the theatres frequently.

The bourgeois theatres were, like the theatres at court, designed to include theatre boxes, which divided the spectators according to their social position. The high-ranking, aristocratic, noble, or wealthy public took their seats in the boxes; ordinary citizens (at first men only, but from *circa* 1775, men and women) sat in the stalls, and the workers (in Hamburg, often including sailors and dockers) watched from the gallery. The class which set the tone in the cities, nevertheless, sat in the stalls: scholars, students, literati, aesthetes and critics. Johann Friedrich Schütze reports on this section of the audience in Hamburg in *Hamburgischer Theater-Geschichte* (*A History of Theatre in Hamburg*, 1794):

The audience showed an unusual enthusiasm for its theatre as never before, at least never before more justified. This was due, not least, to a certain, not inconsiderable group of friends of the theatre, who formed an audience within an audience, a status in statu, a stalls within the stalls and who, no matter what one may otherwise remember, considerably encouraged theatre, art and the improvement of tastes. This group was increasingly composed of connoisseurs and dilet-tantes but also fervent admirers of theatre, including lawyers, learned and simple craftsmen who, none the less, had broadened their horizons through travel and reading beyond the mere status of merchants. They came together for the daily visit to the theatre, to give their vote before and after the performances, to provide applause and condemnation during the plays, to promote morals and order in the theatre. Generally, they occupied the front rows in the stalls, and it seemed as if this privilege of seating was given to them willingly, in silent agreement, so that those visitors in the stalls who did not belong to the club often offered their own seats up to those members of the club who arrived late. These self-appointed men set the tone and applauded good new plays or single, well-performed scenes, or even well-spoken speeches; they demanded quiet, order and silence when unjustified praise, spiteful censure, or any kind of improper comments were voiced in the audience, regardless of whether it came from the boxes or from the gallery. We cannot remember that this self-appointed prerog-ative of the few to the disadvantage of the rest of the audience was ever abused. No one seemed to object when, as we remember the situation, a voice from such a club piped up that a certain play was a good one and so on.

(pp. 398f)

Without doubt, theatre functioned as the forum of bourgeois public life. It was this func-tion which was supported and strengthened by the newspaper theatre critics. In the 1720s, various 'moral' weeklies were founded, at first after the model of the English weekly papers such as *The Spectator* and *Tatler* (thus, in 1725, Gottsched's *Die vernünftigen Tadlerinnen – Ladies of Sense*), which focussed on the prob-lems of bourgeois community life such as charity events and schools for the poor, the family and methods of raising children and so forth. These were followed by the so-called 'Gelehrten Anzeigen' – 'Learned Reports' which arose independently in the 1730s; they included articles and critiques which opened discussion on philosophy and science. Following

Gottsched's efforts in the 1750s, literary critical journals began to appear, such as that founded by Nicolai in 1757 in Berlin, *Bibliothek der schönen Wissenschaften und der freyen Künste* (*Library of the Sciences and Arts*). In 1750, Lessing and his cousin, Christlob Mylius, published *Beiträge zur Historie und Aufnahme des Theaters* (*Reports on the History and Reception of Theatre*) which gathered a wealth of documents and eye-witness accounts of the reception of dramatic literature in theatre:

> The amateur judgement of the responsible audi-ence, or those who consider themselves respon-sible, are organised into institutes of art criticism including literature, theatre and music. This new profession has been given the name 'art critic' in contemporary jargon. He undertakes a strangely dialectic task: he sees himself as the mandatory representative of the audience and, at the same time, as its teacher. The art critic sees himself as … spokesman for the audience because he is not aware of any other authority other than argument and feels himself to be one with all those who can be persuaded by argument. At the same time, he can turn against the audience when he appeals, as expert, against 'dogma' and 'fashion', to the judgement of those who are poorly educated … The art critic has something of the amateur about him; his expertise rests on revoking opinion; it is the organised, amateur judgement which has not specialised, however, into anything other than the judgement of a private man amongst all other private men, who in the last instance, hold no judgement other than their own to be valid … The journal . . [is] the journalistic instrument of this critique.[5]

The founding of the Hamburg National Theatre in 1767 was programmatic of the new demand that theatre should be the forum of bourgeois public life. Alongside its initiator and first artistic director, Johann Friedrich Löwen, both Lessing and Conrad Ekhof were extensively involved. The project was borne financially by several businessmen and managed by a 'direc-torium'. Lessing was engaged as adviser, dramaturge and critic. He also prepared the publication of *Hamburgische Dramaturgie* (*The*

*Hamburg Dramaturgy*) – a 'critical register of all plays to be performed' (in advance) – an institutionalised, in-house critique. The first piece appeared on 1 May 1767, the last on 19 April 1768; it thus embraced the first performance season of the National Theatre.

As stated in the prologue read by Madame Löwen at the opening of the National Theatre in Hamburg (22 April 1767), it was the aim of the theatre 'Through bitter-sweet fear and moderate horror / To tame all evil and strengthen the soul; / In order to succour the state to transform the angry, wild man / Into a human being, citizen, friend and patriot.' The theatre was to become a moral institution. The repertoire from 1767–9 which lived up to this ideal consisted, to a large extent, of new German plays by Johann Friedrich Cronegk, Johann Willhelm von Brawe, Christian Felix Weiße, Johann Christian Brandes, Johann Friedrich Löwen and Pastor Schlosser, who mainly structured their plays on foreign models. The most successful play was Lessing's *Minna von Barnhelm*, which was performed sixteen times. French plays were still, nevertheless, in the majority: comedies by Molière and Marivaux, *comédies larmoyantes* by Destouches and La Chaussée, the new genre of the 'drame' with Beaumarchais' *Eugénie* (performed ten times between April 1768 and January 1769) and Diderot's *Le Père de Famille* (*The Father of the Family*), translated by Lessing (it had twelve performances between July 1767 and January 1769). By comparison, the English plays were more modest in number: George Colman the elder, James Thomson, George Lillo and, above all, Edward Moore's *The Gamester* and Lillo's *The London Merchant*.

'Bourgeois' plays clearly dominated the repertoire for the first time; Gottsched's *The Dying Cato* had completely disappeared, Racine was no longer represented. Corneille's *Rodogune* was only kept in the repertoire because of its star role, Cleopatra, performed by Marie Hensel, and Corneille's *Essex*, the showcase of all travelling troupes, was only performed twice. Similar tendencies can be seen on stages in other cities: a bourgeois repertoire slowly began to develop.

A special importance was laid, in this respect, on the new genre of the *bürgerliche Trauerspiel* (domestic tragedy), which came from England. Its prototype was considered to be George Lillo's *The London Merchant: or, The History of George Barnwell* which, however, did not introduce this generic name. It was given by the French translator of the play (1748) and maintained by the German translator Henning Adam von Bassewitz, who translated it from the French in 1752. The play was premièred at the Drury Lane Theatre on 31 June 1731 and was an immediate success. In 1731 alone it was performed seventeen times in London.

Lillo was well aware of the enormous reform which his play *The London Merchant* had introduced. For the first time in the history of European drama, he had created a tragic hero from the ranks of the bourgeoisie and his drama told 'a tale of private woe' (Prologue l. 20). In the dedication, which he addressed to 'Sir John Eyles, bar, member of parliament for, and Alderman of the City of London, and sub-governor of the South Sea Company', he justifies his method with an argument which points to an aesthetics of affective response:

> What I wou'd infer is this, I think, evident truth; that tragedy is so far from losing its dignity by being accommodated to the circumstances of the generality of mankind, that it is more truly august in proportion to the extent of its influence and the numbers that are properly affected by it.

That is, tragedy demands a middle-class audience and, thus, a middle-class hero as well.

In his drama, Lillo combines material from an old ballad on the apprentice George Barnwell, who falls into the hands of an older mistress and allows himself to be seduced into stealing from his master and murdering his uncle, with an explicit thematicisation of the status of the merchant. The London merchants, represented by the character of Merchant Thorowgood, are the actual heroes. In Act I (1), Thorowgood explains to his apprentice, Truman, that generous merchants have saved their nation by clever financial and trade politics; they are, thus, to be put on a level with the aristocracy: 'As the name of merchant never degrades the gentleman, so by no means does it exclude him' (I, 1, p. 221).[6]

In Act III (1), Thorowgood openly praises trade as the source of all virtue and as a science which is in a position to correct and even expel inequalities which nature has created:

Methinks I would not have you only learn the method of merchandise and practise it hereafter, merely as a means of getting wealth. 'Twill be well worth your pains to study it as a science. See how it is founded in reason, and the nature of things; how it has promoted humanity, as it has opened and yet keeps up an intercourse between nations, far remote from one another in situation, customs and religion; promoting arts, industry, peace and plenty; by mutual benefits diffusing mutual love from pole to pole. ...

'Tis justly observed: the populous East, luxuriant, abounds with glittering gems, bright pearls, aromatic spices, and health-restoring drugs. The late found Western world glows with unnumbered veins of gold and silver ore. On every climate and on every country, Heaven has bestowed some good peculiar to itself. It is the industrious merchant's business to collect the various blessings of each soil and climate, and, with the product of the whole, to enrich his native country.

(III, 1, pp. 238–9)

Thorowgood's words reflect a middle-class self-awareness, an awareness which knows how to embody and realise the higher values of its own social class.

Surprisingly, this aspect seems to have played a rather subordinate role in its reception by the German audience. The play was first performed in April 1754 by Koch's company in Leipzig; a performance by Schönemann's company in Schwerin followed as early as October; finally, Lillo's drama was taken up into the repertoire of all the important acting societies. From documents on its reception, it can be seen that a particularly enduring effect on the audience was created by Barnwell's murder

of his uncle. The Viennese court actor, Johann Friedrich Müller, reports in his memoirs on the effect of a performance given by the Ackermann society in Magdeburg (1755):

I saw this performance and I was so enraptured at the end of the third act where Barnwell, in disguise, draws the dagger to murder his cousin at pray, that I called out loud, 'Stop him! It is his uncle!' ... Men of feeling and dignity, and much affected ladies sitting near me praised my attentiveness, my thorough participation and attempted, since tears were pouring down my cheeks, to comfort me.[7]

In the novel, *Das Leben des Soufleurs Leopold Böttiger* (*The Life of Leopold Böttiger, Prompt*), the actor and later director of the Berlin Royal Theatre, August Wilhelm Iffland, wrote:

I still recall as if it were yesterday the painful condition which the play the *London Merchant* caused in me. Of course, I could only see my own father in old Barnwell. How he prayed for the young man, only to be murdered by him; I was no longer in control of my senses. I was driven from the theatre, I ran home crying loudly and threw myself onto the bed 'Father – my father! – my dear honest father!' – I called out, thus, again and again.

On a performance in Hamburg in 1755, Johann Heinrich Vincent Nölting relates:

By the end of only the first act, our eyes were filled with tears – after the lengthy battle between innocence and the attractions and persuasions of the loathsome mistress Milwoud, Barnwell is ultimately defeated in an unlucky moment and hurries on her arm to her house which was like a murderer's cave. Fine, sensitive and upright souls, when they see this tragic drama for themselves, can easily imagine how intensely our emotions must have increased with every act, and how moved and shaken we were by the end of the tragedy.[8]

In accordance with the audience reception in the theatre, the theme of the merchant's status was not picked up by the critics, either. The first *bürgerliche Trauerspiele*, which clearly orientate themselves on the *London Merchant,* Lessing's *Miss Sara Sampson* and Johann Gottlob Benjamin Pfeil's *Lucie Woodwill* (both 1755) not only make no mention of the professional status of their characters, but also even admit doubt that the characters are even middle class at all. Middle-class self-awareness is articulated in the German *bürgerliche Trauerspiel* in quite another way: it is directly related to the representation of the family, familial and domestic relationships, and family values.

As can be seen from the popular writing of the time, particularly the widely propagated moral weeklies, the family in general became the centre of interest in the eighteenth century. It was assumed that the family represented an original, naturally given system of ideal community life and interrelations between people. In *Ideen zur Philosophie der Geschichte der Menschheit (Ideas on the Philosophy of the History of Mankind,* 1784/5), Johann Gottfried Herder sees it, in opposition to the form of government developed much later, as 'the eternal work of nature ... the growing household in which the seeds of the humanity of mankind are planted and raised'.

The patriarchal organisation of the family is also viewed as something given by nature. In the first half of the century, patriarchy was interpreted as one form of leadership and consequently the father's power was emphasised. Thus, one definition of the term 'family' in Zedler's universal dictionary of 1734 reads, 'The family is a number of people who ... are subordinate to the power and control of the father' (vol. 9).[9] More succinctly, in 1721, in Christian Wolff's *Vernünfftigen Gedancken von dem Gesellschaftlichen Leben der Menschen (Rational Thoughts on the Social Life of Man)* it states: 'The father of the house is in command of the whole household' (Section 195), and even in 1784, the *Deutsche Enzyklopädie* records, 'Since the creation of the world, the father of the house has been provided with certain powers in the home which have not changed despite the constitution of Republics' (p. 487).

The principle of the domestic power of the father determines not only the relationship between husband and wife, but also that between father and child. The mother of the house, in her turn, is in an in-between position. She may act on behalf of the father, but in so doing, she is denied any independence of her own. For even here, the father of the house must 'himself inspect the tasks he has given her ... so that he can see to what extent he can rely on her' (Christian Wolff, Section 204). In addition, she does not have equal rights to the father in exerting authority for, 'it often happens that the children do not take so much notice of the mother as the father, because the mothers turn a blind eye to being strict where it would be needed and are so close to them that they do not see their errors – these are some of the reasons for this' (Section 159). To maintain the order of the patriarchal family, the father of the household must ultimately deal with everything and keep a watchful eye on all members of the family, 'This watchfulness over everything which happens in the household is called a father's vigilance' (Section 203).

In the second half of the century, relationships between family members which were strictly controlled by the patriarchal hierarchy were greatly emotionalised. The emotional distance between father and child decreased. Whilst until well into the middle of the century the father kept a considerable distance from his children – as the Hamburg 'Patriot' complained in 1724, 'How many houses do I know here in Hamburg where the children ... remain among the servants and barely have the luck once a week to be allowed to see their parents until their ninth or tenth year' (p. 18) – the father now began to enjoy the children's presence. Thus, in Campe's *Sittenbüchlein für Kinder aus gesitteten Ständen (Little Book of Manners for Children of Good Standing,* 1777), the father says of his children, 'I always feel so content when they are about me' (p. 8), and the general atmosphere at familial gatherings is described as, 'The hearts of all flowed in silent feeling'. In *Umgang mit Menschen (Polite Intercourse,* 1788), Adolph Freiherr von Knigge judges any distance between parent and child to be 'unnatural and irresponsible' and describes the ideal conditions in the following way, 'What can be more charming than the expression of a beloved father amongst his grown-up children who, through his wise and friendly manner, are keen not to hide any thought of their hearts from him, their truthful adviser, their most considerate friend.' In these works, the family appears, above all, as something which is emotional, as a unit of feelings, rather than a system of leadership. Even if its general definition and understanding had changed, the family continued to lie at the centre of interest and attention.

However, this was not true of all social classes. The new ideal of the family community is related more to the middle class who set themselves clearly apart from both the upper and the lower classes. Thus, Knigge writes that the kind of family life based on the interchange of feelings as he suggests is 'only applicable to persons of the middle classes' for 'the very high ranking and very rich people rarely have a sense for homely happiness, feel no longing in the soul and live, for the most part, in very distanced relations to their spouses'. The middle classes who follow the ideal of 'homely happiness' consist of, on the one side, professionals, such as officials, scholars, lawyers, priests, merchants, managers, and, on the other side, of the gentry, the lower rural aristocracy, that is, noble landowners. For this group, the family values of subordination to the patriarch as well as showing tender bonds of emotion towards him are both obligatory and exemplary.

It is from members of this group that the majority of the theatre audience stem. Having come from the homely community of a tender and loving family, the spectator finds himself confronted with his actual reality in the theatre. The heroes of countless stirring comedies, 'portraits of the family', and bürgerliche Trauerspiele who act on the stage are, to him, fathers and daughters, mothers and sons who belong, as he does, to the middle class. Similarly, the role figures portrayed in the Trauerspiele are no longer kings and princes but people who 'like us, are made of the same husk and corn as we are', as Lessing claimed in the seventy-fifth section of the Hamburg Dramaturgy. Consequently, the character should not be chosen 'from the plebeians'. As Johann Gottlob Benjamin Pfeil explains in Vom bürgerlichen Trauerspiel (On Domestic Tragedy, 1755), this is because:

> no tailor, no cobbler … is capable of a tragic way of thinking. There is a certain middle level between the ordinary people and people of significance. The merchant, the scholar, the nobleman, in short, anyone who has had the opportunity of improving his heart or enlightening his mind, belongs to the same. It is from this class that we must derive the characters for the roles who are to act in the drama. These people are always capable of the necessary degree of virtue and depravity demanded by the tragic stage if it intends to fulfil its goal.
>
> (Section 12)

The middle-class family maintained its presence both on the stage and in the auditorium. From this moment, the German theatre progressed unchallenged for more than 150 years to become one of the most important socialising institutions of the 'middle classes'.

## The loving father and his virtuous daughter

The family in the bürgerliche Trauerspiel consisted predominantly of a father and daughter. The mother is either long dead (as in Lessing's Miss Sara Sampson, 1755, and the first bürgerliche Trauerspiel, Lillo's The London Merchant, 1731) or she plays a subordinate role (as in Lessing's Emilia Galotti, 1722, and Schiller's Kabale und Liebe [Intrigue and Love, 1784]). In this case, she is presented in a, more or less, negative light: Claudia Galotti is disapproved of by her husband as 'a vain and foolish mother' (Emilia Galotti [II, 4, p. 51][10]) and Frau Miller is even accused by her husband of being an 'infamous procuress!' who with her addiction to 'coffee and snuff' – i.e. for expensive luxuries – drives her 'daughter's face to market' (*Intrigue and Love* [I, 1, p. 5][11]). The mother's minor importance allows all interest to focus on the relationship between father and daughter.

This relationship is determined in all *bürgerliche Trauerspiele* by mutual, affectionate love. This is constantly stressed and explicitly emphasised in the first German *bürgerliche Trauerspiel, Miss Sara Sampson*. Thus, Sara never speaks of her father other than of her 'tender father', calls him 'a father who never yet let me sigh for a mother' (*Sara*, IV, 1, p. 58).[12] Accordingly, Sir William longs for his daughter as 'she is the support of my age ... if she loves me still, her error is forgotten' (I, 1, p. 10). The servant, Waitwell, accurately characterises the relationship between father and daughter when he assures Sara, 'Ah, Sir William is still the same fond father, as his Sara is still the same fond daughter that she was' (III, 3, p. 44).

Even if the delicate exuberance, which determines the relationship between Sir William and Sara, may be foreign to Odoardo Galotti and Emilia, they do not love each other any less. Odoardo characterises himself convincingly to his daughter as a father who 'loves you so dearly' (*Emilia Galotti* [henceforth, *Emilia*], II, 4, p. 50) and Emilia shows her love for her father silently in her behaviour: in her disappointment that her father did not wait for her on the morning of her wedding ('And he would not wait for me!' [II, 7, p. 56]) and in her complete trust that her father will free her from the hands of her seducer ('I, alone in his hands? Never, father. Or you are not my father' [V, 7, p. 101]).

Finally, in *Intrigue and Love*, which concludes the development of the *bürgerliche Trauerspiel* in the eighteenth century, Musikus Miller loves his daughter 'idolatrously': 'You were my idol. Listen, Luise, if you still have room for a father's feelings ... you were my all' (*Intrigue and Love* [henceforth, *Intrigue*], V, 1, pp. 78, 81). Luise, likewise, also loves her father, 'She loves her father ... even to idolatry' (III, 1, p. 46). She refuses to leave her father for Ferdinand ('I have a father who has no fortune beyond his only daughter' [III, 4, p. 52]) and is even prepared to sacrifice her love for Ferdinand in order to save her father ('It is my honourable name ... it is Ferdinand ... it is the entire bliss of my life that I now place in your hands ... I am a beggar' [III, 6, p. 60]).

There can be no doubt about the intense love which binds father and daughter together in all these dramas. Nevertheless, the relationship between them is not entirely secure. It is challenged at precisely the moment when another man attempts to form a relationship to the daughter or has already done so. The fathers in the *bürgerliche Trauerspiele* permit their adult daughters the right to choose their own husbands freely. Thus, Odoardo agrees with his wife when she says of the city, 'It was only here that love could join together two people who were made for each other: it was only here that the Count could find Emilia – and he found her' (*Emilia*, II, 4, p. 50).

Musikus Miller understands it to be a matter of course that the daughter should choose her future husband for herself. He rejects the father's mediation as an 'old-fashioned channel' and accuses the lover, 'There! Behind her father's back he has to present his business to the daughter; he has to act so the girl will sooner send father and mother to the Devil than let him go' (*Intrigue*, I, 2, p. 8).

Therefore, the adult daughter's right to choose her husband freely can hardly be a cause for concern for these fathers. On the other hand, they live in the constant fear that their daughters' virtue is threatened, that they might be seduced. Although they love their daughters dearly, they tend to mistrust them on the smallest provocation. On the news that Emilia has gone alone to Mass, Odoardo sweeps aside Claudia's appeal, 'Those few steps ... One is enough to put a foot wrong!' (*Emilia*, II, 2, p. 47). When Claudia tells him how attentive and sympathetic the Prince acted towards Emilia, he is beside himself: 'Ha, when I think – that would be the very place to strike a fatal blow! – A rake, admiring, lusting – Claudia! Claudia! The mere thought of it sends me flying into a rage' (II, 4, p. 51).

In a similar way, Musikus Miller is outraged

by his wife's naïve belief that Ferdinand is only concerned about Luise's 'sheer beauty of soul'. He sees Luise exposed to the threatening danger of seduction:

Just you watch out, just you watch out: even if you had an eye in every knothole and stood guard over every drop of blood in her blushes, he'll wheedle her right out from under your nose, and give the girl one, and take himself off, and there'll be the girl with a bad name for the rest of her life and left an old maid; or else, if she relished the trade, she'd carry it on.

(*Intrigue*, I, 1)

The father views the daughter's virtue as highly valuable goods which must be protected and guarded with great care. If these goods are endangered, a conflict breaks out between father and daughter. The natural order of the family is upset.

This dangerous situation can occur when the father fails in his duty to guard his daughter's virtue. Thus, Sir William accuses himself of causing his daughter's downfall:

I myself am most to blame in this misfortune. But for me Sara would never have made the acquaintance of this dangerous man. I admitted him freely into my house on account of an obligation under which I believed myself to be to him. It was natural that the attention which in gratitude I paid him, should win for him the esteem of my daughter. And it was just as natural, that a man of his disposition should suffer himself to be tempted by this esteem to something more. He had been clever enough to transform it into love before I noticed anything at all, and before I had time to inquire into his former life.

(*Sara*, III, 1, p. 40)

Whilst Sir William blames himself for not fulfilling the paternal duty of vigilance in guarding his daughter carefully enough, Odoardo and Miller are prevented from doing so by their wives. Claudia not only hides the Prince's growing attentions to Emilia from her husband ('You should have told me about it straight away' [*Emilia*, II, 4, p. 51]), she even explicitly commands Emilia to keep her meeting with the Prince in the church a secret from him. Thus, the watchfulness of the father of the family is pre-empted by a mother who forgoes her duty to the family.

Similarly, Frau Miller keeps quiet from her husband that a relationship is beginning to develop between Ferdinand and Luise:

You knew before I did. You should have given me a hint. The girl would still have listened to reason. There still would have been time … but no! … there had to be some dickering, there had to be some fishing. And you went and added fuel to the fire!'

(*Intrigue*, II, 4, p. 37).

If Miller had been warned in time he could have made use of his power as father of the family and thus averted the threatening danger: 'I was the master of the house. I should have kept my daughter more strictly in line. I should have talked turkey to the Major' (I, 1, p. 3). It is only when the vigilance of the patriarch, such as Odoardo and Miller, has slipped, or is abused, that a situation can arise which causes conflict.

This conflict can only be resolved by saving the daughter's virtue. In *Miss Sara Sampson*, this is made possible by giving up the strict concept of virtue held in the period of early Enlightenment and replacing it with a more subjective concept of virtue. Thus, Sir William refuses to see his daughter's mistake as a sin which can only be atoned for by life-long exile from the family. He understands it far more as the 'error of a tender-hearted maiden, and her flight was the result of her remorse' (*Sara*, I, 1, p. 10). A single mistake by his otherwise virtuous daughter can surely be forgiven by a father for, 'a child may err for once and remain a good child in spite of it' (III, 3, p. 47). Sir William is, therefore, determined to forgive his daughter and accept her seducer Mellefont as 'his son' (III, 3, p. 49). In his view, Sara's virtue is thereby wholly reconstructed.

Sara, on the other hand, sees her mistake as a 'crime' (III, 3) which can never be forgiven. It can only be made good in part by turning the 'depraved' relationship between Mellefont and herself into marriage:

> I am yours in my heart and will remain so forever. But I am not yet yours in the eyes of that Judge, who has threatened to punish the smallest transgressions of this law ... Another woman, after having forfeited her honour by an error like mine, might perhaps only seek to regain a part of it by a legal union. I do not think of that, Mellefont, because I do not wish to know of any other honour in this world than that of loving you. I do not wish to be united to you for the world's sake but for my own.
>
> (I, 7, p. 17)

If her subjective feelings find harmony with 'eternal' order, then Sara could believe her virtue restored. Until that time, the word 'virtue', which otherwise once 'sounded sweet', will roll like 'terrible thunder' (I, 7, p. 18).

It is only in her confrontation with Marwood that Sara finds another opinion of her mistake. Now it seems to her a 'mistake' and no longer a 'crime'. For, 'it is one thing to fall into vice from ignorance; and another to grow intimate with it when you know it' (IV, 8, p. 76). It is only in confrontation with a genuine seducer that Sara realises that one mistake alone cannot turn a virtuous girl into a depraved one. Now, she sees it far more as the sign of her 'weak virtue' and accordingly justifies her early death through Marwood's poison, 'God must let the virtue which has been tested remain long in this world as an example; only the weak virtue which would perhaps succumb to too many temptations is quickly raised above the dangerous confines of the earth' (V, 10, p. 91). Sara dies as a virtuous daughter, as 'an angel' who even forgives her murderer. Her last words are for her father, 'my father –' (V, 10) after she has bequeathed his 'fatherly' love to Arabella, the daughter of Mellefont and Marwood. The relationship between the affectionate father and his virtuous daughter becomes a model of interpersonal relations in general. It has no need of a biological basis.

In *Emilia Galotti*, Emilia's virtue is threatened by the Prince's desire. He has ordered that she be abducted and agrees to Marinelli's plan to kidnap her and bring her into the house of the chancellor Grimaldi on the excuse of bringing her mother and father to trial. In this way, he has the opportunity of seeing Emilia whenever he wants. Emilia attempts to escape this situation by suicide. She is determined to save her virtue at any price – even death. Her father, Odoardo, intends to prevent her suicide, because, at first, he does not understand her:

ODOARDO: What? Is that what we have come to? No, no! Remember: for you too there is nothing more precious than life.

EMILIA: Not even innocence?

ODOARDO: That can resist any tyrant.

EMILIA: But not any seducer. Tyranny! Tyranny! Who cannot stand up to tyranny? What men call tyranny is nothing; the seducer is the true tyrant. I have blood in my veins too, father, warm young blood like any other girl. My senses are senses too. I cannot promise anything; I cannot vouch for myself. I know the Grimaldis' house. It is a house where pleasure is all. An hour there, and in my mother's sight, and my soul was in such a tumult that weeks of prayer, and all our religion teaches us, could scarcely calm it.

(*Emilia*, V, 7, pp. 101–2)

Emilia sees her virtue less threatened by the power of the Prince than her own willingness to be seduced. She is not afraid of a weak will which would allow her to give in to the power of the Prince, but rather her own drive, her own senses, which can no longer be controlled under such sensual surroundings. Her virtue could no longer be saved.

Virtue does not appear here as a naturally given characteristic, but rather something which is constantly in danger because it can only be upheld as the result of a fierce battle with sensual nature. Emilia wants to continue to acknowledge it as something which she, in agreement with her father, has placed on the top of her hierarchy of values. Therefore, she must not only try to suppress her desires as well as she can and, thus, fight against her own sensual nature, but she must even destroy this very nature when the battle threatens to end in defeat for her. Since Emilia's virtue is endangered by her own physical nature – and less through the power of the Prince – the saving of it requires her life.

It is in this sense that Emilia appeals to her father to carry out his 'fatherly duty' and defend her virtue even at this great cost,

> Long ago I believe there was a father who, to save his daughter from shame, took steel, the first that came to hand, and plunged it into her heart – gave her life a second time. But all such deeds are deeds of long ago! There is no such father in the world today!'
>
> (V, 7, p. 102)

Odoardo now understands his daughter and stabs her. She dies gratefully kissing his hand with his name on her lips, 'Ah – my father –' (V, 8). The daughter's virtue remains intact for both father and daughter.

Musikus Miller sees the virtue of his daughter threatened to the extreme by Ferdinand. Luise, however, has already confronted this danger by rejecting Ferdinand at the beginning of the drama,

> I do not want him now either, my father. This scanty dewdrop of time ... a dream of Ferdinand already drinks it rapturously up. I renounce him for this life. Then, mother, ... then, when the barriers of discrimination collapse ... when all the hateful husks of rank burst from us ... and human beings are only human beings ... I shall bring nothing with me but my innocence. Father has so often said, you know, that adornment and splendid titles will be cheap when God comes, and hearts will rise in price.
>
> (*Intrigue*, I, 3, p. 11)

Because Luise has adopted her father's understanding that the barriers of class will never be overcome, and that marriage to Ferdinand is completely out of the question, she feels she must renounce 'an alliance that would rend asunder the seams of the bourgeois world and bring the universal and everlasting order down in ruins' (III, 4, p. 53). She believes she has been put before the choice of either failing in her 'obligations' to religion, her social class and her father (III, 6, p. 55), or of having to give up Ferdinand in the here and now. She decides in favour of her obligations, 'Father, here is your daughter once more' (II, 5, p. 37).

Luise freely chooses to deny herself – even after a difficult inner battle ('To *lose* you! O the thought is beyond limits horrible ... monstrous enough to pierce the immortal spirit and to fade the glowing cheek of joy ... Ferdinand! To lose you!' [III, 4, p. 53]) without, however, giving up hope that she is loved by Ferdinand and that she will be tied to him in eternity. But she is even betrayed in this hope. For, in the further course of the drama, she is forced to repeat her rejection twice more. The first time, Wurm gives her the choice of allowing her father to die or writing the letter to the Chamberlain von Kalb who will compromise her and separate her from Ferdinand forever. Luise decides to save her father and writes the letter, 'Take it, Sir. It is my honourable name ... it is Ferdinand, ... it is the entire bliss of my life that I now place in your hands' (III, 6, p. 60).

The second rejection occurs when Miller seeks to save Luise from her death pact with Ferdinand, which was supposed to reconcile her to Ferdinand and bind them together in eternity: 'Go on! Load all your sins upon you, load also this last and most horrible one upon you, and if the load is still too light, then let my curse make up the weight ... Here is a knife ... pierce your heart, and (*as he starts to rush away loudly weeping*) your father's heart!' (V,1, p. 82). For a third time, Luise is put before the choice between Ferdinand and her father. Bowing to the obligations of fatherly love ('tenderness compels more barbarously than tyrant's fury'), she decides ultimately for her father ('Father, so be it! ... Ferdinand ... God is looking down! ... Thus I destroy his last memorial' [V, 1, p. 82]). From the beginning of the drama, Luise already sacrificed her love for Ferdinand in this world for the sake of her father's scale of social values. Now she even sacrifices the chance of their reunion in eternity for his religious values as well. Luise's virtue and pure soul are – from the father's viewpoint – saved. The daughter has restored the order of the middle-class family which her love to Ferdinand threatened to explode.

The temporary disagreement between father and daughter in *Miss Sara Sampson* is restored by mutual forgiveness and reconciliation; in *Emilia Galotti,* by the death of the daughter, and in *Intrigue and Love* through total renunciation. As far as the system of values is concerned, this agreement is, *de facto*, never seriously endangered. For, both fathers and daughters consider virtue to be the highest value which stands above and beyond the individual's expectation of happiness; it is even higher than life itself ('Luise: Your daughter can die for you, but not sin for you' [*Intrigue*, III, 6, p. 57]). The absolute denial of physical nature and its needs, that is, suppression of desire and renunciation, thus become the obligation and fate of all daughters – in total accordance with the principle of the inner-worldly asceticism which Max Weber emphasised as the pillar of Protestant ethics. The father is obliged to create and maintain the inner and outer conditions which allow the daughter to actualise this principle permanently – on the one hand, by affection and, on the other hand, by vigilance.

In the figures of the loving father and his virtuous daughter, the theatre offered its spectators a form of identification which was of great significance to the bourgeois self-understanding of the middle classes between 1750 and 1770, who distanced themselves from the court and developed a different, specific way of life. Here, the emotional intimacy of the small patriarchal family and the daughter's virtue are foregrounded as the most important and effective potential. The emotionally binding relationship between father and child should help the children to accept and internalise the father's scale of values and thus encourage the growth of an appropriate *Über-Ich* ('super-ego'). The father's affection plays a role in the initiation of middle-class self-understanding which cannot be over-stressed. In particular, it is strongly emphasised in the early *bürgerliche Trauerspiele* and only seriously criticised in *Intrigue and Love*. The tenderness of the father expresses itself here, above all, towards the end of the drama in a language which stems from the field of economy and finance.

Now you are no longer disposing of your own possessions. I, too, have all to lose. You see my hair is beginning to turn grey. The time is gradually coming on for me when the capital will stand us in good stead that we laid up in our children's hearts. ... Will you cheat me out of that, Luise? Will you make off with your father's goods and chattels?

(*Intrigue*, V, 1, p. 81)

'I've spent my whole cash-supply of love on this daughter' (V, 3, p. 88). Thus, emotional relationships appear as nothing more than relationships of ownership; the 'tenderness' of the father compels 'more barbarously than tyrant's fury' (V, 1, p. 82); it prevents the daughter's self-determination and self-realisation which are only possible for her in the death pact with Ferdinand. The emotional unit of the natural order of the family is perverted into an instrument of control and suppression.

The virtue of the daughter, on the other hand, remains a consistently positive leitmotif in eighteenth-century bourgeois drama. How deeply it marked middle-class self-understanding is shown, above all, in the confrontation with the court lifestyle. Thus, Miller triumphs over the President with the words, 'Saving Your Grace, my name is Miller, if you want to hear an adagio ... with strumpets I cannot serve you. As long as the court has its own stock of them, the supply is not up to us middle-class people. Saving Your Grace' (II, 6, p. 40). Similarly, Luise draws her self-confidence in her opposition to Lady Milford from awareness of her 'bourgeois innocence', 'what torture of the rack for you to read in your serving girl's face the *serene repose* with which innocence is wont to reward a pure heart' (IV, 7, p. 71). A daughter's virtue provides the middle-class man with a priceless advantage over the 'highness of a ruler' for even the 'meanest labourer … at least receives, in his wife, a whole body by way of dowry' (Ferdinand, I, 7, p. 20). It is the virtuous daughter who secures the indisputable moral superiority of the middle classes over members of court society. Middle-class self-confidence can rest on this moral superiority, even when – as in Germany – the middle classes were still excluded from any participation in political power. In this sense, it was the sacrifice of the daughter – the sacrificial virgin – on which the bourgeois community was founded.

## The court as counterworld: the seducer and the mistress

In the *bürgerliche Trauerspiel*, the natural unit of the family, based on emotion and virtue, is contrasted with the court as a place of depravity and intrigue. The positive identification figures of the loving father and his virtuous daughter are set in opposition to the negative figures of the mistress and the seducer, their antagonists, who belong to the court. Whilst the mistress sees the virtuous daughter as rival in her efforts to win the favour of the seducer, the seducer rivals the loving father for the love and, above all, the virtue of the daughter.

Marwood, the first *Buhlerin* (paramour, mistress) in the German *bürgerliche Trauerspiel*, *Miss Sara Sampson*, is, like her prototype Millwood in *The London Merchant*, characterised as a depraved schemer. She spins the web of intrigue which sets the whole drama in motion in order to drive her rival, Sara, away from Mellefont and it is she who conceives the trick which separates Mellefont from Sara at the decisive moment. When her intrigues fail, however, she turns into her rival's murderer.

Marwood appears, at each point, as Sara's negative, or opposite image. While Sara seeks to restore her virtue, Marwood mocks virtue as 'a silly fancy, which brings one neither happiness nor guilt' (*Sara*, II, 7, p. 36). Whilst Sara does not 'wish to be united' to Mellefont 'for the world's sake', but for her 'own' (I, 7, p. 17),

Marwood tries to win back her 'good name' from him in 'the eyes of the world' (II, 7, p. 36). And although the virtuous Sara wants to welcome Arabella into the family, Marwood, who is Arabella's own mother, a 'voluptuous, egoistic, shameful strumpet' (Mellefont, II, 7, p. 36), threatens to kill her to take revenge on her father:

Behold in me a new Medea! …

Or, if you know a more cruel mother still, behold her cruelty doubled in me! Poison and dagger shall avenge me. But no, poison and dagger are tools too merciful for me! They would kill your child and mine too soon. I will not see it dead. I will see it dying! I will see each feature of the face which she has from you disfigured, distorted, and obliterated by slow torture. With eager hand I will part limb from limb, vein from vein, nerve from nerve, and will not cease to cut and burn the very smallest of them, even when there is nothing remaining but a senseless carcass! I – I shall at least feel in it – how sweet is revenge!

(II, 7, p. 37)

By calling upon the ancient heroine, Medea (also the title heroine of Corneille's drama), and in the wild passion of her desire for revenge, Marwood is placed in a tradition which points to the type of heroine actualised in classical French tragedies. She seems, thus, to be the representative of that era (and its lifestyle) from which heroic drama stems: the era of court absolutism. Marwood is not linked to the court through her social standing – all the figures in the drama belong, as far as it can be made out, to the lower and middle aristocracy– but, instead, through a complex of values and forms of behaviour which are sharply criticised in this thoroughly negative figure. The family, whose middle-class scale of values could have resolved their conflict by accepting the seducer as a son, is endangered to the extreme in its collision with the court lifestyle. The virtuous daughter dies as the victim of her opponent, whom she forgives in dying. Even when the mistress's own catastrophe is revealed, the middle-class lifestyle proves to be superior, for Sara forgives her and offers up Arabella as substitute for her father's love: the daughter of the depraved Marwood becomes the virtuous daughter of the loving father, Sir William.

Depravity and heroic gesture characterise the figure of the mistress in later examples of the genre. The figure undergoes considerable change, however, in Orsina (*Emilia Galotti*) and Lady Milford (*Intrigue and Love*). Depravity no longer appears – as in Marwood – as a characteristic trait, but rather as the direct result of the court lifestyle. Depravity stems from the unnatural form of life at court, not the character of the mistress *per se*, who, in this respect, is considered the victim of the court (*Intrigue and Love*, II, 3). For this reason, the dramatic function of the schemer or intriguer is lifted from the figure of the mistress and transferred onto another representative of court lifestyle: in *Emilia Galotti*, to the chamber master, Marinelli, in *Intrigue and Love*, to the sovereign's private secretary, Wurm. It is these characters who set the machinery of intrigue in motion which, at the end of the drama, results in the death of Emilia, Luise and Ferdinand.

The heroic element in Orsina (*Emilia Galotti*) and Lady Milford (*Intrigue and Love*) is no longer focused on taking revenge on the seducer who discards them for another. The reason Orsina wants to kill her seducer is because she feels he insulted her honour when he left her because he was weary of her. ('How can a man love a creature that insists, as if to spite him, on having her own thoughts? A woman who thinks is as distasteful as a man who paints himself. She should always be laughing, simply laughing, to keep the mighty lord of creation in a good humour' [*Emilia*, IV, 3, p. 81].) For the same reason she forces Odoardo to take her dagger, 'For we have both been wronged; wronged by the same seducer' (IV, 7, p. 89). Orsina even dreams that all the girls who have been insulted by the Prince will unite and destroy him to restore their honour: 'Ah! … what a heavenly fantasy! If we one day – all of us, his victims – a whole army of deserted women – transformed into Bacchantes, into furies – if we could have him in our midst, tear

him to pieces, dismember him, hunt through his entrails to find the heart that he promised to every one of us, the traitor, and gave to none! Ah! What a dance that would be!' (IV, 7, p. 89).

Because she accepts the courtly canon of values and sees her honour as the highest object of value, Orsina desires the death of her seducer; in order to save her virtue, Emilia intends to kill herself. Even in this constellation the opposition between the virtuous daughter and the mistress remains intact.

Finally, in Lady Milford (*Intrigue and Love*), the heroic element causes a reversal in the figure: she ultimately decides to renounce love and honour in favour of virtue:

> Ha! Emilia! Was it for *this* that you overstepped the bounds of your sex? Was it for *this* that you had to vie for the glorious name of the great British *woman*, to have the ostentatious edifice of your *honour* collapse beside the higher virtue of a forsaken bourgeois wench? … I, *too*, have the strength to renounce … It is done! … burst are all bonds between me and the Duke, this wild love is wrenched out of my heart! – Into thy arms I throw myself, Virtue! … Take her to thee, thy repentant daughter Emilia!
>
> (*Intrigue*, IV, 8, pp. 74–5)

Lady Milford gives up Ferdinand and leaves the court and its life of depravity. Calling upon her 'heart', Lady Milford – who has no relationship, no family – chooses virtue as her own model, in the same way that Luise, focused on religion and family, has done from the beginning. The opposition between the two figures can, at least in this respect, be annulled because virtue has been lifted from a middle-class value to a universal, human value.

The *Verführer* (seducer) enters as the courtly opponent to the loving father: whilst the latter tries to watch over the virtue of his daughter and to protect it, the former threatens to destroy it. Mellefont (*Miss Sara Sampson*) seems to have succeeded in this: he has seduced Sara and has eloped with her from her father's house. He presents himself as the court representative of a typically libertine sexual moral: 'I associated with vicious women; that may be. I was myself seduced more often than I seduced others; and those whom I did seduce wished it' (*Sara*, I, 3, p. 13). But in the course of the drama, the same Mellefont is drawn away from the court lifestyle and its scale of values and is led towards the middle-class, familial scale of values as they are represented by Sara and Sir William. He takes his first step with insight into the criminal nature of his actions: 'I still had no ruined virtue upon my conscience' (I, 3, p. 13); and he becomes fully aware of the value of Sara's virtue: 'you are still the virtuous Sara that you were before your unfortunate acquaintance with me' (I, 7, p. 18). His love for Sara has changed him. As confirmation of his transformation, Mellefont weeps, 'See, the first tear which I have shed since my childhood is running down my cheek' (I, 5, p. 14). None the less, he tries to put off marriage to Sara and already feels himself 'fettered for life' (IV, 2, p. 60) when, after reconciliation with Sir William, marriage can no longer be delayed: 'Sara Sampson, my beloved! What bliss lies in these words! Sara Sampson, my wife! The half of the bliss is gone! And the other half – will go' (IV, 2, p. 60). It is extremely difficult for Mellefont to loosen his ties to the courtly scale of values forever. He only achieves this at the end of the drama after Sara, dying, bequeaths her father's love to him and Arabella and after Sir William honours Sara's 'last wish': 'Let me embrace you, my son, for whom, I could not have paid a higher price!'. Mellefont stabs himself and dies as the son (of Sir William) and as the father (of Arabella) with a declaration of belief in family values: 'If now you will call me your son and press my hand as such, I shall die in peace. (*Sir William embraces him*) You have heard of an Arabella, for whom Sara pleaded; I should also plead for her; but she is Marwood's child as well as mine' (V, 11, pp. 92–3).

Mellefont's ultimate conversion from the courtly to the middle-class, familial, lifestyle can be seen as proof of the optimism of the Enlightenment in the 1750s. It was a widely held belief that court values could be replaced by middle-class ones through education: the natural emotions of an individual – including individuals at court – (i.e., Mellefont's love for Sara) will inevitably lead that individual to recognise family values and virtue.

This optimism has disappeared in *Emilia Galotti*. Accordingly, the function of the future son (Appiani) is sharply differentiated from that of the seducer (the Prince). Appiani does indeed belong to the court thanks to his birth. But he decides against the court and prefers to lead a middle-class life of retirement, 'in the valleys where his fathers lived'. He is welcomed into the middle-class Galotti family as a son ('Everything about him delights me' [*Emilia*, II, 4, p. 49]).

Nor is the seducer represented as a thoroughly depraved person. His love for Emilia allows him to take on some middle-class values, 'When that was the way my thoughts went, I was always so gay, so happy, so carefree. Now I am quite the opposite of all that. – But no, no, no! Freer or less free, I am still better off as I am' (I, 3, p. 35). The scale of values against which he measures his emotions leads, temporarily, to a middle-class way of life: 'I have pined and sighed for long enough; but done nothing! And for all this amorous idleness, I was within a hair's breadth of losing everything' (I, 7, pp. 44–5). It is not as a *man* of feeling that the Prince is a danger to Emilia's virtue, even if he succeeds in causing fear and confusion in Emilia with his confession of love in the church. She remains firmly bound to the protective unity of the family. As *prince*, however, as master of intrigue and machinations at court, he represents the greatest danger.

His approach during the Mass is scourged as the intent of a 'seducer' (II, 6). But depravity alone is not enough to rip Emilia from her family and seriously threaten her virtue. This is only possible after Marinelli's trick. It leads to Appiani's death and seeks to separate 'Mother and daughter and father' (V, 5, p. 98): the natural order of the family is upset. It is only depravity, in whose service the intrigue is spun, which allows the Prince to actually become antagonist to the father.

Not only is the court lifestyle criticised in the figure of the seducer but also the political system on which it rests: absolutism. Even if the Prince has human feelings, the system which gives him all the means of power in his hands, leads him to disrespect the middle-class values of virtue and the family which confront him, for the sake of satisfying his own wishes and desires. 'Is it not enough, and the misfortune of so many that princes are but men; must there be devils too to pretend they are their friend?' (V, 8, p. 103). As long as absolutism rules, the natural order of the family and the virtue of its daughters will be threatened.

This critique is taken up in *Intrigue and Love* and even strengthened:

The debauchery of the great of this world is the insatiable hyena that seeks victims with its ravening hunger ... Dreadfully had it already raged in his country ... separating bride and bridegroom ... even rending asunder the divine bond of marriages ... here it had wiped out the tranquil happiness of a family ... there exposed a young, inexperienced heart to ravaging pestilence, and dying learners hissed forth their teacher's name amid curses and spasms.

(*Intrigue*, II, 3, p. 32)

The critique of absolutism is, here, however, separated from the figure of the 'seducer'.

As son of the President, Ferdinand belongs by birth to the sphere of the court. He has, however, released himself from the court scale of values,

Because my notions of greatness and good fortune are not quite yours ... *Your* good fortune seldom manifests itself except in destruction. Envy, fear, execration are the sorry mirrors in which the highness of a ruler smiles at itself ... My ideal of good fortune withdraws more contentedly within myself. All my desires lie buried within my *heart*.

(I, 7, p. 19)

The 'conventions' of court life seem to him only a 'fashion' because they have fallen out with 'nature' and he pits the demands of 'humanity' against them (II, 3, p. 34). Equally, however, he has little faith in the middle-class family values of

love for one's children or children's obedience: 'There is a region of my heart where the word *father* has never yet been heard' (II, 6, p. 41). The 'abominable father' (I, 7, p. 18), '*alien* figure' (II, 5, p. 36), 'murderer's father' (V, 7, p. 98), is confronted with 'the bond-note of filial duty ... torn to pieces' (II, 6, p. 40). Unlike Luise, Ferdinand knows no duties to religion, to social class, or family:

FERDINAND: *You*, Luise, and *I* and *love*! ...
    Does not all heaven lie within that circle?
    ... My fatherland is where Luise loves me.
LUISE: And can you have no other obligation
    besides your love?

(III, 4, p. 52)

The values which Ferdinand 'brought back from the universities' (III, 1, p. 43) collide both with the court and with the middle-class family lifestyle. Ferdinand becomes antagonist to both father figures: Miller, the middle-class father, concerned for the virtue of his daughter, and the President, worried about his son's career at court. The worlds of the fathers and the opposition represented by them are no longer his. Ferdinand's ideals revolve far more around a 'greatness of soul and personal nobility' (III, 1, pp. 43–4) whose actualisation is neither tied to a specific social class nor to any particular class boundaries.

Because his love for Luise is driven by such ideals, it stands in perfect harmony with 'virtue'. For it does not demand the 'pleasure' which Miller fears (I, 5) and which the President takes for granted, but rather, 'adoration' (IV, 3). 'My wildest wishes were silent. Before my spirit stood no thought but eternity and that girl' (IV, 2, p. 62). Such a love can never endanger the virtue of the one who is loved – but it can upset the middle-class family order which is exploded by its absolute demands. For it excludes any thought beyond, or other than, love, 'The moment that parts these two hands will also rip asunder the thread between *me* and *creation*' (II, 5, p. 38).

The only authority which Ferdinand allows and to which alone he refers is his heart:, 'All my desires lie buried within my *heart*' (I, 7,

p. 19). The demands of the 'heart', the autonomous self, are higher than any other demands made by religion, social class or family. The heart becomes the single guarantee of the figure's self-realisation. Ferdinand holds, thereby, a similar scale of values to those held by the middle-class intellectuals of the *Sturm und Drang* (*Storm and Stress*) movement in the 1770s. The identity of the self is no longer confirmed in relation to the family role (as it is in the characters and the spectators of middle-class drama), but only through the certainty of the own personal value. It is a question of realising the individual, own self.

It was through this shift in the concept of values in Ferdinand that Schiller upset the traditionally negative figure of the seducer. The figure of the loving father whose tenderness obstructs the self-determination of the daughter is taken over by a new identificatory figure – the young admirer and idealist, who stands beyond all social class and sees a duty towards his heart alone – and, thereby, towards 'mankind'.

## The body as 'natural sign' of the soul – the reception of the *bürgerliche Trauerspiel* and the development of a new art of acting

The new genre, the *bürgerliche Trauerspiel*, was a sensational success with the public. *Miss Sara Sampson* was premièred on 10 July 1755 in Lessing's presence by the Ackermann troupe in Frankfurt an der Oder. Ramler reported in a letter to Gleim (25 July 1755) on the unusually powerful effect of the play: 'Herr Lessing's tragedy was performed in Frankfurt, and the audience sat for three and a half hours, silent as statues, weeping.'

Shortly after the première, Koch performed *Miss Sara Sampson* and on 6 October 1756 it was premièred by the Schönemann society in Hamburg. Johann Friedrich Löwen noted in *Geschichte des deutschen Theaters* (*History of German Theatre*, 1766): 'Lessing's *Miss Sara Sampson* has been performed on all stages, whether good or bad; the best performance was that by the Schönemann society. How knowledgeably does Miss Starke perform Sara. Not

the tiniest nuance of character or the situation in which she must find herself escapes her. The fear, the unrest, nervousness and partial self-doubt which shadows her after Marwood confesses to her; whom does it not stir to the innermost part of the soul?' (p. 48). At the Hamburg première, the role of Mellefont was played by the leading German actor, Conrad Ekhof.

In Berlin, *Miss Sara Sampson* was performed on 19 October and 4 November 1756 by the Schuch society. Friedrich Nicolai gave a detailed account of it in a letter to Lessing, dated 3 November. Before going into the weaknesses and strengths of individual actors, he spoke of the effect which the performance had had on him:

> Before I tell you about the performance in more detail, I must let you know that I was extremely affected; up to the beginning of the fifth act, I was often in tears, but by the end of the same act and throughout the whole scene with Sara, I was far too moved to be able to cry any more. This has never happened to me at any other drama, and confounds, to a certain extent, my own system which generally resists being moved by tragedy. My feelings and my critical annotations both on your play and the actors were mixed in a wonderful confusion in my head.

Lessing's first *bürgerliche Trauerspiel* clearly provoked an unusually strong emotional response in the spectators. Documents on audience reception repeatedly record how affected the audience was, sobbing and crying. The sensitive reaction of the audience seems to manifest a deep emotional acceptance of the values propagated and dealt with on the stage: familial love as the model of relationships between all human beings in general, and virtue. The middle-class spectator seemed to find himself reflected in the identificatory figures of the loving father and the virtuous daughter and to understand the specifically middle-class nature of their moral claims on each other. Middle-class consciousness was 'articulated' through the communal experience of being moved.

Not one record of such feelings exists in

accounts on the reception of *Emilia Galotti*. The dominant trend in reports and reviews on the performance is to recount the acting methods of the better performers in as much detail as possible. *Emilia Galotti* was premièred on 13 March 1772 in Braunschweig by the Doebbelin society. Its première in Berlin by the Koch society followed on 6 April 1772. The roles were not well cast except that of Claudia, who was played by Madame Starke (the 'moving' Sara in Hamburg). Johann Friedrich Schink describes her style of performance in *Dramaturgischen Fragmenten* (*Dramaturgical Fragments*, 1781):

I can still see the intoxicated joy in her eyes, the overflowing delight in her heart when she tells her husband of the prince's outstanding praise for her dear Emilia – I can still see her worry, her maternal anxiety at Emilia's fear; her sense of foreboding when she hears who is speaking to her and what it is he says to her; her quick comprehension, her peace; I can still hear the convincing tone of her voice, full of love and tenderness with which she calms Emilia. – And then, her great impression of maternal fury, her wild storming into the room in Battista, her outpouring of pain in the tight tones of fear ... what powers would I have to own to act in the way she does, in the way I hear her speak, in the way those tones still ring in my ears![13]

Whilst the critics unanimously praise Madame Starke's performance and give details of her acting without questioning the meaning and function of the role in the play, Lessing turns against the actress in a letter to Nicolai (dated 22 April 1772), who had reported to him that the audience's interest let off after the scene with Claudia and Marinelli:

that the interest after that scene does not always hold: I did not know. Madame Starke might perhaps in all her excellent playing, have played a little too superbly. For that is also an error: and an understanding actor must never raise his acting of a role, where it is not necessary, to the disadvantage of all others.

At the performance in Weimar, by the Seyler society, Odoardo was played by Ekhof and Orsina by Sophie Friederike Hensel, both actors of whom Lessing was thinking when he wrote the final version. Friedrich Nicolai saw the performance in 1773. In an article entitled 'Ueber Ekhof' ('On Ekhof'), he describes Ekhof's performance as Odoardo when he meets Orsina (IV, 7):

In the excellent scene ... between Orsina and Odoardo where the latter, after being given the dagger by the countess only gradually discovers her identity, Ekhof began this discovery by pulling repeatedly at the feathers of his hat which he held in his left hand, while looking meaningfully at the countess from the side, from time to time. One understood the thought which he speaks out in the following scene very clearly from this mimic action, 'What has insulted virtue got to do with the revenge of a scoundrel?' It gripped him from within and increased as Orsina expressed her desire for revenge more emphatically.[14]

Like Schink and Nicolai, other reviewers also thoroughly analyse the means of acting used by the performers to express the various mental states and thought processes of their roles. Clearly, the theatre critic's interest is now concentrated on the art of acting and, in this respect, it can be evaluated as an integral element of the discussion on a new 'natural' art of acting which was debated with great vehemence in the 1760s and 1770s.

Whilst Lessing's *bürgerliche Trauerspiele* were positively received by the audience and critics, the judgement of both on Schiller's *Intrigue and Love* – at least in part – differs widely. The première took place on 15 April 1784 by the Großmann troupe in Frankfurt am Main. The performance in Mannheim, for which the play was written, occurred two days later in Schiller's presence. Schiller's friend, Andreas Streicher, reports it was a great success:

The second act was very lively and the end of the same presented so excellently, with so much fire, and gripping truth that even after the curtain had fallen, all the spectators rose to their feet in a way never seen before, and broke out in stormy and unanimous cheering and applause. The poet was so surprised by it, that he got up and bowed in return.[15]

There followed performances in all the great theatre cities (August in Göttingen, December in Berlin, February 1785 in Breslau, and November in Leipzig). Up to the turn of the century, the play had an almost permanent place in the repertoire of all the great stages of the time. It only met with political resistance in Stuttgart and Vienna.

Neither the actors nor the spectators apparently took notice of the change of values Schiller had made to the role-types. They received the characters of Luise and Miller in the sense of well-known identificatory figures, the virtuous daughter and the loving father. Thus on 3 August 1784, the critic in the *Berliner Litteratur- und Theatre-Zeitung für das Jahr 1784* wrote on the performance by the Großmann troupe:

Madame Albrecht as Louise [moved] ... everyone to silent enchantment through her masterly declamation, perfect to the last syllable ... Never had I seen a more simple, natural action as hers; she is always and always *completely* within her role: one forgets with her more than with any other, that one is only watching the stage, and not something real. She sketched the innocent girl who loves Ferdinand for *himself* and not as the Major; the battle between her love for him and for her father; and in uttering one word which said everything which was to be expressed, showed herself to be a true connoisseur of nature and of the heart. Her glowing, tender expression, her gentle look, her interesting figure, all was united: one must see her for oneself to be enraptured and to understand exactly how much the art of acting has gained through her! – Herr Stegmann played alongside as the old honest Miller excellently and caused great emotion through his warm-hearted portrayal.[16]

The same critic, however, ranked *Intrigue and Love* on the same level as Gemmingen's *Hausvater* (*Father of the Family*), a trivial family melodrama, and criticises Ferdinand accordingly: 'the otherwise noble Ferdinand should

neither sink to the level of poison mixer nor offend the respect owed his father – who, despite his despicable behaviour, is nevertheless still his *father* who loves him' (p. 180).

The move away from the ruling scale of values as it had been created within the genre of the *bürgerliche Trauerspiel* could not prevent the majority of spectators from continuing to prefer the figures of the loving father and his virtuous daughter above all other identificatory figures offered by the theatre until the beginning of the nineteenth century. Here, degenerated into trivial stereotypes, they were presented as dominant identificatory figures in countless family dramas by Friedrich Ludwig Schröder, August Wilhelm Iffland and August von Kotzebue, to an audience who clearly never tired of seeing itself and its own excellence celebrated.

Thus, although the audience continued to enjoy *Intrigue and Love* without restriction and unproblematically as a further example of 'family melodrama' genre, the intellectual critics were irritated by the whipped-up pathos of the play. Karl Philipp Moritz's merciless and slating review is representative of their critique:

In truth, yet another product which drives our times to shame! What sort of brain does a person need to write and print such nonsense, and what must his heart and mind look like if he can observe this birth of his imagination with pleasure! – But we do not want to declaim. Whoever is able or wants to read through 167 pages of disgusting repetitions and blasphemies, a fop cautiously arguing over a silly, affected girl, full of crass, plebeian jokes and incomprehensible gibberish – he should see it for himself. To write like this is to trample on taste and healthy critique; and in so doing, the poet has surpassed himself. Something might have come of some scenes, but everything that this writer touches turns to foam and bubbles in his hands.[17]

The theatre reviewers and reports on the performance mentioned here show the increasing interest in the 1760s for the art of acting. At Ekhof's actors' academy, it was already the object of theoretical discussion. Rémond de Sainte Albine's treatise, *Le Comédien* (1747), and Francisco Riccoboni's *L' Art du Théâtre* (1750), were read and discussed at various meetings.

It was Lessing above all, with a wealth of translations and own works, who drove the discussion towards the development of a psychological-realistic style of acting in place of a purely rhetorical-decorative one. In 1754, he translated extracts of Sainte Albine's article and published it with extensive critical notes in the first part of the first section of his *Theatralischen Bibliothek*. In 1760, he published his own translations of two of Diderot's bourgeois dramas, *Le Fils Naturel* (*The Natural Son*, 1757) and *Le Père de Famille* (*The Father of the Family*, 1757), as well as some theoretical annotations, *Entretiens sur 'Le Fils Naturel'* (1758) and *Discours sur la Poésie Dramatique* (1758), under the title *Das Theater des Herrn Diderot*. At the same time, he worked on an article which was to remain only a fragment: *Der Schauspieler. Ein Werk worinnen die Grundsätze der ganzen körperlichen Beredsamkeit entwickelt werden* (*The Actor. A work in which the basic tenets of a whole bodily expressivity shall be developed*). The *Hamburg Dramaturgy* also contains many observations and thoughts on the art of acting. Lessing's suggestions were taken up and developed by the mathematician and philosopher, Georg Christoph Lichtenberg. In *Briefen aus England* (*Letters from England*, 1775), he delivered detailed descriptions of how the most famous contemporary actor, David Garrick, interpreted his roles, and he also evaluates him on a theoretical level.

The leading interest which underlies all these studies is primarily the question of the true bodily expression of the feelings in the soul. This question also occupied Lessing as he wrote his plays. Countless clues of such bodily signs can be found in the speech text of *Miss Sara Sampson* and in the speech and secondary text of *Emilia Galotti*. Thus, in *Miss Sara Sampson* there are constant repetitions that someone is crying ('Ah, you are weeping again, again, Sir!' [I, 1, p. 9]; '[Sara] remains the whole day long locked up in her room, and cries' [I, 2, p. 11]; 'See, the first tear which I have shed since my childhood is running down my cheek'

[I, 5, p. 14], and so on). In *Emilia Galotti*, bodily actions are mostly shown in a wild look ('And you look about you so wildly?' [II, 6, p. 52]; '*Looking about him wildly*' [IV, 7, p. 88]), trembling ('And you are trembling all over?' [II, 6, p. 52]) and exaggerated movements ('*Enter Emilia in anxious confusion … falling into her [the mother's] arms*' [II, 6]; '*stamping his foot and foaming*' [IV, 7, p. 88]). In all these instances, bodily actions function as signs of feelings experienced by the figure. The body is not spoken of as sensual nature, but, rather, as a complex of signs.

In the Enlightenment, theatre theoreticians – as well as philosophers, linguists, anthropologists, psychologists and ethnologists – interpreted and understood the human body as a natural system of signs. Lichtenberg echoes the ruling thought of the time when he describes gestures in *Über Physionomik; wider die Physiognomen* as 'natural signs of the movements of emotion' whose entirety forms 'a spontaneous language of gesture … which speaks out the passions in all its gradations to the whole world. Man learns to speak it in its totality in general before his 25th year. It is Nature who teaches him and with such emphasis that it becomes an art to make a mistake in it.'[18] The human body is, thus, not by nature a sensual body but a complex of 'natural signs of the emotions'.

It is in this sense that the body of the actor on the stage is employed. Since 'the art of acting is to imitate nature through art and to come so near to it that appearance is taken for reality or things that happen are given so naturally it seems as if they had only just happened', as the most significant actor of the German Enlightenment, Conrad Ekhof, explained, the actor must 'imitate with his gestures that spontaneous gesture' which he observes in 'nature', that is, in the 'ordinary man', in the 'child' and in the 'savage' who are not deformed by cultivation or social behaviour and, thus, consciously form their bodies as signs. In *The Paradox of The Actor*, Diderot demanded that the actor must know 'the outward signs of feeling' in order to apply them on the stage in the right places.

> All his talent consists ... in giving such a scrupulous rendering of the outward signs of feeling that you're taken in. His cries of pain are marked out in his ear. His gestures of despair are memorised and have been prepared in a mirror ... That tremor in the voice, those halting words, those stifled or lingering sounds, that trembling in the limbs, that shaking of the knees, those swoons, those furies; pure imitation.[19]

Whilst in France, the body was only understood in terms of the emotions as a system of natural signs, the German theoreticians saw it as a natural sign of the character and changing mental conditions of the person as well. Thus, the philosopher and, later, theatre director in Berlin, Johann Jakob Engel, tries to differentiate and describe different bodily poses as signs of specific characters in *Ideen zu einer Mimik* (*Ideas on Mime*, 1785/6). He suggests that 'a head bent down from the neck' is characteristic of a 'stupid and lazy' man, for example:

> open lips which let the chin fall as it will; eyes half covered by the lid; bent knees; a stomach pushed out in front; feet turned in; hands pushed deep into the pockets of the coat, or freely swinging arms. Who will not recognise at first sight the loose, inactive soul who is incapable of focusing attention, or interest; a soul not wholly awake, who has not the least energy nor brings the slightest tension into his muscles to hold his body in such a way as to bear his limbs properly.[20]

The theatre of Enlightenment in Germany consequently interpreted and shaped the human body as a sign of the character and feelings of the dramatic figure. The body of the actor is, thus, not presented as sensual nature, but rather as a complex of signs, as a 'text', written in the 'natural language of the soul'. In an ideal situation, while the spectator is reading this text, he will not even acknowledge the body of the actor as sensual nature at all. However, actors and particularly actresses, often sought very hard to prevent precisely this situation arising.

The focus on the 'natural' bodily expression of emotion stands in direct relation to the declared goal of the aesthetics of affective response as celebrated in theatre of the middle classes: it should awaken feelings in the spectator and, thus, strengthen the human ability to feel. This was predominantly true of the first, and original feeling of humanity – empathy. In a letter to Nicolai, in November 1756, Lessing explains:

> The meaning of tragedy is this: it should develop our *ability to feel empathy*. It should make us so empathetic that the most tragic characters of all times and among all people overtake our emotions. *The man of empathy is the most perfect man*; among all social virtues, among all kinds of generosity, he is the most outstanding. A person who can make us feel such empathy, therefore, makes us more perfect and more virtuous, and the tragedy which moves us also makes us thus – or, it moves us in order to be able to make us thus.

The emotions which direct physical expression release in the spectator favour – more than mere linguistic presentation – an emotional readiness to identify with those figures with whom one first feels empathy – with the loving father and his virtuous daughter – and thus also indirectly encourage the goals of the bourgeois theatre of the Enlightenment.

The re-interpretation and reorganisation of the human body on the stage into a complex of 'natural' signs of psychological processes remains the principal characteristic of the middle-class theatre of illusion up to the intervention by the avant-garde movements at the turn of the nineteenth century. The norms and scale of values explicitly formulated in the early drama of the middle classes are, in this respect, implicitly decisive for all bourgeois theatre: the negation of the sensual nature of the body on the stage and its increasingly perfect development as a natural sign system up to its ultimate perfection through Stanislavsky, made it capable of stimulating in the spectator a wealth of feelings which allow his own 'empathy' and identification with the dramatic figure, but which force him none the less towards a high degree of suppression of his own drives. The contribution made by theatre in the process of civilisation on which bourgeois society was founded, has barely been appreciated until now.

## THE MUTILATED INDIVIDUAL

### 'Nature! Nature! Nothing is so like Nature as Shakespeare's figures'

'I, who mean everything to myself! Everything I know, I know only through myself! Thus exclaim those who have self-awareness.' These words from Goethe's speech, *Shakespeare: A Tribute*,[21] in autumn 1771, outline the heart of the programme of the *Sturm und Drang* movement as well as the way its followers saw themselves. The new literary movement was formed as a critique and radicalisation of the Enlightenment and articulated itself in an explosive way in the relatively short time between 1771 and 1776 (excluding Schiller's later, youthful works such as *Die Räuber* [*The Robbers*], *Fiesko* and *Intrigue and Love*). It was led by a group of young, middle-class intellectuals (including Herder, Johann Wolfgang von Goethe, Jakob Michael Reinhold Lenz, Friedrich Maximilian Klinger, Heinrich Leopold Wagner, Johann Anton Leisewitz, and Friedrich Müller known as Maler Müller) who – with the exception of Goethe – strove to liberate themselves from an oppressive, narrow background and secure an existence as free poets.

This new generation of middle-class intellectuals no longer found self-confidence in belonging to the bourgeoisie, nor in distinguishing themselves from the 'plebeians' by adopting middle-class morals and scale of values in opposition to the court lifestyle. Instead, they discovered a new awareness of the unique nature and originality of their own individual selves as something beyond membership of any social class and outside any consideration of class whatsoever. Unique individuality

replaced the middle-class family as the most important reference point.

The 'discovery' of the individual occurred alongside a rediscovery of Shakespeare. In his Shakespeare speech, Goethe writes:

> The first page I read made me a slave to Shakespeare for life. And when I had finished reading the first drama, I stood there like a man blind from birth whom a magic hand has all at once given light. I realised and felt intensely that my life was infinitely expanded. Everything seemed new to me, unfamiliar, and the unaccustomed light hurt my eyes ... I struggled free – and knew for the first time that I had hands and feet.
>
> (pp. 163–4)

The encounter with Shakespeare is experienced as the restoration of the own self, as a liberation towards the self. The confrontation with Shakespeare, thus, leads to the formulation of a new self-understanding and thereby to the demand for a new kind of drama.

The young members of the *Sturm und Drang* movement admired the 'genius' in Shakespeare who did not need to imitate nature by following certain rules (*natura naturata*) but could produce his works from within himself through the power of a genius creative ability, in the same way that nature creates itself (*natura naturans*). 'I feel, when I read [Shakespeare] that the theatre, the actors and the set have disappeared! Like countless, individual leaves from the Book of Events, of prophecies, of the world, fluttering down in the storm of our times!'. Thus Herder's article on Shakespeare (1771/3) emphatically shows how Shakespeare's dramas were understood less as artistic products and more as world creations. In this sense, Goethe compared him with Prometheus: 'He challenged Prometheus, followed him trait for trait in creating his figures, but in his case with *colossal greatness*.' Goethe also saw in Shakespeare's characters, therefore, not artificially created people, but pure nature. 'Nature! Nature! Nothing is so like Nature as Shakespeare's figures' (p. 165). Neither are they condensed into types or roles, instead they represent individual characters, each of whom appears in his own, quite specific uniqueness. Shakespeare's characters are individuals. In this sense, his plays seemed to Goethe to revolve around 'an invisible point which no philosopher has discovered or defined and where the characteristic quality of our being, our presumed free will, collides with the inevitable course of the whole' (p. 165).

The *Sturm und Drang* movement found their understanding of mankind embodied in Shakespeare's dramatic figures. Jakob Michael Reinhold Lenz, for example, defined human uniqueness in *Anmerkungen übers Theater* (*Notes on Theatre*, 1771, printed in 1774):

> We are ... or at least we want to be, the first rung on the ladder of a freely acting independent creator and, since we see a world around us which is the proof of an eternal free, active being, the first drive which we feel in our souls is the desire to imitate him; since however the world has no bridges and we have to satisfy ourselves with that which already exists, we can at least experience the growth of our existence and happiness in imitating him, of creating his creations in small.

Lenz also bases the demand for character drama as the drama of the future on this definition: 'It is a question of characters who create their own occurrences, who independently and unchangingly turn the great machine themselves, without needing the gods up in the clouds for anything but as spectators, not of pictures, or marionette plays, but – of people.' The protagonist of a drama such as this is a unique character who presents his individuality in his actions; a self who is alive to the self-awareness of his individual character as well as his individual freedom. Thus, the 'hero' will become an autonomous self, 'the sole key to his own fate'.

The individual who acts freely, who is creatively occupied, the all-round, complete personality, became the leitmotif of this generation. They demanded uncompromising recognition of the validity of each individual and struggled towards the unrestricted development of the personality. This right should not be given to extraordinary people only, but should be respected as the basic right of every man. For, in the sense that this model was understood to determine mankind *per se*, any man could be considered a genius. Consequently, Herder introduces this concept in *Vom Erkennen und Empfinden der menschlicher Seele* (*On Recognition and Experience of the Human Soul*, 1778): 'The genius sleeps in man as the seed in the tree: it is the individually fixed measure of depth, and the unfolding of all powers of recognition and feeling of *this* person, as the word shows, it is his life-force and *nature*.'

Middle-class intellectuals of this generation demanded the emancipation of the self not merely from the inhuman obligations of court absolutism but also from the functionalisation and reification of middle-class life which did not allow an all-round unfolding of personality. The individual should be set free and restored to himself.

## From the mutilation of the hand to the mutilation of freedom

Goethe's eponymous hero in *Götz von Berlichingen* (1773), a 'man whom the princes hate and to whom the oppressed turn' (I, 2, p. 14), seemed to his contemporaries to be the ideal embodiment of the new image of man.[22] Götz understands and describes himself, 'determined to die before we owe anyone but God for the air we breathe and before we pay loyalty and service to anyone but the emperor' (I, 3, p. 26). His freedom will be fulfilled in one self-determined, self-responsible action:

> The best knight can't do anything when he is not master of his actions. They came against me once before this way, when I had promised to serve the Count Palatine against Konrad Schotte. He handed me a memorandum from the Chancery about how I was supposed to ride and behave. I threw the paper back at the Councillors and said I wouldn't know how to follow its directions; I didn't know what I might run into, *that* wasn't in the memorandum; I had

to keep my own eye peeled and see for myself what I had to do.

(III, 4, p. 68)

To be able to act is, for Götz, in his nature. If the opportunity to act is taken from him, he cannot realise himself, 'Oh! Writing is busy idleness, I find it sour. While I am writing about what I have done, I am annoyed at the loss of the time in which I could be doing something' (IV, 5, p. 105). The urge to act is as elementary as the need for food, drink and sleep.

The character of Götz shows us that human nature cannot be split into the spiritual-moral versus the physical. In refreshing the sensual-bodily nature, at the same time he also restores his spiritual-moral being:

MARTIN: When you have eaten and drunk, you are as new born, you are stronger, more courageous, more fit for your work. Wine rejoices the heart of man, and joy is the mother of all virtues. When you have drunk wine you are everything twice over that you are supposed to be. You think twice as easily, you are twice as enterprising, twice as quick at execution. ...

When you, Sir, return inside your walls with the consciousness of your bravery and strength which no weariness can affect, and for the first time after a long interval stretch out unarmed on your bed, safe from enemy attack, and relax in sleep that tastes sweeter to you than drink tastes to me after a long thirst – then you can talk about happiness.

(I, 2, pp. 10, 11–12)

The profound, naturally assumed relationship between bodily functions such as eating, drinking and sleeping, and Götz's active occupations points to his vital, unique nature which only exists as a given whole, which cannot be pulled apart by different natures fighting against each other.

The unnaturalness of a split nature as it was propagated, and even made a precondition in the *bürgerliche Trauerspiel*, can be read, above all, in the figure of Martin: 'but we, when we have eaten and drunk, are precisely the opposite of what we are supposed to be. Our sleepy digestion attunes the head to the belly, and in the weakness of an over-copious repose desires are engendered which quickly grow higher than their mother's head' (I, 2, p. 11). Here, in Martin's comments, a critique of civilisation is unmistakable. The loss of an original, active lifestyle which creates and cares for the self, leads to a perversion of human nature: natural needs turn into depraved 'desires' which must be suppressed with force.

Eating and drinking, therefore, play an important role for Götz and his followers (I, 1, 2, 3; II, 8; III, 14, 18, 19, 20). In Act IV, when Götz's freedom is decisively restricted, the motif of eating and drinking disappears (apart from Götz's last appeal for a 'drink of water' [V, 4]). Götz himself points explicitly to the close relationship between the fulfilment of his bodily needs and his moral demands for freedom when he pours the last bottle of wine:

GÖTZ: And when our blood starts on its decline the way the wine in this bottle runs first feebly and then drop by drop ... (*he lets the last drops fall into his glass*) ... what shall our last word be?
GEORG: Long live Freedom!
GÖTZ: Long live Freedom!
ALL: Long live Freedom!

(III, 20, p. 88)

Keeping physical nature intact and free from bodily harm and allowing it to regenerate itself as vital force through eating, drinking and sleeping seems, thus, to represent and embody the vital, active nature of the free autonomous individual.

In this respect, Götz's iron hand has particular importance – it is the manifest symbol of a physical injury Götz suffered before the drama begins: he has no right hand. Many functions are accorded the human hand, principally the right hand, in the course of the drama. It first appears as the seat and organ of the power to act, so that its readiness for use guarantees the possibility of action and unfolding oneself as a free, self-determining being. Alongside this, it is used in the 'solemn hand-clasp' (II, 6, p. 51) which morally obliges the parties concerned as a 'knightly word' (IV, 4, p. 101) to keep to the contract sealed by it. Not least, the hand is also sensitive to 'the pressure of love' (I, 2, p. 13). The 'hand' is directly related to the 'heart' which is characterised by Götz and his followers as the seat of natural feeling ('a full heart, a heart totally filled with one emotion' [I, 5, p. 39]; 'whose hearts rejoiced' [III, 20, p. 88], as 'a cheerful heart' [I, 3, p.23], or 'a free and noble heart' [IV, 1, p. 92]). This bond between 'hand' and 'heart' is further deepened in the court scene (V, 11): 'Whatever man whose heart is pure, whose hands are pure', 'My heart is pure of wrongdoing, my hands of innocent blood' (p. 126).

In Maria's tale, finally, the right hand is described as the healing hand which is in a position to cure through mere touch (I, 3). The hand seems, in this form, to be an organ in which both the physical and sensual-moral nature of man is manifested in a special way. The fact that Götz is missing precisely this hand is of great importance. It points unmistakably to the fact that he is far from representing an 'original', bursting with vitality. The mutilation of the body is far more a sign of the mutilation which has been done to the autonomous individual. Götz has, from the very beginning, a damaged nature. The action of the drama is executed as a process in which the mutilation carried out on Götz's hand leads to the total eradication of his identity. 'Were you looking for Götz? He is long since gone. Little by little they have maimed me – my hand, my freedom, my property, and my good name' (V, 13, p. 127).

If one reads the drama retrospectively from this aspect, it is obvious that Götz's first entrance presents less a vital, powerful, young man, and more a tired one: 'I have to keep walking back and forth or sleep will overtake me ... It sours the little life and freedom a man has' (I, 2, p. 8). The 'little life' is regenerated (until III, 20) through eating, drinking and sleeping; freedom is defended by permanent battle. When Götz's freedom is first restricted

(IV, 5) and then finally taken away in prison (V, 13), his 'life' is not restorable: 'his wounds' (V, 10, 13) and his 'age' (V, 10) expose his physical nature to destruction. Just as bodily intactness guarantees the freedom to act, freedom also creates the conditions for vital 'life'. Both are dependent on each other. The mutilation of the body and the mutilation (silencing) of freedom thus appear as two sides of the same process which leads to the destruction and dissolution of the autonomous individual. The missing right hand – and that means the iron hand – signals, therefore, the beginning of a development at whose end the whole, self-determining, freely acting personality has ceased to exist.

The symbolism of the hand is now related in a significant way to the two antagonists who seek to induce Götz's downfall: Weislingen and Adelheid von Walldorf. Weislingen is introduced as 'the Bishop's right-hand man' (I, 1, p. 5). Nevertheless, Götz tells him that after the loss of his own hand, he 'hoped that Adelbert would be my right hand' (I, 3, p. 24). And, in fact, Weislingen does go back and forth between the Bishop and Götz just like the Bishop's hand in Götz's tale: 'the bishop ... said "I did indeed give you my hand because I did not recognise you." Then I said, "Sir, I clearly saw that you didn't recognise me, and here you have your hand back again"' (I, 3, p. 20). Weislingen is bound both to the Bishop and then to Götz as a 'hand' and he is therefore disposable like Götz's iron hand: 'Last night I thought I gave you my right iron hand, and you held me so tight that it came out of the brassarts as if it had been broken off' (I, 5, p. 35). Weislingen is reduced to one single function: to act as the 'hand' of another person.

Although Götz points out to him that he is 'as free, as noble born as any man in Germany, independent, subject only to the Emperor' (I, 3, p. 24), Weislingen cannot rouse himself to any kind of self-determined action. Adelheid accuses him, 'Instead of the active man who enlivened the affairs of a princedom, who did not lose sight of himself and his fame in so doing, who had climbed to the clouds over a hundred great enterprises as over mountains piled one on top of the other, I saw all of a sudden someone complaining like a sick poet, as melancholy as a healthy girl, and idler than an old bachelor' (II, 9, p. 57). Weislingen has no inner energy. When he dreams that Götz draws a sword against him and challenges him, he reaches for his own, but 'my hand failed me' (V, 10, p. 122). Weislingen is incapable of acting independently and on his own decisions, and prefers to act only as the tool of another being. He has become the 'disposable' hand which allows itself to be used first by the Bishop and then by Adelheid.

In Weislingen, a contradiction has taken shape which was characteristic of the German middle classes of the time. On the one hand, Weislingen is as much attracted to the life at court, the 'flirting and dawdling after women' (I, 3, p. 24), as he is to the chance of making himself indispensable so that he can gain influence and power. On the other hand, after becoming engaged to Maria, he enthuses to Götz about an isolated life away from court (as did Appiani in *Emilia Galotti*): 'To be all yours, to live only in you and in the sphere of the Good; far away, cut off from the world, to taste all delights that two such hearts can furnish to each other!' (I, 5, p. 34). The life at court seems to him now to estrange him from himself, to eradicate his identity: 'The way I hung on those wretched people whom I fancied I controlled, and on the glances of the Prince, and on reverential approval around me! Götz, dear old Götz, you have given me back to myself' (I, 5, p. 36). However, after he has been chained to the court life again through Adelheid's clever seduction, he believes his identity can only be secured by this kind of existence and finds, 'I am once again Weislingen' (II, 9, p. 57). The hand which has failed, and the heart which is 'shut' (V, 10, p. 125), thus become signs of a split personality which, by giving up self-determining action and reducing itself to the role of operating as the organ of action for someone else, has given up the own self and its right to develop freely.

Despite this opposition, Götz and Weislingen

are closely related to one another. Both die almost simultaneously and both rationalise their deaths with exactly the same words: 'my strength is sinking toward the grave' (V, 10, p. 123; V, 14, p. 129). In their youth at Margrave's court they were named after the twin brothers 'Castor and Pollux'. Now they attempt, though enemy brothers, but obedient 'sons', to win the favour of the father figure of the Emperor, in whom German national unity is manifested. Both show different aspects and values of the German middle classes. Götz is based on the ideal of the autonomous individual, which the middle-class intellectuals claimed as the *leitbild* of the man of the future – despite represented here in the shape of someone from the past. The figure of Weislingen is coloured with the real conditions of middle-class life: he sways between trying to achieve self-realisation through the realisation of a new (old) ideal and dependence on and subordination to the conditions of the court which he serves as tool of action.

In this regard, it is Adelheid who appears as the actual opponent to Götz, for she embodies the prototype of nobility (her name means 'of noble kind'). She fights Götz for possession of the 'German burgher', Weislingen, whom she finally manages to entice onto her side. On the one hand, Adelheid represents a continuation of the traditional role-type of mistress. In this sense, her depravity, unscrupulousness and obsession with court power are deeply criticised. She seduces the 'true citizen', Weislingen, and binds him to the interests of the court solely through her powers of erotic seduction. Like the traditional mistress role (above all, in Lillo's Millwood and Lessing's Marwood), sexual seduction represents merely the first step of a development whose end is marked by death. In this figure, therefore, as in the earlier *bürgerliche Trauerspiel*, court lifestyle is uncompromisingly condemned.

On the other hand, Adelheid shows some signs of similarity to Götz. She tries to win back her land and to defend her 'freedom' (V, 8). Unlike Götz, she does not fight these battles 'single handedly'. She makes use of other 'helping hands' – first by regaining her land through Weislingen, and later, by defending her freedom through Franz, whom Weislingen should poison on her behalf. On both occasions, Adelheid uses her powers of seduction to win someone else as her 'helping hand': in a way, it is almost a question of 'her hand' in exchange for the man who stands at her disposal to serve her as helping 'hand'.

The struggle for freedom and independence is expressed in the male figure, Götz, as the original feeling for life in the autonomous individual. In the female figure, Adelheid, it is turned into the expression of an abnormally powerful woman. Whilst for Götz, eating, drinking and sleeping are described as natural bodily needs, whose satisfaction serves the recovery of vitality, sexuality in Adelheid is seen in a negative way as the instrument of depravity. Because Adelheid is shaped as the representative of court life, the right to develop the personality freely in a woman of her type is denied. The ideal of the autonomous individual seems, thus, to be exclusively a male *leitbild*, which lacks a female counterpart.

The three figures, Götz, Weislingen and Adelheid, are related to one another through the motif of the hand and yet, at the same time, sharply differentiated from one another by it. The motif of the injured hand points to a relation between the individual fate of Götz and the political fate of the empire: both Götz and the empire have a 'crippled body' (III, 20, p. 87). Mutilation appears, in this form, as a sign and stigma of a time of change which situates and is the basis of the failure of the autonomous individual in a historical-social context.

The emperor 'has to catch mice for the estates of the empire while the rats are gnawing away at his possessions' (*Götz*, III, 20, p. 87). The empire is worn down by individual princes who put their own advantage before the collective interest of the empire. The emperor is described as 'old', 'peevish' (IV, 4, p. 101) and 'very ill' (IV, 5, p. 106). He is incapable of preventing the egotistic actions of the princes. Upon his death, the empire will collapse into principalities which are at war with one another for their own advantage and leadership. Götz

describes the moral situation which will then rule in the empire just before he dies: 'Lock up your hearts more carefully than your doors. The times of Betrayal are coming, and to him free rein is given. The base will rule by cunning, and the noble man will fall into their snares' (V, 14, p. 130). The emperor, 'the soul of such a crippled body' which represents the empire, and Götz share 'one and the same fate' (III, 20, p. 87). The death of the emperor and the collapse of the empire thus coincide with the destruction and extinction of the autonomous individual:

GEORG: These are critical times. For a week now there's been a fearful comet visible, and all Germany is in terror that it may mean the death of the Emperor, who is very ill.

GÖTZ: Very ill! Our road is coming to an end.

(IV, 5, p. 106)

The socio-political situation of the empire is, thus, directly related to the mutilation and collapse of the autonomous individual: Götz fails as a whole, freely acting personality not because of reasons within him, but rather because of specific socio-political conditions which do not allow a free unfolding of the individual.

If one examines this situation more closely, it appears identical to that which determined political and social life in the many absolutist principalities of Germany during the final years of the eighteenth century. The times prophesied in *Götz* as a warning of the future are revealed to exist in the present age. And, thus, the call of 'woe' that Goethe gives to Maria, a middle-class, sensitive soul '(Woe to the age that rejected you!') and Lerse, the classless man of action ('Woe to posterity that fails to appreciate you!'), to end the drama, refers to the actual present time, which in some ways, had only just 'discovered' the autonomous individual.

This contradiction is inscribed in the figure of Götz. It is indeed based on the ideal of the middle-class intellectual as a self-determining individual who acts freely. But, at the same time, it undergoes a double explosion. It is first projected into a distant past which appears to be a backward-looking utopia: the ideal can only be realised in a very distant future. On the other hand, in this distant past, the hero is no longer a pure embodiment of the ideal. The mutilation of his hand points far more to damage which socio-political developments and obligations have effected on his nature from which he cannot withdraw. The real situation at the time of writing *Götz von Berlichingen* has such an impact that it leaves its traces even in a figure which should embody fighting spirit and openness, simplicity and independence, according to the declared intention of its creator. 'And now my dear Götz! I rely on his good nature, he will progress and endure' (Goethe to Kestner, August 1773).

The figure of Götz, therefore, appears to be the embodiment of a new *leitbild* of a freely acting, whole individual and, at the same time, as the embodiment of the impossibility of realising it under contemporary political and social conditions. The individual identity has been discovered – but in the real society of eighteenth-century Germany it can only exist at the price of considerable mutilation, which ultimately destroys it.

### The self-castration of creative nature

In *Über Götz von Berlichingen* (*On Götz von Berlichingen*, 1773), Lenz emphasises that 'action, action is the soul of the world, not taking pleasure, not feeling, not splitting hairs, it is only through action that we become God-like, like one who acts eternally and delights himself eternally with his own creations; what we learn from it is that the power of action is our spirit, our greatest gift'. Consequently, he wanted a character drama for the drama of the future in which the hero is 'creator of his own nature' (*Anmerkungen übers Theater* [*Notes on Theatre*]). However, Lenz did not write any such drama, for he believed character drama was only possible in the form of a tragedy. 'In my opinion, the main thought of a comedy should be the *event*, of a tragedy, the *person*.' However, he felt tragedy in this form was

barely possible in his lifetime. Thus, in *Pandaemonium Germanicum* (1775), he answers Lessing's question on modern tragedy:

> O, I may not even look up to those heights. The high tragedy of today, can you not guess? Go back in history, see a rising demi-god ride on the last rung of his greatness or a benevolent god die in disgrace ... Give them all the depths and prophetic wisdom of the Bible which penetrates space and time, give them all the effectiveness, fire and passion of Homer's demi-gods and your heroes shall stand before you in spirit and body. If only I could witness such times!

Instead, Lenz wrote comedies in which

> the characters are there for the sake of events – for the sake of the happy successes, effects, counter-effects, which turn in a circle around one main idea ... for the sake of an unfortunate marriage, a foundling baby, some mad notion of a rare brain (who must remain unknown to us so that we cannot imagine how such a character could have come up with this notion, idea, or even this whole plot; we do not demand to know everything about him.
>
> (*Anmerkungen übers Theater*)

In *Hofmeister* (*The Tutor*), Lenz draws on the form of the *bürgerliche Trauerspiel* and converts it into a grotesque comedy.[23] Whilst members of the middle classes rose for the first time to the level of tragic heroes in the *bürgerliche Trauerspiel*, the nobility in Lenz's comedy sink to the level of comic figures. Lessing put the middle-class citizen on the same level as the nobility in that he declared both equally capable of tragedy; Lenz cancels out the differences between them and offers them both up to ridicule.

From the *bürgerliche Trauerspiel*, Lenz adopted not only the problematic of the family, but also that of seduction, and changes both in a very specific way. The families he introduces to the stage in *The Tutor* all find themselves, without exception, in a condition of greater or lesser decay and dissolution.

The Major's 'noble' family is ruled by his wife, a 'vain patroness' (I, 2, p. 138), whose puffed-up self-importance and heartlessness cannot be surpassed. Both her husband and her daughter suffer from her rages (II, 1). She persecutes Gustchen ('here in isolation subject to a barbaric mother' [II, 5, pp. 157–8]) and treats her husband with scorn and contempt. She even discloses intimacies about her husband to Graf Wermuth ('You are already acquainted with my husband's ridiculous side' [II, 6, p. 169]).

The Major is all too aware of the deep rift in the patriarchal order of the family: 'My wife makes me miserable. She always has to have the upper hand, and she can because she's cleverer and more cunning than me' (I, 4, p. 143). But he is unable to stand up for himself and thus can only 'follow the line' which his wife 'has laid down' (I, 2, p. 138). Even when he triumphs over the tutor, '*I* am the master in this house' (I, 4, p. 143), it barely covers up the fact that he is a weak and, therefore, laughable patriarch and she is a domineering, vain matriarch.

The relationship between the Major and Gustchen seems, at first, to reproduce the father–daughter relationship of the *bürgerliche Trauerspiel*. He calls Gustchen 'my only consolation' (I, 4, p. 142), and explains to his brother, 'You know how I've made the girl my idol. And now I must watch while she's wasting away and dying under my care. – [*weeps*] Brother, Privy Councillor, you have no daughter. You can't know the feelings of a father with a daughter' (III, 1, p. 164). For her part, Gustchen loves her father so tenderly that after her fall and ensuing escape from her father's house, it is only the thought of her father which upsets her: 'My conscience is driving me to leave here. I have a father who loves me more than his life and soul. In a dream last night, I saw him, with bloodshot eyes, tearing out his white hair. He must think I'm dead' (IV, 2, p. 175). None the less, before her escape, she felt rejected by the family: 'Nobody asks after me; nobody cares about me; none of my family can abide me any

longer; not even my father. I don't know why' (II, 5, p. 158). The dissolution of the family is long complete and, thus, it is merely a natural consequence that the Major declares, 'I'll leave my wife and die in Turkey … There is no family; we have no family. Poppycock! The Russians are my family. I'll become a Russian Orthodox' (IV, 1, p. 173).

The situation in the middle-class Pätus family is no less chaotic. Old Pätus has already twice deeply offended the system of family values. Greedy for money, he has chased his blind mother out of the house and treated his good-hearted son with cruelty and meanness. No longer a member of a humane order, he has become a 'tiger' (V, 12, p. 201) as he acknowledges after his conversion, 'My son, embrace again your father who, for a while, cast off his humanity and degenerated into a wild animal' (V, 12, p. 203).

Even if the upset to the family order does not seem so severe in other cases in the play, they are none the less significant enough. Thus, Pastor Läuffer does not want to give out the money which his son needs to become a civil servant ('My father says: I'm not suitable to be a lecturer. But I believe the fault lies in his purse' [I, 1, p. 137]), and he must suffer the criticisms of the Privy Councillor, 'You want to be a good father to your child and yet you close your eyes, your ears, and mouth when his happiness is at stake?' (II, 1, p. 147).

Musikus Rehaar has so little courage that he does not dare revenge himself for the honour of his daughter. For 'a musician must be devoid of courage, and … a musician with a heart who draws his sword is a scoundrel who will never accomplish anything on any instrument' (IV, 6, p. 181). He is not in a position to undertake the patriarchal function of vigilance so that the virtue of his daughter is better protected by an old aunt than by her father (V, 7).

Even the Privy Councillor, who at the start seems to have an ideal father and son relationship with Fritz, in which care and strictness are well balanced (I, 6), allows himself to be stirred up by slander and intrigue against his son and temporarily withdraws paternal care and help:

there is not one single true model father-figure in the sense of the *bürgerliche Trauerspiel*, not one intact family in this comedy.

Even the *Sturm und Drang* movement saw the family as a natural system of interpersonal communal life. The total collapse of the family in *The Tutor* thus points to a social condition which diverged from the naturally given system of interpersonal communal life in a shocking way and transformed its members into 'beasts' (II, 3), into 'wolves in sheep's clothing' (V, 10). Neither the aristocratic nor the middle-class family could provide asylum for developing 'human nature' (V, 12). In this respect, there is no difference between the nobility and the bourgeoisie, the critique falls equally bitingly upon them both.

A marked difference is revealed however, in terms of the real social consequences which result from this unnaturalness. Whilst it in no way touches upon, let alone questions, the supremacy of the nobility, it can bring social demotion for the middle classes in its trail. If the Rehaar daughter's maiden virtue and honour are not successfully protected, she is in danger of losing her good name and being cast out from middle-class society. When Pätus receives no more money from his father to repay his creditors, he must 'rot in jail' (II, 7), unless his friend Fritz will vouch for him.

Since Pastor Läuffer does not want to spare money for a civil servant, his son must become a tutor. The Privy Councillor tries to make clear to him how degrading this position is:

Let the lad learn something which might be of use to the state. Hell's teeth, pastor, you surely didn't bring him up to be a servant, but what else is he but a servant when he'd sell his freedom as an individual for a handful of ducats? He's a slave over whom his masters have unlimited power. Only he has learned enough at the academy to be able to anticipate their capricious demands, and thereby to apply a fine veneer to his servitude. What a nice, polite fellow, an incomparable fellow; what an incomparable scoundrel.

(II, 1, p. 148)

While the decay of the family remains without consequence for the nobility, it endangers the good name of the middle-class daughter and robs the middle-class son of his freedom. The loss of freedom in middle-class life appears, thus, not only as a general human problem or an individual problem, but rather a social one which solely affects the middle-class individual.

Lenz also upsets the motif of seduction in *The Tutor*, where the seducer is middle class and the victim daughter comes from the aristocratic family. The seduction cannot be justified from the seducer's point of view as the noble right of disposal over middle-class females, nor from the point of view of the seduced as the desire for social elevation through possible eventual marriage. Equally little is it motivated by love. Gustchen only loves her 'Romeo', Fritz (I, 5), to whom her words and loving gestures are aimed when she is together with Läuffer:

GUSTCHEN: [*Taking his hand*] ... O Romeo! If this were but your hand – And yet you leave me, ignoble Romeo! See you not your Juliet dies for you – by all the world, her family too, hated, despised, cast out. [*Presses his hand to her eyes*] Oh, inhuman Romeo! ...

You have forgotten me ... Perhaps you were concerned for me. – Yes, yes, your tender heart could see that which threatened me was worse than that I suffer now. [*Ardently kissing Läuffer's hand*] Oh, divine Romeo!

(II, 5, p. 158)

For Gustchen, Läuffer simply represents a body which stands as a substitute through which she can satisfy her tender desires towards the absent 'Romeo', Fritz.

In turn, Läuffer does not love Gustchen either, and is as little interested in her as a person, as she is in him. When they are together, he is exclusively occupied with his situation and his problems ('I'll have to resign' [II, 5, p. 157]). On hearing the name 'Julie', he does not think, as Gustchen does, of 'Romeo and Juliet', but of 'Abelard and Heloise', a love story which surpasses all class boundaries and which ends in the emasculation of the middle-class seducer, ('What happened to Abelard could happen to me too' [II, 5, p. 158]). For Läuffer, Gustchen's only special appeal is that she is, at present, the only approachable female. Since he was refused the carrot which was promised him, 'I was promised a horse, so I could visit Königsberg every three months' (II, 1, p. 151), he is forced to do without the acquaintance of other females. On neither side does the seduction have anything to do with love. It 'happens' far more as an outpouring of long suppressed sexual instincts. In this, it seems at first to be the result of the human sexual urge in general – that is, in both middle and noble classes – which demands satisfaction. Such urges are not seen as the unnatural product of a libertine sexual moral, as was believed typical of court lifestyle, but rather as an inalienable element of human nature, whose demands even the middle classes cannot deny. The moral supremacy of the citizen claimed by the *bürgerliche Trauerspiel* ultimately proves to be mere self-deception: everyone is subject to their sensual nature.

Although no difference exists between nobility and the middle class in this respect, the real social consequences which result from such natural sexual urges are considerably different. It is of no social significance if members of the aristocracy satisfy their sexual drive. Thus, after the 'seduction' is discovered, Gustchen has no need to leave her parents' home: 'If only you'd told me about all this before, I could have bought the lout a title. Then you could have crept off together' (IV, 5, p. 179). In aristocratic society, the satisfaction of the sexual drive remains entirely without consequence.

The situation is very different for the middle classes, however. In its critique of *The Tutor*, the *Göttinger Gelehrten Anzeigen* (*Göttingen Learned Advertiser*) asked which other occupation Lenz proposed for young middle-class intellectuals if tutelage was done away with. Lenz, who was himself temporarily occupied as tutor in Königsberg, replied in the *Frankfurter Gelehrten Anzeigen* (*Frankfurt Learned Advertiser*) in 16 June 1775: 'As my conviction, or prejudice against this profession increased, I gave it up and dragged freedom back into my arms.' Simply the position of tutor in itself, which was widespread among middle-class intellectuals of the time, already implied the rape of man's physical nature. Here the Privy Councillor explains:

> Spending the noblest hours in the day sitting with a young gentleman, who has no desire to learn but with whom he may not fall out. And the hours that remain, which should be kept sacred to eating and sleeping – to the preservation of life – he sighs away like a chained slave … eating when he's full, and fasting when he's hungry, drinking punch when he'd like to piss, and playing cards when his luck's out. Without freedom a man's life deteriorates sharply. Freedom is Man's element, as water is for fish, and a man who surrenders his freedom poisons the noblest spirit in his blood, nips the sweetest joy in life in the bud, and destroys himself.
>
> (II, 1, p. 147)

As in *Götz*, physical intactness or wholeness, and freedom are two mutually interdependent elements of human nature. The tutor's profession obliges both to be given up and thereby represents a brutal attack on human nature.

The village school teacher, Wenzeslaus, on the other hand, has been able to maintain his freedom, 'I am after all my own master and will have no one accuse me of shirking' (III, 4, p. 170). He can eat and drink when he wants ('my diet' [III, 4]) and is careful of his health and bodily intactness or wholeness. He is concerned when Läuffer wants to drink water when he is overheated ('Are you aware, Herr Almond, that a glass of water is as detrimental to your health after violent emotion as after violent physical exercise?' [III, 2, p. 166]) and quite beside himself when Läuffer picks his teeth: 'But … but … but … [*wrenches the toothpick out of his mouth*] What's this then? Hasn't the great man acquired enough knowledge to care for his own body? Picking your teeth is suicide, yes, suicide, a wanton destruction of Jerusalem carried out on your teeth' (III, 4, pp. 171–2).

On the other hand, his low income restricts him in certain ways, 'I haven't yet presumed to think about a wife, for I know I couldn't support one' (III, 2, p. 167). It forces him to split his sensual nature. Whilst he can eat and drink as much as he wants within the limits of his financial powers ('I've grown thick and fat thereby' [III, 4, p. 170), he has to suppress his sexual drive as 'evil urges' through 'diet', 'cold water' and the pipe: 'tobacco is also said to contain a narcotic, sleep-inducing, stupefying oil ... but the persistent fogs we have in these parts in addition to the continual dampness in the air in autumn and winter, and the marvellous effect I feel from it, while it simultaneously lulls to sleep those evil urges' (III, 4, p. 171).

Since Wenzeslaus does not perceive that simply his position as village school teacher – and that means the conditions of his middle-class existence – makes the suppression of his sexual drive necessary, he transforms it into something devilish in the middle-class tradition of Enlightenment, as an 'evil desire' whose control he declares to be a moral act. And it is this which leads to his paradoxical behaviour. On one hand, he damns Läuffer for picking his teeth, 'a wanton destruction of Jerusalem', and, on the other hand, praises his self-emasculation as the 'heroic resolve' of a 'second Origen' (V, 3, p. 186) in admiration and delight. Sexuality in middle-class life has no place outside marriage. It prevents the citizen from carrying out a profession and destroys any possibility of social elevation. The middle-class citizen may only secure an existence if he can suppress his sexual drive. The human sexual urge remains, thus, for him, of vital social consequence.

In this sense, Läuffer's self-castration represents the climax and, in a way, the final act in a chain of violent acts of aggression which the citizen is forced to inflict (or allows to be inflicted) on his own nature if he wants to secure an existence in society. His social position makes it not only impossible for him to develop his nature freely, it even obliges him to

deform it, so that he will fit into the 'niche' which society has created for him. The deformation of creative nature appears, thus, to be a symbolic act ingrained in the condition of middle-class life. The individual is only fit to be a member of absolutist-bourgeois society if he destroys his own human nature unrecognisably. His urges must be suppressed, he must give up his freedom, lose his creativity and renounce his claim to a free, self-determined profession. He must stop wanting to be a person and instead bow down and castrate himself, becoming a well-oiled cog. Middle-class life, as Lenz wrote at the beginning of his article, *Über Götz von Berlichingen*, seems to follow this pre-determined pattern:

We are born – our parents give us bread and clothing – our teachers drill us with words, language, knowledge – some lovely girl awakes in our hearts the desire to possess her, to hold her in our arms as our own, if our animal needs do not intervene – and a space is made in the Republic for us to fit in – our friends, relations, benefactors get going and push us happily into it – we turn around a while in this place like other cogs in the machine, and push and drive – until we are so blunted, however systematically it happens, that finally we have to give way to a new cog – that is, Gentlemen! without boasting, a report of our lives – and what is left to man other than being a little model artificial machine, which fits, for better or worse, into the great machine, which we call the world, world events, or ways of the world.

The free unfolding of human nature in its totality, which is founded both on the reproduction of life as well as on freedom of action, is closed to the bourgeois individual. The ideal of the autonomous, freely acting personality stands diametrically opposed to the real conditions of middle-class existence – which functionalises and reifies. Whilst the nobility's blind, puffed-up self-importance follows a lifestyle which runs contrary to nature and, thus, willingly gives up the right to self-realisation as a person – in the sense of an autonomous individual – the middle-class man is denied this right because of his social situation, which forces him to deceive himself and others and mutilate his own human nature. Being a middle-class citizen means being prevented from being a person.

There seem to be worlds between *Emilia Galotti* and *The Tutor* which are, however, only separated by a mere two years. Odoardo kills his daughter in the knowledge that he is sacrificing her life for a higher worth – virtue. In this act he proves a moral greatness which points an accusing finger at absolutism which obstructs, and is ready to destroy, the realisation of middle-class values. The tutor, on the other hand, does not castrate himself for the sake of a moral goal or value – even if Wenzeslaus interprets it in this way when he praises him as a 'pillar of our sinking church' (V, 10, p. 198) – but simply in order that his sexual drive no longer hinders him from setting up a middle-class existence ('Perhaps I may start my life anew and be reborn as Wenzeslaus' [IV, 3, p. 188]). The middle-class citizen is no better than the noble, let alone morally superior to him; he must however, exist under the considerably worse conditions of the need to earn his daily bread and the dependence which results from this. Läuffer's self-castration does not throw the light of transfiguration on the citizen but points, critically, to the whole social situation which denies him the chance of self-realisation.

It is hardly conceivable that an audience which identified with the figures of the *bürgerliche Trauerspiel* could see themselves reflected in Lenz's middle-class figures, too. It is, therefore, not surprising that after a positive, almost effusive reception by the literary critics ('I could never get over the belief that a German could ever successfully compete with Shakespeare, but *Götz von Berlichingen* and now *The Tutor* have persuaded me otherwise' – Johann Georg Scherff, 29 September 1774 to Friedrich Justus Bertuch), *The Tutor* was none the less rejected by the majority of the audience. Friedrich Ludwig Schröder gave the première in 1778 in Hamburg and, although he took the role of the Major himself, and was greatly successful in it, he was not able to win the audience over to his favourite play, either at the première or at later performances in Hamburg, Berlin and Vienna. The audience which shed such tears at the fates of the fathers and daughters of the *bürgerliche Trauerspiel* were certainly 'amazed' and 'horrified',[24] but firmly refused to see themselves reflected in the broken image of Lenz's figures.

Friedrich Schröder was the only theatre director who consistently worked towards putting on works by the new *Sturm und Drang* movement. Although he produced nearly all the movement's most important plays in Hamburg, he only found mediocre success. The audience could not warm to the figures of Julius (in Leisewitz's *Julius von Tarent*, 1776), Guelfo (in Klinger's *Die Zwillinge* [*The Twins*], 1776) or Götz. Even the performance of *Götz von Berlichingen*, which Schröder gave in 1774, shortly after the première by the Koch troupe in Berlin (17 April 1774), was a financial disaster. Although the audience was moved, they let themselves believe that it was an unpolished experiment and did not attend further performances. Whilst *Götz von Berlichingen* found extraordinary success with the élite reading audience, and thus helped the *Sturm und Drang* movement towards its breakthrough, the new type of freely acting, autonomous individual seemed to remain foreign to the general public.

This was also evident in the reception of Shakespeare. Between 1776 and 1780, Schröder produced *Hamlet*, *Othello*, *Macbeth*, *King Lear*, *Richard II*, *Henry IV*, *The Merchant of Venice* and *Measure for Measure*. He based these productions on the prose translations by Christoph Martin Wieland (1762–6) and Johann Joachim Eschenburg (1775–7), which he also thoroughly reworked. Whilst his production of *Hamlet* was a sweeping success, the audience was deeply shocked by *Othello*. 'Faint followed faint … the doors of the boxes fell open and shut, they either left or if necessary were carried out and, according to eye witness accounts, the unfortunate miscarriage of this or that well-known Hamburg lady was the result of seeing and hearing this dreadful tragedy.'[25] The productions which followed *Othello* – *The Merchant of Venice*, *King Lear* and *Measure for*

*Measure* – were keenly received. The price which Schröder had to pay for even daring to present Shakespeare to the middle-class public was high. His adaptations did not just entail cuts – whole acts were cut completely and replaced by short, recounted summaries – but he also falsified the plays considerably. The plays generally had to end happily. Thus, it was not only out of the question that Hamlet, Laertes, Othello, Desdemona, Cordelia or Lear should die; they must also participate in a general reconciliation at the end. Neither the German audience nor the English audience of the era could have tolerated the 'true' Shakespeare. Goethe's judgement, from his speech *Shakespeare A Tribute*, seems to represent accurately the attitudes of his contemporaries: 'And how can our century dare judge Nature? How should we know nature, we who from childhood have felt in ourselves and seen in others nothing but restraint and artificiality? ... He guides us through the entire world, yet we pampered novices cry out at the sight of a grasshopper, "Master, it's going to eat us alive!".'[26]

The new *leitbild* of the middle-class intellectuals was not accepted by the broad middle-class audience. The critique of civilisation and the social situation implied by the ideal of a freely acting personality and its grotesque-realistic counterpart of the citizen deformed and turned into a marionette, remained largely without echo. The majority of the middle-class audience clearly approved of the opportunity of social elevation created by the continuing process of civilisation. The demand it made to suppress the sexual drive was already so widely internalised as a moral maxim that its fulfilment was judged to be a moral quality for which the bourgeoisie was to be given special credit.

## SYMBOL OF THE SPECIES

### From fragment to whole

The contradiction between the ideal *leitbild* and real social relations articulated both implicitly

and explicitly by the *Sturm und Drang* movement was also fundamental to the age of German classical drama. Thus, the demand initiated by Goethe and Schiller, that every man should have the right to develop his personality in freedom, continued to be of vital importance. At the same time, insights into the condition of the ruling social order became more perceptive. It was soon realised that the achievement of the ideal was far beyond the reach of the ordinary citizen. In Goethe's *Wilhelm Meisters Lehrjahren* (*Wilhelm Meister's Apprenticeship*, 1795–6), Wilhelm Meister echoes Goethe's own ideas, to a large extent, in analysing the real conditions of contemporary society thus:

> To speak it in a word; the cultivation of my individual self, here as I am, has from my youth upwards been constantly though dimly my wish and my purpose ... but in Germany, a universal, and if I may say so, personal cultivation is beyond the reach of any one except a nobleman. A burgher may acquire merit; by excessive efforts he may even educate his mind; but his personal qualities are lost, or worse than lost, let him struggle as he will. ...
>
> If the nobleman, merely by his personal carriage, offers all that can be asked of him, the burgher by his personal carriage offers nothing, and can offer nothing. ... The former does and makes, the latter but effects and procures; he must cultivate some single gifts in order to be useful, and it is beforehand settled, that in his manner of existence there is no harmony, and can be none, since he is bound to make himself of use in one department, and so has to relinquish all the others.
>
> Perhaps the reason of this difference is not the usurpation of the nobles, and the submission of the burghers, but the constitution of society itself.
>
> (Fifth Book, Chapter 3, pp. 243–4)[27]

Thus the problem is seen to be a basic social issue. The real social situation is biased in favour of the nobleman; it automatically affords him the opportunity of cultivating his personality freely, even if he does not actually make use of this opportunity. Goethe differentiates very carefully between the generally given potential to cultivate the personality as a whole and the use made of it by actual representatives of the nobility; if such men of advantage do not bother about the cultivation of personality, they fall victim to his biting scorn. Thus in 'Confessions of a Fair Saint' in *Wilhelm Meister* it states: 'The people I lived among had not the slightest tinge of literature or science: they were German courtiers; a class of men at that time altogether destitute of culture.'[28] Whilst the nobleman had only himself to blame if he neglected the all-round development of his character, the ordinary citizen was denied the opportunity of doing so altogether because of his low social position and function. Goethe addressed the question as to how the citizen could be put in a position where he could fulfil the ideal concept of man (as a freely cultivated personality).

Schiller viewed the problem not only in terms of the class society in Germany at the time, but also within the more embracing context of world history, in the rapidly growing process of civilisation. Before the 'artificial condition called culture' began, he believed there was no opposition between the demand for the free development of the individual and the real condition of society.

As long as man is pure – not, of course, crude – nature, he functions as an undivided sensuous unity and as a unifying whole. Sense and reason, passive and active faculties, are not separated in their activities, still less do they stand in conflict with one another. His perceptions are not the formless play of chance, his thoughts not the empty play of the faculty of representation; the former proceed out of the law of *necessity*, the latter out of *actuality*.[29]

The age of which he speaks is one where Greek culture was formed. It was an age in which man is found, 'raising his individuality to the level of the race' (*On the Aesthetic Education of Man*, 2nd letter, 1795, p. 26)[30] and, 'in which Man in time can be made to coincide with Man in idea' (4th letter, pp. 31–2). The advancing process of civilisation made the

'stricter classification of the classes and society necessary' and

split up human nature ... That zoophyte character of the Greek States, where every individual enjoyed an independent life and, when need arose, could become a whole in himself, now gave place to an ingenious piece of machinery, in which out of the botching together of a vast number of lifeless parts a collective mechanical life results. State and Church, law and customs, were now torn asunder; enjoyment was separated from labour, means from ends, effort from reward. Eternally chained to only one single little fragment of the whole, Man himself grew to be only a fragment; with the monotonous noise of the wheel he drives everlastingly in his ears, he never develops the harmony of his being, and instead of imprinting humanity upon his nature he becomes merely the imprint of his occupation, of his science.

(6th letter, p. 40)

According to Schiller's three-stage model of history, this process does not lack a certain historical necessity, if man is to develop as a whole being. Even the Greeks could not maintain the level they reached, 'and if they wanted to advance to a higher state of development they were, like ourselves, obliged to surrender the wholeness of their being and pursue truth along separate roads' (6th letter, p. 43). The fragmentary education of modern man can be seen, in this respect, as the inevitable result of the process of civilisation which drives man forward to unfold all the potential within him. By the end of the eighteenth century, however, this process was so developed that the mental trauma to which it exposed the individual became intolerable; man is no longer prepared to tolerate that which he once accepted as inevitable fate, 'men have awoken from their long lethargy and self-deception, and by an impressive majority they are demanding the restitution of their inalienable rights' (5th letter, p. 34). Schiller saw his age as a period of change in which the goal of all human effort must be to win back the right of every individual to cultivate the personality freely.

But can Man really be destined to neglect himself for any end whatever? Should Nature be able, by her designs, to rob us of a completeness which reason prescribes to us be hers? It must be false that the cultivation of individual powers necessitates the sacrifice of their totality; or however much the law of nature did have that tendency, we must be at liberty to restore by means of a higher Art this wholeness in our nature which Art has destroyed.

(6th letter, pp. 44–5)

What is this higher Art which should be in a position to realise the ideal of the total man and even to defeat society which is so set against him? A political solution, in the sense of a change in society, is considered by both Goethe and Schiller to be out of the question. Thus, Wilhelm Meister continues: 'whether it will ever alter, and how, is to me of small importance: my present business is to meet my own case, as matters actually stand; to consider by what means I may save myself and reach the object which I cannot live in peace without' (Book 5, Chapter III, p. 244). Wilhelm strives to find an individual solution which is tailored to his own individual needs without intending to influence directly the real social situation.

This solution cannot satisfy Schiller. It was all too clear to him that the basic possibility of the free development of the personality would not be possible without a new political order. It is only when the state allows man to develop himself in an all-round way that he will be in a position to fulfil this need: 'Because the state is to be an organization which is formed by itself and for itself, it can really become such only insofar as the parts have been severally attuned to the idea of the whole' (4th letter, p. 33). There is, therefore, an interdependence between individual or personal freedom and political freedom, which raises the question of priority. Schiller answers it in favour of the individual: 'I hope to convince you … that we must indeed, if we are to solve that political problem in practice, follow the path of aesthetics, since it is through Beauty that we arrive at Freedom' (2nd letter, p. 26).

Thus, it is aesthetic education, and not revolution, that creates the conditions which would allow every citizen the potential of cultivating his personality freely. In this, the theatre (as art in general) is given a wholly new function: it should recover the totality, or wholeness, once lost in historical-social reality, for each and every citizen, that is, mankind in general.

## The ideal society of autonomous individuals

Goethe's *Iphigenie auf Tauris* (*Iphigenia in Tauris*, final version 1787) proceeds from the real relations of power in the family and society which deny and withhold the individual his right to autonomy. Unlike *Götz von Berlichingen* or Lenz's *The Tutor*, it is not presented through an example from history or social reality, but in the form of Greek mythology. Against the background of discussion on the exemplary nature of Greek art which was carried out with intense passion in Germany in the second half of the century (in part as continuation of the much earlier 'querelle des anciens et des modernes' in France), this choice of material takes on an almost programmatic character. This is because figures from Greek mythology (for example, from Euripides) presented the reader or spectator of the time not with real people who lived in a past or present age, but with ideal figures from a mythical, early age in which history and culture originate, an age in which, it was widely believed, the individual could still actualise the ideal concept of man.

The history of the house of Tantalus symbolises the total distortion of interpersonal relations in the family. Since the members of the house of Tantalus are driven by selfish passions and urges – 'desires', 'jealousy', 'hate' (I, 3 p. 92), 'rage and vengeance' (I, 3, p. 93), 'evil passion' (II, 2, p. 107) – the 'first deed' (I, 3, p. 92) of fratricide defines their relations with one another.[31] This results, in turn, in Thyestes' 'plotting evil', Atreus' 'unexampled deed' (p. 93), Agamemnon's 'grave deed' (II, 2, p. 107), Clytemnestra's 'wicked act' (III, 1, p. 111), and the 'deed' by Orestes 'that I would gladly / Leave hidden in the dull and soundless realms of night' (III, 1, p. 110). In this family, interpersonal relations are ruled by 'deeds' which degrade the other into an object of the own desires and actions, and which generally lead to his physical destruction.

On the one hand, the 'deed' unlike that in *Götz*, takes on an unmistakably negative meaning. It does not arise as the result of an act of free self-determination, but as the expression of brutal violence, driven by passion, which robs others of their autonomy. On the other hand, it explicitly shows that the natural order of the family is deeply disturbed. The unnaturalness of this situation is emphasised even more when the relationship between 'near relations' is described as the result and manifestation of a 'curse' by which the gods pursue the members of the house of Tantalus.

The distortion of public relations is represented both in the image of the state of Scythia and in the way in which the Scythians and the Greeks react to strangers. The Scythian state is an authoritarian state. As King, Thoas is used 'to orders and to action' (I, 2, p. 87); his subjects are bound to 'obey in silence' (I, 2, p. 86). Whilst the king acts through 'words', 'A word / From you and it will be in flames' (V, 5, p. 139), his subjects, the Scythians, must carry out acts which are merely the execution of his orders, and thus which only manifest their dependence and lack of freedom.

Before Iphigenia's arrival in Scythia and after her refusal to marry Thoas, foreigners were sacrificed on the altar to Diana: 'No stranger pays our shore a happy visit; / In past he always faced a certain death' (I, 3, p. 96). Foreigners are not only denied their right to self-determination, but even physical existence. The Greeks, on the other hand, meet foreigners if not with the 'sword' (V, 2, p. 134) then with 'cunning' and 'stratagems' (III, 1, p. 112). These are put to use in 'artful' words (IV, 4, p. 126; V, 3, p. 137) and 'false words' (III, 1, p. 112) which turn others into objects of their own actions and allows them to be manipulated to their disadvantage.

The specific use of 'word' and 'deed' by the Greeks and Scythians seems, thus, to indicate the total distortion of relationships in the family and society. In the course of the play, these private and public power-dominated relationships are transformed through Iphigenia's mediation and initiative into forms of equal communication. Orestes' healing crystallises this process (in terms of family relationships); Iphigenia's return home does the same for social relationships.

Madness, which is a result of his 'deed', the matricide, has made Orestes strange to himself. He allows Pylades to plan their rescue. Yet, on his first meeting with Iphigenia, he feels 'constrained' by her 'sweet lips' (III, 1, p. 110) to give up the strategy of 'deceiving' and 'artful words' which Pylades used to win the foreign priestess over for his plans (robbing the image of the God and returning to Delphi).

> I can't endure that someone of great soul,
> Like you, should be misguided by false words.
> A web of lies is fit to be the snare
> That strangers set before the feet of strangers,
> Cunning and used to stratagems. Between us
> Let there be truth!
> I am Orestes!
>
> (III, 1, p. 112)

In exchanging the 'false word' for the 'truth', Orestes cancels out the distorted relations to the foreign priestess caused by Pylades. Although he does not know it, at the same time he also creates a condition for the 'weighty deeds' which stand for the perverted relationships among members of the house of Tantalus, to be changed into peaceful communication. Iphigenia greets the brother she now recognises with 'a friendly word' (III, 1, p. 113), 'the innocent sister's word of blessing' (III, 1, p. 114), which she explicitly opposes to the 'weighty deed' of matricide which caused his madness.

> Oh, if the voice of mother's blood once shed,
> Can call in somber tones, far down to hell,
> Shall not an innocent sister's word of blessing
> Call, from Olympus, gods of help and rescue?
>
> (III, 1, p. 114)

Iphigenia and Orestes change the structure of human relationships in two important ways: the 'false word' is replaced by 'truth', the 'weighty deed' by 'the friendly word'. After this condition of communication is accepted by the whole house, Orestes is healed: his heart is 'liberated' (IV, 4, p. 125) and he is restored to his own self.

This process occurs through the healing sleep into which Orestes falls after the revelation scene with Iphigenia. As in a vision, he feels transported to the underworld amongst his ancestors:

Thyestes strolling,
Immersed in friendly talk with Atreus; 'round
   them
All their boys, running back and forth ...

I honor you, Atreus; you too, Thyestes;
All of us here are freed of hostility. ...

Is it you, Father?
And Mother, walking with you in friendship?
If Clytemnestra may give you her hand,
Orestes then may go to her, too,
And say to her: Here is your son!
The son of both of you! Offer him welcome!
On earth, in our house, a salutation
Served always as the password to murder. ...

You bid me welcome and you accept me.
                              (III, 2, pp. 117–18)

As Orestes' dream shows, the relations between members of the house of Tantalus have fundamentally changed: in place of the 'password to murder' are greetings of welcome and the handshake, in place of the 'wicked act' as manifestation of 'hostility', men are 'immersed in friendly talk' as a sign of 'peaceful' and 'trusting' communal life. Human relationships, once so perverted, are transformed into authentic communication, in which the autonomy of the individuals concerned is taken for granted and respected. The natural order is restored within the family – the curse annulled.

Just as the family relationships of violence are cancelled in the relationship between Iphigenia and Orestes, so the social relations of power undergo a qualitative change in the relationship between Iphigenia and Thoas. Even before the drama begins, Iphigenia has modified the authoritarian structure of leadership in the state of Scythia:

Does not each person feel his lot improved
Now that the King, who for so long has led us,
Wise and bravely, finds his pleasure too
In the grace of your presence, lightening
For us the duty to obey in silence?
                              (I, 2, p. 86)

She was also able to influence Thoas to abolish the sacrifice of foreigners and thus 'in death's inhospitable shore secure / The stranger's safety and his voyage home' (I, 2, p. 87). Although Iphigenia succeeds in modifying the violence perpetrated on subjects and foreigners in Scythia, she still feels at the mercy of Thoas' power.

So Thoas keeps me here, a noble man,
In solemn, holy bonds – of slavery.
                              (I, 1, p. 84)

The right to self-determination or to cultivate her personal qualities freely is denied her. It is only in the 'fatherland' (I, 1, p. 84) among 'those I love' (I, 1, p. 83) and 'my own people' (I, 1, p. 84), that she feels she can realise herself. She needs a society open to communication which is founded on 'love' (III, 1, p. 114), trust and 'words' (IV, 3, p. 127):

How precious is the presence of a friend,
His words of certainty, whose heavenly power
The lonely person lacks and, lacking, sinks
   back
Listless. Locked in the heart, thoughts and
   decisions
Ripen slowly; having someone near,
Who cares, will bring them swiftly to fruition.
                              (IV, 3, p. 127)

Thoas and the citizens of Scythia, on the other hand, remain foreign to Iphigenia: 'But I am still what I was then: a stranger' (I, 1, p. 83).

She is forced to lead 'a lonely life' (I, 1, p. 83) which seems to her nothing more than a 'second death' (I, 1 p. 84) because it denies her right to self-realisation. Only the return home can secure Iphigenia's right to self-determination and the free cultivation of her personality.

In this sense, Thoas' promise effects a basic change in his relationship with Iphigenia:

If hope of going home exists for you,
Then I'll declare you free of all demands.
But if it be your way is blocked forever,
If your line is banished, or by some
Calamitous blow of evil blotted out,
Then you are mine – and by more laws than
  one.
Speak frankly, and you know I'll keep my
  word.

(I, 3, p. 91)

With this promise, Thoas admits at least the possibility of a return home. At the same time, he sets a condition on her return which does not lie within his power, but which is dependent on circumstances which exist outside his influence. Finally, and most important, his promise transforms the hierarchical relationship between himself and Iphigenia into one of equality: the future of both depends on the conditions he sets in the promise. In making the promise, the one who holds power has willingly renounced part of that power. The promise prevents him from acting on the basis of a whim or desire, if the promise was indeed made in earnest. Thoas has restricted his actions to the situation when and if the conditions laid down by him occur.

However, after Iphigenia turns down his offer of marriage (since to accept would mean giving up her right to self-realisation), Thoas revokes the equal relationship between two autonomous subjects and returns to the hierarchical, functional relationship between 'priestess' and 'prince' (I, 3, p. 96). Their relationship again appears as one of power which is now extended over other foreigners, too. Thoas orders Iphigenia to sacrifice the two foreigners, Orestes and Pylades. In the same way that members of the house of Tantalus are driven

by their desires and passions, he is driven to apply force.

Iphigenia's identity is not threatened by the external power of royal command alone but also by Pylades' powers of persuasion. Although she rejects deception and cunning ('The pure in heart will neither need nor use it' [V, 2, p. 134]), she allows Pylades to persuade her to manipulate the 'foreign' Scythians using the Greek strategy of 'artful words' (IV, 4, p. 126). She tells Arcas a tall story in order to steal the idol and rescue her 'loved ones'. She does not treat Arcas as a 'person' but as an instrument whom she seeks to manipulate to carry out her wishes in a specific way. The urgency of the situation seems to force even Iphigenia to renounce herself: if she refuses to use 'cunning' she endangers the rescue of her brother and his friend and her own long yearned-for return home. If she deceives the Scythians, she will relinquish being 'a pure soul' forever.

She is protected from this internal split by Arcas' words. He reminds her, 'that I leave human beings' (IV, 3, p. 124). And, thus, she rejects the strategy of the 'false word' and seeks a solution which secures autonomy for all those concerned.

Who has the right to unexampled action?
Men alone? They clutch the impossible
To great heroic hearts. Only they? ...

Now my heart
Rises and falls with a bold undertaking.
I shall not escape severe reproach,
Nor deep misfortune either, should I fail.
Still I leave it in your hands, and if
You truly are as you are praised, then show it,
Gods by your support, and glorify
Through me the truth. Yes, Sire, hear what I
  say:
A secret chain of guile is being forged.

(V, 3, pp. 135–6)

Iphigenia's 'unexampled deed' is the speaking out of a word which exposes the 'truth' to others. This 'deed' stands in opposition both to the 'false word', which manipulates others, and, also, to the 'weighty deed', which uses physical violence against others. This marks a climax in the process of change to the concept of 'deed' since *Götz von Berlichingen*; the exemplary 'deed' which allows all individuals their right to self-determination is actually a word or words which reveal the truth. The physical act has been changed into a pure speech-act which, in its turn, is able to symbolise the physical act (by annulling it, keeping it and raising it into a symbolic act). The speech-act has replaced the physical act.

In carrying out this 'unexampled deed', Iphigenia creates the condition on which the right to self-determination need not be restricted to anyone. For, with her 'true word' she tells Thoas that the conditions on which he made his promise to release her have occurred. Her 'word', the 'truth', obliges Thoas to transform the word he has given into deed,

I know you'll keep your word: You swore if ever
Chance of return to kin and home were granted
Me, to let me go; and now it has been.
(V, 2, p. 137)

Iphigenia relies on Thoas to keep his promise. It is a demand that the 'voice of truth and true humanity' be heard:

It's heard
By anyone, born under any sky,
If through his heart the springs of life flow pure
And unimpeded.
(V, 3, p. 136)

Because Iphigenia can trust in the unspoilt human nature of Thoas, her 'unexampled deed' succeeds in transforming their relations to each other into authentic communication. This later also includes both foreigners and, particularly, Orestes. Those who fight put their swords away and peaceful talk begins, in the course of which all the remaining issues of debate (as to where the idol should remain, for example) are settled to the satisfaction of all

and laid aside. In the end, a forgiving departure takes place,

IPHIGENIA: Farewell! Oh, look at us; and in return
Grant to me a kindly word of parting.
For then the wind will swell the sails more gently,
And from our eyes as we take leave the tears
Will flow less painfully. Farewell! Give me
In pledge of lasting friendship your right hand.
THOAS: Farewell!
(V, 6, p. 143)

The 'right hand', which connotes physical, free, self-determining action in *Götz von Berlichingen*, is a symbol of power-free understanding. In place of a community based on shared action stands a community grounded on communication.

The right to self-determination and the free cultivation of the personality seem, thus, open to all mankind as long as conflicts in the family and society are solved through a kind of communication which is free from domination and violence. This passes the death sentence on any form of society contemporary to Goethe: none could allow the actualisation of the ideal. Goethe was certainly aware of this dilemma. The oft quoted passage from his letter to Charlotte von Stein (of 6 March 1779) points to the distance between the ideal nature of his drama and his own social reality all too clearly: 'My play is making no progress here; it's devilish; the king of Tauris has to speak as if no stocking-weaver in Apolde were starving.'[32]

Consequently, the figures of the drama are no longer 'of the same husk and corn as we are' but, as Lessing declared, idealised figures which symbolise mankind *per se*. This is shown not only in their origin in Greek mythology but also in their language, and is particularly obvious in a comparison with *Götz von Berlichingen*. Goethe re-worked his first version because 'everything in it is thought out' (Letter to Herder, July 1772).[33] He changed the discursive language extensively into a characterising, expressive language which was individual to each figure. In *Iphigenia*, on the other hand,

Goethe used the reverse principle. He transformed what was, at least in design, the individualising prose of the first (1779) and the third versions (1781) into careful, highly polished iambics, which smothered any individual differentiation. This abstraction and de-individualisation in the language make the figures seem idealised.

The idealised figures are, as symbols 'of' man (of the species), in a position to transform real relationships of power in the family and society into a situation of ideal communication. At the same time, this defines the goal towards which the development of the species strives: to allow reality, which could only be represented at the time as an ideal in drama, to come true. Although Orestes (through the discovery of his real identity) and Thoas (through giving and keeping to his promise) certainly have a part in the creation of power-free relations, the decisive turn is brought about by Iphigenia and her 'unexampled deed'. In some senses, therefore, Iphigenia can be perceived as embodying the ideal.

The drama emphasises the deep contrast and distance between this ideal and every historical or social reality. Iphigenia is repeatedly shown to be cut off from the real conditions of human life, well 'protected' (IV, 4, p. 128) in the temple. It is only because of this particular situation that she is in a position to risk the 'unexampled deed'. On the other hand, she is carefully differentiated from the men who, in reality, dominate the family and society ('Men are the masters still, at home, at war; / Far from home they need no help from others' [I, 1, p. 83]) as well as from dependent, subordinate women who have more or less been forced to renounce their basic human right to self-determination ('Her duty, yes, her solace to obey / Even a brutish husband' [I, 1, p. 84]). She neither makes use of male strategies – 'Thus / Shall power and cunning, highest boast of men, / Be shamed by truth, the truth of her great soul' (V, 6, p. 142) – nor of 'sweet request' (V, 3, p. 135), the only socially sanctioned means by which a female may influence men and, thus, reality. She rejects both alternatives as unsatisfactory since both either

challenge the own or another's autonomy. Iphigenia can only renew society because she does not belong to any of the real communities (men and women, or ruler and subjects). In this respect, it seems significant that Goethe oriented her character on a religious image:

> In the Palazzo Ranuzzi, I discovered a painting of St Agatha by Raphael … He provided her with a healthy, steadfast virginity, unattractive, and yet not cold, or raw. I observed it carefully, and I will read my 'Iphigenia' out loud to this statue and will not allow my heroine to say anything that this holy saint could not have said.
> (Diary for Charlotte von Stein, 19 October 1786)

In the figure of Iphigenia, woman stylised as a saint becomes the new ideal. As self-determining, freely cultivated personality who knows neither passion nor desire – as 'pure soul' – she should be able to awaken the 'voice of truth and humanity' in man and to 'ennoble' his raw physical actions into symbolic deeds (the handshake) and speech-acts. She must initiate a process of education in man which will lead to the annulment of all relationships of power in the course of the history of the species, and which will create society anew as an ideal community of autonomous individuals.

*Iphigenia in Tauris* did not captivate contemporary audiences. Although the first version was premièred shortly after being written, on 6 April 1779, in an amateur theatre in Weimar in which Corona Schröter played Iphigenia, Goethe the role of Orestes and Prince Constantine – later also the Duke Karl August – the role of Pylades, the final version was premièred much later, on 7 January 1800 in Vienna at the invitation of Kaiser Franz II. The next performance took place on 15 May 1802 in Weimar, and was directed by Schiller. These latter performances were received with respect but had little success. Goethe blamed the actors' poor training and the fact that the audience was insufficiently prepared:

> I really had the notion once that it was possible to form a German drama. Nay, I even fancied I myself could contribute to it, and lay some foundation-

stones for such an edifice. I wrote my *Iphigenia* and my *Tasso*, with a childish hope that thus it might be brought about. But there was no emotion or excitement – all remained as it was before. If I had produced an effect, and had met with applause, I would have written a round dozen of pieces such as *Iphigenia* and *Tasso*. There was no deficiency of material. But, as I said, actors to represent such pieces with life and spirit were lacking, as was a public to hear and receive them with sympathy.

(27 March 1825)[34]

Ultimately, it is hardly surprising that the audience remained aloof. The ennobling of human urges introduced and demanded by the drama (the rawness of which ignites the violence in the play) could be understood up to a certain point as the suppression of such human drives as proposed by earlier, bourgeois dramas where, however, these human urges were placed in a direct relationship to the real lives of the bourgeois spectators. In these plays, moreover, understanding was guaranteed through the possibility of identification with the dramatic figures. In contrast, the new ideal of the 'pure soul' in *Iphigenia* was not only totally removed from the bourgeois lifestyle, but the strong idealisation also directly prevented any identification based on emotion. Understanding the play demands a certain level of cultivation (in the Goethean sense) which could not be found in a broad public who were occupied with the profane business of earning their daily bread. The drama could not 'cultivate' where 'cultivation' had not already taken place and, thus, it was to remain without impact on the general masses as Goethe later also recognised: 'My works cannot be popular. He who thinks and strives to make them so is in error. They are written, not for the multitude, but only for individuals who desire something congenial, whose aims are like my own' (*Conversations with Eckermann*, p. 271). The solution which *Iphigenia* offers in answer to the problem of autonomy within an absolutist-bourgeois society can only be one isolated and individual potential solution to individual cases (as Wilhelm Meister, for example), which can only be realised in the élite circle of a few chosen people and not in larger social groups, nor in society in general, even if it is shaped in the drama as a general, social achievement. Goethe's classical drama never resolved this contradiction for the audiences of his time.

## 'The transition from man into God'

The enormous popularity of the bourgeois dramatis personae among the actors and the audience who were loathe to accept ideal figures speaking verse repeatedly, provoked both Goethe and Schiller to compose biting scorn. In the poem *Xenien*, Goethe writes:

> We can only be moved by the Christian moral,
> Or that which is popular, homely and bourgeois ...
> What? May no Caesar appear in your theatres,
> No Antony, Orestes or Andromeda?
> ... Nothing! All you can see are priests, commercial
>    advisers,
> Sergeants, secretaries or cavalry officers.

(*Xenien*, pp. 402–4)

Schiller emphasised even more emphatically than Goethe that his dramatic figures were, as in Greek drama, 'more or less idealistic masks and not actual individuals' (Letter to Goethe, 4 April 1797). In order to represent his concept of man, he preferred historical material. For it was in history that Schiller saw private motives provoke public happenings and individual passions cause political events even if the historical outcome was something which happened above and beyond the individual despite his wishes and plans and despite the specific goal which the individual had in mind when setting the process in motion. The individual and the general are intertwined in such a way that the individual is principally seen from the perspective of the general. Kings and princes, commanders and rebels thus become the representatives of mankind.

In *Mary Stuart* (premièred 14 June 1800 in Weimar; first published April 1801), these conditions are set in an almost idealised way in the conflict between the queens: Mary and Elizabeth are both rivals for the English throne as well as for the love of a man (the Earl of

Leicester). They are opponents both as queens and as women.

Although Schiller creates Mary and Elizabeth as opposites from the very beginning, in a way he also gives them a shared point of departure: both are 'mixed characters', at the start of the drama neither has succeeded in freely unfolding her personality and neither has realised herself as queen or as woman.

Elizabeth, the Protestant, has been raised in the ethics of renouncing pleasure and fulfilling one's duty:

> You were brought up in harsh adversity.
> Life hid its joyous face from you; you saw
> No throne awaiting, but an open grave.
> At Woodstock and within the Tower's gloom,
> The gracious father of this kingdom let
> You find your way through suffering to duty.
> No flatterers could reach you there. You
>    learnt,
> Beyond distraction of the giddy world,
> In youth to gather up your inward strength,
> To seek true peace of mind within yourself
> And know what lasting good life has to give.
>                           (II, 3, p. 232)[35]

Even as queen, Elizabeth has willingly kept to the morals and behaviour forced upon her earlier:

> I too could just as well as she have claimed
> The right to earthly joys and happiness,
> But I preferred the duties of a king.
>                           (II, 9, p. 250)

Self-denial and the work ethic have enabled Elizabeth to be a good ruler,

> This island has not known such prosperous
>    days
> In all its native princes' many reigns.
>                           (II, 3, p. 230)

Thus Elizabeth seems to be an almost typical ideal embodiment of the bourgeois social character. She will be given future reward in compensation for successfully controlling her urges in the form of success in her career;

as the 'people's joy' (II, 3, p. 230), her self-realisation as queen is almost totally successful. However, this self-realisation cannot be brought into harmony with the 'natural law' (II, 2, p. 173) of the female sex which Schiller, in the tradition of the bourgeois age, determined as dependency on the male: for it is 'this natural law / That binds one half of our humanity / In bondage to the other' (II, 2, p. 226). On the contrary, Elizabeth seems to view her 'virgin freedom' as her 'highest ware'. If she wants to remain a queen without a 'master' then she must reject marriage.

> A queen has nothing, after all,
> More than the meanest of her subjects' wives!
> Like tokens mark a like obedience,
> A like devotion: rings make marriages,
> And ring is joined to ring to make a chain.
>                           (II, 2, p. 227)

According to bourgeois-patriarchal under-standing, the status of the queen will inevitably collide with female 'nature'. Elizabeth cannot give herself up to a man: 'Mortimer: Never on man did you true love bestow' (II, 6, p. 227). Rather, she tries to transfer her status as queen to status as female and make man subject to her, contrary to the rules of 'nature', as she did with Leicester, who 'Obeyed each fancy of her despot's mood / As if I were an Eastern slave' (II, 8, p. 244). Because Elizabeth only wants to see herself as ruler, her self-realisation as woman is denied her. Reduced to the 'business' of ruler, she has neglected the human quality of her nature and has remained, like the citizens, 'fragmented'.

The Catholic Mary, on the other hand, has lived out every aspect of her sensual nature without restriction:

> She
> Was sent, a tender child, to France, and to
> The court of folly and of frivolous joy.
> There in eternal gaiety
> She never heard the sterner voice of truth,
> And dazzled by the glittering show of vice
> Was carried on the flood that heads to ruin.
> The idle gift of beauty she enjoyed,
> She was the foremost woman in the land.
>                           (II, 3, p. 232)

Mary's physical beauty is only empty appearance, because it does not correspond to a beauty of the soul which stems from the harmony between her moral and sensual nature. Mary sacrificed her moral nature in favour of her sensual one:

> But when you let him die, then you were not
> Yourself, you did not know what you were
>   doing.
> Blind passion had enslaved your will, you were
> Beneath the yoke of Bothwell, the seducer –
> ... that fearful man! ...
>
> Your cheeks no longer blushed in purity,
> But glowed with hectic fires. You threw the veil
> Of secrecy away, his shameless vice
> Had conquered you, you flaunted openly
> Your degradation, let the murderer,
> Amongst the curses of the people, bear
> The royal sword of Scotland through the
>   streets
> Of Edinburgh triumphing before you,
> Surrounded by the arms of Parliament;
> In justice's own temple made the law
> In shameless farce pronounce him innocent.
>
> (I, 4, p. 202)

Depravation has persuaded Mary into committing a crime – just like the mistress in the *bürgerliche Trauerspiel*. Following only her urges and passions, she has allowed her lover to murder her husband. Because Mary only wanted to be a loving, giving woman, she has abused her position as queen, and unafraid of the 'people's curse', forced her parliament to break the law. She has failed as queen.

Even though this is all past history when Mary enters the drama, she is far from appearing 'saintly' in any way. Instead, she seems to be a passionate young woman who gives herself up to the hope of finding rescue and new happiness in a man whom she loves, the Earl of Leicester. She clings so much to life that she can hardly stand Mortimer's long narration of his journey to France:

> O spare me, sir, I beg you, do not spread
> This tapestry of life before my eyes!

> No more, I am an exile and a captive.
>
> (I, 6, p. 206)

Mary loves life and is full of vitality, as Mortimer declares:

> *She* only bears delight's true name –
> About her in unending melody
> Hover the gods of grace and youthful joys;
> There at her breast is bliss that never cloys.
>
> (II, 6, p. 240)

Schiller was clearly very concerned to emphasise Mary's sensual nature, right up to her abdication in Act V:

> My *Mary* will not excite any tender feelings, and I did not intend that she should; I mean in all cases to regard her as a physical character, and the pathos must be more a general, deep emotion than a personal or individual feeling of sympathy. She feels and excites no affection, her fate in life being only to experience and kindle violent passions herself.
>
> (Letter to Goethe, 18 June 1799)[36]

Dominated by sensual nature, Mary is not in a position to bring out the whole human nature within. Like Elizabeth she is but a 'fragment'. The opposition between Elizabeth and Mary seems to pick up the old opposition in the *bürgerliche Trauerspiel* between bourgeois and court lifestyles. Whilst Elizabeth's denial of her urges and her sense of the work ethic point to the bourgeois social character, Mary's sensual nature and earlier depravity seem to refer to the court lifestyle. Unlike the *bürgerliche Trauerspiel*, however, in *Mary Stuart* this opposition is severed from the reality of absolutist-bourgeois life. Instead, it represents two different kinds of the fragmentary character of modern man in an idealised, typified way. The conflict of the drama (signing and carrying out the execution) contains for both women the possibility of overcoming their limitations and 'raising themselves up to the level of humanity'.

Elizabeth fails in this process. She is not only unable to lift herself to the moral greatness which she would need to pardon Mary; even her virtues thus far prove to be hypocritical and questionable. Elizabeth has only ever been an exemplary queen for the sake of keeping the throne:

> With my virtue
> I must attempt to patch my tattered rights
> And cover up the stain upon my birth,
> The shame that my own father laid upon me.
> (IV, 10, p. 290)

Thus, she gave the appearance of being a just ruler in order to divert attention from the stigma of her illegitimate birth which lessens her right to the English throne. Her sense of justice proves to be mere clever political strategy:

> But did I choose it of my own free will,
> When I was just? Necessity, that rules
> Our every act, yes, even those of kings,
> Inexorable, forced this virtue on me.
> (IV, 10, p. 290)

Neither insight into the moral necessity of a just government, nor even her own nature has persuaded her to act with 'virtue', but simply her concern not to be unpopular with the 'plebeians' and thereby endanger her claim to the throne. Her virtue as ruler, thus, has not sprung from her own free will (she would have decided otherwise) – 'When shall I sit in freedom on my throne?' (IV, 10, p. 290), but solely as a result of her determined desire for power. Her virtue as ruler is simply the means, not the end.

The same is true of Elizabeth's feminine virtues. She does not stop herself from marrying the man whom she loves either out of duty or her own desire. Political cleverness alone drives her to this 'virtue': the people would have been repelled by her choice and perhaps remembered that her claim to the throne is not entirely secure. In order to satisfy the wishes of the people, Elizabeth considers marriage to the French prince. She subjects her feelings to a strict discipline in order not to lose her position as ruler. If she did not need to care – as Mary does not – about what her subjects will think of her, she would behave very differently, as is shown in her envy and outburst of hatred for Mary:

> The Stuart could permit herself
> To give her hand away as she desired,
> She was allowed all she could wish for, she
> Has drunk and drained the cup of earthly
>     joys. …
>
> She took no notice of the world's opinion.
> She went by easy paths, she never felt
> The heavy yoke to which I bent my neck.
> (II, 9, p. 250)

In order to appear virtuous in public, Elizabeth is forced to bear the yoke which suppresses her desires. Like her implementation of justice, the suppression of her desires also represents a tactical, rather than a moral value. She uses the semblance of virtue in order to disguise her secret wishes and desires which, if they were made public, would weaken her power. It is Mary who gives Elizabeth the decisive push by bringing these secret wishes to light, and in so doing, who highlights Elizabeth's questionable right to the throne at the same time.

> The world knows all the worst of me and I
> Can say that I am better than my name.
> But woe to you, that day when all your deeds
> Are stripped of their disguise, the virtuous
>     cloak
> That you have cast about your secret lusts!
> It was not virtue that your mother left
> To you: all know the honour for whose sake
> Anne Boleyn met her death upon the block!
> …
>
> A bastard sits on England's throne, and dupes
> This noble race with cunning and deceit.
> If right was might, then you would crawl
>     before
> My feet this moment, for I am your Queen.
> (III, 4, p. 264)

Since, as woman and queen, Mary makes use of better arguments, she will have to die if Elizabeth wants to escape the danger of losing power:

> A bastard am I then? Unlucky wretch,
> Only as long as you are living still!

What doubts remain upon my princely birth,
They are stamped out, when I have stamped
on you!
As soon as England can no longer choose,
My blood is pure, my birth legitimate!

(IV, 10, p. 291)

Elizabeth signs the death sentence in order to
keep the throne herself and, at the same time,
to rid herself of a hated female rival: 'She tears
away the man I love, / She robs me of a
husband!' (IV, 10, p. 291).

All Elizabeth's thoughts and energies are
directed towards power, respect and success. To
achieve these goals, she employs her seeming
virtue as an effective instrument without hesitation – just as Adelheid von Walldorf employs
depravity in *Götz von Berlichingen*. Until the very
end, Elizabeth tries to keep up this appearance
and to unload the responsibility for Mary's death
onto others. After she is forced to sign the death
sentence (because no one is willing to assassinate
Mary), she tries to pretend that the signature was
purely a formal act forced upon her by parliament and the people:

It was meant
For me to sign. I have. A piece of paper
Is no decision, and no name can kill.

(IV, 11, p. 292)

In answer to Davison's objection, '*Your* name,
my queen, beneath this document / Does
decide all, it kills' (IV, 11 p. 292), Elizabeth
tries to shift the responsibility back onto him,
her subject. When he implores her to decide
what to do with the paper ('It costs you but a
single word. O speak, / This paper, say what
must become of it' [IV, 11, p. 293]), she carefully avoids the single clarifying word: she
agrees to the act, which remains ambiguous,
but not the word, which points to individual
responsibility and, thus, blame. Right up to the
end, Elizabeth refuses to speak about her decision in public and even after Mary's death, tries
to keep up the appearance of magnanimity:
'My fears are in their grave, and who can say / I
did it? I shall not lack tears to weep / For her,
now she is dead' (V, 12, p. 313).

Elizabeth keeps her power but ultimately
loses 'majesty'. 'Mere power, however terrible
and boundless it may be, can never bestow
majesty on anyone. Power will only impress a
creature of the sense, but true majesty is absolutely compelling for the Spirit.'[37] Elizabeth
cannot lift herself to this majesty because she
remains chained to her desire for power; and 'to
will from desire is only to desire in a more round-
about way' (*Anmut und Würde*, p. 58). Her
'virtues' thus do not prove real 'moral autonomy'
but 'the preponderance of some other emotion'
(namely the addiction to power) which keeps 'a
present emotion under control' (*Anmut und
Würde*, p. 71). Elizabeth is unable to transgress
the boundary of the 'sensual being' and constitute herself as a 'human' person by one truly
moral action – such as pardoning Mary.

Although Elizabeth at first appears to be an
almost ideal-typical embodiment of a bourgeois
social character, her behaviour provides a sharp
critique of the bourgeois way of life in the
further course of the tragedy. Schiller recognised perceptively that the bourgeois virtue of
suppressing one's desires and upholding the
work ethic are not exclusively derived from
having a moral character and, thus, naturally
represent a moral value as was assumed in the
earlier *bürgerliche Trauerspiel*. If such virtues are
only employed as strategic means in the battle
for social elevation (through a favourable
marriage or success in one's career), they are to
be judged critically. For, by behaving in this
way, man gives up his sensual nature and
renounces his basic right to realise himself as a
human being.

In the figure of Elizabeth, Schiller continues
his critique of the bourgeois lifestyle already
outlined in *Intrigue and Love*. In the earlier play,
he revealed the distortion of family love to be
an instrument of oppression; in *Mary Stuart* he
exposes the hypocrisy which pretends that the
means employed towards pure self-preservation
(in the broadest sense) are virtuous and should
be admired. Schiller saw through the disguise
of double morals in its earliest form which
grew to be a thoroughly bourgeois pattern of
behaviour in the nineteenth century.

Through her imprisonment, Mary is denied any possibility of self-realisation either as queen or as woman. In the words of Mary and her followers, the prison almost seems to foreshadow death: Mortimer speaks of her 'dank prison' (I, 6, p. 209), Talbot of 'the darkness of her prison grave' (II, 4, p. 237) and Mary herself of being 'imprisoned here for ever / ... in this endless night' (I, 6, p. 209); she calls her prison a 'loathsome prison' (III, 1, p. 253) and Kennedy suggests she is 'walled up here in living death' (I, 1, p. 196). The withdrawal of bodily freedom creates an enormous mental trauma, because it represents for Mary a brutal suppression of her sensual nature: 'I am an exile and a captive' (I, 6, p. 206). Schiller evokes the violent, unnatural element of this situation in the image of the fire which, despite the most careful watchkeeping, repeatedly threatens to career out of control – to the terror of her enemies. Burleigh describes Mary:

She sits, the Ate of this endless war,
Who sets this realm on fire with brands of
   love.

(II, 3, p. 229)

He cannot be persuaded that she wants peace:

You chose a wicked path to your desires:
To raise rebellion, and to climb the steps
Of England's throne through bitter civil strife.

(I, 7, p. 216)

The same image is used by Paulet, her keeper:

And yet her arm could reach
Out far enough to stir up civil war,
To set this realm alight.

(I, 1, p. 195)

In these words, Mary appears almost as an elemental, natural force which seeks to free itself from its chains with all its strength. In fact, the force of life in her is so strong that up until her meeting with Elizabeth she is only concerned about winning her freedom and saving her life. For her, however, not every means is allowed to achieve this goal. Unlike

Elizabeth she refuses under any circumstances to be a guilty party and thus seeks to avoid endangering Elizabeth's life or the peace of the kingdom at any price. The paths which Mary chooses are certainly legitimate. At first, she hopes to win the support of the Earl of Leicester, whom she loves, later also, Mortimer. She seeks an audience with Elizabeth because a personal meeting between the two queens could only end in a pardon. Life and freedom would then be saved even if Mary must renounce her claim to the throne and her self-realisation as queen would be temporarily put aside.

This is a position counselled by political cleverness which Mary actually supports with great self-will at the beginning of the confrontation with Elizabeth, despite her 'burning consciousness' of suffering and a 'heart ... turned with hate against her' (III, 3, p. 256); ('*Mary gathers her strength and approaches Elizabeth but stops halfway, trembling; her gestures express a violent conflict of emotions*' [III, 4, p. 258]). Ultimately, Mary gives it up in the further course of the discussion. Wounded by Elizabeth's insults, she scorns the strategies of 'restraint' and 'subjugation' which were prescribed to her by cleverness.

This, restraint! I have
Endured as much as any may endure.
And now farewell, meek lamb-like resignation,
Fly to the heavens, patient suffering,
Break from your bonds, come out from your
   dark lair,
Bitter resentment, all too long confined –
And you who gave the angry basilisk
The look that kills, lay now upon my tongue
The poisoned dart!

(III, 4, p. 264)

Well aware that she is putting her life at risk, she tells Elizabeth the truth which makes her sign the death sentence, 'She goes, enraged, and death is in her heart' (III, 5, p. 265). None the less, Mary feels free for the first time:

Oh Hannah, this is joy! At last, at last,
After the years of misery and shame,

A single moment of revenge and triumph!
A mountain's weight is lifted from my heart,
I thrust the knife into my enemy.

(III, 5, p. 265)

As queen, and as woman, she has shown herself superior to Elizabeth even at the cost of her
own life. Filled with intense emotion, she abandons physical nature for the sake of the moral
self and proves herself to be a 'sublime soul',
something which the stage directions also indicate: 'Glowing with rage, but with noble dignity'.
For, according to Schiller, the sublime is given
expression through the emotions:

This is done by having all the sides of a human
being that simply obey nature – sides that the will
is able to manage either never at all or at least not
under certain circumstances – betray the presence of suffering, while no trace of this suffering
or only a slight trace of it is evident in those sides
not subject to instinct's *blind* violence and not
necessarily observing nature's laws. The latter
sides of a human being thus appear free to a
certain extent.

(*Über das Pathetische*, pp. 52–3)[38]

Afterwards, Mary does hope to be liberated by
Mortimer ('Hope waves to us, the sweet desire
for life / Awakes unbidden and omnipotent' [V,
1, p. 297]). But after her death has become
incontrovertible certainty, she finally succeeds
in the transformation into a sublime soul:

We cannot ease ourselves away from life!
But in a moment, swiftly, we must make
The change between this life below and life
Eternal; and my lady was vouchsafed
By God to cast all earthly hopes away
With fortitude, and in this moment set
Her faith in Heaven with a courageous soul.

(V, 1, p. 297)

Thus the sublime affords us an egress from the
sensuous world in which the beautiful world
gladly holds us forever captive. Not gradually (for
there is no transition from dependence to
freedom), but suddenly and with a shock it tears
the independent spirit out of the net in which a

refined sensuousness has entoiled it, and which
binds all the more tightly the more gossamer its
weave.

(*On the Sublime*, pp. 201–2)[39]

Mary has regained her freedom by successfully
overcoming her strong and vital desires and
willingly giving up her life. Now she radiates
dignity, which is 'the expression of the sublime
Spirit' (*Anmut und Würde*).

MARY [*Looking about her with calm dignity*]:
   Why do you weep? What is this grief? You
   should
   Rejoice with me, that all my sufferings
   Are now to end, my fetters to be loosed,
   My prison opened and my joyous soul
   On angel's wings soar to eternal freedom.
   …
   I feel the crown once more upon my head,
   And seemly pride within my noble soul!

(V, 6, pp. 300–1)

Simultaneously to this transition towards the
sublime, the regaining of spiritual freedom and
majesty in the moral sense, Mary has pacified
the wild emotions which once stirred her soul.
She no longer feels hatred towards Elizabeth
('Take to the Queen of England / The greetings
of her sister' [V, 8, p. 309]) and in withstanding
the 'fearful struggle' (V, 7, p. 306) has overcome her 'sinful love' (V, 7, p. 306) to
Leicester. Free of passion, her sensual and
moral natures can now be reconciled in the last
hour of her life. Her physical beauty ('She is
clad in white as for some festivity; around her neck
she wears an Agnus Dei on a necklace of small
beads, and a rosary hangs at her waist; she has a
crucifix in her hand and a diadem on her head,
and wears a long black veil, thrown back' [V, 6,
p. 300]) has become the symbol of the beauty
in her soul. She has gained 'gracefulness and
dignity' ('Anmut' and 'Würde'). 'If grace,
augmented by architectonic beauty, and
dignity, backed by a store of moral energy, are
*joined* in the same person, the expression of
humanity in that person is perfect; he is there,
with the full rights of citizenship in the world of
the Spirit, and a free man in the world of

phenomena' (*Anmut und Würde*, p. 72). Mary has realised the true concept of humanity.

In so doing, she has succeeded in 'the transformation of man into God' (Letter from Schiller to Wilhelm von Humboldt, 29 November 1795). This utopian vision of the beautiful and, at the same time, sublime soul in which man achieves wholeness – that is, both as a sensual-moral being as well as one whose 'human nature' is will (*Über das Erhabene*) – and thus, transforms himself from human into god, can hardly be presented on stage. Schiller overcomes this difficulty by giving the supernatural a sensual form in the scene of the Holy Communion. The bodily union with God understood to occur in taking the Holy Communion, therefore, can be presented on the stage in an aesthetic manner, rather than in a religious way, and become a poetic-theatrical symbol of Mary's 'transformation into God'.

As you believe, so let it be to you! [*Giving her the Host*]
Take this, the body of Christ who died for you!
[*He takes the goblet …* ]
Take this, the blood that Christ did shed for you! …

And as you now, in this your earthly body,
Are joined with God, by this great mystery,
So in that realm of everlasting joy,
Where sin shall be no longer, neither weeping,
You shall be changed, and take on heavenly shape,
An angel, safe for ever in His keeping.

(V, 7, p. 308)

Schiller's highest ideal has taken form in the figure of Mary, and has become aesthetic reality on stage.

Because that which is moral-rational is represented in a sensual manner, it opens the way for the spectator to understand 'the whole of our sensuous and intellectual powers in the fullest possible harmony' in the reception process (*On the Aesthetic Education of Man*,

20th Letter, p. 99).[40] For this, it is important that the spectator's mind remains free, even in the most moving passion, so that he is able to distance himself from the emotions which move him.

The spectator can only do this if he does not succumb to the temptation of mistaking the work of art (the process on stage) for real life. Theatrical processes must be clearly differentiated from the processes of daily life and emphasise their own autonomous laws. In the classical drama, these conditions are partly created by the rationally ordered, strictly symmetrical structure, and partly by the introduction of verse speech. Like Goethe, Schiller was convinced that the transition from 'prose into a poetico-rhythmical form' (Letter to Goethe, 24 November 1797)[41] would bring about a transformation from 'meagre representation' to something 'general and purely human'. In this process, the dramatic figures lose any individuality and become 'symbolic beings', who 'as poetic figures … have invariably to represent and to express what is general in man' (Letter to Goethe, 24 August 1798). Since the spectator cannot identify himself in the same way with 'symbolic beings' as with 'priests, commercial advisers, sergeants, secretaries or cavalry officers' or even fathers and daughters, mothers and sons, his freedom from emotion, or detachment, must be secured. The reception process could be carried out without hindrance as an 'aesthetic education' in Schiller's sense, and modern man, whose education is only fragmentary, could be led towards the experience of wholeness.

The great success of *Mary Stuart* with audiences (as with most of Schiller's dramas) suggests this is an unlikely outcome. For even if the aesthetic reality of the stage events is clearly differentiated and set apart from the bourgeois way of life, a considerable level of cultivation is required before one can find the spiritual freedom, or detachment, which Schiller demands. This is particularly true in terms of the dramatic figure of Mary since, for the audience of the turn of the century (that is, early nineteenth century), she represents in many ways an ideal figure of identification.

The demonic nature of Eros, which Mary embodies as inflamed and inflaming nature up to Act V, was irresistibly attractive to the spectators who had suffered so long under the Puritan moral yoke. But unlike the Romantic view, where Eros should develop into a wild, uncontrollable, elementary power, in *Mary Stuart* it is brought into relation with the bourgeois scale of values. Mary's rejection of life and her subjugation of sensual nature can be reinterpreted in the light of the bourgeois virtue of suppressing desire, and seen as the confirmation of the bourgeois lifestyle. The process of reception in this case, would create considerable spiritual relief. For, while through Elizabeth the increasingly rigorous demands made by the ethics of economy and the suppression of desire, which was something people suffered in real daily life, may be rejected and hated with great vehemence, identification was easily made with Mary, who in an ideal way embodied the counter-image of both the much longed-for sensual-erotic as well as the 'true' virtue of the suppression of desire, transfigured into the sublime.

It is therefore unlikely that many spectators resisted the temptation of such an identification and managed to keep their emotions entirely detached and open. A considerable level of cultivation was necessary to do this, but only relatively few spectators would have been in such a position. The aesthetic cultivation which Schiller wanted for all was actually reserved for a few chosen people.

This conclusion is supported by documents of reception from the period. After *Intrigue and Love*, it could be seen that critical judgement by the literati was, in part, considerably different from that by theatre critics and theatre audiences. This development became increasingly marked as time passed. Amalie von Voigt reports that at the première in Weimar, the audience was deeply offended by the 'squabble between the two queens, and even more so at the scene of the Holy Communion'.[42]

The spirit of opposition which came from the audience, as well as from court, was so intense that Schiller felt it necessary to change the Holy Communion scene. The literary critics, however, made at least some individual attempts to justify the scene within the poetic context of the play. Thus, Ferdinand Huber wrote on the opposition between Mary and Elizabeth:

Mary, the *queen* held in chains, subjected to a kangaroo court and death on a blood-drenched scaffold only needs to feel herself a queen in order to be, in the fullest sense, a tragic being. As for Mary, the *woman*, there were some voices among the audience who wished that some of her actions would have been more ambiguous. This would mean, however, which was not the intent, to wish for something quite other than Schiller's tragedy. One forgot that the *queen* who suppresses and ruins Mary is, as a *woman*, a hypocritical, cold prude and that the nature of the whole drama lies in the contrast between these two women … and that remorseful depravity belongs just as much to the tragic charm of Mary as prudish coquetry which dissolves into dark, political egoism belongs to the tragic hatefulness of her enemy.[43]

A long article in *Allgemeinen Literatur-Zeitung* (*Universal Literature Journal*, 1 and 2 January 1802), places Mary Stuart in the context of Schiller's aesthetic theory in order to soften the growing criticism from audiences and critics. The critic explained how the Holy Communion scene was neither 'unpoetical' nor 'irreligious' and concluded with a general comment on the audience:

On the other hand, since the audience which most frequently comes to the theatre lacks any understanding of the arts; since it neither seeks nor finds anything in the performance other than a way of passing the time, one might think that the authorities who control public entertainment would find the representation of that scene on the stage somewhat questionable, that it might make that which is Holy seem like a musical toy to the great rabble. Such criticism points to problems in the audience, however, not the author.

Schiller's claim that his classical theatre would lift the audience to an aesthetic level of 'harmony' and 'wholeness' could clearly not be realised. The audience continued to receive his dramas according to the patterns and conventions of the bourgeois theatre of illusion even if his dramas blatantly contravened them. The empathy with the processes on stage, in which bourgeois self-awareness around the middle of the century 'articulated' and manifested itself in a new and powerful way, began to degenerate into pure escapism.

## Middle-class *Bildungstheater*

In January 1791, Goethe was made director of the Weimar theatre. He used his position to encourage a style of acting which would complement the intentions of his own classical drama. As the Weimar actor, Anton Genast, reports, Goethe turned 'his greatest attention to the art of performance and noble pathos'. In so doing, he was opposing not only the 'affected beings and the bombastic tone' which the old actors 'followed from the French tragedy', but also the psychological-realistic acting style developed by Conrad Ekhof and his successor, Friedrich Ludwig Schröder. As Genast notes, Schröder restricted 'rhetoric and performance art … to everyday life. His ensemble succeeded best in conversation plays and middle-class dramas; their tragedy was devoid of power and poesy … Goethe in contrast, strove towards the rhetoric, the plastic and mimic arts of ancient times and this drove him, unlike Schröder, towards idealism.'[44]

Goethe wrote 'Rules for Actors'[45] in order to discuss the art of declamation – principally the speaking of verse – and the bodily pose, gesture and movements of the actor. In it, he adopted many of the concepts formulated by Franciscus Lang. Thus, Goethe impressed upon the actors: 'The actor ought also to take particular care never to speak upstage, but always toward the audience' (Section 40, p.

219). And with regard to dialogue, he imposed the following basic rule:

> When two actors are engaged in dialogue, it is very important that the one speaking lean back slightly while delivering his lines, and when finished, lean forward. If the actor uses this technique prudently and practices it until it becomes natural, he will achieve the best results both in regard to the visual effect of his delivery and intelligibility. Actors who have become masters in this will produce gratifying results and enjoy a great advantage over those who have not.
>
> (Section 41, p. 219)

Goethe also noted that, 'It is highly incorrect to place one hand on top of the other, or to rest them on the stomach or stick one or both into the vest' (Section 46, p. 219). Instead, he suggested,

> The hand itself must neither be clenched in a fist nor held flat against the thigh, like a soldier standing at attention. Rather, some fingers must be half bent, the others kept straight, but they must never appear cramped.
>
> (Section 48, p. 219)

Goethe's adoption of the rules of the baroque art of acting in a slightly modified form were intended to restrict the sense of illusion on stage. Diderot's theoretical work, *On Dramatic Poetry*, set out the basic rule of the middle-class theatre of illusion: 'One should imagine a great wall right at the very edge of the stage, which separates it from the auditorium. One should play as if the curtain has not yet been drawn' (Chapter XI, 'On Interest'). But Goethe had no interest in such a 'fourth wall', 'For the actor must always remember that he is there for the sake of his spectators' (Section 38, p. 218). Since Goethe tried to prevent the illusion of reality being created on stage, he explicitly denied his actors the 'natural' way of acting practised by Schröder's company: 'Above all, the actor must remember that he should not only imitate nature but also present it in an idealised way. That is to say, in his presentation he must unite reality with beauty' (Section 35, p. 218).

This style of acting should make it difficult for the spectator to feel direct empathy with the dramatic figures and the processes on stage. It guaranteed a certain aesthetic distance which should enable the spectator to receive the performance as a learning, cultivating experience. Goethe assumed that the Weimar audience was capable of such a reception:

One can show the audience no greater respect than by not treating them as mere rabble. Such crowds rush to the theatre unprepared, demanding anything that can be instantly digested, they want to look, be amazed, laugh and cry and they force the theatre directors, who are more or less dependent on them, to descend to their own level. On one hand, they expect too much from the theatre, and on the other, they destroy it. We are fortunate that we can assume that our audience, particularly if we include those from Jena, brings more than just their ticket money with them, and that those for whom the first careful production of important plays remained somewhat dark and indigestible, are none the less interested in allowing themselves to be educated and drawn into the intentions of the play the second time round. It is only because our situation allows us to perform plays which an élite audience enjoys, that we can be in a position to work towards those productions which will eventually please all.[46]

Even if Goethe was merely trying to flatter his audience, he based his work in theatre on the concept of performing for an 'élite', that is, a cultivated audience, which also demanded in return further intellectual and spiritual cultivation from the theatre.

Goethe also planned the repertoire according to this maxim. He complained that the usual repertoire in regular German theatres contained too much trivial, daily material which was quickly outdated. He strove to find a repertoire that 'could be passed on to the world to come'. This would mean, however,

That the spectator should learn to perceive that not every play is like a coat which must be tailored precisely according to his own current needs, shape

and size. We should not think of satisfying our actual spiritual, emotional and sensual needs in the theatre, but we should far more often see ourselves as travellers, who visit foreign places and lands, to which we travel for the sake of learning and delight, and where we do not find all those comforts which we have the time at home to shape to our own individual needs.[47]

As a consequence, Goethe began to develop a repertoire which, alongside literary advanced productions of his time (principally his own and those by Schiller) and the unavoidable trivial plays by Iffland and Kotzebue, also embraced the most important dramas in European theatre history. Thus, Sophocles' *Antigone* was accompanied by Shakespeare's *Hamlet, Henry IV, Romeo and Juliet, Macbeth, Julius Caesar* and *Othello*; Calderón's *The Constant Prince* and *Life is a Dream* accompanied Corneille's *Le Cid*, Molière's *The Miser* and Racine's *Phaedra*, as well as comedies by Goldoni and Gozzi's *Turandot*, and tragedies by Voltaire and Lessing.

The theatre was to cease being a moral institution of the 'middle classes' and instead become a means of mediating world literature. The plays should no longer serve to represent the daily lives of the spectators, but instead function as 'food for intellectual and spiritual development'. In order to be able to do this, care must be taken that the 'foreign places and lands' to which they lead the spectator are not too foreign. Goethe was prepared to make extensive changes and modifications and was vigorously supported in this by Schiller. In consideration of the moral ideas and norms of the Weimar public, Schiller allowed the porter's scene, which he found obscene and insulting, to be deleted from *Macbeth*; it was replaced by a devout song. For similar reasons, Goethe reworked *Romeo and Juliet* – so extensively that his version would later be described as an 'amazing travesty'.[48]

In a letter to Caroline von Wolzogen of 28 January 1812, Goethe explained his method:

The maxim I have followed was to concentrate on all that is interesting and bring it into harmony, since, according to his genius, his age and his public Shakespeare was able, even forced, to put together much disharmonious Allotria, in order to appease the theatre genius ruling at the time.

Goethe's method seemed to succeed in mediating a foreign culture to the Weimar audience, at least in making them receptive to it. After his production of *The Constant Prince*, he wrote to Sartorius (on 4 February 1811): 'This time … we have revived a play that was written nearly two hundred years ago under quite different skies and for a quite differently educated audience with so much vitality, that it seems to have come straight out of the oven.'

With this repertoire, Goethe realised a programme which he described in the following, now famous, words to Eckermann, 'National literature is now rather an unmeaning term; the epoch of World-Literature is at hand, and everyone must strive to hasten its approach' (31 January 1827).[49] Goethe could only achieve this ambitious programme on the Weimar stage with certain restrictions: non-European drama was excluded. Goethe had read the drama *Sakontala* by the Indian author, Kalidasa, in a German translation of 1791 by Georg Forster, and he recorded the impression it made on him in *Italian Journey* as 'the greatest influence on my whole life'. His enthusiasm was expressed in the poem:

Wouldst thou the blossoms of spring, as well
  as the fruits of autumn,
Wouldst thou what charms and delights,
  wouldst thou what plenteously feeds,
Wouldst thou include both heaven and earth
  in one designation,
All that is needed is done, when I Sakontala
  name.[50]

Goethe's enthusiastic reception of the play also found expression in his own work – he took the idea of the 'Prelude in the Theatre' in *Faust* from the Indian drama. None the less, he shied away from adapting it for the Weimar stage and including it in the repertoire. In the *Tag- und Jahresheften* of 1821, Goethe regretfully notes that, 'our emotions, customs and mentality have grown so apart from those in that far-eastern nation, that this important work can only win a few admirers here'. Something which appeared too foreign would not be in a position to stimulate intellect and spirit and was, therefore, unsuitable 'food for intellectual and spiritual development' for the stage.

Under Goethe's direction, the Weimar theatre was fundamentally different from other middle-class theatres of the time, which largely saw themselves as moral institutions to propagate the middle-class values of virtue and family love, and show the spectator the path towards emotional identification. Goethe, in contrast, designed the Weimar theatre as an institution which addressed the cultivated élite and which promoted further intellectual and spiritual development. The middle-class *Bildungstheater* stepped forward to take the place of the middle-class theatre of illusion.

With the demise of classical theatre, the great age of middle-class theatre drew to an end. Schiller's death (1805), the deaths of two of the most significant middle-class theatre directors, Iffland (1814) and Schröder (1816), as well as Goethe's retirement as director of the Weimar theatre (1817), marked the end of an era in which, for the first time, the middle classes turned the theatre into one of the most important elements of public life and culture. After this era, the court theatre in Germany became reinstated. Theatre was no longer a public forum for middle-class culture or middle-class self-understanding. It was now a place for private entertainment and edification.

# 4 Dramatising the identity crisis

## THE ENIGMATIC PERSONALITY

### Personality as a social category in the nineteenth century

The eighteenth-century concept of personality as an autonomous individual, which defined the bourgeois theatre – principally *Sturm und Drang* and German classical theatre – refers to a potential inborn in man, given by nature. In this sense, Herder defined 'genius' as the embodiment of personality. 'Genius lies dormant in mankind as the tree in its seed', and Goethe complained, through Wilhelm Meister, of the enormous difficulties encountered by the citizen who is forced to earn his daily bread – an activity which hinders the development of his personality.

Personality as an aspect of human nature, as something guaranteed by nature, represented one of the key concepts of the philosophy of the Enlightenment. The struggle to achieve the right to cultivate the personality freely and overcome the obstructional and lamentable conditions of social reality was thought to have been the cause of the French Revolution. In Germany, however, following a process initiated by classical drama and the *Bildungsroman*, it would come about through a growing aesthetic awareness and knowledge. The general disillusionment which set in after the Revolution, the effects of the industrial revolution, and particularly the social mobility which was introduced with the development of industrial capitalism at the beginning of the nineteenth century, led to a considerable and sustained change in the concept of personality. In *The Fall of Public Man*, Richard Sennett describes such changes in the following way:

> Personality came in the nineteenth century to diverge from the Enlightenment belief in natural character in three important ways. First, personality is seen to vary from person to person, whereas natural character was the common thread running through mankind. Personality varies because the appearances of emotion and the inner nature of the person feeling are the same. One is what one appears; therefore, people with different appearances are different persons. When one's own appearances change, there is a change in the self. As the Enlightenment belief in a common humanity is eclipsed, the variation in personal appearance becomes tied to the instability of the personality itself.
>
> Second, personality, unlike natural character, is controlled by self-consciousness. The control an individual practised in relation to his natural character was the moderation of his desires; if he acted in a certain way, modestly, he was bringing himself into line with his natural character. Personality cannot be controlled by action; circumstances may force different appearances and so destablilise the self. The only form of control can be the constant attempt to formulate what it is one feels. This sense of controlling the self is mostly retrospective; one understands what one has done after the experience is over. Consciousness always follows emotional expression in this scheme. Personalities, therefore, are not only composed of variations in rage, compassion, or trust between people; personality is also

the capacity to 'recover' one's emotions. The nineteenth century bourgeois is always remembering what it was like when in youth he was really alive. His personal self-consciousness is not so much an attempt to contrast his feelings with those of others as to take known and finished feelings, whatever they once were, as a definition of who he is.

Modern personality, finally, diverges from the idea of a natural character in that freedom of feeling at a given moment seems like a violation of 'normal' conventional feeling … The awareness of difference suppresses the spontaneity of expression.[1]

From this concept of personality, two fundamentally different, but mutually complementary, possibilities arise as to how to appear in public: as actor or as spectator. The actor puts his idiosyncrasy on show in an artistic way, giving public expression to his emotions. In so doing, he temporarily enables intense emotion to be evoked in the spectator, but he becomes isolated from the spectator in the long term. The spectator, on the contrary, only participates in public life through observation. For he is unsure of his own emotions, and lives in the fearful conviction that the emotions, whatever they may be, will be expressed independently of his will. Such a split within 'public man' explains why performing artists such as Paganini and later, Liszt, were seen to be the embodiment of personality. The performing artist became almost the sole public actor. It was only during the Revolution in 1848 that his role was challenged by politicians.

Inevitably, this development had far-reaching consequences for public institutions like the theatre. The actor, who could barely achieve social recognition or civic reputation at the end of the eighteenth century, now became widely admired and was enthusiastically celebrated as a star. This was particularly true of outstanding actors such as Ludwig Devrient (1704–1832) in Berlin, Edmund Kean (1787–1833) in London and Frédérick Lemaître (1800–76) in Paris.

These actors were a sensation – that is, they simultaneously shocked and filled their audience with enthusiasm – by concentrating on the details of the *mise-en-scène* and replacing the usual stage clichés with 'natural' or unexpected elements. In Germany, since the première of Schiller's *The Robbers*, it had been customary for Franz Moor to be played in a red coat, a red wig with a red cock's plume, and as a hunchback with a squint. But Ludwig Devrient 'created' the role anew in 1824 by presenting him as a splendid gentleman in a heavily embroidered, black velvet dress of the eighteenth-century nobility with lace collar and cuffs, the sword of gallantry at his side and the elegant, noble manners of the *ancien régime*. The aspect of 'rogue' was expressed purely by mimic and gestic means and by an 'incredibly sweet, wicked smile, feverishly restless, insecure facial expressions, beautiful deceptive black eyes, a creeping walk, hypocritical gestures, a wheedling voice'.[2] The effect on the public was astounding. Frédérick Lemaître achieved a similar reaction a decade later when he took over the role of the villain in popular melodramas. Previously, the villain would enter the stage with tiny tripping steps as if he were afraid to be seen by the audience. Lemaître entered, however, with a natural stride which the audience celebrated as a sensation, a *grande geste* in which the creative personality of the actor was expressed to perfection.

Indeed, such actors as Devrient, Kean or Lemaître held a certain 'power' over their audiences because they were bold enough to disobey the theatre conventions (concerning expression) and thus knew how to evoke in the spectator the conviction that he was experiencing the direct and genuine expression of real, true emotions. Karoline Bauer, who appeared as a young actress with Ludwig Devrient, describes this process in her memoires:

I had already admired several great artists performing King Lear, but none came even comparably close to Devrient. His wonderful physiognomy reflected the changing emotions in a shocking way. When he wandered randomly around the heath in his madness his body seemed to be powerlessly driven back and forth by the elements of the storm, but when he did rouse himself again and was aware of his royal strength, he suddenly grew at least a head taller; his chest became broader, his limbs turned to iron and, in a last energetic and impressive magnificence, his eyes flashed. He was indeed, 'every inch a king'. The terrible, shattering tragedy in his whole appearance was stunning ... There was a deathly silence in the great theatre; all one could hear was the hushed sobbing of the trembling audience until a real storm of applause broke out at the end of the scene.[3]

Devrient held the audience in his power by giving them the feeling that they were being exposed to the expression of authentic emotions which in turn released intense emotions in them.

Not only did the actor express his 'incomparable personality' in the embodiment of classical roles to this effect (frequently Shakespeare or, as Devrient, from Schiller), but also in the representation of standard role-types from trivial dramas. The 'personality' of the actors increased the value of the text to such an extent that even critical minds no longer noticed the mediocre quality of the text. Thus Théophile Gautier describes *Robert Macaire*, the most popular play of the 1830s in Paris, as a clever elaboration of one of the most sorry efforts thrown together one could imagine (*L'Auberge des Adrets*).

> 'Robert Macaire' was the great triumph of revolutionary art which followed on the July Revolution ... There is something special about this particular play, and that is the sharp, desperate attack it makes on the order of society and on mankind as a whole. Around the character of Robert Macaire, Frédérick Lemaître created a genuinely Shakespearean comic figure – a terrifying gaiety, sinister laughter, bitter derision ... and on top of all that, an astonishing elegance, suppleness and grace which belongs to the aristocracy of vice.[4]

Because Frédérick Lemaître succeeded in transforming a poor text into one of significance by the power of his 'extraordinary personality', the shortcomings Gautier would have had difficulty in overlooking should he have read the text, eluded him.

In this respect, an extraordinary paradox can be identified which accords the theatre of this era a rather unglorious, and unworthy position in European theatre history. Although the exceptional actor was permitted to display the 'demon' of his 'unique personality' in the stereotype, standard roles of trivial drama as well as the heroes of classical literature without reserve, he was denied the great roles of contemporary drama. Heroes such as the Prince of Homburg, Manfred, Lorenzaccio and Danton were not seen on the European stage within the lifetimes of their authors.

A rift seems to have arisen between the public institution of theatre and aesthetically advanced dramas. Drama became – mostly against the will of the dramatists – dramas to be read. Despite the fact that theatre had exceptional actors at its disposal for even the toughest of roles, the stage remained closed to the most significant dramatists of the era.

In the case of Byron, this fact seemed particularly odd. For his readers across Europe tended to identify him not only with the heroes of his verse narratives – as Childe Harold, The Corsair, Don Juan – but also with his dramatic heroes – such as Manfred, Cain, Sardanapalus – and elevated the poet, already mystified and stylised as *the* romantic personality *per se*, to a glorified and much-imitated idol. Nevertheless Byron's dramas were never performed in his lifetime.

Instead, melodramas (in England and France) were introduced onto the stage and *Schicksalsdramen* (tragedies of fate) and *Schauerdramen* (Gothic-style tragedies) (in Germany), whose figures consisted of eternally repeated stereotypes, to which the concept of personality could not even remotely be applied – unless Frédérick Lemaître were to take them on. However, although these plays were not able to bring the new model of personality to the fore, they none the less articulated – however trivially, pathetically and inadequately – experiences and emotions which had deep significance for the people of the early nineteenth century and which were closely related to the cult of personality. In them, the citizen heard articulated his fear of committing actions against his will, and without his knowledge – actions which would debase him in the eyes of the public and allow him to sink in 'shame', as well as the equally great fear of being interrogated by inquisitive people, persecuted and driven into disaster. These trivial dramas fulfilled the important function of providing a safety valve for middle-class agonising over the destabilisation of the self.

The heroes of the *Schicksalsdramen* and *Schauerdramen* commit the most terrible crimes: patricide, fratricide and incest. Since, however, they act in ignorance and involuntarily, their responsibility is lifted. Not they, but the coincidence of time (for example, *24 February* by Zacharias Werner [1810] or *29 February* by Adolph Müllner [1812]), of space (cemetery, mountain ravine and so on) or fatal weapon (dagger, pistol) triggered the event. In this way, a sense of the 'uncanny' was introduced onto the stage. And through it came the awareness that the self is not master in one's own house, but is driven by dark, unknown powers which make the characters of the *Schicksalsdramen* seem strange and mysterious to themselves: 'I am a mystery to myself – difficult to solve' (Hugo, from Müllner's *The Debt*, 1812 [II, 1]). The dark powers can certainly be understood as the vague cipher of a growing identity crisis. The danger of a destabilisation of the self hovers threateningly in the air.

In melodrama, which shows a similarly changeable plot and seeks to produce strong emotional effects, the motif of persecution is given a prominent position. The oppositions of good and evil, villainy and innocence, victim and tormentor are played out in extreme contrast. 'Evil,' as it tries to destroy innocence, represents a central category of melodrama. In both genres, the guaranteed happy ending disperses the fears raised in the audience during the course of the plot, or at least weakens those fears and turns them into the thrill of the gruesome. The spectator was released in the comforting certainty that his fears are, in the end, groundless – the self will emerge untouched by threat, his personality will remain stable in the public arena.

The brusque refusal of theatre directors to put the works of Kleist, Byron, Shelley, de Musset, Grabbe and Büchner on the stage in their authors' lifetimes suggests that these dramas contained a basic contradiction of the social values of the time, or that they even threatened a vital taboo of the way in which society saw itself. Since personality (in the sense described at the beginning of this chapter) represented a central category of public life in England, Germany and France – despite other greater differences between the three nations – it seems reasonable to assume that the new concept of personality, as it was determined and articulated by the aesthetically advanced dramas of the era, contradicted the formerly widely accepted and propagated concept of personality in several crucial ways. Should this concept of personality not be in a position to weaken or refute the people's latent, or openly admitted, fear of the destabilisation of the self effectively, then the drama could not be performed. This is because it could not satisfy the most important function of theatre for the bourgeois society of the time – which was to provide its members with confirmation of the self.

**The discovery of the unconscious**

Although Kleist was certainly aware of the unique nature of his dramas and their anti-classical thrust, he continually sought to win the acknowledgement and even the admiration of the great Goethe. Goethe had commented benevolently to varying degrees on Kleist's novels, but he brusquely rejected the dramas. He did produce *Der zerbrochene Krug* (*The Broken Jug*) once in Weimar in 1807, but it was a spectacular flop. Goethe blamed the audience's rejection and lack of understanding, expressed in uncouth whistling in the presence of the duke and his wife, on the fact that, 'the play also belongs to the invisible theatre' (letter to Adam Müller, 28 August 1807). Kleist sent Goethe the *Phoebus* booklet with the fragment of *Penthesilea,* on 'my heart's knees' (letter to Goethe, 24 January 1808) and received the reply: 'I cannot get acquainted with Penthesilea. She derives from such a wonderful lineage and moves in such a foreign world, that I must take time to find myself in both' (letter to Kleist, 1 February 1808). Goethe is even said to have thrown his own copy of *Käbchen of Heilbronn* (completed in 1808 and printed in 1810) into the stove after he read it, saying that it was steeped in more of that 'cursed nature'. It was clear to him that 'the present Kleist is intent on confusing the emotions'. He felt that Kleist had created an image of man in his dramas which no longer had anything in common with classical drama.

In his final work, *Der Prinz von Homburg* (*The Prince of Homburg*),[5] which Kleist completed just months before his suicide in 1811, the poet set himself apart from the image of man in German classical drama in a programmatic way. He adopted its formal scheme of construction, such as the division into five acts, symmetrical composition, action and counteraction of hero and antagonist, and perfected it in a way never achieved before. In a formal sense, *The Prince of Homburg* is constructed with the greatest precision according to the principles of the German classic and shows a nearly perfect, symmetrical composition which extends even as far as the details of metaphor. As if to emphasise its connection with German classical drama, many direct allusions and references to Goethe's *Egmont* and more to his *Tasso* are worked into the text. Even the relationship between the protagonist (the Prince) and the antagonist (the Elector) is structured in such a way that it refers to the relationship between Kleist and Goethe.

Within this very direct reference to German classical drama, Kleist unfolds a figural conception that actually negates the principles of German classical drama. It determines all dramatic characters and is particularly noticeable in the changing relationship between the Prince and the Elector.

Such far-reaching change to all the characters is found in their enigmatic, mysterious natures. Whilst Iphigenia and Tasso, Wallenstein and Mary Stuart, allow the actor, and the audience/reader to gain insight into the reasons and motives behind particular decisions (at least in monologues) through extensive reflection and argumentation, Kleist's heroes are silent on the matter. All we learn is *that* a decision has been made, the reasons and motives behind it remain hidden.

When Homburg decides to write a letter to the Elector which will irrevocably change the situation, neither Natalie nor the spectator/reader learn how he arrived at this decision. Whilst it can be reasoned from his gestural behaviour – '*Sits down again, elbows bent upon the table, and pores over the letter*', '*Thinking hard*', '*taking up the pen*' (IV, 4, p. 330); '*writing*', '*concluding*', '*Seals the letter in an envelope*', '*standing up*' (IV, 4, p. 331) – that a process is occurring within him which leads to the decision, the decision is not weighed up, nor are the arguments for and against expressed on a linguistic level. Even the words themselves only point to the fact that the process is underway without, however, giving it any remotely linguistic form: 'It's becoming clear to me what I must write'; 'Yes, I'm listening. What is it?' (IV, 4, p. 330), 'I don't care' (IV, 4, p. 331). The decision itself was made somewhere at a point beyond language.

Even the Elector's decision-making thought process occurs without language. Thus, in Act IV, 1, on the basis of Natalie's report, he decides to show mercy to the Prince without making his decision transparent to Natalie or, in a later monologue, even the audience. The decision is made not as a consequence of an argumentative process, but rather, seems to have arisen spontaneously out of the moment ('*surprised*' [p. 321], '*utterly shocked*' [IV, 1, p. 322]). Nor are these decisions rationalised or grounded by language retrospectively, after they have been made. After reading Homburg's letter, the order is given immediately, 'Oh Prittwitz, let me have / the order for the Prince's execution. Also / bring me, if you would, the safe-conduct / for the Swedish envoy, Count von Horn' (V, 4, p. 336), which shows the Elector has already made the decision to pardon the Prince. The arguments brought by the officers, Kottwitz and Hohenzollern, in the next scene no longer influence this decision. The decision has fallen – without any reason being given.

If the decision-making process is no longer expressed verbally, the reasons and motives behind such decisions can only be assumed. This Natalie does in Act IV, 1 (p. 324):

> I've no idea, and shan't
> inquire what it was that moved you to be so
>     merciful
> so suddenly. But I am sure, Sir, in
> my heart I'm sure you never would descend
> to playing jokes on me. Let the letter say
> whatever it may say, my faith is, he
> is saved – and for that I have yourself to
>     thank!

The various deeply conflicting motives depend entirely on attitude and perspective. Whether the Elector wants the Prince executed because he is determined to carry out the law or whether he wants to be rid of a dangerous young rival who seeks to win his power and 'daughter', can no longer be divined with certainty. Equally puzzling is the question of whether he pardoned the Prince because he wants to fulfil the Prince's dream and elevate his position or, on the contrary, because he intends to humiliate the Prince by denying him a 'free death' and making him dependent again. Since the reasons for these decisions remain in the dark, the character can no longer be judged according to his actions. Whether such actions derive from magnanimity or petty spitefulness, from tried and tested principles, or from an emotional outburst, cannot be determined. Seen in terms of action alone, man remains a mystery to his fellow men. This fact is the cause of the lack of communication, permanent misunderstandings and the loneliness of Kleist's characters.

In place of action, the appearance which the individual shows his fellow men is significant. The Elector shows others the appearance of solid stability. He is always in control of the situation, even when it seems as if a revolution has broken out: 'Damnation! Every arrow I let fly / his armor turns aside' (V, 3, p. 335), the initiative mostly stems from him. He knows how to surprise others through his actions (I, 1), to shock them (III, 10) and to impress them (IV, 9), without revealing his own desires and feelings. He only shows a hint of feeling when he learns that the Prince led the cavalry (II, 10) – and thus is subject to the laws of war – and as Natalie tells him, 'All he thinks / of now, the only thing, is being saved!' (IV, 1, p. 321). The stage directions read, '*surprised*' (p. 321), '*utterly shocked*' (p. 322), '*in a state of confusion*' (p. 322). A more forceful emotional expression does not occur. The Elector has not only the situation but also himself so well under control, that his appearance in public always remains stable.

In contrast, the appearance presented by the Prince to the world changes all the time. In the very first scene, the court society is confronted with an image of the Prince which does not fit their idea of a 'hero' (I, 1, p. 272), and even less so their image of 'The Prince of Homburg, our gallant cousin, / who's led the cavalry in a hot chase / of the flying Swede for three whole days and only / now is back again, quite out of breath, / here in headquarters at Fehrbellin' (I, 1, p. 271). In place of a sword-wielding daredevil they face a 'somnambulist' (I, 1, p. 272), '*bareheaded and with his shirt open at the throat, nodding half asleep*' (I, 1), 'lost in dreams, he acts / posterity's part and himself weaves the glorious / crown of fame to set on his own head' (I, 1, p. 272). As somnambulist, the Prince discloses his most secret desires to those around him, desires which do not just concern 'the victor's crown' in 'Tomorrow's battle' (I, 1, p. 273). Society can accept this wish, even if they are alienated by the fact that the Prince openly reveals it in a dream and weaves himself the wreath of victory somewhat precipitously. The wordless scene in which the Elector tests 'how far gone the fellow / is' (I, 1, p. 273), shows, however, that the Prince's secret desires go far beyond that which the Elector and society are prepared to concede. Homburg dreams of Natalie's hand, 'Natalie! Dear girl!

My bride!' (I, 1, p. 274), of equality with the Elector, 'Prince Frederick! / My own father!' (p. 274), and of being accepted into the Elector's family, 'Oh, mother dear!' (p. 274). When they discover this, the court society withdraws in panic.

In this scene, the Prince shocks the court in two ways. On the one hand, he shows himself to those around him who think of him as a 'hero' as a sleepwalker and dreamer, and on the other hand, he creates and reveals an image of himself which takes him far beyond that which is sanctioned by society.

The Prince is, however, unaware of the identity construed, confirmed and revealed in a dream, which aims to gain fame, to win Natalie's hand and equal status with the Elector. This is apparent when, awakened from his somnambulist state by Hohenzollern, who calls him by his second name, 'Arthur', he remembers the incident devised by the Elector and tells Hohenzollern of a 'strange dream' (I, 4, p. 277). His narration of the dream is significantly different from the actual event in important ways. These aberrations concern, above all, the actions and characters of the Elector and Natalie. Whilst the Elector only took the wreath from Homburg's hand and gave it to Natalie so that she could show it to the Prince, then withdraw with him, the Prince remembers that the Elector gave it to Natalie in order that she could 'place it on my brow' (I, 4, p. 278). Furthermore, Natalie does not raise the wreath in her hand as she withdraws, but 'her purpose was to set a crown / on a hero's head' (I, 4, p. 279). At that moment, the Elector appeared to him as 'lofty-browed as Zeus' (I, 4, p. 278) and Natalie 'Aloft, just like / the spirit of glory' (I, 4, p. 279). This deification of the two people most important to him fits with his vision of the end, 'Endlessly, right up to Heaven's / door, the ramp … seems to reach' (I, 4, p. 279). These godlike figures, who clearly desire to reward him and elevate him to their level, are carried away into the palace as if it were heaven. Alongside these changes, it is particularly noticeable that the Prince, even with all the will in the world, can no longer

recall the name of the 'dream-figure' and cannot even remember Natalie's name.

The remembered 'dream', thus, only contains those elements which concern the Prince's generally accepted role as leader of the cavalry, as 'hero' (I, 4, p. 279): the desire for fame, which is put on the same level as deification, with being accepted in the circle of heavenly beings, through the framework created by the story. Everything to which society might object – the desire for Natalie's hand and equal status with the Elector – is carefully set aside. The Prince is unaware of the identity he has created for himself. His need to be assimilated into the world around him, above all, into the world of the Elector, and his desire to live up to the image that they have made of him, has led to a total subconscious suppression of his own desires. Once he returns to reality and consciousness, the Prince knows nothing more about them and, restricting himself to the role of the hero, he remains a mystery to himself.

It is only with the supposed death of the Elector that the obstacle which stands between his desires and his consciousness is removed. Conflict with the Elector appears out of the question. The Prince's secret desire to fulfil his potential can now be shifted over the threshold into a conscious desire for fulfilment. After the victory, the Prince does indeed put himself in the position of the Elector:

The Elector hoped, before the year was out,
to see the Marches, every corner, free.
Well, then – I'll be the executor of his
last will!

(II, 6, pp. 298–9)

He becomes engaged to Natalie and asks the Elector's wife for Natalie's hand in marriage. All his desires have been fulfilled. As victor in battle, successor to the Elector, and betrothed to Natalie, the Prince has seemingly realised the image of himself that he unconsciously created for himself; from his subjective point of view, nothing seems to stand in the way of his being accepted into the circle of those heavenly beings described in the narration of his dream:

'O *Caesar divus*, I / have stood my ladder up against your star!' (II, 8, p. 303).

From the heights of this apparently successful self-fulfilment the Prince plummets suddenly, with imprisonment and the death sentence imposed on him for insubordination. Since he is now entirely dependent on the mercy of the Elector, 'The court had no choice but to find / for death; the law by which it acts requires / that' (III, 1, p. 311), his desire for equal status with the Elector reveals itself as pure wishful thinking. Even his engagement to Natalie, instead of providing the guarantee of self-fulfilment, seems to be the very cause of his downfall: 'It's clear now, everything; the Swedish offer / is my ruination. I'm to blame / for her refusal; we're engaged, we two!' (III, 1, p. 313). The Elector reduces the Prince's self back to the image of hero: 'from the pulpit you were named, for so / His Majesty commanded, the victor of the day' (III, 1, p. 309). Since the Prince deceived himself so completely, not only in his 'idea' of the Elector, but also in his own idea of himself, his direct confrontation with death makes the possibility of such an identity seem worthless. Because the Elector and reality are alienated from him, he becomes alienated from himself. Thus, the Prince falls apart when faced with his grave, he sees himself reduced to bare physical existence: 'These eyes' and 'this breast' (III, 5 p. 316) become the only factors that seem to prove his existence. In this primal fear of death, the Prince denies all that has made up his identity until now:

Since I've seen my grave my only thought
is, Let me live, I don't care how! ...

No longer have I any wish
for Princess Natalie's hand, and don't fail to tell
him that – the tenderness I felt for her
is now extinguished, utterly.

(III, 5, pp. 316, 317)

The appearance of the Prince in the death scene (III, 5) suggests a total self-alienation which extends as far as giving up the self for the sake of sheer physical survival.

The Elector's letter provides the Prince with a potential new definition of the self, 'He leaves it up to me – *I* must decide!' (IV, 4, p. 330). It makes him independent of the Elector's further plans and reflections – 'He can do just as he pleases, let / him – I must do just as I should' (IV, 4, p. 331), and thus puts them both on the same level: 'I shouldn't want to act / a dishonorable part before a man / who acts so honorably toward me' (IV, 4, p. 331). On the basis of equal status to the Elector, the Prince can create a new identity for himself. He chooses absolute self-determination, 'by freely choosing death!' (V, 7, p. 345). With this act, he gains possession of the two other factors on which the self-fulfilment of the dream scene depended: victory in battle and Natalie's hand:

Every word you utter
is the promise of a victory whose flowering
will crush our enemy into the dust! She is
the Prince of Homburg's bride, I'll write so now
to Sweden; his, no other's, who forfeited
his life, for Fehrbellin, on the altar of the law.

(V, 7, p. 346)

In recognising the fact that self-fulfilment is only possible in total autonomy, even when this demands the high price of death, the Prince finally gains superiority over the Elector. For, whilst he calls upon him the 'blessing' of the 'seraphim' (V, 7, p. 347), he himself rises to the heavenly ranks as one of them:

Now immortality, you're mine, entirely
mine! Your light shines through my blindfold
with the brilliance of a thousand suns! On
   either shoulder
wings unfold, my soul mounts up into the silent
upper spheres; and as a ship, borne
forward by the wind, sees dropping fast behind
the busy port, so all life sinks
and fades for me into the haze – and now
I still can make out shapes and colours,
and now all's shrouded in a thickening mist.

(V, 10, p. 349)

Total self-fulfilment is, in the 'faulty, or imperfect structure or order of the world' (*Marquise of O*),[6] only possible in death.

The changing images of the Prince do not demonstrate an actual destabilisation of the self, but rather a change in the consciousness, through which the self can finally define itself and be realised.

His appearance is variously made up of language and body as expressions of the state of consciousness. In the state of unconsciousness, the 'dream', the desires and feelings of the Prince are expressed through body and language, spontaneously and directly: 'Natalie! Dear Girl! My bride!', 'Prince Frederick! / My own father!', 'Oh, mother dear!', 'My darling! Don't, please, run away from me! / Oh Natalie!' (I, 1, p. 274). The stage directions describe how he '...blushes ... jumps up ... the Prince follows after her with outstretched arms, ... snatching at the wreath' (I, 1, pp. 273–4).

Once the state of consciousness is reached, language and body fall apart; only the body can now express the Prince's desires and feelings spontaneously and directly. In Act I, 4, 'The Prince collapses ... looking at the glove in his hand ... Recovering himself' (pp. 276–7); and in Act I, 5, 'The Prince ... stares sideways at the women ... steals a glance toward the ladies ... He pulls the glove out of his doublet ... stands thunderstruck; then turns and marches triumphantly back among the officers ... The Prince is staring dreamily at the ground' (pp. 282, 283, 286, 287), and so on. Language, however, is no longer capable of spontaneous and direct expression in this state, becoming, instead, a pose. The use of language as role-play can be taken as measure of the crisis of identity. In order to assimilate himself into the various situations he confronts, the Prince uses, in turn, the language of transfiguration (I, 6), the jargon of the culprit (II, 2), conventional rhetoric (II, 6), emotional and critical speech (III, 1), until, in the death scene (III, 5), all his previous speech gestures fall apart and, from the letter scene on, he gradually finds a new kind of language. It is only in the state of total self-fulfilment, in the monologue on immortality (V, 10), that the Prince is able to express himself in language 'honestly' and show himself in a direct and genuine light.

Change in appearance thus becomes the dramatic-theatrical sign for the journey 'all around the world' (Über das Marionnetten-theater)[7] which the protagonist makes in his search for the self. There can be no doubt that Kleist viewed a personality which expresses itself through such changing images as greater than one which presents those around it with an unchanging, stable image. The apotheotic end of the drama springs, in this sense, from

> Poor Heinrich Kleist's dream of the lucky Prince of Homburg, who, delicate and powerful, close to death, lives out his greatest desires and ideals in the face of the restrictive conditions of life at the time and who finally, as in a miracle, experiences their paradisical fulfilment. And, at the same time, the cold, weak state, which only functions on a formal level, turns into a vital, humane political community in which the outsider, the judged, the social 'outcast' rises to become the first hero.[8]

Kleist's contemporaries, however, were of a different opinion. After The Prince of Homburg was published in 1821 (in Hinterlassenen Schriften, edited by Tieck), the character of the Prince was criticised as 'sick' (Hegel in 1828, Fontane as late as 1872!) and 'cowardly' and was fiercely rejected. For the audience, the image of the 'hero' was incompatible with somnambulism, spontaneous expression, and mortal agony. Such a changeable identity could only mean a total destabilisation of the self. Consequently, the play was only produced on stage when certain scenes (I, 1; III, 5) were omitted – or at least when the Prince's mortal agony was changed into the fear of shameful death by execution. Accordingly, the résumé written by Heinrich Laube in 1875 on the first fifty years of the production of the drama is somewhat gloomy:

> The Prince of Homburg has, despite great poetic appeal, never found wide distribution because the character of the Prince, as a soldier who suffers mortal agony to the point of misery, makes a rather too embarrassing impression, and because

his morbidity, even if it is handled poetically, appears so unflatteringly on the stage.[9]

It was only in 1878 that the Meiningen company risked presenting an unabridged version of *The Prince of Homburg* on stage, with Josef Kainz in the main role. In so doing, they began a process which would lead to a fundamental new appraisal of the play and its hero in the twentieth century. One can certainly say that the outstanding production of the play by Jean Vilar at the Théâtre Nationale Populaire (1951), with Gérard Philippe in the main role, turned Kleist's hero into the absolute, prototypical embodiment of 'modern' consciousness.

**Decaying values**

The experience of the 'uncanny' and 'evil', articulated in a minor way on the European stage at the end of the eighteenth century and beginning of the nineteenth century in the almost conveyor-belt productions of *Schicksalsdramen*, *Schauerdramen* and melodramas, had already led to the constitution of a new literary genre in mid-eighteenth century England: the gothic novel. The new genre was founded overnight in 1765 with Horace Walpole's *The Castle of Otranto*. The novel was an immediate success; it was reprinted twenty times before 1800 and countless imitations appeared after it. *The Castle of Otranto* contained all the elements which would later define the genre: a medieval castle, which provides a sinister setting with secret corridors and a labyrinthine network of underground passages; a mysterious crime, an unwitting patricide, fratricide or infanticide etc., often coupled with a forbidden and, as it mostly turns out in the end, incestuous love affair; an aristocratic rogue and arch-villain, who wantonly lusts after an innocent, angelic young maid; and a charming young gentleman who seeks to expose the evildoer and release the innocent victim from his claws. The gentleman is usually allowed to do this before the end of the novel, so that he can celebrate his marriage to the happy girl whilst the evildoer either atones for his sins in a monastery, or as is more

commonly the case, is driven into the devil's arms, having made a pact with him to die a miserable death. After Walpole, other writers such as William Beckford (*Vathek*, 1786), Anne Radcliffe (*The Mysteries of Udolpho*, 1794; *The Italian*, 1792) and Mathew Gregory Lewis (*The Monk*, 1796) developed these basic elements even further.

The main theme of the gothic novel in all its varieties is 'inescapable fear'.[10] It is the presentiment of the 'dark side' of the human soul which is reflected and expressed. Although one might suppose that the existence of such a dark side stood at variance to the image of man as created by the Enlightenment, the gothic novel did not, in fact, contradict the values which prevailed in the enlightened bourgeois society of the eighteenth century.

This is principally due to three factors. First, the arch-villain came from the nobility. The evil incarnated by him – like the evil aristocratic seducer in the *bürgerliche Trauerspiel* – pointed to the corruption and depravity of his class rather than an inborn human tendency towards evil. Man could still be viewed as intrinsically good. The second factor supports this idea. The innocent victim, like the virtuous daughter in the *bürgerliche Trauerspiel*, remained steadfast even under the most threatening conditions. She does not fall into temptation, but protects her angelic virtue even when her innocence has been violently robbed. Evil, in the form of the aristocratic villain, proves incapable of touching, besmirching or even spoiling the naturally given good in mankind. Third, the action had an effect on the emotions (in the sense of the soul) and so generated an increased sensitivity in the reader. Thus, the gothic novel did not step beyond the horizons fixed by the values of eighteenth-century bourgeois society, though individual works may well have contravened its sense of 'good taste' with detailed descriptions of horror scenes and excesses (for example, in *Vathek* and, in particular, *The Monk*).

The enormous popularity of the gothic novel would suggest that it fulfilled an especially important function within the Puritan-bourgeois society. The work ethic and ascetic sexual abstinence characterised the bourgeois lifestyle in England far more than elsewhere. Industrialisation occurred considerably earlier in England than in the rest of Europe (around 1770). It is hardly surprising, therefore, that it was in England that the increased pressure of the advancing process of civilisation gave rise to fears of losing control. By reading a gothic novel, this destructive potential could be unloaded in the reader's inner world; moreover, the reader was effectively led towards an affirmation of the prevailing value system by the novel's ending. Public life in bourgeois society was, in this way, barely affected by the fears of its members, and its smooth functioning was certainly not restricted in any way.

The *gothic novel* not only served as the source of *gothic drama*, or melodrama, of the turn of the century, by providing a large fund of material, but also fed into the aesthetically advanced drama of English Romanticism.

In the 'dramatic poem' *Manfred* (1817), Byron incorporated elements from well-known gothic novels – his hero bears the name of the gothic hero in *The Castle of Otranto*. The Abbot who seeks to convert Manfred in the last Act similarly refers to the novel, as does the setting of the very first scene, '*a gothic gallery*'. Act II, 4, which plays in 'The Hall of Arimanes', is a direct quote from one of the most important sections of the conclusion of *Vathek* – the apotheosis of Satan. Like Eblis, Arimanes, 'the evil principle', sits 'upon a Globe of Fire' (letter to Thomas Moore, 25 March 1817). Byron deliberately adopts the constitutive elements of the gothic novel in the form of the aristocratic villain and his fate, but he changes them in a marked way. The *gothic villain* is transformed into the absolute embodiment of the Byronic hero.

The fundamental experience for Manfred – as for most Byronic heroes – is the clear awareness of difference from others:

From my youth upwards
My spirit walk'd not with the souls of men,
Nor look'd upon the earth with human eyes;

The thirst of their ambition was not mine,
The aim of their existence was not mine;
My joys, my griefs, my passions, and my
    powers,
Made me a stranger; though I wore the form,
I had no sympathy with breathing flesh, ...

I said, with men, and with the thoughts of men,
I held but slight communion ...

(II, 2, 50–7, 60–1)

The knowledge of his difference from others leads to Manfred's lack of interest in human company. To the Abbot's question, 'And why not live and act with other men?', he counters:

I disdained to mingle with
A herd, though to be a leader – and of wolves,
The lion is alone, and so am I.

(III, 1, 121–3)

The proud 'bird of Prey' refutes the approaches of the 'brute of burthen' with the words: 'I am not of thine order' (II, 1, 36–7). Manfred is alienated from all kinds of human contact through his insatiable 'thirst of knowledge' (II, 2, 95), and it leads him to 'Conclusions most forbidden' (83) and enables him to subjugate widely differing spirits so that even they are forced to acknowledge that:

This man
Is of no common order ...
his sufferings
Have been of an immortal nature, like
Our own; his knowledge and his powers and
    will,
As far as is compatible with clay,
Which clogs the ethereal essence, have been
    such
As clay has seldom borne; his aspirations
Have been beyond the dwellers of the earth ...

(II, 4, 51–9)

In spite of his unique nature, Manfred was originally not alone. In Lady Astarte, whom we can view as his sister, he found a female alter-ego:

She was like me in lineaments – her eyes,
Her hair, her features, all, to the very tone
Even of her voice, they said were like to mine;
But soften'd all, and temper'd into beauty;
She had the same lone thoughts and wander-
  ings,
The quest of hidden knowledge, and a mind
To comprehend the universe: nor these
Alone, but with them gentler powers than
  mine,
Pity, and smiles, and tears – which I had not;
And tenderness – but that I had for her;
Humility – and that I never had.
Her faults were mine – her virtues were her
  own –
I loved her, and destroy'd her!
                              (II, 2, 105–17)

The love for his sister, for his female alter-ego, enables Manfred to experience the joy of total self-fulfilment. Here, Byron uses conscious and desired incest as the metaphor for successful self-fulfilment and in so doing offers a provocative countermodel to the gothic novel.

Manfred's love for Astarte gains him the paradise of total self-awareness from which his own secret guilt, which is the cause of Astarte's death and which robs him of his second self, has expelled him:

I lov'd her, and destroy'd her!

WITCH: With thy hand?
MANFRED: Not with my hand, but heart –
  which broke her heart –
  It gaz'd on mine, and withered. I have shed
  Blood, but not hers – and yet her blood
  was shed –
  I saw – and could not staunch it.
                              (II, 2, 117–21)

The loss of the beloved alter-ego gives expression to the central experience of every Byronic hero: the sudden realisation of self-alienation. At the same time, its coupling to a secret guilt exposes the hero's paradoxical existential situation. He can only find self-fulfilment in his love for Astarte. However, this love is directly and indissolubly bound to the guilt which leads to self-alienation. Thus the hero must either relinquish the idea of self-fulfilment, or his self-fulfilment will inevitably result in self-alienation brought down upon him through his own sin, for which only he is to blame:

If I had never lived, that which I love
Had still been living; had I never loved,
That which I love would still be beautiful –
Happy and giving happiness …
                              (II, 2, 193–6)

Since that 'all-nameless hour' (I, 1, 24) Manfred feels alienated, 'My solitude is solitude no more,/ But peopled with the Furies' (II, 2, 130–1).

Unlike the Prince of Homburg, this process is irreversible and cannot be lifted by a 'journey around the world'. The paradise of successful self-fulfilment remains closed to Manfred forever. From now on it is impossible for Manfred to 'restore thee to thyself' (Gemsenjäger, II, 1, 89) or 'To reconcile thyself with thy own soul' (Abbot, III, 1, 99). This is the source of Manfred's 'brotherhood of Cain' (I, 1, 249) – he must live in the full consciousness of an 'own Hell' (I, 1, 251), self-induced, inescapable and inevitably self-alienating.

Manfred does make several attempts to free himself from this knowledge. He begs the spirits to give him 'Forgetfulness' (I, 1, 136), 'Oblivion, self-oblivion' (144), but they are not able to help him. He also tries to resolve his sense of self in finding empathy with nature:

How beautiful is all this visible world!
How glorious in its action and itself;
… Oh, that I were
The viewless spirit of a lovely sound,
A living voice, a breathing harmony,
A bodiless enjoyment – born and dying
With the blest tone that made me!
                              (I, 2, 37–8, 52–6)

He realises, however, the impossibility of his dream:

But we, who name ourselves its sovereigns,
  we,

Half dust, half deity, alike unfit
To sink or soar, with our mix'd essence make
A conflict of its elements.

(I, 2, 39–42)

This 'mixed essence' makes it seem impossible to find resolution either in the material or in the spiritual world – the knowledge of self-alienation remains. Finally, Manfred seeks to escape it by committing suicide: 'Earth! Take these atoms!' (I, 2, 109), but his plans are thwarted by Gemsenjäger.

Although Manfred is to live with the knowledge of irreversible and self-induced alienation, 'I dwell in my despair – / And live – and live for ever' (II, 2, 149–50), and self-fulfilment will be forever denied him, the very same knowledge allows him the possibility of limitless self-determination. He calls upon the 'Promethean spark' (I, 1, 154) within himself to reject any kind of subjugation. He refuses to obey the spirits (II, 2, 158–69) – a precondition which they had set before agreeing to free him from his 'doubts'. Unlike Vathek, who throws himself down to Eblis, or Satan, Manfred proudly refuses to 'Bow down and worship' (II, 4, 30) before Arimanes:

Bid him bow down to that which is above him,
The overruling Infinite – the Maker
Who made him not for worship – let him kneel,
And we will kneel together.

(II, 4, 46–9)

Similarly, unlike the gothic villain Manfred in *The Castle of Otranto*, who allows himself to be converted by the Abbot to a life of repentance in a monastery, Byron's Manfred rejects the Abbot's mediation 'between Heaven and myself' (III, 1, 53–4):

there is no power in holy men,
Nor charm in prayer …
The innate tortures of that deep despair,
Which is remorse without the fear of hell,
But all in all sufficient to itself
Would make a hell of heaven …
there is no future pang
Can deal that justice on the self-condemn'd

He deals on his own soul.

(III, 1, 66–7, 70–3, 76–8)

An uncompromising Manfred holds true to himself, to that which he is ('that I / Am what I am' [III, 1, 151–2]), and to that which he has done ('What I have done is done' [III, 4, 127]). He remains true to himself and his own nature, 'I could not tame my nature down; … / And be a living lie' (III, 1, 116, 119). Thus, he defies the demon who comes to fetch him at the end (like the devil Ambrosio in *The Monk*):

The mind which is immortal makes itself
Requital for its good or evil thoughts –
Is its own origin of ill and end – …

Thou didst not tempt me, and thou couldst
  not tempt me;
I have not been thy dupe, nor am thy prey –
But was my own destroyer, and will be
My own hereafter.

(III, 4, 129–31, 137–40)

Until the very end, Manfred demands radical autonomy: the joy of self-fulfilment is denied him; neither man nor spirit, heaven nor hell, can give any sense to the guilt and sorrow which follow from the resulting self-alienation. All that is left is for Manfred to be his own 'damnation', his own 'destroyer', with consequent self-determination. He is not prepared to confer value on any system of order, any authority, other than that of his Self. The only quality to which he attaches great importance is his autonomy: this he realises with a rebellious gesture against any who contend his right of self-determination. The aristocratic villain of the gothic novel, who in the end is forced to recognise the existence of higher values, is transformed into a metaphysical rebel for whom all values outside his own self-autonomy are utterly meaningless.

In *Manfred*, Byron began an open conflict with the bourgeois society of the time, which *Cain* (1821) was to intensify. The new quality of this conflict is apparent when compared to the *Sturm und Drang* movement. Through the great rebel heroes of *Sturm und Drang* dramas such as Götz von Berlichingen or Karl Moor, the poets force society to see that the values which it officially proclaims and enforces as its foundation are, *de facto,* betrayed daily in social reality. Criticism of society thus occurs on the basis of a fundamental consensus and must be dealt with openly. Byron's *Manfred,* on the other hand, represents a radical negation of the values and opinions that were binding for the bourgeois society of his time, which gave its members the feeling of security and order they demanded in the form of morals and religion. Although Manfred – just as Byron's other heroes – gave expression to the lifestyle of an entire generation of young intellectuals across Europe, negotiation or compromise with bourgeois society was out of the question.

Byron was very well aware of this contradiction – and perhaps even celebrated it. He wrote *Manfred* without the slightest intention of having it performed ('I have at least rendered it quite impossible for the stage' [*Letters and Journals IV*]), although his enthusiasm for Edmund Kean's tragic acting skill has clearly left traces on Manfred's actions. The play was conceived as 'mental theatre' – even if Byron only introduced the term for his later dramas.

After Byron's death, it was, however, performed, as a spectacle, and of course, in a much modified form. The Covent Garden production (1834) – like the two following productions (1863 in Drury Lane, 1873 in the Princess Theatre) – omitted the allusions to incest, and presented Manfred shrouded in mystery, as a 'great personality', ending the play with the apocalyptic battle of the powers of good and evil: 'The Glaciers of the upper Alps! / partly / Borne down by a violent Thunderstorm, / And exhibiting in their ruins, the Evidences of / Crime and Punishment, with the moral of the drama.'[11] Of course, the powers of good were victorious and brought the moral of the play and the moral understanding of the audience into harmonious agreement. *Cain,* on the other hand, was banned from the stage throughout the nineteenth century. It was finally premièred in New York in 1925.

Like *Manfred,* Shelley's *The Cenci* (1819) was also not performed for some time. Although Shelley was not generally interested in theatre, he wrote this play for the stage with a particular actress in mind, whom he especially admired. He asked Thomas Peacock, fellow poet and friend, to bring it to Covent Garden: 'What I want you to do is, to procure for me its presentation at Covent garden. The principal character, Beatrice, is precisely fitted for Miss O'Neill, and it might even seem written for her (God forbid that I should ever see her play it – it would only tear my nerves to pieces), and, in all respects, it is fitted only for Covent garden. The chief male character, I confess, I should be very unwilling that anyone but Kean should play – that is impossible, and I must be contented with an inferior actor' (July 1819). Not only was the play rejected by Covent Garden, Miss O'Neill was not even shown the text lest it shock her too greatly. Finally, in 1886, *The Cenci* was premièred under the patronage of the Shelley Society at a private showing at the Grand Theatre, Islington, London. Despite the success of the production, the play was not put on again.

Shelley bases *The Cenci* on two particularly popular literary genres, the *domestic play* and the *gothic novel.* From the domestic play, he adopted the relationship of the father and child, principally father and daughter. From the gothic novel, he took the relationship between the aristocratic villain and the innocent victim. Shelley bound these two ideas to one another and turned them around: the tender father, who protects the virtue of his daughter from her seducer turns into the fiend who threatens the daughter's virtue himself; the innocent victim, who protects her virtue under the most hideous of circumstances, commits patricide.

Moreover, Shelley also made a further important change to this reversal. From the very beginning, the opposition between Count Cenci and his daughter, Beatrice, is accorded a cosmic dimension. Thus, Cenci is not only introduced as an evil and unnatural father who prays God for the death of his sons and who cruelly tortures his family without reason, but also through the images attributed to him, as one who belongs to the sphere of darkness. He is described as 'dark and bloody' (II, 1, 55) and as a man who was 'dark and fiery' (I, 1, 49) in his youth. Beatrice, on the other hand, not only appears as the innocent victim, but is also allocated the sphere of light. She is a 'bright form' with an 'awe-inspiring gaze, / Whose beams anatomise [Orsino] nerve by nerve, / And lay [him] bare' (I, 2, 84–6). Cenci's attempt to rape his daughter and 'to poison and corrupt her soul' thus, finally, appears as the battle between darkness and light in a Manichaean sense.

In the character of Cenci, the fundamental concept of bourgeois society that 'from the beginning of time … the patriarch may employ a certain domestic violence where needed' (*Deutsche Enzyklopädie*, 1784), is taken to the extreme *ad absurdum*. Cenci abuses his patriarchal power to torture those dependent on him in a sadistic way:

I the father
Look on such pangs as terror ill conceals,
The dry fixed eyeball; the pale quivering lip,
Which tell me that the spirit weeps within
Tears bitterer than the bloody sweat of Christ.
I rarely kill the body, which preserves,
Like a strong prison, the soul within my power,
Wherein I feed it with the breath of fear
For hourly pain.
(I, 1, 109–17)

Cenci wins the perverse pleasure of an inflated view of himself from his knowledge of the unlimited power which he holds over others. After God apparently hears his prayer for the death of his sons, his feeling of omnipotence knows no bounds. He can no longer bear the fact that his daughter, who previously stood with her 'firm mind', 'Like a protecting presence' between him and his victims as the only 'refuge and defence' (II, 1, 48–9), now raises her voice against him in front of his guests. His self-confidence, which stems from the awareness of his unassailable omnipotence, is wounded to the core. Cenci believes he can only regain his position by transforming his sole antagonist, his daughter, into an image of himself. To do this, he must enact a 'deed

which shall confound both night and day' (II, 2, 183), a deed which will 'poison and corrupt her soul' (IV, 1, 45).

In raping his daughter, Cenci attempts to alienate her, and thus himself, from the elements 'light', 'warmth', 'brightness', which are identified with her:

'Tis she shall grope through a bewildering mist
Of horror: if there be a sun in heaven
She shall not dare to look upon its beams;
Nor feel its warmth. Let her then wish for night.
(II, 1, 184–7)

Sensing his regained omnipotence after raping Beatrice, Cenci curses her in order to ensure that he will continue to triumph over her even after his death:

God!
Hear me! If this most specious mass of flesh,
Which Thou hast made my daughter; this my blood,
This particle of my divided being;
Or rather, this my bane and my disease,
Whose sight infects and poisons me; this devil
Which sprung from me as from a hell, was meant
To aught good use; if her bright loveliness
Was kindled to illumine this dark world;
If nursed by Thy selectest dew of love
Such virtues blossom in her as should make
The peace of life, I pray Thee for my sake,
As Thou the common God and Father art
Of her, and me, and all; reverse that doom!
Earth, in the name of God, let her food be Poison …
All-beholding sun,
Strike in thine envy those life-darting eyes
With thine own blinding beams!
(IV, 1, 114–29, 134–6)

It is only when there is no longer light in Beatrice, to 'illumine this dark world', no 'virtues' to make the 'peace of life', that Cenci can be sure that he is ubiquitous and omnipotent. For, if he succeeds in this, the whole world will be like him:

There shall be lamentation heard in Heaven
As o'er an angel fallen; and upon Earth
All good shall droop and sicken, and ill things
Shall with a spirit of unnatural life
Stir and be quickened ... even as I am now.
(IV, 1, 185–9)

In fact, after the rape, Beatrice is not herself. Lucretia notices, 'Thou art unlike thyself' (III, 1, 81). Beatrice recounts her traumatic experience:

I am choked! There creeps
A clinging, black, contaminating mist
About me ... 'tis substantial, heavy, thick,
I cannot pluck it from me, for it glues
My fingers and my limbs to one another,
And eats into my sinews, and dissolves
My flesh to a pollution, poisoning
The subtle, pure, and inmost spirit of life!
(III, 1, 16–23)

Beatrice experiences the rape in a fundamentally different way to that experienced by the violated innocent girl of the gothic novel (for example, Antonia in *The Monk*) who sees the act as a violence done to the body which does not, however, touch upon her 'angelic' being in any way. Beatrice, on the contrary, experiences it as a distortion, poisoning and dissolution of her body in which something has occurred 'which has transformed me' (III, 1, 109). She has been wounded to the innermost self: 'Oh, what am I? / What name, what place, what memory shall be mine?' (III, 1, 74–5). Beatrice senses that the only way to find her self again, to halt the process of self-alienation caused by the violation, is to banish it at once, otherwise she will fall into the danger of a total loss of self, a total 'metamorphosis':

Ay, something must be done;
What, yet I know not ... something which
    shall make
The thing that I have suffered but a shadow
In the dread lightning which avenges it;
Brief, rapid, irreversible, destroying
The consequence of what it cannot cure.
Some such thing is to be endured or done:

When I know what, I shall be still and calm,
And never anything will move me more.
(III, 1, 86–95)

When Beatrice decides to kill her father in order to recover her self, it becomes apparent to what extent her 'metamorphosis' has already begun: her speech contains almost exact echoes of sentences uttered previously by Cenci. Beatrice informs Lucretia and Orsino of her intentions with the words, 'I pray, / That you put off, as garments overworn, / Forbearance and respect, remorse and fear' (III, 1, 207–9). In I, 1, Cenci elevated himself above others with the words, 'I have no remorse and little fear' (84). Beatrice appeals to God in the crime of patricide (III, 1 65), just as her father appealed to God for the death of his sons (I, 3, 65). As Marcio and Olympio, the hired killers, shrink back from the deed, Beatrice reviles them as 'Base palterers' (IV, 3, 25), in the same way that Cenci cursed Lucretia, 'Vile palterer' (IV, 1, 73) when she refused to fetch Beatrice. When Beatrice thinks about the completion of the deed, she realises, 'My breath / Comes, methinks, lighter, and the jellied blood / Runs freely through my veins!' (IV, 1, 42–4). In a similar way, Cenci comments on the curse of his daughter, 'My blood is running up and down my veins' (IV, 1, 161). After the murder of her father, Beatrice heaves a sigh of relief, 'Let us retire to counterfeit deep rest; / ... I could even sleep / Fearless and calm' (IV, 3, 61, 64–5). In anticipation of his curse being fulfilled, Cenci withdrew with the words: 'I will go / First to belie thee with an hour of rest, / Which will be deep and calm' (IV, 2, 180–2). Beatrice has begun to change into her father, that is, to reflect his nature within herself.

After killing her father, Beatrice believes she has found herself again, she thinks she has escaped 'Darkness and Hell' (IV, 3, 41) and been given back the 'sweet light of life' (42):

The deed is done, ...

I am as universal as the light;
Free as the earth-surrounding air; as firm
As the world's centre.
(IV, 4, 46, 48–50)

In this conviction, she insists that she is 'innocent' and 'guiltless' (IV, 4, 112, 143, 159, 162, 184; V, 2, 59, 80, 138, 140, 152; V, 3, 24; V, 4, 110). Beatrice's words should evoke a self which is, however, ultimately lost through the very action which should have recreated it. The only way to avoid self-alienation has, in fact, led to its irreversible reinforcement. This is the tragic fate of Beatrice.

None the less, she does succeed in convincing others that she is 'innocent' and thereby herself again. Marcio, the murderer explains: 'She is most innocent' (V, 2, 165); Camillo calls her and those around her, 'most innocent and noble persons' (V, 2, 187); her brother Giacomo acknowledges, after he has confessed, that she is 'the only one thing innocent and pure / In this black guilty world' (V, 3, 101–2); and her brother Bernardo weeps over 'That perfect mirror of pure innocence' in her (V, 4, 130), the 'light of life' (V, 134).

After the confessions of Lucretia and Giacomo, the Pope irrevocably turns down the plea for clemency and Beatrice realises that she will never recover her self again: 'I am cut off from the only world I know, / From light and life, and love, in youth's sweet prime. ... my heart is cold' (V, 4, 85–6, 89). The self-alienation initiated and enacted by her father can no longer be made retroactive. In this sense, he is the final victor:

> For was he not alone omnipotent
> On Earth, and ever present? Even though dead,
> Does not his spirit live in all that breathe,
> And work for me and mine still the same ruin,
> Scorn, pain, despair.
>
> (V, 4, 68–72)

In the battle of the powers of darkness and light, evil can gain victory because the world in which the battle takes place is intrinsically evil and bad. The patriarchal figure of this society, the Pope, even appears as the source of such evil. His perverse desire for power and possession induce him to cover up even the most dreadful of Cenci's crimes. His fear of losing 'authority and power' makes him decide to deny Beatrice a pardon. He does not act as a

'person' but as 'the engine / Which tortures and which kills' (V, 4, 2–3). His decision not to make Cenci answer for his crimes and to allow Beatrice to be executed for the murder of her father embraces the beginning and the end of the play: evil asserts itself in the world in the body of the Pope. Beatrice's self-alienation is not caused by the *conditio humana* – as is Manfred's – but is grounded in real social conditions. The patriarchal society is the root of all evil. It creates violence and hate which are continuously self-perpetuating and incontestable. Self-alienation is the necessary consequence. The annulment of the patriarchal order of society seems to be a precondition to self-alienation being eradicated.

In this, the abolition of patriarchal society is simultaneously shown to be the precondition of the ultimate victory of good and the power of light in the cosmic battle. For, as long as human society maintains its patriarchal structure, evil will continue to hold power. The victory or defeat of the cosmic battle is, in this sense, considerably affected by the social system.

It seems incredible that Shelley could have thought even for a moment that Covent Garden would produce his play. A more annihilating stroke against the foundations of bourgeois society and patriarchal order than *The Cenci* is inconceivable.

## The outsider: the noble robber and the artist

The heroes in Kleist, Byron and Shelley all stand outside society. Occupied with their own selves, their desire for self-fulfilment, the shock of sudden self-alienation and their insistence on self-determination, they are only aware of society in terms of how it relates to their own, individual selves and problems – society only either confirms or denies the hero his right to self-determination. To the world around them, such heroes remain a total mystery. Accordingly, society plays only a peripheral role for Kleist's hero; for Byron's heroes, a subordinate one. Shelley does present a relationship between the problem of identity and social conditions, but he focuses more on the traumatic experience of self-alienation, on the moment of 'infection' by things which are quite other and the consequences such contact brings.

The playwrights of the French Romantic movement, on the other hand, positioned the outsider in direct confrontation with society, its expectations of individual behaviour and its conventions. Their primary interest is to investigate the extent to which the self-alienation, which made the outsider the way he is, is a social problem. Thus, they choose their heroes principally from a milieu which, by definition, is distanced from 'normal' social life: from amongst those outcast by society, such as outlaws and bandits, or artists, poets and actors.

Since drama was going to raise the question of social problems, a public forum, or stage was needed. Thus, it is hardly surprising that Hugo, de Vigny and Dumas (père) wrote their dramas explicitly for the theatre, even with particular actresses and actors in mind, and that they were eager to see their plays performed. Unlike in Germany and England, in France, the controversy over a new kind of drama took place on the stage. It was here that the most important battles were (literally) staged between 1830 and 1840. Only de Musset, after the spectacular flop of his comedy *La nuit vénétienne* (1830 at the Odéon Theatre), worked on the idea of a 'spectacle dans un fauteuil' ('armchair theatre'). The irony of history has willed that the only remaining dramas from the French Romantic theatre are examples of precisely such 'armchair theatre'.

In *Préface de Cromwell*, the manifesto of the French Romantic movement, published in 1827, Victor Hugo quashes any doubts that the long overdue aesthetic revolution, the liberation from the imposed rule of classicism, could achieve the same heights gained by the revolution in society, in the arts. Accordingly, in his prologue to *Hernani* (1830), he declared that everyone should have free access to art and thus proposed an important change to the constitution of the theatre audience: 'The principle of literary freedom, already understood by those who read and meditate, has not been less completely adopted by the huge crowds greedy for the pure emotions of art, who inundate the theatres of Paris every night. This loud and mighty voice of the people which is like that of God, would wish that poetry should hereafter have the same motto as politics: TOLERANCE AND LIBERTY.' Art should no longer be the exclusive possession and privilege of the social *élite*, but belong to the people: Hugo conceived his theatre as a theatre for the people.

The search for an audience for his newly found people's theatre led Hugo to the Boulevard du Crime (which Marcel Carné transformed into an unforgettable monument in the film, *Enfants du Paradis*, 1945), where the public streamed into vaudeville shows and melodramas. He wanted to write his drama for just such an audience, though he clearly saw them in an idealised way. For 'the audience ... has never been so enlightened, nor so serious, as now' (Preface to *Marion de Lorne*). Thus, Hugo hoped this audience would fulfil the 'mission' of drama, a mission he viewed as 'a national mission, a social mission, a humane mission'. 'When, each night, he [the author] sees such intelligent and progressive spectators, who have made Paris the central city of progress, pack themselves together as a crowd with such concentration and curiosity ... he knows he is responsible, and he does not want this crowd to be able to bring him to account one day for that which he should have taught them' (Preface to *Lucrèce Borgia*).

Even though Hugo assumed that the audience for whom he wanted to write was 'intelligent' and 'progressive', he was well aware that he would only be able to fulfil his 'mission' if he was able to find a path between his high artistic expectations and the needs of the audience. He was forced to go some way towards compromising with other theatregoing habits and tastes. This taste was largely determined by melodrama.

Melodrama can, in certain ways, be seen as a product of the revolution. It was created in the ten years from 1790 to 1800, although whether it began in 1792 with Lamartellière's reworking of Schiller's *The Robbers* as *Robert*, *chef de brigande* or later, in 1800, with Pixérécourt's *Coelina*, whose plays ruled the Boulevard du Crime unchallenged until 1830, is somewhat irrelevant. The new theatrical genre, whose preferred sources were *Sturm und Drang* poetry and the gothic novel, stepped into the vacuum left behind by the terror of revolution amongst the lower social classes.

In melodrama, a stable moral order is established on the foundation of a Manichaean world view – a moral order ruled by a high form of justice, where good always gains victory over evil. In order to help the audience member to orientate himself, straightforward, instantly identifiable signs are presented on the stage. These enable the spectator to attribute benevolent or evil powers to the characters at their very first appearance, without any danger of misinterpretation – the villain, the innocent victim, her saviour and his helper.

Although the audience was, at first, made up of soldiers, young men and workers, as time went on melodrama increasingly attracted the educated middle classes. The people's theatre of which Hugo dreamt was at last realised – at least in the composition of the audience. This may have given him the idea of developing the form and adapting it for his particular uses and requirements by making carefully considered changes.

To a large extent, Hugo maintained the basic character constellation: villain, innocent victim, saviour and helper, but altered the fixed attributions determined by the plot. This had the result that, on the one hand, the affiliation of a character to good or evil was no longer constant throughout, and this meant, on the other hand, that the signs referring to appearance could no longer be deciphered and understood in a straightforward way. In *Hernani*, whose performance at the Théâtre Français (25 February 1830) achieved a breakthrough in romantic drama, Hugo introduced a leading hero, similar to one of Byron's heroes, onto the French stage. He furnished the role with the melodramatic function of saviour. Hernani who, like all Byronic heroes, is described as 'pale' and 'sombre', is given the same characteristics which constitute the figure of Manfred:

I must be alone …
I am a force that moves!
Blind and deaf agent of dark mysteries!
Unhappy soul created in darkness!
Where do I roam? I do not know. But I feel
  myself being blown
By an impetutous breath, by an insane destiny.
I am falling, I am falling, and cannot stop.
If, perhaps, breathless, I dare to turn my head,
A voice tells me: Go on! And the abyss is deep,
And I see the reddening flames or blood in
  the depths!
And in the course of my wild journey,
All shall be dashed to pieces, all shall die.
  Misfortune to any I touch!
(Lines 987, 992–1002)[12]

In Manfred, the negative characteristics of loneliness, feeling cursed and damned all stem from his existential situation, that is, they have to do with his self; in Hernani, however, they are caused by society. Hernani's family has been bitter enemy to the king's family for centuries. The father of the present king had Hernani's father executed and continued to threaten the family with his hatred. Because of this, Hernani is poor, persecuted, deprived of rights, and has been forced to hide in the mountains since childhood. Despite his noble birth, he has become the leader of a band of robbers. His identity problem, which is rooted in the injustice of society, is fittingly expressed in make-up and costume. With a false name and in the 'costume de montagnard d'Aragon, gris', Hernani is forced to conceal his true identity. His deceptive appearance thus points to the 'mask' of rank in society behind which the 'true' identity of the soul is hidden as Doña Sol determines:

Yield to the bandit, king; if men were graced,
Not as their birth, but as their virtues placed
Their separate rank – if honour drew the line –
His were the sceptre, and the poniard thine.
(II, 1, p. 317)

If Hernani seems a mystery to those around him, this is because of the injustice of society which forces him to hide behind a false identity. His damnation, 'Banished – proscribed – contagious' (Act II, p. 323), is inflicted upon him by society. This is the reason why Hernani, unlike Manfred, always refers to society in his thoughts, words and deeds. Since the king has forcefully expelled his true identity, he can only find himself again through revenge. The metaphysical rebel in Byron has become the 'King's rebel' (III, pp. 1, 2, 3, 6).

Like Manfred, Hernani believes he can only find fulfilment in love. This, however, unlike Manfred, is denied him by society. Marriage to Doña Sol is not only out of the question because of his supposed low social status, but is also refused him by the king, who kidnaps Doña Sol. It is the king who stands in the way of Hernani's self-fulfilment, yet again. As the representative of social order, the king is cast, all too appropriately, in the role of schemer and tyrannical villain, which follows the basic character constellation in melodrama.

Since Hernani's identity problem is caused by society, it can only be solved by a fundamental change in that society. Don Carlos, who represents the unjust, tyrannical hereditary kingship (the side-swipe against the Bourbons, just a few months away from the Revolution of 1830, can barely be missed), is transformed into the democratically disposed Emperor Charles V, freely elected in accord with the will of the people. Instead of the role of villain, he now takes over the role of the helper. After Hernani has announced himself as Juan d'Aragon, not only does Don Carlos return to him all the rights and dignity to which he is entitled, he even raises his status to Knight of the Golden Fleece and confers Doña Sol's hand in marriage. The feared bandit has risen to become the most important man in the state. His integration into society has succeeded perfectly, the identity of the hero has been reinstated.

Thus far, however – unlike melodrama, which would end here – the cosmic battle between the powers of light and darkness has not yet been decided. At the beginning,

Hernani belongs to both worlds: 'Demon or angel' (p. 307). He stands between the incarnation of light, Doña Sol, who always appears in white and is distinguished by the epithets 'angel', 'innocent and pure', 'dove', and the representatives of darkness, embodied at first by the king and, after his transformation, by Ruy Gomez, Doña Sol's uncle. After he is cast in the role of the helper in Act III, he takes over the role of villain, in a black Domino, and is continually described as 'demon'. It is certainly of importance that after the fundamental change in society, this function falls upon the representative of conservative power, of 'Castillian honour' *per se*.

Ruy Gomez wants to separate Hernani forever from Doña Sol, the very incarnation of goodness and light. Calling upon the vow that Hernani swore to him at the end of Act III when he rescued Doña Sol from the clutches of the king, Ruy intends to force Hernani to commit suicide with his own 'voice', the horn, on his wedding night. Hernani's vow appears, in retrospect, to be a melodramatic pact with the devil. The question of identity surfaces again – Hernani returns in Juan d'Aragon:

Call me Hernani; – I must re-assume
That fatal name of vengeance and of gloom.

(p. 356)

Now, however, it is a question of Hernani's metaphysical identity. Will he succumb to the satanic realms, or can he yet be saved? Doña Sol decides the battle when she dies of a broken heart. Death unites them both in eternity ('Was not this head to sleep upon thy breast / To-night? What matters where it sinks to rest?' [p. 361]) and finally gives Hernani salvation:

Our wings expand
Towards the blest regions of a happier land.

(p. 361)

Ruy Gomez dies as one 'damned'.

Unlike the heroes in Kleist, Byron and Shelley, Hernani finds a solution to the question of identity on a social, as well as a metaphysical level. Love is accorded a new and special function as a redeeming power. Even while Hernani is still socially an outcast, and even though he still sways between the satanic and the angelic, his self-realisation and salvation through love is, at least temporarily, anticipated. In the lyrical, in part rapturous, love dialogues (I, 2; II, 4; III, 4), time comes to a standstill, and the moment stretches to eternity. 'Dearest, is't not sweet / To love … thus to be two where not a third is nigh' (p. 323). Indeed, it is partly because of these love duets that Hugo's drama was given a place in the history of the genre between melodrama and *grand opéra*.

The première, on 25 February 1830 in the Théâtre Français, brought the play unprecedented success. In a well-prepared 'bataille d'Hernani', it was not only the romantics who drew victory over the classicists. The audience eagerly welcomed the model of identification in the form of Hernani. From this moment, it became fashionable to imitate at least the outward appearance of Hernani; 'It became the fashion in the romantic school to look pale … sickly green. … It created a fatal air, Byronic, *giaour*, devoured by passion and remorse.'[13]

However, Hugo's drama transformed Byron's hero in significant ways. For example, the hero's awareness of the negative aspect of being 'chosen' is reduced to a stylised pose, the metaphysical revolt is turned into a rebellion against an unjust and envious society by which alienation of the self can partly (as in love) be avoided. This interpretation made him a popular and undisputed figure of identification for Jeunes-France just before and after the Revolution of 1830. The figural type inaugurated by Hernani became at once the most popular hero on the French stage in the 1830s. He appears time and again in countless variations by Hugo and Dumas (*père*) – and less than a year later (1831) in Dumas' exemplary and successful *Antony*, during the première of which 'the auditorium was truly delirious, they applauded, sobbed, wept, cried out. The burning passion of the play inflamed their hearts.'[14]

De Vigny's 'pale' youthful poet, *Chatterton* (1834), also shares significant features with Hernani. He is a 'handsome genius' (III, 3), one who is chosen. However, he is not chosen by Satan, nor is he torn between the regions of light and darkness. Rather, he is chosen by 'providence' (I, 5), by 'God', who 'created him in this fashion' with intent (I, 5). None the less, he bears 'on his forehead' the 'fatal' mark of Cain (I, 5), which is represented in contradictory physical reactions: if 'his hands are burning', his face is 'pale' (I, 5); if his hands are 'icy cold', his head 'burns' (III, 1):

> I will always find a fatal enemy, born with me, between my work and myself – a wicked fairy found, no doubt, in my cradle, distraction, poetry! – She appears everywhere; she gives and takes all; she charms and destroys everything for me; she has saved me … she has made me lose myself!
>
> (I, 5)

Poetry, which distinguishes Chatterton from others and raises him above them, is at the same time, the source of his tragedy: 'I sense inevitable misfortune all around me' (II, 1). Like Manfred, Chatterton has aged because of it, despite his actual youth: 'I've lived a thousand years!' (I, 5). This experience separates him from his fellow men, isolates him and turns him into a kind of leper: 'Have you ever seen men who suffer the plague, lepers? Your first wish is to separate them from their fellow humans. – Expel me, spurn me, leave me alone; I would rather exile myself than infect anyone with the disease of my misfortune' (II, 1). The poet is condemned to be an outsider in society. Thus he is continually 'running away' (II, 1; II, 2; II, 4). Despite this, however, his passion and work are drawn from that very society, and create social qualities of the highest level:

> And yet, don't I also have a right to the love of my brothers, I work for them day and night; I search with so much effort among national ruins for some blossoms of poetry from which I may extract a lasting perfume; I only wish to add another pearl to the

English crown, and I dive into all oceans and rivers in order to find it?

> (I, 5)

The poet's work is a 'pearl' in the 'English crown'.

Chatterton must take up the 'cross' of loneliness upon his shoulders – 'Men of imagination are perpetually crucified' (III, 2) – because it is only by so doing that he can fulfil the mission in society for which God 'created' him in this way. For the poet is born to lead society along the path towards a better world. It is only he, as he 'manoeuvres' the 'state ship of England', who can 'read in the stars the path which will show us the Lord's way' (III, 6). The poet sacrifices his desire for companionship, for personal happiness, for the sake of the well-being of society, which can only discover its future path through him. The poet as seer and leader of his people demands nothing more than the recognition of the poet's works, material support, and a place in society appropriate to his standing.

The society into which Chatterton is born has not the slightest sensitivity, however, to the poet's calling. The only quality society values is money. In the image of early eighteenth-century capitalist society in England and its representative John Bell, de Vigny characterises the situation in French society after the July Revolution as the start of ruthless industrialisation. John Bell represents the credo of a calculated rationale, a utilitarian positivism:

> That which is done is done. – If only every man would behave as I do! ... Toby was a skilful labourer, but had no foresight. – Someone who truly calculates things allows nothing useless to exist around him. – Everything is in harmony, both things animate and inanimate. – The soil is fertile and money is equally fertile, and time is in harmony with money.
>
> (I, 2)

Only possessions are important, for ownership is power:

> The land is mine, because I bought it; the houses, because I built them; the inhabitants, because I gave them shelter; and their labour, because I pay for it.
>
> (I, 2)

John Bell is 'just, according to the law', even if this law is 'unjust according to God' (I, 2). A godless society which dances around the Golden Calf cannot understand the heavenly mission of the poet. For them, poetry is at best 'entertainment' (II, 3). But since 'the most beautiful muse in the world is not enough to nourish a man' (III, 6), such a muse is ultimately 'useless', as 'the most honest and one of the most enlightened men in London' (III, 2), the Lord Mayor of London, remarks. He denies the social mission of the poet and instead of a privileged position in society, offers Chatterton the post of chief valet in his household.

Moreover, society even denies Chatterton recognition of his work: he is defamed in the newspaper as a forger of old manuscripts and labelled a criminal. In such a society, there is no room for a poet:

> My name has been smothered! My glory extinguished! My honour is lost! ... Damnable land! Land of scorn! Cursed be it forever!
>
> (III, 7)

If the poet, in a society which demands of him that he 'should be another man than the one you are' (I,5), has decided,

> Never to hide from being myself up to the very end, to listen, in everything, to my heart in all its outpourings and indignations, and to resign myself to following my own laws.
>
> (I, 5)

all he can do is to lie low and avoid recognition if he is to fend off society's destructive demands and, though outwardly mute, poeticise in silence, as Chatterton does, after he takes lodgings under a false name with the Bells who know nothing about him or his poetry. When society disputes his poetry, however, and negates the mission given to him by God, any chance of self-realisation is dashed. He can only choose to die of hunger, to perish in the debtor's prison, or to commit suicide.

Not even love can change this state of affairs. However, since Kitty Bell's love springs from a 'maternal soul' (II, 5; III, 7), which is similar to 'divine charity' (III, 8), perhaps she can make God 'pardon' him (III, 8), although Chatterton knows, 'I am condemned' (III, 8). Nor is there any place for this kind of love in the purely profit-orientated society where possessions are deified: Kitty Bell dies as a result of a martyrdom she is forced to suffer in this society: 'Lord, receive these two martyrs!' (III, 9).

De Vigny further radicalised, and complexi-fied, the problem of the antithetical relationship between an extraordinary personality and the broad masses (who neither desire nor are able to recognise their special right to self-realisation) in the poet's confrontation with a brutally capitalist society exclusively oriented towards economic utility. The poet's quasi-religious mission places him, as one chosen by God in a totally secular society, in a direct relationship to the indifferent masses and their fate. For it is only his work which can 'save' the people, if only they would listen to him. But the people deny his claim and push him coldly away. In denying the poet the right to self-realisation, society also closes the only way towards a better future for itself. The poet's suicide seems, in this respect, to be revenge on a world not worthy of his like. Society passes its own death sentence.

One would suppose that the audience, as part of, or representatives of, this criticised and defamed society, would give the play a some-what frosty reception. In fact, the opposite was the case. The première, on the 12 February 1835 at the Comédie Français, was a resounding success – a triumph thanks, in large part, as de Vigny also acknowledged, to the actors and in particular Marie Dorval, who performed the part of Kitty Bell. In 'Notes' on the performance, de Vigny wrote:

No play has ever been acted better than this, I believe, and it is of great merit for, behind the written drama, there is a second drama which the written words cannot reach, which words cannot express. This drama rests in the love shared by Chatterton and Kitty Bell; a love which always anticipates and never expresses itself; a love between two such pure beings, that they dare not ever speak of it, only alone in the moment of death; a love which can only be expressed in timid glances, its only message, the Bible; as messengers, two children; as caresses, only the line of the lips and the tears which these inno-cents carry from the young mother to the poet.

The actors intensified the already strong tendency of the play to allow the tragic love story to take precedence, and thus, it was prin-cipally Marie Dorval's incomparable skill in silent, expressive acting which she developed in performances of melodrama on the Boulevard du Crime, which made it possible to ease the audience into a sympathetic, almost enchanted, reception of the play. In this context, the prob-lematic relationship between the artist and society could be readily appreciated. For some members of the audience, it made the identifi-cation with the suffering poet complete. For,

the stalls in front of which Chatterton made his speeches were full of pale adolescents with long hair, who firmly believed that there never was a more acceptable occupa-tion on earth than that of writing verse or painting – than art, as they said – and they looked down upon the *bourgeois* more than did the *sly foxes* of Heidelberg or Jena on the *philistines*. The bourgeoisie! That was just about the whole world ... Never had such glorious thirst burned on human lips. As for money, they didn't think of that.[15]

As it later turned out, at the première of *Kean, ou désordre et génie* (*Kean; or, Disorder and Genius*) by Alexandre Dumas (*père*) on 31 August 1836 in the Théâtre des Variétés on the Boulevard du Crime, this theme had immense audience appeal, and great potential for success, particularly when it was set in a whirlpool of love intrigues, scenes of jealousy, and gossip among the higher echelons of society. An actor outcast by society because of a scandal and exiled by the king proved – next to the young heiress Anna Damby, whom he ultimately married, and the Prince of Wales – to be the sole decent person in thought and deed, in a corrupt and hypocritical society. Even Heinrich Heine could not resist the effect of the performance in which Frédérick Lemaître played the title role:

This play ... is conceived and performed with a vitality I have never seen before, ... a fable, whose threads unwind in a most natural way, an emotion that comes from the heart and speaks to the heart ... I thought I saw the ghost of Kean himself, whom I ... saw perform so often, in person before me. Of course, the actor playing the role of Kean contributed to this deception, although his outward appearance, the great figure of Frédéric Lemaître is so unlike the small stocky build of Kean. But there was something in his character as well as in his acting, that I found again in Frédéric Lemaître. A wonderful kinship unites them both. Kean was one of those exceptional types, who brings to outward expression not so much the general simple feelings as more the unusual, bizarre, and extraordinary, which can fill the human breast through surprising movement of the body, inconceivable tone of voice, and yet more inconceivable glance of the eye. It is the same with Frédéric Lemaître. ... Kean was one of those people, ... who was made, I will not say of better stuff, but rather of quite different stuff than we are, ... filled with an unrestricted, unfathomable, unconscious, devilish godly power, which we call demonaical. To greater or lesser degree, the demonic exists in all great men of word and deed.[16]

The extraordinary actor, played by another extraordinary actor, became the very epitome of great personality as interpreted by the Romantic movement.

## The demontage of 'personality' in the Vienna Volkstheater

It seems rather ironic that the great actor-writers of the Vienna Volkstheater, Ferdinand

Raimund and Johann Nestroy, set about to dismantle the personality and its 'demonic' nature. In *Der Alpenkönig und der Menschenfeind* (*The King of the Alps and the Misanthrope*, 1828) Raimund showed how the demonic can be a disruptive factor in the safe, daily lives of the bourgeois family. Nestroy, however, denounced it thoroughly in *Der Zerrissene* (*The Torn One*, 1844) as the empty posturing of rich good-for-nothings, who neither acted according to real experience, nor were able to feel the true emotions of *Weltschmerz* ('world-weariness').

In the 1820s and 1830s, a person who was at odds with himself and the world (in a meta-physical and/or actual social sense) became an extremely significant figure of identification for young intellectuals across Europe. The experience of alienation from the self, surrounded by an indifferent, if not hostile society, seems to have been crucial to this age; their *Weltschmerz* became the *mal du siècle*. Whatever the reason for this interpretation of life, it certainly found fertile soil in the new political and social Europe after 1815.

A total, all-embracing period of restoration in nearly all areas of life – excluding the economy – choked any demand for personal or political freedom, whether this was enforced by the police, censorship or other institutional measures, or through openly brutal violence, such as the Decembrist uprising in Russia (1825) or the November Revolution in Poland (1830). At the same time, the process of industrialisation spread explosively from the West and, in a compensatory way, focused on speeding up economic development and expansion. In a world such as this, there was no opportunity for young intellectuals to develop awareness of the self. 'The former idols [Napoleon, the French Revolution] lay in pieces, and new ones had not yet been born' (Dostoyevsky, *Diary of a Writer*, 1877). The result was disgust and a world-weariness: the Byronic hero became the figure of identification of the moment, the *Hero of Our Time* (Lermontov, 1840), and his experience of life is found over and over again in countless diaries, notes, letters and poems of this epoch, as well as in the heroes of verse epics, novels and dramas. On the European stage, however, – with the exception of France – he was only to be seen in a somewhat harmless form in trivial drama.

The type of Byronic hero, or at least the figure of *Der Zerrissene* (the 'torn one', one who suffers from inner conflict, as Klinger's Blasius described himself in 1778), was a well-known figure on the Vienna stage. The first 'true' figure of inner conflict to suffer the experience of self-alienation appeared in Vienna as early as 1817 in the Theater an der Wien: the robber Jaromir, in Grillparzer's *Die Ahnfrau* (*The Prophetess*). The play sailed under a false flag, however, against the will of its author – it was celebrated by audiences as a *Schicksalsdrama*. Its success made it one of the most popular plays of the nineteenth century. The critics, however, reviled and criticised it as a plagiarism of Müllner's *Guilt*. The Byronic hero achieved a second great success in Vienna when, in 1828, he appeared on stage in the character of Raimund's Rappelkopf, as a comic figure.

This rather odd metamorphosis is very important. Raimund – like Grillparzer – was not spared the '*mal du siècle*', as is shown by his remark in a letter to Antonie Wagner, 'I have seen through the ugliness of this world and it seems to me too wretched ever to wish to make a longer stay in it.'

Raimund's theatre, on the other hand, contained a thoroughly consolatory element. It propagated 'positive values' (such as self-denial, contentment, honesty, love between parents and children, and between friends), which stabilised the predominantly petit-bourgeois milieu of the audience, though it was occasionally peppered with members of the educated upper classes and nobility. It confirmed the audience's positive view of itself and thus reconciled the members of the audience to their world. He activated the magical apparatus of the spiritual and fairy world in order to combat any disruptive factors which might otherwise threaten the milieu.

Raimund's 'misanthrope' in *The King of the Alps and the Misanthrope*, Herr von Rappelkopf, a patriarch from a noble family, is in dishar-mony with himself and his world. When he looks into the mirror, he 'smashes' it 'with his fists', and cries out: 'Agh! This ugly face,[6] / I can't bear it any more. So! There lies the hero, / And his armour is smashed' (I, 14). Since he feels unjustly persecuted and cheated by the world around him, he decides to withdraw from human society: 'I'll give the whole world the sack at Michaelmas. … It's over! The world is nothing but deadly nightshade, I have had a bite, and gone quite mad. I need nothing from anyone, and no-one'll get anything from me, nothing good, nothing bad, nothing sweet, nothing sour' (I, 11). Nature seems to be the only possible refuge:

> Alone at last and so I hope to stay,
> I shall take loneliness tenderly to my bed,
> I don't want any friends to lean on as moun-
>   tains and cliffs,
> I'll swat the scrounging riffraff away as if they
>   were but mosquitoes,
> I shall no longer have to endure the prattling
>   of old wives,
> I'd rather listen to the gushing waterfall.
> I'll have the four elements as pages,
> They shall keep themselves busy with their
>   giant hands.
>
> (I, 17)

Herr von Rappelkopf obviously shares significant characteristics with the Byronic hero. None the less, he is a comic figure because he bases his opinions on false premises. The society in which he lives is not against him, but actually very willing to accept him, even lovingly. Although a few false friends have deceived him out of a large sum of money, his family – his wife, his daughter Malchen and her fiancé, August, respect him deeply and love him. Because he feels such despair at being hated by the family and overruled by it, the gentle, devoted patriarch turns into a despotic tyrant: he refuses to allow his daughter to marry; suspects his wife of attempting to kill him; bullies and tortures his family mercilessly and brutally; and finally deserts them – the sacred world of the bourgeois family has broken apart because of a quirk, an unjustified misanthropy.

The King of the Alps heals Rappelkopf from his 'sickness' by playing his part and showing him the shamefulness of his behaviour in a dramatic way. Like the villain of the gothic novel, he curses wife and child and throws himself off the cliff, 'my life ... is worth nothing to me, I throw it away, the tasteless left-overs of an aged being, I don't need it' (II, 14). In the 'Temple of Knowledge', Rappelkopf realises that he was an 'unreasonable animal, a tiger'; he is reconciled with his family and even regains his fortune. The troubled milieu of the bourgeois family is calmed, the disruptive factor disarmed: the 'demonic' which empowered the patriarch, which transformed him into a merciless despot and thus distanced him from himself and his family, is exposed as groundless misanthropy and is exorcised by spiritual forces. The sacred world of the bourgeois family, in which mutual love, tenderness and care reign, is restored once again, the correctness and legitimacy of the patriarchal order of the family is confirmed.

The première of *The King of the Alps and the Misanthrope* (17 October 1828) brought Raimund possibly the most stormy success of his career – both as an actor (in the role of Rappelkopf) and as a playwright. This success was repeated during Raimund's tour through Germany. The play was even translated into English and, in 1831, played nightly for three months in London's Adelphi Theatre to thunderous applause. *The King of the Alps and the Misanthrope* was a true dramatic success.

However, its ideological thrust was more than a minor element of its success. Both for Raimund and his audience, the values of the bourgeois family acted as a basic guideline. If a Byronic hero is transferred to the milieu of the family, he acts either as threat (to insiders) or as comic figure (to outsiders). In both cases, he disrupts the bourgeois order. A figure like this is no longer capable of acting as patriarch – nor can he be the manager of an expanding business. He is a threat to the smooth running of the bourgeois system. Under such circumstances, the figure cannot represent an appropriate figure of identification. Thus, he is only allowed to set foot on the bourgeois stage as a negative example, as a comic figure.

Nestroy's *Der Zerrissene* (*The Torn One*) forfeited its potential danger to the bourgeois system very early on. In the dramatis personae, the titular hero's name, 'Herr von Lips' is explicitly labelled '*a capitalist*'. Clearly, he is a successful capitalist, 'My money lies safe, my houses insured, no one can steal my real estate' (I, 5). Bourgeois society is only too eager to integrate the capitalist figure of inner conflict:

A rich man cannot have affairs. Do we have to start at the bottom? No, they open doors and gates to us wherever we go! – Would anyone throw us down the stairs? No, maids and butlers look up to us with respect. Are the dogs put on us? Is anything emptied out over our heads? No, Father and Mother beg us to honour their house again. – And even the husbands – are mostly good men. How seldom does anyone demand revenge? Corsican acts of revenge shall stay, where they belong, under the deck. When have you ever heard of a husband picking up a gun and shooting at one of us? No, they're more likely to advance us some money.

(I, 5)

The figure of inner conflict, like this vituperative society, recognises one basic value system – money: 'Poverty is without doubt the most dreadful thing. You could put ten million down, but if I had to be poor to get it, I wouldn't take it' (I, 5).

For the sake of riches, he is even prepared to bear 'boredom' and, through the stance of one undergoing inner conflict, to confer it with a higher solemnity – the obsession with *Weltschmerz*. The 'English sickness', the '*mal du siècle*' appears, thus, as the privilege of noble, rich good-for-nothings.

Nowhere lacks fools, but they are mostly poor fools, so you don't have to mention them, and even then they are fools who wrap themselves up in the fog of cleverness with a pitiful anxiety! The Englishman has enough money to realise his idiotic ideas and the courage to display his frivolity; that's the difference, that's where *renommee* comes from.

(I, 6)

Only a rich man can afford to contemplate inner conflict. When he does, however, he presents an interesting image and will certainly not remain 'lonely' and 'alone' for long. If he has the fortune – albeit undeserved – to fall in love with a sweet, gentle, ordinary country girl like Kathi, despite the adverse circumstances he calls down upon himself, there is a good chance that he will give up his notion of inner conflict and become a normal patriarch:

Now I see it … that I really was a torn soul. The whole married side was missing, but praise God, I've found it now, if a little late. Kathi! Here stands one who has lived life to the full, full of love, your fiancé, here stands my bride!

(III, 11)

The deconstruction of the great personality as represented by the Byronic hero could hardly have turned out to be more malicious or more destructive. Inner conflict becomes a pose; *Weltschmerz* becomes simply the quirk of one who can afford it. A population which has to work hard day in, day out, which must fight to gain social position and to maintain status, had nothing but resounding laughter for an attitude of this kind. 'Salvoes of applause, thunderous applause, endless curtain calls!' in all possible variations were among the comments after the première (9 April 1844, in the Theater an der Wien). In Nestroy's lifetime alone, the play was performed in Vienna 106 times. Inner conflict and *Weltschmerz,* apparently, were no longer problems which the bourgeois society of the period from 1815 to the March Revolution of 1848 must struggle to deal with – rather it had degenerated into an occasion for enjoyable entertainment in which the 'great' actor Johann Nestroy (as the Torn One) celebrated great triumphs. In fact, among the bored *haut volée* inner conflict became such a fashion as a parlour game that in the satirical announce-

ments of the *Wiener Tageszeitung* a 'Louis Spleen, famous for his inner conflict' could advertise extra coaching in the rules of suffering inner conflict. He promised he would 'teach' his customers 'in a short time, how to become a complete, thoroughbred "torn soul", and to show what unearthly distance exists between the pathetic natural "torn soul" and the "educated torn soul".[17]

*The Torn One* fought only a rearguard skirmish with the enemy, however. The principal thrust of Nestroy's work aimed far more at exposing the concepts and ideologies which served the bourgeois capitalist society of his time as a kind of fig leaf, with which to cover their ugliest nakedness: brutal egoism as the foundation and condition of the way society functioned, which disguised it unrecognisably and protected it from too close examination. Thus, by 1840, the generally widespread concept 'personality' was given a cardinal function: 'Personality created by appearances, controlled if at all by self-consciousness about one's past, spontaneous only by abnormality: these new terms of personality began to be used in the last century to understand society itself as a collection of personalities.'[18]

Nestroy took aim on the concept of personality defined in this way in *The Talisman* (premièred in Vienna 1840). He begins from a straightforward syllogism: if society represents a collection of personalities, then it is only a personality who can reach a position and play a role. Since personality can only be proven in outward appearance, everything will depend on the 'coherency' of outward appearance, right down to the smallest detail. *Ergo*: red hair is an obstacle to gaining a good career and position, because 'red hair always indicates a foxy, scheming disposition' (III, 4, p. 159)[19], as everyone knows. *Second conclusion*: if the person concerned can get hold of a black curly wig, the crucial fault in his outward appearance is overcome, and nothing stands in the way of a glorious rise to fame.

With this thought, the hero of the play, the beggarly poor and ragged Titus Foxfire, despite his foxy red hair and trusting his lucky mascot, the black wig, begins his career with great hope as head gardener (and presumptive candidate for the hand-in-marriage of the gardener's widow, Flora), only to find he has been promoted to the post of Huntsman within a few hours (and potential candidate for the hand of Constantia, the chambermaid) and from thence to secretary of the lady of the castle and authoress, Frau von Cypressenburg. Owing to the blond wig that he mistook in the darkness, this latter believes him to be a genius. For, 'Your blond curls indicate an Apollonian temper' (II, 17, p. 148). Titus' outward appearance, so advantageously judged ('You have a good carriage, an agreeable manner' [II, 17, pp. 147–8]) – which is magnificently perfected by the suits of the three departed husbands which he puts on and takes off in turn – is further perfected by his use of a cleverly fitting language and his skill in placing himself in a good light in different circumstances, or in different conversations with different women. From a flowery language based on gardening ('[I am] an exotic species, not indigenous to this soil, but uprooted by circumstance and transplanted by chance in the amiable parterre of your home, where, warmed in the sun of your graciousness, the tender plant hopes to find nourishment' [I, 7, p. 127]), he climbs to impressive gallantries ('This lofty carriage of forehead; this haughty batting of eye; this autocratic swing of elbow' [I, 20, p. 130]), to the metaphoric 'language of the poet' ('[My father] plies a quiet, retiring trade, whose only stock is that of peace. Though bound to a Higher Authority, he is nevertheless quite independent, and free to mold himself – in short, he's dead' [II, 17, p. 148]). Frau von Cypressenburg observes, 'The person obviously has an aptitude for literature' (II, 17, p. 148).

Titus has succeeded: his 'coherent' outward appearance, right down to the last detail, has shown him to be a personality who can claim an influential position for himself on one of the higher rungs of the social ladder. However, since Titus' magnificent promotion and the position which gives grounds for his greatest hopes to be realised depends exclusively on his hair, that socially sanctioned coherency of his appearance, it is the revelation of his real hair

colour that makes him tumble cruelly from his high pride. A 'carrot-top' (II, 27) cannot be a personality.

Nevertheless, Titus is lucky in his misfortune. His uncle, an excessively rich beer merchant, has finally been persuaded by the brew master to take his nephew on, buy him a shop in town, provide him with a few thousand Taels and make him his sole heir in order to save him from becoming a 'blot on the family honour' (III, 4, p. 161). Promoted by an employee to 'Herr von Titus' ('Honour to whom honour is due' [III, 10, p. 164), he is catapulted back into the marriage market as a highly desirable bachelor. For, even red hair can be 'excused' in a sole heir.

*Third conclusion*: even though one all-decisive detail in his outward appearance is not considered correct under normal circumstances, a sole heir can be courted from all sides. For money makes personality.

Nestroy, thus, totally deconstructs the idea of personality as a social category. Either it is reduced to the ability to concentrate on the important details of appearance without making a mistake and thus to cast the right strategy for social promotion, or it is reduced quite simply to a question of possessions. If promotion does not succeed, if a fortune is lost, then there is no personality. The actual circumstances of position are wholly irrelevant. For, personality is expressed either in the ability to gain capital or the ability to keep and increase capital. Mystery and secrecy do not surround personality because no one is interested in how someone has come into possession of the things which define him as a personality. The only fact that counts is that he possesses these things. The only mystery a personality may have is the actual size of his fortune.

According to Nestroy, personality in bourgeois, capitalist society is not something demonic, unique or distinctive which allows one person to stand out from another. This concept is nothing but a super-elevated ideology which veils the dirty facts of bare reality. Personality can be reproduced *ad infinitum*. There are even experts in the field, who are especially cunning in their own creations: actors and businessmen.

Actors are experts in producing an appearance which is coherent right down to the last detail – the businessman produces added value. Therefore, it is only right and proper to regard and respect such occupations as the epitome of personality. Since the actor, however, only reproduces the conditions without which a poor man cannot rise to becoming a personality, the prize goes to the businessman: he is the real hero of bourgeois society, he represents personality *per se*.

Nestroy's critical-satirical diagnosis of the society of his time from a Viennese perspective is confirmed by Gautier from a Parisian point of view. On the occasion of a performance of *Chatterton* in 1857, he writes in *Moniteur*:

John Bell, precise, positive, fair according to the law, with his practical reasoning which is almost irrefutable, provokes on the other hand, [at the première in 1835] violent disgust; one hates him as a traitor of the melodrama, full of darkness and crimes, … Now, John Bell, who does not want them to destroy his machines and maintains he must pay his share in the banquet of life with hard labour, or, rising from the table without any money, as severe towards others as he was to himself, seems to be the only reasonable character in the whole play.[20]

The businessman who calculates to the last penny has become the true hero of the times.

When a businessman like this went to the theatre after a long working day with his family, he wanted to relax and be amused. He did not need heroes, or a figure of identification on the stage – for he has even taken over this role himself in social reality – but instead, light comedy, such as the 'moral dramas' and comedies of intrigue written by Scribe, Dumas (*fils*), Augier, Labiche, Sardou (in France) and the social comedies of Birch-Pfeiffer, Bauernfeld and Benedix (in Germany). The audience found themselves confronted with their own milieu which may have been presented ironically, but was never seriously questioned. The bourgeois classes were the actual heroes of the stage. Thus, the comic theatre of the time confirmed to its audience, time and again, that a crisis of identity was not possible even in a changing world as long as the individual understood his role as representative of his class and identified with that class. His self would remain stable as long as he made the ideologies of his social class his own and if he kept to the general rules of the same. In the context of bourgeois order, the phenomenon of self-alienation is thus automatically excluded, it can only be conceived of as a strange sickness of the soul.

In 1872, Theodor Fontane commented on the *Prince of Homburg*:

I believe such Arthurs do exist … but *they don't interest me* and *shouldn't* interest any sensible person. They are vain, sick, pretentious washcloths, not heroes, but fellows who only sow disaster in the families of bourgeois society or state life, they are only celebrated in sick times or by other sick souls.[21]

## IDENTITY AND HISTORY

### The power of history to define identity

'Inner conflict and politics have been, for some time, the material of poetry which has alone created quite a sensation.' In 1843, Friedrich Theodor Vischer began his great critique of poets from the period 1815 to the March Revolution of 1848 with this comment. He criticises them for a political zeal which, in his opinion, is nothing more than a kind of act stemming from 'whining inner conflict', and a narcissistic 'reflection of the self in pain and wrath'.[22]

The relation Vischer makes between inner conflict and political engagement – even if malicious and coloured by undisguised negative derision, cannot, however, be easily dismissed. For many poets and intellectuals of the first half of the century, the question of the self seemed to be closely linked to political events in Europe – though each may have interpreted this relation differently. Some wanted, therefore, to change these relations from the viewpoint and unspoken premise that in so doing, the process of self-alienation could be halted and annulled.

This situation is already present in the *Prince of Homburg*. The Prince shows his autonomy – gained by deciding for suicide – to be the explicit condition for the return of national autonomy, 'May he be humbled in the dust, the foreign Prince / who seeks to bend us to his yoke, and the Brandenburger / live a free man on his native ground' (p. 345). The supposed liberation – first by the Swedish army, then the French – is referred to as the pre-condition for the construction of an ideal state in which the freedom of every individual is guaranteed.

Shelley also raises the question of self-alienation in *The Cenci* in the all-embracing context of world history. Self-alienation is the result of a few men becoming over-powerful which allows the power of evil to gain victory over good. Since this is encouraged by various social systems such as patriarchy, only a radical change to social relations can support the power of good and help it to a permanent victory which would lead to the end of self-alienation.

In *Hernani*, through the example of Spanish history, Hugo deals with actual political relations in France and exposes the change from hereditary kingdom to an empire based on free election and the will of the people as one possible way of disposing of the self-alienation of the individual, the personality. In all these examples, a direct relationship is made – though grounded differently in each case – between the phenomenon of self-alienation and certain political events. History as national or world history is seen to be something which has the power to stabilise the self and to recon-struct the threatened identity of the individual. However, the reference to history in individual cases is somewhat peripheral, as in the *Prince of Homburg* or *The Cenci*, despite the fact that these plays originate in historical events.

In the first half of the nineteenth century, at a time of great social change, the awareness of the historicity of events gained rapidly in significance. It is certainly no coincidence that in all areas of the humanities, even in biology, a historical view of things gained in importance. The origins of language, literature, art, religion, law, and the constitution of the own culture and of other cultures were researched according to the historical concept of develop-ment already formulated in different ways by Vico, Montesquieu, Voltaire, Turgot, Möser, Winckelmann and Herder. The field of history studies was created, whose beginnings in Germany are associated with the names Ranke, Gervinus and Droysen. Behind these efforts lay – at least in the case of the German Romantics – the concept of a *Volksgeist* ('national spirit'), which manifested itself in all expressions of the spiritual life of the nation and thus could be understood as key factor of identification. Since it only became obvious through the process of history, the recourse to history seemed to be the most important, and most promising, method by which to guarantee the 'higher' identity as postulated by the 'national spirit'. If the personal identity of an individual was shadowed by doubt, then history would provide the security of a well-ordered, all-embracing identity.

The preoccupation with the past was an attempt to solve a double need that had arisen in all sectors of society through the process of industrialisation. It allowed, on the one hand, escape from an increasingly complex and depressing reality and satisfied, on the other hand, a deep-seated desire to find orientation and identity in a changing world.

The newly created literary genres of the historical novel and the historical drama met these needs perfectly. It is therefore hardly surprising that they were taken up by audiences with great enthusiasm. Walter Scott's *Waverley* (1814), which founded the new genre of the historical novel, not only provoked a flood of followers in England and the rest of Europe, but it also succeeded in rapidly ousting the gothic novel from first position in the favour of English readers. In the process of this new liter-ary fashion in the 1820s, Schiller's 'historical' dramas, *Fiesko, Don Carlos, Wallenstein* and *Maria Stuart,* experienced an overwhelming renaissance, despite monstrous changes by the censor. In 1821, they were translated into French, received warmly (by Hugo and Dumas (*père*) among others) and achieved great success on the French stage – though in mostly pitiable adaptations.

Anyone who was anyone in Germany and France wrote historical dramas. It is therefore understandable that the poets of inner conflict, the prophets of the Byronic hero, also emerged as writers of historical drama and often realised the two themes in the same play. The most important condition a historical drama should fulfil when it was to be performed was that it should represent history as an all-embracing system and as a force which helps to define identity.

In *König Ottokars Glück und Ende* (*King Ottocar's Rise and Fall*) which, after great conflict with the censor in 1825, was finally successfully premièred at the Burgtheater in Vienna, Grillparzer compares two different views of history. The King of Bohemia, Ottocar, who in many characteristics imitates – almost denunciates – Napoleon, can only perceive history through those events which he has changed and achieved consciously through his own powers. History, for him, is a subjective category which refers only to himself. In comparison, Rudolph of Hapsburg understands history as an event which points to something higher, which has nothing to do with the wishes of an individual, and he identifies with this idea after his election and coronation as German Emperor. Whilst Ottocar loses his self through the false strategies of his personal plans and intrigues, Rudolph's ego is maintained and protected by the all-embracing order of history:

RUDOLF OF HAPSBURG: No longer Hapsburg and not Rudolph more;
The blood of Germany flows through these veins,
The pulse of Germany throbs in this breast.

All that was mortal, I have laid aside;
To be the Emperor who never dies.

(III, 3, p. 97)[23]

Whilst, in Grillparzer, history enables the self to be protected, because it is understood as the manifestation of a higher power with which the hero can identify – as Rudolph I – in Grabbe, history seems to be random fate that is controlled by coincidence – 'That the Fate of France can depend upon the stupidity, carelessness or misdeeds of one single wretch' (*Napoleon or the Hundred Days*, V, 5), as a simple process of nature, in which the strongest body dominates, 'The world is happiest when the greatest nation dominates, maintains itself and its laws everywhere' (I, 4). People, however, do not represent historical power. People are simply the material from which or with whose help the great historical figures in history make history. They are 'great' because they realise their nature ruthlessly. They prove themselves to be the strongest through action, through mercilessly destroying anything which stands in their way. In making history in this way, they determine and maintain their selves. 'Napoleon: … In the future, you shall leave out the terms "We" and "by God's Mercy" from all official documents. I am I, that is, Napoleon Bonaparte, who created himself in two years' (III, 3). A hero such as this cannot be brought down because he fails or makes a mistake – only a coincidence, an oversight for which he is not responsible, can be the cause of his downfall: 'General, it is my luck which is failing, not me' (V, 7). In this way, the downfall of such heroes does not illuminate some mysterious meaning, but rather manifests, with brutal clarity, the fact that history is nothing more than a simple, natural process which follows its course blindly and violently without referring to a higher ideal or power.

Of course, to his Biedermeier contemporaries, Grabbe's play, written in 1830/1, seemed, like his other historical dramas, impossible to perform – even if the hero defines and maintains a self in the story.

The playwrights of the period between 1815 and 1848, on the other hand, were very careful to provide their plays with a meaningful relation to tradition which the spectator could understand and with which he could identify. The heroes of the historical dramas by Karl Gutzkow and Heinrich Laube (later director of the Burg-theater) between 1839 and 1847 are mostly bourgeois heroes (such as Uriel Acosta, Friedrich Schiller, Struensee) who represent the ideals of the bourgeois revolution as it was first formulated in the Enlightenment. Their down-fall is caused by an unjust political system in which the nobility scrupulously uses and exploits the state as a means to enforce and justify its own privileges and egotistic concepts of power.

Even though these plays were banned by the censors many times, and even if they did not become great dramatic successes, they none the less found a large enough audience in the oppositional bourgeoisie of the period who found their own place in the continuity propa-gated by them.

Success was achieved, however, by historical trivial dramas by Ernst Raupach, particularly his monumental drama cycle on the nobles of the Hohenstaufen clan. A broad public was invited, even tempted, to identify itself with German greatness of the past and thus to recover from the pitiable situation of the time. The frequency with which they were performed suggests that these plays knew how to satisfy and affect the general and deep needs of the bourgeois and noble audience effectively.

In France, the situation was different in that the traditional concept of history which defined identity and meaning generally avoided having the church and throne as structuring factors. Conservative historians in the reign of Louis XVII and Charles X did try to go back to such traditions. However, it had no effect on the creation of historical dramas. Here, the histor-ical elements which provided continuity and national feeling were the traditions of anticleri-calism and hatred of tyranny founded by the Revolution. Moreover, the manicheistic battle between good and evil was shown to be of more importance. This characteristic is also true of the historical dramas by Hugo and Dumas (*père*) but most particularly of plays by Casimir Delavigne – the French Raupach.

Delavigne understood that in order to have success with a wide public one should not only turn to recent history but also present the bour-geois audience with an extremely flattering and idealised picture of themselves and their past with which they would identify only too will-ingly. More than this, he also preferred themes which would compensate for the frustration of those who had experienced the humiliating experience of losing to a foreign occupation. His recipe was unsurpassed, and led to regular triumphant successes. After the performances of his plays, the atmosphere described in *La Quotidienne* after the première of *Marino Falieri* (1829) was common: 'The theatre was still full more than half an hour after the end, they called for the author with great shouts. They were reluctant to leave, especially when they heard that M. Delavigne was moved by their enthusiasm' (1 June 1829). In Delavigne's dramas, history was, for the bourgeois audi-ence, without doubt a self-confirming and thereby identificatory and meaningful power.

Despite this enthusiasm for history and for historical drama the most significant examples of the genre were banned from the stage throughout the nineteenth century. Alfred de Musset's *Lorenzaccio* (written in 1833 and published 1843) was finally performed in 1896 with Sarah Bernhardt in the title role; Georg Büchner's *Dantons Tod* (1835) was not performed until 1902. Both dramas clashed dramatically with the basic demands of the time – which Delavigne and Raupach fulfilled in ideal ways – that history is only conceivable, presentable and can only uplift when it is a power which defines identity.

## The dissolution of the self in history

Musset's *Lorenzaccio* largely keeps close to its source, *La Storia Fiorentina* by Benedetto Varchi. Varchi, who lived in Florence between 1527 and 1536, was commissioned by Como de Medici to write a history of the Medicis from 1527 to 1538 – the period leading up to his own enthronement. Varchi might even have spoken personally to the murderer of

Alexander de Medici (1536) – Lorenzo de Medici – and discovered the motives behind the deed. Just how closely Musset was familiar with this source is shown in a comparison with George Sand's 'scène historique', *Une conspiration en 1537*, which the author entrusted to him. George Sand also drew upon Varchi as a source, but limited herself to the fifteenth book. Musset not only corrected the small historical mistakes and inaccuracies which had slipped by George Sand (such as the date of the conspiracy, which was 1536 not 1537, and the name of the 'reigning' Pope – Paul III rather than Clemence VII), he also brought Varchi significantly more into play. He must also have read, at least in part, the ninth to the fourteenth books, from which he gathered material and characters for new side plots and further information on Lorenzo de Medici. Whilst George Sand deviated from Varchi in that she made Lorenzo into an avenger of his honour and the murderer of a tyrant – following the general trend of the mood a year after the revolution of 1830 – Musset kept close to Varchi even in giving five possible reasons for the killing – of which three at least are not wholly morally sound, even reprehensible – without explicitly deciding finally for one or the other. The character of Lorenzo de Medici in Musset's source remains an unsolved mystery.

Since Musset treats the historical facts so carefully, the moments where he does vary from his source gain all that much more weight. He kills off Lorenzo shortly after he murders Alexander, although we know that he lived fourteen years after the murder, before he finally fell into the hands of the henchman of Como de Medici.

In Musset's drama, the political situation in Florence in 1536 is not merely a backdrop before which the hero can evolve and act out his search for identity and his ultimate deed. Rather, the political situation is an integral element of the dramatic event. Only three of the thirty-nine scenes of this unusually lengthy drama do not mention the state. Its political situation is tightly bound to the individual problems which face the hero.

Florence is an occupied city. The Pope and the Holy Roman Emperor have imposed the Pope's illegitimate son, Alexander de Medici as ruler, against the will of the people, and have strengthened his position with German troops who reside in the citadel and control the city. Although the population grumbles about the wild ways of the depraved duke and the foreign occupation, they do not openly oppose it. Criticism is repeatedly voiced by the bourgeoisie, craftsmen and traders (I, 2; I, 5), and patriotic feeling and a mood in favour of a republic is gradually growing amongst the other powerful families in the city such as the Strozzis, the Pazzis and others. However, good business skills (I, 2; II, 4) and greed for influence and power (II, 4) maintain the upper hand and suffocate any subversive movement in its seed. After Lorenzo's deed has created the conditions for a republican uprising, it is the students who allow themselves to be shot down for citizens' rights, while the great families and bourgeois middle classes do nothing. They willingly allow themselves to be manipulated by the secret agent of the Pope, Cardinal Cibo, and vote unanimously for the candidate chosen by the Pope and the Holy Roman Emperor, Como de Medici. The murder of a tyrant and the change of power has altered nothing. The political situation in Florence remains, to a large extent, unchanged.

The references and allusions to the actual situation in France in 1833 cannot be overlooked. For here, too, the power change caused by the revolution effected no real changes – whether in home or foreign policy. The merchant classes felt themselves strengthened in their desire to expand without, however, participating directly in political power. The uprising initiated by the workers and students was put down. France depended, as before, on the goodwill and consent of the 'Holy Alliance' – just as Florence depended on the alliance between Emperor and Pope.

Clearly, Musset used the historical example to take a critical look at the actual social and political situation. There are various reasons as to why he should seek his example in the Renaissance period. On one hand, the parallels between Florence in 1536 and Paris in 1833 were already explicitly laid out for the reader in George Sand's work, so that an adaptation for the stage seemed an obvious development. On the other hand, there was a great passion for Italy in Paris in the late 1820s and early 1830s, which also inspired, among many other new publications and adaptations, an adaptation of *The Cenci* for the two actors Frédérick Lemaître and Marie Dorval – though from a literary point of view it was utterly deplorable. Finally, in turning to the Renaissance, Musset could take up themes and motives of his great idol, Shakespeare, and rework them so that they would be 'relevant' to the times: hypocrisy and disguise, political intrigue, regicide and the shift of power. Moreover, the historical source offered the ideal potential of dealing in an explicitly distant and confrontational way with themes which were otherwise sure of success: patriotism, tyrannicide and anticlericalism, so constitutive of romantic and historical dramas such as Delavigne's.

The city of Florence gains a key function in the process, not only on the historical-political level, but also on a symbolic level. The city is repeatedly referred to as 'mother' of its citizens, 'Our Mother Florence is sterile. She has no more milk for her sons!' (I, 6, p. 110), a 'mother' who 'is nothing but a *catin*' (II, 6), who even sucks the 'blood' of her 'sons' (II, 5).[24] The once gentle, beautiful mother has turned into a bad mother. Raped by the 'bastard' Alexander de Medici, into whose lustful and brutal hands the two father figures, the Pope and the Emperor, have delivered her, Florence has become a 'bastard', a 'loathsome phantom which, as it murders you, still calls you by the name of mother' (I, 6, p. 108). Thus, it is finally these invisible fathers who are responsible for the depravation of Mother Florence and the perversion and tragedy of her children. In this way, the political situation is shown to be like a broken family and the relations between those in power and those without power in terms of perverse sexual relations. The problem of Lorenzo de Medici draws directly upon this constellation, for his natural mother,

Marie Soderini, saw him in his youth as an ideal 'father of the nation' whom, however, the wicked mother Florence 'corrupted' (I, 6) and allowed to degenerate into a depraved, effeminate Lorenzaccio.

Lorenzo's identity seems to slip constantly between the masculine and the feminine. This is shown both in his changing name as well as in his changing physical appearance. Lorenzo not only forfeits the name Medici when he faints in an effeminate way when he sees the drawn dagger: 'Duke: Shame on you! You disgrace the name of Medici. And *you're* legitimate! I'm only a bastard, but I would honour it better than you' (I, 4, p. 100), but he is also forced to accept the mutilations and transformations of his first name: 'Lorenzo' becomes 'Renzo', 'Lorenzino', 'Renzino', 'Lorenzaccio' ('The people call Lorenzo by the infamous name of "Lorenzaccio"' [ I, 4, p. 98]), 'Rezinaccio'. Slicing off the syllable 'Lo' and the affectionate and pejorative additions '-ino' and '-accio' belittle and undermine him; his feminisation is concretised in the name 'Lorenzetta' (I, 4). The same effect is achieved in the terms 'mignon' and 'femmelette' which Alexander imposes upon Lorenzo. A homosexual relation, in which Lorenzo takes on the female role is clearly implied. The mutilation of the name 'Lorenzo' functions as the symbolic castration of the man. This corresponds to his weak physical state:

THE DUKE: See that puny little body, this walking aftermath of last night's orgy! See his leaden eyes, his feeble little hands, scarce firm enough to lift a fan. That gloomy face, which sometimes smiles but never finds the strength to laugh.

(I, 4, p. 99)

Not only hypocritical fainting before Alexander and his entourage, but also the fact that his whole body shakes when his mother mentions that she has seen his ghost, 'What's wrong? You're shaking all over' (II, 4, p. 125), reveal a somewhat tender constitution. In the fencing scene with Scoronconcolo (III, 1), this 'feminine', physical image is placed in opposition to a somewhat animalistic, almost cannibalistic, 'masculine' image:

I'll stick you like a pig, I'll bleed you! Run him through the heart! He's ripped open! – Go on Scoronconcolo, shout! Hit him, then, kill him! Tear his guts out! Let's cut him in pieces and eat him. Eat him! I'm in up to the elbow! Now dive into his throat! Roll him over! Let's bite him, get our teeth in! Devour him!

(p. 140)

However, after such outbursts, Lorenzo sinks 'exhausted' to the ground and finally 'falls' into a 'swoon'. His body is not able to transform the masculinity it postulates and takes on into appropriate behaviour. It can be done through language alone.

In this context, the killing of Alexander seems to be an attempt to regain his lost masculinity: 'Oh, day of blood, my marriage night.' On this 'marriage night' Alexander is first given the part of bridegroom: 'Lorenzo: Hey, mignon, mignon! Put your best clothes on, and wear your new gloves! Tra la la! Look your finest for your beautiful bride! But let me whisper in your ear: watch out for her little knife!' (IV, 9, p. 192). With the help of the 'little knife', Lorenzo then undergoes a role change. He consummates the 'marriage' by stabbing Alexander with the dagger, an explicitly phallic symbol. At this moment, Alexander slips the wedding ring on Lorenzo's finger: 'Lorenzo: See where he bit my finger. I shall carry till death this ring of blood, this diamond without price' (IV, 11, p. 195).

The political act of tyrannicide which liberates the 'violated' Mother Florence from the degenerated perverse father-figure, her rapist, appears in this way as a sexual act in which the 'castrated' Lorenzo regains his masculinity. It is realised as a bloody *rite de passage* which Lorenzo tries, at least temporarily, to bring into harmony with nature: 'What a beautiful night! How clear and pure the air. Now my heart bursts with joy. I can breathe again … The evening breeze is soft and scented. How the wild flowers are unfolding! Resplendent Nature and eternal peace!' (IV, 11, p. 195).

The question of Lorenzo's true identity is only posed in terms of gender: the story of his life seems to divide into separate stories of different people. At least four different individual identities can be clearly differentiated:

- the 'étudiant paisible' who is only interested in art and nature;
- the patriot who weeps for 'poor Italy' and makes an oath in the Coliseum to murder one of his nation's tyrants;
- the virtuous young man who is prepared to sacrifice the 'lily-white purity' for a patriotic deed and to 'kiss' Alexander, the 'butcher's boy', 'on his thick lips', in order to 'grapple with a live tyrant at close quarters' (III, 3, p.154) and be able to kill him;
- Lorenzaccio, the lover, drinking companion and pimp to Alexander, a 'débauché' and a 'ruffian'.

Each of these four personalities is mirrored in a *Doppelgänger*:

- the peace-loving student in the artist Tebaldeo, who lives only for his art ('I am an artist' [II, 2, p. 118]);
- the patriot in Philippe Strozzi, who is imbued with the ideals of a republic: 'We need a word like "Republic". And were it nothing but a word, then still it would be something, for the people rise up as it echoes through the air' (II, 1);
- the young man who sacrifices his purity is mirrored in the Marchesa Cibo who commits adultery and hopes her love will transform the lecherous Alexander, who has ravaged both Florence and her daughters, into a 'father of the nation' who can tear the state out of the hands of the evil Emperor and the Pope and who will take her in a 'holy marriage' as his legal wife;
- the depraved Lorenzaccio in his 'cousin' Alexander, the 'libertine'.

As the mirroring of the different dramatis personae underlines, Lorenzo's divergent personalities are not held together by some superordinate, integrated ego, nor do they represent the single stages of development of an originally unified self. Instead, they show four different images as manifestations of various different selves. Lorenzo's identity is dissolved into a sequence of different personalities. With the decision to execute the historical deed of patricide, to enter history as a new 'Brutus', he puts the disintegration of his self in motion.

In order to carry out his intent, Lorenzo considers the moral depravity of Alexander, and uses the strategy of putting on the mask of depravity – as Richard III puts on a mask of love for Lady Anne, Iago a mask of devoted love for Othello, Hamlet a mask of madness, or Hernani the robber's disguise. But Lorenzo, unlike these figures, makes the shocking discovery, 'Once I wore vice like a garment; now it's stuck fast to my skin. I'm a pander now all right' (III, 3, p. 158). Depravity is not a disguise which can be put on and taken off; it soaks into the skin – like the rape of Beatrice Cenci – it permeates the whole body: 'Has vice, like Dejaneira's tunic, infected the very fibres of my being? I was on the point of corrupting Catherine. I believe I'd defile my own mother if my brain once set itself the task' (IV, 5, p. 183). Lorenzo's body and language are transformed; in place of the patriotic youth is a debauched lecher.

Lorenzo finds himself in a paradoxical situation. The decision to commit tyrannicide, which initiated the dissolution of his identity is, paradoxically, the only element which still ties his present self to his former self. Although Lorenzo as Lorenzaccio believes in the political meaninglessness of his original plan – i.e. the patriotic motive has become irrelevant – he still intends to carry out the killing so that he can at least re-integrate his self. In his double, Alexander, he aims to kill the 'débauché' Lorenzaccio and, thus, go back to being the virtuous patriot, Lorenzo.

If I am but the shadow of myself, would you rather I broke the last thread that links my heart today with the few remaining fibres of my former self? Don't you see that this murder is all that's left of my virtue? ... It's high time the world found out about me,

and about itself. ... Whether I am understood or not, whether men take action or abstain, I will have said my piece ... They can call me what they like, a Brutus or an Erostratus, but I don't wish them to forget me. My whole life hangs on the point of my dagger.

(III, 3, p. 160)

The deed proves, in this respect, a total failure: 'I wear the same clothes, I still walk with the same legs and yawn with the same mouth. Only one wretched thing in me has changed. I feel more hollow and more empty than a tinpot statue' (V, 6, p. 211).

The murder has not disposed of the debaucher – 'I still love women and wine' – but rather created 'emptiness' and 'ennui'. Even Lorenzo's hope that he will be 'acknowledged' by his contemporaries and immortalised is destroyed. No one talks about him in Florence and, even before the new heir has taken Alexander's throne, Lorenzo has fallen into oblivion – thrown into the Venetian lagoons by hired assassins. His name is erased from history. (In order to bring about this turn, Musset was obliged to diverge from Varchi and bring Lorenzo's death forward fourteen years.)

Lorenzo's historic deed neither annulled the disintegration of his self, nor did it constitute – let alone secure – a historical identity for him amongst his fellow citizens in posterity as, for example, a new 'Brutus', as Philippe Strozzi calls him after the murder. The deed remains wholly without consequence in terms of the self.

Moreover, the deed also proves to be inconsequential in terms of the political situation in Florence. The reigning tyrant of the city has been disposed of, but he is immediately replaced by a new tyrant, through secret agents working undercover for the invisible fatherfigures, the Pope and the Emperor: the drama ends with the coronation of Como de Medici. He receives the crown from the hand of Cardinal Cibo, 'which the Pope and Caesar have charged me to entrust you' (V, 7, p. 213) and swears an oath (which Musset took directly from Varchi's *Storia*).

It is only the physical presence of the father-figure that has been exchanged; the political power structures have not even been seriously challenged. Neither a 'lonely assassin' like Lorenzo, nor a fully idealistic patriot like Philippe Strozzi, who has lost all touch with reality, nor the poor masses, nor a population which is, in principle, indifferent, and only concerned with private advantage, are able to change them. The invisible father-figures maintain their positions unchallenged, they can corrupt the 'mother', the state, which is dependent on them, and castrate their 'sons', the people. History shows the perpetuation of patriarchal structures to be a destructive force – it is wholly unable to secure the identity of an individual, let alone act as a higher authority which might provide a general meaning to life.

## The 'fatalism of history' and the concrete utopia of physical nature

As the 21-year-old Georg Büchner was writing his first drama *Danton's Death*, accomplished in an extremely short time of five weeks in January/February 1835, he was in constant danger of being arrested. It was only after the drama was finished that he escaped this fate by fleeing over the border on 9 March 1835.

A year earlier, Büchner had founded the 'Gesellschaft für Menschenrechte' ('Society for Human Rights') in Giessen. This was a secret society, whose aim was to educate the peasants politically and to practise the use of weapons in order to be prepared for a revolution. At the same time, Büchner contributed to a revolutionary pamphlet, the *Hessische Landbote*, together with the Butzbach rector, the theologian Friedrich Ludwig Weidig. Leaflets were printed in July and distributed among the peasant community. Afraid of being caught with such dangerous pamphlets in their pockets, however, the peasants handed them over to the police. A trusted friend of Weidig betrayed the enterprise. Many members of the 'society' were arrested, although Büchner was at first spared, since a thorough house search failed to reveal any incriminating evidence. In January 1835, he was twice summoned to court – as witness.

On 21 February, Büchner sent the finished manuscript of *Danton's Death* to the literary editor of the magazine *Phoenix*, Karl Gutzkow, and begged him to recommend the drama to the publisher, Sauerländer. Three months after his escape, he was put on the wanted list for treason. *Danton's Death* appeared at the end of July in a heavily re-worked version made by Gutzkow, in some places so changed that the meaning was wholly distorted.

In this context, it appears that the mere act of writing *Danton's Death* could be seen as one more revolutionary activity by its author. Moreover, his choice of subject – an episode from the French Revolution – makes it seem likely that Büchner's drama followed a specific historical tradition and that he intended to evoke certain comparisons in the minds of his German readers. In a letter of 28 July 1835 to his parents, directly after the drama was published, Büchner explicitly states his documentary intentions:

> The dramatic poet, in my view, is merely someone who records history. He stands above history, however, in that he creates history for a second time and places us directly in the life of a certain time, instead of providing a dry account; he provides characters instead of characteristics, and figures instead of descriptions. It is his greatest task to come as close as he can to history as it really happened.

He seems to achieve this goal in his careful evaluation of various historical sources and the number and diversity of citations from them in his play. Approximately one-sixth of the drama consists of direct or paraphrased citations from various sources, amongst them, Thier's *Histoire de la Révolution française* in ten volumes, Paris 1823–7 (quotations derive from volume VI); *Galerie historique des Contemporaines*, eight volumes, two supplements, Brussels 1818–26 (quotations are taken from articles entitled *Danton* and *Desmoulins* in volume IV); and *Die Geschichte unserer Zeit*, edited by Carl Strahlheim, thirty volumes, Stuttgart 1826–39 (quotations derive principally from volume XII). Thus, it would seem as though Büchner intended to paint an accurate picture of the French Revolution for his readers/audience, not least of course, if one looks at the context of the drama's creation, with the aim of stimulating them towards revolutionary actions or towards a positive, approving attitude.

In this case, the refusal of theatre managers to produce the play can be seen to be politically motivated. No German court theatre was permitted to produce a play which contained a call to revolution. A careful reading of the drama, however, refutes this interpretation and conclusion. Political actions which aim to cause a revolution are critically, even pessimistically assessed, and this is predominantly concretised in the two leading figures of Danton and Robespierre.

Neither Robespierre nor Danton are able to bring about the goals of the revolution through their political deeds. For Robespierre, the social revolution is most important:

> The social revolution is not yet accomplished ... The society of the privileged is not yet dead. The robust strength of the people must replace this utterly effete class.
>
> (I, 6, p. 22)[25]

Since Danton opposes this process, he must be disposed of, 'When a crowd is pressing forward, a man standing still is as big a nuisance as if he were pushing in the opposite direction. He is trampled underfoot' (I, 6, p. 23). The assassination of Danton's followers is intended to push the social revolution on, 'bread' should be obtained for the people. But even after Danton's death, the social revolution does not happen. The people remain hungry. Robespierre's actions are not in a position to influence the path of history.

For Danton and his followers, the goal of the revolution is represented by the greatest happiness of each individual:

> Every individual must carry weight; every individual must be free to assert his nature. Whether he's reasonable or unreasonable, educated or uneducated, good or bad, is no concern of the state. We are all fools and no

one has the right to impose his particular brand of folly on anyone else. Everyone must be able to enjoy himself in his own way – but not at others' expense, not if he interferes with other people's enjoyment.

> (I, 1, p. 7)

The Dantonists represent the view that, 'We must call a halt to the revolution, and start the republic!' (I, 1, p. 7). With this demand, however, they compromise their own goals. For, at the moment, the common people are excluded from enjoyment, 'they don't enjoy it. Hard work blunts their senses' (I, 5, p. 21). Under these circumstances, when Danton and his followers claim their right to enjoy their natures as they please, they do so at the cost of others, i.e. the common people, whose 'hunger' makes them 'whore and beggar' (I, 2, p. 10). Their political actions cannot achieve the goals they proclaim for the revolution. The historical process happens over their heads.

Neither political action nor inaction from either protagonist has any effect on the process of history. As if this were not enough, it even alienates those who take action themselves. Robespierre identifies himself with history. According to him, the individual's wishes, needs and drives must take second place to history's needs; he must even be prepared to undertake actions which go against his own nature, if this is required, in the process of history. In this sense, Robespierre accepts the title of 'bloody Messiah':

> Yes, a bloody Messiah who sacrifices and is not sacrificed. *He* redeemed men with His blood, and I redeem them with their own. He invented sin and I take it upon myself. He had the joys of suffering and I have the pangs of the executioner. Who denied himself more, He or I?
>
> (I, 6, p. 26)

Identification with history erases the identity of the individual. Robespierre is prepared to pay this price because he believes himself to be in accord with the historical process. The self-denial which results from this is, however, barely justified.

Danton also understands history as a power beyond the individual whose goals are served by the individual and the individual's actions, which takes no consideration of the individual as individual:

'It must needs be that offences come, but woe to that man by whom the offence cometh!' *It must needs be* – this was that *must!* Who will curse the hand on which the curse of *must* has fallen? Who spoke that *must?* What is it in us that lies, whores, steals, murders? We are puppets and unknown powers pull the strings. In ourselves, nothing.

(II, 5, pp. 75–6)

Like Robespierre, Danton sees history as something which happens beyond the individual and which in the process destroys the individual self by allowing the individual to operate as its tool. But, contrary to Robespierre, he is no longer prepared to identify himself and his deeds with the process of history, even if he acted in 'self-defence', as in the case of the September murders.

In Robespierre and Danton lies proof of the concept of the 'fatalism of history' on which Büchner wrote to his bride in spring 1834 – when the 'Society for Human Rights' was founded:

I have been studying the history of the Revolution. I feel as though I had been annihilated by the dreadful fatalism of history. I find a terrible uniformity in human nature, an inexorable force, conferred upon all and none, in human circumstances. The individual: mere foam on the wave, greatness pure chance, the mastery of genius a puppet play, a ridiculous struggle against an iron law to acknowledge which is the highest good, to defeat the impossible.[26]

Whilst Büchner opposes his view of the fatalism of history in the revolutionary action of founding the 'Society for Human Rights' and in writing for the *Hessische Landbote*, he

makes his protagonist Danton react quite differently to a similar experience. Danton wants to 'drop out' of the history which is destroying his self and use all the valid aims of the Revolution to realise his own nature in a 'private' anticipation:

There are only Epicureans, coarse ones and fine ones. Christ was the finest. That's the only difference between men that I've been able to discover. Everyone acts according to his own nature – in other words he does what does him good.

(I, 6, p. 23)

It is, however, the stigma of the historical situation in which Danton finds himself which prevents people from achieving self-realisation outside history. Without caring whether the individual conceives himself to be the willing tool of history or whether he withdraws from it in disgust, history has the effect of destabilising the self.

Each character in the drama offers several different appearances of the self, which Büchner particularly conveys in the language used by each. All these appearances assert themselves with the same rights as manifestations of the self. In Danton, this dissolution of the self into various different personalities is taken to its furthest extreme. At least six different appearances can be identified:

- the Epicurean and unscrupulous hedonist who likes to express himself in obscene language filled with sexual innuendo (I, 5; II, 2);
- the philosopher suffering from *ennui*, disgust with life, and world-weariness who delights in cynicism, nonsense sentences and paradox (I, 1; II, 1; III, 7; IV, 2);
- the demagogue and agitator who styles himself as a man of personality with effective and unerringly accurate rhetoric, whose powerful prose draws the people to him (III, 4; III, 9);
- someone who suffers from nightmares and a bad conscience who, for the sake of a deed which gains him fame among the

people as politician, racks his brains in a language full of imagery (II, 5);

- the lover who speaks of his love for Julie in the metaphor of death and who seeks reassurance of her love as he dies (I, 1; IV, 3);
- the sympathetic friend who works himself up into a poetic delirium with great pathos together with his friend, who is sentenced to death (IV, 5).

Whilst Musset used the motive of the *Doppelgänger* to strengthen the idea that the different – in his case sequential – appearances of the self are equally justified manifestations of one divided self, Büchner introduces the old topos of the *theatrum mundi* or *theatrum vitae humanae*, for the same purpose: 'We can play-act all the way through, even though we're stabbed in good earnest at the end' (II, 1, pp. 28–9). The different appearances of the self can, thus, be understood as the expression of different roles which the individual takes on. Some act with decency and honour, even with amusement – such as Danton or Camille – others with dry seriousness – such as Robespierre or Saint-Just, and yet others get in a muddle and mix their different roles up into each other, like the prompter Simon and the Citizen:

You're turning away? Can you ever forgive me, Portia? Did I strike you? Not my hand, not my arm did it, but my madness.

'His madness is poor Hamlet's enemy.

Then Hamlet did it not, Hamlet denies it'.

Where's our daughter, where's our little Suzon?

(I, 2, p. 12)

CITIZEN: My good Jacqueline – I mean Corny ... You know, Cor –
SIMON: Cornelia, citizen, Cornelia.
CITIZEN: My good Cornelia has blessed me with a little boy.
SIMON: Has borne a son to the republic.

(II, 2, p. 29)

Unlike in theatre, however, the individual persona of the actor does not put on the role and change it according to his pleasure, but rather each role has replaced the self. If one were to rip away the various 'masks' then the 'faces will come away with them' (I, 5, p. 20). Their identity is not unified, whole any more, only the change from one role to another, into which the identity has become dissolved. If beyond these roles a 'superordinate' authority can be identified as a unifying base, then it is basic human nature shared by all:

We should all unmask; then it would be like a room full of mirrors, we'd see everywhere the same age-old indestructible sheep's head repeated to infinity. Nothing else. The differences are so small. We're villains and angels, geniuses and boneheads, all in one. There's room for all four in the same body; they're not on the scale some people can imagine. Sleep, digest, and make babies – we all do these things. What's left is only variations; the key changes, but the theme's the same.

(IV, 5, p. 66)

The idea of someone who is special, or clearly different from another, has become obsolete. There is only the same human nature on the one side and, on the other, a spectrum of different roles prepared by the various historical and social conditions and put on by the individual. An individual, whole self, does not appear anywhere on this map of mankind.

The female figures in the drama are given a special function, however. Either Büchner invented them completely (Marion, and the *grisettes*) or he presents them in a different way than in their historical sources (Lucile and Julie: Julie, Danton's wife who was really called Louise, married again after her husband's execution and survived not only Danton, but also Büchner by several years!). Marion, Julie and Lucile seem untouched by history: Marion, because she lives in total harmony with her nature, and Julie and Lucile because, for them, there is no reality beyond their love for their husbands, Danton and Camille. The destabilisation of the self from which all the male figures in the drama suffer, does not apply to the female roles. Lucile goes mad after Camille's arrest, but the madness does not have the effect of alienating her from herself, and actually creates the conditions under which she can remain wholly herself – i.e. true to her love to Camille – despite the fact that politics and history have interfered with her life to such a great extent.

The self-realisation for which Julie and Lucile strive and achieve in their love is, however, deeply threatened by the real historical situation in which they find themselves from start to finish. It is not for nothing that love is always put alongside death. The beginning and end of the drama are stamped with the relationship between love and death:

DANTON: No, Julie, I love you like the grave ... They say there is peace in the grave; the grave and peace are one. If that's so I'm already underground when I lie in your lap. Sweet grave, your lips are passing bells, your voice is my knell, your breast my burial mound and your heart my coffin.

(I, 1, p. 5)

[*Lucile enters and sits on the steps of the guillotine.*]

LUCILE: You silent angel of death, let me sit in your lap. ... You cradle, who rocked my Camille asleep and stifled him among your roses. You passing bell whose sweet tongue sang him to his grave.

(IV, 9, p. 71)

Self-realisation in love is only attainable during this historical period at the price of life. The death scenes become love scenes because the love scenes can only be realised as death scenes, as is mirrored in Julie's words as she brings out the phial of poison: 'Come, dear priest. Your Amen sends us to bed' (IV, 6, p. 68). Thus Lucile and Julie must die if they want to maintain their sense of self. The women of the drama appear in this way as a kind of utopian alternative to the self-alienating

existence of the men which is thoroughly determined by politics and history against their will.

This is especially true of the whore, Marion. Whilst Danton and his Epicurean friends vainly attempt to live their lives to the full and enjoy every moment, Marion really does live as her nature determines: 'For me, every partner was the same; all men merged into a single body. Well, it's the way God made me; nobody can get out of that' (I, 5, p. 17). Because she is in harmony with her own nature, love becomes a place where she can find herself and maintain her sense of self. For Marion, life and love have become one thing, so that her life appears to be an act of permanent self-realisation which cannot be disturbed or threatened by anything, once she has freed herself from the social corset, 'That was the one big gap in my life ... I know nothing about divisions or changes. I'm all of a piece, just one big longing and clinging. I'm a fire, a river' (I, 5, p. 18). In Marion exists the utopia which should have been the goal of the revolution for the Dantonists and of every political act.

Without doubt, Büchner follows on from the literary tradition of the *Sturm und Drang* movement with this dramatic 'rehabilitation' of human nature. However, he goes far beyond its aims and ambitions. Whilst the poets of the *Sturm und Drang* movement appealed for harmony in the vital bodily functions and natural human instincts with a moral differentiation between virtue and vice, and intended to promote virtue in this way, Büchner is far from such differentiation. The *Sturm und Drang* poets aimed to achieve a radical autonomy of the individual, but for Büchner, the mere idea of an individual – still less one who is autonomous – has become obsolete.

At this time, such plays as Goethe's *Götz*, for example, or Lenz's *Hofmeister*, could still be performed and openly discussed, even if the majority of spectators ultimately rejected them and prevented them from being played again. *Danton's Death*, on the other hand, was too much for a bourgeois and aristocratic audience – and this was not because, as the actor and director Eduard Devrient criticised, 'the characters' are 'simply sketched out' and therefore there is 'little for the actor to do' (diary entry, 29 September 1837).[27] The image of mankind created in *Danton's Death* contradicts the demands made by the spectators of the time concerning a dramatic hero in *all* significant aspects: in place of the confirmation of the self through history, Büchner sets the dissolution of the self; in place of the unique, exceptional personality, the ever-same physical human nature.

Gutzkow's reworking of the drama for publication (!) suggests that in fact it was less political reasons that spoke against publishing it in its original form than the image of mankind set out in it. For the changes he made barely concern the 'revolutionary tendencies' of the drama – so that the scenes in the Jacobin Club and in the National Convention remain almost untouched. On the other hand, Gutzkow erased everything which concerned the physical nature of mankind, particularly all references to sexuality. Every allusion to coitus and sexual desire is generalised and toned down. Particularly offensive, and thus removed, were considered the terms: 'genitalia', 'back', 'Venus mound', 'whore', 'brothel', 'sexual epidemic', 'fornication', 'go brothelling', 'to do it', 'have it licked' and 'make babies'. Beyond this, elementary bodily functions were paraphrased with supplementary words, particularly if they were felt to be improper in terms of social standing: thus a plebeian might have breath that 'stinks', but a woman who has exerted herself by dancing does not 'stink'. The trend of the reworking is clear: the physical nature of mankind may not be exposed to a bourgeois audience, even in literary form.

Whilst dramas by Kleist, Byron, Shelley and de Musset could at least appear unadulterated in print, *Danton's Death* was only made available to the reading public as a 'ravaged ruin' (Karl Gutzkow). The chasm that had grown in the early nineteenth century between bourgeois society and the most aesthetically advanced dramatists, could not even be bridged by a reading public.

Other eras have existed where the theatre public clashed with the leading dramatists of the time, where such clashes have also led to open and violent condemnation of a play. Thus the theatregoers in Athens were neither able nor willing to recognise themselves in many of Euripides' tragedies – as little as the court audience of Louis XIV could see themselves in some of Molière's comedies. Such dissent was, however, usually carried out in the theatre and the audience expressed its dislike with appropriate reaction either during or after the performance – to some extent with drastic clarity. The theatre was generally recognised as a proper and appropriate place in which the current or newly introduced ideals of behaviour, the norms and values of society could be brought under discussion – whether as critical analysis (as in the case of Sophocles, Euripides, Shakespeare, Molière, Lenz), or more propaganda (as in the case of Aeschylus, Calderón, Racine, Lessing, Goethe). Mostly, the audience was fully prepared to tolerate images with which it disagreed on stage as negative examples. Common agreement on valid ideals of behaviour was reached in the theatre in this way until the end of the eighteenth century – even if the audience responded frostily to the dramas of the *Sturm and Drang* movement and showed uncomprehending respect for other heroes of German classic drama.

At the beginning of the nineteenth century, the theatre lost for more than fifty years its most vital and legitimate social function in England and Germany – to some extent also in France. The discussion raised by drama of the time concerning a new image of mankind was prevented from approaching the stage. One can only surmise what the reasons for such a spectacular amputation of this most vital function may have been.

The beginning of the industrial revolution saw a social change which, in a relatively short time, demanded an all-embracing and totally new social adaptability. The result was an inevitable crisis in identity. It was thought that it could be dealt with if, on the one hand, the traditional values given by the patriarchal family, the bourgeois morals and Christian religion were rigidly upheld, and on the other, if a certain spiritual relief was guaranteed by offering the individual the chance to escape temporarily the stress of reality which so threatened the self. The needs and hopes of the potential audience – from the petit-bourgeois craftsman, whose existence was threatened, to the bourgeois, capitalist entrepreneur and noble landowner – would hardly have been fulfilled if they were confronted in theatre with heroes who are themselves at the mercy of the process of the destabilisation of the self, who stubbornly deny the current values and in their place set negation, nihilism and sensualism. It would not have been tolerated. On the other hand, theatre was supposed to divert the audience's attention from reality by amusing and entertaining them, providing the kind of temporary escapism as was excellently provided in the popular genres of ballet and opera, or it should explicitly reassure the spectator that his self would remain stable and would thus confirm him to be a personality. First and foremost, the theatre was obliged to relieve the audience from stress, before such stress became too great, and thus to stabilise its members, at least for a while – that is, until the next theatre visit.

The moral institution which was bound to the bourgeois public of the eighteenth century was followed by a therapeutical institution which was based upon the psyche of the individual. Clearly, the theatre was able to fulfil this function to general satisfaction. The numbers of spectators reached record heights, new theatres experienced a veritable boom. At the same time, the most widely differing forms of school and amateur theatres developed, theatre was performed with great passion in both bourgeois and noble circles. The need for the therapeutic institution 'theatre' was great in nearly all classes of society and grew to a true addiction. It was common to go to the theatre every evening. In this context, the exclusion of the most significant dramas of the era from the stage seems to indicate a deep social and cultural crisis.

# THE FALL OF THE BOURGEOIS MYTHS

## The stage as a public forum of the bourgeoisie

As the nineteenth century progressed, the situation in theatre across Europe grew more and more desolate. By about 1880, the literary level of theatre had reached an all-time low. This was a time in which shallow, commercial, entertainment theatre celebrated great triumphs. At the same time, the higher demands of the educated classes were placated with hollow, declamatory theatre, which drove out the last traces of relevance and intellectual stimulation from the classics and stuffed them with boring text. This was after the censor had mercilessly removed every possible offensive snippet – whether it offended political, religious, traditional, or moral mores – and every hint of encouragement towards provocation had been eradicated. Literature and theatre were separated by a deep chasm.

This intellectual and artistic drought was brightened, none the less, by a shimmer of hope in the Meiningen theatre. George II, Duke of Saxe-Meiningen was obsessed with theatre and, as early as the 1870s, had introduced decisive reforms to his small provincial court theatre. The reforms challenged the extensive censorial attacks to the texts of classical dramas as well as the 'star' system in theatre so typical of the nineteenth century. For, as Max Grube, a long-standing member of the Meiningen company describes in his memoirs, the 'stage art' of the Meiningen court theatre was 'based' on the 'great principle that the stage is obliged to reproduce an overall image of poetry in which both the living and the dead apparatus must submit themselves to the decisions of one single director. This was the great and new thing that the Duke gave the theatre.'[28] Following these very principles, the Duke was the first theatre director to adhere to the law of being 'true to the work'. Three things followed from this:

1   The poet's text should not, as far as possible, be cut. If cuts are necessary due to the length of the play, then these are to be made according to the immanent logic of the poetry and not for censorial reasons.

2   The actor is subordinate to the poetry. He must see himself as a member of an ensemble, and not as an exception, a star. Attendance at rehearsals is obligatory, as is the undertaking of minor roles or even appearing as extra. No solo tours are permitted.

3   The costumes and sets must derive from the poetry. Details of time, place, the social class to which certain roles belong, etc., must be upheld. Historical and socially correct sets and costumes, right up to the smallest details are, therefore, imperative.

As mentioned earlier, the Meiningen company produced an unabridged version of the *Prince of Homburg* based on these principles.

In extensive tours, from 1874 to 1890 through all the major cities of Europe, the Meiningen company presented well-considered productions – mostly of the classics – to a wider public for discussion. Wherever they went, they enjoyed a 'monstrous, unmatchable success never seen before'.[29] From the point of view of the history of theatre, the positive, even enthusiastic, reactions which the Meiningen company provoked in the majority of audiences and critics, suggest some interesting conclusions to be drawn. Such widespread approval of a theatre which negated the basic principles of the usual theatre practices would not have been possible if the audience were really satisfied with the regular theatre offerings. It is not too extreme an assumption, therefore, to suppose that a large percentage of the audience had begun to express expectations and demands (for whatever reasons) which could not be met by the regular, shallow entertainment theatre on the one hand, nor by the heavily censored performances of the classics offered to the educated classes, on the other. The Meiningen company thus began their tour through Europe at a time in which the call for a new theatre already existed, but was not yet clearly or extensively articulated. Their function was in a sense to act as catalyst which enabled audiences and critics to become aware of their new hopes and desires for theatre and to formulate these demands.

In this regard, the Meiningen company seem to be forerunners and pioneers of the art-theatre movement which appeared throughout Europe at the end of the 1880s. This thesis is supported by the fact that the most prominent representatives of the movement, such as Otto Brahm in Berlin, André Antoine in Paris, or Constantin Stanislavsky in Moscow, all repeatedly and explicitly referred to the Meiningen company.

The art-theatre movement arose as a demonstrative protest against a general theatre practice which denied confrontation with real burning issues of the time. Wherever a dramatist engaged in such issues, his play, if it even reached production, would be mutilated unrecognisably by the censor. Theatre, as a public forum, remained closed to issues such as women's rights, social Darwinism, genetics, atheism, socialism, and so forth. One way out of this dilemma was opened by the founding of theatre societies which, through membership or season tickets, could offer 'closed' – i.e. private performances, for members only and in this way circumvent the censor. It was their aim to encourage young dramatists and engage in discussions which the court, state and commercial theatres had avoided.

In 1887, André Antoine founded the 'Théâtre libre' in Paris, which was principally devoted to naturalistic drama. This was countered by the 'Théâtre d'art' founded by Paul Fort in 1890 which, from 1893, was continued by Aurélien Lugné-Poë as a theatre of symbolism under the name 'Théâtre de l'Oeuvre'.

In Berlin, the 'Freie Bühne' was founded in 1889 with the help of Otto Brahm. This society sponsored Gerhart Hauptmann, and it was followed by many other theatre societies. In 1890, Bruno Wille opened the 'Freie Volksbühne' where Otto Brahm was also a committee member. In the same year the 'Deutsche Bühne' was created, and among the leaders were such famous names as the Hart brothers, Karl Bleibtreu and Conrad Alberti. In 1892, the 'Fresco Bühne' was born; in 1895 the 'Verein Probebühne' by Arthur Zapp and finally, in 1897, the 'Dramatische Gesellschaft' directed by Ludwig Fulda and Bruno Wille.

In London, J.T. Greins founded the 'Independent Theatre Society' in 1891, and this led to a series of other club theatres being founded which reformed the English theatre system as the 'Repertoire Theatre Movement'. As successor to the 'Independent Theatre Society', the 'English Stage Society' was created in 1899. In the same year, in Dublin, the 'Irish Literary Theatre' opened, one of its founders being William Butler Yeats, followed in 1902 by the 'National Theatre Society'. Both were later absorbed into the 'Abbey Theatre' which A.E. Horniman founded in 1904.

As early as 1888, Constantin Sergeyevitch Alexeyev founded the 'Society for Literature and Art' in Moscow under the artistic name of Stanislavsky. It was succeeded by the 'Moscow Art Theatre' in 1898 which was opened by Stanislavsky and Nemirovitch Danchenko. In the first year of its existence, its legendary reputation was built upon their production of Chekhov's *The Seagull*. This production established Chekhov's career in the theatre.

These art-theatres, created entirely as private stages, set the goal of closing the gap between literature and theatre which was so characteristic of theatre at the end of the nineteenth century. Their repertoire consisted almost exclusively of dramas by contemporary poets. It was on these stages that dramas by Ibsen, Björnson, Strindberg, Turgenev, Tolstoy, Chekhov, Gorky, Hauptmann, Hofmannsthal, Maeterlinck, Wilde, Yeats, Galsworthy and Shaw could be produced. Nearly all these performances provoked violent reactions, both among audiences and critics – whether in the form of enthusiasm, or determined, uncompromising condemnation. The most significant critics of the time – such as Fontane in Berlin and Sarcey in Paris – reported on the plays and performances in the leading newspapers and thus continued the discussion theatre had

provoked amongst a wider public. Thus, with the art-theatre movement, the aesthetically most advanced contemporary dramas won back the stage as a public forum.

The dramas of Henrik Ibsen gained special importance in this process. As early as 1869, after Ibsen turned the actual situation in Norwegian politics into a theme for the stage in *The League of Youth*, gave up verse speech and introduced the realistic language of every day life into the theatre, the nearly 50-year-old dramatist turned to the new genre of social drama with *Pillars of the Community* (1877). 'Photographic' reproductions of the real situation of the time and society, the exposure of weaknesses and defects, became, from this point on, the centre of his dramatic creations. Although *Pillars of the Community* did not employ the innovations of the genre to perfection and, from a contemporary viewpoint, can certainly be seen as the weakest of Ibsen's social plays, it was his greatest success. The première in Teatret Odense (14 November 1877) was followed two weeks later by the Norwegian première in Det Norske Teater in Bergen. In 1878, a series of performances came to Germany. In Berlin alone, the play was performed in February 1878 by five theatres in three different translations. The audiences in Germany and Scandinavia were enthusiastic, if in part deeply shocked by the play. Paul Schlenther writes in his memoirs on the extraordinary impression made by the play on him and many others of his generation:

Any man who ... as I, has experienced two of the greatest artistic revelations in *Pillars of the Community*, cannot forget this capturing and illuminating drama. In 1878, it was performed in Berlin in three different suburbs at a time when the fashionable court theatre still stuck to Lubliner and Gensichen and the sensationalist dramas of Sardou and Dumas. Despite all that dazzling and glittering theatricality round about us, our youthful eyes were opened. We shuddered and cheered. It was not in the Faustian sense that we shouted to those close to Karsten Bernick, 'That's a world! That really is a world!'. We went back to the theatre again and again; during the day we read the play in Wilhelm Lange's dreadful German. Neither the unpoetic, bookish translation nor the stiff souls of the provincial players could hide the power of this work. Schiller's *Intrigue and Love* must have had the same effect on the not-so-innocent youth ninety years ago.[30]

Ibsen's play succeeded in achieving that which the art-theatre movement would only achieve on a broad base in the 1890s: in turning the stage back into a forum where the bourgeois public was confronted with, and invited to discuss, the problems which actually moved them.

The discussion opened in theatre was taken up not only in the press, but also in the bourgeois salon, with great vehemence. This can be seen from invitations to members of society in Copenhagen and Berlin in the 1880s, which explicitly stated the request that on that evening, the play *Nora* should *not* be discussed. As Conrad Alberti, one of the founders of the 'Deutsche Bühne' jokingly remarked, 'the ladies of our educated circle ... were mad about the play and never tired of speaking of it ... In families living to the west of Berlin, there reigned a real *Nora*-mania for several weeks.'[31] The problems taken up in Ibsen's plays – such as corruption in *Pillars of the Community* or women's rights in *Nora* – became the subject of heated debates which were carried out amidst much controversy in the bourgeois salons of the time.

Indeed, the example of *Nora* – or *A Doll's House* as the play was originally called – made the function and needs of the art-theatre movement very apparent. Whilst at its première in Copenhagen (21 December 1879), the first performances in Norway (20 January 1880 in Oslo, 30 January 1880 in Bergen) as well as a month later at the Münchner Hoftheater (3 March 1880), the play was performed in Ibsen's original version, Ibsen was forced to write a conciliatory ending for the rest of the German performances in Flensburg (6 February 1880), Hamburg, Berlin and Vienna, because the theatres were not prepared to present a drama to the public which ended

with a woman who left her husband and children for the sake of finding herself.

In some ways, Ibsen drew on the tradition of the bourgeois theatre as it was shaped by the Enlightenment and the *Sturm und Drang* movement. Like them, he understood and used theatre as a moral institution in which the ruling norms and values of the bourgeois society could be reflected. But whilst, in the eighteenth century, Lessing and Diderot turned the stage into a public forum on which bourgeois family life was promoted, Ibsen used the forum of the stage to expose the hypocrisy of this style of life.

Like Goethe, Lenz and Schiller, Ibsen also dealt with the idea of potential self-realisation which remains open to the bourgeois individual within society. Whilst the poets of the *Sturm und Drang* movement did not question the family as the natural arena for self-realisation but denounced the rigid class system of absolutism as the cause of the destruction of the natural order of the family which thus made self-realisation impossible, Ibsen demonstrated precisely how the bourgeois institution of the family hinders its individual members from gaining self-realisation. By referring to the beginnings of bourgeois theatre in this way at the end of the bourgeois era, he not only raised consciousness of the rapid changes which the bourgeois theatre and the bourgeois society had continually suffered since the mid-eighteenth century, but at the same time, he also held up a mirror to the audience which clearly showed them the monstrous discrepancy between the actual situation and the original ideal which once lay behind it.

## The family

### The lie of family life

No other period created such a cult around the family as that of the bourgeoisie in the eighteenth and nineteenth centuries. That which was propagated by the eighteenth century seemed, in the idyllic Biedermeier period, to have become reality, at least in the 'middle classes': the family was a gentle community which, although it recognised the father as the natural leader, none the less created necessary opportunity for each member to develop and express his own particular individuality. In the course of rapid social changes catalysed by the industrial revolution, the family understood in this way increasingly became the intimate refuge from the various changes in public life and a stabiliser of a self which was threatened with destabilisation in dangerous ways by general social developments.

From approximately the middle of the nineteenth century, however, the family seemed increasingly less able to fulfil this function. It was more and more exposed to attacks from widely differing areas. Radical feminists believed the family could be done away with entirely; utopian socialists planned a substitute; and Marxists diagnosed its exploitative, hypocritical character and thus damned it to destruction. These critics belived that the family was a thing of the past and, in this respect, a superfluous phenomenon. Attacks by the conservatives were not more merciful in their judgement either, though it resulted in a diametrically opposite argumentation. They saw the family as a holy shrine – but at the same time, however, as a centre of infection; an asylum from ugliness, materialism, and immorality, yet weakened by every decline, whose prevention should actually be its greatest and most meaningful task.

In *Die Familie* (*The Family*), which appeared first in 1855 (in 1881 it was reprinted for the ninth time and it continued to be reprinted until the 1930s), the family sociologist Wilhelm Heinrich Riehl never tires of lamenting the lost idyll of harmonious family life and profusely curses the imminent downfall of the family. The cause of this downfall of the family, the 'most universal sub-system of the people's personality', is in his opinion the widespread attempt to undermine the natural authority of the patriarch. Riehl apportions not a little blame on the emancipation of women in this development: 'The history of our political misery runs parallel to the history of the blue-stocking.' Their strides must

be curbed, 'This is ... the only sensible political emancipation which women should strive towards: a far reaching respect for the family in the state. The emancipation of women can briefly be summarised as the 'state recognition of the family'.

The family sociologist, Frédéric Le Play, came to a similar conclusion. For him, it was clear that the emancipation of women was the root of all evil. He argued that: 'the domestic hearth is, in some respects, a world of its own, the control of which demands the total energy of the mother'.[32] For this reason, women must be brought back to the domestic hearth through the force of male authority. Of course, the family should ensure the freedom of its individual members, but it was understood only in so far as they are 'aware' of 'the greatest measure of paternal authority over them'.[33] Accordingly, Riehl's ideal vision of the family in the twentieth century culminated in the dream of unqualified restoration of authority to the patriarch; 'The citizen of the twentieth century has won back the honour of the home priest: he has regained the courage to pray together with the whole house, and to go to church in one procession with the whole house.'

Riehl, Le Play and many of their contemporaries never tired of reiterating in books, newspapers, lectures and sermons, ideas which were not considered to be new or 'revolutionary', rather they were commonplace concepts which were certainly familiar to members of the bourgeois society across Europe; concepts which the great majority of the bourgeoisie confirmed without reservation. It was amid this thought and value system, which dominated the cultural climate of the time, that Ibsen wrote his first family dramas: *A Doll's House* (1879), *Ghosts* (1881) and *The Wild Duck* (1884).

The family situation which forms the basis of Ibsen's *The Wild Duck* is, in some respects, comparable to the constellation of the family in the bourgeois tragedies of the eighteenth century. Love and tenderness seem to determine the relationships between individual members of the Ekdal family. Hjalmar Ekdal, the patriarch, cares for his old father, who suffers the shame of a prison sentence, 'My poor, unfortunate father lives with me, of course. He has no one else in the world to lean on' (Act 1, p. 120);[34] he appreciates the domestic skills of his wife Gina, 'She's as capable and good a wife as any man could wish for' (Act 1, p. 122); and he clings with his whole soul to his daughter Hedvig, 'Our greatest joy ... And also our greatest sorrow ... There is a grave risk that she may lose her eyesight. Oh, it will be the death of me' (Act 2, pp. 145–6). In return, his wife and daughter busy themselves with ensuring Hjalmar's mental and physical needs, and try to make him feel as 'at home' as possible, for, 'we love you very, very much, father' (Act 2). The tender relationship between father and daughter is given central significance. Like the fathers in the *bürgerliche Trauerspiel*, Hjalmar confesses that his love for his daughter is deeply important to him, 'I loved that child beyond words. I felt so incredibly happy every time I came back to this humble home and she ran to greet me with those sweet eyes peering at me' (Act 5, p. 211).

Alongside the typical tenderness of the eighteenth-century family, the components of family life which were particularly important to the nineteenth century also seem to be beautifully realised. The authority of the patriarch, Hjalmar, is not questioned by any of the family members, instead it is recognised as self-evident. He is admired as an 'inventor', as an exceptional personality, 'Hjalmar isn't just an ordinary photographer, you know' (Act 3, p. 164); he seems to be regarded with considerable gratitude as the 'breadwinner', a 'man besieged by a host of sorrows' (Act 2, p. 144), who none the less finds time to play the flute amongst his loved ones. In this respect, too, the Ekdal family seems to be a model family in the sense that Riehl envisioned: 'In the poor photographer's home the roof is low, I know that well. And the circumstances are narrow. But I am an inventor, Gregers – the breadwinner for my family – and that lifts me above the poverty of my surroundings' (Hjalmar, Act 3, p. 170).

This moving and perfect portrait of the

family is clouded by individual members of the Ekdal family who reveal strongly divergent appearances of themselves in different contexts. This holds true, above all, for Hjalmar, but also for his wife, Gina. In both, there is a wide discrepancy between speech and action. After presenting himself to Gregers Werle as the devoted son who sacrifices all his energies into brightening the last days of his 'poor, white-haired father', a few minutes later he disowns his father to Werle's evening guests because he is ashamed of him. Whilst Hjalmar cannot find enough words to express his love for and care of Hedvig, he forgets to bring her something from the evening out which he greatly enjoyed. The man who, according to his own statement, is 'crushed' by fear for Hedvig's sight, is glad to allow her to retouch the photographs so that he can be free of a tedious job. The appearance of a devoted son and loving father which Hjalmar creates around himself in great detail stands in opposition to his actions as a cowardly, lazy and amoral egotist.

In a similar way, the image of the breadwinner of the family and great inventor is also pulled apart. In fact, it is Gina who runs the business and brings in the money to keep the family. Hjalmar is even too lazy to touch up the photographs and prefers to mess about in the attic building things with his father. Whilst officially, after supper, he meditates on his inventions, he actually lies down on the sofa for a digestive nap. The scientific journals, for which his wife and daughter scrimp and save, because they are urgently needed for inventing, remain unopened. Hjalmar Ekdal, cared for by his wife and idolised by his daughter is, in truth, a weak, morally corrupt egotist who plays the part of the tender, responsible patriarch from an eighteenth-century sentimental melodrama.

Gina Ekdal, who works very hard to take care of the running and economy of the household and business, and who fulfils her duties as spouse and mother to the best of her abilities, is, as the spectators learn as early as Act 1, even before Gina has appeared on stage, 'a woman with a past': before her marriage, she was the senior Werle's lover. She has kept this a secret all these years from Hjalmar, as well as the resulting possibility that Hedvig is Werle's child (which, in the light of the genetically transmitted blindness which threatens both Werle and Hedvig, seems likely). Gina also keeps from her husband the fact that the sum of money which Old Ekdal receives for copying business papers from Werle's office is so high that it covers his keep and a small amount of pocket money.

The harmonious family life of the Ekdals does not rest on the fact that they actually fulfil the socially sanctioned ideal of the family. Rather, it is only made possible by the fact that the Ekdals have succeeded in persuading both themselves and public opinion that their lives are determined by this ideal and at the same time are able to live according to their desires which somewhat contradict this same ideal. Thus Hjalmar is a master at lazing about without taking on any responsibility, and allowing himself to be pampered without limit by his wife and daughter (as he was by his two aunts who raised him as a child). Yet he can also convince himself that he deserves love and respect from his family as the tender loving father and responsible breadwinner of the family. Thus, Gina can bring in the material income needed to keep the family single-handedly and yet still give Hjalmar the feeling that as 'inventor' he has the right to special consideration, recognition and gratitude. The Ekdals are a 'happy family' because despite their moral instability, or even insufficiency, with the greatest of ease they are able to unite appearances of the self which totally contradict each other and even cancel each other out.

The bourgeois family as portrayed by Ibsen in theatre is like a 'swamp' (Act 4). The family members are not able to fulfil the ideal demands which society asks of them in the form of public opinion. Since society insists on these demands, however, because it is thought they are 'natural', the individual is forced to build a family life on the foundations of a lie: s/he must hide behind an image of herself/himself which society has determined and created for her/him in the role of housewife or patriarch. This lie in private and public life

which has become the basis for the bourgeois-patriarchal family leads to the moral impoverishment of the individual and the dissolution of the self.

In *Die conventionellen Lügen der Kultur-menschheit* (*The Conventional Lies of Mankind*), which appeared in summer 1883 and was reprinted four times by November of the same year, Max Nordau proposed that 'all social transactions' have 'the character of hypocrisy', that 'everything which surrounds us is hypocrisy and lies' and that 'we are acting a deeply immoral comedy'. In his thesis, he refers to the 'religious lie', the 'monarchic-aristocratic lie', the 'political lie', the 'economic lie' and the 'marriage lie', each of which forms one chapter, thus emphasising that all aspects of social life in the bourgeois society at the end of the nineteenth century were based on nothing but lies. The lie in private and public life presented by Ibsen as the basis of family relations seems, in this context, to be a phenomenon which is determined by the structure of bourgeois society. Interestingly, in the foreword, Nordau emphasises the 'need to reproduce faithfully the views of the majority of those who have a certain level of education'. The insight that social conditions alienate the individual from the self could no longer be suppressed.

For the children who grow up in these bourgeois families, the 'lie' has catastrophic consequences. Ibsen makes this clear in an artistic device which in fact derives from comedy. In the form of a truth-fanatic and idealist Gregers Werle, he introduces the figure of troublemaker into the self-sufficient milieu of the Ekdal family. Because Gregers is plagued by a 'guilty conscience' owing to his father, he tries to 'find a cure' (Act 3, p. 175) by revealing Gina's past to Hjalmar and destroying the illusion that he is the breadwinner of the family. The system of family order and peace which has until now functioned perfectly, regulating itself, is deeply upset. As in the comic tradition, those who have suffered try to restabilise the turbulent milieu and recreate the old sense of balance.

To do this, Hjalmar uses a well-tried model of behaviour. He attempts to fulfil, in his words, the ideal image of himself which Gregers has created of him: 'A time comes when a man can no longer ignore the command of his ideals. As the family breadwinner I am continually tormented by this command ... it isn't easy for a man of small means to repay an old debt on which ... there has settled the dust of oblivion. But there's no other way. I must do what is right' (Act 4, p. 190). In his actions, on the contrary, he concentrates on not endangering his comfortable life too much: although he claims he wants to move out, he readily allows Gina to put a rich breakfast before him and eagerly agrees to her suggestion to move into the sitting room first until he has planned his 'move' more thoroughly. Hjalmar and Gina's attempts to recreate the old conditions step by step using well-tried models of behaviour are within the well-established framework of the comic tradition.

Hedvig reacts quite differently to the changed situation, however. For her, there is no difference between speech and act, image of self or appearance and reality. The lie behind the bourgeois lifestyle is still alien to her for she is only an adolescent. And thus, she concludes from Hjalmar's theatrical-rejectional behaviour ('Get away, get away, get away! [To Gina] Get her away from me! ... During my last minutes in what was my home, I wish to be spared the presence of outsiders' [Act 5, pp. 205, 206]), that her idolised father no longer loves her. She interprets his tearful, pathetic speech literally, 'If they came to her with their hands full of gold and cried to the child: "Leave him! We can offer you life!" – ... If I were to ask her: "Hedvig will you sacrifice your life for me?"' (Act 5, p. 212), and believes she must prove her love for her father through death. She dies as a victim of the lie which undermines the bourgeois family lifestyle.

A comparison with the bürgerliche Trauerspiel of the eighteenth century makes it clear how far-reaching the changes to the family had been since the days of Lessing and Diderot. Whilst Emilia Galotti seeks to die at the hand of her father in the secure knowledge of her father's

love for her, in order to save her virtue from the burdens of the courtly lifestyle, and in this way to realise the bourgeois system of values, Hedvig dies in order to satisfy the self-love of her egotistic and amoral father. Whilst in Emilia Galotti the potential self-realisation of the individual, only possible within the family, is hindered by the control of the court which tears the family apart, in The Wild Duck, it is the structure of the patriarchal-bourgeois family itself which proves to be the responsible factor in sabotaging the self-realisation of its members, in crippling them mentally and morally and pulling them down into actual physical ruin. Amongst Ibsen's family dramas, Nora is the only character who finds the strength to break away from the family and give herself up to the search for her own self. She is the only one for whom there is hope that she will find self-realisation. For all others, the family is the ill fate which ultimately destroys the self.

In a letter to Björnson, Ibsen writes: 'to realise oneself is the highest goal that a man can reach. We all are faced with this task, each and every one of us: but most of us make a mess of it' (August 1882). Since the family is the principal reason for this, Ibsen felt, the goal will only be in reach when some basic changes have been made to the structure of the family. The bourgeois-patriarchal form of the family was considered obsolete.

With this diagnosis, Ibsen put himself in stark juxtaposition to the generally accepted idea of the family repeated ad infinitum like a prayermill, and reproduced in works by Riehl and Le Play. The enormous success of his plays – principally in Germany – and the unending discussions they provoked seem to suggest that at least part of the audience – consciously or not, willingly or not – identified with his characters and recognised their own situation in the dramas. Long before Freud (who dedicated a long essay to Ibsen's drama, Rosmersholm) had shocked the bourgeois public with his merciless analysis of the effect of the consequential and catastrophic family relations on the development of the personality, that same public could study the inevitable consequences of the patriarchal family on the individual self in the concrete example of Ibsen's plays.

## The battle of the sexes

The family constellation in Strindberg's early tragedy *The Father* (1887) in some respects accords with the family constellation in the *Wild Duck* and the *bürgerliche Trauerspiel* in general: the core of the family consists of father, mother and daughter. Here, too, it is a question of how the daughter can develop her personality within the family and how she can achieve self-realisation.

At the beginning of the play, the Captain tries to persuade his brother-in-law, the Pastor, of his view that his daughter must leave the family if she is to develop in her own way:

> This house is full of women who all want to bring up my daughter. My mother-in-law wants to make a spiritualist of her; Laura wants her to be an artist; the governess wants to make her a Methodist; old Margret, a Baptist; and the maids, a Salvation Army lass. It's no earthly good trying to mould a character like a piece of patchwork – especially when I, who should have most voice in her upbringing, meet with nothing but opposition.
>
> (Act 1, p. 27)[35]

The family seems to be an inappropriate place for the adolescent daughter to grow up in because the father cannot implement his views on her upbringing within it. As in Lenz's *The Tutor*, it is the 'women' who 'reign' in the family of the Captain (Act 1). This is what upsets the order necessary for the development of the child. On the other hand, it seems to be the Captain himself who actually hinders his daughter's search for self-realisation. For, after his wife has raised doubts on his fatherhood because she wants to 'have control over the child' and 'raise her herself' (Act 2), he demands that Bertha should identify herself solely with him: 'You must only have one soul, or you will never have any peace, and nor shall I. You must have one thought only, the child of

my thought; and only one will – mine!'. When Bertha claims the right to be her own self ('I want to be myself'), her father even reaches for his revolver to kill her, 'You see, I'm a cannibal, and I want to eat you. Your mother wanted to eat me, but she couldn't. I am Saturn, who ate his own children because it had been foretold that otherwise they would eat him. To eat or be eaten' (Act 3, p. 69).

Neither father nor mother act on behalf of their daughter and her right to achieve self-realisation; rather it is Bertha who represents an important strategic factor in the battle for power between her parents: 'It's man versus woman the whole day long in this house, without a break' (Captain, Act 1, p. 29).

The battle over Bertha's future seems to be a dramatic pretext to crystallise and express the issues in the battle of power. The battle held between the Captain and Laura is a battle between life and death.

CAPTAIN: I realise that one of us must go under in this struggle.
LAURA: Which?
CAPTAIN: The weaker, of course.
LAURA: And the stronger will be in the right?
CAPTAIN: Naturally, since he has the power.
(Act 2, p. 60)

The elements which Strindberg adopts from the tradition of family drama – such as the patriarchal structure of the family, the weaknesses of the patriarch, the intrigues of the mother, problems of raising and educating the children and so forth – only function in terms of the battle of wills which rages between the married couple.

This battle does not spring from any particular element of individual character. On the contrary, it seems to deform character, as the words of the nurse seem to show: 'But, my goodness, why must two people plague the life out of each other? Two people who are so good and kind to everyone else. The mistress is never like that with me – or with anyone else' (Act 1, p. 39). Later, Bertha says to her father, 'But Papa, you must be kind to Mama, you know. She does cry such a lot' (Act 1, p. 41). If by character we mean the unity of a person, then the permanent battle for power has long dissolved the character of the protagonists involved. Depending on how the battle progresses, the Captain and, above all, Laura, play different roles both to the adversary as well as to those who are apparently uninvolved (such as the Nurse, the Doctor, the Pastor); they put on different masks according to the needs of the battle. Laura and the Captain are no longer individuals with specific characteristics and a distinguishable identity, but rather a set of many roles which is organised and structured according to each situation. It is noticeable that at crucial moments, neither protagonist speaks in the first person. The Captain justifies his position by that which 'a man' or 'a father' must do, Laura, on the other hand, by that which 'a mother' believes to be necessary and correct. The set of roles into which the character is split is not held together or structured by a superordinate self, but is determined by a general underlying relationship which is implied in the opposition of 'a man' with 'a mother'.

This basic, underlying relationship is not created or legitimised by real social conditions, nor can it be tied down to any moral category. Logically, the Captain's appeal to the socially sanctioned rights of fatherhood, or the doubt sown by Laura on his fatherhood, function solely as weapons which are strategically employed in the battle, though not as serious arguments which might affect this underlying relationship.

The battle between 'a mother' and 'a man' is grounded far more in biological differences. It stems, as the Captain notes, from a 'racial prejudice'. 'If it's true that we're descended from apes, it must have been from two different species. Certainly there's no resemblance between us' (Act 2, p. 59). In this context, it is interesting to note that the Captain still describes the similarities which none the less exist between man and woman in exactly the same words as Shylock from Shakespeare's *The Merchant of Venice* describes the similarities

between Christian and Jew. The citation is not marked as such:

Has not a man eyes? Has not a man hands, organs, dimensions, senses, affections, passions? Fed with the same food, hurt with the same weapons, warmed and cooled by the same winter and summer as a woman. If you prick us, do we not bleed; if you tickle us, do we not laugh?

(Act 2, p. 57)

The biologically based power battle between Laura and the Captain is now interpreted on a mythological level. When the Captain, tricked by the Nurse, finds himself in a straitjacket, he calls out when he sees Laura enter, 'Omphale! Omphale! Playing with the cub while Hercules spins your wool!' (Act 3, p. 71). In so doing, he draws a parallel between his situation and that of Hercules, who is bought by Omphale as a slave and forced to carry out the humiliating, 'feminine' task of spinning.

The name Omphale means 'navel' and makes a direct reference to the Ur-mother. Omphalos was the sacred stone which the Greeks thought was the navel of the world. It was also the seat and symbol of Gaia, the earth mother. Hercules succeeds in liberating himself from slavery to Omphale and thus tears the umbilical cord which binds him to the mother earth. The Captain, on the contrary, proves himself to be a kind of Hercules who lacks the strength to make this decisive step.

In *The Father*, the image of Omphale, the earth mother, is divided up into four women: the Captain's mother-in-law, Margret the Nurse, the Captain's biological mother and his wife, Laura. Neither the mother-in-law nor the mother actually appear on stage. Bertha says that her grandmother, the Captain's mother-in-law, is forcing her to write messages from the ghosts. She has direct access to the world of the invisible, 'But Grandmamma says there are things that she can see and you can't' (Act 1, p. 41). The mother-in-law communicates with the ghosts of the dead and the unconscious and exercises her secret power over others from a hidden position. In this way, she represents the negative components of the maternal constellation – the jealous, threatening, cannibalistic mother. These components are also shared by the Captain's biological mother, 'My mother, who didn't want to bring me into the world because my birth would bring her pain, she was my enemy: she starved my unborn life of its nourishment, till I was nearly deformed' (Act 3, p. 71).

The Nurse, on the other hand, represents the positive components, the nourishing and protective mother, from whom the Captain does not wish to separate himself, 'I even have my old nurse here, treating me as if I still wore a bib. She's a dear old soul, heaven knows, but she oughtn't to be here' (Act 1, p. 28). When the Nurse succeeds in seducing the Captain into the straitjacket with the same, loving, tender words with which she would have persuaded the young boy into his clothes, the Captain gives in to his fate, after a brief outburst of anger: 'Let me put my head on your lap. There! Ah, that's warmer. Lean over me, so that I can feel your breast. Oh, it's good to sleep on a woman's breast – a mother's or a mistress's, but a mother's is best.' He ends his life with a prayer to the mother-god: 'put me to sleep. I'm tired – so tired. Good night, Margret! And blessed be thou among women' (Act 3, p. 73).

Laura embraces both components. At the beginning of their relationship she was the loving, protective mother:

Do you remember that, when I first came into your life, it was as a second mother. Your great strong body had no fibre, you were like an overgrown child, as if you'd come into the world too soon, or perhaps were unwanted … That's true, and that's why I loved you as if you were my own child. But you must surely have noticed how embarrassed I was whenever your feelings altered, and you presented yourself as my lover. The pleasure of your embraces was always followed by remorse, as if my very blood were ashamed. The mother had become the mistress. Ugh!

(Act 2, p. 58)

The mother takes revenge for this 'incest' by attempting to castrate him. Laura orders, 'Nöjd, have you taken all the cartridges out of the guns and emptied the pouches?' (Act 3, p. 61) and this represents an obvious symbolic castration. On a metaphysical level, all her attempts to intercept the Captain's post and to boycott the books which are sent to him, must also be seen as similarly castrating acts. For, they obstruct the Captain in his research with which he seeks to prove the existence of signs of organic life in meteors and thus construct a relationship with heaven. On the mythical level, therefore, he appears somewhat as a hero who reaches towards light, a higher level of consciousness, whilst Laura and the other mothers represent the earthbound powers of the unconscious, which tie him down to the earth and want to keep him in darkness. The Captain is destroyed because he cannot tear himself away from the good mother and thus falls victim to the bad mother.

*The Father* is always understood and interpreted as the expression of Strindberg's private, biographically founded obsession, as the document and manifestation of his notorious misogyny. This viewpoint has, for a long time, distorted the idea that precisely in these early tragedies, fears are articulated which can be seen as more than typical of their era.

In 1861, a sensational work, *Das Mutterrecht* (*Mother Right*), was published by Johann Jakob Bachofen. In it, the author sought to prove that the patriarchal society only developed after a matriarchy. Strindberg became familiar with this work in 1886, and in the foreword to the second edition of his narrative stories, *Married*, agrees with a quotation from an essay published by Paul Lafargue in *La Nouvelle Revue*, entitled *Le Matriarcat*, as commentary on Bachofen's work: 'The patriarchal family is therefore a comparatively new form of society and its creation was accompanied by as many crimes as we can expect, perhaps, in the future, if society should attempt to return to a matriarchy.'

Hidden behind these words is the fear of a whole generation of men who feel their manhood threatened by the somewhat shy attempts at women's emancipation – the fear of the 'man-killing woman'. This fear is not only expressed in the fine arts in a notable preference for certain subjects such as Delilah, who cut Samson's hair, Judith, who kills Holofernes, Salome, who dances with the head of John the Baptist, the Sphinx, who is finally overcome by Oedipus, or the death of Marat (*Samson und Delilah* by Max Liebermann, *Salome II* by Eduard Munch, *The Climax* by Aubrey Beardsley, *Oedipus and the Sphinx* by Gustave Moreau, *Marat's Death* by Eduard Munch). It is also apparent in the numerous attempts to reveal the ridiculous nature of emancipated women and their potential male allies in caricatures and satires as, for example, a complaint in the *New York Herald* that 'masculine ladies' are 'like hens wanting to sing cockadoodle doo', or the accusation that 'the majority of the male sex' who attended the feminist conferences were 'henpecked heroes' who should really 'be wearing aprons'. This fear also lies behind the directly furious attacks on the women's movement, as is clearly seen in Stephen Archer's speech against women's votes to the House of Representatives on 30 May 1872: 'A monstrous army is now coming down upon us – a hundred thousand 'whirlwinds in petticoats' – which we must meet firmly, or be overwhelmed by the storm'.[36] Woman, created by God to be gentle, has become violent and aggressive, she has discovered sharp claws and can tear man down. 'The little boy concealed in the nineteenth-century man looked up at his powerful unpredictable mother and was afraid.'[37] Not least, it was this fear which was the cause of various castration nightmares which apparently troubled many men in this era. Thus, on the night of the anniversary of the storming of the Bastille, the epitome of patriarchal authority, Edmond de Goncourt dreamed of a naked dancing actress who 'exposed her private parts: they were fitted out with the most horrible jaw bones one could think of, they snapped open and closed continually and revealed two rows of teeth' (14 July 1883, *Journal*, XII, p. 45f).

Strindberg's dramatisation in *The Father* of a Hercules who does not succeed in cutting the umbilical cord to mother earth and who, thus, is 'eaten' by her, seems, in the light of these documents, to be less the manifestation of the private obsession of a misogynist than the creation of a collective male fantasy, typical of its time. In his later marital drama, *Dance of Death I* (1900), which Strindberg wrote after his so-called inferno crisis, the male fears of this period are no longer taken up. Strindberg does keep the battle between the married couple as the central motif and basic situation which determines the relationship between the protagonists Edgar and Alice. But he gives them a new interpretation by referring to another myth – the myth of the Fall of Man.

ALICE: Yes, sometimes I think our stock is cursed.
KURT: Since the Fall, yes, that's so.
ALICE: [*With a venomous glance, sharply*] What fall?
KURT: Adam and Eve's.

(I, 1, p. 147)[38]

In referring to the mythology of the Fall, the question of the two protagonists' personal guilt is dismissed as inappropriate. They despise and fight one another not because of any mistake, regrets, insults, malice, or unkind actions, but because they are *a priori* 'cursed' to do so. For this reason, the emphasis in Edgar and Alice is different to that in Laura and the Captain. Whilst the Captain must fall victim to the stronger Laura because he is the 'weaker', Edgar and Alice stand in equal opposition to each other. Whilst Laura obstructs the Captain's attempts to reach a higher state of consciousness, and pulls him back down to earth, in *Dance of Death* it is rather the male who is marked by a materialist character, who constantly thinks about gourmet meals (broiled mackerel with a glass of white burgundy, or the *Nimbs navarin aux pommes* in Copenhagen), whiskey and cigars. Alice, on the contrary, is presented as a 'woman of taste' who remembers the 'concerts in Tivoli' (Act 1). Part of the curse laid on them is to prefer things which are diametrically opposite to each other:

ALICE: You don't like my repertoire.

THE CAPTAIN: Nor you mine.

(I, 1, p. 127)

The couple reveal themselves to be 'damned' when they are unable to part from each other despite many attempts, 'Now only death can separate us. We know it, so we wait for him as the deliverer' (I, 1, p. 145).

In the fortress, a former jail, cut off on an island, Edgar and Alice live in total isolation from their surroundings. They are fixated on their hatred and battle against each other. First, they drive away each other's friends and family:

ALICE: First he uprooted my brothers and sisters from the house – 'uprooted' is his word for it – and after that my girlhood's friends ... and the rest.

KURT: But what about *his* relatives? Did you uproot them?

ALICE: Yes.

(I, 1, p. 145)

Next, the children are sent away from the house:

ALICE: ... They couldn't stay at home. He set them against me ...

KURT: And you against him.

ALICE: Yes, naturally. Then it came to taking sides, canvassing, bribery ... So, in order not to destroy the children, we parted from them.

(I, 1, p. 147)

Finally, the servants leave the fortress. Alice and Edgar remain alone with each other. All that is left is the daily battle against one another, eye to eye without any allies, 'What's going on here? The very walls smell of poison – one feels sick the moment one comes in. ... There's a corpse under the floor ... and such hatred that one can scarcely breathe' (Kurt, I, 1, p. 144). It is this situation which is continually described as 'hell': 'This is hell!' (Alice, I, 1, p. 153); 'Don't you believe in it – you who are right in it?" (Kurt to the Captain, I, 1, p. 157); 'You know that people call this island "Little

Hell"' (Alice, II, 1, p. 172). At the end of their inevitable battle against one another, Alice and Edgar interpret their situation in a similar way:

ALICE: And We ... ?

THE CAPTAIN: We're destined to torment one another, so it seems.

ALICE: Haven't we tormented one another enough?

(II, 2, p. 186)

Because the permanent fight between Edgar and Alice is a result of their being damned to hate and torture each other, the role-play in their relationship is more deeply emphasised than it was in that between Laura and the Captain. Every response, every action represents a move in a game whose rules have been dictated to the players, rules which they cannot alter. Edgar and Alice are unable to make their own decisions or to act with their own self-determination in any way. They are only able to choose between two or more possible moves in the game. To end the game, or to choose another game is not within their power.

The drama is opened by the Captain's words which typify the situation: 'Won't you play something for me?' (I, 1, p. 127). The ritualised communication between the two is continued in a game of cards (symbolic of the ongoing battle between them) and finally thematised by the Captain:

Don't you realise we go through the same rigmarole ever day? When you repeated your old dig just now: 'In *this* household at any rate', my cue was to retort: 'The household isn't just *my* affair.' But as I've already said this five hundred times, now I yawn instead.

(I, 1, p. 135)

After Kurt arrives, the game is no longer played with ritualised gestures, but with ritualised battle actions: each player's defeat is inevitably followed by the defeat of the other, without, however, actually ending the fight. Finally, the two sit once more opposite one another – not without pity for one another ('He is to be pitied – for being like this' [Alice, I, 2, p. 165]) and not without understanding of the essence of the battle ('We're destined to torment one another', 'Haven't we tormented one another enough'), but without the strength, means or potential to end it all:

ALICE: ... Is there no end?
THE CAPTAIN: Yes, but we must have patience. Perhaps when death comes, life begins.
ALICE: Ah, if that were so ... !

(II, 2, p. 186)

The prospect of death, which alone might bring an end to the absurd game, is the sole hope which the two opponents have left. In this *danse macabre* or 'end game' they are more played upon than players themselves. The true player – and creator – of this game in which Edgar and Alice are little more than figures on a board, or marionettes for whom a different voice speaks the predefined text, remains hidden. The *deus absconditus* does not show himself. Since the game seems to be a result of the Fall, however, it is surely not wrong to suspect the punishing God of the Old Testament. In place of the cannibalistic Great Mother in *The Father*, a revenging, merciless God appears in *The Dance of Death* who punishes the disobedience of his first children, Adam and Eve, in every human couple again and again by forcing them into the eternal game of a mutual battle of destruction. He makes each person the other's 'hell' from which only death can provide salvation – if at all. Even when God the father remains hidden, he is none the less almighty. A new rebellion against him is completely impossible.

The attack on the patriarchal system is established on the mythological level of the 'Fall'. It can apparently only be avenged and perhaps atoned for by the severest punishment: through the 'eternal suffering' of people who are forced to torment one another into eternity. The suffering of mankind through mankind thus becomes a sign of the almighty power of the avenging father and of the ultimate return to the patriarchal system which must not be upturned. Whilst the Mother god in *The Father* swallows her son, the Father god in *Dance of Death* hands out eternal torture to his children.

An escape from the mythical, overpowerful, destructive parent figure seems to be out of the question. The destruction of the self continues in unending family suffering.

The 'sacred' nature of the institutions of marriage and family, as conservatives such as Riehl and Le Play never tired of preaching, in which the majority of the bourgeois classes at least pretended to believe, is revealed by Strindberg to be a lie, a dangerous illusion. For him, the relationship between the sexes represents a biologically or mythically founded relationship of violence from whose power the individual is unable to escape. A 'hell' has been created out of the 'eternal work of nature' in which 'she has planted the seeds of humanity and cultivates them', as Herder explained in *Ideen zur Philosophie der Geschichte der Menschheit* (*Thoughts on the Philosophy of the History of Mankind*), a hell which disfigures the individual unrecognisably, distorts his face into a grotesque animal or vampire mask and totally dehumanises him. A dignified existence, the hope of self-realisation, can only exist beyond hell. The bourgeois myth of the family as the place and refuge of humanity in which the personality of the individual can develop itself in an unobstructed way and in freedom is here, as in Ibsen, not only torn apart and exposed as a lie, but is also replaced by a new mythology: the myth of the 'marriage in hell'. Eternal damnation has become – the other.

*The fatherless family*

The families at the heart of Chekhov's dramas are mostly fatherless. In *The Seagull* (1896), the family consists of mother, son and uncle; the *Three Sisters* (1901) concerns four siblings; *Cherry Orchard* (1904) has a mother, daughter, foster-daughter and uncle. The father's seat remains empty. This characteristic, which is particularly noticeable in the context of the period, is certainly not the result of a disregard for the patriarchal role. Chekhov had experienced the fatal implications of that as a child all too often. In a letter to his two elder brothers, he wrote, 'I want you to remember that despotism and lies destroyed your mother's youth. Despotism and lies so spoiled our childhood, that it frightens and sickens me to think of it even now' (2 January 1889).[39] Chekhov felt that he was coerced into slavery by his father and had to squeeze 'the slavish self' out of his system until he 'awoke one morning feeling that real human blood was flowing through his veins, instead of the blood of slaves' (letter to his friend and publisher, A.S. Suvorin, 7 January 1889).[40]

The absence of the father-figure in Chekhov's dramas does not contradict this experience, rather, it is related to it. In *Three Sisters*, Andrey talks about his father, who died the previous year:

My father – God bless his memory – used to simply wear us out with learning. It sounds silly, I know, but I must confess that since he died I've begun to grow stout, as if I'd been physically relieved of the strain. I've grown quite stout, in a year. Yes, thanks to Father, my sisters and I know French and German and English, and Irena here knows Italian, too. But what an effort it all cost us!

(Act I, pp. 262–3)

The death of the father seems to have physically liberated the son so that he can find himself.

In other respects, too, Chekhov leaves no doubt that the General influenced and determined the lives of his children in a far-reaching way. While he was alive, Olga became a teacher at the grammar school for girls – clearly not at her own wish: 'I suppose I must get this continual headache because I have to go to school every day and go on teaching right into the evening. I seem to have the thoughts of someone quite old. Honestly, I've been feeling as if my strength and youth were running out of me drop by drop, day after day' (Act 1, p. 111). Masha is married off to someone she does not love: 'You see, they married me off when I was eighteen. I was afraid of my husband because he was a school-master, and I had only just left school myself. He seemed

terribly learned then, very clever and important. Now it's quite different, unfortunately' (Act 2, p. 276).

Not only did the father have a deep effect on the education of his children, he also influenced their whole lifestyle. Thus, at the beginning of the drama, the anniversary of his death seems to have great significance. The problem of self-realisation is formulated in a radically new way: the brother and sisters are now independent of their father, they are free to live according to their own desires and are responsible for their own lives.

The greatest dream of all the siblings is to leave the administrative capital where they moved with their father eleven years previously, and return to Moscow. Olga would then give up her job and marry ('I suppose everything that God wills must be right and good, but I can't help thinking sometimes that if I'd got married and stayed at home, it would have been a better thing for me' [Act 1, pp. 251]). Irena dreams of finding her true love in Moscow ('I've been waiting all this time, imagining that we'd be moving to Moscow, and I'd meet the man I'm meant for there. I've dreamt about him and I've loved him in my dreams' [Act 3, p. 306]) and, at first, makes concrete plans as to how she will find happiness and satisfaction in her work. For 'Man must work by the sweat of his brow whatever his class, and that should make up the whole meaning and purpose of his life and happiness and contentment … You know how you long for a cool drink in hot weather? Well, that's the way I long for work' (Act 1, p. 252–3). Andrey intends to marry Natasha and dreams 'every night that I'm a professor in Moscow University, a famous academician, the pride of all Russia!' (Act 2, p. 274). Only Masha seems to be content with a vague yearning to go to Moscow and does not make any concrete plans as to how she could change her life.

By the end of the play, all their hopes have been dashed. The siblings remain in the administrative capital. Olga has not married, but has been promoted to headmistress in the job she hates. Irena has worked in the telegraph office and for the government administration, but this work was 'the sort of work you do without inspiration, without even thinking' (Act 2, p. 278), so that she 'hates' and 'despises' every task she is given. Nor has she found the 'right man', and has agreed to enter a loveless marriage to Baron Toozenbach. But even this plan is thwarted: Toozenbach dies in a duel. Andrey has married Natasha, and he has not become a professor but rather a member of the County Council whose chairman, Protopopov, is having an affair with Natasha.

All their plans have come to nothing, all their dreams have dissolved into thin air. Why is this so? Why have they not been able to organise and realise their lives according to their plans and dreams? The father-figure and the patriarchal structure of the family cannot be considered the cause, nor the excuse. Similarly, it was not through financial need or other circumstances for which the siblings were not responsible.

On the other hand, the possible 'inner' situation cannot be blamed on lack of cultivation of the individual personality. Rather, Chekhov lets the audience know, as early on as the first Act, that the brother and sisters have been given an excellent education, and he puts great value on showing each character with the tiniest detail of nuance as a distinctive, individual personality, whose temperament, talent, habits, behaviour, means of expression and speech are unmistakably different from all the others. In this respect, the three sisters represent an almost ideal embodiment of the concept of personality as it was developed in the nineteenth century. They are well aware of this cultivated specialness, their difference from others – not only the 'petit bourgeois' Natasha, but also the 'mass of ignorance' among the 'hundred thousand people in this town' (Vershinin, Act 1, p. 263).

Awareness of the own individuality, and the fixation on the needs which arise from it, seem, in the case of Olga and Irena, to be the cause of their inability to alter their lives according to their desires. When Natasha reproaches the nurse Anfisa and demands that she leave the house, Olga chooses not to interfere directly, but instead defends herself weakly by referring to her individuality:

> You spoke so harshly to Nanny just now … You must forgive me for saying so, but I just can't stand that sort of thing … it made me feel quite faint … When people are treated like that, it gets me down, I feel quite ill … I simply get unnerved … Any cruel or tactless remark, even the slightest discourtesy, upsets me.
>
> (Act 3, pp. 296–7)

Thus the own individuality is shown to be the cause and excuse for the fact that Olga is not able to oppose Natasha effectively.

In another way, the centrality of the own ego and its needs proves, for Irena, to be the greatest obstacle to fulfilling her yearning for the 'true, beautiful life' (Act 3). She complains about her work at the telegraph office, that it is a job which can be done 'without inspiration and without even thinking', and she says this directly after telling Masha how she herself has chased 'inspiration' and 'thought' out of her work:

> A woman came into the post office just before I left. She wanted to send a wire to her brother in Saratov to tell him her son had just died, but she couldn't remember the address. So we had to send the wire without an address, just to Saratov. She was crying and I was rude to her, for no reason at all. 'I've no time to waste', I told her. So stupid of me.
>
> (Act 2, p. 278)

Irena expects something back from her work which she must actually invest herself first, if she is to find satisfaction. Consideration for others would create 'inspiration' and 'thought'. Since for Irena the only thing which exists is her own desire for happiness and the utopia of Moscow and nothing else, she fails to meet the expectations demanded of her from the real people who surround her.

This is also true of her relationship with Toozenbach. Although Irena is firmly convinced that she can only meet the 'right' man in Moscow, she finally agrees to marry the baron if this is the only way to Moscow: 'I'll agree to marry him, if only we can go to Moscow! Let's go, please do let's go! There's nowhere in all the world like Moscow. Let's go, Olia! Let's go!' (Act 3, p. 310). Thus, even after the engagement, Toozenbach does not become a true companion for whom she can raise real interest, nor will she even listen to him. Although she suspects that something has happened between Toozenbach and Solenyi, she cannot prevent the duel because she does not know anything to say which would betray a deeper concern for Toozenbach as an individual.

TOOZENBACH: I'll take you away tomorrow. We'll work, we'll be rich, my dreams will come to life again. And you'll be happy! But – there's only one 'but', only one – you don't love me!

IRENA: I can't help that! I'll be your wife, I'll be loyal and obedient to you, but I can't love you ... What's to be done? [Weeps.] I've never loved anyone in my life. Oh, I've had such dreams about being in love! I've been dreaming about it for ever so long, day and night ... but somehow my soul seems like an expensive piano which someone has locked up and the key's got lost. [A pause] Your eyes are so restless.

TOOZENBACH: I was awake all night. Not that there's anything to be afraid of in my life, nothing threatening ... Only the thought of that lost key torments me and keeps me awake. Say something to me ... [A pause] Say something!

IRENA: What? What am I to say? What?

TOOZENBACH: Anything.

IRENA: Don't, my dear, don't ... [A pause]

TOOZENBACH: ... I must go, it's time ... Look at that dead tree, it's all dried-up, but it's still swaying in the wind along with the others. And in the same way, it seems to me that, if I die, I shall still have a share in life somehow or other. Goodbye, my dear ... [Kisses her hands] Your papers, the ones you gave me, are on my desk, under the calendar.

IRENA: I'm coming with you.

TOOZENBACH: [Alarmed] No, no! [Goes off quickly, then stops in the avenue] Irena!

IRENA: What?

TOOZENBACH: [Not knowing what to say] I didn't have any coffee this morning. Will you tell them to get some ready for me? [Goes off quickly]

(Act 4, p. 321)

Toozenbach's words 'say something', may be understood as an appeal to Irena to turn to him. But Irena refuses three times to accept a relationship with him: through silence ('pause'), through her return question, 'What am I I say?', and through explicit rejection ('Don't ... don't!'). Despite this, Toozenbach tries, after he has spoken of his presentiment of death, a final appeal – he calls her by name. This call is simply an address, a show of affection, and at the same time it is Toozenbach's last attempt to move Irena to open up to him as a person. But Irena does not understand his appeal. With her question 'what?' she transports the mention of her name from an interpersonal communication to a simple informational one. Toozenbach's escape into banality represents the end of all dialogue between them.

Indeed, Irena is like an 'expensive piano' which remains closed; the encounter with the other, which can only occur when two people meet, takes place in her innermost being. The path to the other is blocked because she is wholly sunken into her own subjectivity and only obsessed with her own personality.

Irena is unable to step beyond the central focus on herself and turn to her fellow human beings. She is unable to grasp the potential of the moment to open up to others and thereby perhaps find happiness herself because she believes her character is only suited to the imaginary people she will find in the utopia of Moscow. Irena's loneliness is a result of making her own special personality the centre, it is a result of the cult which she builds around her own personality.

This becomes very clear in a comparison with Masha. Masha is as sensitive and cultivated a person as her sisters. She finds rudeness and lack of sensitivity as repulsive as Olga: 'Vulgarity upsets me, it makes me feel insulted, I actually suffer when I meet someone who lacks refinement and gentle manners, and courtesy. When I'm with the other teachers, my husband's friends, I just suffer' (Act 2, p. 276). This sensitivity has, however, not prevented Masha from being open to others and showing an interest in them. Whilst Olga and Irena only care about the fact that Vershinin comes from Moscow and, thus, represents an ambassador from their dream world, Masha remembers his earlier nickname and notes how old he has become in the last eleven years since she saw him. Gradually she finds herself becoming warm to Vershinin – not because he is a Don Juan, irresistible, nor because she gives herself up to the utopian dream of true happiness. With the opening verses of Pushkin's poem *Ruslan and Ludmilla*, a classic Russian love story, which Masha often quotes, 'A green oak grows by a curving shore, And round that oak hangs a golden chain ...', Masha signals that she is not happy in her marriage and perhaps dreams of a great love as Irena does. But this yearning does not make her blind to the real people whom she meets in the present. Thus, unlike her sisters, she is able to welcome Vershinin with openness and interest in him as a person – rather than merely seeing the fact that he comes from Moscow.

I thought he was queer at first, then I started to pity him ... then I began to love him ... love everything about him – his voice, his talk, his misfortunes, his two little girls ... If I love him, well – that's my fate! That's my destiny ... He loves me too. It's all rather frightening, isn't it? Not a good thing, is it? [*Takes Irena by the hand and draws her to her*] Oh, my dear! ... How are we going to live through the rest of our lives? What's going to become of us? When you read a novel, everything in it seems so old and obvious, but when you fall in love yourself, you suddenly discover that you don't really know anything, and you've got to make your own decisions.

(Act 3, pp. 307–8)

Chekhov reveals the decision made by Masha and Vershinin in the form of a dialogue which takes place without, in the main, words:

VERSHININ: [*Sings*] 'To love all ages are in fee, The passion's good for you and me.' ... [*Laughs*]
MASHA: [*Sings*] Tara-tara-tara ...
VERSHININ: Tum-tum ...
MASHA: Tara-tara ...
VERSHININ: Tum-tum, tum-tum ... [*Laughs*]

(Act 3, p. 302)

True, genuine feelings can only find appropriate expression outside language. In this respect, Chekhov was filled with a deep scepticism about language, similar to that experienced by Hofmannsthal as he expressed it in a well-known letter to Lord Chandos in 1902. Chekhov also expressed himself thus:

Above all, speech, as beautiful and deep as it may be, only has an effect on the indifferent, and often it cannot satisfy those who are happy or unhappy; that is why the highest form of expression of happiness or unhappiness is mostly silence: those who are in love understand each other better when they are silent, and a burning memorial speech for the deceased only touches strangers, to the widow and the children of the deceased, it seems cold and empty.[41]

In the 'tara-tara-tara' dialogue, Masha and Vershinin have found their own 'language' which is equivalent to silence and which is a fitting expression of their emotions. Both succeed in this moment in finding total self-realisation; both experience the 'true and beautiful life' of which Irena only dreams. They are happy – even if only for a short time – because they are open to each other and truly participate in the lives of their fellow beings; because they are prepared to leave the centrality of the self and to move to a world which exits *between* self and the other. This is only possible, however, because Masha has not made a cult of her individual, special personality, but instead is open to the world and others.

If language is useless in expressing the emotions of those who are either happy or unhappy, as is suggested by the 'Tram-tam-tam' dialogue between Masha and Vershinin, the question arises as to what extent language can stimulate togetherness at all – and in doing so, dispel loneliness. In Act 2, Andrey has the following conversation with the very deaf Ferapont:

ANDREY: If you could hear properly I don't think I'd be talking to you like this. I must talk to someone, but my wife doesn't seem to understand me, and as for my sisters … I'm afraid of them for some reason or other, I'm afraid of them laughing at me and pulling my leg … I don't drink and I don't like going to pubs, but my word! How I'd enjoy an hour or so at Tyestov's or the Great Moscow Restaurant! Yes, my dear fellow, I would indeed!

FERAPONT: The other day at the office a contractor was telling me about some business men who were eating pancakes in Moscow. One of them ate forty pancakes and died. It was either forty or fifty, I can't remember exactly.

ANDREY: You can sit in some huge restaurant in Moscow without knowing anyone, and no one knowing you; yet somehow you don't feel that you don't belong there … Whereas here you know everybody, and everybody knows you, and yet you don't feel you belong here, you feel you don't belong at all … You're lonely and you feel a stranger.

FERAPONT: What's that? [A pause] It was the same man that told me – of course, he may have been lying – he said that there's an enormous rope stretched right across Moscow.

(Act 2, p. 275)

Andrey talks about his unsuccessful life, his desires, dreams, fears and yearnings to Ferapont because 'I must talk to someone'. The

presence of another clearly gives him the feeling that he is not quite alone, that he is talking to someone. Speech does not have this function for Andrey alone. Nearly all the characters in *Three Sisters* are lonely, but they do not withdraw into silence because of it – quite the contrary, because they are lonely, they talk. They talk about daily things or the future of mankind, they talk for the sake of talking, for only talk can take away their feelings of loneliness. Andrey believes that loneliness can be dissipated and communication is possible; but he transports the realisation of it to his utopia of Moscow – the same Moscow across which, as Ferapont relates, a rope is tied – a sign of separation and isolation.

For Andrey, speech has yet another function. In Act 4, Andrey has a last dialogue with Ferapont. After complaining once more about his failed life in particular and the meanness and baseness of life in general, and after Ferapont's interruption that Petersburg in winter was minus two hundred degrees, he continues:

I hate the life I live at present, but oh! the sense of elation when I think of the future! Then I feel so light-hearted, such a sense of release! I seem to see light ahead, light and freedom. I see myself free, and my children, too, – free from idleness, free from *kvass*, free from eternal meals of goose and cabbage, free from after-dinner naps, free from all this degrading parasitism!

(Act 4, p. 323)

In his speaking of the distant future, in which he will overcome his problems, Andrey has liberated himself from the responsibility of undertaking anything concrete in the present to overcome those problems now. He does not talk for the sake of doing something, but rather to avoid doing something. Speech, thus, is a substitute for action.

The same is true of Toozenbach's and Vershinin's philosophising. Vershinin always philosophises with different people, though mostly with Toozenbach. Each gives his opinion without letting himself be influenced by the other's view. When Vershinin speaks of his conviction that, 'In two or three hundred years life on this old earth of ours will have become marvellously beautiful. Man longs for a life like that, and if it isn't here yet, he must imagine it, wait for it, dream about it, prepare for it' (Act 1, p. 263), he liberates himself from the need to do anything in the real situation in which he finds himself. For Andrey, talk becomes a substitute for action, where, none the less, another person is needed. In philosophising to another being, Vershinin makes the other person witness to the action substituted by philosophising. Whilst he sits and talks of a better future in two or three hundred years' time, the present is left uncondi-tionally to the 'petit bourgeoisie' like Natasha and Protopopov, who will ensure that triviality, baseness and meanness will continue to deter-mine the style of life.

In the course of the play, Natasha trans-forms from a shy, awkward girl, who runs away from the table in embarrassment, into the mistress of the Prozorov household. The most effective weapon she uses in her elevation to this position is speech. Her words always concern concrete situations, unlike those of the others. In Act 2, she succeeds in banning the carnival singers, which everyone anticipated would bring them fun, entertainment and something new, with her speech on the theme of 'Bobik'. It also chases Irena from the room. In Act 3, she achieves the same in a similar way by driving the nurse Anfisa and Olga out of the house. Natasha's flow of speech reveals itself each time as a process of the gradual overpow-ering of others (first Andrey, then Olga) who are seen as obstacles in the execution of her own will. Each of her words is used as a weapon to tame those of others and overpower them. For Natasha, to speak is to act – as in classical drama – it is a kind of action, however, which views its fellow humans as objects which must be subjected to the will of the agent at any price. Natasha's speeches are nothing but acts of aggression, to which the others must bow, until there is no one left who can contradict her will:

I'll get Andrey and his old violin to move into your room: he can saw away at it as

much as he likes there. And then we'll move Sofochka into his room … So tomorrow I'll be alone here. [*Sighs*] I'll have this fir-tree avenue cut down first, then that maple tree over there. It looks so awful in the evenings … [*To Irena*] My dear, that belt you're wearing doesn't suit you at all. Not at all good taste. You want something brighter to go with that dress … I'll tell them to put flowers all round here, lots of flowers, so that we get plenty of scent from them … [*Sternly*] Why is there a fork lying on this seat? [*Going into the house, to the maid*] Why is that fork left on the seat there? [*Shouts*] Don't answer me back!

(Act 4, p. 328)

Typically, Natasha's last words are 'Don't answer me back!' For when words are weapons which are used to destroy others, then other people's words cannot be tolerated. All that remains is Natasha's triumphant will, which has driven away all others who are a distur-bance and which has 'liberated' her self from all the others: 'So tomorrow I'll be alone here'. Only by holding power over others, suppressing or banishing them, can Natasha achieve self-realisation. She stops being a human being, as Andrey notices, 'My wife is my wife. She's a good, decent sort of woman … she's really very kind, too, but there's something about her which pulls her down to the level of an animal … a sort of mean, blind, thick-skinned animal' (Act 4, p. 318).

The sensitive, cultivated characters leave their house, their presence, their lives to such an 'animal' because they are totally occupied with their own complex personalities and needs, beyond which they are not able to take anything in and, except for philosophising, they are unable to stir themselves to any action.

The audience was moved to tears at every performance of Stanislavsky's production of *Three Sisters* (premièred 31 January 1901) – much to the annoyance of Chekhov. He told Alexander Tichonov in 1902:

You say you cried over my play. You were not the only one. But I didn't write it for that reason. I intended something quite different. I simply wanted to say, in honesty, look at yourselves! look what poor and boring lives you lead! It is most important that people see this. As soon as they understand, they must begin another, better way of life. I won't live to see it, but I am convinced that it will be a totally different life, incomparable with life today. But in the meantime I shan't stop repeating myself: Look what boring and poor lives you lead! That's nothing to cry about![42]

To see the image of a lazy section of society on the brink of revolution (of 1905) in the *Three Sisters* is, however, as false an interpretation as bewailing an existentially founded loneliness which the individual cannot prevent as the cause of his inability to act while recognising the self in characters who are full of self-pity. As this analysis shows, in the fatherless family of the *Three Sisters* it all depends upon the individual as to what he makes of his life. Membership of a particular social class cannot be made responsible. In similar vein, Chekhov wrote to Gorky:

For a while it is the students – they are an honest, good lot, they are our hope, the hope of Russia. But when they have grown up, our hope and Russia's future turns into smoke, and all that remains in the filter are doctors, landlords, starving bureaucrats and corrupt engineers. ... I do not believe in our intelligence, it is hypocritical, false, hysterical and lazy, I do not even believe in it when it suffers and complains, for its suppresser springs from our own laps. I believe in individual beings who are scattered all over the country whether common people or intellectuals; in them lies the power even if they are only few ... for their work is seen.[43]

Without overlooking or trivialising the social and familial causes for the crisis of identity in the individual in his dramas, Chekhov gives the individual final responsibility for the organisation of his own life. This responsibility cannot be passed on to anyone else.

It is somewhat ironic that Chekhov's dramas were only successful among his contemporaries because they were not received in this way. Stanislavsky's productions, which were produced as 'atmospheric dramas' in which the dramatic figures were relieved of any responsibility for their 'poor and boring lives', and could thus ensure the tearful pity of the spectators, became the model for productions of Chekhov both in Russia as well as the rest of Europe, which only came to know Chekhov's plays when the Moscow Art Theatre toured Europe. The bourgeois audience could resolve itself in pity and tears as they watched, instead of feeling confronted with their 'poor and boring lives'. Chekhov's dramas were successful because they did not shake up the audience, but rather offered weepy consolation for their own 'misery': one could enjoy the cult of the own, highly sensitive personality and the resulting inability to act, be moved and melancholic in an aesthetic atmosphere. 'Look how we are destroyed, misunderstood and innocent in our beauty.' Seldom was a playwright so deeply misunderstood by his time as Chekhov in his.

## The great personality – the artist

### The charismatic artist and the 'femme fatale'

The bourgeoisie not only made a cult out of the family, but also out of the great personality. What began in the *Sturm und Drang* movement as the cult of genius increasingly became, in the course of the nineteenth century, the cult of the mysterious personality. As Richard Sennett suggests, 'the sheer revelation of someone's inner impulses became exciting; if a person could reveal himself in public and yet control the process of self-disclosure, he was exciting. You felt he was powerful but couldn't explain why. This is secular charisma.'[44] It is hardly surprising, therefore, that the artist – and more particularly the performing artist, the star – became the epitome of this mysterious personality. Equipped with just such charisma, the poet Lamartine succeeded in drawing the crowds on his side in the February Revolution of 1848, for example, so that they became passive and forgot their own interests in the matter.

In aesthetically advanced drama, the mysterious personality had been embodied by a kind of Byronic hero – principally an artist, such as de Vigny's Chatterton – who falls into ruin because society does not recognise his mission and denies him an appropriate public status. This chasm between the individual and society, which is typical and characteristic of the drama of the Romantic movement, seems to have been done away with in Ibsen's later play *The Master Builder* (1892). Halvard Solness is a successful builder who has not only won the recognition of society, but also leads a bourgeois lifestyle. He manages an office with three employees, he is married and lives in a representative house in which the honoured members of the city, such as Dr Herdal, and ladies of good society are welcomed.

Despite this, Solness has certain traces which are reminiscent of the artist in the romantic drama. That he should be thought of as an outstanding personality is indicated by Ibsen's choice of name. 'Sol' means 'sun' and 'ness' means 'promontory, spit of land'. Solness does actually count among the 'happy few'. Not only has he been, according to Dr Herdal, 'unbelievably lucky' (Act 1, p. 259), but he also lives in the knowledge that he has been chosen:

SOLNESS: [*confidentially*] Don't you think, Hilde, that there are people singled out by fate who have been endowed with grace and power to wish for something, desire it so passionately, will it so inexorably that, ultimately, they must be granted it? ... No man can achieve such things alone. Oh, no. There are – helpers and servers – who must be at our side if we are to succeed. But they never come of their own accord. One must call on them with all one's strength. Silently, you understand.

(Act 2, pp. 290–1)[45]

The feeling of being chosen grows out of the special ability to influence other people and change reality merely through intensely desiring it. As Freud showed, this literally fairy-tale ability embraces a relict from ancient times, 'when desire still had effect' ontogenetically since childhood, and phylogenetically since the time of magical, nature religions. In *Totem and Taboo*, written in 1912/13, Freud

called it 'the almighty power of thought'. As early as 1907 in a lecture on the *Poet and the Imagination*, Freud characterised the activity of the poet as daydreaming which serves the desire and in this way described the 'almighty power of thought' as a typical characteristic of the poet, though he did not explicitly use this phrase. It seems an interesting parallel that fifteen years earlier Ibsen introduced this same characteristic as the most significant one which affects Solness' awareness that he is the chosen one, that he has a mission to fulfil as an artist.

This ability to change reality by mere desire clothes Solness in a kind of magical power over others. Kaja Fosli becomes dependent on him, even enslaved, and it seems simply because of the magic of desire: 'Solness: I just stood and looked at her – and kept wishing from the bottom of my heart that I had her here' (Act 1, p. 257). Kaja comes and stays. She lives only for Solness, protects herself from the influence of anyone else with her green shade and bows before Solness as if he were a god:

KAJA: [*Drops on her knees*] Oh, you're so kind to me! So wonderfully kind!

(Act 1, p. 252)

Kaja's dependence on Solness, who in fact exploits and uses her as a tool to eliminate his rival, her fiancé Ragnar, is the result of his magic ability, his charisma. In *Wirtschaft und Gesellschaft* (*The Theory of Social and Economic Organization*), written between 1899 and 1919, Max Weber describes charisma in the following terms:

The term 'charisma' will be applied to a certain quality of an individual personality by virtue of which he is set apart from ordinary men and treated as endowed with supernatural, super-human, or at least specifically exceptional powers or qualities. These are such as are not accessible to the ordinary person, but are regarded as of divine origin or as exemplary, and on the basis of them the individual concerned is treated as a healer. ... How the quality in question would be ultimately judged from any ethical, aesthetic, or other such point of view is naturally entirely indifferent for purposes of definition. What is alone important is how the individual is actually regarded by those subject to charismatic authority, by his 'followers' or 'disciples'. ...

It is recognition on the part of those subject to authority which is decisive for the validity of charisma. This is freely given and guaranteed by what is held to be a 'sign' or proof, originally always a miracle, and consists in devotion to the corresponding revelation, hero worship, or absolute trust in the leader. But where charisma is genuine, it is not this which is the basis of the claim to legitimacy. This basis lies rather in the conception that it is the *duty* of those who have been called to a charismatic mission to recognise its quality and to act accordingly. Psychologically, this 'recognition' is a matter of complete personal devotion to the possessor of the quality, arising out of enthusiasm, or of despair and hope.[46]

Halvard Solness certainly possesses this kind of charisma. He not only uses it to exude power over Kaja but also over Knut and Ragnar Brovik, his wife Aline and Hilde Wangel.

Solness' feeling of being chosen is not the only thing which places him in the tradition of the mysterious personality of romantic drama, but also his Promethean rebellion against God.

SOLNESS: He wanted to give me the chance to be a real master in my own field, and build greater churches to His glory ... It was so that I should have nothing to bind me. No love or happiness or anything, you see. I was to be a master builder – nothing else. And all my life was to be spent building for Him. [*Laughs*] But that wasn't the way it worked out ... Then, like Him, I did the impossible ... And as I stood high up there, right at the top, and placed the wreath over the weathercock, I said to Him: 'Listen to me, mighty One! Henceforth I, too, want to be a free master builder. Free in my field, as You are in Yours. I never want to build churches for You again. Only homes, for people to live in.'

(Act 3, p. 314)

Solness not only refuses to do service to God, he even puts himself on a level with God. Like God, he intends to create and, like Prometheus, the fruits of his creation should benefit the people. But, like Prometheus, he is punished with a wound which will never heal. As Solness comments: 'It feels as though the skin had been flayed from my breast. And the helpers and servers go round taking the skin from other people's bodies to cover the wound. But it can't be healed. Never, never!' (Act 2, p. 291). Solness' 'wound' marks the conspicuous difference between Solness and Prometheus, Solness and the Promethean hero of the Romantic or *Sturm und Drang* movement. For while they pay for their rebellion with their own suffering, Solness' rebellion has results both for him and for others. In order to close his wounds, the 'servants and helpers' tear yet more skin from other bodies. The difference lies in Solness' relationship to his fellow human beings and to society.

On the one hand, his sense of being chosen has rewarded him with extraordinary success and an outstanding position in the bourgeois society: 'You began as a poor country lad, and here you are, the top man in your profession' (Herdal, Act 1, p. 260). On the other hand, however, – and the pun on shreds of skin that the 'servants and helpers' rip from others make this clear – Solness pays for these 'services' with a deep feeling of guilt towards his wife and an over-exaggerated fear of the young who will one day replace him, at first in the form of Ragnar Brovik.

Both his feelings of guilt, his fears – and the knowledge of his being chosen – are a direct consequence of Solness' special ability to wish intensely. His success as a master builder is founded on the fire which destroyed Aline's family's house and which was indirectly the cause of her twin children's death: 'If it hadn't been for that fire, I wouldn't have been able to build homes' (Solness, Act 2, p. 285). Solness had wished for this fire with all his heart and soul; he was none the less as surprised as anyone by it, and yet he had *de facto* nothing to do with starting it. Despite this, he is plagued by feelings of guilt as though he had laid the fire himself, for he is firmly convinced that it was his wish alone which caused it. In thinking this, he also burdens himself with guilt for Aline's ruined life. He is tormented by doubt as to whether his calling as artist is actually so great that he may draw from it the right to sacrifice Aline's calling to build 'the souls of children. So that they might grow into something noble, harmonious and beautiful. So that they might become worthy human beings' (Act 2, p. 287). Solness' rise as artist is, from one point of view, bought in exchange for a severe social misdemeanour – it is built on the destruction of the basic foundation of a family. Solness is not always able to defend his existence as artist in the face of the demands society makes of him, and which he totally accepts, that a man must have a wife and that the wife exists solely to bear and raise children. By internalising the social demands made upon him, his conscience has become, as Hilde comments, 'frail. Over-sensitive, won't get to grips with things. Can't carry a heavy burden' (Act 2, p. 292), and it fills him with feelings of guilt which are expressed in physical – and symbolic – symptoms of vertigo. The master builder 'dare not – cannot – rise as high as he can build' (Hilde, Act 2, p. 299). He feels vertiginous even on the balcony of a first floor.

Socially, Solness cannot live up to the image which he creates of himself as an artist. His feelings of guilt make him giddy just facing it. Only in the moment of his Promethean absolution from God is he able to overcome feelings of guilt and vertigo and to realise his own image of himself in an appropriate way – as a free, independent artist who, from the knowledge of his artistry, can draw the strength to be himself in a radical way without needing to consider others.

The myth of personality proves to be an illusion in a bourgeois society. It is not society which is the outer, oppositional force preventing Solness from achieving self-realisation as was in the case of the Byronic heroes or the artists of romantic drama. Rather, he is prevented by his own internalisation of the many social demands concerning the family so that he no longer experiences it as an external command but as a command led by his own

conscience. Disobeying this command, therefore, releases feelings of guilt in terms of his own failure and ruin and this stops his personality from being able to develop freely. Under such conditions, the idea of 'personality' can be nothing more than an illusion.

Since Solness believes that his rise as an artist is only thanks to his ability to dream, he has reason to fear that his artistry will be over as soon as the magic of his dreaming has no power because 'I'm afraid the helpers and servants won't obey me any longer' (Act 2, p. 295). He would be not in a position to execute any further great works. However, if the 'proof of his charismatic qualification fails him for long, the leader endowed with charisma tends to think his god or his magical heroic powers have deserted him. If he is for long unsuccessful, above all if his leadership fails to benefit his followers, it is likely that his charismatic authority will disappear.'[47] Solness would forfeit his charisma and lose his power over others. He fears this day as the day of 'retribution' (Act 2, Act 3.). It will be a day on which someone will enter and 'demand: "Make way for me!" And then all the others will storm after him shaking their fists and shouting: "Make way! Make way!"' (Act 1, p. 260). It is for this reason that Solness is afraid of Ragnar, the young, talented builder whom he knows how to keep under his power and influence, and whom he will not allow independence: 'He is the youth who is waiting ready to bang upon my door. And make an end of master builder Solness' (Act 2, p. 295). It is not a coincidence that Ragnar's name is reminiscent of 'Ragnarök', the day of *Götterdämmerung* and the end of the world in Nordic mythology. Ironically, Solness' ruin is not initiated by Ragnar, but by Hilde Wangel, with whom Solness begins to build 'palaces in the air' and with whom he had hoped to start a new phase in his artist's career.

Hilde's name also evokes associations with Nordic mythology. It is similar to the name of one of the Valkyries who bring the dead heroes to Walhalla. It also has the same root as the substantive 'hulder' which describes a siren-like being in a Norwegian folk-tale, which itself points to the specifically literary connotation 'femme fatale'.

By the turn of the century, the figure of the 'femme fatale' already had a long tradition in European literature, and grew to an unexpected significance in the second half of the nineteenth century. Whilst in Romanticism, until approximately the middle of the century, it was the type of the demonic male, particularly in the form of the Byronic hero who had dominated in the second half of the century, the demonic female took over as the one who attracts and destroys. Particularly prominent examples of this kind are shown in Keats' *La Belle Dame sans Merci* (as early as 1819), Gautier's Cléopatre from *Une Nuit de Cléopatre* (1845), Swinburne's Dolores in *Our Lady of Sensual Pains* (1863), Wilde's *Sphinx* (1894) and D'Annunzio's *Pamphilia* (1893). From these examples, it is clear that these figures appear exclusively in poems, verses and novels. The femme fatale found no embodiment in drama of the nineteenth century (if one excludes Mallarmé's fragment of a lyrical drama, *Hérodiade*, published in 1869). Clearly, the image of a woman who draws a man to her through sexual attraction and thereby destroys him, is a figure which no one dared to show on the nineteenth-century stage because, according to the ideas of bourgeois morality, such a figure could not even exist. It was only as the women's movement increasingly mobilised the collective male fear of the man-murdering female, the cannibalistic mother, that the figure of the femme fatale was viewed not only as the private problem of an individual, perverse person, but as a general problem. This opened the way to dramatic representation. In 1891, Oscar Wilde wrote the tragedy *Salomé* in French. He had Sarah Bernhardt in mind for the main role when he wrote it, but the censor banned the performance. On 11 February 1896, *Salomé* was finally premièred at the Théâtre de l'Œuvre. Although Sarah Bernhardt played the main role, the production had only mediocre success. In 1901, a year after Wilde's death, *Salomé* was performed in Berlin with Gertrude

Eysoldt as Salomé. The play's success after this could not be stopped. It was translated into Czech, Dutch, Greek, Hungarian, Polish, Russian, Catalan, Swedish, Italian and even Yiddish. Since its musical interpretation by Strauss (1905), it has become one of the most popular dramas of the early twentieth century.

Frank Wedekind worked on the Lulu tragedy from 1891 which was to have been entitled *Pandora's Box*. In 1895, the first part was published under the title, *Earth Spirit*, and was premièred on 25 February 1898 in the Kristallpalast in Berlin. The drama was a great success throughout Germany, particularly with the actress Mathilde (Tilly) Newes, Wedekind's wife, in the role of Lulu. The figure of the femme fatale was well established on stage.

Hilde Wangel shares single details of appearance with the lyrical and epic representation of this figure such as, for example, the 'veiled look' (end of Act 2), and moreover, the most important feature: she destroys the man who has fallen under her spell. The master builder, Solness, falls from the tower of his new house which he only climbed in order to hang the garland for the raising the roof feast because Hilde, who knew of his vertigo, demanded of him 'the impossible' (Act 3). The fact that sexual attraction plays a role in the relationship between Hilde and Solness – as is typical of the femme fatale – is not even questioned. Not only do the phallic symbol of the tower, and the symbolism of climbing it, point to their desire, but also to the dreams of Solness and Hilde as they fall from a 'frightfully high, steep cliff' (Act 2, p. 279), and hug their knees up under them as they fall, as well as the ever-recurrent call of the Troll, hiding in Hilde and Solness, to their urges, 'And it's the troll, you see, that calls to the powers outside! And we have to submit whether we like it or not' (Solness, Act 2, p. 292). Solness submits to Hilde's magic in the same way that others fall victim to his magic: the demonic-charismatic male (of the Romantic movement) and the demonic female (of the end of the nineteenth century) are attracted to each other, and the female proves to be the stronger of the two. In this respect it is justified to see in Hilde Wangel the embodiment of the form of the femme fatale typical of its time.

But the relationship between Hilde and Solness is not defined by sexual attraction alone. Hilde demands of Solness the 'kingdom' which he promised her ten years earlier. If he really is 'a king', someone who has been chosen, then it should not be difficult for him to create a kingdom for her. If he cannot, then it is the 'probationary test' of which Max Weber speaks. But what is this kingdom which Hilde demands of Solness actually like?

HILDE: You owe me this kingdom. And a
    kingdom's got to have a castle, hasn't it?
SOLNESS: [*More and more exhilarated*] Yes,
    they usually do.
HILDE: Good. Build it for me then! At once!
SOLNESS: [*Laughs*] Within the hour?
HILDE: Yes! The ten years are up now. And I
    don't intend to wait any longer. I want my
    castle master builder!
SOLNESS: It's no joke to have you as creditor,
    Hilde.
HILDE: You should have thought of that
    before. Now it's too late. Now then!
    [*Thumps on the table*] Where's my castle?
    It's my castle!

(Act 3, p. 307)

Hilde describes the castle in more detail as a 'castle in the air' which both will build together, 'with a firm foundation' as Solness adds. In this, a new phase in his artistic career as building master begins.

At first, Solness had built churches as the builder to the 'powerful'. After his Promethean rejection of God he gave up sacred art and built 'homes for people', 'Bright, peaceful, comfortable homes, where mothers and fathers could live with their children secure and happy in the knowledge that it is good to be alive' (Act 2, p. 285). Solness thus gives his services to the social world; his work should encourage and ensure the happiness of the family. Now, however, he realises that 'Building homes for people isn't worth twopence, Hilde ... Because I realise now that people have no use for the homes they live

in. They can't be happy in them' (Act 3, p. 315). Art cannot fulfil its social contract because the general social conditions prevent mankind from being happy. Even social art has become functionless. With this recognition, Solness turns to quite another kind of art:

SOLNESS: Now I shall build the only place
    where I believe happiness can exist.
HILDE: (*Looks at him*) Master builder – you
    mean our castles in the air.
SOLNESS: Yes. Castles in the air.
HILDE: I'm afraid you'll get giddy before
    we've climbed halfway.
SOLNESS: Not when I can go hand in hand
    with you, Hilde.

(Act 3, pp. 314–15)

In his essay, *The Poet and the Imagination*, Freud calls the poet's fantasy 'castles in the air' which serve the yearnings of dreams and which represent a correction of reality. They relate to two principally different kinds of wish, 'either ambitious desires which serve to promote the personality, or they are erotic desires'.[48] When Solness wants to build castles in the air, he shifts the process of his self-realisation from the social arena to that of art. His art should now serve his desires, his self-realisation.

Hilde, on the other hand, insists that this self-realisation should also take place in real life. For it means 'more than life itself' to her 'To see you great! See you with a wreath in your hand! high, high up on a church tower!' (Act 2, p. 295). The image that she has created of Solness accords perfectly with the image which Solness created for himself in the church tower of Lysanger with his Promethean rejection of God. It has parallels to God: 'No one but you should be allowed to build. Only you' (Act 2, p. 281), and is unmistakably oriented around the ideal of the autonomous individual, around the image of the great personality. When Hilde demands of Solness, 'Then let me see you stand up there, high and free! ... Just once more, master builder! Do the impossible again!' (Act 3, p. 315), she is asking nothing less than that he should be able to realise his image of himself free from feelings of guilt and fears, free from vertigo. Solness does manage to climb the tower and, for a moment, to show the others how he would like to be ('Hilde: Now I see him great and free again!'). But he cannot hold this self-image for long: he falls.

From this perspective, Hilde can hardly be seen as the epitome of the femme fatale. To a greater extent, she represents youth 'with its clear conscience' which has not yet internalised the demands of society and, thus, she is one who does not believe the self-realisation of a great personality to be an illusion. Hilde does not use her attraction to destroy Solness, but on the contrary, to bring him back to himself, she wants to persuade him to realise the image that both she and Solness have made of his true self. And it is Solness who decides to take on the challenge. He is destroyed because he is not in a position to realise this image in reality under the present social conditions. Even the artist cannot realise himself as a great personality in real life. This can only be achieved, at the end of the nineteenth century, in 'castles of air'.

The première of *The Master Builder* was held on 7 December 1892 at the Haymarket Theatre in London. Both this production and one performed a little later at the Trafalgar Square Theatre (20 February 1893), met with little understanding and less success. Under the headline 'Ibsen's *The Master Builder* – A Feast of Dull Dialogue and Acute Dementia at the Trafalgar Square Theatre', the *Evening News and Post* critic wrote:

> The chief lunatic is Halvard Solness, a gentleman who appears to have a monopoly of all the best building contracts in his native town. ... The man is really a coward and subject to fits of dizziness, and has once in his life ventured to a respectable distance from the ground, but his vanity induces him to yield to Hilde's persuasion: He climbs the tower, hangs his wreath, and tumbles down a hundred feet or so, killing himself comfortably and ending the play, and a good job, too. ... In his latest play Ibsen has fully demonstrated that he is a great man. No one but a great man could get a clever actor and actress to accept and produce

upon stage such a pointless, incoherent and absolutely silly piece.

> (21 February 1893)

The critic of *The Times* declared his total bafflement and concludes his review:

> All this, say the admirers of the Norwegian dramatist, is symbolism and symbolism as applied to Mr. Ibsen's own work. He had begun by building churches – that is, by writing orthodox plays; the houses for human beings to live in were the Ibsenite drama proper. What the castle in the air is they do not, so far as we are aware, explain, but if it should be the symbolical drama over which its author comes to grief, no impartial-minded person who witnesses this crazy performance of *The Master Builder* will be disposed to say them nay.

> (21 February 1893)

It is notable that in most reviews, mention is made in some way of Solness' feeling of being chosen. Equally, no critic fails to point out Hilde's attractiveness as a woman and this is mostly received negatively. Clearly, the critics have not missed the fact that Solness and Hilde are prototypes of the charismatic personality and the femme fatale. But they were not in a position to understand the far-reaching and significant changes that Ibsen made to these two types. This general lack of understanding need not be a surprise. For one should not forget that Ibsen wrote *The Master Builder* at the end of the nine-teenth century, at a time when the figure of the femme fatale and the great personality had not yet really 'blossomed'. The femme fatale as vamp in film history and the charismatic personality as leader had yet to leave their mark on the history of the twentieth century.

It was only the production of the play by Lugné-Poë at his Théâtre de l'Œuvre (1894) which opened the eyes of his contemporaries to at least a few important aspects of the work.

Lugné-Poë placed his emphasis on the 'duel d'amour et de génie' which is played out with great passion. In October of the same year, Lugné-Poë showed his production to Ibsen in Christiana. Ibsen was at first very restrained, but gave up his reservations by Act 2: 'It was, the resurrection of my piece. A passionate author must be played with passion, not otherwise.'[49]

The person who came nearest to understanding the work of the 74-year-old Ibsen, however, was probably Hugo von Hofmannsthal. In his essay published in 1893, *Die Menschen in Ibsens Dramen* (*The Characters in Ibsen's Dramas*), he writes about *The Master Builder*:

> The artist, the great master builder, stands between the two kings from *The Pretenders*. For, Ibsen's kings are also master builders and the master builders are kings. ... He has the devil's luck of one, and he is eaten alive with worry like the other. His genius, his inborn calling, his mastery in building comes from the grace of God, the right and duty to see it through comes from King Hakon, 'who has the thoughts of a king'; and his petty fears, gnawing conscience and the yearning for strength and ease of life comes from King Skule, who has no right to be king. The artist within is like these kings and master builders ... Next to the creative artist stands Life and its demands, which mocks, which confuses. And next to the anxious master builder stands Princess Hilde ... Her kingdom lies in the ... miraculous. There, in the dizzy heights. There, where a strange power lifts you up and carries you off. He too, has this longing in his soul to stand on tall towers where, in the wind and dawning loneliness, it is incredibly beautiful, where you can talk to God and from where you can fall and die. But he suffers vertigo: he is afraid of himself, afraid of happiness, afraid of life, the whole, puzzling life. It is even his being afraid of Hilde which attracts him to her, a single tempting fear, the artist's fear of nature, the merciless, demonic, sphinx-like quality embodied in woman, the mystic fear of youth ... In Hilde he meets himself: he demands the miracle of himself, forces it from himself and, at the same time, watches and experiences the shudder 'when life comes upon you and makes poetry'. Then he falls to his death.[50]

Hofmannsthal's lyrical drama, *Der Kaiser und die Hexe* (*The Emperor and the Witch*, 1897) seems, from this perspective, to offer a response to *The Master Builder*. After the emperor has been subservient to the witch for seven years, the artist seeks the fulfilment of his desires in art, so he withdraws from her power and turns to social concerns. He follows the reverse path to that taken by Solness and his art.

## The search for the self

The myth of personality, which was so fundamental and significant to the bourgeois era, was deconstructed by writers at the turn of the century, long before such writers as Max Weber and Sigmund Freud attempted to expose it on a theoretical level (in Weber's *Wirtschaft und Gesellschaft*, and Freud's *Die Zukunft einer Illusion* [1927] and *Der Mann Moses und die monotheistische Religion*, published in 1937). This seems even more astounding when we consider that according to popular belief in the nineteenth century, the poet was thought to be the ultimate representative of the species' 'great personality'. Nevertheless, exceptional dramatists such as Ibsen, Strindberg and Chekhov judged it harshly. Strindberg analysed it particularly mercilessly, or rather dissected it. It brought him results which prophesy far into the twentieth century.

The protagonist of his first dream play, *The Road to Damascus 1* (1898), is a poet who is not only held to be a 'great man' (the Stranger, Scene 2) and a famous poet (the Doctor, Scene 2) by others, but who has also convinced himself that he is 'a famous person' (Scene 1). Accordingly, all the characteristics which mark the great personality, particularly the artist in romantic drama, are true of him. Because of his Promethean tendency he is at odds with the family and society.

STRANGER: I couldn't endure to see men suffer. So I kept on saying, and writing, too: free yourselves, I will help you. And to the poor I said: do not let the rich exploit you. And to the women: do not allow yourselves to be enslaved by the men. And – worst of all – to the children: do not obey your parents, if they are unjust. What followed was impossible to foresee. I found that everyone was against me: rich and poor, men and women, parents and children.

(Scene 1, p. 30)[51]

Moreover, the Stranger is a metaphysical rebel. Like Byron's Manfred or Cain, he rebels against God and his authority. He has a 'devilish spirit of rebellion', he is a 'child of the devil' (Scene 10, p. 88) which made him 'blasphemously' shake his fist 'at heaven' (Scene 1, p. 30). His rebellion against God not only marks him outwardly with the sign of Cain and the 'curse of the damned' ('You see this scar on my forehead? That comes from a blow my brother gave me with an axe, after I'd struck him with a stone' [Scene 1, p. 29]), but he also identifies himself with Lucifer because Lucifer challenged God: 'The challenge has been thrown down; now you shall see a conflict between two great opponents. [*He opens his waistcoat and looks threateningly aloft*] Strike me with your lightning if you dare! Frighten me with your thunder if you can!' (Scene 4, p. 58). And thus it is not surprising that he also appears to others as Satan:

OLD MAN: It was no angel after all.
MOTHER: No good angel, certainly.
OLD MAN: Really! [*Pause*] You know how superstitious people are here. As I went down to the river I heard this: a farmer said his horse shied at 'him'; another that the dogs got so fierce he'd had to tie them up. The ferryman swore his boat drew less water when 'he' got in.

(Scene 7, pp. 70–1)

In good romantic tradition, the Stranger is not satisfied with only rebelling against God. He also seeks to put himself in place of God. The Stranger becomes the creator:

STRANGER: ... And I feel my spirit growing, spreading, becoming tenuous, infinite. I am everywhere, in the ocean which is my blood, in the rocks that are my bones, in the trees, in the flowers; and my head reaches up to the heavens. I can survey the whole universe. I *am* the universe. And I feel the power of the Creator within me, for I am He! I wish I could grasp the all in my hand and refashion it into something more perfect, more lasting, more beautiful. I want all creation and created beings to be happy, to be born without pain, live without suffering, and die in quiet content.

(Scene 4, p. 56)

The Stranger not only puts himself in place of the Creator, he proclaims himself as a better creator who is in a position to correct the incompleteness of godly creation.

This almost perfect embodiment of the great artist-personality suffers, however, from a disintegration of the self which goes far beyond the level of self-alienation which marked the romantic characters of Manfred or Lorenzaccio, for example. The Stranger not only appears to himself as 'the Stranger' as the description reads in the dramatis personae; his self is actually split into different aspects of personality which have materialised in doubles.

De Musset used a very similar method in order to recreate the dissolution of the self dramatically. In Lorenzaccio, however, the *Doppelgänger* act as mirrors in which the different images of personality of the hero are reflected, but they maintain the quality of independent dramatic characters which have important functions to fulfil in the process of the action. In *The Road to Damascus 1*, on the other hand, the *Doppelgänger* have almost no dramatic existence independent of the Stranger. Their function consists entirely of embodying the pieces or aspects of his personality which have split from the conscious self.

The Beggar who, like the Stranger, also bears a scar on his forehead, enjoys wine from the Mosel and persuades the Stranger to 'take the words out of your mouth' (Scene 1, p. 32) against his will, seems to be a projection of his fear that one day he will no longer be celebrated as a famous poet for his rebellion, but will end as a beggar in the gutter. The Beggar embodies the Stranger's fear that he will be socially outcast. He has, however, thoroughly suppressed this fear and wants to know nothing about it.

BEGGAR: For instance, can you guess who I am?

STRANGER: I don't intend to try. It doesn't interest me.

(Scene 1, pp. 31–2)

The Doctor represents a much more complex projection of the Stranger. At first sight he appears to be a *Doppelgänger* like the Beggar because of his rebellion; he also challenges God:

STRANGER: That pile of wood, for instance.

DOCTOR: Yes. It's been struck by lightning twice.

STRANGER: Terrible! And you still keep it?

DOCTOR: That's why. I've made it higher out of defiance.

(Scene 2, p. 46)

Whilst the hubris of the Stranger is founded in his proclaimed spiritual-creative equality with God, the Doctor challenges God on a mechanical-materialistic level. His hubris lacks all spiritual dimension – as does his view of death, which seems to him simply the deliverer of 'medical material … specimens' which are destined 'for the authorities' (Scene 2, p. 47). The Doctor embodies the materialistic, animal-istic side of the Stranger: he is a 'werewolf'.

On the other hand, deep-seated, tormenting feelings of guilt are multiplied and have taken shape in the character of the Doctor. The Doctor became 'a werewolf because, as a child, he lost his belief in the justice of heaven, owing to the fact that, though innocent, he was punished for the misdeeds of another' (Scene 8, p. 76). This other was, however, the Stranger.

Thus, it is all the more understandable that the Stranger 'suffocates' in the presence of the Doctor, that he 'suffers', feels 'persecuted' and 'entrapped'. In him, he finds himself con-fronted with an early childhood guilt which draws on the materialistic-animalistic side of his personality. He tries to escape the guilty feelings which result from this by fighting this part of his personality with great violence and aggression: 'I'd rather have fought it out with him here' (Scene 2, p. 50). Despite this, the Stranger is unable to suppress these feelings entirely: he even sees the face of the werewolf in the pattern of flowers in the wallpaper in the hotel room.

The severity of this early childhood guilt seems to be so great that it produces a further *Doppelgänger*: the Madman. The Doctor named him Caesar, thus giving him the same nick-name given to the Stranger by his schoolmates after the prank for which the Doctor was blamed and punished. Caesar suffers from megalomania: 'He's free to wander in the garden and re-arrange creation' (Scene 2, p. 47) – just as the Stranger seeks to do with his poetry. On the one hand, the Madman embodies the Stranger's personality, by linking his early childhood feelings of guilt with his conscious image of himself as god-like creator and, on the other hand, through his fear of being called 'mad' (Scene 1). This aspect seems to be deeply repressed: the Doctor has to lock him in the cellar, that is, in the depths of his unconscious.

The split pieces of personality personified by the Beggar, the Doctor and the Madman refer primarily to those aspects which can barely be brought into harmony with the self image of the Stranger. The idea of the great personality which the Stranger has of himself is not compatible with an early childhood, materi-alistic, animalistic nature filled with guilt, nor with social downfall and madness which can arise from such guilty feelings. They are thus repressed. Guilty feelings and fear create split parts which cannot be integrated into the cons-cious self-image and, thus, lead to the disinte-gration of the self. The unity of the person, in the case of the Stranger, is lost because of the same spiritual impulses as those which hinder the master builder Solness in his self-realisation. Strindberg places them, however, in a different relation. The Stranger is aware of the fragmen-tation of his self:

STRANGER: … I feel as if I lay hacked in pieces in Medea's cauldron. Either I shall be sent to the soap-boilers, or arise renewed from my own dripping! It depends on Medea's skill!

LADY: That sounds like the word of an oracle. We must see if you can't become a child again.

STRANGER: We should have to start with the cradle.

(Scene 1, p. 36)

Although the unity of character has resolved into different aspects, there is clearly the possibility of returning to the 'maternal bosom' (Scene 1) and reintegrating the split pieces. It does not appear to be in the hands of the Stranger, but rather depends upon 'Medea', an embodiment of the Great Mother. The Stranger is not in a position to become aware of the split, repressed aspects of his personality, to acknowledge them as integrative components of his self and thus to rebuild the unity of his character. What hinders him from being 'reborn' as himself is the idea of himself as a great personality. It is this which defines his whole conscious self and he considers it final. From it arises the Stranger's hubris which must reject even the merest thought of early childhood guilt or the fearful idea of social misery and madness as unacceptable. The leading concept of the great personality in the nineteenth century could hardly be challenged more radically or more firmly negated: it is the image of the self as a great personality which necessarily leads to the disintegration of the self.

*The Road to Damascus 1* is organised into seventeen scenes which are strictly symmetrical, or cyclical:

<table>
<tr><td colspan="2" align="center">Street Corner</td></tr>
<tr><td align="center">Doctor's House</td><td align="center">Doctor's House</td></tr>
<tr><td align="center">Room in an Hotel</td><td align="center">Room in an Hotel</td></tr>
<tr><td align="center">By the Sea</td><td align="center">By the Sea</td></tr>
<tr><td align="center">On the Road</td><td align="center">On the Road</td></tr>
<tr><td align="center">In a Ravine</td><td align="center">In a Ravine</td></tr>
<tr><td align="center">In a Kitchen</td><td align="center">In a Kitchen</td></tr>
<tr><td align="center">The 'Rose' Room</td><td align="center">The 'Rose' Room</td></tr>
<tr><td colspan="2" align="center">Asylum</td></tr>
</table>

The drama begins and ends on the street corner; the asylum is the sole station which is only passed once. The first nine stations confront the Stranger with the repressed, rejected sides of his personality and lead him ever deeper into his unconscious and the past from which all these aspects arise. On the return journey, he slowly succeeds to at least a partial acceptance of the repressed aspects of his personality and thus to a partial reintegration of his self.

The Stranger begins his journey towards the self in the same way as the heroes of early sagas and medieval tales: 'Count on me. Killing dragons, freeing princesses, defeating werewolves – that is Life!' (Scene 1, p. 40). Unlike these heroes, he does not make the journey alone, but is accompanied on the first eight stations by the Lady. The relationship of the Stranger to the Lady can be read from the name which he gives her: although she is called Ingeborg, he calls her Eve. In this he proposes a fourfold relationship between himself and the Lady: (1) the Stranger places himself in the position of her creator and God: 'By inventing a name for her I made her mine. I wanted to change her' (Scene 7, p. 68). As far as this relationship is concerned, the fact that the Lady allows herself to be persuaded by the Mother to read the Stranger's last book seems to be a repetition of the original sin: 'Since I've got to know your terrible book ... I feel as if I'd eaten of the tree of knowledge. My eyes are opened and I know what's good and what's evil, as I've never known before' (Scene 8, p. 77). (2) The Stranger appears as Lucifer who seduces Eve–Ingeborg, 'Lady: Tell me, what have you done to me? In the church I found I couldn't pray. A light on the altar was extinguished and an icy wind blew in my face when I heard you call me' (Scene 1, p. 40). (3) The Stranger sets himself as Adam's equal who allows himself to be tempted by Eve and is expelled with her from the garden of paradise for his sin. 'Stranger: We've been driven from the garden, and must wander over stones and thistles. And when our hands and feet are bruised, we feel we must rub salt in the wounds of the ... other one' (Scene 14, p. 98). (4) The Stranger is Cain, Eve's son: 'Lady: Where are you? What are you doing? Why did you call me? Must you hang on a woman's skirts like a child?' (Scene 1, p. 39). The Lady plays with this mother–child relationship when she, in turn, wants to define her relationship to the Stranger: 'Lady: And now I see how evil you are, and why I am to be called Eve. She was a mother and brought sin into the world: it was another mother who brought expiation. The curse of mankind was called down on us by the first, a blessing by the second … Perhaps I have a different mission in your life' (Scene 8, pp. 77–8). In comparing herself to the Virgin Mary, she places the Stranger in the role of Jesus.

Finally, the Stranger says of the Lady, 'You sit there like one of the Fates and draw the threads through your fingers' (Scene 4, p. 55). Accordingly, the journey accompanied by the Lady becomes a journey into the 'underworld'. Before they can reach the Lady's Mother in the inner depths of the mountains, they must be carried by a ferryman over a river – a river of death or forgetfulness. After this, they have arrived in the land of 'the Mother': both the kitchen and the rose room symbolise the female regions. The kitchen appears as a 'witch's cauldron' (Scene 7) in which Medea, as the Stranger's evil mother, wants to see 'his soul … being ground in the mill ready for the sieve' (Scene 7, p. 71).

The Stranger escapes from the kingdom of the Mother because here he cannot maintain his desire to be a god-like great personality: the Mother treats him like a 'vagabond', a 'fine fellow' whose 'pride should be damped' (Scene 7, p. 69); with her fall into sin, the Lady has revoked her blind obedience and 'recognised' him: 'And now I see how evil you are' (Scene 8, p. 77). In his battle with the father-god, the Stranger now seeks confirmation of the self:

ABBESS: You were found on the hills above the ravine, with a cross you'd broken from a calvary and with which you were threatening someone in the clouds. Indeed, you thought you could see him. You were feverish, and had lost your foothold … Since then you've spoken wildly, and complained of a pain in your hip, but no injury could be found.

(Scene 9, p. 79)

Unlike the Stranger's challenges to God up till now, this feverish battle is carried out with the

symbol of the son – religion, in the sign of the cross: as the 'hip wound' suggests, it is similar to the battle fought by Jacob until God blessed him (1. Moses 32), thereby signalling the possibility of return.

In any case, the Stranger now seems to be in a position to acknowledge the separate aspects of his personality and personifications which have until now played an important role in his life, even if he is not yet up to a direct confrontation with them and sits 'with his back' to them: the Madman, the Beggar, the Doctor, his parents, sister, ex-wife and her two neglected children, and the Lady. In order to 'go to them' and 'greet' them, as the confessor demands of the Stranger, it will need a deep penetration of the own unconscious, and thus the 'mother' Abbess sends him back to the realm of the mother. In the dark kitchen the Stranger experiences the climax of his crisis of identity, his spiritual death:

STRANGER: Soon I felt cold air on my breast – it reached my heart and forced me to get up … To stand and watch the whole panorama of my life unroll before me. I saw everything – that was the worst of it.

(Scene 11, p. 91)

He is submerged deep into his unconscious and has brought back all that he had forgotten and repressed. Now, he is prepared for his 're-birth' at which the Mother as benevolent 'Medea' provides help.

MOTHER: On your knees, my son!
STRANGER: I cannot bow the knee. I cannot. Help me, God Eternal [*Pause*].
MOTHER: (*After a hasty prayer*) Do you feel better?
STRANGER: Yes … It was not death. It was the annihilation!
MOTHER: The annihilation of the Divine. We call it spiritual death.
STRANGER: I see. [*Without irony*] I begin to understand.
MOTHER: My son! You have left Jerusalem and are on the road to Damascus. Go back the same way you came. Erect a cross at

every station, and stay at the seventh. For you, there are not fourteen, as for Him.

STRANGER: You speak in riddles.

MOTHER: Then go your way. Search out those to whom you have something to say. First, your wife.

(Scene 11, pp. 92–3)

This change in direction means that the Stranger is offered a real chance to be born again as 'Paul', someone who acknowledges the existence of the 'power' of his unconscious and thus is able to embrace the separate parts of his personality as integrated components of his conscious self. If the Stranger wants to take this path, he must, however, relinquish the identification with the father-god, the creator, and instead replace it with the role of the suffering, human son of god. The knowledge and acceptance of guilt and fear are preconditions to this.

Through this change of direction, the Stranger is now able to take up the advice of the Beggar, when he meets him, although he maintains his mistrust of him:

STRANGER: [as if to himself] Who is it reads my secret thoughts, turns my soul inside out, and pursues me? Why do you persecute me?

BEGGAR: Saul! Saul! Why persecutest thou Me?

[The Stranger goes out with a gesture of horror. The chord of the funeral march is heard again].

(Scene 13, p. 97)

A total integration of the Beggar into the conscious self is denied the Stranger. However, he can still admit to the Lady: 'I'll take the blame upon me' (Scene 14, p. 99). He is even prepared to rattle 'at the door of the locked chamber' and to admit his hidden guilt to the Doctor, even if it exposes him to the danger of being locked up as 'mad': 'I need an emotional shock, strong enough to bring myself into the light of day. I demand this torture, that my punishment may be in just proportion to my sin, so that I shall not be forced to drag myself along under the burden of my guilt. So down into the snake pit, as soon as may be!' (Scene 15, p. 102). Although the Doctor assures him,

'You need no more worry about the whole thing', he refuses to shake his hand: 'Impossible. And what is the use of my forgiving you, if you lack the strength to forgive yourself?' (Scene 16, pp. 106–7).

However, he has succeeded in a partial reintegration of the self, the separate and repressed elements of his personality are now acknowledged and have, to a certain extent, become united in a new image of the self. A total recreation of the unity of his character has, however, failed – the Stranger does not have the 'strength … to forgive himself', to reconcile himself with his early childhood feelings of guilt. And thus he ends his journey where he began it: on the street corner. He does not return as the same man, as the one who started the journey. But because he has not wholly succeeded in reintegrating his self, he will have to make another journey to the underworld of his past and his unconscious:

LADY: … Let's go.

STRANGER: And hide ourselves and our misery in the mountains.

LADY: Yes. The mountains will hide us!

(Scene 17, p. 108)

A comparison with Kleist's *Prince of Homburg*, which began our examination of the great personality, clarifies the far-reaching changes to this concept made in the course of the nineteenth century. Both dramas are open to comparison in that both recreate the search of the protagonist towards the self in strict symmetrical form, and show the climax of the crisis of identity at the end of the third act in the image of a spiritual death followed by a 're-birth' and thus the beginning of the discovery of the self.

After the father-figure, the Elector, acknowledges Homburg as equal in rank, Homburg achieves self-recognition by choosing total autonomy freely and deliberately – even at the price of his own life. It is precisely through this act that he achieves 'immortality' and rises to the 'heavens'. He achieves a self by becoming equal to the godly father-figure, by becoming a great personality.

The Stranger, on the other hand, only finds

himself in part. Driven by 'powers' and through the escort of the mother-figures of the Lady, the Abbess and the Mother, he achieves partial self-discovery after giving up identification with the father godhead, the creator, and relinquishing the idea of seeing himself as a great personality.

In *The Road to Damascus 1*, Strindberg irrevocably extinguished the concept of personality in the nineteenth century. The concept of person and self as realised here, points far more towards the twentieth century. This is not only true of the literary-aesthetic effect which can be traced in work from German expressionism to Ingmar Bergman's film, *Wild Strawberries* (1957), but, above all, in terms of the concept of the person and the self as developed by psychoanalysis, particularly Freud, with which Strindberg was certainly not familiar.

Thus, Strindberg's concept that the 'great personality' is the result of a total and therefore pathological identification with the father godhead of monotheistic religions, contains striking parallels to Freud's work, particularly those mentioned earlier. More surprising is the similarity, or correspondence presented in all important points between the journeys towards the self as they are presented in *The Road to Damascus 1* and the process of a psychoanalytical cure as was summarised in Freud's *The Outline of Pscyhoanalysis* (1938).

It is notable that Strindberg carries out this process *sub specie*, a polyphone mythological interpretation. The Stranger appears in a changing mythical form: as Adam and Jacob, who fights with God, as the wandering Jew from the Ahasver legends, as Job, Jonah, Cain, Lucifer, Saul/Paul, Christ, Aeneas on his journey to the underworld, as Prometheus, as Hercules. The process of finding oneself, which the Stranger goes through seems, thus, less the healing of a mentally ill person, a 'neurotic' at the turn of the century, and more an archetypal process which finds its basic foundation and source in the general *conditio humana* as the collective unconscious based more on Jung than Freud.

## *Just ordinary people 'like everyone else ...'*

'If a famous astronomer or politician dies, then they print an obituary of about five lines, but whenever an actor or writer dies, then they thump out an obituary of two paragraphs and frame it in black on the front page.' This entry in Chekhov's notebook, which he kept both before and during his work on his comedy *The Seagull*, illustrates, not without irony, the general social situation which forms the basis of his dramas: it was public opinion that actors and poets were the epitome of a great personality. Part of the general understanding of the term was that the great personality was someone of outstanding importance and, in this sense, unique. When Chekhov has actors and poets enter the scene in *The Seagull* in pairs it seems to satirise this public definition.

In *The Seagull*, two routined professionals, the successful actress Arkadina and her somewhat younger lover, the celebrated poet Trigorin, are set in contrast to two novices in the art world: Arkadina's son, Trepliov, who has just completed his first drama, and the young actress, Nina Zaryechnaia, who has her debut in the private performance of his play. Through the example of these four different 'artistic personalities' the validity and justification of public opinion is tested.

The cherished and propagated public concept of the artist as a great personality is explicitly represented and formulated in the comedy by only the youngest of the four, Nina, even before her own career begins. For her, the image of the artist developed by the Romantics is binding: she is convinced that a famous, successful writer like Trigorin must be 'great and wonderful' and that his life cannot be compared with that of ordinary people:

How different people's destinies are! Some just drag out their obscure, tedious existences, all very much like one another, and all unhappy. And there are others – like you, for instance, one in a million – who are given an interesting life, a life that is full of significance. You are fortunate!

(Scene 2, p. 147)[52]

Whilst the masses must be reconciled to an unfulfilled, unsuccessful life without climax or splendour, the artist alone can achieve total self-realisation: he is a chosen person, the only one who has the right to a creative and, thus, happy life. For Nina, this romantic concept of the artist is incompatible with the trivialities of daily life:

How strange it is to see a famous actress crying ... and for such a trifling reason! And isn't it strange, too? Here we have a famous author, a favourite with the public – they write about him in all the papers – they sell pictures of him everywhere, his works are translated into foreign languages – and he spends the whole day fishing and is quite delighted if he catches a couple of gudgeon. I used to think that famous people were proud and inaccessible and that they despised the crowd; I thought that the glory and lustre of their names enabled them, as it were, to revenge themselves on people who put high birth and wealth above everything else. But here they are, crying, fishing, playing cards, laughing and getting angry like anyone else.

(Act 2, pp. 144–5)

It is made clear that the two successful artists, Trigorin and Arkadina, do indeed live most of their lives 'like anyone else' and fill their days with trivial pursuits such as 'fishing' and 'playing cards'. Moreover, it is unlikely that their lives could be described as either 'great', 'lustrous' or 'fortunate'.

Trigorin complains that he has 'no peace' because he must write unceasingly, he is 'devouring' his 'own life'. Furthermore, he does not 'like' himself as a writer. There are two reasons for this. On the one hand, he knows that he is 'talented' but, however, 'no Tolstoy', that he is a 'good writer, but not as good as Turgenev'. He suffers from his own mediocrity. On the other hand, he only feels capable of describing nature and is afraid of failing the higher demands of art:

I'm not a mere landscape painter, I'm also a citizen of my country; I love it, I love its people. As an author, I feel I'm in duty bound to write about the people, their sufferings, their future – and about science, the rights of man, and so on, and so forth. And I write about everything in a great hurry while I'm being prodded and urged on from all sides and people keep getting cross with me, so that I dash about from one side to the other like a fox badgered by the hounds. I see science and society forging ahead, while I drop further and further behind, like a peasant who's just missed his train, and in the end I feel that all I can do is to paint landscapes, and that everything else I write is a sham – false to the very core.

(Act 2, p. 150)

One can hardly speak of Trigorin's self-realisation in art, despite the sense of a certain self-fulfilment which the act of writing gives him which he experiences as 'enjoyable'.

Trigorin has even less success in his private life. He lives with Arkadina though he does not love her, and feels misunderstood by her; he cannot, however, leave her: 'I have no will of my own ... I've never had a will of my own. Sluggish, flabby, always submissive – how can any woman like that sort of thing?' (Act 3, p. 162). He does fall in love with Nina, and lives with her for a while, but he does not really love her deeply and cannot see anything or feel anything for her except 'a subject for a short story'. Trigorin cannot find the 'happiness' of self-realisation in either love or art, 'I should overcome this passion of mine and do nothing but fish' (Act 4, p. 176).

In this respect, Trigorin's life is barely different from the lives of the others, for example, Sorin; both have dreams which are not realised. Their careers allow them no time for true love, for life. Whether writer or councillor, there is no difference – both feel their lives to be unfulfilled and unsatisfactory.

Arkadina is clearly wholly satisfied with herself and her life. At least, she constantly speaks of it – 'What a reception I had'; 'The students gave me a regular ovation' (Act 4, p. 175). Her art increases her sense of self which, however, is barely distinguishable from an almost pathological egocentrism. Trepliov comments that:

You mustn't praise anybody but her, you mustn't write about anybody but her, you must acclaim her and go into raptures over her wonderful acting in *The Lady with the Camellias*, or *The Fumes of Life*. But we can't offer her such intoxicating praise here in the country, so she feels bored and out of humour, and we all seem like enemies, we are all to blame. And then she's superstitious – she's afraid of having three candles alight, she's afraid of the number thirteen. And she's close-fisted too. She has seventy thousand in the bank, in Odessa – that I know for certain. But you try to borrow money from her, and she'll just burst into tears.

(Act 1, p. 122)

The contradictory behaviour shown by Arkadina is caused by her deep-seated fear of age and death: 'And I have a rule – never to wonder about the future! I never think of old age or death' (Act 2, p. 138). For her, acting is an effective means of suppressing these fears. When she is 'fit to take the part of a fifteen year old girl' (Act 2, p. 139), the public and critics praise and celebrate her achievement, then she feels her eternal youth ratified, and feels wholly alive. In this sense, she does indeed need theatre like 'a drug'. It not only increases her sense of herself but it also liberates her from the fear of the ageing process and dying.

This fear also dominates her private life. It makes Arkadina unjust towards her son because she feels he attacks her as the representative of an old, outlived generation of artists. He has struck her Achilles heel.

He wanted to show us how we ought to write plays and what plays we should act in. Really, this is becoming tedious! These perpetual jibes at my expense, these pin-pricks – anyone would get tired of them, surely you'll grant me that! He's a conceited, difficult boy! ... Here we have pretensions to new creative forms, to a new era in art ...

Let him write what he wants to and as he is able to, if only he leaves me out of it.

(Act 1, pp. 131–2)

Fear also lies beneath the surface of Arkadina's relationship to Trigorin:

Am I really so old and ugly that you can talk to me about other women without embarrassment? [*Embraces and kisses him*] Oh, you must have gone mad! My beautiful, my wonderful ... You – the last page of my life! [*Kneels before him*] My joy, my pride, my happiness! ... [*Embraces his knees*] ... You're mine ... mine ... This forehead is mine, and these eyes, and this beautiful silky hair is mine, too ... All of you is mine.

(Act 3, p. 161)

Arkadina cannot achieve self-realisation, either in art or in her private life. All her actions are dictated by her fear of growing old and her fear of death; it is a fear which prevents her from giving her art meaning and from turning to those around her as independent people not merely as subjects devoted solely to her. Her life is no less miserable and empty than that of the quite ordinary Polena who torments Doctor Dorn with her caring, jealousy and her possessiveness. With the constant reminder, 'now we're so near the end of our lives' (Act 2, p. 144), she determines to win him finally for herself alone.

The successful, famous artists, Arkadina and Trigorin, do not fulfil in any way their own ideal of the great personality. Rather, they live their lives in a way that, as Chekhov commented to Tochonov, is just as 'miserable and boring ... as anybody else'. The representatives of the coming generation of artists, however, do not have anything in common with the concept of the great personality as it was created by the nineteenth century, either. Trepliov begins his writer's career with a 'Promethean' protest against 'these high priests of a sacred art'. He wants to write because, 'We need new art forms. New forms are wanted, and if they aren't available, we might as well have nothing at all.' For only with a new form of art will it be possible 'to depict life as it is, or as it ought to be, but [also] as we see it in our dreams' (Act 1, pp. 123, 126). Trepliov is clearly ambitious enough to want to cause a revolution in art and replace realistic art with a new art which is not oriented on real life, but rather on dreams. He does not succeed in turning his ideas on art into works, however. Right until the end, he floats about 'in a chaotic world of dreams and images, without knowing what use it all is' (Act 4, p. 181). He refuses to set himself a concrete goal and thus cannot create the 'new form' by which it could finally be realised: 'Yes, I'm becoming more and more convinced that it isn't a matter of old or new forms – one must write without thinking about forms, and just because it pours freely from one's soul' (Act 4, pp. 177–8). Although Trepliov is a writer in a social sense because he has published work and is paid for his publications, he has failed as an artist.

As if that were not enough, his private life is a string of disasters. Trepliov is unable to step out of his role of adolescent boy away from his mother. He still seeks to gain her attention and love by temper tantrums or sweet-talk. Right to the end he is unable to release himself from this Oedipal relationship, which is already suggested in Act 1 quite explicitly with the citation from *Hamlet*. Even his last thoughts before his suicide are turned towards his mother: 'It won't be very nice if someone meets her in the garden and tells Mamma. It might upset Mamma' (Act 4, pp. 182).

This infantile dependency on the object of love is carried over by Trepliov onto Nina, 'I can't live without her' (Act 1, p. 124). Beyond this love, he is unable to give his life any meaning:

It's not in my powers to stop loving you, Nina. Ever since I lost you, ever since I began to get my work published, my life's been intolerable. I'm wretched ... I feel as if my youth has been suddenly torn away from me, as if I've been inhabiting this world for ninety years. I call out your name, I kiss the ground where you've walked; wherever I look I seem to see your face, that sweet smile that used to shine on me in the best years of my life ... I am lonely. I've no one's love to warm me, I feel as cold as if I were in a cellar – and everything I write turns out lifeless and bitter and gloomy. Stay here, Nina, I entreat you, or let me come with you!

(Act 4, pp. 179–80)

Since Trepliov cannot find fulfilment either in art or love, he sees no other way out of his misdirected life than suicide.

His way of escaping reality, however, barely deserves more respect than the path Masha chooses: she drinks 'in mourning for my life' (Act 1, p. 119) to forget her unrequited love for Trepliov. In similar ways, both suicide and alcoholism prove the inability of the individual to face life and accept it as it is. Trepliov has not helped his talent in writing.

In certain ways, Nina begins in a position quite similar to that of Trepliov or Masha. She, too, suffers from unrequited love: 'When you see Trigorin don't tell him anything ... I love him. I love him even more than before ... Yes, I love him, I love him passionately, I love him desperately!' (Act 4, p. 182). Like Trepliov, at the start of her career she doubted her own talent and was tormented by her own poor artistic means, 'when I acted I did it stupidly ... I didn't know what to do with my hands or how to stand on the stage, I couldn't control my voice ... But you can't imagine what it feels like – when you know that you are acting abominably' (Act 4, p. 181). Nina has in the meantime learned her trade, 'Now I am a real actress, I act with intense enjoyment, with enthusiasm; on the stage I am intoxicated and I feel that I am beautiful' (Act 4, p. 181), although she is still a long way from 'being a great actress'. She will only be able to find engagements in seasonal or provincial theatres in the future. Although for Nina, 'Life is coarse' (Act 4, p. 179), she has faced it and given her life meaning through her profession:

I think I know now, Kostia, that what matters in our work – whether you act on the stage or write stories – what really matters is not fame, or glamour, not the things I used to dream about – but knowing how to endure things. How to bear one's cross and have faith. I have faith now and I'm not suffering so much, and when I think of my vocation I'm not afraid.

(Act 4, p. 181)

In giving her life sense and purpose through her vocation, she is also successful in gaining self-fulfilment.

The idea of the artist as a man of personality is taken *ad absurdum*. It is not the opposition between artist and 'the others' which counts, but rather, simply, the difference between people who lead 'uninteresting and boring' lives and those who set themselves a life goal and try to give life a purpose – whether they are artists, such as Nina, or representatives of the professional classes such as Dorn who, in principle, is satisfied with his life because he has lived a life 'full of change and taste' and can look back on his professional career with pride and satisfaction, 'Ten or fifteen years ago, you remember, I was the only good obstetrician in the whole district' (Act 1, p. 127). The concept of a great personality is exposed as pure fiction – there are only 'ordinary people'. The really significant differences between people exist in the way in which they lead their lives. In this, the situation from which each person begins plays only a minor role. It all depends exclusively on the individual as to what he does with his life and whether he finds self-fulfilment. If he makes a mess of it, if his attempt at self-fulfilment fails, then this is not the great tragedy of a 'mysterious' (Act 4) personality, but rather the everyday farce of ordinary people.

The age of the great personality is irrecoverably past: the 'death of tragedy' (George Steiner) cannot be reversed after Chekhov. The theatre of the twentieth century will belong to ordinary people and their everyday comedies.

## THE COMPLETION AND END OF THE BOURGEOIS THEATRE OF ILLUSION

To Chekhov's great annoyance, Stanislavsky interpreted these comedies of ordinary people as

tragedies and his public wept copiously. The intended effect was precisely the reverse. In this sense, Chekhov's criticism is only too understandable. On the other hand, one must not overlook the fact that it was principally thanks to Stanislavsky that Chekhov's dramas were successful on the stage during the author's lifetime: whilst *The Seagull* was booed at its première in St Petersburg (17 October 1896), it won triumphant success at the Moscow Art Theatre (17 December 1898). To explain this success on the basis of a misinterpretation of the drama seems only partly plausible, however. The particular art of acting developed and used by Stanislavsky certainly contributed to a great extent, since this style of acting was particularly appropriate for presenting the specific individuality of the dramatic characters as portrayed in Chekhov's concept of character.

The so-called 'method' of acting which Stanislavsky developed over many years, and whose most important aspects are described in his two works *An Actor Prepares* and *Building a Character*,[53] places the concept of the individual in the centre: 'Every living person has his/her own character. The actor who cannot mediate character – even in the smallest role – is a poor and boring actor'.[54] For Stanislavsky, the task of acting consists of presenting the character of the role in its individuality. Stanislavsky clarifies this in the following example:

Of course one can put 'generalised' characters on stage – for example, the merchant, the soldier, the aristocrat, the peasant, and so on. Even a superficial glance allows recognition of certain obvious kinds of behaviour, manners and habits which are typical of each profession to which people belong.

Thus, for example, the soldier 'generally' holds himself upright; he marches, rather than walks like other people; he turns his shoulders so that his epaulettes shine: he clicks his heels, he speaks and clears his throat loudly in order to appear tougher and more manly, and so on ...

These are all stereotyped, 'general' features which supposedly create the characteristic ... This is how 'one plays' ... [the soldier] in all theatres. It belongs to the conventional acting ritual. Other actors who may have a finer, more accurate talent for observation are able to pick out a *particular sub-group* amongst the mass of merchants, soldiers, aristocrats or peasants; they differentiate between a foot soldier and a guard, between cavalrymen, infantry or other soldiers, between officers and generals. ...

The third type of character actor has an even finer talent for observation. These actors are able to pick out one single Ivan Ivanovich Ivanov out of all the possible soldiers, out of the whole regiment of foot soldiers, and they can clothe him with characteristics that are individual to him alone and not to be found in any other foot soldier. Undoubtedly, such a person is also 'generally' a soldier, he is also a foot soldier, but over and above this, he is the wholly concrete personality Ivan Ivanovich Ivanov.[55]

Or, one could add, Alexander Ignatyevich Vershinin or Nikolai Lvovich Toozenbach or Vassily Vassilich Soliony and so on.

If the task of acting is to represent individual characters, the first issue to be addressed is the way in which the actor will express an individual's way of thinking, feeling and being in each different role. In answer to this question, Stanislavsky developed the idea of 'physical action'.

Since the 'inner feelings ' are 'incalculable, invisible, inaccessible, labile' (vol. 1, p. 174), the actor cannot begin with these things. Stanislavsky assumes that 'the line of the body and the soul are dependent on each other'.[56] From this it follows that, on the one hand, 'the *reflection* of every emotion arising from inside, every feeling, every experience is [mirrored] on the outside' (vol. 2, p. 233). On the other hand, it is the case that 'the outside has an effect on the inside' (vol. 2, p. 172), and thus outward changes can bring about 'an almost invisible change even in the psyche, without the actor having to do anything' (p. 174). Thus a relationship of mutual exchange exists between the body and the soul: not only 'is the life of the spirit reflected in the life of the body, but the reverse: the life of the body can be reflected in the life of the spirit'.[57]

Stanislavsky's teaching on physical action is built on this condition. For:

It is easier to control the body than it is to control emotion. Therefore, if the *spiritual life* of the role does not arise by itself, then at least we can create the *physical life* ... See for yourself whether your feelings remain untouched when you really experience the physical actions of your body ... You will see, that if you believe in your physical life on stage, you will also experience appropriate feelings and a logical connection between them. And then the *physical life* which has been taken out of the role brings forth an analogical *spiritual life*.

(p. 38)

The task of the actor consists of organising his role into a sequence of physical actions which are 'logical and consistent'.[58] The 'unbroken line of physical action' can become 'the tracks that lead towards the role' (p. 120). In this way, the actor will be able to create the physical *and* spiritual life of the role and thus present it as a unique, individual character. In this, the audience is opened to the possibility of identifying with the role and its 'inner life': s/he is 'more moved than the actor' (vol. 2, p. 193) and weeps, as at the Chekhov productions, bitter tears.

Stanislavsky's 'system' rests principally on two basic conditions:

1  the actor should present the role as an individual character, and
2  the body of the actor is engaged in the total expression of the soul of the role and is able to do so because a relationship of exchange exists between the physical actions and their spiritual impulses.

These two premises reflect back to the early days of the bourgeois theatre of illusion as it slowly developed from the middle of the eighteenth century. Lessing, for example, demanded of theatre that it should present 'individual characters' and not deteriorate into presenting 'unnatural' 'misshapen beings' (*The Hamburg Dramaturgy*, Part 9). Similarly, all performance theoreticians, from St Albine, Riccoboni, Diderot, Lessing and Lichtenberg to Engel, agreed that the human body disposed of an 'instinctive repertoire of gestures' which 'speaks of passions in all its gradations across the whole world' (Lichtenberg, *On Physiognomy*). Thus the basis of Stanislavsky's system was already valid for the earliest representatives of the bourgeois theatre of illusion. What they demanded, without really convincing the actors and theatre directors of their time, is realised by Stanislavsky to the last detail: his actors were able to find an identifiable physical expression of the tiniest inner nuances of the role. Thus, the actor was capable of speaking the words 'last night' in forty-five different ways, each of which carried a different meaning to the audience. Consequently, Stanislavsky can be viewed as someone who completed the performance art of the bourgeois theatre of illusion.

Of course, several important differences exist between Stanislavsky and the theoreticians of the eighteenth century. Diderot, for example, was convinced that the actor only had to know the 'outward signs' of inner processes in order to be able to present the role as an individual character:

> all his talent consists not in feeling … but in giving such a scrupulous rendering of the outward signs of the feeling that you're taken in … That tremor in the voice, those halting words, those stifled or lingering sounds, that trembling in the limbs, that shaking of the knees, those swoons, those furies: pure imitation.[59]

Thus, the actor produces only the illusion of feeling and stimulates emotions in the spectator whilst he himself remains detached. Lessing, on the other hand, assumes a certain interaction between body and soul which creates certain changes in the body, 'the modification of the soul, which causes certain changes to the physical body, is itself then affected by such physical changes' (*The Hamburg Dramaturgy*, Part 3). But this interaction relates mostly to the relationship between spontaneous and deliberate expressions of feeling. It does not go so far as to say that the execution of specific actions, which are usually tied to an emotional

cause, makes these feelings actually felt. If, for example, the actor realises the deliberate signs to be expressed for anger,

> the hasty tread, the stamping feet, the rough, part screeching part bitter tone, the play of the eyebrows, the quivering lips, the gnashing of teeth, etc. – if he … just imitates well such things that can be imitated, if you will, then a dark feeling of anger will certainly fall upon him which itself then works upon the body and brings about those changes which are not simply under our control; his face will glow, his eyes will flash, his muscles tense; in short, he will appear to be really angry without yet being so and without understanding in the least why he should be so.
>
> (*The Hamburg Dramaturgy*, Part 3)

Stanislavsky not only assumed there was an analogy between body and soul, as did the theoreticians of the Enlightenment, but also proposed a psycho-physical unity of man in which the possibility of the psychological realism of his performance art is grounded. Despite this fundamental difference, even the leading ideas of the bourgeois theatre of illusion formulated in the Enlightenment are valid for Stanislavsky:

1   Theatre should present an illusion of reality.
2   The materials of performance art are the spiritual condition and mental processes of an individual.
3   The body of the actor is, by nature, empowered and able to express the soul.

Stanislavsky is the last significant European theatre artist to acknowledge this manifesto and follow it without question. The moment the individual makes his exit from the stage, the manifesto of the bourgeois theatre of illusion exits with him.

# 5  Theatre of the 'new' man

## Theatre as art – the actor as Über-marionette

At the beginning of the twentieth century, Western European theatre, which was traditionally determined by its dramatic text, was radically changed. The avant-garde movement made the de-literarisation of theatre their programme. Stanislavsky still saw the 'task of theatre' as giving 'form to the inner life of the play and the roles within it and to embody on the stage the kernel, essence and basic thoughts from which the work of the poet stems'.[1] In contrast, Edward Gordon Craig wrote in 'First Dialogue on the Art of the Theatre', first published in 1905, that, 'the poet is not of the theatre, has never come from the theatre, and cannot be of the theatre'[2], and out of this discovery formed a demand for 'unfinished' drama. This demand was echoed between 1900 and 1930 by nearly all representatives of the avant-garde movement, by Futurists and Constructivists, Dadaists, Surrealists, and the Bauhaus, by Meyerhold, Tairov and Artaud.

This bold liberation of theatre from the chains of literature was certainly linked to an oft repeated distrust of language at the time. As early as 1876, Nietzsche noted in reference to Wagner,

First of all he recognized a state of distress extending as far as civilization now unites nations: everywhere *language* is sick, and the oppression of this tremendous sickness weighs on the whole of human development. Inasmuch as language has had continually to climb up to the highest rung of achievement possible to it so as to encompass the realm of thought – a realm diametrically opposed to that for the expression of which it was originally supremely adapted, namely the realm of strong feelings – it has during the brief period of contemporary civilization become exhausted through this excessive effort: so that now it is no longer capable of performing that function for the sake of which alone it exists: to enable suffering mankind to come to an understanding with one another over the simplest needs of life. Man can no longer really communicate at all: and under these dimly perceived conditions language has everywhere become a power in its own right which now embraces mankind with ghostly arms and impels it to where it does not really want to go. As soon as men seek to come to an understanding with one another, and to unite for a common work, they are seized by the madness of universal concepts, indeed even by the mere sounds of words, and, as a consequence of this incapacity to communicate, everything they do together bears the mark of this lack of mutual understanding, inasmuch as it does not correspond to their real needs but only to the hollowness of those tyrannical words and concepts: thus to all its other sufferings mankind adds suffering from *convention*, that is to say from a mutual agreement as to words and actions without a mutual agreement as to feelings.[3]

The dramatists also suffered from this inability of language, diagnosed by Nietzsche as the sickness of civilisation. Thus Hugo von Hofmannsthal, in *The Lord Chandos Letter* (1902), complains to the editor:

It gradually became impossible for me to converse on any higher or general subject ... I felt inexplicably loath even to say 'Mind' or 'Soul' or 'Body'. I found myself incapable of passing an opinion on the affairs at Court, events in Parliament, or whatever else. And this not through caution or regard – you know I am candid to the point of recklessness: but those abstractions which the tongue has to pronounce in making judgement fell apart like rotten mushrooms in my mouth.[4]

The linguistic qualities and possibilities which were constitutive of the drama of the previous century, and which were founded on the dominance of the language, are no longer available to Hofmannsthal's Lord Chandos. He must renounce all further linguistic expression:

Because the language in which it might perhaps have been given to me not only to write, but also to think, is neither Latin nor English nor Italian nor Spanish, but a language of which I do not know even one word, a language in which dumb things speak to me, and in which I may once, in my grave, have to account for myself before an unknown judge.

(*Ibid.*, p. 20)

Because Hofmannsthal finds 'true language' a language of 'dumb things', in *Die Bühne als Traumbild* (*The Stage as Dream Image*, 1903), he challenges theatre 'to create an image in which not one inch is empty of meaning'. Bodies and objects are transformed into language whilst (word) language renounces its semantic qualities. Hofmannsthal drew certain consequences from this conclusion: he turned away from language and towards music and began a close collaboration with Richard Strauss for *Elektra* (from 1905/6) and then the 'Comedies with Music'. Accordingly, it is not in *Elektra*'s speech that the tragic dimension gains its shape and reality but in her silence, in the intoxicated frenzy of her 'nameless dance' at the end of which she falls down dead.

Hofmannsthal's de-semanticisation of language and the semanticisation of the body and world of objects are mutually determining. Artaud argued in a similar way, in 1932 in his *Letter on Language*:

For a gesture culture also exists side by side with word culture. There are other languages in the world besides our Western languages which have decided in favour of despoiling and dessicating ideas, presenting them in an inert, stale manner, unable to stir up in their course a whole system of natural affinities, as do Oriental languages.[5]

The demand to de-literarise the theatre was, in this sense, to a considerable extent founded on the crisis in language during this era. However, the main impulse to de-literarise theatre stemmed from quite another cause: the idea or fundamental concept that theatre represents an art *sui generis* and does not serve the mediation of works in other arts, that is, dramatic texts.

Edward Gordon Craig argued that every art is defined by the unique quality of its material. Drama, as a work of literature, uses words:

The poet's imagination finds voice in words, beautifully chosen; he then either recites or sings these words to us, and all is done. That poetry, sung or recited, is for our ears, and, through them, for our imagination. It will not help the matter if the poet shall add gesture to his recitation or to his song; in fact it will spoil all.

('The First Dialogue', *op. cit.*, p. 139)

The theatre uses material, on the other hand, which consists of movement, scenic design and voice. It is necessary that the director, 'acquire the mastery of action, line colour, rhythm, and words' so that 'the Art of the Theatre' can win back 'its rights, and its work would stand self-reliant as a creative art, and no longer as an interpretive craft'. (Craig, p. 178). The art of theatre stemmed from movement, gesture and dance. Thus, Craig felt it was time to reflect back on what was thought to be its origins, to release the theatre from the chains of literature and to re-theatricalise it. This argumentation can be found in different permutations in works by the entire avant-garde movement.

The key term, 're-theatricalisation of theatre' (Georg Fuchs, 1904), became the password of the era.

The demand to re-theatricalise the theatre had far-reaching consequences. It abandons the leading principles of middle-class theatre of illusion because it specifically attacks any kind of stage realism:

> The actor looks upon life as a photo-machine looks upon life; and he attempts to make a picture to rival a photograph ... He tries to reproduce Nature ... he never dreams of *creating*. ... This is to be an imitator, not an artist. This is to claim kinship with the ventriloquist.[6]

If theatre is understood as an art, its task cannot be simply to imitate nature and produce an illusion of reality. Instead, Craig demands that theatre should give up its mimetic intentions and proceed in a creative way; only in this way will it be capable of evoking, 'beautiful things from an imaginary world' which 'catch some far-off glimpse of that spirit which we call Death' and make an 'ideal world' visible, a life peopled by 'strange, fierce and solemn figures, pretty figures and calm figures, and those figures impelled to some wondrous harmony of movement' (p. 74). As an art form, theatre can only be satisfying not by imitating reality but in the act of creation and evoking worlds which are invisible or imaginary. This meant that the art of acting must be newly defined. In 'The Ghosts in the Tragedies of Shakespeare' (1908), Craig attempts to illustrate this new definition through the example of *Macbeth*. He proposes the thesis that the appearances of the ghost in Shakespeare's tragedies not only represent an episodic ingredient, but they are also the central, or key theme of the work. For it is through the ghost that Shakespeare succeeds in presenting the figures not as individuals but as the hapless media of invisible powers:

> I seem to see him in the first four acts of the play as a man who is hypnotised, seldom moving, but, when he does so, moving as a sleep-walker. Later on in the play the places are changed, and Lady Macbeth's sleep-walking is like the grim, ironical echo of Macbeth's whole life, a sharp, shrill echo quickly growing fainter, fainter, and gone. ... [Macbeth] is not the man some actors show him to be, the trapped, cowardly villain; nor yet is he to my mind the bold, courageous villain as other actors play him. ... While his wife lived he was not conscious of his state, he acted the part of her medium perfectly, and she in her turn acted as medium to the spirits whose duty it ever is to test the strength of men by playing with their force upon the weakness of women ...
>
> What we *should* see is a man in that hypnotic state which can be both terrible and beautiful to witness. We should realise that this hypnotism is transmitted to him through the medium of his wife, and we should recognise the witches as spirits, more terrible because more beautiful than we can conceive except by making them terrible.[7]

According to Craig, Macbeth and Lady Macbeth do not represent characters who are conscious of or responsible for their thoughts and actions, but those who act in a trance. To reinforce this concept of man, Craig draws explicitly on the Belgian symbolist Maurice Maeterlinck. There is, however, a fundamental difference between the two. In his early one act plays, *L' Intruse, Les Aveugles* (1890) and *Intérieur* (1891), Maeterlinck attempted to show that man is not able to have insight into the fate which falls upon him. Death (which Craig conceives as a beautiful imaginary world) is, for Maeterlinck, the inescapable fate of all men; it is neither caused by human action nor can man be held responsible for it. Under these circumstances, action is paralysed and turns into mere situation; action turns into waiting. Because no deed (act) and no speech (dialogue) can liberate man from his fate, the dramaturgy is totally static.

In Craig, on the other hand, it is a question of becoming aware of; things we are not normally aware of; 'we are not only conscious of the influence of these "sightless substances"; we are somehow conscious of their presence' (p. 272). For him, therefore, theatre does not have to show man being overtaken by his fate, but it should rather expose and make visible the invisible powers which use man solely as medium to work their effect.

Craig is not interested in human beings on the stage either as individuals or as representatives of a species ruled by fate, but only in the extent to which they are part of a transindividual power which manifests itself through them. In his essay, 'The Artists of the Theatre of the Future' (1907), he expands this idea:

I believe not at all in the personal magic of man, but only in his impersonal magic. ... For the impersonal in man is his best side and personality comes second. At first glance, it may seem as though the personal nature of a thing makes its character, even creates its identity. But if one thinks about it more carefully, one sees that in doing away with the personal, one wins a great power which is different from all other powers, and superior to any other power.[8]

The theatre, then, must not only stop wanting to imitate reality, it must also stop representing people as individuals, as personalities. The object of its creative efforts has to be an impersonal power which Craig describes in the following way:

There is a thing which man has not yet learned to master, a thing which man dreamed not was waiting for him to approach with love; it was invisible and yet ever present with him. Superb in its attraction and swift to retreat, a thing waiting but for the approach of the right men, prepared to soar with them through all the circles beyond the earth – it is Movement.[9]

The theatre of the future which Craig proclaimed should be a theatre of movement – a theatre which makes visible the invisible powers of movement and gives them presence. For this task, the theatre must first discover various instruments of presentation – and this raises the question as to whether the actor's body can be suitable material.

In his article, 'The Actor and the Über-Marionette' (1907), Craig answers this question with a definite 'no'. He argues that:

Art arrives only by design. Therefore in order to make any work of art it is clear we may only work in those materials with which we can calculate. Man is not one of those materials ...

But with the actor, emotion *possesses* him; it seizes upon his limbs, moving them whither at will. He is at its beck and call, he moves as one in a frantic dream or as one distraught ... As with his movement, so it is with the expression of his face ... Therefore the body of man ... is *by nature* utterly useless as a material for an art.

(pp. 55–6, 61)

The actor may overcome this dilemma of facial expression by putting on a mask. Thus, Craig recommends the use of masks wherever the actor – for whatever reason – cannot be dispensed with. But the actor can only rise above his body '*if*' he can turn himself into a 'machine' (p. 70). As long as the actor dominates in theatre, it will not be able to transform itself into an art form and will remain incapable of expressing the power of movement. For Craig this has one ultimate consequence: 'The actor must go, and in his place comes the inanimate figure – the Über-marionette we may call him' (p. 81). If the theatre of the future is to happen, an artificial figure, Craig's Über-marionette, must be created, because

The Über-marionette will not compete with life – rather it will go beyond it. Its ideal will not be the flesh and blood but rather the body in trance – it will aim to clothe itself with a death-like beauty while exhaling a living spirit.

(pp. 84–5)

Thus, it will become an instrument through which the theatre can reveal the 'spirit of movement'. Craig's theatre of the future not only repudiated the middle-class theatre of illusion and the middle-class concept of personality – it annihilated the idea of the individual altogether – a concept which had increasingly spread in modern Western culture since the Renaissance, and manifested itself on all European stages. Craig consequently proposed not only the beginning of a new era in theatre history, but also in the history of European culture, if not entire humanity:

And I like to suppose that this art which shall spring from movement will be the first and final belief of the world; and I like to dream that for the first time in the world men and women will achieve this thing together ... And as this is a new beginning it lies before men and women of the next centuries as a vast possibility.

('The Artists of the Theatre of the Future, p. 52)

It is interesting that in describing the Über-marionette which should begin this new era in theatre, Craig refers to non-European cultures in which the concept of the individual is either unknown or held to be a temporary condition, to be overcome as quickly as possible:

In Asia, too, the forgotten masters of the temples and all that those temples contained have permeated every thought, every mark, in their work with this sense of calm motion resembling death – glorifying it and greeting it. In Africa ... this spirit dwelt, the essence of perfect civilisation. There, too, dwelt the great masters, not individuals obsessed with the idea of each asserting his personality as if it were a valuable and mighty thing, but content because of a kind of holy patience to move their brains and their fingers only in that direction permitted by the law – in the service of simple truths.

('The Actor and the Über-marionette', pp. 86–7)

The new era created by Craig's theatre of the future will no longer recognise the individual. In presenting the 'spirit of movement', time (like Einstein's Fourth Dimension in his work on the theory of relativity, *On the Electrodynamics of Moving Bodies*, 1905), breaks through space; the dualism of life and death, female and male will be annulled: an era of the non-individual, integral 'new' man will begin.

Craig was acutely aware that the theatre of which he dreamed could not be realised immediately and that one must therefore 'work under the conditions which are to-day offered us' ('The Artists of the Theatre of the Future', p. 53). None the less, the number of productions which he actually realised as director was notably small. He was repeatedly invited to collaborate with such influential theatre artists

as Otto Brahm, Max Reinhardt, Eleonora Duse and Beerbohm Tree. But most of these projects failed because of major artistic differences and Craig's refusal to make compromises. In fact, he was more sought after as a scenic designer than as a director. It was only in collaboration with the most pronounced representative of stage realism, Stanislavsky, that he produced a result: Craig's production of *Hamlet* was finally produced after four years of preparation, in 1912 at the Moscow Art Theatre.

In 1913, Craig founded a theatre school in Florence for which he had worked out a comprehensive training programme with a view to his idea of a theatre of the future. Notably, it did not include the subjects 'role-study' or 'art of acting'. When the First World War broke out in 1914, the school was forced to close.

Craig's practical theatre work had no lasting effect nor was he able to establish a specific school or style of performance. But his theoretical work has become increasingly influential and provides productive inspiration even today – elements of it can be seen in contemporary theatre, particularly in the work of Peter Brook and Robert Wilson, among many others.

## Theatre as production – the actor as engineer

The early years at the beginning of the century when Craig drafted his theory of the theatre of the future were, in many respects, decisively important in the development of modern culture as a whole.

In 1900, Max Planck published his Quantum theory, followed in 1905 by Albert Einstein's theory of relativity in *On the Electrodynamics of Moving Bodies*. The mechanical worldview of physics prevalent since Galileo was destroyed at one blow. In 1902, Hugo de Vries discovered natural mutation which amended Darwin's evolutionary theory in important ways. In psychology, Freud's *Interpretation of Dreams* (1900) was published, followed by, in 1905, *The Origin and Development of Psychoanalysis*, in which he radically challenged the basic principles of classical psychology of the nineteenth century.

In 1906, Ferruccio Busoni published *Sketch of a New Aesthetic of Music*, in which he challenged the composer to venture towards 'indistinguishable tones' in order to overcome the limitations of tonal music customary since the Renaissance; the first a-tonal work, by Schönberg, was published in 1908–9. In 1907, Picasso's *Girls from Avignon* started the Cubist movement and undermined the perspectival interpretation of the spatial image which had been valid since the Renaissance. In 1910, Vassily Kandinsky's *First Abstract Watercolour* represented a radical rejection of any kind of mimetic objective in the fine arts. Modes of perception which had defined ways of seeing and listening in art for over three hundred years were thereby declared invalid.

As early as 1890, James George Frazer's ethnological-sociological-religious historic work, *The Golden Bough. A Study in Comparative Religion*, was published in two volumes (by 1936 it was expanded to thirteen volumes). The 1907–15 edition in twelve volumes was entitled, 'A Study in Magic and Religion'. Drawing on a wide range of materials, Frazer attempted to prove that notable analogies existed between the concepts and actions of so-called 'primitives' and the morals and institutions rooted in the collective unconsciousness of Western culture. The undoubted cultural superiority of nineteenth-century Europeans was exposed as a mere illusion.

A whole sequence of relations and parallels can be drawn between such discoveries or reformations and Craig's theory on theatre. Craig's theoretical concept agreed with the most advanced trends in science and art of his time; in the world of *theatre*, however, it was ahead of its time. This was because many of the pioneering changes described above had very little immediate effect on the lives of ordinary people. The self-understanding and lifestyle of the middle-class audience on which the theatre at the beginning of the twentieth century depended were not remotely affected by these decisive changes in science and art. Whilst this fact did not prevent scientists, composers and artists from continuing along this new path which they had created, it had catastrophic consequences for the 'revolutionary' and relatively isolated theatre artists. It meant that they were unable to find either a theatre or an audience prepared to accept their utopia and experiments. Without a basic social change which would either transform the consciousness of every man or create a new social class to support the new theatre, a radical renewal in theatre was unthinkable.

One consequence of the second industrial revolution (the electric motor was already in use by the turn of the century) was the electrification and automatisation of communications, economy and administration. In fact, it was so much a part of life that the Futurists praised it as a 'source of inspiration'. Thus, in Marinetti's manifesto, *Le Futurisme*, which appeared on the front page of *Le Figaro* on 20 February 1909, he states:

> We say that the world's magnificence has been enriched by a new beauty; the beauty of speed. A racing car whose hood is adorned with great pipes, like serpents of explosive breath – a roaring car that seems to ride on grapeshot – is more beautiful than the Victory of *Samothrace*. ...
>
> We will sing of the vibrant nightly smoke-plumed serpents; factories hung on clouds by the crooked lines of their smoke; bridges that stride rivers like giant gymnasts, flashing in the sun with a glitter of knives; adventurous steamers that sniff the horizon; deep-chested locomotives whose wheels paw the tracks like the hooves of enormous steel horses bridled by tuning; and the sleek flight of planes whose propellers clatter in the wind like banners and seem to cheer like an enthusiastic crowd.[10]

It would seem, then, not unreasonable to draw a relation between the machine-produced speed to which the Futurists paid homage and the 'spirit of movement' that Craig conjured. Nor can it be overlooked that Craig's proposal for an ideal theatre has striking similarities to the birth of film technique and film art, 'cinematography', which also happened at about the same time. Cinematography actualised several of the principal conditions of the theatre of the future: it could certainly be described as an art mediated by technical means or as a technical process by which movement can be produced, recorded and re-produced.

However, these developments (automatisation, the birth of film) were still too new in the first years of the century to have a lasting effect, either on the theatre or on the great middle classes which might lead to a fundamental renewal in theatre.

The First World War changed political and social relations across most of Europe in a fundamental way: the multi-ethnic Austro-Hungarian Empire was dissolved into several small independent states which were formed either as republics or monarchies; in Germany, the Kaiser was forced to abdicate and the Republic was born. The most decisive changes, however, were in Russia. After a bourgeois revolution in April 1917, led by the Mensheviks, disposed of the Tsar, the Bolsheviks disempowered the bourgeois parliament in October 1917 and established their own council of workers' and soldiers' deputies.

The new society which they intended to build needed a new theatre. The political revolution was to be followed by a revolution in theatre art. In Autumn 1920, when civil war was still rife in the regions, Vsevolod Meyerhold proclaimed the 'October in the Theatre'.

Meyerhold began his career as an actor at the Moscow Art Theatre. In the famous opening performances of *The Seagull* he played Trepliov. Despite success as an actor, he quickly became dissatisfied both with his own work and the leading principles of the Art Theatre. As early as 1902, Meyerhold withdrew from the ensemble. At different provincial theatres, in Moscow, St Petersburg and in studio work, he attempted to clarify his still somewhat vague concepts of theatre and try them out by way of experiment on the stage. His basic demands were not vastly different from those of Craig, even if Meyerhold did not formulate them in such a radical way. He agreed with the de-

literarisation of theatre without, however, wanting to be rid of the poet's drama altogether. Theatre should no longer be a 'servant of literature' (*Balagan* 1912), but should be able to develop as an art with its own laws. Meyerhold turned against the naturalistic theatre of illusion with its psychological style of acting, however, in the same, uncompromising way as Craig. He defined the basic elements of his anti-illusionist, 'stylised' theatre as mask, gesture and movement.

Alongside this actual, fundamental agreement between the two artists, the considerable differences which separate Meyerhold's 'stylised' theatre from Craig's theatre of the Über-marionette must not be forgotten. Meyerhold's renewal of theatre was based on his interest in precisely those human relations which the theatre of illusion, obsessed with human psychology, simply ignored if they could not be reduced psychologically. In *On the History and Techniques of Theatre* (1907), he wrote:

> Gestures, poses, looks and silence determine the *true* relationships between men. Words cannot say everything. Thus a *structure of movement* on the stage is indispensable in transforming the spectator into a keen-eyed observer in order to hand him the same material which the two dialogue partners give the third who observes them.[11]

Out of this fundamentally different emphasis, Meyerhold proceeds in an entirely opposite direction. On the one hand, he includes the spectator which Craig excluded from his considerations to a great extent. Thus, in the above-mentioned essay he complains that:

> The spectator experiences only *passively* what happens on stage. 'The stage acts as a barrier between the spectators and the actor, dividing the theatre into two mutually foreign worlds: those who act and those who watch – and there are no arteries which might bind these two separate bodies into one circulatory system'. The orchestra brought the spectator close to the stage. The forestage was constructed where the orchestra

had been and separated the audience from the stage.

(pp. 131f)

On the other hand, one consequence of Meyerhold's different emphasis is that the actor maintained his central position. He attempted to develop an art of acting which would be in a position to represent human relationships (rather than the inner workings of an individual's mind) and, in the process, drew upon some very different traditions: on Russian *Skomorokhi* and the showbooths, on ancient masked theatre and medieval mystery plays, on Elizabethan drama and theatre from the Spanish *siglo de oro*, on *commedia dell'arte*, puppet theatre, Molière and on Japanese and Chinese theatre. Meyerhold gave particular importance to his experiments with Japanese theatre and *commedia dell'arte*.

In the Japanese theatre, Meyerhold saw an almost perfect paradigm of anti-illusionist theatre and he took from it the convention of the stagehand, clothed in black and the 'flower-path' or *hanamichi* for various productions. It may well be that his first acquaintance with the Japanese theatre was not only mediated by an article in a German journal,[12] but also in 1902 during the first European tour by a Japanese troupe (Kawakami Otojiro and his wife, Sada Yakko), after which he repeatedly referred to Japanese stage practices as exemplary. In a talk with the guild of amateur artists in 1933, he introduced the Japanese theatre as an example from which to learn:

In Japanese art we might see that the Japanese, knowing the conventional nature of theatre, are not shy of playing without a curtain, or of building a 'flower path' through the auditorium. They are not concerned if, during a monologue, a neutrally clothed man holding a candle on a long stick approaches the actor quietly to light the actor's face so that his expression is more clearly seen. The spectator is not amazed; he knows that it is just a 'stage assistant' who simply lights the actor's face.[13]

Inspired by figures from Schnitzler's *Der Schleier der Pierette* (*The Veil of Pierette*), Meyerhold began to experiment with masks from the *commedia dell'arte* in directing the play *Columbine's Scarf* in 1910, and to develop a new style of movement for his actors. He continued his efforts in a production of Molière's *Don Juan* (1910) in which Meyerhold also employed stage assistants, following the Japanese model. The social function of the mask clearly stood at the centre of his interest, as is clearly to be seen in his interpretation of the figure of Don Juan:

For Molière, Don Juan is no more than a wearer of masks. At one moment, we see on his face a mask which embodies all the dissoluteness, unbelief, cynicism and pretensions of a gallant of the court of Le Roi-Soleil; then we see the mask of the author-accuser; then the nightmarish mask which stifles the author himself, the agonising mask he was forced to wear at court performances and in front of his perfidious wife.[14]

Each of the theatre traditions with which Meyerhold experimented up to the outbreak of the October Revolution had, despite their great differences, something in common: they represented man not as an individual but as a type, role, functionary or agent and they demanded a high degree of physical control, even acrobatic skill of the actor. Despite intensive efforts, Meyerhold did not succeed in developing from this historic material an art of acting which would realise his ideal or satisfy his demands. In fact, it was only the October Revolution which created the context in which Meyerhold could pull together the findings of his experiments and create a new, fruitful direction. In autumn 1920, he began to develop his theory of *biomechanics*.

The group of left-wing artists in the Soviet Union to which Meyerhold also belonged, aimed to close the gap between life and art which was characteristic of the bourgeois condition as well as to create life and art in a new way according to scientific principles. Thus, Boris Arvatov, a theoretician of production art, defined 'theatre as production' as a 'tool of the reorganisation of life', as 'a factory of qualified men and a qualified way of life'.[15] The theatre should become an 'experimental laboratory which co-operates with social practice' whereby its 'material' will be 'man, who moves in a material environment' (p. 84).

These principles were also binding for Meyerhold and he developed his biomechanics accordingly through recourse to techniques and scientific directions which were also fundamental to the new organisation of other social areas: on the basis of Taylorism and reflexology.

Designed by American engineer Frederick Taylor, Taylorism was a scientific system of organising labour in order to increase work efficiency on the basis of the exact calculation of the period of labour and refreshment break. The system was propagated by the Central Institute of Labour in Moscow from 1920 and spread across the country as the basis of a new 'labour culture'. This 'labour culture' was seen as a universal instrument in modifying the backward nation into an electrified, industrial state and it would both need and create a 'new man' with new attitudes towards 'cultural values'. A 'strictly utilitarian "Taylorised" style of life' (Arvatov, p. 71) became the new ideal.

Reflexology also contributed to the same goal in that it researched the laws which determined human reflex actions and behaviour. Bechterev strove to replace the current psychology with a system of reflexology because it would not only enable human motivation and behaviour to be understood and foretold according to unchanging biological and social laws, but it could also change them under laboratory conditions.

Meyerhold founded his new theatre on Taylorism and reflexology as the fastest and most effective method by which to stimulate the desired reaction in the audience. In order to reach this goal, he developed a biomechanics. In a lecture of 12 June 1922, 'The Actor of the Future and Biomechanics', Meyerhold explained the connection between Taylorism and biomechanics in the following way:

> Apart from the correct utilisation of rest periods, *it is equally essential to discover those movements in work which facilitate the maximum use of work time.* If we observe a skilled worker in action, we notice the following in his movements: (1) an absence of superfluous, unproductive movements; (2) rhythm; (3) the correct positioning of the body's centre of gravity; (4) stability. Movements based on these principles are distinguished by their dance-like quality; a skilled worker at work invariably reminds one of a dancer; thus work borders on art. The spectacle of a man working efficiently affords positive pleasure. This applies equally to the work of the actor in the future.
>
> In art our constant concern is the organisation of raw material. Constructivism has forced the artist to become both artist and engineer. Art should be based on scientific principles; the entire creative act should be a conscious process. The art of the actor consists in organising his material; that is, in his capacity to utilise correctly his body's means of expression.
>
> The actor embodies in himself both the organiser and that which is organised (i.e. the artist and his material). The formula for acting may be expressed as follows:
>
> $N = A_1 + A_2$ (where $N$ = the actor; $A_1$ = the artist who conceives the idea and issues the instructions necessary for its execution; $A_2$ = the executant who executes the conception of $A_1$).
>
> The actor must train his material (the body), so that it is capable of executing instantaneously those tasks which are dictated externally (by the actor, the director).
>
> In so far as the task of the actor is the realisation of a specific objective, his means of expression must be economical in order to ensure that *precision* of movement which will facilitate *the quickest possible realisation of the objective.*
>
> The methods of Taylorism may be applied to the work of the actor in the same way as they are to any form of work with the aim of maximum productivity.[16]

Thus, the actor must specially train his body into an economical, efficient and easily managed 'work machine' which can produce any randomly desired movement on demand without difficulty (a possibility which Craig excluded from his considerations as unrealistic).

Meyerhold developed a sequence of exercises for this training programme which should train different muscles and reflexes, for example, the 'dactyl', stone-throwing, boxing the ear, stabbing with a dagger, building a pyramid, kicking, jumping on the chest, falling, horse and rider, carrying a sack, jumping from someone's back, the circle. Interestingly, these exercises for actors are closely correlated to exercises which Gastev, the founder and director of the Central Institute of Labour, had listed as the 'Catechism of Work Exercises':

Taking up weights from the ground, lifting weights over one's head, setting heavy weights on the shoulders without the help of an assistant, lifting a beam of 819 kilogrammes in a team of four, weight-bearing of all kinds to practice stamina and weight-bearing endurance, turning movements both horizontally and vertically, swings of the arm – forceful and gentle with smaller and greater swings; jumps and throws, which – unexpected – must be sure and fast.[17]

The biomechanic exercises which Meyerhold made his actors carry out were not intended to be reproduced on the stage (even if one or the other sometimes found use in a production), but should enable the actor to produce any movement at will. With the help of this training programme, Meyerhold finally succeeded in developing an art of acting which would be able to represent human relations.

Alongside Lyubov Popova's Constructivist stage gantry, which provided a working contraption for the actors, this new art of acting gave Meyerhold's production of Crommelynck's *The Magnanimous Cuckold* (1922) its particular characteristic.

The actors, without make-up and dressed in uniform grey or blue overalls, worked with carefully synchronised movements, each of which was designed and carried out as part of an organised pattern. Single movements were structurally supported and strengthened by

their relation to the gantry structure of the stage. Thus, an outstretched arm or leg was not to be seen as an isolated gesture, but as an echo of one of the characteristics of the stage architecture: the bodies of the actors and the stage construction, and the movements of the actor and the stage architecture (windmill sails, wheels, revolving doors) were so harmonious with one another, that together they created a constantly changing structure.

The same was also true of the acting style of the three main figures (Igor Illinksy, Boris Zaichikov and Maria Babanova) who moved as a collective, in a totally synchronised way. Although each was given an individual movement, it was employed as part of a superior whole into which each actor fitted.

In this way, gesture functioned to create relations: between the actor and the stage architecture, between the actor and the objects, between the actor and other actors, between the actor and the stage figure, between the stage figure and objects, between the stage figure and the stage architecture and, not least, between the actor and the audience.

The movements of the actor were not employed as signs which are given a specific meaning (as mental state x of a certain character y), but instead, as bearers of signs which could be accorded a different meaning according to the relationship which was being produced at any one moment. Presented in this way on stage, man appears as a being who defines himself exclusively through the relationships into which he enters or is forced. Since such relationships constantly change, however, man also changes: to attribute him with an individual, determinable identity is thus impossible.

The spectator, on his part, is constantly challenged to find new meanings for the movements of the actors (as well as for the other scenic elements such as the uniform costume, its variants, the props, etc.) and is, therefore, stimulated into a condition of permanent activity. A 'new' man is born, both on the stage and in the auditorium. As Meyerhold comments, 'For through this play he can define himself as co-player and *creator of a new meaning*, because for him as a living being (as a new man, already changed by Communism) the whole essence of theatre lies in enjoying the reflective excitement of the *joy of new life*, now and again.'[18] Man, the centre of Meyerhold's theatre, is the 'creator of a new meaning'.

Meyerhold's theatre enjoyed enormous popularity. Even in the most remote cities of the Soviet Union, the workers' assemblies demanded that Meyerhold's revolutionary theatre come to perform. Despite this, Meyerhold's theatre was repeatedly accused of being too abstract to be understood by the proletarian spectator. These accusations developed into furious attacks against Meyerhold's 'formalism' in the 1930s and finally led to the closing of the Meyerhold theatre (1938), to Meyerhold's arrest (1939) and his execution in a Moscow jail (1940). The doctrine of socialist realism thoroughly negated Meyerhold's aesthetic: in place of the man open to the future, the 'creator of a new meaning' who permanently changed himself and his surroundings through creative acts, should stand the ideologically fixed, normative positive hero, in whom the spectator could empathise and whom he could mimetically imitate. Biomechanics was therefore declared formalistic game-playing and Stanislavsky's 'method' became the single legitimate foundation of the art of acting.

## Theatre as ritual – the actor as hieroglyph

Antonin Artaud defined the re-theatricalisation of theatre demanded by all avant-gardists in a fundamentally new way. His essays and lectures on theatre between 1931 and 1936 (which were collected and published under the title *Le théâtre et son double* in 1938, only partly translated as *The Theatre and its Double*) are marked by the awareness of a deep crisis. Thus in *Third letter on Language* (9 November 1932), he writes:

We probably live in a unique period of history where a riddled world sees its old values crumbling away. If the foundations of burnt-up life dissolve, on an ethical and social level this is expressed in a

monstrous unleashing of lust unbridling the basest instincts, and the crackling of burnt-out lives prematurely exposed to the flame.[19]

Artaud particularly emphasises logocentrism, rationalism and individualism as the main reasons for the 'false concept of life ... inherited from the Renaissance' which is deeply destructive to mankind (*Le Théâtre et les dieux*, Lecture of 29 February 1936, held at the University for Mexico City[20]). Western logocentrism has paralysed thought:

It is understood that word language is the major language, it is definitely accepted, has become part of our customs and mentality and has an established intellectual value. Yet even from a Western point of view we must agree words have become fossilised, words, all words are frozen, strait-jacketed by their meanings, within restricted, diagrammatised terminology. Written words have as much value in theatre as it is performed here as the same words spoken ... Everything relating to the particular enunciation of a word escapes them, the vibration it can set up in space, and in consequence everything it can add to thought. A word thus understood has only little more than an indirect, that is to say, a clarificatory meaning. Under these conditions it is no exaggeration to say that in view of their clearly defined, limited terminology, words are made to stop thought, to surround it, to complete it, in short they are only a conclusion. [21]

Rationalism has led to a mechanical science, 'which ... has quartered Nature' and 'prevented us from believing ourselves people' (*L' Homme contre le destin*, p. 188). Individualism is not interested in 'man as great as nature' (*Le Théâtre et les dieux*, p. 198), but only in man 'as individual being' and in his psychological conflicts. Psychology, however,

persists in bringing the unknown down to a level with the known, that is to say with the everyday and pedestrian. And psychology has caused this abasement and fearful loss of energy which appears to me to have really reached its limit.

(*The Theatre and its Double*, p. 58)

To overcome the crisis of logocentrism, ration-alism and individualism in the West, Artaud proposed to re-theatricalise theatre. In taking theatre back to its pre-logic, pre-rational, pre-individualistic origins, the theatre will be transformed into a magical ritual which will initiate a process of healing in the spectator. For, in a theatre conceived in this way, man found himself indivisible with Nature, and the so-called gods were natural, subtle powers which modern man could win for himself anew. Re-theatricalisation would allow the theatre healing properties – even if radical ones – to cure man of the disease of civilisation by putting it in a position to 'recreate' 'life' and 'humanity' in the spectator[22] – not 'psycholog-ical man with his clearcut personality and feelings', nor 'social man submissive to the law, warped by religions and precepts' but 'man in his totality' (*The Theatre and its Double*, here-after *TAD*, p. 82).

This gives Artaud's plan to re-theatricalise theatre a decisively different drive from that in Craig, or even Meyerhold. Artaud's concept of re-theatricalisation should not make the theatre an independent art, nor should it propose a new concept of man, but it should conjure up a new state of consciousness in the spectator, a new way of being, and help him towards it. Artaud's re-theatricalisation is exclusively aimed at the *effect* which theatre should have on the spectator.

In order to achieve the desired cathartic effect, the theatre should create a 'trance' state so that the spectator can access his uncon-sciousness directly and more easily. For,

a real stage play upsets our sensual tranquillity, releases our repressed subconscious, drives us to a kind of potential rebellion (since it retains its full value only if it remains potential), calling for a difficult heroic attitude on the part of the assem-bled groups.

(*TAD*, p. 19)

In order to achieve this goal, Artaud wanted to change the relationship between stage and auditorium in a fundamental way and develop a 'sign language' of theatre that would consist of noises, cries, gestures, poses and signs which would only include words as 'incantations' (*TAD*, p. 70).

The audience would take their seats on revolving chairs in the centre of the room and the 'stage event' would occur around them, 'in all four directions' both in the auditorium as well as on a gallery running around the whole room. In this way, the spectator would not be able to take up the perspective of either a distanced – or empathetic – observer, but would find himself in the middle of the event, encircled on all sides and directions by events of noise and movement.

The events of noise and movement would be organised in such a way that they would draw the spectator into the desired trance state and alter his subconscious so that the healing process could begin. In Artaud's draft to 'The Theatre of Cruelty' as he called it, he uses the word cruelty 'in the sense of hungering after life, cosmic strictness, relentless necessity, in the Gnostic sense of a living vortex engulfing darkness' (*TAD*, p. 80). Artaud orients himself on the model of the Balinese theatre, whose performances at the World Exhibition in Paris (1931) deeply impressed him. Here he found the 'magic power' ('4th Letter on Language') which his theatre should also exercise:

In fact the strange thing about all these gestures, these angular, sudden, jerky postures, these syncopated inflexions formed at the back of the throat, these musical phrases cut short, the sharded flights, rustling branches, hollow drum sounds, robot creaking, animated puppets dancing, is the feeling of a new bodily language no longer based on words but on signs which emerges through the maze of gestures, postures, airborne cries, through their gyrations and turns, leaving not even the smallest area of stage space unused. Those actors with their asymmetrical robes looking like moving hieroglyphs ...

These mental signs have an exact meaning that only strikes one intuitively, but violently enough to make any translations into logical, discursive language useless. ... [They result from] the very automatism of the unleashed subconscious.

(*TAD*, p. 37)

Accordingly, Artaud intended his theatre to be made of 'exact symbols' which are 'immediately. legible', where the 'human body' would create 'hieroglyphic characters' (*TAD*, p. 72). The actor on stage should not represent the new ideal of a 'total man'; instead, he should act as a 'living hieroglyph', which has immediate effect on the spectator. In this way, the theatre would be in a position to provide the audience with 'truthful distillations of dreams where its taste for crime, its erotic obsessions, its savageness, its fantasies, its utopian sense of life and objects, even its cannibalism, do not gush out on an illusory, make-believe, but on an inner level' (*TAD*, p. 70). In this process, the 'l'intensité des formes'[23] should encourage the spectator 'to become conscious and also be in command of certain predominant powers … governing everything' (*TAD*, p. 60).

Artaud conceived the theatre, thus, as a *rite de passage* – as a magical cleansing ritual or exorcism in which the 'devils' (*TAD*, p. 42) which possess modern man are called up so that he is aware of them and can 'possess' them as productive energies – or is destroyed by them. In this sense, Artaud compared the theatre to the plague: 'Like the plague, theatre is a crisis resolved either by death or cure' (*TAD*, p. 22).

Artaud's aim in re-theatricalising the theatre is to bring about the 'death' of the 'old' European man (a particular psychological and social individual) and his rebirth as 'total man' – in the spectator, not on the stage! In this sense, re-theatricalisation came to be the most important instrument of the revitalisation of Western man who had become a stranger to himself and his crumbling culture:

> Theatre should emulate life, not individual life where the CHARACTERS triumph, but a kind of liberated life, which sweeps aside human individuality and where man is nothing more than a reflection. The true object of the theatre is to create myths, to translate life into its universal, immense aspect, and to extract from this life

images in which we would like to find ourselves again.[24]

Artaud's radical rejection of individualism and rationalism, his passionate yearning for dream, magic and myth provoked contradictory interpretations among his contemporaries and later artists. Whilst his critics and opponents understood it to be proof of his regressive mentality which, in a naïvely adoring way, yearns to regress into pre-civilised irrationality, to his followers it seemed to be a prophecy of a new age. Both interpretations overlook the historic position of Artaud's concept of theatre in the context of the avant-garde movement of the first decades of the century and the way he continued and, in part, radicalised a trend which had already been formulated by others such as Craig and Meyerhold. Thus, Craig's negation of the personality. and his approach towards non-European cultures are certainly comparable to Artaud's rejection of the individual, even if Craig articulated his in a presentational aesthetics or aesthetics of the work of art and Artaud in the framework of effect aesthetics. On the other hand, the transition from a purely representational to an effect aesthetic had already been realised in Meyerhold's theatre where man as 'creator of new meaning' was both represented on the stage and created in the spectator. However, in arguing exclusively around the effect which theatre should exercise on the spectator, Artaud actually goes far beyond the position taken up by Meyerhold.

Following the radical nature of his conception, Artaud did not succeed in realising it for the theatre, which makes him certainly comparable to Craig. In the 1920s, at the Théâtre Alfred Jarry, which Artaud and Roger Vitrac founded, he experimented with voice, sound, light and gesture in order to 'excavate' that which, in earlier times, led to the creation of theatre. But his main interest in these years was far more to provoke the middle-class audience either through the theme of the play performed (as in Vitrac's *Victor* on which Artaud wrote: 'This part lyrical, part ironic, part direct drama was aimed at the family and used its adultery, incest, scatology, rage, surrealistic poetry, patriotism, madness, scandal and death as discriminators'), or through actions which directly attacked the audience. Thus, at the French première of Strindberg's *Dreamplay* (2 June 1928) for which the Swedish community in Paris provided extensive financing, Artaud suddenly appeared from behind the wings, cleared himself a path through the speechless actors and declared, 'Strindberg is a rebel, just like Jarry, Lautréamont, Breton, and me! We shall perform this play as emetic for his Fatherland, for all Fatherlands, for society.' It is unnecessary to add that such provocations were always guaranteed a huge success.

Artaud's concept of a 'theatre of cruelty' was most closely achieved in his production of *Les Cenci* (after Shelley's drama and Stendhal's chronicle), which had its première on 7 May 1935 at the Théâtre des Folies Wagram. For this production, a wide range of recorded sounds were used: the bells of the cathedral at Amiens, machine noises, trumpet fanfares, steps, metronomic beats, birds twittering and voices calling out 'Cenci' with increasing and decreasing volume, supported by an electronic instrument with monodic claviature. These sound recordings were sent out from different directions through loudspeakers: the loudspeakers were set in all four corners of the auditorium so that the spectator was totally surrounded by sound and could be moved towards a trance-like state.

The actors, whose human characteristics Artaud endeavoured to abolish ... [became] live hieroglyphs; he organised all the dialogue scenes with the strictness and precision of clockwork: thus, for example, Beatrice moved the two murderer automata like chess figures, turned them into walking mummies (Act 4 Scene 1); there was the call of the bird of prey, the conjuring, suggestive gesture of the hypnotist, the pendulum movement which described a circle of guards – the whole play followed a 'secret gravitation'. Light and sound, rhythms, incantations, repetitions, the same monotonous tone dominated over the word, logos, whereby the voice supported the gestures

and the gestures seemed to be the plastic extension of the voice.[25]

Artaud played Cenci as a madman. In *Paris Soir*, Pierre Audiard wrote that he was, 'a dreadful actor, but despite this: with his absurd intensity, his rolling eyes and his barely feigned frenzy, he carried us along with him, beyond any sense of good and evil, into a desert where the thirst for blood burned in us'. The production found no resonance among audiences and was savaged by the critics, who found the text impossible to understand acoustically, the noises terrible, the music cacophonous. In sum, they considered the production was an insult to theatre.

Artaud's Theatre of Cruelty was, like Craig's theatre of movement at the time of its creation, a theatre of the future. Much of that which Artaud demanded has only been realised in the last thirty years in modern theatre – by the 'poor theatre' of Jerzy Grotowski, by the 'Living Theatre' of Julian Beck and Judith Malina and by Robert Wilson's 'theatre of images'.

If one views the theatre of the avant-garde – above all the conceptions of Craig and Artaud – as a theatre of the future, then, in a historical context, it really does seem to be a clear and deliberate reaction to the bourgeois-realistic theatre and to the crisis of the individual in bourgeois society of the time. The great playwrights at the turn of the century certainly exposed the idea of the unique, great personality as an illusion. They sharply criticised bourgeois society in general as well as the institution of the family in particular because they denied the individual any possibility of cultivating the self and achieving self-realisation. But their lamentation was unquestionably based upon their yearning for an integrated, cultivated, individual personality.

This ideal was sharply attacked by the avant-garde movement. They declared the individual to have resulted from a continuing false development in mankind which – according to Artaud – started with the Renaissance and with its progression over the centuries had led European man and his culture to the edge of self-destruction and annihilation. Salvation, thus, cannot be achieved by reforming bourgeois society and its institutions but only by 'abolishing' the individual. This determined and radical negation of the individual was understood and propagated as the single possible answer to a catastrophically false way of life.

The rejection of the individual led to a theatrical re-evaluation of language and body. In that language used to function as the most important means of expression to show the unique nature and individuality of a personality, it now retreated into the background or found new functions (for example, as signs for social relationships as in Meyerhold, or as 'incantations' as magic sound-symbols in Artaud). The human body which had been limited to serving as the natural sign of an individual's soul, now became a theatrical sign system which would be eminently suitable for expressing and presenting widely different phenomena, conditions and processes. Thus, for Craig – to the extent that he would tolerate the actor on stage at all – the human body was conceived as a sign of 'invisible forces' which use men as media through whom they communicate (as in his *Macbeth* interpretation); Meyerhold formed and presented the human body as a sign of various human relations; Artaud wanted to use it as a 'living hieroglyph' which had direct, sensual effect as a magic sign on the subconscious of the spectator. In all these cases, the human body on stage was released from the idea of the individual and made and used as a sign of the 'impersonal' in man.

The re-theatricalisation of theatre seems, in this respect, to be a direct and logical result of the negation of the individual. For the avant-garde movement, the age of middle-class theatre of illusion and the era of the modern individual was irrecoverably and finally, over.

## BEYOND THE INDIVIDUAL

### The dead as the curse of the living – repeating the Ur-performance

The idea of man beyond the mere definition as an individual, unique personality became the deci-

sive leading argument in the theatre between the two world wars. Like the theatre avant-garde movement, the playwrights of this era also uncompromisingly rejected the theatre of illusion and psychological characters, even if some strove towards a more metaphysical theatre and others towards a more socially critical one. The historical situation with which they were confronted did not permit a return to nineteenth-century middle-class theatre under any circumstances – its hero was irreparably torn apart.

It was science which first challenged man as an individual in that it explained man's behaviour by taking recourse to general laws – in psychoanalysis to basic human urges, in sociology to economic, social and political laws, in anthropology and ethnology to phylogenetic development. Next, the use of human life as fodder in the First World War degraded the individual to an interchangeable object, something to be replaced and reproduced at any time as well as a pure instrument of destruction. Ultimately, man was annulled by fascism and Stalinism into a no longer identifiable element of the great masses called people's community (*Volksgemeinschaft*) or communist society. Defined in this way, the masses usurped the place of the individual and became the generally valid and, ultimately, the only recognised factor of identity; anyone who did not let himself be subsumed by this concept was mercilessly excluded – even if it meant physical destruction. The search towards a 'new', non-individual man had fallen on a dangerous, misguided path which led to the regressive annihilation of the self and total submersion in a faceless crowd, which released the individual's basest instincts, stimulated his childish fantasies of power in an irresponsible way and provoked his regression into unlimited it barbarity.

In opposition to these torn and nightmare images of a non-individual man, the theatre presented images developed according to models passed down from ancient, or foreign, dramatic forms: Greek tragedy, the mystery plays of the Middle Ages and the Spanish baroque, baroque tragedy, in customs, entertainments and feasts from folk culture (for example, in Poland, Ireland, Spain) and in

Japanese *no* theatre. Thus, Greek tragedy was the model for Hugo von Hofmannsthal's *Elektra* (1905), Eugene O'Neill's *Mourning Becomes Electra* (1929–31) and T. S. Eliot's *The Family Reunion* (1939). The form of the mystery play was revitalised by Hofmannsthal in *Jedermann* (*Everyman*, 1903–11) which Max Reinhardt premièred in 1911 in Berlin at the Schumann Circus, and the *Salzburger großes Welttheater* (*Salzburg Great Theatre of the World*), which was premièred at the Salzburg Festival 1922 in the Collegiate Cathedral; by Vladimir Mayakovsky with his revolution drama, *Mysterium Buffo* (*Mystery-Bouffe*, 1918), and by Paul Claudel in his psychological Christian drama, *Le Soulier de Satin* (*The Satin Slipper*, 1929). The form of the baroque tragedy was the foundation for Hofmannsthal's second adaptation from Calderón, *Der Turm* (*The Tower* 1925). Stanislaw Wyspianski turned to Polish folk culture with *The Wedding* (1901); John M. Synge referred to Irish folk culture in nearly all his dramas (for example, *Riders to the Sea*, 1904, and *Playboy of the Western World*, 1907), and Federico García Lorca turned to the Spanish puppet theatre with his dramatic romance, *Mariana Pineda* (1928), and lyrical tragedy, *Bodas de sangre* (*Blood Wedding*, 1933). The form of the Japanese *no* play was taken up by W. B. Yeats and formed the basis for his *Plays for Dancers* (1914–20).

Despite their great differences, these ancient or foreign dramatic forms and theatrical traditions are similar in one important detail (already emphasised by Meyerhold): they were neither designed for the perspectively organised stage (as the box-set stage) nor were they developed for the theatre of illusion; the figures which they presented were neither individuals nor psychological characters.

This latter characteristic had already been described by Nietzsche in *Die Geburt der Tragödie aus dem Geiste der Musik* (*The Birth of Tragedy*), published earlier, in 1872, when he examined the hero of Greek tragedy:

> In truth, however, the hero is the suffering Dionysus of the Mysteries, the god experiencing

in himself the agonies of individuation ... In this existence as a dismembered god, Dionysus possesses the dual nature of a cruel, barbarised demon and a mild, gentle ruler. But the hope ... looked toward a rebirth of Dionysus, which we must now dimly conceive as the end of individualisation. It was for this coming third Dionysus that the epopts' roaring hymns of joy resounded. And it is this hope alone that casts a gleam of joy upon the features of a world torn asunder and shattered into individuals; this is symbolised in the myth of Demeter, sunk in eternal sorrow, who *rejoices* again for the first time when told that she may *once more* give birth to Dionysus. This view of things already provides us with all the elements of a profound and pessimistic view of the world, together with the *mystery doctrine of tragedy*: the fundamental knowledge of the oneness of everything existent, the conception of individuation as the primal cause of evil, and of art as the joyous hope that the spell of individuation may be broken in augury of a restored oneness.[26]

Not least because of this interpretation, Greek tragedy was seen to be a particularly suitable point of departure for the development of a new anti-perspective, anti-illusionist, anti-individualist drama.

Referring to Nietzsche's interpretation of Greek tragedy (which was translated into English in 1909), Eugene O'Neill conceived a new theatre which was to transform the American theatre beyond the 'sawdust realism', pure entertainment and commercialism of 'show business' into an art form and, at the same time, make it an integral component of Western theatre. In a letter written in 1928, he stated that his theatre

> will dig at the roots of the sickness of today as I feel it – the death of the old God and the failure of science and materialism to give any satisfying new one for the surviving primitive religious instinct to find a meaning for life in, and to comfort its fears of death with.[27]

O'Neill already had this goal in mind in his early dramas. He attempted to realise it on stage in his collaborative work with the theatre group, the 'Provincetown Players' from 1916 (continued after 1923 under a different director as the 'Experimental Theatre'), whose founders wanted to transform the theatre back into a 'sacred' institution – however, he did not refer to Greek tragedy here. But such references were increasingly emphasised in the dramas written in the first half of the 1920s, such as *The Hairy Ape* (1921), *Desire under the Elms* (1924) and *The Great God Brown* (1925). *The Great God Brown*, which was premièred in January 1926 at the Greenwich Village Theatre and transferred to Broadway after only a few performances, where it ran with great success for eight months, has Dionysus as the hero of a play which deals with initiation into manhood, death and re-birth in the dramatic figures of Dion Anthony and William Brown. O'Neill printed large passages of Nietzsche's *The Birth of Tragedy* in the programme notes.

However, *Mourning Becomes Electra* (1929–31) was the first play in which O'Neill deliberately and explicitly dealt with the form of Greek tragedy. In 1926, he read an English version of Hofmannsthal's *Elektra* based on the Sophocles' tragedy and tried to persuade Kenneth McGowan and Robert Edmond Jones, with whom he shared the directorship of the Experimental Theatre, to produce it. The following entry in his work diary stems from this time:

Modern psychological drama using one of the old legend plots of Greek tragedy for its basic theme – the Electra story? The Medea? Is it possible to get modern psychological approximation of Greek sense of fate into such a play, which an intelligent audience of today, possessed of no belief in gods or supernatural retribution, could accept and be moved by?[28]

O'Neill decided to take the story of Electra. He shaped it into a trilogy which explicitly drew upon Aeschylus' trilogy, *The Oresteia*. With *Mourning Becomes Electra*, O'Neill consciously picked up the origins of Western drama.

The plot of the two first parts of his trilogy, *The Homecoming* and *The Hunted*, to a large extent correspond to the plots of *Agamemnon*

and *The Libation Bearers*. In *The Homecoming*, the Yankee General, Ezra Mannon (Agamemnon), returns from the American Civil War to his home in a small harbour town in New England and is murdered by his wife Christine (Clytemnestra) with the help of her lover, Adam Brant (Aegisthus). The background history of the plot is explained in dialogue: Ezra's father, Abe Mannon (Atreus) has exiled his brother David (Thyestes), because he had an affair with the Canadian nanny, Marie Brantôme. Adam Brant, the son of David and Marie, who left the house at the age of 10, only a few years after his father's suicide, swore before the corpse of his starving mother to take revenge upon the Mannons on his return. By coincidence, he becomes acquainted with Christine and becomes her lover.

In *The Hunted*, Lavinia (Electra) persuades her brother, Orin (Orestes), to kill Adam Brant in revenge for the murder of her father. Christine kills herself on the news of her lover's death.

In the third part, *The Haunted*, O'Neill deviates widely from the third part of *The Oresteia*. Whilst in *The Eumenides* Orestes finds redemption (and Electra does not even appear), Orin commits suicide in atonement for the death of his mother for which he is responsible and Lavinia locks herself up for the rest of her life in the darkened Mannon household.

O'Neill also took the theme of physical family similarities from Aeschylus which, as 'natural' identity in *The Oresteia*, prove who are the members of the house of Atrides. O'Neill, however, expands it into an important meaning-producing system. All members of the Mannon family – Abe, David, Ezra, Adam and Orin – have the same facial features, '[an] aquiline nose, heavy eyebrows, swarthy complexion, thick straight black hair, light hazel eyes' (*The Homecoming*, Act 1; *The Hunted*, Act 1). The women who marry into the family, such as Marie Brantôme and Christine, or who are born into it, such as Lavinia, also share many physical characteristics: they all have 'thick curly hair, partly a copper brown, partly a bronze gold, each shade distinct and yet blending with the other', 'deep-set eyes, of a dark violet blue', 'black eyebrows [which] meet in a pronounced straight line above her strong nose', 'a heavy chin' and 'a large and sensual mouth' (*The Homecoming*, Act 1). Moreover, female and male members of the Mannon family are similar in that their faces at rest give the impression of a 'life-like mask'.

O'Neill binds these physical similarities to mental similarities. All members of the family are driven by incestuous desire. The men suffer from an Oedipus complex, the women from Jocasta and Electra complexes.

O'Neill was often criticised for using these complexes without encoding them and yet allowing his figures to talk about them explicitly. Thus Christine accuses her daughter Lavinia, 'You've tried to become the wife of your father and the mother of Orin! You've always schemed to steal my place!' (*The Homecoming*, Act 2). In fact, O'Neill employs these complexes so systematically that it is hardly likely that he intended to give dramatic form to a psychoanalytical handbook. Instead, he used them as a key device in structuring another problem.

The chain of these complexes can be seen in the following way. Ezra is in love with the nanny, Marie Brantôme, who is a kind of mother-figure to him:

He was only a boy then, but he was crazy about her, too, like a youngster would be. His mother was stern with him, while Marie, she made a fuss over him and petted him ... but he hated her worse than anyone when it got found out she was his Uncle David's fancy woman.

(*The Homecoming*, Act 3, p. 261)

Ezra marries Christine because she is similar in appearance to Marie. Adam falls in love with Christine for the same reason. Orin loves his mother and, in killing Adam, kills his rival (and father); in the last part of the trilogy, he desires his sister because she is similar to his mother. Christine falls in love with Adam because he reminds her of her son; Lavinia lusts after Adam because he looks like her father.

O'Neill employs this system of physical and mental similarities and correspondences in order to remove any individuality from the figures. Each character is nothing more than a repetition of another who, in his turn, is the double of yet another. There is no 'original' and therefore no individual personality. Every figure is the repetition of another, who repeats another, who repeats another, and so on *ad infinitum*. The figures, thus, do not appear to be individual selves, but instead, are substitutes for another who is absent – just as Orin discovered in war:

Before I'd gotten back I had to kill another in the same way. It was like murdering the same man twice. I had a queer feeling that war meant murdering the same man over and over, and that in the end I would discover the man was myself! Their faces keep coming back in dreams – and they change to father's face – or to mine.

(*The Hunted*, Act 3, pp. 304–5)

Accordingly, the figures do not act of their own free will – as self-determining individuals – but are driven by 'another' or are forced to repeat an action which another has done in the past.

This is particularly clear when comparing the situation of decision-making with those in *The Oresteia*. Aeschylus explicitly shows the deeds of his figures – Agamemnon's sacrifice of Iphigenia, Clytemnestra's murder of Agamemnon, Orestes' murder of Clytemnestra and Aegisthus – to be the result of a consciously taken decision. O'Neill's figures, on the other hand, act as people who are driven by others, as a kind of medium through which another acts. Thus, the thought of poisoning, which moves Christine to kill the husband she does not love, is not a conscious decision, 'I've been reading a book in Father's medical library. I saw it there one day a few weeks ago – it was as if some fate in me forced me to see it!' (*The Homecoming*, Act 2, p. 257). Apparently she cannot escape from this fate.

Orin leaves his mother before her suicide as if directed by an invisible hand:

LAVINIA: ... Leave her alone! Go in the house! [*As he hesitates – more sharply*] Do you hear me? March!

ORIN: [*Automatically makes a confused motion of military salute – vaguely*] Yes, sir. [*He walks mechanically up the steps – gazing up at the house ...*].

(*The Hunted*, Act 5, p. 327)

Lavinia lies to Orin in order to stir up his jealousy, though she has not planned it and does not do so consciously:

LAVINIA: [*Strangely shaken and trembling – stammers*] Yet – it was a lie – how could you believe I – Oh, Orin, something made me say that to you – against my will – something rose up in me – like an evil spirit!

(*The Haunted*, Act 2, p. 356)

Two key decisions which differ from Aeschylus in the third part of the trilogy – Orin's decision to commit suicide and Lavinia's decision to give up Peter and lock herself in the dark Mannon household – are also not consciously made. Orin finds himself in a kind of trance state:

Yes! That would be justice – now you are Mother! She is speaking now through you! [*More and more hypnotised by this train of thought*] Yes! It's the way to peace – to find her again – my lost island – Death is an island of Peace, too – Mother will be waiting for me there – [*With excited eagerness now, speaking to the dead*] Mother! ... [*His mouth grows convulsed, as if he were wretching up poison*] ... You've heard me! You're here in the house now! You're calling me! You're waiting to take me home! [*He turns and strides towards the door*].

(*The Haunted*, Act 3, pp. 365–6)

Orin finally shoots himself, and the very moment when Lavinia decides consciously for Peter, love and life, she is caught up by her obligations to the dead:

Listen, Peter! ... Kiss me! Hold me close! Want me! Want me so much you'd murder anyone to have me! I did that – for you! Take me in this house of the dead and love me! Our love will drive the dead away. It will shame them back into death! [*At the topmost pitch of desperate, frantic abandonment*] Want me! Take me, Adam! [*She is brought back to herself with a start by this name escaping her – bewilderedly, laughing idiotically*] Adam? Why did I call you Adam? I never even heard that name before – outside of the Bible! [*Then suddenly with a hopeless and deadly finality*] Always the dead between! It's no good trying any more!

(*The Haunted*, Act 4, p. 374)

The decision to isolate herself in the Mannon household is beyond Lavinia's consciousness and it was made outside her free will. She ultimately carries out that which was decided elsewhere.

These acts, driven by another force, are not only carried out as if by others, but also appear to be the precise repetition of deeds carried out by others as, for example, the little gesture with which Ezra, Adam and Orin try to touch the hair of Marie, Christine and Lavinia, or even whole sequences of behaviour by Orin and Lavinia in the third part of the trilogy:

ORIN: So you kissed him, did you? And that was all?

LAVINIA: [*With a sudden flare of deliberately evil taunting that recalls her mother in the last act of 'The Homecoming' when she was goading Ezra Mannon to fury just before his murder*] And what if it wasn't? I'm not your property! I have a right to love!

ORIN: [*Reacting as his father had – his face grown livid – with a hoarse cry of fury grabs her by the throat*] You – you whore! I'll kill you! [*Then suddenly he breaks down and becomes weak and pitiful*]

... [*With a quiet insistence*] Can't you see I'm now in Father's place and you're Mother! That's the evil destiny out of the past I haven't dared predict! I'm the Mannon you're chained to! So isn't it plain

LAVINIA: [*Putting her hands over her ears*] For God's sake, won't you be quiet! [*Then suddenly her horror turning into a violent rage – unconsciously repeating the exact threat she had goaded her mother to make to her in Act Two of 'The Homecoming'*] Take care, Orin! You'll be responsible if –! [*She stops abruptly, terrified by her own words*].

ORIN: [*With a diabolical mockery*] If what? If I should die mysteriously of heart failure?

(*The Haunted*, Act 2, pp. 335–6)

In their physical appearance, desires, words and deeds, the figures repeat those of others who came before; they are neither identical to themselves or the others – they have no own self, no definable identity. The living are repetitions of the dead and the dead prove to be a curse on the living.

This curse can, however, only be fully effective because the living offer themselves up to serve an instrumentalised reason, a perverted logic. This is particularly true of the two female figures, Christine and Lavinia. After the momentous decisions to kill Ezra (Christine), to kill Adam and give up Peter (Lavinia), are forced upon them or happen to them unconsciously, uncontrollably, as if they were under pressure, and certainly without consent of their free will, they go about their plans with a high measure of planning and precise rationality: 'I've planned it carefully' (Christine, *The Homecoming*, Act 2, p. 258); 'You've got to do everything exactly as we've planned it' (Lavinia, *The Hunted*, Act 4, p. 320).The expression 'calculatingly' is repeatedly used in the stage directions for Christine and Lavinia (Christine in *The Homecoming*, Acts 2 and 4, pp. 256 and 275; Lavinia in *The Hunted*, Act 4, p. 321) or 'with calculated coarseness' (Lavinia in *The Haunted*, Act 4, p. 375).

Moreover both rationalise their actions by calling it an 'act of justice', 'That would only be justice' (Christine, *The Homecoming*, Act 2, p. 256); 'You know it was justice', 'It is your justice, Father' (Lavinia, *The Hunted*, Act 5, pp. 327, 328); 'there was only justice' (Lavinia, *The Haunted*, Act 3, p. 365).

It is only when reason is made subservient to decisions made in the unconscious and instrumentalised accordingly so that explanations are found which deny the living insight into their true relationship to the dead, that they can maintain their illusion that their actions are reasonable, and morally justified. This is seen in the way Lavinia evaluates her mother's suicide, 'She could have lived, couldn't she? But she chose to kill herself as a punishment for her crime – of her own free will!' (*The Haunted*, Act 1, Scene 2, p. 344). Reason instrumentalised in this way prevents the living from understanding themselves as repetitions of the dead, as 'bound' (the leitmotif of the shanty song 'Shenandoah'), although their bodies are steeped through and through with this aspect.

This is not only true in terms of the similarities in facial feature, eye or hair colour, but more importantly, in the 'mask-like' expression on all the Mannon faces and movements which are repeatedly described with the same attributes: 'stiff', 'wooden', 'mechanical', 'automatical', 'like some tragic mechanical doll' or 'like an automaton'.

It can hardly be overlooked that these characteristics correspond extensively to Craig's theory of a theatre of movement. Like Craig, O'Neill rejects the individual mimic, facial expression of the actor; from the 1920s, O'Neill experimented with the use of masks in his dramas and, in the process, turned to Far-Eastern theatre and African cultures:

At its best, it [the mask] is more subtly, imaginatively, suggestively dramatic than any actor's face can ever be. Let anyone who doubts this study the Japanese No masks, or Chinese theatre masks, or African primitive masks.[29]

Like Craig, O'Neill based the use of masks on the need to create an 'imaginative theatre' which would be in a position to make invisible, impersonal powers visible and thereby – as Artaud proposed – to respond to what was felt to be a deep social crisis:

I mean the one true theatre, the age-old theatre, the theatre of the Greeks and Elizabethans, a theatre that could dare to boast – without committing a farcical sacrilege – that it is a legitimate descendent of the first theatre that sprang, by virtue of man's imaginative interpretation of life, out of his worship of Dionysus. I mean a theatre returned to its highest and sole significant function as a Temple where the religion of a poetical interpretation and symbolical celebration of life is communicated to human beings, starved in spirit by their soul-stifling daily struggle to exist as masks among the masks of living!

(*Ibid.*, p. 166)

In the same way, the 'mechanical' and 'automatic' movements of the figures in *Mourning Becomes Electra* point to the mechanised movements of Craig's Über-marionette. Whilst Craig, however, proclaimed the Über-marionette as ideal, O'Neill makes the 'mechanical' movements appear somewhat ambivalent by opposing them to movements by Marie ('with something free and wild about her like an animal', *The Homecoming* [Act 3, p. 261]) and Christine ('she moves with a flowing animal grace' [Act 1, p. 230]) which he declares to be expressions of an animalistic being.

This ambivalence is manifested in the relationship created by O'Neill between the mask-like facial expression, or mechanical movements, and death, which Craig apostrophised as a kind of positive metaphor of the invisible world which the theatre should make visible. O'Neill describes Lavinia in the stage directions for the first part of the trilogy as, 'an Egyptian statue' (Act 3, p. 260), Ezra's stance betrays 'attitudes that suggest the statues of military heroes' (p. 263), and in the third part of the trilogy, Orin's movements and posture are emphasised as having 'the statue-like quality that was so marked in his father' (Act 1, Scene 1, p. 340). In the second part of the trilogy, the statue-like nature of the Mannon family is explicitly characterised as the expression of death in the description of Ezra's corpse: 'His mask-like face is a startling reproduction of the face in the portrait above him,

but grimly remote and austere in death, like the carven face of a statue' (Act 3, p. 303).

O'Neill shows the invisible forces which use men as a medium through whom they can act, as Craig suggested in his interpretation of *Macbeth*, as forces of death and life which have materialised in the 'tomb' or 'sepulchre' of the house (*The Homecoming*, Act 1, p. 237) and in the 'Blessed Isles of the South Sea'.

Death is bound to the Mannons and their Puritanism in a special way: 'That's always been the Mannons' way of thinking. They went to the white meeting-house on Sabbaths and meditated on death. Life was a dying. Being born was starting to die. Death was being born' (*The Homecoming*, Act 3, p. 269). The Mannon house, built as a 'temple of hatred', the portrait gallery of the ancestors, their actions always oriented around their Puritan duty and moral ideas, appear as manifestations of death, which controls the Mannons. It is opposed to the motif of the South Sea islands, the image of life, longed for by all Mannons. Adam describes it in the first part of the trilogy as the 'Garden of Paradise before sin was discovered' (*The Homecoming*, Act 1, p. 242) and Lavinia as a place of fulfilled presence:

There was something there mysterious and beautiful – a good spirit – of love – coming out of the land and sea. It made me forget death. There was no hereafter. There was only this world – the warm earth in the moonlight – the trade wind in the coco palms – the surf on the reef – the fires at night and the drum throbbing in my heart – the natives dancing naked and innocent – without knowledge of sin!

(Act 1, Scene 2, p. 348)

The battle of the impersonal forces of life and death in, or rather, through the Mannons is carried out simultaneously as the battle between patriarchy and matriarchy. The 'gravestone' of the house becomes identified with the male Mannons – with Abe, who had it built as the 'temple of his hatred', with Ezra and all their ancestors. The islands, on the other hand, are identified with the matriarchs – with Marie, whose eyes are as 'blue as the Caribbean Sea', with Christine and with Lavinia, who says of the Isles, 'They finished setting me free' (*The Haunted*, Act 1, Scene 2, p. 348). For Orin, the Isles and his mother are one and the same thing:

those Islands came to mean everything that wasn't war, everything that was peace and warmth and security. I used to dream I was there ... There was no one there but you and me. The breaking of the waves was your voice. The sky was the same colour as your eyes. The warm sand was like your skin. The whole island was you.

(*The Hunted*, Act 2, p. 300)

For Ezra, Adam and Orin, the patriarchal demand for death, represented by war and Puritanism, stands in opposition to longing for the pre-birth condition in the mother's womb. But this longing is only to be fulfilled at a high cost – if the difference between death and life is wiped out, if house and island, 'tomb' and 'womb', are united into one and death is desired as the return to the mother, as actually happens through Orin's suicide. But even here, the powers of death prove to be stronger and force Orin to repeat the deed of others – that of his dead mother, and that of his uncle David. The compulsion to repeat, which controls the behaviour of the Mannon family, appears thus as a sign of victory of death over life, a victory of the patriarchy over the matriarchy. It is only Lavinia, who moves between the two systems, who finally succeeds in breaking the compulsion to repeat. She is not, however, able to break the power of the dead over the living. Though she will no longer repeat the actions of the dead, she now accepts the power they exert over her, the living:

I'm bound here – to the Mannon dead! ... I'm not going the way Mother and Orin went. That's escaping punishment. And there's no one left to punish me. I'm the last Mannon. I've got to punish myself! Living alone here with the dead is a worse act of justice than death or prison! I'll never go out or see anyone! I'll have the shutters nailed so close so no sunlight can ever get in. I'll live alone with the dead, and keep their secrets, and let them hound me, until the curse is paid out and the last Mannon is let die! [*With a strange cruel smile of gloating over the years of self-torture*] I know they will see to it I live for a long time! It takes the Mannons to punish themselves for being born!

(*The Haunted*, Act 4, p. 375)

The identification with the matriarch – with Christine and Marie Brantôme – must be reversed and replaced by a new identification with the patriarch – the male Mannons. In the battle between Eros and Thanatos, between matriarchy and patriarchy, death and the father-figure are proved stronger. But despite this, Lavinia succeeds in maintaining her dignity. Just as Oedipus withdraws back into the house as into the mother's womb, after becoming aware of his true identity, and deliberately punishes himself for a crime which he committed unknowingly – as another, a 'stranger' – so Lavinia shuts herself up in the patriarchal 'grave' and deliberately punishes herself for the crime of even being born in a world of others – the dead and the fathers. Whilst Oedipus, however, is immediately re-born out of the house into the public eye of the polis, the action of closing the door of the house means Lavinia's final 'burial', from which there will be no resurrection, no rebirth: life with the dead is the end.

In its plot, figures and actions, *Mourning Becomes Electra* repeats the Aeschylean *Oresteia*, the 'first' Western drama. Such repetition highlights the fact that any drama which can be produced on stage is always only a drama of the same impersonal powers. Man is only given a particular role in it when – like Orestes and Oedipus, Beatrice Cenci and Lavinia – he recognises this trans-individual relationship and is able to break the compulsion to repeat set by it. O'Neill's theatre, in this respect, 'repeats' the Greek theatre.

In another way, however, it is significantly different. In the *Oresteia*, insight into trans-individual relationships leads to Orestes' redemption and to the transformation of the

Furies into Eumenides because the recognition of a patriarchy founded on logos must be a blessing for the polis. In *Mourning Becomes Electra*, however, atonement is out of the question; this is because the patriarch, founded and supported by a perverted logic, will irrevocably infect everyone on whom it breathes. O'Neill's changed ending explicitly marks the historical distance dividing the democratic polis of Athens of the fifth century BC and twentieth-century democratic America – or Western culture, in an age between the two world wars. Here, theatre can only become a 'symbolic celebration of life' if the death-bringing patriarchal system, which Shelley uncompromisingly denounced in *The Cenci* in a similar way, is disempowered.

*Mourning Becomes Electra* was premièred on 26 October 1931 by the Theatre Guild on Broadway. The six-hour performance, which began in the afternoon and was interrupted for a long 'dinner-break' in the early evening, was given an enthusiastic reception by both the critics and the audience. In the *New York Times* (27 October 1931), Brook Atkinson named the play a 'dance of death' and explained:

Using a Greek legend as his model Mr. O'Neill has reared up a universal tragedy of tremendous stature – deep, dark, solid, uncompromising and grim. It is heroically thought out and magnificently wrought in style and structure ... Although Mr. O'Neill has been no slave to the classic origin of his tragedy, he has transmuted the same impersonal forces into the modern idiom, and the production, which has been brilliantly directed by Philip Mueller, gives you some of the stately spectacle of Greek classicism. Lavinia in a flowing black dress sitting majestically on the steps of Robert Edmond Jones's set of a New England Mansion is an unforgettable and portentous picture. Captain Brant pacing the deck of his ship in the ringing silence of the night, the murdered Mannon lying on his bier in the deep shadows of his study, the entrances and exits of Christine and Lavinia through doors that open and close on death are scenes full of dramatic beauty.

Other critics also saw the impersonal, trans-individual aspect of the dramatic figures and

were united either in declaring it, 'a tragic melodrama of heroic proportions' (John Mason Brown, *New York Post*, 27 October 1931) or in criticising the figures and rejecting them as 'melodramatic figures' (Eugene Burr, *Billboard*, 43 [7 November 1931]).

Despite its length, the production ran for over three months on Broadway. In the light of this, it might not be wrong to suppose that the spectators could see themselves and their own problems in the non-individual dramatic figures and, at least emotionally, come to the conclusion: *tua res agitur*. If one considers that O'Neill's work was based on popular knowledge and categories of psychoanalysis, which were widely propagated in the 1920s in the United States, he certainly succeeded in creating for his audience a convincing picture of trans-individual man.

## The multiplicity of roles in the theatre of life or the multiple personality

The première of Luigi Pirandello's *Sei personaggi in cerca d'autore* (*Six Characters in Search of an Author*) on 10 May 1921 in Rome triggered one of the greatest theatre scandals of the century. Actors, critics and spectators came to blows with one another on stage; after the performance, members of the audience pulled together and threatened the author. Even hours after the performance, passionate discussions of the play took place in the market squares of Rome. It was the greatest disaster imaginable. None the less, a few months later, the theatre in Milan risked a new production and indignation was transformed into enthusiasm. The play was declared the theatre sensation of the century and, within three years, had won over nearly all the stages in the world. In 1922, it was performed in London and New York; in 1923, George Pitoeff produced it in the Théâtre des Champs-Elysées in Paris (and began a new era in theatre, according to Lugné-Poë), and in 1924, Max Reinhardt directed it in Berlin. John Ford saw the need to finance an American tour of Pirandello, commenting that, 'I believe that one can make good money out of him ... Pirandello is a man of the people'. *Six*

*Characters in Search of an Author* had become the greatest theatre success of the 1920s.

Pirandello, at the age of 54, had only begun to write for the theatre in 1916 after he had already made a name for himself with novellas and novels, most notably the novel, *Il fu Mattia Pascal* (*The Late Mattia Pascal*, 1903). Encouraged by Nino Martoglio, the director of the Sicilian theatre, 'Teatro del grottesco', he wrote *Pensaci, Giacomino* (*Think! Giacomino*, 1916) and, after its success, provided many other plays for them. None of the nine plays which Pirandello brought to the stage between 1916 and 1921 was unsuccessful. None however, had anywhere near the success of *Six Characters in Search of an Author*. The play, which deals with its own impossibility, proved to be highly dramatic.

The six characters, whose drama the author refuses to write because he has not succeeded in discovering any 'sense' in them, no matter 'how much' he has 'searched' (Foreword), turn to a theatre group who are in the process of rehearsing Pirandello's *Il giuoco delle parti* (*The Rules of the Game*, 1918) and try to persuade them to produce the play. At first, the director agrees to their plan and the actors begin to rehearse a scene; but it proves impossible to play the drama. It neither comes into being as manuscript nor as performance. Each reader/spectator is thus forced to consider the grounds upon which it is impossible to write and produce the drama of the six characters.

The play, which can neither be written nor performed, is a melodramatic domestic play. Its main figures are the Father, Mother, Step-daughter, Son, Boy, Girl and the brothel-keeper, Madame Pace, who is 'later called upon'. It is readily apparent from the energetic discussions between the six characters – above all between the Father and the Step-daughter and the director and his actors – that the drama should begin with the scene where the Father meets the Step-daughter, who works as a prostitute to keep her fatherless family, at Madame Pace's brothel. Before 'incest' can take place, the Mother bursts in and there follows a scene of recognition. The Father takes the Mother, the Step-daughter and the two children into his household. The Son rejects them as intruders. The drama ends with the death of the Girl who drowns in a pond while playing, the Boy's suicide and the Step-daughter's escape. Between the recognition scene in the brothel and the catastrophe at the end, the background history must be revealed – perhaps in an Ibsen-like way; events prove the Father's attempt to plan his life in great detail as well as the lives of others – the Mother, the Son, the Secretary, the Step-daughter, the two children – to be a misguided and thus fatal failure.

The story of the six characters is dramatic in that it can be reconstructed as a chain of single actions which can be considered acts in a Hegelian sense:

The act is something simple, determinate, universal, to be grasped as an abstract, distinctive whole; it is murder, theft, a benefit, a deed of bravery and so on, and what it *is* can be *said* of it. It *is* such and such, and its being is not merely a symbol, it is the fact itself. It *is* this, and the individual human being *is* what the act *is*. In the simple fact that the act *is*, the individual is for others what he really is and with a certain general nature, and ceases to be merely something that is 'meant' or 'presumed' to be this or that …

Individuality, which commits itself to the objective element, when it passes over into a deed no doubt puts itself to the risk of being altered and perverted. But what settles the character of the act is just this – whether the deed is a real thing that holds together, or whether it is merely a pretended or 'supposed' performance, which is in itself null and void and passes away. Objectification does not alter the act itself; it merely shows what the deed *is*, i.e. whether it *is* or whether it is *nothing*.[30]

The entire question of modern drama since Shakespeare rests on precisely this quality of the act. In the dispute between the director and the six characters it is severely challenged, however. For the argument proves that an act is not 'simply determined' but is 'multiply determined', something which is seen and interpreted differently by everyone:

FATHER: Her [the mother's] drama lies entirely, in fact, in these four children ... The children of the two men that she had.

MOTHER: Did you say that I had them? Do you dare to say that I *had* these two men? ... to suggest that I wanted them? [*To the Producer*] It was his doing. He gave him to me! He forced him on me! He forced me ... he forced me to go away with that other man!

STEP-DAUGHTER: [*At once, indignantly*] It's not true!

MOTHER: [*Startled*] Not true?

STEP-DAUGHTER: It's not true! It's not true, I say.

MOTHER: And what can you possibly know about it?

STEP-DAUGHTER: It's not true! [*To the Producer*] Don't believe her! Do you know why she said that? Because of him. [*Pointing to the Son*] That's why she said it! Because she tortures herself, wears herself out with anguish, because of the indifference of that son of hers. She wants him to believe that if she abandoned him when he was two years old it was because he [*Pointing to the Father*] forced her to do it.

MOTHER: [*Forcefully*] He forced me to do it! He forced me, as God is my witness! [*To the Producer*] Ask him [*Pointing to her husband*] if it's not true! Make him tell my son! She [*Pointing to her daughter*] knows nothing at all about the matter ...

SON: [*Without moving from where he is, speaking coldly, softly, ironically*] Yes! Listen to the chunk of philosophy you're going to get now! He will tell you all about the Daemon of Experiment.[31]

The battle between the six characters suggests that the acts are not 'simply determined'; everyone interprets them in a different way and, consequently, judges the creator of the action in a different way. The Father, Mother, Step-daughter and Son – the two children have no spoken text – each one gives a different interpretation of the action. Similarly, no single interpretation of the creator or his motives can be drawn from the action. Consequently, the characters themselves refuse the director's will to judge and determine them by a firmly fixed action:

FATHER: My drama lies entirely in this one thing ... In my being conscious that each one of us believes himself to be a single person. But it's not true ... Each one of us is many persons. ... Many persons ... according to all the possibilities of being that there are within us ... With some people we are one person ... With others we are somebody quite different ... And all the time we are under the illusion of always being one and the same person for everybody ... We believe that we are always this one person in whatever it is we may be doing. But it's not true! It's not true! And we see this very clearly when by some tragic chance we are, as it were, caught up whilst in the middle of doing something and find ourselves suspended in mid-air. And then we perceive that all of us was not in what we were doing, and that it would, therefore, be an atrocious injustice to us to judge us by that action alone ... To keep us suspended like that ... To keep us in a pillory ... throughout all existence ... as if our whole life were completely summed up in that one deed. Now do you understand the treachery of this girl? She surprised me somewhere where I shouldn't have been ... and doing something that I shouldn't have been doing with her ... She surprised an aspect of me that should never have existed for her. And now she is trying to attach to me a reality such as I could never have expected I should have to assume for her ... The reality that lies in one fleeting, shameful moment of my life. And this, this above all, is what I feel most strongly about. And as you can see, the drama acquires a tremendous value from this concept.

(pp. 25–6)

Here, the Father exposes the paradox on which the six characters and their drama rests: although each is aware that the others interpret their actions differently, and although none wants to be fixed by his actions, they all insist on playing the drama as a sequence of precisely such actions:

FATHER: [*Solemnly*] The eternal moment, as I told you, sir. She [*He points to the Step-daughter*] … She is here in order to fix me … To hold me suspended throughout all eternity … In the pillory of that one fleeting shameful moment of my life. She cannot renounce her rôle … And you, sir, cannot really spare me my agony.

(p. 52)

The drama can only have a 'big effect' if the characters are tied to 'dramatic' action and defined by it, in the Hegelian sense, as individual characters (*personaggio*). In order to put their drama onto the stage, the six characters – or more precisely, the Father and the Step-daughter – reduce the multiplicity of 'possibilities of being' presented to the director to 'one' single meaning 'expressed' by one particular action. It is such actions which, as in every melodrama, once and for all fix the characters and their interrelationships.

The author finds the drama of the six characters irrelevant and unacceptable. He is only interested in and fascinated by

the impossibility of understanding one another which is the irreversible consequence of empty definitions of the word; the ambiguity of the personality, corresponding to all the possibilities of being, which is found in each of us; and, finally, the tragic, immanent conflict between life, which is constantly moving and changing, and form which holds it immutably.

(Foreword)

The author believes that it is impossible to understand and define the individual on the basis of his actions. For, as a living being, man is capable of infinite change; he cannot, therefore, be understood as a defined, finished being, but rather as potential which will be actualised in forever different ways. A definable, individual character cannot exist. Since the six characters want to act out their drama as individual characters, it is only natural that the author refuses to write it. Since, on the other hand, in the dispute with the Producer, they explicitly refuse to be identified with their actions, the author is in a legitimate position to write a drama about the impossibility of their drama. This is because he sees the ambiguous, multiple personality as the key element of drama.

Pirandello thus decisively overturns the baroque topos of the *theatrum vitae humanae* which certainly underlies his theatre. In Calderón's *Great Theatre of the World*, the Director declared the roles in which he cast the individual people in the theatre of life to be mere appearance, in contrast to the soul, which will ultimately be judged on the basis of deeds, or actions. The author of *Six Characters in Search of an Author*, on the other hand, refuses to write a play in which a character is determined and judged by his deeds because his being (*Sein*) is not identical to his actions – which are pure appearance (*Schein*) – but rather with a multiplicity of different 'roles' which he intends to perform, 'corresponding to all the possibilities of being' which he discovers within himself.

The constitutive relations in the baroque theatre between author/director (God) – role (social class) – actor (man) are fundamentally redefined in *Six Characters in Search of an Author*. Pirandello is careful to introduce the six characters as dramatic figures in the sense of roles (*personaggi*):

It is imperative that the producer should use every means possible to avoid any confusion between the SIX CHARACTERS and the ACTORS … the most effective and most suitable method of distinguishing them that suggests itself, is the use of special masks for the CHARACTERS, masks specially made from some material which will not grow limp with perspiration and will at the same time be light enough to be worn by the actors playing these parts. They should be cut out so as to leave the eyes, the nose and the mouth free ... The masks will assist in giving the impression of figures constructed by art, each one fixed immutably in the expression of that sentiment which is fundamental to it. That is to say, in REMORSE for the FATHER, REVENGE for the STEP-DAUGHTER, CONTEMPT for the SON and SORROW for the MOTHER. Her mask should have wax tears fixed in the corners of the eyes and coursing down the cheeks, just like the paintings of the Mater Dolorosa that are to be seen in churches. Her dress, too, should be of a special material and cut. It should be severely plain, its folds stiff, giving in fact the appearance of having been carved.

(p. 6)

In this way, the six characters are – despite their physical presence, which for obvious reasons cannot be overlooked – unmistakably shown to be 'roles' which require actors in order for their embodiment. For, as the Producer remarks, it is not the roles which 'play' in the theatre 'but the actors. The roles are written in the script [He points to the prompt-box] ... when there is a script!' (p. 33). If the roles 'want to live', they are dependent on their embodiment through the actor. The non-identification between actor and role, the process of the actor's 'embodiment' of the role can be described as the definition and constitution of theatre.

The issue of non-identity becomes problematic in *Six Characters in Search of an Author*. The Father and Step-daughter neither can nor will accept it. Their difficulties begin with the question of who should play which role:

PRODUCER: [To the Juvenile Lead) You, the Son ... (To the Leading Lady) And you'll play the Step-daughter, of course ...

STEP-DAUGHTER: [Excitedly] What! What did you say? That woman there ... Me! [She bursts out laughing]

PRODUCER: [Angrily] And what's making you laugh?

LEADING LADY: [Indignantly] Nobody has ever dared to laugh at me before! Either

you treat me with respect or I'm walking out!

STEP-DAUGHTER: Oh no, forgive me! I wasn't laughing at you ... I was laughing about myself ... Because I can't see myself in you at all. I don't know how to ... you're not a bit like me!

FATHER: Yes, that's the point I wanted to make! Look ... all that we express ...

PRODUCER: What do you mean ... *all that you express*? Do you think that this whatever-it-is that you express is something you've got inside you? Not a bit of it ... The things that you express become material here for the actors, who give it body and form, voice and gesture.

(p. 34)

A significantly larger problem is thrown up by the question of representation:

FATHER: I think that however much of his art this gentleman puts into absorbing me into himself ... However much he wills it ... [He becomes confused] ... Even if he makes himself up to look as much like me as he can ... I should say that with his figure ... [All the ACTORS laugh] ... it will be difficult for it to be a performance of me ... of me as I really am. It will rather be ... leaving aside the question of his appearance ... It will be how he interprets what I am ... how he sees me ... If he sees me as anything at all ... And not as I, deep down within myself, feel myself to be.

(p. 35)

The Father conceives the disembodied role-self as his true self. The embodiment by an actor threatens to falsify it, to distort and deform it. The greatest danger to the true self is clearly in someone else's gaze. The Son, therefore, rejects the actor's comment on the six characters at the same time as their petrifying and depersonalising gaze. The Son comments:

Not even the tiniest vestige of us is to be found in you ... And all the time your actors are studying us from the outside. Do you think it's possible for us to live confronted by a mirror which, not merely content with freezing us in that particular picture which is the fixing of our expression, has to throw an image back at us which we can no longer recognise? ... Our own features, yes ... But twisted into a horrible grimace'.

(p. 65)

The actor's gaze, as the gaze of the other, cannot pierce through to the true self of the person, it remains superficial and thus objectifies the person on whom it is directed. Embodiment through an actor can only falsify the true self of the person and produce a stiff, deformed mask in which the person cannot recognise himself. As the Father notes: 'They're certainly not us!' (p. 48).

Instead of finding embodiment and thereby identity in the actor's play, the true self remains unembodied in the role. The six characters view the self which is embodied by the actors as a false self which they do not recognise as their own, let alone willing to accept. The situation of the six characters is, in this respect, comparable to that of schizophrenia, as Ronald D. Laing describes in *The Divided Self*:

In this position the individual experiences his self as being more or less divorced or detached from his body. *The body is felt more as one object among other objects in the world than as the core of the individual's own being.* Instead of being the core of his true self, the body is felt as the core of a *false self*, which a detached, disembodied, 'inner', 'true' self looks on at with tenderness, amusement, or hatred as the case may be.

Such a divorce of self from body deprives the unembodied self from direct participation in any aspect of the life of the world, which is mediated exclusively through the body's perceptions, feelings and movements (expressions, gestures, words, actions, etc.). The unembodied self, as onlooker at all the body does, engages in nothing directly. Its functions come to be observation, control, and criticism *vis-à-vis* what the body is experiencing and doing, and those operations which are usually spoken of as purely 'mental'.[32]

The condition of a conscious split into a true, but unembodied self and a false, but embodied self can only be resolved when the body is 'experienced' again as 'core of its own self'. Because the actor and role (character) cannot be identical to each other, the division into an unembodied, true self and an embodied, false self cannot be reconciled. Paradoxically, the very act which should give 'life' to the character – embodiment by the actor on the stage - prevents him from ever coming alive. It not only falsifies him, but it also depersonalises him, turns him into stone. His true self can never find embodiment.

The non-identification between role and actor, which Calderón's Director defines as the non-identity between appearance (*Schein*) – role, social position and being (*Sein*) – actor/man, which was the fundamental thesis behind the mere possibility of a world theatre, thus turns out to be the very reason and cause of the impossibility of staging the drama of the six characters. Their being (*Sein*) – role/person, remains incommensurable to their appearance (*Schein*) – as the gaze of other and as embodiment by the actor: the roles must indeed 'play themselves' or become identical to the actors if the drama of the six characters is to be performed.

The impossibility of writing and performing the drama of the six characters is founded on the recognition of a premise initiated by baroque theatre, but which had since become totally invalid in the twentieth century. If the stage figures are reduced to, and judged by, their actions, the author cannot write their drama because man is multiple and escapes any ultimate definition. In insisting that the roles do not play themselves and, thus, cannot be identical to the actors, the Producer makes the performance impossible because the actors deform and distort the true selves of the role.

The actor on the stage of the world theatre in the twentieth century played many roles 'corresponding to all the possibilities of being which he discovers within himself' and he is identical to all of them without being absorbed, determined, fixed or judged by any one of them.

Pirandello created an exemplary figure of this kind in *Enrico IV* (*Henry IV*). The play was written in the same year as *Six Characters* and draws radical consequences from the impossibility of their drama.

The title figure, 'Henry IV' – the 'correct' name for the Italian noble is neither included in the list of dramatis personae nor named in the dialogue – is described as an actor who has become identical with his roles. Following an accident twelve years earlier, when he represented the Salian emperor Henry IV in a masked procession and fell from his horse, he believes himself to be Henry IV. But one day he wakes up totally cured and consciously decides to continue playing the role of a madman who believes he is Henry IV. In so doing, he creates a freedom for himself which would be unattainable in 'normal' social life. On the one hand, he can direct and control the behaviour of others who see the madman in him and thus prevent their gaze from deforming and fossilising him into the torn image of a madman:

Don't you understand? Can't you see how I treat them? How I make them dress themselves up, just as my fancy takes me! How I force them to appear before me? Miserable, frightened clowns that they are! And what is it they're frightened of? This ... and this alone ... that I shall tear off their fool's mask and show up their disguise for what it is! As if it wasn't *I* myself who had forced them to assume that mask ... so that my taste for playing the madman might be satisfied!

(Act 2, p. 73)[33]

On the other hand, 'Henry' can also resist in this way the attempts by others to tie him to a specific role. Only as an apparent madman does he have the freedom to actually realise all the possibilities of being which he discovers within.

In wanting simply to heal the 'madman', the others resolutely insist on rehabilitating the 'cured one' into a 'normal' life – that is, one which

is fixed and determined by others. 'Henry's' right to 'ambiguity', to the multiplicity of roles according to the possibilities which lie within him, collides with the demands of society to define him once and for all by the gaze of others – who see in him either the poor madman or the sham artist. 'Henry's' tragedy lies in the fact that he can only defend this right with an action which binds him forever to the role of madman: the murder of Belcredi. The freedom won by his creation of the role turns into absurdity. His polyvalent role-play deteriorates into laughable farce. Stiff social convention and the norm have irrevocably killed off a life which is 'moving', 'continually changing'.

In *L' Umorismo* (*Humour*), in which Pirandello revealed the foundations of his aesthetic in 1908, he writes:

Life is a continual flux which we try to halt, to fix, in us and around us. ... The forms ... are terms ... the ideals ... are all the fictions we create, the conditions, the situations in which we seek to find stability. But the flowing continues within ourselves, inside that which we call spirit, and that which is life within us, indeterminate, slipping underneath the dams, over the banks which we fix by building a conscience, by constructing personality.

It is this idea of an *élan vital*, the conception of life as an irrational, natural power beyond all moral and social values, in which Pirandello coincided with the basic concepts of the Italian Fascist movement. In 1924, he joined the Fascist Party and published his application for Party membership in the Fascist newspaper, *L' impero* (*The Empire*). In a gesture of gratitude, Mussolini invited him to a personal interview. Six days after his visit, Pirandello addressed Mussolini in public as one who can 'only be blessed' because 'he clearly shows that he senses this double and tragic need of form and movement and desires it with such force, that movement is bridled to an organised form and that form is no longer a proud, vain idol, but accommodates life, pulsating and thundering, so that it recreates at every moment and is ever ready to act, in confirmation of itself and convincing others'. A more

enthusiastic apology for the Fascist dictatorship is barely imaginable.

None the less, it would be a dangerous conclusion to misinterpret the trans-individual self which Pirandello created for the theatre and label it a Fascist prototype. This would hardly accord with our interpretation of *Six Characters in Search of an Author*. The reception of Pirandello in Europe, particularly in Germany, and in America also contradicts this theory.

In the 1920s, Pirandello was a highly successful author whose work received great enthusiasm from audiences. Max Reinhardt's production of *Six Characters in Search of an Author* was performed 131 times. In Germany, twelve plays by Pirandello were performed in three years. In 1925, Pirandello was given his own theatre with state funding, the Teatro d'Arte di Roma. He performed with this company at the state theatre in Berlin from 12 to 14 October 1925. The programme included *Six Characters in Search of an Author, Henry IV* and *Il Piacere dell'Onestà* (*The Pleasure of Honesty*). Whilst in the Reinhardt production of *Six Characters in Search of an Author*, the critics preferred the acting skills of Pallenberg (Director), Lucie Höflich (Mother), and Gülstorff, who played the Father ('dull, tortured, well-meaning, mischief-making, clumsy and lumpy, and yet rising and sinking from the depths with great feeling' – Kurt Pinthus), to that of the Italian acting, Pirandello's troupe was able to win reasonable success. Even the critics were impressed. One such critic, Alfred Klaar, noted that:

The Father, Lamberto Picasso, and the Daughter, Marta Abba … increasingly grow from shadow beings into ones with impetuous, eccentric passions. Whilst Picasso's first entrance reminds us of our Gülstorff and the figure wriggles out of its embarrassment and shyness, here, (forced by the plot) it becomes ever more clear in its passionate pleading and Marta Abba grows with it in bridle-less emotions, in gushing inner emotions, right up to the final ecstasy.

Enthusiasm for Lamberto Picasso as 'Henry IV' was even more unanimous, 'Picasso's Henry did not play tragedy, he is tragedy' (Julius Knopf). And yet Picasso also gave the comic a place in his role, 'We are never lectured on the mental state, it is always vibrant movement. Wherever possible, the heaviness of the events are balanced out by comedy, it even goes as far as buffoonery' (Fritz Engel).

After this tour, the Pirandello fever in Berlin reached another highpoint in 1926 when Alexander Moissi played the title role in *Henry IV* at the 'Tribüne' theatre. 'The courtly ties of this play king seem to be bloody irony, his piercing eyes penetrate the helplessness of the unwilling players, the lurking barb of his observations tears the mask from their faces' (Alfred Kerr). Alfred Kerr complained, however, that Moissi showed 'the representation of pain rather than pain', which, none the less, did not affect an overall enthusiastic response: 'In short, he gives rather the outline than the heart of the matter – and yet a magnificent outline.'

For a further two years, Pirandello remained the most popular dramatist on the German stage. Whilst the Fascist movement in Germany steadily grew, however, enthusiasm for Pirandello waned dramatically and ended abruptly with a new theatre scandal. Pirandello was not able to perform his third play of the theatre-in-the-theatre trilogy (after *Six Characters* and *Ciascuno a suo modo* [*Each His Own Way*, 1924], *Questa sera si recita a soggetto* [*Tonight We Improvise*, 1929]) at any Italian theatre. He finished writing it in Berlin and dedicated it to Max Reinhardt, 'whose incomparable creative powers gave magical life to *Six Characters in Search of an Author* on the German stage'. In 1930 it was premièred at the Lessing theatre in Berlin in the presence of the author. In the concluding scene, where the acting skill of the leading actress once again appeals to the identificatory participation of the audience, tumult broke out: the audience had had enough of Pirandello's mirror battles between being (*Sein*) and appearance (*Schein*), actor and role; they began to riot, reacting with rage and anger. The actress who played Mommina – who played the role so grippingly that she almost died of a heart attack herself – burst into tears, and the director angrily scolded the audience, calling them a 'disrespectful crew'. This scandal meant, as a deeply satisfied Herbert Ihering realised, the ultimate end of the 'fashion for Pirandello' in Germany.

## Dialectic of the Enlightenment: the 'new man' in the theatre of the future

In Bertolt Brecht's lecture, *On Experimental Theatre*, which he gave in 1939 for members of the student theatre of the University of Stockholm, the self-declared opponent of middle-class theatre emphasised one important model function of the middle-class theatre of the Enlightenment:

> Bourgeois revolutionary aesthetics, founded by such great figures of the Enlightenment as *Diderot* and *Lessing*, defines the theatre as place of entertainment and instruction. During the Enlightenment, a period which saw the start of a tremendous upsurge of the European theatre, there was no conflict between these things. Pure amusement, provoked even by objects of tragedy, struck men like Diderot as utterly hollow and unworthy unless it added something to the spectator's knowledge, while elements of instruction, in artistic form of course, seemed in no wise to detract from the amusement; in these men's views they gave depth to it.[34]

Brecht criticised the theatre of his time, for having 'an increasingly marked conflict between ... entertainment and instruction'. The problem which his own theatre should resolve was this:

> How can the theatre be both instructive and entertaining? ... How can the free, ignorant man of our century, with his thirst for freedom and his hunger for knowledge; how can the tortured and heroic, abused and ingenious man of this great and ghastly century obtain his own theatre which will help him to master the world and himself?
>
> (*Ibid.*, p. 135)

Accordingly, Brecht voiced the demand for a theatre of the scientific age. In his *Notes on a Society for Inductive Theatre*, written in 1937,

which he projected as a programme for the founding of a 'Diderot society', he explained:

> The production of depictions of the world which might contribute to making the world controllable naturally encounters great difficulty and forces the artist to change his techniques to reach the changed goal. If the 'inner eye' had no need of either microscope or telescope, then the outer one needs both. Other people's experiences are useless to the visionary. The experiment does not belong to the tradition of Seer.[35]

Thus, one of the key concepts in Brecht's theatre aesthetic in the mid-1920s – the concept of experiment – is announced.

Since the age of Galileo, the experiment has been one of the most important epistemological methods of exact science. Since knowledge was no longer conceived as something given in God's order, but something to be gained by human effort, man had to find a means to refute or challenge the mere appearance of things: the experiment. Nature is put to the test by artificially isolating certain processes and devising an experimental apparatus which, though unnatural, should make transparent the way in which natural processes function and expose the conditions and laws from which they derive. Brecht intended to transfer this methodology, characteristic of the exact sciences (in which Artaud saw the detrimental development of European civilisation and which his theatre should reverse), back into society and base his theatre upon it. The view of Shakespeare's theatre in a metaphorical sense as 'laboratory' and 'experimentation', is meant in Brecht's theatre quite literally: his theatre should *actually* become a laboratory in which experimentation shall provide the conditions in which man's communal life, and his interrelations with others will be determined and on which they will depend.

It is in this context that Brecht felt Marxism could be given meaning and function. In 1926, Brecht began to study Marx while he was planning a new play about events on the Chicago corn exchange, entitled *Joe Fleischhacker*. He read up on national economic journals and interviewed people who worked at the stock exchange:

> I thought I could quickly acquire the knowledge I needed by asking various specialists and practitioners. No one, not well-known economic writers nor businessmen … could explain to me clearly what goes on at the Corn Exchange. I had the impression that it is something which cannot be explained, that is, it cannot be rationally understood, and that means it is quite simply irrational. The way in which cereals are distributed around the world was utterly inexplicable. From every point of view, other than that of a handful of speculators, the Corn Exchange was a quagmire. I didn't write the play I had planned, but instead I began to read Marx, only now, really read Marx.[36]

The relationship between Brecht's understanding of theatre and Marxism is thereby already sketched. Brecht's theatre does not serve either as illustration or institution of propaganda for Marxist theories, nor is Marxist theory employed to lift the probability of the dramatic plot or the efficiency of the performance. Instead, Brecht needed Marxism as a foundation on which to base his experiments as he designed his models. Marx's social theory allowed him to formulate precisely the issues his theatre should test for their truth and to isolate the key responsible elements. Brecht's claim of developing a theatre for the scientific age, to become the Galileo of theatre, was, in this respect, only possible through initial recourse to Marxist theories.

From the very beginning, Brecht's theatre took an experimental stance. Brecht began his career as dramatist by challenging an issue constitutive of and inalienable to middle-class society and its theatre from the very beginning: the issue of individual personality. His first drama, *Baal*, was written as a counter-model to Hanns Johst's expressionist play *Der Einsame* (*The Lonely Man*, 1917), which indulged and styled the genius Christopher D. Grabbe into a world-saving 'god-the-father' personality in the tradition of dramas on the romantic artist. Recalling the open form of the *Sturm und Drang* dramas, in which Goethe's *Götz von Berlichingen* had founded the tradition of 'great', individualist 'power men' as dramatic heroes, Brecht construed an antithesis. From similar points of departure he arrives at a completely opposite conclusion:

1    The absolute self-realisation of the vital individual, liberated from all moral scruples is impossible in bourgeois society, since this form of society forces everyone to fit in and its conventions stand in total opposition to the individual's claim to happiness and eradicate individuality.
2    The individual who sets himself up to be absolute, who lives out his insatiable sexual lust, his incontinent consumption of food and drink, is a monstrous social being who either falls into the realms of the mythic or becomes part of the circle of nature – from the 'white mother's womb' to the 'dark womb' of the earth – and dissolves his own individuality.

Like O'Neill and Pirandello, Brecht, in *Baal*, comes to the conclusion that there can be no individuality. Whilst O'Neill and Pirandello, however, assume that the impossibility of individuality is determined by all-powerful forces of impersonal life and death, and that it is this which makes the tragedy of human existence (O'Neill), or blame it on the collision with the demands and norms of society (Pirandello), Brecht turns his conclusion into a positive one – something only Hugo von Hofmannsthal had recognised at that time. In a prologue which he wrote for the performance of *Baal* at the Theater an der Josefstadt (12 March 1926), Hofmannstahl has the art critic Egon Friedell, the editor of *Kulturgeschichte der Neuzeit* (*Modern Cultural History*) appear and interpret *Baal* in the following way: 'I would go so far as to maintain that all ominous processes in Europe which we have experienced in the last twelve years, are nothing more than an inconvenient way of burying the European individual in the grave which he dug out for himself.'

Unlike O'Neill and Pirandello, however, Brecht does not want the spectator to identify or feel empathy with his 'heroes'. In 1922, he noted in his diary:

I hope in *Baal* and *Jungle* I've avoided one common artistic bloomer, that of trying to carry people away. Instinctively, I've kept my distance and ensured that the realisation of my ... effects remains within bounds. The spectator's 'splendid isolation' is left intact; it is not *sua res quae agitur*.[37]

Consequently, Brecht draws quite different conclusions from the concept of the impossibility of individuality in *Baal* than do O'Neill or Pirandello in their work. Brecht opposes the idea of the ever-constant – tragic or polyvalent – absurd being (*Sein*) of man with the theorem of man's changeability. He designed the comedy *Mann ist Mann* (*Man Equals Man*) as a kind of experimental apparatus which would demonstrate the basic pre-conditions of re-assembling one 'personality' into another.

Herr Bertolt Brecht maintains man equals man
– A view that has been around since time began.
But then Herr Brecht points out how far one can
Manoeuvre and manipulate that man.
Tonight you are going to see a man reassembled like a car
Leaving all his individual components just as they are.[38]

The play seeks to prove the changeability of man and deals with the transformation of the packer Galy Gay into the 'human fighting-machine', Jeraiah Jip (*Man Equals Man*, p. 75). It was written in 1924/5 and repeatedly reworked in later years (1927, 1929, 1931, 1936, 1954). In the Preface to the 1927 radio version, Brecht clearly saw positive value in the possibility of re-assembling the packer who 'can't say no' (p. 11) into a 'human fighting-machine' driven by 'ancient urge to kill / Every family's breadwinner / To carry out the conquerors' / Mission' (p. 76). *Man Equals Man* is based on the creation of this new type:

It struck me that all sorts of things in *Mann ist Mann* [*Man Equals Man*] will probably seem odd to you at first – especially what the central figure, the packer Galy Gay, does or does not do – and if so it's better that you shouldn't think you are listening to an old acquaintance talking about you or himself, but to a new sort of type, possibly an ancestor of just that new human type I spoke of. ... I imagine also that you are used to treating a man as a weakling if he can't say no, but this Galy Gay is by no means a weakling; on the contrary he is the strongest of all. That is to say he becomes the strongest once he has ceased to be a private person ... No doubt you will go on to say that it's a pity that a man should be tricked like this and simply forced to surrender his precious ego, all he possesses (as it were); but it isn't. It's a jolly business. For this Galy Gay comes to no harm; he wins.[39]

In the Preface, Brecht clearly shows the positive aspect of the process described in the comedy which is that the individual does not define himself in opposition to the collective but rather, is defined by the collective and strengthened by it. With the growing strength of the Fascist 'movement' in Germany, however, a negative aspect of Galy Gay's re-assembly increasingly came to the foreground, namely the degradation of the individual into a mindless, irresponsible, inhuman animal member of a herd whose basest instincts are given free rein by becoming part of the collective. The change in evaluation of the character is reflected in Brecht's re-writing in 1931 and particularly in 1936. It is characteristic of Brecht's experimental theatre that it is not closed and can react quickly to changes to the experiment on stage.

All of Brecht's re-writes began from the insight gained from *Baal*, that man is nothing without his social and economic relations ('One is none') and that it is only through relationships that he becomes something; these relationships prove to be not primarily human ones but rather relationships based on commodity exchange. Such relationships of ownership turn man into an object which can be used in a negative or positive way, according to the situation, and this can be demonstrated experimentally. The experiment shows how each change in the relationship leads to a change in the person (as object). Man is thus, in principle, changeable – *Quod erat demonstrandum*. The dramatist appears to be the organiser of these social experiments and explicitly emphasises its evidential, demonstrative character which forbids the audience empathy and keeps them at a reflective, if cheerful distance. The 'new type' is thus not represented on the stage as an ideal (nor as a negative example) which the spectator should emulate, but is instead designed and presented as an 'ancestor' of this new type whom the spectator must critically change and complete, that is, as a specific task of reception.

As is evident from reports on the performances in Darmstadt and Düsseldorf in 1926, Berlin 1928 (with Heinrich George as Galy Gay) and 1931 (with Peter Lorre as Galy Gay), on both occasions designed by Engel, Neher and Brecht, the audiences were not in a position to understand the task demanded of them, let alone fulfil or do justice to it.

The relationship between the individual and the collective, between the 'Individual and the Masses' (*Gesammelte Werke*, vol. 20, p. 60) remained even after (and precisely because of) Brecht's central interest in Marxism.

> One result of the growing collective is the destruction of the person. The suspicions of the old philosophers that man is a split nature have become true: thought and being are mirrored in man in the form of a monstrous disease.
>
> The personality falls into tiny pieces, it runs out of breath. It overflows into something else, it is nameless, it has no face any more, it flees into a minuscule size from being over-expanded – from being useless into nothing; but in its tiniest form, it breathes deeply and realises its new and actual indispensability to the whole.
>
> (*Gesammelte Werke*, vol. 20, p. 61)

This complex and complicated relationship determines Brecht's *Lehrstücke* which, by and large, were created between 1928 and 1931. At the heart of them lies the issue of 'consent', either given or withheld by the individual to being erased in the collective, or for the sake of the collective.

The *Lehrstücke* represent a special kind of theatrical experiment. They were not written for the existing professional theatre, but for amateurs – for school performances – and exclude one of the most important elements of theatre for Brecht – the audience.

> The *Lehrstück* instructs by being played, not by being watched. In principle, no spectator is necessary for the *Lehrstück*, but of course, a spectator can be put to good use. The *Lehrstück* is based on the premise that the players can be influenced socially by executing specific actions, taking up specific attitudes, and reproducing specific speeches, and so on.
>
> The imitation of highly qualified patterns plays an important role, as does the critique which is practised on such patterns when careful consideration results in playing it differently … just as the reproduction (the best that can be achieved) of a-social actions and attitudes can also have an instructive effect. …
>
> Particularly individual, unique characters are excluded, unless the individual unique qualities are an aspect of the intended instruction.
>
> (*Gesammelte Werke*, vol. 17, p. 1024)

Brecht developed the form of *Lehrstück* in response to a very specific problem which repeatedly confronted his theatre in the course of the 1920s. It concerns, on the one hand, the 'new type' and, on the other, the middle-class audience response to it.

Brecht presumes that there can be no individuality in the way conceived by the former bourgeoisie, and that no definitive statements can yet be made on 'new' trans-individual man since it can only arise as the result of a lasting process of development. Brecht felt supported in this view by Marxism, which defines man as a changeable and world-changing being, whose consciousness is determined through his social being. The 'new' man, who will be formed as a product of a situation where there is no bourgeoisie, in a classless society, thus cannot be defined and fixed in advance. Consequently, the stage cannot present him as the new ideal whom the spectator should emulate through identification.

Long before Brecht worked out his theory of epic theatre in any detail, he 'instinctively' attempted to keep the spectator at a distance in order to give him the possibility of actively developing the 'new' man from the actions and attitudes performed on stage. However, the audience rejected Brecht's plays (*In the Cities' Jungle*) or reacted with lack of understanding (*Baal, Man Equals Man*). Alternatively, they identified with them (*Drums in the Night*) and even celebrated them (*The Threepenny Opera*). There was certainly no productive reception in the Brechtian sense, so that Brecht felt the productions had no effect on society.

The *Lehrstücke* seemed to indicate a way out of this dilemma. They excluded the spectator altogether and concentrated their efforts on the changes experienced by the actors: instruction takes place when they take on different attitudes in a playful way, realise different ways of behaving and express critical views of themselves through play.

It has been rightly shown that Brecht's *Lehrstücke* stand in a relationship to the 'Music in Schools' movement, which is not only suggested by the genre description 'school opera' for *Der Jasager* (*He Who Says Yes*) and *Der Neinsager* (*He Who Says No*). Thus, at the Festival of New Music in Berlin in 1930, alongside Brecht and Weill's *He Who Says Yes*, four other school operas were performed: Hindemith and Seitz's *Wir bauen eine Stadt* (*Let's Build a City*), Höffer and Seitz's *Das Schwarze Schaf* (*The Black Sheep*), Toch and Döblin's *Das Wasser* (*The Water*) and Dessau and Seitz's *Das Eisenbahnspiel* (*The Toy Train*). But it is precisely this comparison between Brecht's *Lehrstücke* and the other musical plays for children which shows up enormous and fundamental differences. In the school operas and child-cantatas mentioned above, the children were taught specific bourgeois judgemental and behaviour patterns, or were directly influenced by a philosophical way of looking at the world. That is, the desired result was fixed from the beginning. Brecht's *Lehrstücke*, on the other hand, encouraged the players to look critically at the roles and attitudes they were being asked to perform.

Similarly, there is no 'positive hero' in the *Lehrstück*, no ideal for the actor to imitate through empathy and identification. Neither agreement – saying yes – nor rejection – saying no – are introduced *per se* as either ideal or negative patterns of behaviour which the players should rehearse or to which they should be made resistant. In trying out these attitudes in a critical way in the play, the player is exposed to the possibility of either developing new attitudes and ways of reacting other than those determined by the fixed conditions of the play, or to change the conditions – the given experimental apparatus. The result of the experiment is in no way fixed beforehand. If, according to Brecht, the *Lehrstück* has the task 'of creating, on the widest and most vital basis, even only for minutes, a counter-balance to the collectives which forcefully tear apart the people of our age' (*Gesammelte Werke*, vol. 17, p. 1028), then the 'liquidation of individuality' by the masses can hardly be the desired result. An appropriate new relationship between the individual and the masses will need to be created. The final result of the experiment is, in principle, open.

With the *Lehrstück*, the centre of interest shifts from the processes represented and the reaction of the spectator to them, to the side of the actors. The experiment is carried out with them and its aim is to change them: the act of performing should open the actor to the possibility of developing a 'new man' in himself, or out of himself, as part of an all-embracing, social process.

Much disputed however, is the question of whether Brecht conceived the *Lehrstücke* as a weapon against middle-class society or in utopian anticipation of a socialist/communist social system. From 1929 comes the following note, attached to the *Lehrstücke*:

our attitudes come from our actions, our actions arise from need.

if need is well-ordered where do our actions come from?

if need is well-ordered our actions shall come from our attitudes.[40]

The change in those who act aimed at by the *Lehrstücke* through the playful taking on of attitudes can, in this respect, only be possible in a society in which need is already 'well-ordered'.

It must be emphasised, however, that Brecht strove to have his *Lehrstücke* performed immediately. *He Who Says Yes* and *He Who Says No* were performed forty-eight times between 1930 and 1932 (after which they were banned), mostly by schools and amateur theatres. *Ozeanflug* (*Ocean Flight*) and *Das Badener Lehrstück vom Einverständnis* (*The Baden Lehrstück on Consent*) were both premièred at the Music Festival of Baden-Baden (27 and 28 July 1929). Here, Brecht tried to draw in the audience as a crowd and make them sing along – which was described by the critics as 'social music' and met with puzzlement:

> If Herr Brecht thinks he can abuse the spectators then the latter also have the right to resist and we are pleased that indeed they made use of this right by helping themselves with whistling and jeering ... because there was something rather sadistic in the way the nerves of the people, who were already somewhat irritated, were very heavily trampled upon.[41]

A performance of *Die Maßnahme* (*The Measures Taken*) was rejected by the new artistic directorship of the New Music Berlin in 1930; it was 'created by those for whom it is intended ... and for whom alone it has a use: workers' choirs, amateur theatre companies, school choirs and school orchestras' (*Gesammelte Werke*, vol. 17 p. 1030). But the performance given by the International Tribüne (13

December 1930) was a sensational success. Further performances followed in 1931 and 1932 in Berlin and Vienna, albeit in professional theatres.

If one considers the performance history of the *Lehrstücke*, it is hard to estimate whether the performances actually did function as 'exercises' towards changing those who played them or whether they were planned as a provocation against the bourgeois institution of professional theatre and its audiences.

On 28 February 1933, one day after the burning of the Reichstag, Brecht left Germany with his family and went into an exile which was to last fourteen years. During this time, he wrote his 'great' epic works, such as *Leben des Galilei* (*Galileo*, 1938/9) *Mutter Courage und ihre Kinder* (*Mother Courage and Her Children*, 1939), *Der gute Mensch von Sezuan* (*The Good Person of Setzuan*, 1939–41) and *Herr Puntila und sein Knecht Matti* (*Puntila and his Man Matti*, 1940), as well as the most significant work on the theory of epic theatre, including the magnificent *Messingkauf* (1937–43/1951). Disconnected from any possibility of real theatre work, Brecht suffered tremendously ('it is impossible to finish a play properly without a stage, the proof of the pudding ... only the stage can decide between possible variants'[42]). He developed a theatre of the scientific age uncompromisingly as a theatre of the future, 'for a desk drawer you need make no concessions'.[43]

As Brecht had already remarked in the notes to the opera *Aufstieg und Fall der Stadt Mahagonny* (*The Rise and Fall of the City of Mahagonny*, 1930), the 'object of the investigation' in the epic theatre is 'man' who is presumed to be 'changeable and world-changing' ('On Experimental Theatre', p. 132). Since man is only constituted as man through the relationships into which he enters, as Brecht's plays until then had shown, the theatre has a prime role to play in exposing different kinds of relationship which determine and produce different types of men. The object of investigation in the epic theatre is thus more precisely expressed as relationships between men.

In analysing such relationships, Brecht always starts from one thesis or idea which was formulated in the course of European culture and theatre history and which still held validity for twentieth-century bourgeois society. To test this thesis, Brecht designed a specially tailored experiment.

The parable play, *The Good Person of Setzuan*, with which Brecht wanted finally 'to get back up to standard again',[44] was to test the idea that a good person is always, and under all circumstances, good and will act for the good, since everything is entirely dependent upon free will. Calderón had exemplified this thesis in his *auto sacramental, The Great Theatre of the World* (compare Chapter 2, 'The great theatre of the world'), in which the law of mercy whispers into every ear, 'Love your neighbour as yourself, / Do good, for God is the Lord' (l. 666–7). Goethe took up this thesis in *Faust*. In the 'Prologue in Heaven', the Lord says, 'A good man in his dark, bewildered course / Will not forget the way of righteousness.'[45] In both these dramas, it is God as director who puts the play of human lives on stage and who, at the end of the play, makes a judgement on the actors.

In designing the experiment *The Good Person of Setzuan*, Brecht included similar starting conditions and framework: (1) There is a prologue in which three gods appear; (2) the gods are responsible for the 'play' in that they donate a sum of a thousand silver dollars to Shen Te, the good person of Setzuan, and this action propels the rest of the play; (3) at the end, the gods hold judgement over Shen Te. There is, however, a significant deviation: whilst Calderón's Master and Goethe's Lord remain in heaven, Brecht's gods have climbed down to earth, and though in Calderón and Goethe, God *knows* that man

can be good in this world, Brecht's gods must find proof of it for themselves.

How did the resolution read? … 'The world can stay as it is if enough people are found … living lives worthy of human beings.' Good people, that is. These atheists are saying, 'The world must be changed because no one can *be* good and *stay* good.' No one, eh? I say: let us find one – just one – and we have those fellows where we want them!

(*The Good Person of Setzuan*, pp. 7–8)[46]

These altered starting conditions make a decisive change to the function of the play which follows: it is shown as an experiment set up less to test man, the 'good person of Setzuan', and rather, to challenge the godly commandments and the way the world has been created. If the experiment shows a negative result, the world must be changed.

On the other hand, Brecht did everything in his power to overcome any doubt about Shen Te's good qualities: not only 'can't' she 'say no' (p. 8), but it is actually her 'nature' to be good:

Isn't it hard work
To trample on your fellows? The veins
In your forehead swell with the strain of being
so greedy.
Naturally extended,
A hand reaches out and welcomes with the
same lightness. Only
Grabbing greed must exert force. Ah,
What joy it is to give! How easy
It is to be friendly. A good word
Slips out like a contented sigh.[47]

The experiment cannot fail because Shen Te lacks goodness. In this, the optimal condition is created to prove the thesis that it is possible for man to be good if he wants to: Shen Te is a heroine who is good by nature and the gods give her a large gift of money which allows her to buy a small tobacco shop; 'I hope to do a lot of good here' (p. 13).

None the less, the experiment fails. Shen Te is overwhelmed by so many people seeking her help that even by the first evening, her shop is threatened with ruin:

The little lifeboat is swiftly sent down.
Too many men too greedily
Hold on to it as they drown.

(Scene 1, p. 21)

Shen Te is only able to keep her shop, the basis for her good deeds, if she goes along with the trick suggested by her nephew of inventing a cousin who cares for the 'business'. In order to be good and live respectably at the same time, Shen Te divides into two people, Shen Te, the 'angel of the slums', and the cousin, Shui Ta, who becomes the exploitative tobacco king and the 'scourge of the slums'.

Your injunction
To be good and yet to live
Was a thunderbolt:
It has torn me in two.

(Scene 10, p. 107)

Shen Te only wants to do good, and so she needs the 'bad' cousin Shui Ta – not because 'two souls' (*Faust, I*) live in her breast, but because her circumstances leave her no other option, although she is good and wants to be good. In this, the thesis is defeated: man cannot be good under all circumstances, just because he wants to, but he can be good under the condition that he is, at the same time, bad.

Brecht designed the experiment *The Good Person of Setzuan* in such a way that the sequence of actions exposes the reasons behind these conditions – that is, the causes behind division of the good person into Shen Te and Shui Ta: the system of human relationships which dominate the people of Setzuan.

These relationships are certainly determined by object and commodity. Each person is, for the other, solely a means of relieving one's own needs, of finding a job, rising in social circles and making profits.

Both the former shopkeeper, Mrs Shin, who deceived Shen Te when she bought the shop from her and Shen Te's former landlord, who threw her out onto the street when she could

no longer pay the rent, squeeze every last penny out of Shen Te for the sake of their own survival.

The pilot, Sun, with whom Shen Te falls in love, wants to sell her shop although he knows that in so doing he will ruin her and others, because he needs the money to bribe his way into a job as pilot. The barber, Shu Fu, wants to buy Shen Te's love with a blank cheque by providing her protégés with barracks which are so damp that his stores of soap go mouldy. The landlady, Mi Tzu, is only prepared to offer Shui Ta the necessary rooms to enlarge his factory if he gives her his manager Sun in return, 'She wouldn't let me have her premises unless she had him to stroke her knees' (Scene 10, p. 105).

Whenever Shen Te tries to create humane interpersonal relationships she is ultimately forced to transform herself into Shui Ta who perverts these relationships into ones of object and commodity exchange. When Shen Te's generosity threatens to ruin the shop, Shui Ta puts up a notice of marriage in order to sell Shen Te to a rich man.

When Shen Te falls in love with Sun and is prepared to give up her shop for love:

I want to go with the man I love
I don't want to count the cost
I don't want to consider if it's wise
I don't want to know if he loves me
I want to go with the man I love

(Scene 5, pp. 64–5)

Shui Ta tries to marry her off to the barber, Shu Fu, instead. When Shen Te realises that she is pregnant and wants to secure a good quality of life for her son:

To be good to you, my son,
I shall be a tigress to all others
If I have to.

( Scene 7, p. 81)

Shui Ta fills out Shu Fu's blank cheque and starts a tobacco factory in which he ruthlessly exploits Shen Te's protégés as workforce and sets up Sun, whom he has forced to work through bribery, as the merciless slavedriver over them.

Even if she wants to be good, Shen Te cannot, because every attempt to create human relations necessarily distorts them into relations between objects. The split of the good person into Shen Te and Shui Ta appears, thus, to be a theatrical model for the division of middle-class man into a private, and a business, self. Through 'being bad', the business self guarantees the possibility that the private self can be good. Such distortion of human relationships is, thus, conditioned socially: the bourgeois-capitalist 'world' is evil, and it must therefore be changed. The trial held by the gods over Shen Te/Shui Ta in the last scene, thus, becomes a trial of their own selves and world, 'For your great, godly deeds, I was too poor, too small' (Scene 10, p. 108). But the gods try to manipulate the results. Since they have found Shen Te in Shui Ta again, they declare their search for a good person at an end and are satisfied that the world should continue unchanged, 'Should the world be changed? How? By whom? The world should *not* be changed!' (Scene 10, p. 109). Before the helpless Shen Te, begging for advice, for she does not know how go on living, they withdraw on their pink cloud back up to heaven:

> Unhappily, we cannot stay
> More than a fleeting year,
> If we watch our find too long
> It will disappear.
>
> (Scene 10, p. 112)

For the gods, the experiment is thus at an end, but it has not finished for the designer of the experiment nor for the spectators. All they know is that the primary premise has been refuted; but what consequences are to be drawn from this fact?

> You're thinking, aren't you that this is no right Conclusion to the play you've seen tonight? …
>
> We feel deflated too. We too are nettled
> To see the curtain down and nothing settled.
> How could a better ending be arranged?

> Could one change people? Can the world be
>   changed?
> Would new gods do the trick? Will atheism?
> Moral rearmament? Materialism?
> It is for you to find a way, my friends,
> To help good men arrive at happy ends.
> *You* write the happy ending to the play!
> There must, there must, there's got to be a way!
>
> (Epilogue, p. 113)

The 'open ending' of the play shifts the centre of interest from the processes taking place on stage to the processes taking place within the spectator, from the designer who set up the experiment to the observer of the experiment who, unlike the gods ('we're only onlookers, you know' [Scene 6a, p. 75]), should observe carefully and with long consideration before making a final conclusion. This shift of focus is not surprising, for the interaction between what happens on stage and what happens in the spectator represents the constitutive structural principle of the parable play. It is repeatedly achieved in the course of the play through the technique of *Verfremdung*, or alienation, the so-called A-effect. Brecht explains:

> What is involved here is, briefly, a technique of taking the human social incidents to be portrayed and labelling them as something striking, something that calls for explanation, is not to be taken for granted, not just natural. The object of this 'effect' is to allow the spectator to criticise constructively from a social point of view.
>
> ('Street Scene', in *Brecht on Theatre*, p. 125)

Brecht designed the experiment in such a way that the processes shown to the spectator – even well-known ones – seemed foreign, so that the spectator could not empathise with the figures being represented – but, instead, could be critical of them and their behaviour. *Verfremdungseffekt* allows the spectator to 'develop that detached eye with which the great Galileo observed a swinging chandelier. He was amazed by this pendulum motion, as if he had not expected it and could not understand its occurring, and this enabled him to come on the rules by which it was governed' ('Small Organum for Theatre', Section 44, in *Brecht on Theatre*, p. 192). It is *Verfremdungseffekt* which transforms the theatre into a 'scientific institution'.

In *The Good Person of Setzuan*, *Verfremdung* is brought about by many different processes: by the way in which the figures turn directly to the audience (above all Shen Te, but also Sun, Shu Fu, Wang and Mrs Yang), by the figures' self-introduction ('I sell water here in the city of Setzuan. It isn't easy' [Prologue, p. 5]), by flashbacks, as in Scene 8 where Mrs Yang reports on her son's rapid promotion in the last three months in Shui Ta's tobacco factory ('There's something I just *have* to tell you: strength and wisdom are wonderful things. The strong and wise Mr. Shui Ta has transformed my son from a dissipated good-for-nothing into a model citizen' [p. 87]). *Verfremdung* is also created by mime, as when Shen Te takes her unborn son by the hand in Scene 7 and teaches him to steal cherries and to conceal the theft ('Take a look at the world, my son' [p. 79]), and through the songs which accompany the play: 'The Song of Smoke' (Scene 1, p. 20), which is used as an allegory of the fate of the eight-person family; 'The Song of the Water Seller in the Rain' (Scene 3, p. 39), which functions as a parable of economic progress of the play; 'The Song of the Defenceless' ('Why is it the gods do not feel indignation / And come down in fury to end exploitation / Defeat all defeat and forbid desperation / Refusing to tolerate such toleration?' [Scene 4a, pp. 53–4]). This complaint to the gods shows dialectically that people must be reliant on themselves – Shen Te sings it whilst she dresses as Shui Ta; 'The Song of St. Nevercome's Day' (Scene 6, pp. 72–3). It plays on the long overdue trial, at which the last shall be the first; and 'The Song of the Eighth Elephant' (Scene 8, p. 90), describes a model of the hierarchic structures of exploitation.

These alienating devices, set in a 'non-Aristotelian dramatic structure', ensure a shift in focus from the stage towards the spectator. They are supported and strengthened in this through the *Verfremdung* techniques of the epic theatre, particularly in the 'new art of acting'. 'In order to produce A-effects the actor has to discard whatever means he has learnt of getting the audience to identify itself with the charac-ters which he plays. Aiming not to put his audience into a trance, he must not go into a trance himself' ('A Short Organum', in *Brecht on Theatre*, p. 193). He must instead split himself and appear on stage 'in a double role' (*ibid.*, p. 194): as the actor X who shows his conception of figure A and what he thinks about figure A and as figure A. Brecht suggests three main means of doing this:

> Given this absence of total transformation in the acting there are three aids which may help to alienate the actions and remarks of the characters being portrayed:
>
> 1  Transposition into the third person.
> 2  Transposition into the past.
> 3  Speaking the stage directions out loud.
>      ('Short Description of a New Technique
>        of Acting', in *Brecht on Theatre*, p. 138)

These well-calculated *Verfremdung* techniques built into the experiment, *The Good Person of Setzuan* – and its performance – demand a wholly new way of spectating. Instead of being seduced into empathetic identification with the figures represented, the spectator is given the opportunity of distancing himself from them and judging critically both behaviour and the underlying conditions for it identified in the experiment. The *Verfremdung* effects in the performance and the open ending allow the spectators the chance to intervene permanently with new thoughts. 'Intervening thought. Dialectics as division, organisation, or observation of the world, which exposes its radical contradictions in such a way as to allow intervention.'[48]

Thus, the theatre refers the spectator to a reality in which he should continue the experiment. In the theatre he has learned that, 'To let no one perish, not even oneself / To fill everyone with happiness, even oneself / Is so good' (Scene 5a, p. 66), is an impossible goal even for the good person because every man must turn himself into an object if he wants to 'fill' others 'with happiness' and must turn others into objects if he wants to 'fill' himself 'with happiness'. Furthermore, he has also learnt that objectified relations between people are determined by the ruling model of the middle-class society and, thus, comes to the conclusion that such object relations can only be transformed into humane, authentic, interpersonal relations if this situation is changed. How man will act after a change in the social situation the spectator cannot know: this can only be found out in the future through further experiment.

In this way, Brecht's epic theatre determines the relations between theatre and reality as dialectic. Theatre confronts the 'thesis' of existing relations with the 'antithesis' of its models; the spectator must create a synthesis from both of these things through concrete changes to which the theatre, in its turn, can reply with another antithesis, and so on *ad infinitum.*

Even the epic theatre, which Brecht preferred in his last years to call 'dialectic theatre', does not introduce the 'new man' as ideal onto the stage. The new man remains – as in Brecht's early theatre and in his *Lehrstücke* – unknown and hidden; he is, however, in no way identical to the positive hero of the social realism.

Brecht's theatre starts with man in the existing bourgeois situation and demands that the spectator must change 'the world' through dialectic processes of mediation which he actively carries out between reality and processes on stage and vice-versa. That is, he must create the social conditions which would enable man to stop being a wolf to other men and allow him to enter into authentic human relations – the condition underlying the birth of a new man.

Brecht's epic-dialectic theatre for the scientific age is – and it is this which is so very new about him – in a radical sense, a theatre of the spectator. Although Meyerhold had already conceived of the spectator as the 'creator of a new meaning', he also showed this 'new type' as really existing on stage. Despite concentrating all his efforts on the spectator, Artaud intended to change them into new men through a *rite de passage.* Brecht, on the contrary, makes the 'arrival' of the new man depend entirely on the spectator: it is only his interventional thinking released on stage by his

experiment and the actions which lead from it which really change the social reality and create the conditions under which, in the long run, the new man can appear as product of such dialectic processes. Whilst in the *Lehrstück* theatre the new man should be built out of the act of playing, in the dialectic theatre, the location of his birth is neither on stage nor in the actor but solely to be found in social reality: the new man is *strictu sensu* the result of the productive reception of the spectator.

However, as long as this spectator does not yet exist – and at least at the moment he seems to belong to a largely unknown species – the theatre of the scientific age will remain a theatre of the future.

## DISMEMBERMENT AND RE-BIRTH

### End plays

Euripides' *The Bacchae* marks the end of the Greek polis and Greek tragedy. All that remains on stage at the end is the dismembered corpse of Pentheus, symbolising the dismembered 'body' of the human community from which the polis and the tragedy stem. Any sense of re-birth is out of the question.

Shakespeare wrote *King Lear* during another time of transition – the start of the new age – as an apocalyptic tragedy. The systems of family, society and state, founded on natural 'bonds', were pulled apart, and there was no prospect of a new order arising in or by mankind. Instead there is chaos, created and caused by the individual self and his desires. The images and metaphors in the tragedy repeatedly conjure a 'human body in anguished movement, tugged, wrenched, beaten, pierced, stung, scourged, dislocated, flayed, gashed, scalded, tortured and finally broken on the rack', and point to an apocalyptic end of the world as the result of the uncontained, bestial aggression which humans practice on one another.

Strindberg's *Dance of Death I*, written at the end of the bourgeois era, defined and described the family as something based on biological or mythically founded power struggles. This meant the end of the bourgeois family, the 'seed' of bourgeois society. The 'eternal workings of nature' which plants 'the seeds of humanity' in mankind 'to be cultivated' have become a 'hell' which dehumanises all members of the family, principally the male (Father) and the female (Mother). There is no end to the 'eternal tortures' which each sex exert on each other in battles which constantly repeat themselves – unless that end is death.

Samuel Beckett's *Fin de partie* (*Endgame*, 1954–6) undoubtedly belongs to this tradition of 'apocalyptic plays'. At the end of the 1920s, Beckett began to write poems, essays, stories and novels in his mother tongue, English. After the Second World War, he began to write for the theatre in French. Beckett offered various reasons for changing to the French language: 'To make *me* noticed' (1948), 'I just felt like it … It was more exciting for me' (1956), 'So I could write without style' (1956), 'To make me even poorer. That was the real reason' (1968). He explained his interest in theatre in the following way, 'Theatre is for me first of all relaxation from the work on a novel. It deals with a fixed space and with the people in this fixed space. That is relaxing' (1967).

Beckett wrote two 'great' (that is, longer) dramas, *En Attendant Godot* (*Waiting for Godot*, 1948) and *Endgame*. Despite multiple efforts by Beckett and Roger Blin, it was 1953 before Blin could finally première *Waiting for Godot* at the Théâtre du Babylone in Paris, making Beckett famous almost overnight. Beckett also wrote two plays without words, *Actes sans paroles I* and *II* (which were first performed after the première of *Endgame* on 3 April 1957 in London), and the short *Fragments de théâtre I* and *II* (1960) written in French. After *Krapp's Last Tape* (1958), Beckett mostly wrote plays in English.

In some respects, *Endgame* stands at the end of modern drama and Western culture as a whole. In a wealth of parody, allusions and quotations, Beckett makes permanent reference to some of the most significant texts in Western culture.

The drama takes place after an unspecified catastrophe which has destroyed the entire world but for the apparently only surviving people, the former landlord Hamm, his parents Nagg and Nell, and his servant Clov, who have found shelter in a 'refuge'. Using a telescope from the window which looks out onto sea and land, Clov delivers a report on the situation in a kind of *teichoscopia*:

CLOV: [*He gets up on ladder, turns the telescope on the without*] Let's see. [*He looks, moving the telescope*]. Zero … [*He looks*] … zero … [*He looks*] … and zero.
HAMM: Nothing stirs. All is —
CLOV: Zer-
HAMM: [*Violently*] Wait till you're spoken to! [*Normal voice:*] All is … all is … all is what? [*Violently:*] All is what?
CLOV: What all is? In a word? Is that what you want to know? Just a moment. [*He turns the telescope on the without, looks, lowers the telescope, turns towards Hamm*] Corpsed. [*Pause*] Well, content?
HAMM: Look at the sea.
CLOV: It's the same.
HAMM: Look at the ocean!
[*Clov gets down, carries ladder over and sets it down under window left, gets up on it, turns the telescope on the without, looks at length. He starts, lowers the telescope, examines it, turns it again on the without*]
…
HAMM: And the horizon? Nothing on the horizon?
CLOV: [*Lowering the telescope, turning towards Hamm, exasperated*] What in God's name could there be on the horizon?
[*Pause*]
HAMM: The waves, how are the waves?
CLOV: The waves? [*He turns the telescope on the waves*] Lead.
HAMM: And the sun?
CLOV: [*Looking*] Zero.
HAMM: But it should be sinking. Look again.
CLOV: [*Looking*] Damn the sun.

HAMM: Is it night already then?

CLOV: [*Looking*] No.

HAMM: Then what is it?

CLOV: [*Looking*] Grey. [*Lowering the telescope, turning towards Hamm, louder*] Grey!
[*Pause*]
[*Still louder*] Grrey!
[*Pause. He gets down, approaches Hamm from behind, whispers in his ear*]

HAMM: [*Starting*] Grey! Did I hear you say grey?

CLOV: Light black. From pole to pole.

HAMM: You exaggerate.

(pp. 44–8)[49]

The situation in the world outside described by Clov is characterised by the lack of sunlight, by the impossibility of distinguishing between day and night. Everything is grey, as in the story of creation,

And the earth was without form, and void; and darkness was upon the face of the deep. And the spirit of God moved upon the face of the waters. And God said, Let there be light: and there was light. And God saw the light, that it was good: and God divided the light from the darkness. And God called the light Day, and the darkness he called Night.

(*Genesis* 1, 2–5)

In *Endgame*, there is 'no nature any more' and nothing grows:

HAMM: Did your seeds come up?

CLOV: No.

HAMM: Did you scratch round them to see if they had sprouted?

CLOV: They haven't sprouted.

HAMM: Perhaps it's still too early.

CLOV: If they were going to sprout they would have sprouted. [*Violently*] They'll never sprout!

(p. 24)

And the Bible reads, 'And God said, Let the earth bring forth grass, the herb yielding seed, and the fruit tree yielding fruit after his kind, whose seed is in itself, upon the earth. And it was so' (*Genesis* 1, 11).

The unmistakable allusions to the story of creation, the 'first' text of our culture, are thoroughly destructive: creation has been reversed and annulled. The 'last' text, *Endgame*, quotes from the 'first' text purely for the sake of denouncing and destroying it.

Other textual passages are evoked in a similar way, for the same purpose: texts from the Bible include: 'Mene; God hath numbered thy kingdom, and finished it' (*Daniel* 5, 26); the Flood and Noah's Ark (*Genesis*) as well as the Commandment, 'Thou shalt love thy neighbour as thyself' (*Matthew* 19, 19; 'Lick your neighbour as yourself' [p. 96]). The paradox of the pre-Socratic philosopher, Zeno of Elea, is alluded to three times (pp. 10, 98, 116). Shakespeare is quoted in passages from *Richard III* (V, 4, 7) ('My kingdom for a horse' [p. 36]) and *The Tempest* (IV, 1, 148) ('Our revels now are ended' [p. 80]). From Descartes' *Discours sur la méthode* stem several allusions to the sense of 'being' ('He's crying ... Then he's living' [p. 88]), and logic (pp. 69, 93), and the 'infinite emptiness' (p. 54) is derived from Pascale's *Pensées*. Schopenhauer is brought into play in the German version through the joke about the tailor and his trousers (pp. 34/6) as well as by the 'poodle' (p. 59), which however, also refers to Goethe's *Faust*. Nietzsche's 'God is dead!' rings in Hamm's call for the Lord's Prayer, 'The bastard! He doesn't exist!' (p. 80), and Baudelaire is literally cited in Hamm's last monologue ('You cried for night; it falls: now cry in that darkness' [p. 116]). As Karnick (1980) has shown, Strindberg's *Dance of Death* is repeatedly referred to – the 'insect death' of the flea (p. 51), and Hamm's command to kill the rat, 'And you haven't exterminated him?' (p. 78) echo Alice's words, 'First he uprooted my brothers and sisters from the house – 'uprooted' is his own word for it' (I, 1 p. 145); Clov's refusal to touch Hamm, 'I won't touch you' (p. 94), echoes Alice's refusal, 'I can't touch him' (I, 1, p. 150). Hamm and Clov continually repeat the same questions and answers:

HAMM: Do you remember your father?

CLOV: [*Wearily*] Same answer. [*Pause*] You've asked me these questions millions of times.

HAMM: I love the old questions. [*With fervour*] Ah the old questions, the old answers.

(p. 56)

Edgar and Alice have a similar exchange: 'Don't you realise we go through the same rigmarole every day? When you repeated your old dig just now … my cue was to retort … But as I've already said this five hundred times, now I yawn instead' (I, 1, p. 135). Edgar and Alice have been 'in this tower a lifetime … twice we broke off our engagement and since then not a day has passed in which we haven't tried to separate … Now only death can separate us … so we wait for him as the deliverer' (I, 1, 145). Hamm and Clov describe their situation thus,

CLOV: Why do you keep me?

HAMM: There's no one else.

CLOV: There's nowhere else.

[*Pause*]

HAMM: You're leaving me all the same.

CLOV: I'm trying.

(pp. 14–16)

HAMM: All right, be off. [*He leans back in his chair, remains motionless. Clov does not move, heaves a great groaning sigh. Hamm sits up*] I thought I told you to be off.

CLOV: I'm trying. [*He goes to the door, halts*] Ever since I was whelped.

(p. 24)

CLOV: So you all want me to leave you.

HAMM: Naturally.

CLOV: Then I'll leave you.

HAMM: You can't leave us.

CLOV: Then I shan't leave you.

(p. 54)

Whilst Alice calls the tower a 'little hell' and her relationship to Edgar 'hell', Hamm comments, 'Beyond is the … other hell' (p. 40).

These very different truth-seeking texts from Western literature and philosophy, which all had a lasting and profound effect in their time and beyond, are alluded to in *Endgame* like distant echoes where words, sentences, theories and verses which once had deep significance, now only ring hollow and empty. As fragments, they only indicate their derivation from specific texts and are unable to maintain either their original significance or to create meaningful associations to their new context, *Endgame*. They have deteriorated into meaningless, functionless 'cultural trash'.[50] The body of Western texts quoted and evoked in *Endgame* is, therefore, completely incapable of constituting a meaningful whole; it sits within the dramatic text as an irreparable fragment – like Pentheus' corpse at the end of *The Bacchae*, a new birth is out of the question.

The characters in the drama, in their turn, are also made up of fragments. Much puzzlement and speculation has arisen on the meaning of their names. 'Hamm' might be a shortened form of 'Hamlet'; it can be interpreted to mean 'hammer', or it might refer to Ham, the son of Abraham and Hagar, who founded the clan of the blacks; or a 'ham' actor, or it might allude to the blind director, Hummel, who sits in a wheelchair in Strindberg's *The Ghosts*. Clov is interpreted as 'nail' (from the French, *clou*) and as a fragment of the word 'clown'. Nagg is thought to derive from the German 'nagen' (to gnaw) or 'Nagel' (nail); Nell, from the English word 'nail'. All commentators are unanimous in agreeing that these *four letter words* reveal the key issue of shortening names, the issue of fragmentation.

Fragmentation of the name, a classic factor of identification, corresponds to fragmentation of the body, another classic factor of identification. Hamm sits in a wheelchair because he is crippled and blind; Clov moves stiffly like an automaton and cannot sit; Nagg and Nell lost their legs in a tandem accident in the Ardennes near Sedan and are stuck in rubbish bins. Their physical collapse seems to grow deeper and deeper. Nagg complains about a tooth that has fallen out, and the worsening of his own and Nell's sight (p. 26). Hamm warns Clov, 'One day you'll be blind, like me. You'll be sitting there, a speck in the void, in the dark, for ever, like me' (p. 52). It seems that the rudiments of the body and the rudiments of a name can only produce a rudimentary identity.

Even the typical dramatic means of giving a figure an identity – speech and action – are made dysfunctional. Linguistic communication has deteriorated into the exchange of stereotypes; the same questions are asked, the same replies given and the same stories recounted. The dialogue only serves to keep the dialogue going. This is why the continually repeated replies are even exchangeable amongst the figures. Thus, 'Why this farce, day after day?', is spoken once by Nell (p. 26) and another time by Clov (p. 48). Language is entirely unable to convey the feelings or thoughts of a person. The sentences are interchangeable, hollow, empty echoes of sentences which once might have had meaning, which were once perhaps important, but which now have become meaningless.

HAMM: Yesterday! What does that mean? Yesterday!
CLOV: [*Violently*] That means that bloody awful day, long ago, before this bloody awful day. I use the words you taught me. If they don't mean anything any more, teach me others. Or let me be silent.

(p. 62)

In a similar way, the actions represent constant repetitions of stereotypes. On the one hand, they seek to maintain the damaged physis, to survive, actions such as sleeping, waking, eating broth, toast or chocolates, peeing, and lying down to sleep. On the other hand, they also serve to maintain relations already established, such as Nell and Nagg's attempt to kiss or to scratch each other and the different commands and their execution which pass between Hamm and Clov: to climb up the ladder, to fetch the telescope, to bring the dog, to push the wheelchair through the room, and so on.

The stereotyped actions and dialogue emphasise these relationships as simple, fragmentary extracts from a pattern which has

been long overused in the history of drama: as relations between family members and those between master and servant.

It is not only their relations which indissolubly chain them to each other in pairs (Nagg/Nell; Hamm/Clov) – 'nec tecum nec sine te' as Beckett remarked, which are provided by the models given in drama history, but also single characteristics and qualities which belong to each of the dramatis personae.

Hamm is assembled from various tragic heroes, 'Can there be misery – [*He yawns*] – loftier than mine?' (p. 10). His blindness refers back to King Oedipus, to Lear and Gloucester; his name alludes to Hamlet; the citations from *Richard III* and *The Tempest* evoke partial identification with Richard and Prospero. Hamm quotes the mighty *Sturm und Drang* heroes, who rebel against their fathers ('Scoundrel! Why did you engender me? [p. 70]) and against God ('The bastard! He doesn't exist!' [p. 80]). Like the romantic hero, he puts himself both on a level with God – when he warns Clov, 'Yes, one day you'll know what it is, you'll be like me' (p. 54), as well as styling himself on a negative Saviour, on Satan: 'All those I might have helped. [*Pause*] Helped! [*Pause*] Saved. [*Pause*] Saved! [*Pause*] The place was crawling with them! [*Pause] [Violently:*] Use your head, can't you, use your head, you're on earth, there's no cure for that! [*Pause*] Get out of here and love one another! Lick your neighbour as yourself!' (p. 96). Like the romantic hero, Hamm is an artist, a poet who narrates a tale like the blind rhapsodist Homer, 'It's time for my story' (p. 68), and an actor who plays a role, 'Me – [*He yawns*] – to play' (p. 10). And, as with all these heroes, Hamm insists on being the centre of the world, around whom everything must turn:

HAMM: Take me for a little turn. [*Clov goes behind the chair and pushes it forward*] Not too fast! [*Clov pushes the chair*] Right round the world! [*Clov pushes the chair*] Hug the walls, then back to the centre again. [*Clov pushes the chair*] I was right in the centre, wasn't I?

...
CLOV: I'll measure it.

HAMM: More or less! More or less!

CLOV: [*Moving chair slightly*] There!

HAMM: I'm more or less in the centre?

CLOV: I'd say so.

HAMM: You'd say so! Put me right in the centre!

CLOV: I'll go and get the tape.

HAMM: Roughly! Roughly! [*Clov moves chair slightly*] Bang in the centre!

(pp. 38–42)

Hamm's dramatic figure is constituted by fragments of tragic heroes from throughout the history of Western drama. These fragments – the different kings, autonomous individuals and personalities – constitute what Hamm is and is not, in the same kind of paradox that the grains of corn do (and do not) make a pile for Zeno. He is the remains of them – their husk, their parody.

Clov, on the other hand, is patched together from fragments which suggest different servant characters from the comic theatre: the servants in plays by Plautus and Terence, Harlequin and Brighella from the *commedia dell'arte* and the *gracioso* of the Spanish theatre, Shakespeare's fools, the servants in Molière's comedies, Hanswurst and his descendants in the Vienna folk theatre, circus clowns, Charlie Chaplin and Buster Keaton.

Just as the text of *Endgame* stands at the end of a long tradition of texts from Western culture which it now evokes in fragments and in parody, the characters of the play bring to an end certain traditions of modern drama, and the modern concept of individuality, in that they also allude to fragments and rudiments which they parody.

This implied ending is made explicit on different levels of the play. The mere title of the play, *Endgame*, suggests the end of a game of chess – a game played according to certain rules – through the false move by the King (Hamm) and the Knight (Clov). The drama begins after an undefined catastrophe, which seems to imply the end of the world and all life. The dramatis personae see themselves as the last people on earth. What happens on stage, therefore, seems to be the 'promised end' (*Lear* [V, 3, p. 263]) or the 'Last Days of Mankind' (Karl Kraus).

The drama begins with Clov's words, 'Finished, it's finished, it must be nearly finished' (p. 10). Hamm repeats these words in his first monologue, but seems, however, to make the end dependent on his own decision, 'Enough, it's time it ended, in the refuge too. [*Pause*] And yet I hesitate, I hesitate to ... to end. Yes, there it is, it's time it ended and yet I hesitate to – [*He yawns*] – to end' (p. 12). Just before the end of the play, Hamm decides, 'Then let it end!' (p. 108), and assures Clov, 'It's the end, Clov, we've come to the end' (110). The repeatedly echoed ending, which Hamm still believes he can bring about whenever he desires, does not occur. At the end of the play, Clov stands in his travelling clothes near the door as if he intends to abandon Hamm to certain starvation, and die in the desert himself, but he remains, 'impassive and motionless, his eyes fixed on Hamm, till the end' (p. 114). Hamm covers his face 'with his handkerchief, lowers his arms to armrests, remains motionless' (p. 118), but in so doing, he takes up the same position as at the beginning of the play. The drama could practically begin again from the beginning *ad infinitum*. An actual, that is to say final, irreversible, inevitable end seems impossible.

This makes the apocalyptic ending in *Endgame* fundamentally different to the end of the world in other 'apocalypse' dramas. In *The Bacchae*, as in real life, Thebes and the Greek polis did in fact come to an end. In *Lear*, the end of an era is brought to a close and finished forever. In *Dance of Death*, there is always hope that death might bring the desired and longed-for end. In *Endgame*, on the other hand, the end seems to exist in the eternal repetition of the ever-same play. Time has lost any kind of finality.

To Hamm's question, 'What time is it?', Clov answers, 'The same as usual' (p. 12). A little later, the two figures engage in the following dialogue:

329

HAMM: Do you not think this has gone on long enough?

CLOV: Yes! [*Pause*] What?

HAMM: This ... this ... thing.

CLOV: I've always thought so. [*Pause*] You not?

HAMM: [*Gloomily*] Then it's a day like any other day.

CLOV: As long as it lasts. [*Pause*] All life long the same inanities.

(p. 64)

This is a time of deterioration. Thus, although the physical collapse of the figures advances rapidly, the objects which are necessary for their forward movement, to maintain their physis or even assist in their burial (such as bicycles, broth, chocolates, sedatives, coffins) are constantly reduced. But these reductions do not lead to an actual end: it becomes less and less, but it never ends.

Time in *Endgame* is neither the final, eschatological time of the Judaic-Christian culture and modern drama, nor the mythical time of cyclical rebirth, nor the Faustian moment of fulfilment, but an empty present, the timelessness of an eternal 'now'. The 'now' of dramatic time corresponds to the absolute 'here' of the dramatic space: '*Bare interior. Grey light. Left and right back, high up, two small windows, curtains drawn*' (p. 8). Outside is 'death' (p. 18) or 'the other hell' (p. 40). Everything which exists in the world is contained in this interior, the refuge: a journey around the walls of the room is a journey around the world (p. 38). Not without reason does *Endgame* return to the ancient dramatic units of time and space, which were characteristic and constitutive of Greek tragedy and the tragic drama of Racine. Here, however, they point to a situation in which each figure, above all Hamm, is wholly turned in upon himself and has lost every possible reference to the world outside, 'I was never there ... I was never there. ... Absent, always. It all happened without me. I don't know what's happened' (p. 104). Consequently, the interior with its two high windows (eyes) has often been interpreted as an image of the inside of a skull.

It is not known whether this situation is the result of a catastrophe or if, in reverse, the solipsism of the subject caused the catastrophe; in any case, Hamm seems in some way to be responsible. He reacts, none the less, with a further retreat into his own subjectivity; his reality has become that of 'his-story' (*Geschichte, histoire*) which he repeatedly narrates (pp. 72ff, 84ff, 116ff). This story, described by Hamm in the French version as 'roman' and in the English as 'chronicle' (p. 84), can clearly be identified as his biography.

For Hamm, the story has taken over reality. By narrating it as fiction, he makes himself the creator of the world, of the events and figures who act in it as well as his own self. It also gives him the illusion that he can end the world and life at will, 'Moments for nothing, now as always, time was never and time is over, reckoning closed and story ended' (p. 116). When Hamm stops telling the story, the drama will come to an end. Reality, the play and Hamm's story are, in the end, all one. Only Hamm's story can guarantee his existence and that of the world.

This aspect seems to be constitutive for all Beckett's drama. His later plays concentrate on and restrict themselves to playing it out again in increasingly reduced form. In *Krapp's Last Tape* (1958), the old invalid Krapp ('*White face. Purple nose. Disordered grey hair. Unshaven. Very near-sighted (but unspectacled). Hard of hearing. Cracked voice*'[51]) listens to tapes which he made in earlier years of stories of his own life. In *Play* (1962/3), the three protagonists $W_1$, $W_2$ and M are stuck in three grey urns out of which only their faces peer out, '*Faces so lost to age and aspect as to seem almost part of urns. But no masks*' (p. 147).

When the spotlight hits them, they repeat the same old story, the banal story of their triangular relationship without, however, ever coming to an end. In *Not I* (1972), there is only a mouth on the stage, 'upstage, audience right, about 8 feet above stage level, faintly lit from close-up and below, rest of face in shadow' (p. 216), which narrates fragments of the biography of a woman with a female voice, in the third person. In *That Time*, (1974/5), there is only the 'Listener's Face' on the stage *'about 10 feet above stage level midstage off centre. Old white face, long flaring white hair as if seen from above outspread. Voices A B C are his own coming to him from both sides and above'* (p. 228). These three voices repeat the same fragments from three different lifetimes in the second person.

The total centring of the subject on itself and on its life story causes an increased sense of decentring from drama to drama. The subject's unity is dissolved in the melting of physical boundaries (the body becomes pulled apart and only consists of single elements such as the head, or even the mouth), in the division of voice and body (or what remains of the body) and in the impossibility of using the first person and saying 'I'.

Paradox, as it may seem, the existence of the solipsistic subject totally withdrawn into itself, which intends to put its own history in place of the world, is dependent on another: the history must be heard by someone else, the subject must be perceived by another. In *Endgame*, Hamm bribes his father with the false promise of chocolate if he will only listen to his story (pp. 70/2) and manipulates Clov's interested questions on stage in order to be able to narrate the story a second time (p. 84). In *Play*, M ensures the spotlight falls on him, 'And now, that you are … mere eye. Just looking. At my face. On and off … Looking for something. In my face. Some truth. In my eyes. Not even … Mere eye. No mind. Opening and shutting on me. Am I as much – … Am I as much as … being seen?' (p. 157). In *Not I*, the figure of the 'Auditor' is introduced in the stage instructions thus: *'downstage audience left, tall standing figure, sex undeterminable, enveloped from head to foot in loose black djellaba, with hood, fully faintly lit, standing on invisible podium about 4 feet high shown by attitude alone to be facing diagonally across stage intent on MOUTH, dead still throughout but for four brief moments where indicated'* (p. 216). When no other is present, the figure must split into the voice which narrates the own tale and the 'Listener's Face' who listens, as in *That Time*. The de-centralisation of the

subject happens, in this respect, as a consequence of its efforts to be perceived by another, even in absence. For *esse est percipi* ('to be perceived is to exist'), as the Irish empiricist George Berkeley (1685–1733) contests, and whom Beckett often quotes.

The gaze of the other in Beckett's theatre, just as in Pirandello – and, in the seventeenth-century, Racine – is a constitutive category. Whilst in Pirandello, the gaze of the other objectifies the subject, because it tries to reduce the multiplicity of its potential beings (roles) and fix it forever, in Beckett – as in Racine – it functions as one condition of the possibility of existence. This gives the theatre metaphor a fundamentally different meaning.

In *Endgame*, constant reference is made to the question of game, of play and theatre. Hamm opens his first and last monologues with the words, 'Me – [*He yawns*] – to play' (pp. 10, 96, 114). To Clov's question, 'What is there to keep me here?' (p. 82), he replies, 'The dialogue' (p. 84). Hamm acts with knowledge of the underlying theatrical conventions and rules of performance, 'Since that's the way we're playing it … let's play it that way' (p. 118). He teaches Clov, 'An aside, ape! Did you never hear an aside before? [*Pause*] I'm warming up for my last soliloquy' (p. 108). He begins and ends the play theatrically: at the beginning he makes the curtain rise ('*He removes the handkerchief from his face*' [p. 10]) and at the end he lets it fall ('*He covers his face with handkerchief*' [p. 118]).

Hamm is an actor who is identical to his roles – and, in this respect, comparable to Pirandello's Enrico IV. He acts as a director, dictates roles to the others and stages his own life story. As narrator as well as actor and director, he sees himself as creator of the events, and their centre. However, just as he deceived himself into thinking he will narrate his story for the last time, without an audience – Clov has entered in the meantime and stands motionless near the door – so he deceives himself when he thinks he can end the game by covering his face with the handkerchief. He is still present, not only for Clov, but also for the audience. As long as the spectator perceives him, he cannot end. The gaze of the other is, in this sense, filled with double meaning. It not only guarantees the existence of the subject – even the solipsist, wholly introverted – it also stops it at the same time from coming to an end. Beckett's theatre figures can never have the experience of the character Murphy, in Beckett's novel of the same name, shortly before his death when the game of chess was finished:

And Murphy began to see nothing, that colourlessness which is such a rare post-natal treat, being the absence ... not of percipere but of percipi. His other senses also found themselves at peace, an unexpected pleasure. Not the numb peace of their own suspension, but the positive peace that comes when the somethings give way, or perhaps simply add up.[52]

In this way *Endgame* reverses the ancient topos of the *theatrum mundi*: as little as the actor on stage can withdraw from the gaze of the spectator, the subject – no matter how solipsistically it presents itself – can equally little escape the gaze of the other. This other must in no way be a 'rational being' as Hamm imagines, 'Imagine a rational being came back to earth, wouldn't he be liable to get ideas into his head if he observed us long enough. *Voice of rational being:* Ah, good, now I see what it is, yes, now I understand what they're at!' (p. 48). He only needs to be there and to perceive.

It is for good reason that for his own production of *Endgame* at the Schillertheater in Berlin, Beckett cut all the references to the audience and explained it through the principle of naturalistic theatre: 'the play should be performed as if there were a fourth wall instead of the stage'.[53] In this, the role of the spectator is clearly defined: the only expectation is that they will perceive (percipere) and give the actors security through their mere presence, that they are being perceived (percipi), 'Am I as much as being seen?'

It is only in this sense that Beckett's theatre – radically different from Brecht's – referred to the audience. The plays are set after a catas-

trophe: after the phylogenetic-historic catastrophe of the Second World War, the Holocaust and the Hiroshima bomb as well as after the ontogenetic-biographical one of birth. What happens on stage is a fragmentation, reduction and dismemberment of the text-body of Western culture, of the text-body of drama, of the different dramatic heroes from modern drama and not least, the dramatis personae, who increasingly withdraw into themselves from drama to drama. The spectator is only intended to perceive these processes. Whether this self-perpetuating ending in the theatre is experienced by the spectator as the passage into a new age or whether the pulled apart bodies will experience rebirth in the heads of the spectators is a question outside Beckett's theatre. His modus of time is a time of end, his *modus vivendi*, increasing fragmentation, reduction and dismemberment with no possibility of an end – the pre-condition of rebirth. The modus of his perception and reception, however, is neither prescribed nor fixed; it is handed over to the spectators themselves.

## The rebirth of human nature: the redeemed and redeeming body

Beckett's *Endgame* can, in many respects, be read as an apocalyptic drama: it deals with events after a catastrophe which has destroyed mankind and the world; it evokes the 'great' texts of Western culture, in fragmented form and through parody; the dramatic figures end century-old traditions of modern drama and the modern concept of individuality by exposing the fragmentary and rudimentary nature of the world. On the other hand, it seems to have brought to an end the utopia of a new, trans-individual man created by theatre from the beginning of the century in most diverse variations: the fragmented body of texts deriving from Western culture, like the dismembered, individual dramatic hero, cannot be reborn.

The dream of a new trans-individual man engendered by the deep crisis in middle-class culture was irrevocably nipped in the bud. After Fascism and Stalinism had eradicated the idea of individual human life by collectivisation, ideology and stereotypisation, events in the Second World War, especially Auschwitz and Hiroshima, wiped out the idea of individual, human death. The individual had ceased to exist.

The postwar dramatists of the 1950s started from this experience. In ever new variations and evaluations, dramatists such as Jean Genet and Eugène Ionesco in France, Tennessee Williams and Arthur Miller in the United States and Max Frisch and Friedrich Dürrenmatt in Switzerland, performed the play of the impossibility of the individual. Some blamed historical-social conditions, others found existential-anthropological causes; others simply drew attention to it, while yet others made vehement protest and expressed their longing for a return to individuality. Whilst some continued the dramatic traditions of Pirandello, O'Neill and Brecht, who treat man as a non-individual, others drew upon the great dramatists of the earlier bourgeois age, such as Ibsen, Strindberg and Chekhov. They were unanimous, however, in diagnosing the evil of the times as a condition in which the individual cannot exist – for whatever reason. A 'remedy' for Western culture seemed unlikely, if not impossible. Beckett radicalised this gloomy description of the situation by placing it *sub speciem apocalypsis*: the dissolution and dismemberment of the individual is not only to be understood as the end of the Western culture, but at the same time as a standstill, as a perpetual end condition. The future is usurped by empty time. 'Salvation' – which for Beckett means less the absence of *percipere* than that of *percipi* – has no place.

The young Polish director, Jerzy Grotowski, did seek salvation, however. In the late 1950s, he began to conceive of a new theatre which would be in a position to function as remedy of the evil of the times: 'Theatre – through the actor's technique, his art in which the living organism strives for higher motives – provides an opportunity for what could be called integration, the discarding of masks, the revealing

of the real substance: a totality of physical and mental reactions.'[54]

Grotowski thus consciously continues a specifically Polish tradition which finds its origins in Romanticism. The two major Polish Romantic poets, Adam Mickiewicz and Juliusz Slowacki, developed messianic ideas on the determination of the fate of the Polish nation. In *Dziady III* (*Burial Ceremony*, 1832), which Grotowski directed in 1961 with his company, the Theatre of 13 Rows in Opole, Mickiewicz reveals the messianic concept of a resurrection of the Polish people in an analogy to the story of Christ's passion. Just as Christ was resurrected, so the Polish people would also be resurrected. The suffering of the Polish youth in the years after the November Uprising (1830), thus, was given meaning. Slowacki expresses a rather more secular messianism. In his *Kordian* (1833), which Grotowski produced directly after *Dziady*, Poland is described as 'the Winkelried of all nations'.[55] In his final drama, *Samuel Zborowksi* (1844, published in 1901), on which Grotowski based his last theatre production, *Apocalypsis cum figuris* (1968), Slowacki formulated the idea of a 'revolution out of the spirit'. Grotowski continued this tradition not through identification, but instead through confrontation.

Two fundamental concepts underpin Grotowski's idea of the theatre as a 'place of salvation' or, more prosaically, as a therapeutic institution: the idea of the poor theatre and the concept of the performance as a transgression of boundaries. Grotowski developed a 'poor theatre' by experimenting with eliminating everything which seemed superfluous. Through this process, he discovered that theatre can exist, 'without make-up, without autonomic costume and scenography, without a separate performance area (stage), without lighting and sound effects, etc. It cannot exist without the actor–spectator relationship of perceptual, direct "live" communion' (p. 19). The players and the spectators were, therefore, indisputable constituents of theatre: 'We can thus define theatre as "what takes place between spectator and actor"' (p. 32). Following this insight,

Grotowski reduced his theatre laboratory from a theatre which was rich in means and which had always depended on the fine arts, lighting and music, into a poor, ascetic theatre, 'in which the actors and audience are all that is left. All the other visual elements – e.g. plastic, etc., – are constructed by means of the actor's body, the acoustic and musical effects by his voice' (p. 33).

The 'redemptive' effect which theatre should have rests entirely on the relationship between actor and spectator; 'It is therefore necessary to abolish the distance between actor and audience by eliminating the stage, removing all frontiers' (p. 41). This does not mean, however, that the spectator – as later in the American avant-garde – should take part. Nor is the actor to perform '*for* the audience, he must act in confrontation with the spectators, in their presence. Better still, he must fulfil an authentic act in place of the spectators' (p. 182). The actor acts as a representative of the spectator – as Christ acted as a representative of mankind who has sinned. And, as Christ called upon his people to continue his works, so the actor calls upon the spectator: 'This is an excess not only for the actor but also for the audience. The spectator understands, consciously or unconsciously, that such an act is an invitation to him to do the same thing' (p. 37). Thus, for Grotowski, audience participation means the potential of turning the spectator into a 'disciple'.

In order to make this happen, two conditions must be fulfilled: first, the spatial organisation must allow direct confrontation, and second, the actor's performance must be carried out as a 'total act'.

Grotowski created a different spatial arrangement for each production. In the early production of *Kordian*, for example, he set the action in a psychiatric clinic – several years before Peter Weiss wrote *The Persecution and Assassination of Marat as Performed by the Inmates of the Asylum of Charenton under the Direction of the Marquis de Sade* (1964). The entire theatre became the place of action. The spectators sat on iron bunk beds which were arranged in

three different places in the room, and were treated as patients. The patients' beds also served as podia on which the most important scenes of action took place.

The production of Wyspianski's *Akropolis* (1962) was, as the dramatist Ludwig Flaszen reported,

conceived as a poetic paraphrase of an extermination camp. ... The rule of the Theatre Laboratory is to distribute the action all over the theatre and among the spectators. These, however, are not expected to take part in the action. For *Akropolis*, it was decided that there would be no direct contact between actors and spectators: the actors represent those who have been initiated in the ultimate experience, they are the dead; the spectators represent those who are outside of the circle of initiates, they remain in the stream of everyday life, they are the living. The inmates belong in a nightmare and seem to move in on the spectators from all sides.

(p. 63)

In Grotowski's production of *The Constant Prince* (1965), a strict division was made between spectators and actors. The theatre was designed as an arena or operating theatre (as in Rembrandt's 'Anatomy Lesson of Dr. Nicolaes Tulp') so that one could observe what was going on below as 'some cruel sport in an ancient Roman arena or a surgical operation' (p. 82). In this way, the spectators were forced into the role of voyeurs.

Direct confrontation, where the spectator 'is within arm's reach of the actor, can feel his breathing and smell the perspiration' (p. 42), does not permit large numbers of spectators. Whilst for *Kordian*, sixty-five spectators could be seated, their number was reduced in *The Constant Prince* to between thirty or forty. For *Apocalypsis cum figuris*, only twenty-five spectators per performance attended. Grotowski's theatre was, in this respect, to be understood as a theatre for the élite, albeit, 'an élite which is not determined by the social background or financial situation of the spectator, nor even education. The worker who has never had any secondary education can undergo this creative process of self-search, whereas the university professor may be dead, permanently formed, moulded into the terrible rigidity of a corpse' (pp. 40–1).

The spectator, too, must fulfil certain conditions if the theatre is to achieve its therapeutic function. He must experience a 'truly spiritual need' to be 'reborn' as himself. For a spectator who 'fights to keep his mask of lies intact at all costs' (p. 46) will not be in a position to take on the demands of the actors and follow their example.

The most important condition, however, is fulfilled by the actor and his 'total act'. Grotowski developed an entirely new concept, the 'holy actor', who was at the same time a utopian vision of a 'new man'. The holy actor is, in a way, the incarnation of new man. He is 'reborn – not only as an actor but as a man' (p. 25).

Like many other dramatists of the 1950s, Grotowski's point of departure is the impossibility of individuality in present times. This is manifested in the many roles and masks which the individual is forced to put on in everyday life and in the chasm between intellect and instinct, thought and feeling. It should now be the task of the actor to take off the masks and penetrate his 'true substance' and, thus, to integrate his physical and spiritual reactions with one another.

Grotowski explains, 'self-research' is the 'right of our profession, our duty' (p. 200). This causes a serious problem for the actor:

Either (1) he plays for the audience – which is completely natural if we think of the theatre's function – which leads him into a kind of flirtation that means he is playing for himself, for the satisfaction of being accepted, loved, affirmed – and the result is narcissism; or (2) he works directly for himself. That means he observes his emotions, looks for the richness of his psychic states – and this is the shortest way to hypocrisy and hysteria.

(p. 202)

The 'self-research' has nothing to do with narcissism, with being concerned with one's

own private problems and feelings. Grotowski calls such actors 'prostitute' actors because they show off their private nature in an exhibitionistic way.

Rather, the 'holy' actor is one who 'unveils himself, opens and gives himself in an extreme, solemn gesture, and does not hold back before any obstacle set by custom and behaviour' (p. 92). 'It is a serious and solemn act of revelation. The actor must be prepared to be absolutely sincere. It is like a step towards the summit of the actor's organism in which consciousness and instinct are united' (p. 178). Grotowski names these acts carried out in the theatre 'total acts', acts 'modelled in a living organism, in impulses, a way of breathing, a rhythm of thought and the circulation of blood, when it is ordered and brought to consciousness, not dissolving into chaos and formal anarchy' (p. 92).

This 'total act' of self-research and self-opening of the actor can neither be carried out in isolation nor for the sake of self-satisfaction. In order to make the 'total act' authentic, an 'other' is an absolute necessity.

The concept of the other is fundamental to Grotowski's concept of the 'holy' actor and the total act. The actor must carry out the 'total unveiling of one's being' in the presence of another and he must do it for another so that it 'becomes a gift of the self which borders on the transgression of barriers and love' (p. 99). It is only in the process of the act of self-revealing that the actor may make contact with his true self and this must be carried out in the presence of others: another actor, a director, a spectator – an 'other' being.

Grotowski's concept thus does not represent a return to the middle-class sense of the individual who stands apart from others and seeks to exist purely for himself. For Grotowski, that would be nothing but narcissism. He sees the discovery of the self as something which is only possible if an 'other' is part of the equation and which can only be achieved as a transgression of the ego, a transcendence of the self.

In this respect, Grotowski conceives a wholly new concept of role. The actor cannot exist merely in order to embody or present a role.

It is not a question of portraying himself under certain given circumstances, or of 'living' a part; nor does it entail the distant sort of acting common to epic theatre and based on cold calculation. The important thing is to use the role as a trampoline, an instrument with which to study what is hidden behind our everyday mask – the innermost core of our personality – in order to sacrifice it, expose it.

(p. 37)

The author's text is 'a sort of scalpel enabling us to open ourselves, to transcend ourselves, to find what is hidden within us and to make the act of encountering others; in other words to transcend our solitude' (p. 57). The role is no longer the purpose behind the actor's efforts but solely a means towards another goal. For the actor does not transform himself through the total act into a role figure, but rather into a new man.

This new man can be described as 'integral' in that he annuls the dualism of instinct and intellect, thought and emotion, spiritual and physiological reactions through integration; as 'whole' in that he no longer suppresses any components of his human nature but acts them all out in the same way as someone who is 'ego-free'. By neither insisting on the unique nature of the self as an 'ego-centric' modern middle-class individual, nor giving up his ego by regressing to a mythic 'ego-less' condition, he consciously transcends the boundaries of the ego.

The body is given a fundamental function in the transformation of the actor into the new man. For Stanislavsky, with whom Grotowski agrees in the belief in the psycho-physical unity of man, the body of the actor served to express different mental states of the role. For the avant-garde movement, the actor's body represented a material which could be shaped at will – even as far as Artaud's alphabet of hieroglyphic signs. The physical training of the actor was designed according to these views. Grotowski's theatre, on the other hand, aimed towards a technique of 'the integration of all the actor's psychic and bodily powers which

emerge from the most intimate layers of his being and his instinct, springing forth in a sort of "translumination"' (p. 16). This is the reason why the actor's training will not attempt to teach, but rather,

to eliminate his organism's resistance to this psychic process. The result is freedom from the time-lapse between inner impulse and outer reaction in such a way that the impulse is already an outer reaction. Impulse and action are concurrent: the body vanishes, burns, and the spectator sees only a series of visible impulses.

Ours then is a *via negativa* – not a collection of skills but an eradication of blocks.

(pp. 16–17)

The many exercises which Grotowski developed serve this goal: to eradicate the blocks. The training demands an almost unbearable effort which takes the actor repeatedly to the edge of exhaustion. As Grotowski himself explains:

There are certain points of fatigue which break the control of the mind, a control that blocks us. When we find the courage to do things that are impossible, we make the discovery that our body does not block us. We do the impossible and the division within us between conception and the body's ability disappears.

(pp. 204–5)

For Grotowski, the actor's body is not an instrument; it is neither a means of expression, nor a material from which to construct specific signs, nor a means towards transformation. It is, far more, a place in which the transformation of the actor into a new man – integral, whole and ego-free – is concretely present: the material of the body is transformed into energy in the process of self-revelation. It is the actor's body which 'redeems' him and allows his 're-birth'.

The actor Ryszard Cieslak in *The Constant Prince* (translated by Slowacki), came closest to Grotowski's concept of a 'holy' actor. The critic Józef Kelera wrote (in *ODRA XI*, 1965) of the actor:

The essence ... does not in reality reside in the fact that the actor makes amazing use of his voice, nor in the way that he uses his almost naked body to sculpt mobile forms that are striking in their expressiveness; nor is it in the way that the technique of the body and voice form a unity during the long and exhausting monologues which vocally and physically border on acrobatics. It is a question of something quite different. ...

Until now, I accepted with reserve the terms such as 'secular holiness', 'act of humility', 'purificaiton' which Grotowski uses. Today I admit that they can be applied perfectly to the character of the Constant Prince. A sort of psychic illumination emanates from the actor. I cannot find any other definition. In the culminating moments of the role, everything that is technique is as though illuminated from within, light, literally imponderable. At any moment the actor will levitate ... He is in a state of grace. And all around him this 'cruel theatre' with its blasphemies and excesses is transformed into a theatre in a state of grace.

(*Ibid.*, no page ref.)

The new man, as embodied by the actor Ryszard Cieslak in *The Constant Prince*, bears unmistakable messianic traits. Grotowski's theatre continues a historic line which leads back to the religious plays of the Middle Ages.

During the many days of performance of the Passion Plays of the fifteenth and sixteenth centuries, a scapegoat ritual was *carried out*: Jesus the son of God and Man, accepts the violence done to him on behalf of mankind – the violence which the spectator is afraid to confront. The more cruelly the tortures are carried out on the holy scapegoat, the greater the protection accorded the spectator's body in a magical way. The ritual is exclusively directed towards the body – the body of the 'scapegoat', Jesus, and that of the spectator. After the introduction of the concept of modern individuality, the human ego was held to be strong enough for the disciples of Christ to accept suffering willingly themselves. A form of martyr theatre developed in the baroque theatre: the Christian Prince seems, as no other, well suited to act in a quasi-representative way as martyr who reveals this strength of the human ego – so to speak, as

substitute for all other men. In the baroque theatre his martyrdom is *represented* by an actor and, thus, the spectator is encouraged to imitate him.

In Grotowski's theatre, the actor acts as representative for the spectator and *carries out* the transformation into a new man with his body, thus challenging the spectator to imitation. Grotowski consciously continues this tradition. He begins from the assumption that a theatre must be 'national' if it is to have any effect; for it must attack 'what might be called the collective complexes of society, the core of the collective sub-conscious or perhaps superconscious ... the myths which are not an invention of the mind but are, so to speak, inherited through one's blood, religion, culture and climate' (p. 42). In Poland, that means primarily certain Christian and national myths founded on Christianity. Grotowski refers back to the great romantic poets of Poland and to Calderón because these texts 'are like the voices of my ancestors and those voices which come to us from the sources of our European culture' (p. 58). They open the 'possibility of a sincere confrontation'. The vibrant Christian-messianic inheritance is continued in Grotowski.

In creating a poor theatre and in his conception of a holy actor, Grotowski at the same time also conceived a utopian human being, whose realisation should, from the very start, not remain limited to the theatre: the actor transforms himself on behalf of the spectator into a new man and challenges the spectator to follow him. In this respect, Grotowski's admission (from 1970) that 'the ordinary everyday world is a theatre',[56] does not seem surprising. In 1975, his troupe left the theatre and devoted themselves entirely to so-called 'special projects'. Each of these occasions were intended to give a large group of 'quite ordinary people' – who none the less had 'sincere spiritual needs' – the possibility of confrontation with an other in order to find themselves.

The theatrical inheritance of Grotowski was greedily taken up by the American avant-garde. In the United States in the 1960s, in the train of civil rights and the anti-Vietnam movement, deep cultural changes had taken place, which Herbert Marcuse summarises under the term 'cultural revolution':

> In the West, this term first suggests ideological developments which rush ahead of the development of the social *basis*. Cultural revolution – but not (yet) political or economical revolution. Whilst changes have occurred in art, literature and music in forms of communication, in morals and customs, which cause new experiences, a radical re-evaluation of values does not seem to alter the social structure and its political forms of expression very much, or at least lags behind cultural changes. 'Cultural revolution' implies, at the same time, that radical opposition today extends in a new way to the region beyond material needs and aims towards wholly reorganising traditional culture in general.[57]

The theatre avant-garde movement, which included the Bread and Puppet Theatre, the La Mama Theatre, the Performance Group and the Living Theatre, among others, saw themselves as carrying out and being part of this cultural revolution.

In November 1967, Grotowski and Cieslak held a four-week course on methodology at the New York University School of the Arts. The first edition of *Towards a Poor Theatre* was published in September 1968. The same year, Twickenham Studios in London filmed a televised version of *Akropolis* with Grotowski's troupe, which was broadcast on New York television on 12 January 1969. The troupe also made their first US tour in 1969, a year after the American authorities originally refused their application for entry visas. While on tour, Grotowski gave four lectures at the Music Academy in Brooklyn, New York. The troupe's performances and Grotowski's lectures had a unique echo – 'I'm sure that since the time when Stanislavsky came to the United States with his Moscow Art Theatre in 1923 no other foreign theatre has made such a great impression' (Stuart W. Little, *Saturday Review* 7 February 1970). Grotowski's theory and practices were enthusiastically adopted by the American avant-garde, ignoring Robert Brustein's warning that 'the American actors' lack 'the powers of self-denial which Grotowski's techniques demand'.

In fact, however, there are at least a few striking correspondences concerning certain pre-conditions. Like Grotowski, the avant-gardists assumed that people who lived in the industrial society lacked the essential dimensions of humanity: 'Wholeness, process/organic growth, concreteness, religious, transcendental experience'.[58] Richard Schechner, founder of the Performance Group and representative of the Environmental Theatre, drew the conclusion that:

> Links must be discovered or forged between industrial societies and non-industrial ones, between individualistic and communal cultures. And a vast reform in the direction of communality – or at least a revision of individualism – is necessary. This reform and revision will leave no aspect of modern society untouched; not economics, government, social life, personal life, aesthetics, or anything else. Theater takes a pivotal position in these movements because the movements are histrionic; a way of focusing attention and demanding change. The marches, demonstrations, street and guerrilla theaters, arrests of well-known and unknown people were for show: symbolic gestures.
>
> (*Ibid.*, pp. 197f)

Schechner hoped to initiate primary changes through a revival or introduction of a ritual theatre.

In the first production by the Performance Group, *Dionysus in 69* (based on Euripides' *The Bacchae*), which ran from 6 June to 27 July 1969, Schechner tried to actualise his idea of the ritual theatre through recourse to Grotowski's theory and practices.

Like Grotowski, Schechner abolished the division between stage and auditorium: the whole theatre became an 'environment'. The spectator should choose the place to sit and be able to change his seat at will during the performance:

The spectator can change his perspective (high, low, near, far); his relationship to the performance (on top of it, in it, a middle distance from it, far away from it); his relationship to other spectators (alone, with a few others, with a bunch of others); whether to be in an open space or in an enclosed space.

(*Ibid.*, pp. 6f)

Whilst for Grotowski the spatial organisation caused a confrontation between actors and spectators, for the Performance Group it should allow the individual spectator a free choice in changing his perspective and the level of his 'involvement'.

There was also a corresponding shift in emphasis concerning the actor who, in the Performance Group – as generally in the American avant-garde – was termed 'performer'. Calling upon Grotowski, Schechner rejected the idea that the performer should present a role or embody it. 'Rather, there is the role and the person of the performer; both role and performer are plainly perceivable by the spectator. *The feelings are those of the performer as stimulated by the actions of the role at the moment of performance*' (*Environmental Theatre*, p. 166). In *Dionysus in 69*, this idea led to the performer using the role in order to act out his wholly personal problems and feelings. Each actor rewrote the role for himself and worked his personal experiences and private biography into it. One 'performer' of Dionysus gave a personal view of how the process worked:

I am not interested in acting. I am involved in the life process of becoming whole. I do many technical exercises which organically suit that process. They act as catalyst for my ability to let essence flow, to let my soul speak through my mind and body. ... I am acting out my disease, the disease that plagues my inner being, that stops the flow ... *Dionysus* is not a play to me. I do not act in *Dionysus*. *Dionysus* is my ritual.[59]

In *Dionysus*, the actor's self-revelation through confrontation with the other became a self-mirroring or showing of private problems and group neuroses to the spectators.

Grotowski's concept of the other was fundamentally changed. The sense of group and audience participation were now held to be the constitutive element of ritual theatre and a therapeutic measure *par excellence*: 'I think that fundamentally the formation of a group is an attempt to create a family, but a family structured from the assumption that the dominance of the parents can be eliminated and that repression can be reduced if not eradicated' (*Environmental Theatre*, p. 255). It was intended that the group create a community which would take action against the egoism and isolation of the individual on the one hand, and his anonymity and conformity, his feeling of being drowned by the masses, on the other. It was conceived as a 'viable dialectic between solitude and being-with-others'. This community of performers should be extended in the performance to include the spectator through audience participation. 'Participation is a way of trying to humanize relationships between performers and spectators' (p. 60).

Audience participation in *Dionysus* was dependent on two conditions:

First, participation occurred at those points where the play stopped being a play and became a social event – when spectators felt that they were free to enter the performance as equals ... The second point is that most of the participation in *Dionysus* was according to the democratic model: letting people into the play to do as the performers were doing, to 'join the story'.

(Schechner, *Environmental Theatre*, p. 44)

This type of participation began the minute the public was admitted to the theatre with a special 'opening ceremony', which Schechner created on the basis of van Gennep's descriptions of initiation rites in *Rites of Passage*. The spectators could participate in the birth ritual (of Dionysus) at the beginning of the performance and, later, the death ritual (of Pentheus) as well as in the Bacchanalian dance at the conclusion: 'Together we can make a community. We can celebrate together. Be joyous together. So join us in what we do next. It's a circle dance around the sacred spot of my birth' (*Dionysus*).

Schechner designed the birth and death rituals which formed the dominants of the performance according to a ritual of adoption among the Asmati people in New Guinea. In the first performance, the actors wore only minimal clothing, later, none. Moreover, only spectators who were also naked were permitted to attend: a group of men lay on the floor side by side whilst the women stood over them with legs spread out, leaning slightly forwards, so that a tunnel to represent the birth channel was formed. At the beginning of the performance the actor playing Dionysus was reborn as god – he was pushed through the 'birth channel' by their rhythmic hip movements. At the death of Pentheus, this movement was repeated in reverse direction: instead of being ripped to pieces, Pentheus was symbolically swallowed by the community which as an individual he had tried to dominate.

Without doubt, Schechner turned the birth and death ritual into a powerful and effective theatrical symbol of man's rebirth out of the body of the community, or alternatively, of the Dionysian unity of birth and death. But in this symbol something was *represented*, not *carried out*: a 'transformation' of the participants, whether actor or spectator did not take place. It cannot take place. The representatives of a new 'ritual' theatre clearly did not take into account that rituals may not – like articles of consumption – be replanted at will, and that they can only function in a community in which the myths on which they are founded are still a living part of community life. An Asmati adoption rite carried out by young American actors in New York cannot turn Americans into a 'communal being'.

In Grotowski's poor theatre, the body of the actor possessed transforming power because the actor 'annihilates it, burns it … sacrifices it' (*Towards a Poor Theatre*, p. 34). In *Dionysus in 69*, on the other hand – as in other productions by the avant-garde companies – the naked body of the performer and his private neuroses are simply put on show. That which is expressed is merely 'a delight in showing off, in

displaying the body. Coupled with exhibitionism is a certain amount of voyeurism. The one who wants to be looked at is complemented by the one who wants to look. There was understandably a lot of this in *Dionysus in 69*, a play largely based on the relationship between exhibitionists and voyeurs' (Schechner, *Environmental Theatre*, p. 114f.).

Indeed, the naked body played a prominent role in American avant-garde theatre of the late 1960s and early 1970s – if not as transforming power, then at least in 'cultural-revolutionary' protest. 'Going naked' was 'a rejection of the system' and at the same time 'an affirmation of the body' (*Environmental Theatre*, p. 114). The tradition of suppressing human urges as demanded by Protestant ethics and propounded in the Western world in general since the Enlightenment was not only still alive in Puritan America of the 1960s, but also dominant. The vital body filled with desires was excluded from public culture. The nakedness of the avant-garde arose as an expression of opposition. Showing the naked body in theatre, or in public, was meant as a protest against the suppression of human urges and to demand that human nature was recognised. 'In the sixties what we tried to liberate was the actor's body'.[60] This 'liberation of the body' marked a fundamental cultural change in the Western world. Only on the basis of this could the development of a new identity be made available to members of Western culture. For the body, in particular,

the living and lived body, is an element constitutive of the self. Even if (*per impossibile*, I believe) there should seem some way of conceiving of the self as existing independently of its body, yet if we do conceive of it having a body we must conceive of it having it essentially. That is, unlike any other of its actual possessions (e.g. its house), there is no way of conceiving of the self independently of conceiving of its body, if we once conceive of its having a body at all. We can conceive of a person without conceiving of his house, but if we try to conceive of him without his body we can no longer do so … My body is mine *and* me; it is primordially mine; and it is so just insofar as it is not thematized, not identified *as* mine. It does not presuppose the independent identifiability of the self which owns it because it is not a simple owned object. As body-subject it is an element constitutive of the self, the subject.[61]

In some respects, the 'liberation of the body' carried out by the American avant-garde continued Büchner's concrete utopia of physical nature. It created the pre-conditions for a 'rebirth of man 'out of the body' – something which had been suppressed and excluded from public discourse in Western culture for centuries.

## 'Men of new flesh'

> Mankind will only survive the total crash-test on the human collective in this, perhaps our last, century (if resistance runs dry and its place between the poles crumbles) as a collective. The founding Communist principle, NONE, IF NOT ALL is given its ultimate meaning in the context of the possible suicide of the species. But the first step in cancelling out the individual in this collective is tearing him apart, death or caesarean the alternative of the NEW MAN. The theatre simulates this step, pleasure-den and torture-chamber of metamorphosis.[62]

With these words from 1983, Heiner Müller's theatre takes up the thoroughly different strands of tradition started by Nietzsche and Artaud, Brecht and Beckett and the ritual theatre of the American avant-garde.

Heiner Müller had been writing for the theatre since the 1950s. His so-called 'Stücken aus der Production' (production plays), such as *Der Lohndrücker* (*The Wage Squeezer*, 1965), *Die Korrektur* (*Correction*, 1957), *Die Bauern* (*Peasants*, 1956), *Der Bau* (*Building*, 1964), are principally concerned with the problems of socialist reconstruction in East Germany. Alongside these concerns, however, he quickly began to confront the question of the historical conditions responsible for the success (or

failure) of revolution. Müller deals with it partly through recourse to ancient and classical material as in, for example, *Philoktet* (*Philoctetes*, 1958–64), *Herakles* (*Heracles*, 1964), *Ödipus Tyrann* (*Oedipus the Tyrant*, 1965), *Der Horatier* (*The Horatian*, 1968), *Macbeth* (1972), and partly by reflecting on the 'German misery', for example in *Die Schlacht* (*Slaughter*, written in 1951, reworked and published in 1974), *Germania Tod in Berlin* (*Germania Death in Berlin*, 1951/71) and, finally, *Leben Gundlings Friedrich von Preußen Lessings Schlaf Traum Schrei* (*Gundling's Life – Frederick of Prussia Lessing's Sleep Dream Scream*, 1976).

Whilst the 'production plays' continued to a large extent Brecht's dramaturgical theories, and even the plays drawing on the reception of the ancient classics were related to Brecht's model *Lehrstücke* in that the new type of play derived from, and yet criticised Brecht's *Lehrstücke* theory and practice, Heiner Müller broke away entirely with this form of dramaturgy in the mid-1970s.

> I believe we must take leave of the LEHRSTÜCK until the next earthquake. Christian apocalyptic MEASUREMENT has run out of time, history has postponed the trial onto the streets, even the trained choirs do not sing any more, humanism seems to be nothing more than terrorism, the Molotov cocktail has become the ultimate middle-class learning experience. What remains: isolated texts waiting for history.
>
> (Letter to Reiner Steinweg, editor of *Lehrstücke*, 4 January 1977)

Müller's *Germania Death in Berlin* was, to a large extent, an experiment consisting of citations from earlier works and the montage of fragments. From the mid-1970s, Müller explicitly stated this method of working as his programme:

> There is no dramatic literature as rich in fragments as German literature. It has to do with the fragmentary nature of our (theatre) history, with the constant rupture of ties between literature, theatre and audience (society) which results from it. ... The need of yesterday is the virtue of today:

the fragmentation of a process emphasises its procedural character, stops the production being lost in the product, in commercialism, makes the depiction a laboratory, in which the audience can co-produce. I do not believe that a story with 'hands and feet' (the plot in the classical sense) can still cope with reality.

(Letter to Linzer, 1975)

Müller's new dramaturgy draws, in this respect, upon Brecht's epic theatre; the work is declared a 'field of experiment', a 'laboratory' and the active role of co-producer is handed over to the recipient – the reader and/or spectator who will carry out or continue the experiment in his own way. On the other hand, Müller also comes close to Beckett in that both reject the idea of a coherent plot and make that which is fragmentary, broken, into the source of dramatic creation. In Beckett, however, the fragment is a product of reduction and of the history of decay and is employed in the work in such a way that the text lies before the eyes of the recipient as a dismembered body, for whom a rebirth seems impossible – thus quoting the dismembered body of Pentheus at the end of *The Bacchae*. But Müller's fragments gain – as Walter Benjamin's fragments 'which have been exploded out of the homogenous process of history' (*Geschichtsphilosophische Thesen*, XVIII) – a somewhat subversive reference to the future:

The rift between text and author, situation and character provokes / exposes the explosion of continuity. If cinema can watch death at work (Godard), theatre deals with the horror / joy of transformation in the unity of birth and death.

(Letter to Linzer, 1975)

In this sense, Müller's new fragmentary dramaturgy refers not only to Nietzsche and Artaud, but also to Grotowski's 'holy' actor and the ritual theatre of the American avant-garde.

The dramaturgy tried out in part in *Germania Death in Berlin* was further developed from the mid-1970s, principally in *Gundling's Life*, in *Hamletmaschine* (*Hamlet-Machine*, 1977), *Verkommenes Ufer Medeamaterial Landschaft mit Argonauten* (*Waterfront Wasteland Medea-Material Landscape with Argonauts*, 1982) and *Bildbeschreibung* (*Description of a Picture*, 1985). Müller's excessive use of self-quotation – modified in part – makes the individual plays seem less defined, separate works and more different stages of one continuing, self-corrective and expanding *work in progress*. It would be a mistake, however, to assume there is any sense of the random or even aleatoric behind the aesthetic principle in Müller's work. The plays reveal a high degree of structure, even if on the first reading they seem to give the impression of entropy.

The *Hamlet-Machine*, for example, follows strict principles of composition. The short, barely nine-page, text is organised into five scenes which correspond to the five acts of the Shakespearean – and classical – drama. The first and fourth scenes are dedicated to Hamlet, the second and fifth to Ophelia. The Hamlet and Ophelia scenes closely refer to each other through a wealth of allusions, cross-references, quotation, repetitions, etc. The third, middle scene brings Hamlet and Ophelia together. Whilst the other scenes contain only monologue, here a 'dialogue' takes place:

OPHELIA: Do you want to eat my heart, Hamlet. [*Laughs*]
HAMLET: [*Hands covering his face*] I want to be a woman.[63]

Hamlet and Ophelia appear as the protagonists of the play – as citations of figures whose drama has already taken place. Their roles are fixed forever in Shakespeare's text. This raises a problem which confronts Müller's two quotational dramatic figures from the very beginning: should they follow their roles, which were created for them and written down elsewhere or should they break with the roles handed down to them and create new ones?

On his first appearance, Hamlet already seems to have distanced himself from his role: 'I was Hamlet. I stood at the waterfront and talked to the surf BLAH BLAH BLAH, behind me the ruins of Europe' (p. 87). He goes on to relate, in the past tense, the story of Hamlet who 'stopped' the burial procession at the state funeral of his father, opened the coffin, cut up 'the dead father' into pieces and handed it out to the people, the 'wretched creatures' standing hungrily by. This story took place in the past and had nothing to do with Hamlet even then; 'I lay down on the ground and heard the world doing its rounds in step with decay' (p. 87).

The first scene can be divided into five passages. The first narrative passage, distanced through the imperfect tense, follows a montage of quotes or allusions which refer to *Hamlet*, *Richard III*, T.S. Eliot's *Ash-Wednesday* and Heiner Müller's *Der Bau*.

> I'M GOOD HAMLET GI'ME A CAUSE FOR GRIEF / AH THE WHOLE GLOBE FOR A REAL SORROW / RICHARD THE THIRD I THE PRINCE KILLING KING / OH MY PEOPLE WHAT HAVE I DONE UNTO THEE / LIKE A HUMP I'M LUGGING MY HEAVY BRAIN / SECOND CLOWN IN THE COMMUNIST SPRING / SOMETHING IS ROTTEN IN THIS AGE OF HOPE / LETS DELVE IN EARTH AND BLOW HER AT THE MOON.
>
> (p. 87)

This montage functions as a 'monologue' in which Hamlet patches together his justification for being concerned with events and taking action out of ready-made speech fragments. However, this justification cannot persuade him, as the next passage reveals. Hamlet moves from the preterite to the present tense and excuses himself from any kind of historical continuity:

> Here comes the ghost that begot me, the axe still in his skull. You can keep your hat on, I know you've got one hole too many. I wish my mother had had one less when you were still dressed in flesh; it would have spared me myself. Women should be stitched up, a world without mothers. We could get on with butchering each other in peace and quiet, and with some chance of success,

when life gets to be too long, or our throats too tight for our screaming.

> (pp. 87–8)

The end of history of which Hamlet is dreaming seems only possible at the end of humanity: it is only when the women are forcibly prevented from giving birth that the endless chain of violence, counter-violence, killing and being killed can be broken. History will end – but only at the price of human life, 'Dawn will not take place any more' (p. 88).

In the fourth section, Hamlet reflects on another way of bringing history to a standstill and ending violence – the possibility of rejecting the custom and tradition of revenge killing and violence by consciously refusing to carry out the next deed of violence:

> SHALL I / BECAUSE IT'S CUSTOMARY STICK A PIECE / OF STEEL INTO / THE NEXT FLESH OR INTO THE NEXT / BUT ONE FOR ME / TO HANG ON BECAUSE THE EARTH IS / SPINNING ROUND / LORD BREAK MY NECK IN A FALL FROM AN ALEHOUSE BENCH.
>
> (p. 88)

Despite this, Hamlet returns in the fifth section to 'his tragedy'. He accepts his role, 'I am Hamlet', kills Polonius and rapes his mother in the dramatic present of 'now-time':

> MOTHER'S WOMB IS NOT A ONE-WAY STREET. Now I'm going to tie your hands behind your back with your bridal veil, because your embrace makes me puke. Now I'm going to tear the wedding dress to pieces. Now you have to scream. Now I'm going to daub the rags of your wedding dress with the earth my father has become, your face your abdomen your breasts with the rags. Now I'm going to have you, mother, in his, my father's invisible trail.
>
> (p. 88)

Hamlet carries out that which his role in the tragedy (of Shakespeare and of history) prescribes for him and that which the ghost of his father – the Western tradition – demands of him. With the act of violence against his mother, Hamlet has ultimately identified himself with his father (all his 'fathers' as far back as Oedipus) and treads in their 'footprints': history will continue.

Neither Hamlet's distance as narrator, nor his command of literature, nor his insight into the essence of history and the need to bring it to a standstill, nor even his reflection on the possibility of refusing to do the deed of violence demanded of him have prevented him from taking on the role prescribed for him and identifying himself with his father. The intellectual has proved himself incapable of breaking through the endless chain of violence: with the rape of his mother he adds one more link to the chain and thus guarantees its continuity. Unlike in *The Oresteia*, here, *logos* no longer has the power to inspire a new order. The traditional patriarchal order which Shelley and O'Neill expose to be a deadly order, has corrupted him through and through. Although the intellectual Hamlet may have theoretical doubts, ultimately he will confirm it through his own deed of violence. 'THE FAMILY ALBUM' – the title of the first scene – can be continued.

The fourth scene, entitled 'PEST IN BUDA BATTLE OF GREENLAND', shifts Hamlet to the time of the Hungarian uprising: 'Smoke is belching from the stove in a riot-ridden October / A BAD COLD HE HAD OF IT JUST THE WORST TIME / JUST THE WORST TIME OF THE YEAR FOR A REVOLUTION' (p. 90). In this historic situation, as Stalin's 'monument' lies on the floor 'raised three years after the state funeral of the hated and honoured one by his successor to power' (p. 90), Hamlet, the intellectual, abandons history and gives his role back: '[*He takes off his mask and costume*] Hamlet Performer: I am not Hamlet. I have no more role to play. ... My drama does not take place any more ... I'm not interested any more either. I'm not playing any more' (p. 90). The intellectual has not given up his Hamlet role, however, in order to

bring history to a standstill but rather because he does not want to take clear sides in the uprising: 'My place, if my drama were still to take place, would be on both sides of the front, between the front lines, above them' (p. 91). He falls into a conflict of roles, identifies himself both with the 'crowd' who hurl stones at the 'police soldiers tanks bullet-proof glass' as well as with the 'soldiers inside the tank turret' (p. 91); 'I'll string my uniform up by the ankles' (p. 91). The intellectual reacts to this situation by retreating into his subjectivity: 'I go home, and kill time, at one with my undivided self' (p. 92). He pays for avoiding conflict, unity within himself, with the loss of his public role.

As a private man, he can now enjoy the 'privilege' of disgusting himself without hindrance: in front of the television, 'the prefabricated Blah Blah Blah', the 'prescribed cheerfulness' before the 'struggle for office jobs votes bank accounts', before the 'consumer battle' (p. 92) of the wholly revolting capitalist daily life; he can afford the luxury of subversive, anarchic dreams, 'A kingdom / for a killer' (p. 92), in which the notable Macbeth and Raskolnikoff stand as godfathers who committed murder for subjective reasons: one to acquire power, the other to prove his theory of being the chosen one. Disgust for the capitalist world changes into the negation of any sign of life, 'I don't want to eat drink breathe love a woman a man a child an animal any more, I don't want to die any more. I don't want to kill any more' (p. 93). The conclusion, 'I want to be a machine', is not far away.

The 'photograph of the writer' appears before the life-negating phrase; after it comes the stage direction, 'He tears up the photograph of the writer' – possibly a hint that the author has included himself in the description by/of the intellectual up to now, but that with the ripping up of the photograph, however, now wants to disappear and thereby emancipate himself, the play, and the reader from any narrowing down to biographical references.

Finally, the Hamlet Performer withdraws into a total solipsism: 'I break open my sealed flesh. I want to live in my veins, in the marrow of my bones, in the labyrinth of my skull. I retreat into my entrails. My place is in my shit ... my blood' (p. 93). Whilst Beckett's figures only exist as single parts of the body – head, mouth – and withdraw into the rudiments of their life story, Müller's Hamlet Performer escapes into the innermost part of his body, into the veins, the marrow bone, the entrails, the blood. In both cases, the total solipsism leads to a de-centring of the self.

This retreat into the self allows space for the insight that solipsism is paid for at the price of aggression against others: 'Somewhere bodies are being broken so that I can live in my shit. Somewhere bodies are being opened so that I can be alone with my blood' (p. 93). But nothing stems from this recognition; it simply encourages the desire to make oneself like the smooth running apparatus of a technologically equipped industrial society: 'I want to be a machine. Arms to grab legs to walk no pain no thinking' (p. 93). At this point, the Hamlet Performer puts on 'his mask and costume'. Hamlet betrays – as in the first scene – his better insight. 'He steps into the armour' of his father and 'splits the skulls of MARX LENIN MAO with the axe' who appear as naked women and who each in his/her own language, and at the same time, speak the text, 'THE MAIN POINT IS TO OVERTHROW ALL EXISTING CONDITIONS IN WHICH MAN ...' (p. 93).

HAMLET THE DANE PRINCE AND FODDER FOR WORMS STUMBLING / FROM HOLE TO HOLE TOWARDS THE FINAL HOLE IN APATHY / BEHIND HIM THE GHOST THAT DID / BEGET HIM / GREEN LIKE OPHELIA'S FLESH IN / CHILDBED / AND JUST BEFORE THE 3RD CROW OF THE COCK / A CLOWN TEARS / TO SHREDS THE JINGLE DRESS OF THE PHILOSOPHER / AN OBESE / BLOODHOUND CRAWLS INTO THE ARMOUR.

(p. 93)

With his act of violence – once again, against women – Hamlet, the intellectual, has become a traitor to the revolution and mankind: '*Snow. Ice age*'. The dominance of the male – logocentric and phallocentric, the violent ego which identifies itself with the father – has, in history, led mankind towards catastrophe. There is no hope for the future.

Ophelia is placed in opposition to this Hamlet. Each of Hamlet's three- and four-page scenes is followed by a short, half-page scene with Ophelia. Ophelia decisively opposes Hamlet's distanced 'I was Hamlet' with 'I am Ophelia'. The first Ophelia scene bears the title 'Europe of the Woman' (p. 89). The place of action is an 'enormous room', which alludes to the French prison camp in the First World War from the novel of the same name by e.e. cummings. Ophelia attempts to escape from her prison, from the century-old role of woman being destroyed by men and co-operating in her own self-destruction, with which she identifies wholly at the beginning: 'I am Ophelia. The one the river didn't keep. The woman dangling from the rope. The woman with slit arteries. The woman with the overdose SNOW ON HER LIPS. The woman with the head in the gas oven' (p. 89).

When Ophelia recognises that her body belongs to her, when she refuses to continue working on her own self-destruction, her self-liberation begins, 'Yesterday I stopped killing myself. I am alone with my breasts my thighs my womb' (p. 89). Now she can pull down her prison walls, 'I demolish the battlefield that was my home', and free herself from every outside determination, 'I dig the clock that was my heart from out of my breast. I go out on to the streets, dressed in blood' (p. 89).

The image of the clock has particular significance. On the one hand, it shows the degree to which she is determined by others, and under which she suffers: she has internalised the instrument of mechanical time measurement on which modern civilisation of the industrial society is built so totally that it – as her heart – determines her life rhythms. In digging the clock out of her breast she frees her organism from the dictates of the machine. In contrast,

Hamlet wants to be 'a machine'. On the other hand, this act of liberation alludes to Benjamin's *Geschichtsphilosophische Thesen*:

> The awareness that the continuum of history is being exploded is unique to the revolutionary classes in the moment of their action. The great revolution introduces a new calendar. The day which fixes the beginning of the calendar also functions as a historical fast forward. It is basically the same day which constantly returns in the form of anniversaries, remembrance days. Such calendars do not count time like clocks. They are monuments to an awareness of history, something there has not been the faintest sign of for centuries any more in Europe.
>
> (XV)

Müller's allusion to *Geschichtsphilosophische Thesen* reveals Ophelia's self-liberation to be a revolutionary act which explodes the continuum of history. With it begins a new measurement of time. In that Ophelia disassociates herself from her role as a woman suppressed and abused by men, and breaks with her role as victim, she rejects the 'patriarchal' history which rests on the continuity of those who act and those who are acted upon. Her self-liberation leads her, thus, 'onto the streets' – towards the revolutionary masses. Hamlet, in contrast, in the fourth section, will leave the rioting masses on the streets and decide: 'I go home'. Whilst in the identification with his father, Hamlet repeats the past acts of violence which guarantee the continuity of history, against his better judgement, Ophelia explodes it and thus rekindles the flames of hope.

Hamlet and Ophelia represent a sequence of oppositions such as male/female; perpetrator/victim; *logos* (the intellectual)/*physis* (the abused, tortured body); counter-revolutionary/revolutionary; bound to the past/bound to the future.

In the third section, entitled 'SCHERZO', a transposition of these categories is implied. The dead women from the 'ballet' of the dead women, such as 'The woman dangling from the rope. The woman with the slit arteries', tear the clothes from Hamlet's body – as Orsina dreamed of doing in *Emilia Galotti*:

> Ah! … What a heavenly fantasy! If we one day – all of us, his victims – a whole army of deserted women – transformed into Bacchantes, into furies – if we could have him in our midst, tear him to pieces, dismember him, hunt through his entrails to find the heart that he promised to every one of us, the traitor, and gave to none! Ah, what a dance that would be!
>
> (IV, 7, p. 89)

Hamlet wants 'to be a woman', 'puts on Ophelia's clothes' and 'Ophelia smears a whore's mask on his face'.

A similar change in categories in *Gundling's Life* releases an almost Dionysian, world-recreating power: Emilia Galotti and Nathan the Wise recite key passages from their roles ('Force! Force! Who cannot resist force?', and Nathan recites the ending of the Ring parable).

[*Police siren. Emilia and Nathan exchange their heads, undress embrace kill each other. White light. Death of the machine on the electric chair. Stage goes black*]

VOICE (AND PROJECTION)

HOUR OF WHITE HEAT DEAD BUFFALOS FROM THE CANYONS SQUADS OF SHARKS TEETH OF BLACK LIGHT THE ALLIGATORS MY FRIENDS GRAMMAR OF EARTHQUAKES WEDDING OF FIRE AND WATER MEN OF A NEW FLESH LAUTREAMONTMALDOROR PRINCE OF ATLANTIS SON OF THE DEAD.

(p. 78)[64]

The change of sex, coupling, and the killing of Emilia/Nathan is shown through the images of the projection to be a cosmic marriage ('wedding of fire and water') which will create 'men of a new flesh'. Carried out in the 'hour of white heat' and after the 'grammar of earthquakes' – traditional symbols of the appearance of a god – the act receives a utopian dimension which is given further emphasis through the 'Prince of Atlantis'. This utopia alludes both to the apocalyptic end of the old world in 'death of the machine' as well as the beginning of a new one brought about by 'men of a new flesh'. The reversal of opposing categories through Emilia/Nathan's change of sexes (dismemberment), coupling, and death releases an enormous utopian potential.

In *Hamlet-Machine*, by contrast, no such reversal/transformation takes place. Reduced purely to the exchange of clothes and roles, it seems to be a 'scherzo/playful' intermezzo between Hamlet's act of violence against his mother and his betrayal of the revolution. The light of the theophany at the end of the scene radiated from the Madonna with breast cancer: 'The breast cancer shines like a sun' (p. 94).

The title of the final scene after the 'ice age' is a fragment from a late work by Hölderlin: 'Maddening Endurance / Inside the Dreaded Armour / Millennia'. It is set in the 'Deep sea … Fish / wreckage / corpses and limbs drift by' (p. 94). Space and time are only enigmatically given. Do 'millennia' and 'deep sea' mean a return to mythical times and spaces? The dawning of history in nature? Or are they a projection of the four-dimensional 'spacetime' as modern physics describes it: a cancelling of absolute, measurable, time which is the same for all so that instead, 'each individual has his own personal measure of time that depends on where he is and how he is moving'?[65] Does 'deep sea' refer to the sunken Atlantis or rather to water as a symbol of the soul and the sub-conscious, of the pre-birth condition and femininity?

In this polyvalent scene Ophelia announces her revolutionary message, the broken body of her historical existence immobile in the wheelchair, thus alluding to Hamm in Beckett's *Endgame*: 'TWO MEN dressed in surgeons' gowns wrap muslin all around her and the wheelchair from the bottom to the top' (p. 94).

Here speaks Electra. In the heart of darkness. Under the sun of torture. To the metropols of the world. In the name of the victims. I discharge all the sperm I ever received. I transform the milk from my breasts into deadly poison. I take back the world which I gave birth to. Between my thighs I strangle the world that I gave birth to. I bury it in my crotch. Down with the happiness of surrender. Long live hatred, contempt, uprising, death. When it walks through your bedrooms with butcher's knives you will know the truth.

(p. 94)

Ophelia has transformed herself into Electra. The life-giving and life-sustaining parts of her body with which she was 'alone' for the first time in Scene 2 after the men repeatedly abused her – breasts, thighs, lap – have become instruments of destruction. Like Medea in *Medea-material*, Ophelia/Electra takes back 'the world' she 'gave birth to'. The path of human life towards death is a repetition of that towards birth (as in Schechner's birth and death ritual in *Dionysus in 69*). Ophelia carries out a radical reversal of which Hamlet in 'SCHERZO' was incapable. She announces a total break with the past, absolute discontinuity. Her message is aimed at the 'metropols of the world', at industrial society. She speaks in the name of the victims – the women, the exploited masses, the suppressed peoples of the Third World. And she speaks into the future, 'you will know the truth'. In so doing, she inevitably poses the question whether, and to what extent, her announcement of the 'good news' of discontinuity is capable of igniting utopian potential.

*Hamlet-Machine* has been described as 'Heiner Müller's Endgame'. Ophelia remains alone on stage at the end, silent and 'motionless in white muslin wrapping'. Her revolutionary impulse is suffocated and silenced by men who are similar to the psychiatrists busy with straitjackets in *Gundling's Life*. At the end there is only failure.

This interpretation overlooks fundamental differences. *Endgame* and *Hamlet-Machine* do indeed deal with Western history and follow it through to the apocalypse. But whilst in *Endgame* time stands still, in *Hamlet-Machine* it has an unstoppable, futuristic dimension. In this sense, the wrapping up at the end could also be read as cocooning, or a kind of pupation and, thus, as the promise of a future. Furthermore, Ophelia's message is the realisation of a present utopia, for whilst the many quotes and allusions to/from other text(s) in Hamlet's speeches are clearly marked and the sense of his speech can only be understood through recourse to the subject speaking – his situation, intention, reflection – in Ophelia's speech, the different quotes produce a continuous unity with her 'own' words: 'Im Herzen der Finsternis', cites Joseph Conrad's novel, *The Heart of Darkness*, which deals with young Captain Marlow's travels into Central Africa and describes the journey to the 'heart' of the 'dark' continent as a journey of discovery into the un- and sub-conscious. 'The wretched of this earth' refers to Sartre's preface to Frantz Fanon's *The Wretched of the Earth*. 'When it walks through your bedrooms with butcher's knives you will know the truth' is taken from a witness account by the anarchist Susan Atkins who was a member of the Manson 'family' and, at the same time it is reminiscent of Rosa Luxemburg's 'I was, I am, I will be', with which she ended her article in the *Red Flag* in 1919. 'Deep sea' might then also allude to Luxemburg's murder by drowning in the Landwehrkanal.

Ophelia's speech presents itself as a polyphonous text in which the authors have disappeared; 'Work on making the authors disappear is resistance against the disappearance of mankind'. In this sense, Ophelia's speech realises the utopia of the 'universal discourse which excludes nothing and no-one'.[66] Her speech is the *Vor-Schein* (fore-shadow) of a better future – just as is her silence which follows.

Finally, the ending – like the entire text – is open to the reader/spectator and thus each can unfold the utopian potential within himself. For, 'drama is not made on stage, it does not happen on stage, but between stage and auditorium'. Theatre 'is born out of the tension between stage and auditorium, out of the provocation of the text' (Müller, *Rotwelsch*, pp. 110–92).

After the première of *Hamlet-Machine* by Jean Jourdheuil (30 January 1979, at the Théâtre Gérard Phillipe, Saint-Denis), most theatres had difficulties with the play. Some repeated attempts have been made to illustrate the text scenically – in vain, as one can imagine. Robert Wilson was the only artist to refuse to illustrate the text in this way. In his New York and Hamburg productions of the *Hamlet-Machine* (in June and November 1986) with acting students, he unchained the text from its figures or roles, following his own aesthetic principles.

By not illustrating the text scenically, but confronting it with his very American (underworld) figures, [he] forces what is said into the ears and brain. The text is experienced in an acoustic space, where it is mostly difficult to tell if it is created directly or through a microport and loudspeaker. It is only seldom directly spoken by a figure, without this electronic diversion. It is not experienced visually but acoustically. Thereby with great clarity and plasticity. All italicised sections of the text which were held to be scenic directions by other directors (with obvious shortcomings) were only spoken. For example, 'Hamlet puts on Ophelia's clothes. Ophelia smears a whore's mask on his face'. Only one of these italicised sentences remained unspoken, non-verbal. It was interpreted scenically: a figure holds out in front of him a photo of Heiner Müller, 25cms by 25cms, tears it exactly in the middle, from top to bottom ... The text is acoustically produced: through repetitions, overlappings. In the terrible course of things the distortions in tone increase. The scratching fingers of the three beauties on the metal table penetrate the text: 'With my bleeding hands I rip up the photographs of the men whom I loved whom I was used by on the bed on the table on the chair on the floor' (Ophelia, Scene 2).

The American night of Wilson's images and Müller's bitter-German text seem to correspond with each other in such scenes; in the main, however, the gloomy-dark *Hamlet-Machine* is not brightened by the figures and the movements they exercise but instead by the slow, clear, frequently repetitive, textual lecture which makes them very plastic.[67]

Robert Wilson, who himself says, 'I don't understand Heiner Müller's text', clearly agrees in important aspects with Heiner Müller, who confesses, 'The things that I say, I neither can, nor want, to fix to figures any more … It is evermore random who says or plays what' (*Rotwelsch*, p. 185).

Heiner Müller and Robert Wilson first worked together in May 1984 on Wilson's Cologne production of the mammoth project *the CIVIL warS*. Heiner Müller put the text material together for Act IV, scene A, which almost exclusively consisted of quotations: from a letter by Friedrich Wilhelm I of Prussia to his son (later Frederick the Great), *Hamlet*, Kafka's *Letter to a Father*, *Timon of Athens*, *Phaedra*, *The Elf King*, *Empedocles*, Wilson's texts, Naita di Niscemis, and repeatedly from his own texts – *Father* (1958), *Gundling's Life*, *Mauser* (1970) and *Der Auftrag* (*The Contract*, 1979). It was only in the eighth scene, the dying scene (the death of Frederick the Great), that this principle was not adhered to. Here the names of battlefields, bomb targets, concentration camps and prisons which have earned tragic fame in German history were enumerated. The text material was thus chosen and put together to illuminate ever different facets of 'patriarchal violence' and the identification of the son with the violent father as fateful factors in history, particularly German history. Wilson contrasted these texts with widely different images: a giant turtle in the water, an arctic landscape and a spaceship, a volcano and dancing bears, a string of faces, Frederick the Great under a chair, a man and a woman on a bear, a flying eagle, houses collapsing and laughing men, a boat, a row of numbers. There was no possible connection between the text and the images.

The most important aesthetic principles of Wilson since his earliest work in the late 1960s and early 1970s, lie in the unharnessing of the spoken text both from the scenic processes happening on stage as well as from the actors' bodies (the spoken texts are mostly played back on tape or at least electronically transformed); in an enormous slowing down of the actors' movements towards a pronounced form of a slow-motion and in the 'equalisation' of the actor's body with the other objects presented on stage. The actors do not represent figures and do not play roles any more. The body of the actor becomes part of a dreamlike image which floats by, offering no semantic unity.

In this way, the spectator is opened to the possibility of being amazed by the processes on stage – like his own images in a dream – as a unique, at first strange, world, whose elements seem familiar without being bound to one another in any ordered unity of meaning. If the spectator allows himself to become involved in the concrete givens of this world without haste and stress and without the urge to ascribe a meaning to everything at once, the associative relations he makes can release in him new experiences and unlock unforeseen potential meanings.

Heiner Müller clearly recognised in Wilson's work the fundamental principles of his own aesthetic. In a note on Wilson's theatre, he wrote:

Robert Wilson steps out of the room into which Ambrose Bierce disappeared after he saw the terrors of the Civil War. The '*Wiedergänger*' (the resurrected) carries the shock under his skin. His theatre is the resurrection. The redemption of the dead takes place in slow motion. With the wisdom of the fairy-tale that the history of mankind cannot be separated from the history of animals, plants, stones, machines unless at the price of downfall, the *CIVIL warS* formulates the theme of the era: the war of classes and race, between the species and sexes, civil war in every sense. On this stage there is room for Kleist's Marionettentheater, a dance floor for Brecht's epic theatre. An art without effort, each step plants a new path. The dancing god is the marionette, his/her dance creates man of new flesh, which will be born out of the wedding of fire and water, of which Rimbaud dreamed. Just as the apple on the tree of knowledge must be eaten once more so that man can find the condition of innocence again, the Tower of Babylon must be built again so that confusion in languages has an end. A TREE IS BEST MEASURED WHEN IT IS DOWN. But the cut-down forests will continue to grow under the earth. The noise of the stock-exchange will not survive the silence of the stage that is the ground of their language. When the panthers walk between the counters of the World Bank and the eagles in flight rip the banners of separation, the theatre of the resurrection will have found its stage. A TREE IS BEST MEASURED WHEN IT IS DOWN.

The collaboration with Robert Wilson on *the CIVIL warS* has left clear traces on the later work of Heiner Müller – his theatrical practice has become even more radicalised. In *Bildbeschreibung* (*Description of a Picture*, 1985), he states, 'things which I say' are no longer fixed 'to the figures'. A text produced explicitly for the theatre presents itself as a loosely connected prose text without paragraphs or full stops, only divided by commas and colons. It contains neither figures nor situation.

The text starts from a coloured picture drawn by a Bulgarian stage-design student – in this respect it can be subsumed under the genre 'description of a picture', and extensively cites paintings from the Surrealist tradition, among others, René Magritte's 'Transfer', The Domain of Arnheim' and 'Pleasure'. Following the text is the note, 'BILDBESCHREIBUNG can be read as a palimpsest of ALCESTIS, which cites the *no* play KUMASAKA, the 11th song of the ODYSSEY, Hitchcock's THE BIRDS, and Shakespeare's TEMPEST'.[68]

In making excessive reference to foreign paintings and texts without marking the 'citation' as such in the text, *Bildbeschreibung* appears to be a realisation of that 'universal discourse which excludes nothing and no-one', a discourse which speaks with one voice and thus makes the 'individual' authors disappear. A new text body has been reborn out of the fragments of foreign texts – out of the dismembered text corpus of Western culture.

On the other hand, the text material is organised in such a way that it can be read as a reflection on the relationship constituted by theatre 'between stage and auditorium'. By declaring itself to be a description of a painting, the text defines the reception process as a process of production: the reception of the painting is carried out as the production of a text in which, as the simultaneity of the image is translated into linguistic sequences, the two-dimensional space of the painting becomes time. In this way, the unity of reception and production creates a unity of time and space, a time–space.

The theatre which plays in this time–space presents – free of any chronology – the eternal return of the dead, man's 'perhaps daily murder' of 'the perhaps daily resurrected woman' (p. 11); 'the image of an experiment, the rawness of a sketch, the expression of disgust for the laboratory animals man, bird, woman, the blood-pump of daily murder, man against woman and bird, woman against bird and man, bird against woman and man, provides the planet with fuel, blood, ink, which describe his paper life with colour, also threatens his anaemic sky through the resurrection of the flesh' (p. 13). The theatre perpetuates the past for all time through the continual repetition of the ever-same acts of violence. Redemption can only come by breaking the continuity 'wanted: the gap in the procedure, the other in the return of the same, the stutter in the wordless text, the hole in eternity, the perhaps one, redemptive MISTAKE' (p. 13). Such a mistake could be caused by the 'wild gaze of the murderer' or when he 'tests the neck of his victim on the chair with his hands, with the blade of a knife' or by 'a woman's laugh which for a single moment stops the strangling grip, and makes the hand holding the knife shake' and then, perhaps, 'the nose-dive of the bird, attracted by the glistening blade, landing on the man's skull, two pecks of the beak right and left, frenzy and roaring by the blind, blood spurting in the tumult of the storm, which the woman seeks' might actually happen (pp. 13f). A mistake such as this, which so abruptly interrupts the continuity of eternal repetition, would give the spectator the chance to experience 'Fear, that the mistake might happen in the blinking of an eye, the eyeslit in the time between one blink and another ... lightning-like uncertainty in the certainty of the dreadful: MURDER is sex-change, BEING FOREIGN IN ONE'S OWN BODY, the knife is the wound, the nape of the neck the axe' (p. 14). The productive reversal achieved by Ophelia in *Hamlet-Machine*, and by Emilia and Nathan in *Gundling's Life*, depends on the effort of the recipient, 'The first appearance of what is new [is] horror' (Müller, *Rotwelsch*, p. 98). And in that the recipient asks the question, 'who OR WHAT cares for the image', he will be able to include himself in a reversal which releases the future 'LIVING IN THE MIRROR is the man with the dance-step I, my grave his face, I the woman with the wound on the neck, right and left in my hands the split bird, blood on the mouth, I, the bird who shows the murderer the path to night in the writing of its beak, I the frozen storm' (p. 14). The Dionysian-transforming 'ripping apart of the individual' is carried out in the act of reception; it dissolves the unity of the self – the recipient – and unites him with man, woman, bird, the storm. The recipient becomes part of that which is received, into which he becomes integrated – in fragments – into which he disappears. In this way, the act of reception is a preparation for the 'wedding of fire and water' which will create 'men of new flesh'.

'I write in another time from that in which I live' (Müller, *Rotwelsch*, p. 79). For this reason – or despite it – Heiner Müller has denied himself the creation of 'new man' as a reality in the here and now which Grotowski and the ritual theatre of the American avant-garde attempted by making the performance a *rite de passage*. The birth of the 'new man', which the theatre had announced at the turn of the century, can only be anticipated even today, as an aesthetic fore-shadow when carrying out the process of reception/production. 'Theatre has to be a projection of Utopia, or it's not worth anything' (Müller, *Rotwelsch*, p. 92).

# Notes

1 Jean-Jacques Rousseau, *Discours sur les sciences et les arts / Lettre à d'Alembert sur les spectacles*, edited and introduced by Jean Varloot, Paris: Editions Gallimard, 1987, p. 423.
2 See Helmut Plessner, *Die Frage nach der Conditio humana*, Frankfurt: Suhrkamp, 1976.
3 See Helmut Plessner, 'Zur Anthropologie des Schauspielers', in H. Plessner, *Gesammelte Schriften*, vol. VII, Frankfurt am Main: Suhrkamp, 1982, pp. 399–418.
4 Milton Singer (ed.) *Traditional India: Structure and Change*, Philadelphia: American Folklore Society, 1959, pp. xiif.
5 Stephen Greenblatt, *Shakespearean Negotiations. The Circulation of Social Energy in Renaissance England*, Regents of the University of California, 1988.
6 Judith Butler, 'Performative Acts and Gender Constitution', in Sue-Ellen Case (ed.) *Performing Feminism*, Baltimore: Johns Hopkins University Press, 1990, pp. 270f.
7 Max Reinhardt, 'Rede über den Schauspieler', in Heinz Herald (ed.) *Max Reinhardt. Bildnis eines Theatermannes*, Hamburg: Rowolt, 1953, pp. 93–8, 97.
8 Max Herrmann, 'Bühne und Drama', *Vossische Zeitung* 30 July 1918.
9 David de Levita, *Der Begriff der Identität*, Frankfurt: Suhrkamp, 1976.

## 1 RITUAL THEATRE

1 Christian Meier, *Die Entstehung des Politischen bei den Griechen*, Frankfurt am Main: Suhrkamp, 1983, p. 151.
2 Aeschylus, *The Libation Bearers*, trans. Richmond Lattimore, in *The Complete Greek Tragedies*, vol. II, eds David Grene and Richmond Lattimore, Chicago and London: University of Chicago Press, 1960, pp. 1–45.
3 Aeschylus, *The Eumenides*, trans. Richmond Lattimore, in *The Complete Greek Tragedies*, vol. III, eds David Grene and Richmond Lattimore, Chicago and London: University of Chicago Press, 1960, pp. 1–43.
4 Karl Reinhardt, *Tradition und Geist*, Göttingen: Vandenhoeck & Ruprecht, 1960, p. 256.
5 Sophocles, *Antigone*, trans. Elizabeth Wyckoff, in *the Complete Greek Tragedies* vol. I, eds David Grene and Richmond Lattimore, Chicago and London: University of Chicago Press, 1960, pp. 117–228.
6 Sophocles, *Oedipus at Colonus*, trans. Robert Fitzgerald, in *The Complete Greek Tragedies* vol. III, eds David Grene and Richmond Lattimore: Chicago and London: University of Chicago Press, 1960, pp. 107–89.
7 Alfred Heuss, *Propyläen Weltgeschichte*, vol. III, Berlin: Propyläen Verlag, 1965, p. 373.
8 Sophocles, *Oedipus the King*, trans. David Grene, in *The Complete Greek Tragedies*, vol. I, eds David Grene and Richmond Lattimore, Chicago and London: University of Chicago Press, 1960, pp. 107–77.
9 Sophocles, *Antigone*, trans. Elizabeth Wyckoff, in *The Complete Greek Tragedies* vol. I, eds David Grene and Richmond Lattimore, Chicago and London: University of Chicago Press, 1960, pp. 177–229.

10 Sophocles, *Philoctetes*, trans. David Grene, in *The Complete Greek Tragedies* vol. III, eds David Grene and Richmond Lattimore, Chicago and London: University of Chicago Press, 1960, pp. 43–107.

11 *Aristotles' Poetics*, trans. James Hutton, New York: W.W. Norton and Co., 1982, p. 75.

12 Euripides, *Suppliant Women*, ed. and trans. David Kovacs, in *Euripides III*, Harvard: Harvard University Press, 1998, pp. 12–141, 53.

13 Euripides, *Hippolytus*, trans. David Grene and Richmond Lattimore, in *The Complete Greek Tragedies*, vol. I, Chicago and London: University of Chicago Press, pp. 229–91.

14 Euripides, *The Bacchae*, trans. William Arrowsmith, in *The Complete Greek Tragedies*, vol. III, eds David Grene and Richmond Lattimore, Chicago and London: University of Chicago Press, 1960, pp. 189–261.

15 *The Cambridge Guide to World Theatre*, ed. Martin Banham, Cambridge: Cambridge University Press, 1988, p. 631.

16 Rainer Warning, *Funktion und Struktur. Die Ambivalenzen des geistlichen Spiels*, Munich: Fink, 1974, p. 74.

17 Warning, *Funktion and Struktur*, p. 93.

18 Arno Borst, *The History of Manners: The Civilizing Process*, trans. Edmund Jephcott, New York: Pantheon Books, 1982; Norbert Elias, *Über den Prozeß der Zivilisation*, 2 vols, Frankfurt am Main, 1976; Robert Muchembled, *Kultur des Volkes – Kultur der Elite. Die Geschichte einer erfolgreichen Verdrängung*, Stuttgart: Klett-Cotta, 1984.

19 *Sterzinger Passionsspiel* l, pp. 1223–42, in Joseph Eduard Wackernell, 1897.

20 Heinz Wyss, *Das Luzerner Osterspiel*, Bern: Francke, 1967, l.106.

21 *Das Redentiner Osterspiel*, ed. Brigitta Schottmann, Stuttgart, 1975, pp. l. 9–18.

22 Johan Nowé, 'Kult oder Drama? Zur Struktur einige Osterspiele des deutschen Mittelalters', in Herman Braet *et al.* (eds) *The Theatre in the Middle Ages*, Leuven: Leuven University Press, 1985, pp. 269–313, 30f.

23 See in comparison record nos 32–4, 1055, 1944, 1946, 1969, 2106 and 2258 in Bernd Neumann, *Geistliches Schauspiel im Zeugnis der Zeit*, 2 vols, Munich and Zurich: Artemis Verlag, 1987.

24 Peter Burke, *Popular Culture in Early Modern Europe*, Aldershot: Scolar Press, 1978 (reprinted 1994), p. 211.

25 Harold C. Gardiner, *Mysteries' End*, New Haven: Yale University Press, 1946, p. 109 f.

26 Gardiner, *Mysteries' End*, p. 90.

27 Burke, *Popular Culture*, p. 221.

28 Erasmus von Rotterdam, *Supportatio errorum in censuris Beddae Opera IX*, Ledien, 1706 (reprinted by Hildesheim, 1962), l. 516.

29 Martin Luther, *Werke*, vol. 2, Weimarer Ausgabe, Leipzig, 1930, p. 136.

30 Muchembled, *Kultur des Volkes*; Burke, *Popular Culture*.

31 Muchembled, *Kultur des Volkes*, p. 202.

## 2 THEATRUM VITAE HUMANAE

1 This document, as with all others cited above, is from Alfred Harbage, *Shakespeare's Audience*, New York: Columbia University Press, 1941.

2 All citations in this chapter from Shakespeare's work are from *The Arden Shakespeare Complete Works*, eds Richard Proudfoot *et al.*, Waltham on Thames, Surrey: Thomas Nelson and Sons, 1998.

3 Marsilio Ficino, *De amore*.

4 Niccolo Machiavelli, *The Prince*, trans Luigi Ricci, Oxford: Oxford University Press, 1903.

5 In Joseph Wittreich, *Image of that Horror. History, Prophecy and Apocalypse in 'King Lear'*, San Marino, 1984, pp. 29–30.

6 Charles Nicholl, *The Chemical Theatre*, London: Routledge & Kegan Paul: Huntington Library, 1980.

7 Caroline Spurgeon, *Shakespeare's Imagery and What it Tells Us*, Cambridge: Cambridge University Press, 1952, p. 339.

8 Richard Alewyn, *Das große Welttheater. Die Epoche der höfischen Feste in Dokument und Deutung*, Reinbek bei Hamburg, 1959, p. 14.

9 Alewyn, *Das große Welttheater*, p. 50.

10  Calderón, *The Great Stage of the World*, trans. George W. Brandt, Manchester: Manchester University Press, 1976, p. 2.

11  Alewyn, *Das große Welttheater*, p. 70.

12  José Ortega y Gasset, *Papeles sobre Velázquez y Goya*, Madrid, 1950.

13  *The Trickster of Seville*, trans. Roy Campbell, in *Masterpieces of the Spanish Golden Age*, ed. Angel Flores, New York and Toronto: Rinehart and Co., 1957, pp. 287–368.

14  Marcelin Defourneaux, *Spanien im Goldenen Zeitalter. Kultur und Gesellschaft einer Weltmacht*, Stuttgart: Reclam, 1986, p. 34.

15  Emilio Cotarelo y Mori, *Ensayo sobre la vida y obras de D. Pedro Calderón*, Madrid, 1924, p. 135.

16  Walter Benjamin, *Ursprung des deutschen Trauerspiels*, Frankfurt: Suhrkamp, 1963, p. 60.

17  Defourneaux, *Spanien im Goldenen Zeitalter*, p. 167.

18  Jean Tronçon, *L'Entrée triomphante de Leurs Majestés*, Paris, 1662 (no page no.).

19  André Félibien, *Les divertissements de Versailles*, Paris, 1674, p. 23.

20  Charles Cotin, *Réflexions sur la conduite du roi*, Paris, 1663, p. 9.

21  Chappuzeau, *Théâtre français*, ed. P.L. Jacob, Brussels, 1867, p. 60.

22  Edme Boursault, *Artémise et Poliante*, Paris, 1670, p. 3.

23  Donneau de Visé, *Nouvelles nouvelles*, 3 vols, Paris, 1663, 3, pp. 221ff.

24  Norbert Elias, *Die Höfische Gesellschaft*, Frankfurt: Suhrkamp, 1983, p. 120.

25  Elias, *Prozeß der Zivilisation*, vol. 2, p. 370.

26  Elias, *Höfische Gesellschaft*, p. 169.

27  Jean de La Bruyère, *Caractères*, no. 2, Paris, 1922, p. 211.

28  Louis de Rouvroy, Duc de Saint-Simon, *Mémoires*, vol. XVIII, chapter 31, Paris, 1910 (1711), p. 172.

29  Elias, *Höfische Gesellschaft*, p. 152.

30  Alewyn, *Das große Welttheater*, p. 35.

31  Pascal, *Pensées*, trans. A.J. Krailsheimer, Harmondsworth: Penguin, 1966, p. 245.

32  'First Petition Addressed to the King Concerning the Play Tartuffe', in *Molière. The Misanthrope and Other Plays*, trans. John Wood, Harmondsworth: Penguin, 1959, p. 106.

33  Molière, *Don Juan*, trans. John Wood, in *The Miser and Other Plays*, Harmondsworth: Penguin, 1966, pp. 197–249, 203.

34  D'Olivet, *Histoire de l'Académie*, vol. II, Paris, 1729, p. 158.

35  Molière, *The Misanthrope*, in *The Misanthrope and Other Plays*, trans. John Wood, Harmondsworth: Penguin, 1971, pp. 23–77.

36  Saint-Simon, *Mémoires*, vol. XI, p. 84.

37  Antoine Gombaud, Chevalier de Méré, *De la vraie Honnêteté*, in *Oeuvres complèts du Chevalier de Méré*, vol. III, Paris, 1930, pp. 69–102, 70.

38  Documents on the reception of *Iphigenia* and the quarrel on *Phaedra* are cited in Raymond Picard, *La carrière de Jean Racine*, Paris: Gallimard, 1956.

39  *Phaedra*, in *Jean Racine: Four Greek Plays*, trans. R.C. Knight, Cambridge: Cambridge University Press, 1982, pp. 103–111. All quotations in this section are from this text.

40  Pierre Corneille, *The Cid*, translated and introduced by John Cairncross, Harmondsworth: Penguin, 1975.

41  Antoine Gombaud, 'Chevalier de Méré, De la conversation', in, *Oeuvres*, vol. II, pp. 97–133, 107.

42  *The Passions of the Soul, by René Descartes*, trans. Stephen H. Voss, Indianapolis: Hackett Publications, 1989.

43  François de la Rochefoucauld, *Maximes*, in *Oeuvres complètes*, Paris, 1957, pp. 422–4.

44  Georges Montgrédien, *La vie quotidienne des comédiens au temps de Molière*, Paris, 1966, p. 175.

45  P. Franciscus Lang, *Dissertatio de actione scenica*, ed. and trans. Alexander Rudin, Bern: Francke, 1975, pp. 189f.

46  Denis Diderot, *Ästhetische Schriften* (2 vols), ed. Friedrich Bassenge, Frankfurt: Europäische Verlagsanstalt, 1968, vol. 1, p. 11.

47  See Chapter 3, 'From strolling players to moral institution'.

48  F. Taviani and M. Schino, *Il segreto della Commedia dell'Arte, La memoria delle compagnie italiane de XVI, XVII e XVIII secolo*, Florence: La Casa Usher 1982, pp.180f.

49  See K. Richards and L. Richards, *The Commedia dell'Arte. A Documentary History*, Oxford: Blackwell, 1990.

50 Kathleen McGill, 'Women and Performances: The Development of Improvisation by the Sixteenth Century Commedia dell'arte', *Theatre Journal*, vol. 43, no. 1 (March), 1991, pp. 59–69.

51 Garzoni, in Taviani and Schino, *Il segreto della Commedia dell'Arte*, p. 121.

52 Valerini, in Taviani and Schino, *Il segreto della Commedia dell'Arte*, p. 135.

53 Linda Woodbridge and Edward Berry (eds) *True Rites and Maimed Rites*, Urbana and Chicago: University of Illinois Press, 1992, particularly pp. 2–9.

54 See Chapter 1, 'The vital body'.

55 Giuseppe Pavoni, *Diario de Guiseppe Pavoni*, Bologne, 1589, in Richards and Richards, *The Commedia dell'Arte*, pp. 75f.

56 Marsilio Ficino, *De amore*, second speech, Chapter 8.

57 Jane Tylus, 'Women at the Windows: *Commedia dell'arte* and Theatrical Practice in Early Modern Italy', *Theatre Journal*, vol. 49, no. 3 (October) 1997, pp. 323–42.

58 Kristine Hecker, 'Die Frauen in den frühen Commedia dell'Arte Truppen', in Renate Möhrmann (ed.) *Die Schauspielerin. Zur Kulturgeschichte der weiblichen Bühnenkunst*, Frankfurt: Insel-Verlag, 1989, pp. 27–58.

59 Taviani and Schino, *Il segreto della Commedia dell'Arte*, p. 137 (translated into German by Kristine Hecker).

60 Hecker, 'Die Frauen', p. 53.

61 *Tutte le opere di Carlo Goldoni*, 14 vols, Milan, 1935–56, vol. 1, pp. 769f, cited in J. Hösle, *Carlo Goldoni. Sein Leben, sein Werk, seine Zeit*, Munich and Zurich: Piper, 1993, pp. 124f.

62 Preface, cited in Hösle, *Carlo Goldoni*, p. 123.

63 Regola VI, p. 246, in Richards and Richards, *The Commedia dell' Arte*, pp. 132f.

64 Regola VII, p. 273–9 in Richards and Richards, *The Commedia dell'Arte*, pp. 133 and 135.

65 Rudolf Behrens, ' "Son chi sono". Identitätsthematik und Fingieren in Goldonis Komödien', in *Italienische Studien*, book 4, 1993, pp. 53–74.

66 Carlo Goldoni, *The Servant of Two Masters*, trans. J.M. Dent, Cambridge: Cambridge University Press, 1928.

67 Richards and Richards, *The Commedia dell'Arte*, p. 128.

68 See I. Hafner, *Ästhetische und soziale Rolle. Studien zur Identitätspolitik im Theater Carlo Goldonis*, Würzburg: Königshausen & Neumann, 1994.

69 Carlo Goldoni, *The Mistress of the Inn*, trans. Jenny Covan, ed. Oliver M. Saylor, London: The Moscow Art Theatre Series of Russian Plays, Brentano's Ltd, 1924.

70 Hösle, *Carlo Goldoni*, pp. 253f.

## 3 THE RISE OF THE MIDDLE CLASSES AND THE THEATRE OF ILLUSION

1 This and following documents on the situation of the theatre in Germany in the eighteenth century are cited in Sybille Maurer-Schmook, *Deutsches Theater im 18. Jahrhundert*, Tübingen, 1982.

2 Martin Banham (ed.) *The Cambridge Guide to World Theatre*, Cambridge: Cambridge University Press, 1988, p. 435.

3 Johann Christoph Gottsched, *Versuch einer Critischen Dichtkunst vor die Deutschen*, 4th edition, Leipzig, 1751, p. 95.

4 Heinz Kindermann, *Conrad Ekhofs Schauspieler-Akademie*, Vienna, 1956.

5 Jürgen Habermas, *Strukturwandel der Öffentlichkeit*, Neuwied/Berlin, 1962, pp. 57f.

6 George Lillo, *The London Merchant or George Barnwell*, in *18th Century Plays*, selected and introduced by John Hampden, London: J.M. Dent, 1961, pp. 211–67.

7 Johann Heinrich Friedrich Müller, *J.H.F. Müllers Abschied von der k.k. Hof- und Nationalschaubühne*, Vienna, 1802.

8 Johann Heinrich Vincent Nölting, *Zwote Vertheidigung des Hrn. Past. Schlossers in welcher des Herrn Seniors Goeze Untersuchung der Sittlichkeit der heutigen teutschen Schaubühne mit Anmerkungen begleitet wird*, Hamburg, 1769.

9 This and following accounts of the concept of the family in the eighteenth cenutry are taken from Bengt Algot Sørensen, *Herrschaft und Zärtlichkeit. Der Patriarchalismus und das Drama im 18. Jahrhundert*, Munich, 1984.

10 *Emilia Galotti*, in *Five German Tragedies*, trans. and with an introduction by F. J. Lamport, Harmondsworth: Penguin, 1969, pp. 31–105.

11 *Intrigue and Love*, in *Friedrich Schiller, Plays* trans. Charles E. Passage, New York: The German Library Continuum, 1984, pp. 1–103.

12 *Sara*, in *Two Plays, Gotthold Lessing*, trans. Ernest Bell, Bath: Absolute Classics, Absolute Press, 1990, pp. 7–93.

13 Johann Friedrich Schink, *Dramaturgische Fragmente*, Graz, 1781, vol. 2, pp. 428f.

14 Friedrich Nicolai, Über Ekhof, in Iffland, *Almanach fürs Theater*, 1807, pp. 35f.

15 *Andreas Streichers Schiller-Biographie*, ed. Herbert Kraft, Mannheim, Vienna and Zurich, 1974, pp. 104f.

16 *Berliner Litteratur- und Theater-Zeitung für das Jahr 1784*, Part III, Berlin, 1785, pp. 181f.

17 Karl Philipp Moritz, in *Königlich priviligierte Berlinsche Staats- und gelehrte Zeitung*, 87. Section 20.7.1784.

18 Georg Christoph Lichtenberg, *Über Physionomik; wider die Physiognomen*. Zur Beförderung der Menschenliebe und Menschenkenntnis, in Georg Christoph Lichtenberg, *Schriften und Briefe*, ed. Wolfgang Promies, vol. 3, Munich, 1972, pp. 256–95, 278.

19 Denis Diderot, *The Paradox of the Actor*, in *Selected Writings on Art and Literature*, trans. Geoffrey Bremner, Harmondsworth: Penguin, 1994, pp. 100–59, 107–8.

20 Johann Jakob Engel, *Ideen zu einer Mimik*, in *Schriften*, vols VII/VIII, Berlin, 1804 (reprinted, Frankfurt, 1971), vol. VII, pp. 1311f.

21 In *J. W. von Goethe. Goethe's Collected Works*, ed. John Geary, vol. 3, *Essays on Art and Literature*, trans. Ellen von Nardorff and Ernest von Nardorff, New York: Suhrkamp, 1986, p. 163.

22 *Götz von Berlichingen*, trans. Charles E. Passage, Illinois: Waveland Press, 1965/1991.

23 *The Tutor*, in *Lenz. Three Plays*, trans. Anthony Meech, London: Oberon Books Ltd 1993, pp. 135–203. All references in this section are from this text.

24 Berthold Litzmann, *Friedrich Ludwig Schröder. Ein Beitrag zur deutschen Literatur- und Theatergeschichte*, 2 vols, Hamburg and Leipzig, 1890 and 1894, vol. 2, p.239.

25 Johann Friedrich Schütze, *Hamburgische Theatergeschichte*, Hamburg, 1799, p. 454.

26 *Goethe's Collected Works*, p. 165.

27 *Goethe's Wilhelm Meister's Apprenticeship*, in *Translations from the German by Thomas Carlyle*, 3 vols, vols 1 and 2, London: Chapman and Hall, 1871.

28 *Meister's Apprenticeship*, trans. Thomas Carlyle, 1871, Book 6, p. 305.

29 *Naive and Sentimental Poetry* ('The Sentimental Poets' [Die Horen, no. 12], 1795), trans. Julius Elias, New York: Ungar, 1984, p. 111.

30 *On the Aesthetic Education of Man*, trans. Reginald Snell, London: Routledge, 1954.

31 *Iphigenia in Tauris*, in *Johann Wolfgang von Goethe Plays*, ed. Frank G. Ryder, trans. Frank G. Ryder, The German Library, vol. 20, New York: Continuum Press, 1993, pp. 81–145. All references in this section are from this edition.

32 *Letters from Goethe*, trans. M. von Herzfeld and C. Melvil Sym, Edinburgh: Edinburgh University Press, 1957, p. 89.

33 *Goethe's World As Seen in Letters and Memoirs*, ed. Berthold Biermann, London: Peter Owen Ltd, 1951, p. 60.

34 *Conversations of Goethe with Eckermann*, trans. John Oxenford, London: J.M. Dent and Sons, 1935, p. 99.

35 *Mary Stuart*, in *Five German Tragedies*, trans. and with an introduction by F. J. Lamport, Harmondsworth: Penguin, 1969, pp. 191–319.

36 *Correspondence between Schiller and Goethe from 1794–1805*, trans. L. Dora Schmitz, 2 vols, London: G. Bell and Sons, 1914.

37 *Schiller's Treatise 'Über Anmut und Würde'. An annotated translation into English*, Leon Richard Liebner, Northwestern University, PhD, 1979, p. 80.

38 'On the Pathetic', in *Friedrich Schiller Essays*, eds Walter Hinderer and Daniel O. Dahlstrom, New York: Continuum Press, 1933, pp. 45–70.

39 *Schiller. Naive and Sentimental Poetry and On the Sublime*, trans. Julius A. Elias, New York: F. Ungar, 1966.

40 *Schiller. On the Aesthetic Education of Man*, trans. Reginald Snell, London: Routledge, 1954.

41 *Correspondence Between Schiller and Goethe*, vol. 1.

42 Amalie von Voigt, 'Cäcilie: Erste Aufführung der Mary Stuart am 14. Juni 1800', in *Weimars Album zur vierten Säcularfeier der Buchdruckerkunst am 24. Juni 1840*.

43  Ferdinand Huber, 'Mary Stuart und die Jungfrau von Orléans', in *Taschenbuch für Dramen auf das Jahr 1803*, Tübingen, 1802, pp. 115–121.

44  Eduard Genast, *Aus dem Tagebuch eines alten Schauspielers*, Leipzig, 1862/1866, pp. 83 and 85f.

45  In *Goethe's Collected Works*, ed. John Geary, 12 vols, New York: Suhrkamp, 1986, vol. 3, *Essays on Art and Literature*, trans. Ellen von Nardorff and Ernest von Nardorff.

46  Goethe, 'Weimarisches Hoftheater', *Journal des Luxus und der Moden*, March 1802.

47  *Ibid.*

48  W.H. Bruford, *Theatre, Drama and Audience in Goethe's Germany*, London: Routledge & Kegan Paul, 1950, p. 319.

49  *Conversations of Goethe with Eckermann*, 1935, pp. 165–6.

50  *J. W. von Goethe's Works: Poetical Works*, 2 vols, vol. 1, London, 1943.

## 4  DRAMATISING THE IDENTITY CRISIS

1  Richard Sennett, *The Fall of Public Man*, London: Faber and Faber, 1977, p.152.

2  Karoline Bauer, *Aus meinem Bühnenleben*, ed. Arnold Wellmer, Berlin, 1876/7, in Rolf Kabel (ed.) *Solch ein Volk nennt sich nun Künstler ...*, Berlin: Henschel Verlag, 1983, pp. 258–99, 282.

3  *Ibid.*, p. 284.

4  Sennett, *The Fall*, pp. 204–5.

5  *Prince Frederick of Homburg*, trans. Martin Greenberg, in *Heinrich von Kleist, Five Plays*, trans. Martin Greenberg, New Haven and London: Yale University Press, 1988, pp. 269–351. All references in this section are from this text.

6  Heinrich von Kleist, *The Marquise of O – and Other Stories*, trans. David Luke and Nigel Reeves, Harmondsworth: Penguin, 1985, pp. 64–114, 113.

7  Heinrich von Kleist, 'A Marionette Theatre', trans. Dorothea B. McCollester, *Theatre Arts Monthly*, July 1928, pp. 476–84, 481.

8  Botho Strauß, 'Traum', in *Kleists Traum vom Prinzen Homburg*, programme notes, Berlin: Schaubühne am Halleschen Ufer, 1972.

9  In Helmut Sembdner (ed.) *Heinrich von Kleists Nachruhm, Eine Wirkungsgeschichte in Dokumenten*, Munich, 1977, p. 342.

10  Mario Praz, 'Der "gotische Roman" von Mathew Gregory Lewis', epilogue to the German edition of *The Monk*, Munich: Hanser, 1971, p. 566.

11  Martin Meisel, 'The Material Sublime. Byron, Turner and the Theatre', in Karl Krocher, William Walling (eds) *Images of Romanticism: Verbal and Visual Affinities*, New Haven and London: Yale University Press 1978, pp. 211–32, 224.

12  Victor Hugo, *Hernani*, trans. Francis, 1st Earl of Ellesmere, in *Select Poems and Tragedies*, London, New York and Melbourne: Ward Lock and Co., 1890, pp. 301–63. All references in this section *other* than these verses trans. by Jo Riley and given line reference from French text, are from this volume.

13  Théophile Gautier, *Histoire du romantisme*, Paris, 1874, p. 31.

14  *Ibid.*, p. 167.

15  *Ibid.*, pp. 153f.

16  Heinrich Heine, 'Vertraute Briefe an August Lewald', sixth letter, written in May 1837 in a Paris suburb, in Heinrich Heine, *Über die französische Bühne und andere Schriften zum Theater*, Berlin (DDR).

17  Gerhard Thrum, *Der Typ des Zerrissenen. Ein Vergleich mit dem romantischen Problematiker*, Leipzig, 1931, p. 195.

18  Sennett, *The Fall*, p. 153.

19  *The Talisman*, trans. Robert Harrison and Katharina Wilson, in *19th Century German Plays*, New York: Continuum Publishing, 1990, pp. 110–81.

20  Gautier, *Histoire du romantisme*, pp. 157 ff.

21  Sembdner, *Heinrich von Kleists Nachruhm*, p. 575.

22  Friedrich Theodor Vischer, 'Gedichte eines Lebendigen', in *Kritische Gänge*, vol. 2, Tübingen, 1944, pp. 282–340, 282, 292.

23  *King Ottocar, His Rise and Fall*, trans. Arthur Burkhard, Yarmouth Port, Massachusetts: Register Press, 1962.

24  *Lorenzaccio*, trans. Donald Watson, in *Musset, Five Plays*, ed. and introduced by Claude Schumacher, Reading: Methuen, 1995, pp. 79–215.

25  Georg Büchner, *Danton's Death*, in *Danton's Death, Leonce and Lena, Woyzeck* trans. Victor Price, Oxford: Oxford University Press, 1971, pp. 1–73.

26  *Ibid.*, p. xi.

27  Eduard Devrient, *Aus meinen Tagebüchern* (Berlin and Dresden, 1836–1852), ed. Rolf Kabel, Weimar, 1964, p. 26.

28  Max Grube, *Jugenderinnerungen eines Glückskindes*, in *Solch ein Volk nennt sich nun Künstler …* Leipzig, 1917, pp. 463–505, 483.

29  *Ibid.*, p. 503.

30  Paul Schlenther, *Gesammelte Werke*, vol. VI, pp. xviif.

31  *Die Gesellschaft* 6, 1890, pp. 1022f.

32  Frédéric Le Play, *La réforme sociale en France, déduite de l'observation purée des peuple européens*, 2 vols, Paris, 1874, vol. 1, p. 186.

33  Frédéric Le Play, *Les ouvriers européens. Etudes sur les travaux, la vie domestique, et la condition morale des populations ouvrières de l'Europe*, Paris, 1855, p. 286.

34  *The Wild Duck*, trans. Michael Meyer, in *Ibsen Plays: One*, London: Methuen, 1994.

35  Strindberg, *The Father*, in *Three Plays*, Harmondsworth: Penguin, 1958, pp. 21–74.

36  Peter Gay, *The Bourgeois Experience. Victoria to Freud*, vol. 1, *Education of the Senses*, Oxford: Oxford University Press, 1984, p. 192.

37  *Ibid.*

38  *The Dance of Death*, in *Five Plays of Strindberg*, trans. Elizabeth Sprigge, New York: Doubleday, 1960, pp. 121–237.

39  Chekhov, *Plays*, Harmondsworth: Penguin, 1959, p. 10.

40  *Ibid.*, pp. 13–14.

41  *Polnoe sobranje socinenija v dvenadcati tomach* [collected works in twenty volumes], pod obscej redakcij V.V.Ermilova, K.D. Muratovoj, Z.Y. Pepernogo, A.J. Revjakina, Gosudarstvennoe izdatel'stvo chudozestvenoj literatury, Moscow 1963, t.6, str. 30/31.

42  Siegfried Melchinger, *Tschechow*, Velber bei Hannover, 1968, pp. 59, 61f.

43  In Melchinger, *ibid.*, p. 56.

44  Sennett, *The Fall of Public Man*, pp. 269–70.

45  *The Master Builder*, trans. Michael Meyer, in *Ibsen Plays: One*, London: Methuen, 1980, pp. 245–320.

46  Max Weber, *The Theory of Social and Economic Organization*, trans. A.M. Henderson and Talcott Parsons, New York: The Free Press, 1947, pp. 358–9.

47  T. Weber, *Ibid.*, p. 360.

48  Sigmund Freud, *Studienasugabe*, vol. X, Frankfurt, 1969, p. 174.

49  F.L. Lucas, *The Drama of Ibsen and Strindberg*, London: Cassell, 1962, p. 270.

50  Reprinted in *Maske und Kothurn* 24, 1978, pp. 136–42, 141f.

51  Strindberg, *The Road to Damascus. A Trilogy*, trans. Graham Rawson, London: Jonathan Cape, 1939.

52  *The Seagull*, in *Anton Chekhov, Plays*, trans. Elisaveta Fen, London: Penguin, 1959, pp. 117–84.

53  Constantin Stanislavsky, *An Actor Prepares*, London: Methuen, 1980 and Constantin Stanislavski, *Building a Character*, London, 1988, both translated by Elizabeth Reynolds Hapgood.

54  Konstantin Stanislavsky, *Die Arbeit des Schauspielers an sich selbst*, 2 vols., Berlin 1986.

55  *Ibid.* p. 190f.

56  Konstantin Stanislavksy, *Die Arbeit des Schauspielers an der Rolle*, Berlin, 1986, p. 51.

57  *Ibid.*, p. 38.

58  Konstantin Stanislavskij, *Von den physischen Handlungen*, in: Stanislavskij, *Theater, Regie und Schauspieler*, Hamburg, 1958, pp. 120–8, 127.

59  Denis Diderot, 'The Paradox of the Actor', in *Denis Diderot, Selected Writings on Art and Literature*, trans. Geoffrey Bremner, Harmondsworth: Penguin, 1994, pp. 100–59, 107–8.

## 5  THEATRE OF THE 'NEW MAN'

1  Stanislavsky, *Arbeit des Schauspielers an sich selbst*, vol. 2, p. 227.

2  Edward Gordon Craig, 'First Dialogue', in *On the Art of Theatre*, London, 1957, pp. 137–82, 142.

3  Nietzsche, 'Richard Wagner in Bayreuth', in *Untimely Meditations*, trans. R. J. Hollingdale, Cambridge: Cambridge University Press, 1997, pp. 195–254, 214–15.

4 Hugo von Hofmannsthal, *The Lord Chandos Letter*, trans. Michael Hofmann, London: Syrens Press, 1995, pp. 9–10.
5 Antonin Artaud, '1st Letter on Language', in *Collected Works*, trans. Victor Corti, London: Calder and Boyars, 1968, vol. 4, p. 83.
7 Craig, 'The Ghosts in the Tragedies of Shakespeare', in *On the Art of Theatre*, pp. 264–81, 269–70, 274.
8 Craig, 'The Artists of the Theatre of the Future', in *On the Art of Theatre*, pp. 1–54, in part, p. 49. The rest of the quotation comes from a footnote to the French edition.
9 Craig, 'The Artists of the Theatre of the Future', in *On the Art of Theatre*, pp. 1–54, 46–7.
10 Marinetti, *Manifesto of Futurism*, Yale: Sillman College Press, Yale Library Associates, 22 April 1983.
11 Vsevolod Meyerhold, *Schriften*, 2 vols, Berlin (DDR), 1979, vol. 1, p. 129.
12 Adolf Fischer, 'Japans Bühnenkunst und ihre Entwicklung' ['Japan's Stagecraft and its Development'], in *Westermanns Illustrierte deutsche Monatsheft*, vol. 89, 1900/1901, pp. 449–514.
13 Meyerhold, 'Ideologie und Technologie im Theater' (1933), in *Theateroktober. Beiträge zur Entwicklung des sowjetischen Theaters*, Frankfurt, 1972, pp. 159–83, 172.
14 In Edward Braun, *The Theatre of Meyerhold. Revolution on the Modern Stage*, London: Methuen, 1979, p. 114.
15 Boris Arvatov, *Kunst und Produktion*, Munich, 1972, p. 86–94.
16 *Meyerhold on Theatre*, trans. and ed. Edward Braun, London: Methuen, 1991, pp. 197–8.
17 Aleksei K. Gastev, *Kak nado rabotat'*, Moscow, 1966, p. 257.
18 Meyerhold, 'Rezension des Buches "Aufzeichnungen eines Regisseurs" von A.Ja. Tairov (1921/22)', in *Meyerhold Theaterarbeit*, ed. Rosemarie Tietze, Munich, 1974, pp. 63–72, 72.
19 Antonin Artaud, *Collected Works*, 4 vols, trans. Victor Corti, London: Calder and Boyars, 1968, vol. 4, pp. 87–9.
20 In Antonin Artaud, *Messages Révolutionnaires*, in *Oeuvres Complètes d'Antonin Artaud*, 10 vols, Paris: Gallimard, 1971, vol. VIII, pp. 169–207, including 'L'Homme contre le destin', pp. 184–96 and 'Le Théâtre et les dieux', pp. 196–207.
21 Artaud, '4th Letter on Language', in *Collected Works*, vol. 4, p. 91.
22 See *Oeuvres Complètes*, vol. 4, 'Dossier du Théâtre et son Double', II Préface, p. 215.
23 'Le Théâtre et la Culture', in *Le Théâtre et son Double*, *Oeuvres*, vol. 4, p. 12.
24 '3rd Letter on Language', *Oeuvres*, vol. 4, p. 112.
25 Elena Kapralik, *Antonin Artaud. Leben und Werk des Schauspielers und Regisseurs*, Munich, 1977, p. 167f.
26 Friedrich Nietzsche, *The Birth of Tragedy and the Case of Wagner*, trans. Walter Kaufmann, New York: Vintage, 1967, pp. 73–4.
27 George Jean Nathan, *The Intimate Notebooks of George Jean Nathan*, New York; Knopf, 1932, p. 10.
28 'Working Notes and Extracts from a Fragmentary Working Diary', in Barret H. Clark, *European Theories of Drama. With a Supplement of the American Drama*, New York: Crown, 1978, pp. 529–36, 530.
29 'Memoranda on Masks', in George Jean Nathan *et al.* (eds) *The American Spectator Year Book*, New York: Stokes, 1934, pp. 159–67, 161.
30 G.W.F. Hegel, *The Phenomenology of Mind*, trans. J. B. Baillie, London: Allen and Unwin, 2nd ed., rev. 1949.
31 Luigi Pirandello, *Six Characters in Search of an Author*, trans. Frederick May, Melbourne and London: Heinemann, 1954, pp. 14–15.
32 R.D. Laing, *The Divided Self. An Existential Study in Sanity and Madness*, Harmondsworth: Penguin, 1960, p. 69, 'The Unembodied Self'.
33 L. Pirandello, *Henry IV*, ed. E. Martin Browne, trans. Frederick May, Harmondsworth: Penguin, 1962, pp. 11–95.
34 Bertolt Brecht, 'On Experimental Theatre', in *Brecht on Theatre*, trans. John Willett, London: Methuen, 1964, pp. 130–6, 131–2.
35 Bertolt Brecht, *Gesammelte Werke*, Frankfurt, 1967, vol. 15, p. 306.
36 Bertolt Brecht, 'Der Lernende ist wichtiger als die Lehre', in *Gesammelte Werke*, Frankfurt, 1967, vol. 20, p. 46.
37 Bertolt Brecht, *Baal*, trans. Peter Tegel, in *Bertolt Brecht: Plays, Poetry, Prose. The Collected Plays*, vol. 1, part 1, London: Methuen, 1979, p. x.

38 Brecht, *Man Equals Man*, trans. Gerhard Nellhaus, in *Brecht: Collected Plays. Two*, London: Methuen, 1994, pp. 1–76, 38.

39 *Brecht on Theatre*, pp. 18–19.

40 Reiner Steinweg (ed.) *Brechts Modell der Lehrstücke, Zeugnisse, Diskussionen, Erfahrungen*, Frankfurt: Suhrkamp, 1976, p. 47.

41 Elsa Bauer, *Badische Volkszeitung*, Baden-Baden, 30 July 1929.

42 *Bertolt Brecht, Journals, 1934–55*, trans. Hugh Rorrison, London: Methuen, 1993 (30 June 1940), p. 73.

43 *Ibid.* (15 March 1939), p. 25.

44 *Ibid.*

45 Johann Wolfgang von Goethe, *Faust Part One*, trans. Philip Wayne, Harmondsworth: Penguin, 1949, pp. 41–2.

46 *The Good Person of Setzuan*, in *Two Plays by Bertolt Brecht* (rev. edn Eric Bentley), New York: Signet, 1983, pp. 1–114.

47 See Brecht, *Gesammelte Werke*, vol. 4, p. 1570. This passage has been cut from the English translation by Eric Bentley (see note 46).

48 'Beschreibung des Denkens', in *Gesammelte Werke*, vol. 20, pp. 170f.

49 Samuel Beckett, *Endspiel, Fin de partie, Endgame*, Frankfurt: Suhrkamp, 1974.

50 Theodor W. Adorno, *Versuch, das Endspiel zu verstehen*, Frankfurt: Suhrkamp, 1972, p. 167.

51 Samuel Beckett, *Collected Shorter Plays*, London: Faber and Faber, 1984, p. 55.

52 Samuel Beckett, *Murphy*, London: John Calder, 1977, p. 138.

53 *Materialien zu Becketts 'Endspiel'*, ed. Michael Härdter, Frankfurt, 1968, p. 38.

54 Jerzy Grotowski, *Towards a Poor Theatre*, London: Methuen, 1975, pp. 211–2. Page numbers quoted throughout this section refer to this text.

55 At the Battle of Sempach (1386), the Swiss owed their victory over Leopold III of Austria to the personal heroism of Arnold Winkelried, who was said to have deliberately gathered into his own body the lances of the vanguard of Austrian knights.

56 Tadeusz Burzynski/Zbigniew Osinski, *Das Theater Laboratorium Grotowskis*, Warsaw: Interpress, 1979, p. 114.

57 Herbert Marcuse, 'Kunst und Revolution', in Marcuse, *Konterrevolution und Revolte*, Frankfurt: Suhrkamp, 1973, pp. 95–148, 95.

58 Richard Schechner, *Environmental Theatre*, New York: Hawthorn Books, 1973, pp. 196f.

59 *Dionysus in 69*, New York: Performing Arts Journal Publ., 1970.

60 Herbert Blau, *Blooded Thought*, New York: Noonday Press, 1982, p. 29.

61 Bruce Wilshire, *Role Playing and Identity. The Limits of Theatre as Metaphor*, Bloomington: Indiana University Press, 1982, p. 158.

62 Heiner Müller, *Herzstück*, Berlin, 1983, p. 103.

63 Heiner Müller, *Hamlet-Machine*, in *Theatremachine*, trans. Marc von Henning, Boston and London: Faber and Faber, 1995, pp. 85–94. Quotation here, p. 87.

64 *Gundling's Life*, in *Hamletmachine and Other Texts for the Stage by Heiner Müller*, trans. Carl Weber, New York: Performing Arts Journal Publ., 1984, pp. 59–81.

65 Stephen W. Hawking, *A Brief History of Time*, Toronto and London: Bantam Books, 1988, p. 33.

66 Heiner Müller, *Rotwelsch*, Berlin, 1982, p. 98.

67 Henning Rischbieter, 'Deutschland, Ein Wilsonmärchen', in *Theater heute* 12, 1986, pp. 5–6.

68 Heiner Müller, *Bildbeschreibung*, in *Shakespeare Factory 1*, 1985, pp. 7–14, 14.

# Select bibliography

## 1 RITUAL THEATRE

Aeschylus (1972), *A Collection of Critical Essays*, ed. M.H. McCall Jr, Englewood Cliffs, NJ: Prentice-Hall.

Blume, H.D. (1978), *Einfuhrung in das antike Theaterwesen*, Darmstadt: Wissenschaftliche Buchgesellschaft.

Brinkmann, H. (1959), 'Das religiöse Drama im Mittelalter. Arten und Stufen, *Wirkendes Wort* 9, Düsseldorf: Schwann, pp. 257–74.

Cameron, A. (1968), *The Identity of Oedipus the King*, New York/London: New York University Press.

Chambers, E.K. (1903), *The Medieval Stage*, 2 vols, Oxford: Oxford University Press.

De Boor, H. (1967), *Die Textgeschichte der lateinischen Osterfeiern*, Tübingen: Niemeyer.

Diller, Hans (ed.) (1967), *Sophokles*, Darmstadt: Wissenschaftliche Buchgesellschaft.

Gardiner, H.C. (1946), *Mysteries' End. An Investigation of the Last Days of the Medieval Religious Stage*, New Haven: Yale University Press (Yale Studies in English, 103).

Gurjewitsch, A.J. (1986), *Das Weltbild des mittelalterlichen Menschen*, Munich: Beck.

Hardison, O.B. (1965), *Christian Rite and Christian Drama in the Middle Ages. Essays in the Origin and Early History of Modern Drama*, Baltimore, MD: Johns Hopkins University Press.

Hommel, H. (ed.) (1974), *Wege zu Aischylos*, Darmstadt: Wissenschaftliche Buchgesellschaft.

Kitto, H.D.F. (1970), *Greek Tragedy*, London: Methuen.

Kott, J. (1973), *The Eating of the Gods. An Interpretation of Greek Tragedy*, New York: Random House.

Lesky, A. (1968), *Die griechische Tragödie*, Stuttgart: Kröner.

—— (1972), *Die tragische Dichtung der Hellenen*, Göttingen: Vandenhoeck & Ruprecht.

Meier, C. (1988), *Die politische Kunst der griechischen Tragödie*, Munich: Beck.

Melchinger, S. (1974), *Das Theater der Tragödie. Aischylos, Sophokles, Euripides auf der Bühne ihrer Zeit*, Munich: Beck.

—— (1979/1980), *Die Welt as Tragödie*, 2 vols, Munich: Beck.

Murray, G. (1940), *Aeschylus. The Creator of Tragedy*, Oxford: Clarendon Press.

—— (1955), *Euripides and His Age*, Oxford: Clarendon Press.

Neumann, B. (1987), *Geistliches Schauspiel im Zeugnis der Zeit*, 2 vols, Munich/Zurich: Artemis.

Nowé, J. (1985), 'Kult oder Drama? Zur Struktur einiger Osterspiele des deutschen Mittelalters', in Herman Braet *et al.* (eds), *The Theatre in the Middle Ages*, Leuven: Leuven University Press.

Pickard-Cambridge, A.W. (1968), *The Dramatic Festivals of Athens*, rev. J. Gould, D.M. Lewis, Oxford: Clarendon Press.

Reinhardt, K. (1948), *Sophokles*, Frankfurt: Klostermann.

—— (1949) *Aischylos als Regisseur und Theologe*, Bern: Francke.

Seeck, A. (ed.) (1979), *Das griechische Drama*, Darmstadt: Wissenschaftliche Buchgesellschaft.

Segal, E. (ed.) (1968), *Euripides. Twentieth Century Views*, Englewood Cliffs, NJ: Prentice Hall.

Snell, B. (1928), *Aischylos und das Handeln im Drama*, Leipzig: Dieterich.

Stemmler, T. (1970), *Liturgische Feiern und geistliche Spiele*. Studien zu Erscheinungsformen des Dramatischen im Mittelalter, Tübingen: Niemeyer.

Thomson, G. (1955), *Aeschylus and Athens. A Study in the Social Origins of Drama*, London: Lawrence and Wishart.

Warning, R. (1974), *Funktion und Struktur. Die Ambivalenz des geistlichen Spiels*, Munich: Fink.

Webster, T.B.L. (1967), *The Tragedies of Euripides*, London: Methuen.

—— (1970), *Greek Theatre Production*, London: Methuen.

Winnington-Ingram, R.P. (1980), *Sophocles. An Interpretation*, Cambridge: Cambridge University Press.

Young, K. (1933/1967), *The Drama of the Medieval Church*, 2 vols, Oxford: Clarendon Press.

## 2 THEATRUM VITAE HUMANAE

Adam, A. (1954), *Histoire de la littérature française au XVII siècle*, vol. 4, Paris: Domat Montchrestien.

Andrews, R. (1993), *Scripts and Scenarios. The Performance of Comedy in Renaissance Italy*, Cambridge: Cambridge University Press.

Anglani, B. (1988), *Goldoni – il mercato – la scena – l'utopia*, Naples: Liguori.

Apostolidès, J.-M. (1981), *Le roi-machine. Spectacle et politique au temps de Louis XIV*, Paris: Editions de Minuit.

Aubrun, C.-V. (1981), *La comedia española 1600–1680*, Madrid: Taurus.

Baader, R. (ed.) (1980), *Molière*, Darmstadt: Wissenschaftliche Buchgesellschaft.

Baratto, M. (1985), *La letteratura teatrale del settecento in Italia*, Vicenza: Pozza.

Barber, C.L. (1959), *Shakespeare's Festive Comedies: A Study of Dramatic Form and its Relation to Social Custom*, Princeton, NJ: Princeton University Press.

Barthes, R. (1963), *Sur Racine*, Paris: Editions du Seuil.

Bénichou, P. (1948), *Morales du grand siècle*, Paris: Gallimard.

Bradbrook, M.C. (1955), *The Growth and Structure of Elizabethan Comedy*, London: Chatto and Windus.

Bradley, A.C. (1905), *Shakespearean Tragedy*, London: Macmillan.

Bray, R. (1954), *Molière, homme de théâtre*, Paris: Mercure de France.

Brook, N. (1963), *Shakespeare: King Lear*, London: Arnold (Studies in English Literature, 15).

Bryans, J.V. (1977), *Calderón de la Barca. Imagery, Rhetoric and Drama*, London: Tamesis Books.

Cairncross, J. (1963), *Molière bourgeois et libertin*, Paris: Nizet.

Clemen, W. (1968), *A Commentary on Shakespeare's Richard III*, trans. Jean Bonheim, London: Methuen.

Clubb, L.G. (1989), *Italian Drama in Shakespeare's Time*, New Haven, CT and London: Yale University Press.

Deierkauf-Holsboer, S.W. (1960), *L'Histoire de la mise en scène dans le théâtre français de 1600 à 1657*, Paris: Nizet.

Díez Borque, J.M. (1976), *Calderón de la Barca. Sociología de la comedia española del siglo XVII*, Madrid: Ed. Catedra.

—— (1978), *Sociedad y teatro en España de Lope de Vega*, Barcelona: Bosch.

—— (1983), *Una fiesta sacramental barroca*, Madrid: Taurus.

—— (ed.) (1983), *Historia del teatro en España. Vol. 1 Edad Media, siglo XVI, siglo XVII*, Madrid: Taurus.

Frye, N. (1965), *A Natural Perspective: The Development of Shakespearean Comedy and Romance*, New York: Columbia University Press.

—— (1967), *Fools of Time: Studies in Shakespearean Tragedy. The Alexander Lectures*, Toronto: University of Toronto Press.

Gaines, J.F. (1984), *Social Structures in Molière's Theatre*, Columbus: Ohio States University Press.

Goldman, L. (1955; rev. ed. 1970), *Racine*, Paris: L'arche.

—— (1959), *Le dieu caché*, Paris: Gallimard.

Guicharnaud, J. (1963), *Molière, une aventure théâtrale. Tartuffe, Dom Juan, le Misanthrope*, Paris: Gallimard.

Hafner, I. (1994), *Ästhetische und soziale Rolle. Studien zur Identitätspolitik im Theater Carlo Goldonis*, Würzburg: Königshausen & Neumann.

Heilman, R.B. (1963), *This Great Stage. Image and Structure in 'King Lear'*, Washington: Washington University Press.

Hösle, J. (1993), *Carlo Goldoni. Sein Leben, sein Werk, seine Zeit*, Munich and Zurich: Piper.

Jasiniski, R. (1958), *Vers le vrai Racine*, 2 vols, Paris: Colin.

——— (1963), *Molière et 'le Misanthrope'*, Paris: Nizet.

Kantorowicz, E.H. (1957), *The King's Two Bodies. A Study in Medieval Political Theology*, Princeton, NJ: Princeton University Press.

Karnick, M. (1980), *Rollenspiel und Welttheater. Untersuchungen an Dramen Calderóns, Schillers, Strindbergs, Becketts und Brechts*, Munich: Fink.

Katritsky, M.A. (ed.) (1998), 'The Commedia dell'Arte', *Theatre Research International*, vol. 23, no. 2 (Summer), London: Oxford University Press.

Kaufmann, B. (1976), *Die comedia Calderóns. Studien zur Interdependenz von Autor, Publikum und Bühne*, Bern and Frankfurt: Lang.

Kennedy, R.L. (1974), *Studies in Tirso*, Chapel Hill, NC: UNC Dept of Romance Languages.

Kott, J. (1965), *Shakespeare, Our Contemporary*, New York: Barnes and Noble.

Lough, J. (1965), *Paris Theatre Audiences in the Seventeenth and Eighteenth Centuries*, Oxford: Oxford University Press.

Matzat, W. (1982), *Dramenstruktur und Zuschauerrolle. Theater in der französischen Klassik*, Munich: Fink.

Mauron, C. (1969), *L'inconscient dans l'œuvre et la vie de Racine*, Paris: Corti.

——— (1986), *Phèdre*, Paris: Corti.

Molinari, C. (1985), *La Commedia dell'Arte*, Milan: Mondaldori.

Mongrédien, G. (ed.) (1965), *Recueil des textes et documents du XVIIe siècle relatifs à Molière*, 2 vols, Paris: Edition du Centre National de la Recherche Scientifique.

——— (1966), *La vie quotidienne des comédiens au temps de Molière*, Paris: Hachette.

Muir, K. (1972), *Shakespeare's Tragic Sequence*, London: Hutchinson.

——— (ed.) (1984), *King Lear. Critical Essays*, New York and London: Garland.

——— and Schoenbaum, S. (ed.) (1971), *A New Companion to Shakespeare Studies*, Cambridge: Cambridge University Press.

Müller, H.-J. (1977), *Das spanische Theater im 17. Jahrhundert*, Berlin: E. Schmidt.

Müller-Bochat, E. (ed.) (1975), *Lope de Vega*, Darmstadt: Wissenschaftliche Buchgesellschaft.

Neumeister, S. (1978), *Mythos und Repräsentation – Die mythologischen Festspiele Calderóns*, Munich: Fink.

Nevo, R. (1972), *Tragic Form in Shakespeare*, Princeton, NJ: Princeton University Press.

Niderst, A. (1969), *Le Misanthrope de Molière*, Paris: Edition Europe.

Oehrlein, J. (1986), *Der Schauspieler im spanischen Theater des Siglo de oro*, Frankfurt: Verveurt.

Pandolfi, V. (1969), *Il teatro del Rinascimento e la Commedia dell'Arte*, Rome: Lerici.

Picard, R. (1956), *La carrière de Jean Racine*, Paris: Gallimard 1956.

Pörtl, K. (1985), *Das Spanische Theater*, Darmstadt: Wissenschaftliche Buchgesellschaft.

Rennert, H.A. (1963), *The Spanish Stage in the Time of Lope de Vega*, New York: Dover Publications.

Ribner, I. (1965), *The English History Play in the Age of Shakespeare*, 2nd rev. edn, London.

Richards, K. and Richards, L. (1990), *The Commedia dell'Arte. A Documentary History*, Oxford: Blackwell.

Rosenberg, M. (1972), *The Masks of King Lear*, Berkeley: University of California Press.

Ruiz Ramón, F. (1979), *Historia del teatro Español. Desde sus origenes hasta 1900*, Madrid: Ed. Cátedra.

——— (1984), *Calderón y tragedia*, Madrid: Alhambra.

Santomauro, M. (1984), *El gracioso en el teatro de Tirso de Molina*, Madrid: Ed. Revista Estudios.

Scherer, J. (1950), *La Dramaturgie classique en France*, Paris: Nizet.

Shergold, N.D. (1967), *A History of the Spanish Stage*, Oxford: Clarendon Press.

Starobinski, J. (1961), *L'œil vivant*, Paris: Gallimard.

Suerbaum, U. (1980), *Shakespeares Dramen*, Düsseldorf: Bagel.

Sullivan, H.W. (1981), *Tirso de Molina and the Drama of the Counter Reformation*, Amsterdam: Rodopi.

Taviani, F. and Schino, M. (1982), *Il segreto della Commedia dell'Arte, La memoria delle compagnie italiane de XVI, XVII e XVIII secolo*, Florence: La Casa Usher.

Theile, W. (1974), *Racine*, Darmstadt: Wissenschaftliche Buchgesellschaft (Erträge der Forschung, 26).

—— (ed.) (1976), *Jean Baptiste Racine*, Darmstadt: Wissenschaftliche Buchgesellschaft (Wege der Forschung, 402).

—— (ed.) (1997), *Commedia dell'arte. Geschichte – Theorie – Praxis*, Wiesbaden.

Tillyard, E.M.W. (1944), *Shakespeare's History Plays*, London: Chatto and Windus.

Trilling, L. (1972), *Sincerity and Authenticity*, Cambridge, MA: Harvard University Press.

Valbuena Prat, A. (1969), *Historia del teatro español*, Barcelona: Juventud.

—— (1969), *El teatro español en su Siglo de Oro*, Barcelona: Ed. Planeta.

Vinaver, E. (1963), *Racine et la poésie tragique*, Paris: Nizet.

Vossler, K. (1932), *Lope de Vega und sein Zeitalter*, Munich: Beck.

Weimann, R. (1975), *Shakespeare und die Tradition des Volkstheaters*, Berlin: Henschel.

Young, D.P. (1966), *Something of Great Constancy: The Art of 'A Midsummer Night's Dream'*, New Haven, CT: Yale University Press.

## 3 THE RISE OF THE MIDDLE CLASSES AND THE THEATRE OF ILLUSION

Bahr, E. (ed.) (1982), *Humanität und Dialog, Lessing und Mendelssohn in neuer Sicht*, Munich.

Barner, W. (1981), *Lessing. Epoche – Werk – Wirkung*, 4th rev. edn, Munich: Beck.

Berghahn, K.L. (ed.) (1975), *Friedrich Schiller. Zur Geschichtlichkeit seines Werks*, Kronberg, Ts.: Scriptor.

Borchmeyer, D. (1973), *Tragödie und Öffentlichkeit. Schillers Dramaturgie im Zusammenhang seiner ästhetisch-politischen Theorie und die rhetorische Tradition*, Munich: Fink.

—— (1977), *Höfische Gesellschaft und Französische Revolution bei Goethe. Adliges und bürgerliches Wertsystem im Urteil der Weimarer Klassik*, Kronberg, Ts.: Athenaeum.

—— (1980), *Die Weimarer Klassik. Eine Einführung*, 2 vols, Königstein, Ts.: Athenaeum.

Bruford, E.H. (1936), *Die gesellschaftlichen Grundlagen der Goethezeit*, Weimar: Böhlau.

—— (1966), *Kultur und Gesellschaft im klassischen Weimar 1775–1806*, Göttingen: Vandenhoeck & Ruprecht.

Bürger, C. (1977), *Der Ursprung der bürgerlichen Institution Kunst im höfischen Weimar. Literatursoziologische Untersuchungen zum klassischen Goethe*, Frankfurt: Suhrkamp.

Conrady, K.O. (ed.) (1972), *Deutsche Literatur zur Zeit der Klassik*, Stuttgart.

Fischer-Lichte, E. (1992), *The Semiotics of Theatre*, Part II 'Changes in the Baroque Gestural Code During the Early Enlightenment', Indiana: Indiana University Press.

Girard, R. (1968), *J.M.R. Lenz. Genèse d'une dramaturgie du tragicomique*, Paris: Klincksieck.

Glaser, H.A (1969), *Das bürgerliche Rührstück*, Stuttgart: Metzler.

Graham, I. (1974), *Schiller's Drama. Talent and Integrity*, London and New York: Methuen.

Guthke, K.S. (1980), *Das deutsche bürgerliche Trauerspiel*, 3rd rev. edn, Stuttgart: Metzler.

Hinck, W. (ed.) (1978), *Sturm und Drang. Ein literaturwissenschaftliches Studienbuch*, Kronberg, Ts.: Athenaeum.

—— (1982), *Goethe – Mann des Theaters*, Göttingen: Vandenhoeck & Ruprecht.

Hinderer, W. (ed.) (1979), *Schillers Dramen. Neue Interpretationen*, Stuttgart: Reclam.

—— (1980), *Goethes Dramen. Neue Interpretationen*, Stuttgart: Reclam.

Huyssen, A. (1980), *Drama des Sturm und Drang. Kommentar zu einer Epoche*, Munich: Winkler.

Koopmann, H. (1966), *Friedrich Schiller*, 2 vols, Stuttgart: Metzler.

—— (1979), *Drama der Aufklärung*, Munich: Winkler.

Kopitzsch, F. (ed.) (1979), *Aufklärung, Absolutismus und Bürgertum in Deutschland*, Munich: Nymphenburger Verlagshandlung.

Korff, H.A. (1954), *Geist der Goethezeit*, 4 vols, 7th edn, Leipzig: Koehler & Amelang.

Koselleck, R. (1973), *Kritik und Krise, Eine Sudie zur Pathogenese der bürgerlichen Welt*, 2nd edn, Frankfurt: Suhrkamp.

*Lessing Yearbook* (1969–1986) 1–18, Göttingen: Wallstein.

Martens, W. (1968), *Die Botschaft der Tugend. Die Aufklärung im Spiegel der Moralischen Wochenschriften*, Stuttgart: Metzler.

Maurer-Schmook, S. (1982), *Deutsches Theater im 18. Jahrhundert*, Tübingen: Niemeyer.

May, K. (1957), *Form und Bedeutung*, Stuttgart: Klett.

Mayer, H. (1973), *Goethe. Ein Versuch über den Erfolg*, Frankfurt: Suhrkamp.

Müller-Seidel, W. (1983), *Die Geschichtlichkeit der deutschen Klassik. Literatur- und Denkformen um 1800*, Stuttgart: Metzler.

Pütz, P. (ed.) (1980), *Erforschung der deutschen Aufklärung*, Königstein, Ts.: Athenaeum-Hain-Scriptor-Hanstein.

—— (1986), *Die Leistungen der Form. Lessings Dramen*, Frankfurt: Suhrkamp.

Rasch, W. (1979), *Goethes 'Iphigenie auf Tauris' als Drama der Autonomie*, Munich: Beck.

Rilla, P. (1973), *Lessing und sein Zeitalter*, Munich: Beck.

Rudloff-Hille, G. (1969), *Schiller auf der deutschen Bühne seiner Zeit*, Berlin and Weimar: Aufbau Verlag.

Rudolf, O. (1970), *Michael Reinhold Lenz. Moralist und Aufklärer*, Bad Homburg: Gehlen.

Schings, H.-J. (1980), *Der mitleidigste Mensch ist der beste Mensch. Poetik des Mitleids von Lessing bis Büchner*, Munich: Beck.

Sørensen, B.A. (1984), *Herrschaft und Zärtlichkeit. Der Patriarchalismus und das Drama im 18. Jahrhundert*, Munich: Beck.

Staiger, E. (1952–9), *Goethe*, 3 vols, Zurich: Atlantis.

—— (1967), *Friedrich Schiller*, Zurich: Atlantis.

Stephan, I. and Winter, H.-G. (1984), *Ein vorübergehender Meteor? J.M.R. Lenz und seine Rezeption in Deutschland*, Stuttgart: Metzler.

Strich, F. (1957), *Goethe und die Weltliteratur*, Bern: Francke.

Szondi, P. (1973), *Die Theorie des bürgerlichen Trauerspiels im 18. Jarhhundert. Der Kaufmann, der Hausvater und der Hofmeister*, ed. G. Mattenklott, Frankfurt: Suhrkamp.

Ter-Nedden, G. (1986), *Lessings Trauerspiele. Der Ursprung des modernen Dramas aus dem Geist der Kritik*, Stuttgart: Metzler.

Wacker, M. (ed.) (1985), *Sturm und Drang*, Darmstadt: Wisenschaftliche Buchgesellschaft.

Walach, D. (1980), *Der aufrechte Bürger, seine Welt und sein Theater*, Munich: Fink.

Wiese, B. von (1980), *Schiller*, Stuttgart: Reclam.

Winter, H.G., *J.M.R. Lenz*, Stuttgart: Metzler 1987.

## 4 DRAMATISING THE IDENTITY CRISIS

Affron, C. (1971), *A Stage for Poets. Studies in the Theatre of Hugo and Musset*, Princeton, NJ: Princeton University Press.

Anton, H. (1975), *Büchners Dramen, Topographien der Freiheit*, Paderborn: Schönigh.

Arnold, H.L. (ed.) (1979), *Georg Büchner*, 2 vols, Munich: Edition Text und Kritik.

Barricelli, J.-P. (ed.) (1981), *Chekhov's Great Plays. A Critical Anthology*, New York: New York University Press.

Bauer, R. (1965), *La réalité, royaume de Dieu. Études sur l'originalité du théâtre viennois dans la première moitié du 19ième siècle*, Munich: Hueber.

Bayerdörfer, H.-P. (1983), *Strindberg auf der deutschen Bühne: eine exemplarische Rezeptionsgeschichte der Moderne in Dokumenten (1890–1925)*, Neumünster: Wachholtz.

Behrmann, A. and Wohlleben, J. (1980), *Büchner: Dantons Tod. Eine Dramenanalyse*, Stuttgart: Klett.

Benedetti, J. (1982), *Stanislavski: An Introduction*, London.

Berendsohn, W.A. (1974), *Strindberg*, Amsterdam: Rodopi.

Blackstone, B. (1975), *Byron: A Survey*, London: Longman.

Blöcker, G. (1960), *Heinrich von Kleist oder das absolute Ich*, 2nd edn, Berlin: Agon.

Boerge, V. (1974), *Strindberg. Prometheus des Theaters*, Vienna and Munich: Österreichische Verlagsanstalt.

Brinckmann, C. (1977), *Drama und Öffentlichkeit in der englischen Romantik*, Frankfurt: Lang.

Bruford, W.H. (1957), *Anton Chekhov*, New Haven, CT: Yale University Press.

Bryan, G.B. (1984), *An Ibsen Companion. A Dictionary-Guide to the Life, Works and Critical Reception of Ibsen*, Westport, CT: Greenwood Press.

Buss, R. (1984), *Vigny's 'Chatterton'*, London: Grant and Cutler.

Byron, Lord (1969), 'Manfred', *Manfred*, Frankfurt am Main, Heinrich Heine Verlag.

Carlson, H.G. (1982), *Strindberg and the Poetry of Myth*, Berkeley, Los Angeles and New York: University of California Press.

Carlsson, A. (1978), *Ibsen, Strindberg, Hamsun. Essays zur skandanavischen Literatur*, Kronberg, Ts.: Athenaeum.

Castex, P.G. (1979), *Études sur le théâtre de Musset*, Paris: CDU & SEDES.

Chahine, S. (1981), *La Dramaturgie de Victor Hugo*, Paris: Nizet.

Chamberlain, J. (1982), *Ibsen: The Open Vision*, London: Athlone.

Clarke, C.M. (1979), 'Byron's Plays', Dissertation, University of Toronto.

Curran, S. (1970), *Shelley's 'Cenci'. Scorpions Ringed with Fire*, Princeton, NJ: Princeton University Press.

Denkler, H. (1973), *Restauration und Revolution. Politische Tendenzen im deutschen Drama zwischen Wiener Kongreß und Märzrevolution*, Munich: Fink.

Dlugosch, I. (1977), *Anton Pavlovič Čechov und das Theater des Absurden*, Munich: Fink.

Durbach, E. (1980), *Ibsen and the Theatre. The Dramatist in Production*, New York and London: New York University Press.

Egan, M. (ed.) (1972), *H. Ibsen. The Critical Heritage*, London: Routledge & Kegan Paul.

Ehrstine, J.W. (1976), *The Metaphysics of Byron: A Reading of the Plays*, The Hague: Mouton.

Eichler, R. (1977), *Poetic Drama. Die Entdeckung des Dialogs bei Byron, Shelley, Swinburne und Tennyson*, Heidelberg: Winter.

Ellis, J.M. (1979), *Heinrich von Kleist. Studies in the Character and Meaning of his Writing*, Chapel Hill: University of North Carolina Press.

Fletcher, R.M. (1966), *English Romantic Drama 1795–1843. A Critical History*, New York: Exposition.

Fricke, G. (1971), *Gefühl und Schicksal bei Heinrich von Kleist. Studien über den inneren Vorgang im Leben und Schaffen des Dichters*, 2nd edn, Darmstadt: Wissenschaftliche Buchgesellschaft.

Friese, W. (ed.) (1976), *Ibsen auf der deutschen Bühne. Texte zur Rezeption*, Tübingen: Niemeyer.

Gans, E.L. (1974), *Musset et le 'drame tragique'. Essai d'analyse paradoxale*, Paris: Corti.

Gochberg, H.S. (1967), *Stage of Dreams. The Dramatic Art of A. de Musset*, Geneva: Droz.

Goltschnigg, D. (ed.) (1974), *Materialien zur Rezeptions- und Wirkungsgeschichte Georg Büchners*, Kronberg, Ts.: Scriptor.

Graham, I. (1977), *Heinrich von Kleist. Word into Flesh: A Poet's Quest for the Symbol*, Berlin and New York: de Gruyter.

Hahn, B. (1977), *Chekhov. A Study of the Major Stories and Plays*, Cambridge: Cambridge University Press.

Hannemann, B. (1977), *Nestroy. Nihilistisches Welttheater und verflixter Kerl. Zum Ende der Wiener Komödie*, Bonn: Grundmann.

Harding, L.V. (1974), *The Dramatic Art of Raimund and Nestroy. A Critical Study*, The Hague and Paris: Mouton.

Hein, J. (1970), *Ferdinand Raimund*, Stuttgart: Metzler.

—— (1978), *Das Wiener Volkstheater. Raimund und Nestroy*, Darmstadt: Wissenschaftliche Buchgesellschaft.

Hermand, J. and Windfuhr, M. (eds) (1970), *Zur Literatur der Restaurationsepoche 1815–1848*, Stuttgart: Metzler.

Hinderer, W. (1977), *Büchner-Kommentar zum dichterischen Werk*, Munich: Winkler.

—— (ed.) (1981), *Kleists Dramen. Neue Interpretationen*, Stuttgart: Reclam.

Holz, H.H. (1962), *Macht und Ohnmacht der Sprache. Untersuchungen zum Sprachverständnis und Stil Heinrich von Kleists*, Frankfurt: Athenaeum.

Hornby, R. (1981), *Patterns in Ibsen's Middle Plays*, Lewisburg: Bruckwell University Press.

Hoverland, L. (1978), *Heinrich von Kleist und das Prinzip der Gestaltung*, Königstein, Ts.: Scriptor.

Hristič, J. (1982), *Le Théâtre de Tchékhov*, Lausanne: L'Age d'homme.

Hübner, F. (1971), *Die Personendarstellung in den Dramen Anton P. Čechovs*, Amsterdam: Hakkert.

Jacobsen, S.A. (1977), 'Shelley's Idea of Tragedy and the Structure of *The Cenci*', Dissertation, Purdue University.

Jancke, G. (1975), *Georg Büchner: Genese und Aktualität seines Werks. Einführung in das Gesamtwerk*, Kronberg, Ts.: Scriptor.

Kirk, I. (1981), *Anton Chekhov*, Boston: Twayne.

Klotz, V. (1980), *Bürgerliches Lachtheater*, Munich: dtv.

Knapp, G. (1984), *Georg Büchner*, 2nd rev. edn, Stuttgart: Metzler.

Kommerell, M. (1956), *Geist und Buchstabe*, 4th edn, Frankfurt: Klostermann.

Kroeber, K. and Walling, W. (eds) (1978), *Images of Romanticism: Verbal and Visual Affinities*, New Haven, CT and London: Yale University Press.

Laffitte, S. (1955), *Tchékhov par lui-même*, Paris: Hachette.

Lagercrantz, O. (1984), *Strindberg*, Frankfurt: Suhrkamp.

Lawson, T.J. (1972–3), *Structural Patterns in the Plays of Musset*, Cambridge, MA: Cambridge University Press.

Lefebvre, H. (1955), *Alfred de Musset dramaturge*, Paris: L'Arche.

Lessenich, R.P. (1978), *Lord Byron and the Nature of Man*, Cologne and Vienna: Boehlau.

Lindenberger, H. (1975), *Historical Drama. The Relation of Literature and Reality*, Chicago and London: University of Chicago Press.

Lucas, F.L. (1962), *The Drama of Ibsen and Strindberg*, London: Cassell.

Lunin, H. (1962), *Strindbergs Dramen*, Emsdetten: Lechte.

Magarshak, D. (1980), *Chekhov the Dramatist*, London: Methuen.

Martin, P.W. (1982), *Byron: A Poet Before His Public*, Cambridge: Cambridge University Press.

Masson, B. (1974), *Musset et le théâtre intérieur*, Paris: Colin.

Mautner, F.H. (1974), *Nestroy*, Heidelberg: Stiehen.

Mayer, H. (1946), *Georg Büchner und seine Zeit*, Wiesbaden: Liemes.

Moore, D.L. (1976), *The Late Lord Byron. Posthumous Dramas*, London.

Müller-Seidel, W. (1961), *Versehen und Erkennen. Eine Studie über Heinrich von Kleist*, Cologne and Graz: Boehlau.

Northam, J. (1973), *Ibsen. A Critical Study*, Cambridge: Cambridge University Press.

Odoul, P. (1976), *Le drame infini de Musset*, Paris: Pensée Universelle.

Orr, J. (1985), *Tragic Drama and Modern Society. Studies in the Social and Literary Theory of Drama from 1870 to the Present*, London: Macmillan.

Paul, F. (1977), *H. Ibsen*, Darmstadt: Wissenschaftliche Buchgesellschaft.

Poliakova, E. (1971), *Stanislavsky. A Collection of Critical Essays*, Englewood Cliffs, NJ: Prentice-Hall.

Pouillard, R. (ed.) (1979), *Théâtre de Victor Hugo*, Paris.

Reinert, O. (ed.) (1971), *Strindberg. A Collection of Critical Essays*, Englewood Cliffs, NJ: Prentice-Hall.

Rellstab, F. (1980), *Stanislawski Buch*, Wädenswil: Stutz.

Richard, J.-P. (1970), *Études sur le Romantisme*, Paris: Editions du Seuil.

Robinson, C.E. (1976), *Shelley and Byron: The Snake and the Eagle Wrathed in Fight*, Baltimore, MD and London: Johns Hopkins University Press.

Rokem, F. (1986), *Theatrical Space in Ibsen, Chekhov and Strindberg*, Ann Arbor, MI: UMI Research Press.

Roubine, J.J. (1981), *'Lorenzaccio' de Musset*, Paris: Ed. Pédagogie Moderne.

Schlagdenhauffen, A. (1953), *L'univers existentiel de Kleist dans le Prince de Hombourg*, Paris: Les Belles Lettres.

Schmid, H. (1973), *Strukturalistische Dramentheorie*, Kronberg, Ts.: Scriptor.

Senelick, L. (1985), *Anton Chekhov*, London: Macmillan.

Sengle, F. (1974), *Das historische Drama in Deutschland. Geschichte eines literarischen Mythos*, Stuttgart: Metzler.

—— (1971–80), *Biedermeierzeit*, vols 1–3, Stuttgart: Metzler.

Shelley, P.B. (1909), 'The Cenci', *The Cenci* ed. by George Edward Woodbury, Boston, MA and London: D. C. Heath & Co.

Sices, D. (1974), *Theater of Solitude. The Drama of Musset*, Hanover, NH: University Press of New England.

Silz, W. (1961), *Heinrich von Kleist. Studies in His Works and Literary Character*, Phildelphia: University of Pennsylvania Press.

Sprinchorn, E. (1983), *Strindberg as Dramatist*, New Haven, CT and London: Yale University Press.

Steene, B.A. (1982), *Strindberg: An Introduction to His Major Works*, Stockholm: Almquist & Wiksell.

Streller, S. (1966), *Das dramatische Werk Heinrich von Kleists*, Berlin: Ruetten & Loening.

Thorslev, P.L. (1962), *The Byronic Hero. Types and Prototypes*, Minneapolis: University of Minnesota Press.

Törnquist, E. (1982), *Strindbergian Drama: Themes and Structures*, Stockholm: Almquist & Wiksell.

Troyat, H. (1984), *Tchékhov*, Paris: Flammarion.

Tulloch, J.C. (1980), *Chekhov: A Structuralist Study*, Totowa, NJ: Barnes and Noble.

Übersfeld, A. (1974), *Le roi et le buffon. Étude sur le théâtre de Hugo, de 1830–1839*, Paris: L'Information Littéraire.

Valency, M. (1966), *The Breaking String: The Plays of Anton Chekhov*, New York: Oxford University Press.

Volz, R. (1982), *Strindbergs Wanderungsdramen: Studien zur Epoisierung des Dramas*, Munich: Tuduv- Verlagsgesellschaft.

Welleck, R. and Nonna, D. (1984), *Chekhov. New Perspectives*, Englewood Cliffs, NJ: Prentice-Hall.

Wentzlaff-Eggebert, H. (1984), *Zwischen kosmischer Offenbarung und Wortoper. Das romantische Drama Hugos*, Erlangen: Universitätsverbund Erlangen-Nürnberg.

Whitmore, A.P. (1974), *The Major Characters of Lord Byron's Dramas*, Salzburg: Universität Salzburg.

Wren, K.H. (1982), *Hugo, 'Hernani' and 'Ruy Blas'*, London: Grant and Cutler.

## 5 THEATRE OF THE 'NEW MAN'

Ahrends, G. (1978), *Traumwelt und Wirklichkeit im Spätwerk E. O'Neills*, Heidelberg: Winter.

Arnold, H.L. (ed.) (1982), *Heiner Müller. Text und Kritik*, H. 73, Munich: Edition Text und Kritik.

Bablet, D. (1962), *Edward Gordon Craig*, Cologne and Berlin: L'Arche.

—— (ed.) (1979), *Les voies de la création théâtrale. Mises en scène années 20 et 30*, Paris: CNRS.

Baldwin, H.L., *Beckett's Real Science* (1981), Pennsylvania: Pennsylvania University Press.

Barba, E. (1964), *Le Théâtre laboratoire 13 Rzčdow ou le théâtre comme autopénétration collective*, Kraków.

Basnett-McGuire, S. (1983), *Luigi Pirandello*, London: Macmillan.

Benjamin, W. (1978), 'Geschichtsphilosophische Thesen' in *Zur Kritik der Gewalt und andere Aufsätze*, Frankfurt: Suhrkamp.

Berlin, N. (1982), *E. O'Neill*, London: Macmillan.

Bishop, T; Federman, R. (eds.) (1976), *Samuel Beckett*, Paris: L'Herne.

Blüher, K.A. (ed.) (1982), *Modernes französisches Theater*, Darmstadt: Wissenschaftliche Buchgesellschaft.

Bogard, T. (1972), *Contour in Time: The Plays of E. O'Neill*, Oxford: Oxford University Press.

Braun, E. (1979), *The Theatre of Meyerhold: Revolution on the Modern Stage*, London: Methuen.

Brauneck, M. (1986), *Theater im 20. Jahrhundert. Programmschriften, Stilperioden, Reformmodelle*, rev. ed, Reinbek: Rowohlt.

Brecht, S. (1979), *The Theatre of Visions: Robert Wilson*, Frankfurt: Suhrkamp.

Breuer, R. (1976), *Die Kunst der Paradoxie. Sinnsuche und Scheitern bei S. Beckett*, Munich: Fink.

Burzyński, T. and Osiński, Z. (1979), *Das Theaterlaboratorium Grotowskis*, Warsaw: Interpress.

Butler, L. (1984), *Beckett and the Meaning of Being. A Study in Ontological Parable*, London: St Martin's Press.

Carpenter, F. (1979), *E. O'Neill*, Boston.

Chothia, J. (1979), *Forging a Language. A Study of the Plays of O'Neill*, Cambridge: Cambridge University Press.

Cohn, R. (1980), *Just Play: Beckett's Theater*, Princeton, NJ: Princeton University Press.

Costa, S. (1978), *Luigi Pirandello*, Florence: Nuova Italia.

Costich, J.F. (1978), *Antonin Artaud*, Boston: Twayne.

Credico, D.J. (1973), *Towards a Theatre of Cruelty. Artaud, Peter Brook, the Living Theatre, Happenings, Jerzy Grotowski*, Dissertation, University of Alberta.

Eaton, K.B. (1985), *The Theatre of Meyerhold and Brecht*, Boston.

Ebert, H. (1974), *Samuel Becketts Dramaturgie der Ungewißheit*, Vienna and Stuttgart: Braumüller.

Eckardt, J. (1983), *Das epische Theater*, Darmstadt: Wissenschaftliche Buchgesellschaft.

Esslin, M. (1961), *The Theatre of the Absurd*, Harmondsworth: Penguin.

—— (1976) *Artaud*, London: Calder.

Eynat-Confino, I. (1987), *Beyond the Mask. Gordon Craig, Movement and the Actor*, Carbondale, Illinois: Southern Illinois University Press.

Falk, D. (1969), *O'Neill and the Tragic Tension: An Interpretative Study of the Plays*, New Brunswick, NJ: Ruttgers University Press.

Fiebach, J. (1975), *Von Craig bis Brecht. Studien zu Künstlertheorien in der 1. Hälfte des 20. Jahrhunderts*, Berlin: Henschel.

Fletcher, B.S. and Fletcher, J. (1978), *A Student's Guide to the Plays of Samuel Beckett*, London and Boston: Faber.

Floyd, V. (1985), *The Plays of Eugene O'Neill. A New Assessment*, New York: Ungar.

Garelli, J. (1982), *Artaud et la question du lieu. Essai sur le théâtre et la poésie d'Artaud*, Paris: Corti.

Girshausen, T. (ed.) (1978), *Die Hamletmaschine. Heiner Müllers Endspiel*, Cologne: Prometh.

—— (1981), *Realismus und Utopie: Die frühen Stücke Heiner Müllers*, Cologne: Prometh.

Gouhier, H.A. (1974), *Artaud et l'essence du théâtre*, Paris: Vrin.

Grimm, J. (1982), *Das avantgardistische Theater Frankreichs 1895–1930*, Munich: Beck.

Grimm, R. (ed.) (1961), *Episches Theater*, Cologne and Berlin: Kiepenheuer & Witsch.

—— (1971), *Bertolt Brecht*, 3rd edn, Stuttgart: Metzler.

Hecht, W. (ed.) (1974), *Materialien zu Brechts 'Der gute Mensch von Sezuan'*, Frankfurt: Suhrkamp.

Hermand, J. and Trommler, F. (1978), *Die Kultur der Weimarer Republik*, Munich: Nymphenburger Verlagshandlung.

Hinck, W. (1959), *Die Dramaturgie des späten Brecht*, Göttingen: Vandenhoeck & Ruprecht.

Hinderer, W. (ed.) (1984), *Brechts Dramen. Neue Interpretationen*, Stuttgart: Reclam.

Hoover, M.L. (1974), *Meyerhold: The Art of Conscious Theatre*, Amherst: University of Massachusetts Press.

Hoßner, U. (1983), *Erschaffen und Sichtbarmachen. Das theatralische Wissen der historischen Avantgarde von Jarry bis Artaud*, Bern, Frankfurt and New York: Lang.

Innes, C. (1981), *Holy Theatre*, Cambridge: Cambridge University Press.

—— (1983), *E.G. Craig*, Cambridge: Cambridge University Press.

Janvier, L. (1979), *Beckett*, Paris: Editions du Seuil.

Kapralik, E. (1977), *Antonin Artaud. Leben und Werk des Schauspielers, Dichters und Regisseurs*, Munich: Matthes & Seitz.

Karnick, M. (1980), *Rollenspiel und Welttheater*, Munich: Fink.

Kaschel, G. (1981), *Text, Körper und Choreographie. Die ausdrückliche Zergliederung des A. Artaud*, Frankfurt: Haag und Herchen.

Kenner, H. (1979), *A Reader's Guide to Samuel Beckett*, New York: Farrar, Straus and Giroux.

Kiebuziñska, C. (1988), *Revolutionaries in the Theatre. Meyerhold, Brecht and Witkiewicz*, Ann Arbor, MI and London: Microfilms International Research Press.

Klotz, V. (1957), *Bertolt Brecht. Versuch über das Werk*, Darmstadt: Gentner.

Knopf, J. (1974), *Bertolt Brecht. Ein kritischer Forschungsbericht*, Frankfurt: Athenaeum.

—— (1980), *Brecht-Handbuch*, 2 vols, Stuttgart: Metzler.

Kreidt, D. (1968), 'Kunsttheorie der Inszenierung. Zur Kritik der ästhetischen Konzeptionen Adolphe Appias und Edward Gordon Craigs', Phil. Dissertation, FU Berlin.

Laas, H. (1979), *Samuel Beckett: dramatische Form als Medium der Reflexion*, Bonn: Bouvier.

Lüdke, W.M. (1981), *Anmerkungen zu einer 'Logik der Zerfalls': Adorno-Beckett*, Frankfurt: Suhrkamp.

Mailand-Hansen, C. (1980), *Mejerchol'ds Theaterästhetik in den 1920er Jahren: ihr theaterpolitischer und kulturideologischer Kontext*, Copenhagen: Rosenkilde Bagger.

Manheim, M. (1982), *O'Neill's New Language of Kinship*, Syracuse, NY: Syracuse University Press.

Marotti, F. (1961), *E.G. Craig*, Bologna: Cappelli.

Martini, J. (1979), *Das problem der Entfremdung in den Dramen Samuel Becketts*, Cologne: Pahl-Rugenstein.

*Materialien zu Becketts 'Endspiel'* (1968), Frankfurt: Suhrkamp.

May, R. (1973), *A Companion to the Theatre. The Anglo-American Stage from 1920–1970*, Guildford: Lutterworth Press.

Mayer, H. and Johnson U. (eds) (1975), *Das Werk von Samuel Beckett*, Berliner Colloquium, Frankfurt: Suhrkamp.

Meier, U. (1983), *Becketts Endspiel Avantgarde*, Basel and Frankfurt: Stroemfeld.

Mennemeier, F.-N. (ed.) (1965), *Der Dramatiker Pirandello*, Cologne: Kiepenheuer & Witsch.

Mercier, V. (1979), *Beckett, Beckett*, Oxford: Oxford University Press.

Moestrup, J. (1972), *The Structural Patterns of Pirandello's Work*, Odense: Odense University Press.

Müller, K.-D. (ed.) (1985), *Bertolt Brecht. Epoche – Werk – Wirkung*, Munich: Beck.

Newman, L.M. (1976), *Gordon Craig Archives*, International Survey, London: The Malkin Press.

O'Neill, E. (1959), *Three Plays of Eugene O'Neill*, (Desire Under the Elms, Strange Interlude, Mourning Becomes Electra), New York: Vintage Books, pp. 227–376.

Ranald, M. (1984), *The O'Neill Companion*, Westport, CT: Greenwood Press.

Rood, A. (1977), *Gordon Craig on Movement and Dance*, London: Dance Horizons.

Rose, E. (1931), *Gordon Craig and the Theatre. A Record and Interpretation*, London: Low, Marston and Co.

Rössner, M. (1980), *Pirandello Mythenstürzer*, Vienna: Boehlau.

Roubine, J.-J. (1980), *Théâtre et mise en scène 1880–1980*, Paris: Pr. Univ. de France.

Rudnicky, K. (1981), *Meyerhold the Director*, Ann Arbor, MI: Ardis.

—— (1988), *Russian and Soviet Theatre. Tradition and the Avant-Garde*, London: Thames and Hudson.

Rühle, G. (1967), *Theater für die Republik. 1917–1933 im Spiegel der Kritik*, Frankfurt: Fischer.

Rühlicke-Weiler, K. (1968), *Die Dramaturgie Brechts*, Berlin: Henschel.

Scheid, J. (ed.) (1981), *Zum Drama in der DDR: Heiner Müller und Peter Hacks*, Stuttgart: Klett.

Schenk, I. (1983), *Luigi Pirandello – Versuch einer Neuinterpretation*, Frankfurt: Lang.

Schivelbusch, W. (1974), *Sozialistisches Drama nach Brecht. Drei Modelle: Peter Hacks – Heiner Müller – Hartmut Lange*, Darmstadt and Neuwied: Luchterhand.

Schmeling, M. (1982), *Metathéâtre et intertexte. Aspects du théâtre dans le théâtre*, Paris: Lettres Modernes.

Schulz, G. (1980), *Heiner Müller*, Stuttgart: Metzler.

Schumacher, E. (1955), *Die dramatischen Versuche Bertolt Brechts 1918–1933*, Berlin: Ruetten & Loening.

Schwab, G. (1981), *Samuel Becketts Endspiel mit der Subjektivität: Entwurf einer Psychoästhetik des modernen Theaters*, Stuttgart: Metzler.

Sontag, S. (1981), *Under the Sign of Saturn*, New York: Vintage Books.

Steiner, G. (1961), *The Death of Tragedy*, New York: Knopf.

Steinweg, R. (1972), *Das Lehrstück. Brechts Theorie einer politisch-ästhetischen Erziehung*, Stuttgart: Metzler.

Temkine, R. (1972), *Grotowski*, New York.

Teraoka, A.A. (1985), *The Silence of Entropy or Universal Discourse. The Postmodernist Poetics of Heiner Müller*, New York: Lang.

Virmaux, O. (1975), *Le théâtre et son double. Antonin Artaud. Analyse critique*, Paris: Hatier.

Voigts, M. (1977), *Brechts Theaterkonzeption. Entstehung und Entwicklung bis 1931*, Munich: Fink.

—— (ed.) (1980), *Hundert Texte zu Brecht. Materialien aus der Weimarer Republik*, Munich: Fink.

Völker, K. (1983), *Brecht-Kommentar zum dramatischen Werk*, Munich: Winkler.

Wieghaus, G. (1981), *Heiner Müller*, Munich: Beck.

—— (1984), *Zwischen Auftrag und Verrat. Werk und Ästhetik Heiner Müllers*, Frankfurt: Lang.

Wilson, R. (1984), *The Theatre of Images*, Introduction by John Rockwell, New York: Harper and Row.

Winkens, M. (1975), *Das Zeitproblem in Samuel Becketts Dramen*, Frankfurt.

# Index of dramatic works

# General index

Abbey Theatre 246
Ackermann, Konrad Ernst: acting company
146, 150, 153, 165
the act: in Hegelian sense 307–8
acting profession: founding of in Germany 146
acting style: critical reviews of *bürgerliche
Trauerspiel* 165–6; Ekhof and Schröder 198;
Franciscus Lang's rules 126–8; French
tragedy 198; Goethe's classical drama
198–9; Goldoni's dramaturgy 137;
Meyerhold's stylised theatre 290–1, 292–3;
new aesthetic of eighteenth-century theatre
144; Stanislavsky's method 281–3, 294;
stock roles in *commedia dell'arte* 131–2;
theory and criticism in eighteenth century
167–9, 283; at time of Louis XIV 125, 126
acting troupes: *commedia dell'arte* 130–1,
134–6; eighteenth-century Germany 146,
147; increase in seventeenth century 81; in
reign of James I of England 70–1; *see also*
under names of acting companies
actions: in Pirandello's *Six Characters* 307–9;
stereotyped in Beckett's *Endgame* 328
actors: and actresses in *commedia dell'arte* 130,
131, 134–6; Artaud's Theatre of Cruelty
296, 297; concept of personality epitomised
in *Kean* 225; Craig's idea of replacement
with Über-marionette 287–8; cult of
personality 203, 204, 277; de Vigny's tribute
to after *Chatterton* première 224; Diderot on
skills of 4, 168; eighteenth-century theories
of acting style 168–9, 283; figure of Richard
in *Richard III* 56–8; German Enlightenment
theatre 169; Goethe's 'Rules' 199;
Grotowski's theatre 333–4, 334–7, 339, 340;
Hamm in *Endgame* 331–2; Meyerhold's
stylised theatre 290–1, 293; Nestroy's *The
Talisman* 230; Pirandello's *Six Characters*
310–12; relationship with spectators in
medieval religious plays 46–7; in Robert
Wilson's theatre 349; role in Meiningen
theatre 244; Rousseau's ideas 1–2; self-
revelation in Schechner's *Dionysus in 69*

339; stage realism 286; Stanislavsky's acting
method 281, 282–3
Adelphi Theatre 227
Aeschylus 10, 11, 24, 243; theme of the polis
11, 25, 32
aesthetic education: Schiller's ideas 184, 197,
197–8
African cultures: influence on O'Neill 303
*agon* (competition): Great Dionysia festival 8, 9
Alberti, Conrad 246
alchemy: and pattern of transformation in *King
Lear* 79
Alcibiades 8
Alembert, Jean le Rond d' 1
Aleotti, Giovanni Battista 84
Alewyn, Richard 81, 96
Alexeyev, Constantin Sergeyevitch 246
alienation *see Verfremdung*
Alleyn, Edward 70
*Allgemeinen Literatur-Zeitung* (*Universal
Literature Journal*) 198
Alsfeld: Passion Plays 46
Alvarez, João: chronicle of Portuguese history
92
American avant-garde theatre 334, 337–8,
340–1, 342
Anaxagoras 19
ancient drama: Heiner Müller's use of 341; *see
also* Greek tragedy; Roman comedy
Andreini, Isabella 133, 134–5, 135, 136
androgyny: actresses of *commedia dell'arte*
135–6
Anselm of Canterbury, St: *Cur Deus Homo* 42
anthropology: cultural performance and rites of
transition 3
Antoine, André 245
apocalypse: in Beckett's *Endgame* 325, 329–30;
James I's understanding of 72, 80;
references in *King Lear* 72, 79–80, 324, 329;
in Shakespearian tragedies 72; tradition in
drama through the ages 324–5
Archer, Stephen 255

376